THE
SOVIET
TRAGEDY

THE
SOVIET
TRAGEDY

*A History of Socialism
in Russia, 1917–1991*

MARTIN MALIA

THE FREE PRESS
New York   London   Toronto   Sydney

The Free Press
A Division of Simon & Schuster Inc.
1230 Avenue of the Americas
New York, N.Y. 10020

First Free Press Paperback Edition 1996

Printed in the United States of America

printing number

    5   6   7   8   9   10

Library of Congress Cataloging-in-Publication Data

Malia, Martin E. (Martin Edward)
    The Soviet tragedy: a history of socialism in Russia, 1917–1991/
Martin Malia.
        p.   cm.
    Includes bibliographical references (p.   ) and index.
    ISBN-13: 978-0-684-82313-3
    ISBN-10:   0-684-82313-6
    1. Communism—Soviet Union—History.   2. Soviet Union—Politics
and government.   I. Title.
HX311.5.M355   1994
321.9′2′09470904—dc20   93–50128
                                                     CIP

Pages 139 and 491: Excerpts from "Burnt Norton" and "East Coker" in *Four Quartets,* copyright 1943 by T. S. Eliot and renewed 1971 by Esme Valerie Eliot, reprinted by permission of Harcourt Brace & Company and by Faber & Faber Ltd.

To Poland's Solidarity, which began the task of dismantling Communism in 1980, and to Democratic Russia, which finished the job in 1991. The two movements worked in a liberal democratic spirit rarely realized in the painful liberation struggle of the Eastern half of Europe but on this occasion triumphant, a spirit first invoked by the Decembrists and Alexander Herzen with the watchword *za nashu i vashu volnost* ("for our freedom and yours").

Some of the leaders of these two groups I was privileged to call friends during the course of that struggle. Indeed, this book had its inception in a request from certain of them to suggest Western Sovietological literature that might illuminate their plight and point the way out. But since most of this literature in effect sent the message that they should mute their dissidence and wait on the good graces of the system to reform itself, the only way I could meet my friends' request was by subjecting Western Sovietology to the critical examination offered in these pages.

Nor has such a critique been rendered superfluous by the collapse of 1989–1991, for recent events demonstrate that the liberation of the Eastern half of Europe from the Soviet heritage is far from complete, and Western voices will continue to be heard advising retention of the "viable" part of that heritage. Shreds of the poisoned tunic of Nessus that Communism once was still cling, though now with a "democratic socialist" dye, to the emaciated bodies of the nations it enfolded for so long.

CONTENTS

PREFACE

For much of its history Communist Russia was perceived by the outside world to be, in Winston Churchill's famous characterization, a "riddle, wrapped in a mystery, inside an enigma." This verdict was later moderated by an American ambassador to Moscow to yield the judgment that "Soviet Russia is not a mystery; it is only a secret." With the collapse of 1989–1991, the world that Lenin and Stalin built was no longer even a secret. The intimate record of seventy-four years of utopian experimentation is an open book for all to read.

Soviet history is now for the first time really history, and this closure permits us to see the pattern or "logic" of its life course. The present study is an effort to delineate this pattern and to probe the dynamic driving it.

What follows, therefore, is first of all a survey narrative of the evolution of Sovietism over seventy-four years as the system moved from its origins to its end. But even more, this study is an extended essay in analysis and interpretation of the Soviet phenomenon. For we did not perceive that phenomenon directly, but only as through a glass darkly. This was so in part because until almost the end Soviet reality was indeed a well-kept secret, and in part because its universalistic socialist pretensions made it an object of perturbing attraction or repulsion to the rest of the planet.

Thus, Western observers in talking about Communist Russia were almost always talking, if only indirectly, about Western problems and politics as well, a circumstance that made Soviet studies the most impassioned field of the social sciences. This passion focused on the issue of whether the Soviet Union was a unique "totalitarianism," and therefore beyond democratic redemption, or instead was a variant of universal "modernity," and therefore capable of true civilization. Nor did the application of the purportedly value-free categories of social science make the task of resolving this issue any easier. For the very use of such categories constituted a value judgment since they necessarily presupposed the Soviet system to be a social mechanism like any other.

The present book, therefore, is above all an effort to come to terms with the concepts and categories with which the West has attempted to decode the late Soviet enigma. In this sense, it is not only a chronicle of the Soviet tragedy, but also a commentary on much of twentieth-century intellectual history and on the contemporary world's quest for the just society. Given the worldwide role of Soviet socialism, however, the historical autopsy of the experiment and this ideological commentary cannot be disentangled. Yet, given also that the experiment is now a closed historical episode, it should at last be possible to conduct the two inquiries with greater realism than in the past. The task of this book is to effect this conceptual transvaluation.*

---

* The system of transliteration of Russian terms used here is that of the Library of Congress with a few modifications: "Ya" and "Ye" at the beginning of such now familiar names as Yakovlev and Yeltsin, and "y" at the end of such older familiar names as Dostoevsky or Trotsky. The soft sign is omitted.

Introduction
THE HISTORICAL ISSUES
A Time for Judgment

Marxism has been the greatest fantasy of our century.
—Leszek Kolakowski

God, how sad our Russia is!
—Aleksandr Pushkin, anent Gogol's Dead Souls

And along the legendary quay
Approached, not the calendar—
But the real Twentieth Century.
—Anna Akhmatova, anent St. Petersburg, winter 1913

The Soviet socialist revolution was the great utopian adventure of the modern age. Yet, like Janus or the two-headed Russian eagle, this experiment offered to mankind a dual face. To millions it meant the hope of socialism, and to other millions the terror of totalitarianism; but to all it posed a challenge, and no one could escape its fascination. For over seventy years, Marx's "spectre of Communism" in truth haunted the world. Men everywhere had to take a stand for or against the experiment in Russia and measure their domestic politics against its universalistic pretensions. The Soviet spectre thus became the great polarizing force of twentieth-century politics, giving a harsher, redder meaning to the Left and, in answer, hyperradicalizing the Right as well.

It is the positive face of the experiment that first made the affairs of the Soviet Union the affairs of all mankind. For after October 1917,

1

Russia was not just another country: It was the world's "first workers' state" and history's "first socialist society." The land of Lenin thus acquired universal import; for full socialism—not the half-way approximations of Western social democracy—is, at least in aspiration, the acme of democratic equality. And who, in the modern age, can be against equality?

The negative face of Sovietism emerged only progressively, as the dictatorship of the proletariat turned first into the dictatorship of the Party and then into the dictatorship of Stalin, and finally as the resulting totalitarian system expanded into a global, threatening superpower. For throughout its seven decades the Soviet Union was never integrated into the international system as just another state. Thus, the negative consequences of the experiment, though they might be explained by the pressures of capitalist hostility, fascism, and war, also raised the more basic—and for some agonizing—question of whether there was a necessary link between the socialist and totalitarian guises of the Soviet Janus. Was the degeneration of Communism produced by the outside world's hostility and Russian backwardness or by the nature of the Marxist-Leninist project itself? Did the experiment become totalitarian *despite* it being socialist or *because* it was socialist?

Then, after seven decades of tension with the external world, the experiment, spectral to the end, concluded with the greatest social disaster of the modern age. In an event without historical precedent, after forty-five years of peace the Soviet superpower suffered the structural equivalent of defeat in total war. Its backbone, the Communist Party, disintegrated; the Soviet state itself dissolved; and its economy wound up as flattened as those of Germany and Japan in 1945. Indeed, the collapse was such that Russia and the world, for an indefinite future, will be as engrossed with the consequences of the disaster as they once were with the vicissitudes of the experiment.

The heavy heritage of October thus spans, in fact demarcates, Anna Akhmatova's "real Twentieth Century." For centuries are not neatly bounded by round centennial dates; rather, they are defined by long-term political and cultural patterns. Europe's nineteenth century of general peace, economic development, and democratic progress extended from the end of the great French Revolutionary and Napoleonic crisis in 1815 to the outbreak of an even broader world crisis in 1914. Likewise it has often been asserted that the First World War inaugurated our own somber century. Its terminal date has now been revealed by the collapse of Communism and the end of the Cold War in the years 1989–1991. It was only then that we knew that our "short twentieth century" was at last over.[1]

But this short century was also an exceptionally violent and a tragic one. Appropriately, both of the great prophets of our century's most mesmerizing ideology, Hegel and Marx, had as a favorite author the "father of tragedy," Aeschylus. And the burden of Aeschylus' *Oresteia* is that crime begets crime, and violence violence, until the first crime in the chain, the original sin of the genus, is expiated through accumulated suffering. In similar fashion, it was the blood of August 1914, acting like some curse of the Atridae on the house of modern Europe, that generated the chain of international and social violence that has dominated the modern age. For the violence and carnage of the war were incommensurate with any conceivable gain, and for any party.

The war itself produced the Russian Revolution and the Bolshevik seizure of power; its outcome led to a humiliated, revanchist, and ultimately Nazi Germany, as well as to a Fascist Italy. By the 1930s, these three "dictatorships," as they were then called, had between them ideologized and polarized world politics in a hitherto unknown manner, while at the same time eclipsing the power and dividing the societies of the beleaguered constitutional democracies of the Atlantic West.

The Second World War was a direct consequence of the First, and continued the fatal spiral. Begun as Hitler's attempt to undo the defeat of 1918, this new round of bloodshed instead brought Stalin's power into the heart of Europe, and at the same time led to Communist victories in East Asia, thus at last making Leninism a global force. This great Red breakthrough in turn caused the United States to become a countervailing power against Communism, thereby producing still another ideologically polarized struggle: the Cold War. Finally, this hair-trigger yet nonviolent contest between the United States-cum-NATO and the heirs to a now imperial October lasted forty-five years—until the Soviet system collapsed under the strain and gave up the ghost.

So at the end of our centenary cycle, in 1989–1991, the furies unleashed in 1914 were finally appeased. The field was thus left free for the as yet unknown forces of the twenty-first century, which, whatever else it may be, will at least be post–Communist. But what is sure is that post–Communism's beginning will be dominated by digging out from under the rubble—to use Aleksandr Solzhenitsyn's metaphor—left over from the experiment. And the magnitude of this task will be on a scale with the earlier Soviet endeavor.

Together with our short twentieth century, Soviet history, too, is now over. Post-Communist Russia will, of course, remain a major European state and international power, but Leninism, with its world-historical pretensions, is finished. For the first time it is possible to see Soviet Communism as a closed historical episode, with a clear beginning, a middle, and an end. Until 1989–1991, in assessing the erstwhile Soviet enigma, we were always somewhere *in medias res*, and our analyses of Soviet development were accordingly governed by a range of expectations as to how the experiment might turn out. Now that we know the real denouement of the drama the guessing game is over, and most of what we believed we understood about the story's beginning and middle appears far from the mark indeed. Hence, the real process of assessing the Soviet adventure can at last begin: to draw on the historicist wisdom of Hegel, "the owl of Minerva takes flight only as the shades of night are falling."[2]

Because the Soviet adventure ended in disaster, its trajectory since 1917 can be understood only as tragedy. October was just as much a curse of the Atridae as was August: The initial violence of the Bolshevik seizure of power was multiplied many times over as the regime remolded a recalcitrant Russian reality by constant coercion from above. The resulting tragedy is all the more complete because it was produced by the quest for that perfection of justice, equality, and peace which is "socialism," and for that summum of Promethean technological power which defines "modernity." For we should not forget that the aim of October was nothing less than to raise mankind, as Marx put it, "from the realm of necessity to the realm of freedom." We can only understand the Soviet tragedy under the sign of this paradox—that it takes a great ideal to produce a great crime.

What did we think we understood about Soviet history before we reached its end? It is always true that we observe the world through the filter of our analytical concepts and categories. But since direct observation of the self-isolated Soviet Union was so difficult, we were particularly prone to see it as through a glass darkly—indeed through a double glass of political ideology and social-science methodology.

To begin with the latter, in the forty-five years after the Second World War, Western Sovietology grew into an enormous, multidisciplinary enterprise, operating as a "value-free" science. And this investigative effort yielded what are indeed impressive empirical results. By the end of the 1980s, we had built up a vast corpus of literature staking out the details of the Soviet record in all domains, from economics to culture. In fact, we were so successful that during Gorbachev's *glasnost* Soviet publishers took to translating key works of Western Sovietology to help fill in the "blank spots" of their own knowledge. Where the Sovietological enterprise went awry, however, was in making the transition from the details to the deeper dynamic driving Soviet reality.

Briefly put, the Soviet Union portrayed by Western social science represented a variant of "modernity," rough-hewn no doubt, yet in significant measure a success. Most specialists agreed, further, that the system was "stable"; and they considered it normal that it should constitute one of the two great poles of international affairs. Moreover (since ideology could never be entirely excluded from value-free social science), many specialists suggested that the Soviet Union's "mature industrial society" might yet realize its underlying socialist potential. In short, we were presented with a Soviet system that was viable, durable, and, for some, downright promising—and so it was clear that we should all adjust to living with it for good. In consequence, no one was prepared for the system's brusque demise.

Now, it would be too much to expect that anyone should have predicted the precise form of the crash of 1989–1991; and, of course, no one did. Even the dissidents of Eastern Europe, such as the leaders of Poland's Solidarity, who all along saw the system as it really was, were surprised when the moment of their liberation came. But it is not too much to expect that our categories of explanation should be able to account for the collapse of Communism once it has occurred, and on this score mainstream Sovietology clearly fails. Worse still, before the collapse, its theories often intimated, and at times explicitly predicted, the opposite of the actual outcome. Most of our usual "models" presented us with a Soviet system which, although it might not be eternal, was at least permanent: an "urban, industrial, educated" society, as the litany went, that was as much a going concern as its "capitalist" adversary. To be sure, a number of observers, particularly dissidents living under the system, did perceive that it was too fatally flawed to be reformed, but they were usually dismissed by social-science Sovietology. Thus almost everyone, on both the Left and the Right, took Soviet prowess with too grim a seriousness, whether as an ideal or as an adversary.

How could so many have been so wrong about so much for so long? The most general answer is not to be found in Sovietology as such, but in the broader social-science culture through which it perceived its subject. The beginning of systematic study of the Soviet system in the wake of the Second World War coincided with what might be called the behavioral revolution in Western universities. The disciplines of economics, political science, anthropology, and sociology, in gestation since various times in the nineteenth and early twentieth centuries, at last came together in separate faculties of social science and in specialized research institutes to form a third great area of learning alongside the natural sciences and humanities; this development also transformed the venerable discipline of history. All of these disciplines shared, to some degree, the ambition of making the study of man and society as exact and as scientific as possible, an enterprise very much in the positivist spirit of Auguste Comte—though not, of course, in accordance with his precise doctrines. The methodologies of this arsenal of disciplines were soon brought to bear on the burgeoning study of Soviet "society" with the inadequate results that we have seen.

A first reason for this failure is that all of our great social-science theories were devised before the Soviet system came on the scene. To begin with Marx, there is no more misleading guide to understanding Soviet realities than his division of society into a dominant socioeconomic base and a derivative political and cultural superstructure, since in the Soviet situation the relationship between the two is exactly reversed. Nor is Emile Durkheim, for all his commitment to socialism, any more helpful with his categories of "organic solidarity" and "moral" social organization as answers to modern "anomie." Max Weber, though quite aware of the importance of the market, nonetheless held the rather Prussian idea that the essence of capitalism was "legal-rational bureaucracy": he therefore expected that socialism, when and if its day came, would simply carry the rational modern order a step further by replacing the market and private property with hyperbureaucratic planning—at best a half-insight.[3] The only one of the classic theorists who is truly relevant to the Soviet experience is

Alexis de Tocqueville—but the reasons for this must await the next chapter.

When, in the early to mid-twentieth century, the work of the great founders was amplified and institutionalized to produce academic social science, matters were not improved for coping with the Soviet phenomenon. In part this was because the still relatively sparse Soviet data were not fundamental to the new mix of disciplines. But the more important reason concerned the basic premise of the new behavioral culture. Crudely put, the idea of social science posits that, behind the obvious diversity of discrete social formations, something called "society" is the fundamental human reality, and that this "society" is basically the same everywhere, in the past no less than in the present. In other words, although there exist enormous differences in time and place among civilizations, all societies are ultimately governed by the same general laws of structure, function, and development: Were it otherwise, there could not be a science of society but only a jumble of ad hoc observations.

Two consequences follow from this basic assumption. First, culture is a set of "value systems" and thus essentially a function of interests; ideology and politics, therefore, are subsets of the more basic global entity of society. The Marxist dichotomy between superstructure and base is simply one, albeit probably the most influential, expression of this perspective. Thus, the very idea of social science is in some measure reductionist: Politics and ideology are merely reflections of the "social base." Second, the pattern of Soviet development cannot be unique or sui generis, but must be essentially similar to that of other "modern" societies. And this view, once again, subordinates ideology and politics to social process. Thus social-science Sovietology has largely dismissed the Communist regime's declared goal of "building socialism" as transitory utopianism or mere propaganda. As one famous essay put it, what Soviet history really added up to was a process of maturation "from utopia to development."[4]

In this manner, Western Sovietology proceeded to foist on Soviet reality categories derived from a very different Western experience. The Leninist phenomenon was denatured, and the fantastic and surreal Soviet experience was rendered banal to the point of triviality. In the eyes of most Western social scientists the Soviet Union came to appear as "just another society," different only in degree, but not in kind, from other "modern" nations. However, genuinely modernized nations do not disintegrate as the result of a bout of mere reform as the Soviet system did in 1989–1991. What should have been the great social-science case study of the modern age thus was botched, and will now (hopefully) prove to be the starting point for a reexamination of social-science premises.

And so social-science sophistication wound up getting Soviet reality backside to and upside down. As former Soviets used to say, their world was a "looking-glass world," a reversed reflection of the real modernity of Western "capitalism." Or, to adapt Marx's characterization of Hegel's idealism, the Soviet system was an "inverted world," a world "standing on its head." That is to say, it was a world where (contrary to Marx's own sociology) ideology and politics formed the "base" of the system rather than its "superstructure," and where socioeconomic arrangements derived secondarily from this Party base. Thus, commonsense Western social science, in its attempt to set the Soviet system on its socioeconomic feet, in fact stood it quite on its head. The aim of this book, therefore, is to set the inverted Soviet world right-side up by treating it as a structure that was by nature upside down. For in the world created by October we were never dealing in the first instance with a *society;* rather, we were always dealing with an ideocratic *regime.*

The West's inverted perspective on Sovietism may be best illustrated by a look at the history of Western Sovietology. When serious Soviet studies got started in the wake of the Second World War, while Stalin was still in the Kremlin, the problem of understanding Sovietism appeared stark and simple. The prevailing view, which developed the positions of émigré Russian liberal historians, was this: October was not a proletarian revolution, but a coup d'état carried out by a monolithic and disciplined Bolshevik Party. This minority seizure of power was made possible only by the devastating impact of the First World War on the rickety political and social structures of Imperial Russia. The Revolution was therefore not a product of the logic of Russia's historical processes, as Soviet Marxists would have it, but a brutal interruption of the country's development towards constitutional democracy. More devastatingly still, Lenin's Party dictatorship led logically to Stalinism, with its forced collectivization and institutionalized terror.

Since these practices resembled those of the contemporary "dictatorships" of Italy and Germany, the term "totalitarianism"—coined by Mussolini with a positive connotation to designate his new order and first applied in a negative sense to Stalin's Russia by Trotsky—was taken up by Hannah Arendt and other refugees from Nazism to produce a general theory of perverse modernity and degenerate democracy.[5] And they did so because the blander term "authoritarian," seviceable, say, for a Salazar or a Chiang Kai-shek, simply would not do for the gruesome grandeur of Stalin, Hitler, or Mao.

Then, with Khrushchev's de-Stalinization, the Soviet Union began to appear more prosaic; and in the course of the 1960s the "totalitarian model" was displaced by modernization theory. This perspective, which Raymond Aron once described as "Marxism with the class struggle left out," held that the Soviet regime, behind its socialist rhetoric and the macabre trappings of Stalinism, was really a force for "development"—industrialization, urbanization, and mass education—like "authoritarian" regimes in other backward countries. Indeed, the Soviet case might be considered a model of "development economics" for the Third World. And some specialists even held that Soviet Russia would one day "converge" with Western industrial societies, thereby at last realizing its democratic potential and bringing to the new amalgam a socialist sensitivity to human needs that was lacking in the capitalist West. Or at least Russia might do this if the burden of the Cold War were lifted and the corresponding ideological justification—the "totalitarian model"—with its slanderous equivalence of Communism with Nazism, were refuted.

So modernization theory shaded off into a more ideological perspective, and the class struggle came creeping back in. It did so, however, on little cat feet, for this new socioeconomic approach was prosaically academic and positivistic, eschewing all overt value judgments. This new focus was in part due to a larger shift of scholarship at the time to a concern with the base of society and with ordinary people, a generally fruitful expansion of historical horizons best exemplified by the Annales school. The shift in focus was also due, however, to the hopes engendered by de-Stalinization and détente and to the need for a credible Soviet partner in arms control. So it soon became apparent that with modernization theory, no less than with the totalitarian model, a value-free approach to the value-laden pretensions of the Soviet experiment was as ever a contradiction in terms: Overall, one had to be either for or against the Specter.

Thus, for all its austere, empirical exterior, much of the new social history of the 1960s and 1970s in fact turned out to be an ideological effort to explain the Soviet system as the product of popular action, and hence as democratically legitimate. And this entailed a vehement repudiation of the state-centered totalitarian model. The resulting "revisionism" reversed its predecessor's emphasis on politics and ideology, and gave priority instead to social and economic forces; it replaced "regime studies" with "social studies," and purported to explain Soviet developments "from below," as an expression of society, rather than "from above," as an imposition of the state.

In this new historiography two major issues were at stake. The first was the legitimacy of the founding act of the regime, "Great October" itself, as a proletarian and socialist revolution. The second was the question of continuity or discontinuity between Lenin's rule and that of Stalin. And both issues posed the further question of the Soviet regime's capacity for democratic reform after Stalin—which was also the question of the viability of socialism anywhere.

If the Soviet regime originated in a genuinely popular revolution, then Stalin was an "aberration" from the Leninist norm, and the system thus had the capacity, despite a temporary detour into horror, to return to democratic and humane socialism. But if the system was born in a conspiratorial coup, then Stalin was Lenin writ large, and there was no democratic source to return to: Communism therefore could not be reformed; it had to be abolished. By the late 1960s Anglo-American historiography had by and large adopted the first, or "optimistic," perspective and was consequently organized around these questions: What went wrong? When did it go wrong? How might it be set right? This historiography ignored the possibility that these might be false questions: that nothing *went* wrong with the Revolution, but rather that the whole enterprise, quite simply, *was* wrong from the start.

Thus after the mid-1960s Soviet history was systematically rewritten in the West from the "optimistic," social perspective. Briefly, the conclusions of this endeavor run as follows: October was an authentic proletarian revolution, generated by class "polarization" between workers and capitalists, and not a minority coup d'état made possible only by the "accident" of the First World War.[6] The Bolshevik Party in 1917 was not monolithic, but instead undisciplined, diverse, and therefore "democratic."[7] Lenin's recourse to terror and to all-out nationalization during the War Communism of 1918–1921 were temporary expedients made necessary by the emergency of civil war; his true legacy was the "mixed" economy of the New Economic Policy, or NEP, of the 1920s, and Nikolai Bukharin was his legitimate heir.[8] Thus Leninism was not totalitarian, and Stalin was excluded from the authentic canon of Bolshevik history. Indeed, the unity of the Communist phenomenon simply disappeared, and we were left with two totally separate entities, Bolshevism and Leninism on the one hand, and Stalinism on the other, as if there were no such continuing institution as the Party and no such abiding worldview as Marxism-Leninism.[9]

This, at least, was the main current of revisionism, and its cardinal point was the absolute separation of Lenin and October from Stalin. But there was a bolder school of revisionism that suggested that Stalinism, properly understood and pruned of some of its excesses, was the real fulfillment of Leninism. This school held that Stalin's first Five-Year Plan also had democratic origins, in the form of a "cultural revolution" from within the Party and the working class against holdover "bourgeois specialists." Moreover, the consequence of the Plan was massive "upward mobility" from the factory floor that culminated in the "Brezhnev generation." In this view the whole revolutionary process could be summed up as "terror, progress, and social mobility," with the modest overall cost in purge victims falling in the "low hundreds of thousands."[10]* Finally, the politics of this mature Soviet Union was characterized by the interplay of "interest groups" in a pattern of "institutional pluralism," just like in all other "developed societies."[11]

This second revisionist school thus rejoined the totalitarian model's emphasis on continuity between Lenin and Stalin, though with a positive evaluation of their consubstantiality. But the two principal strains of revisionism converged on one point: Gorbachev's *perestroika* would at last produce the crowning of the edifice of Soviet modernity, and thus a return to the True October, with all aberrations overcome and all wrong things set aright.[12]

It is around these theological issues that revisionist scholarship largely turned during the two and one-half decades before the col-

---

* The real figure for executions and camp deaths in 1937–1938 was nearer to three million, and the total number of deaths for the Stalin epoch was probably around twenty million.

lapse. In the introduction to each new monograph, the totalitarian model was ritually excoriated, and the "T-word" was banished from polite academic discourse, its use viewed as virtual incitement to Cold War hostility towards the "Evil Empire." By the onset of *perestroika* in 1985, a pall of political correctness had settled over the field.

And so revisionism wound up by presenting us with a twentieth-century Russia virtually without Communism, a Soviet *Hamlet* without the prince—and also without the tragedy.

After the Great Collapse of 1989–1991, it is apparent that the time has come for a reappraisal of the basic assumptions and the classic problems of Sovietology. To make this new departure, the best place to begin is with the evaluation of Communism that emerged in the East once the Soviet world started to crumble. Ironically, just when the word "totalitarianism" was being expunged from Western Sovietology around 1970, it became current in Eastern Europe; Hannah Arendt was translated in *samizdat*, and by the late 1980s, a label that was once considered calumny in Moscow was openly used by Soviet intellectuals to refer to the whole system, including its Leninist phase. Indeed Gorbachev himself, after his fall, adopted it to describe what he had been trying to undo. To be sure, the fact that after 1970 the forbidden term could be used at all indicated that the system was no longer total. So in recognition of this obvious fact, Eastern European intellectuals differentiated between what might be called the "high totalitarianism" of Stalin and the "classical," or routine, totalitarianism of Brezhnev—"totalitarianism with its teeth kicked out," in Adam Michnik's phrase.[13] In other words, they took a historical approach to defining this vexed concept, recognizing that there could be significant change without fundamental transformation under Communism.

No such sense of nuance marked the controversy over totalitarianism in Western Sovietology, where the debate was almost embarrassingly shallow. The origin of the controversy lay in circumstances as they stood at Stalin's death. In 1956 the initial historical and philosophical approach of Hannah Arendt was codified and made into an abstract "model" by Carl J. Friedrich and Zbigniew Brzezinski.[14] In six famous points they defined totalitarian dictatorship as resting on (1) an elaborate ideology, (2) a single mass party, (3) terror, (4) a technologically conditioned monopoly of communication, (5) a monopoly of weapons, and (6) a centrally controlled economy. All of this, of course, is quite true, especially for high totalitarianism, though just as obviously it is not exhaustive. But this characterization is also static, in part because social-science models by their nature tend to ahistorical abstraction, and in part because the system by the end of Stalin's reign had in fact become a frozen affair. In addition, the general totalitarian model does not distinguish adequately between ideologies of the Left and of the Right and their very different effects. Still, this model can easily be historicized to yield fruitful results when applied to concrete situations, as, notably, in the works of Merle Fainsod, Leonard Schapiro, and Adam Ulam, the three most notable empirical practitioners of the totalitarian approach.[15] All the same, since the general concept is static, it was vulnerable to the obvious mellowing of the Soviet system in the decades after Stalin's death.

But revisionism went too far in exploiting this vulnerability, and in correcting one error it fell into a worse one. This resulted from a conceptual confusion between quantity and quality, or between the degree of control under Sovietism and the nature of the system as such. Thus, since the extent of repression and the dimensions of the Gulag shrank drastically from Stalin to Khrushchev and Brezhnev, the conclusion was drawn that the regime had evolved from totalitarianism to some form of authoritarianism, say, on the model of Greece under the colonels or of Pinochet's Chile. And so, if Khrushchev and Brezhnev could no longer terrorize their economic managers and military officers as Stalin had, then totalitarianism had given way to "pluralism," and the monolithic Party had become a "coalition" of "interests."

To be sure, the quantitative changes after Stalin were most real and, what is more, especially welcome to those who had to live under Sovietism. Nevertheless, those changes did not alter the central fact that the fundamental structures remained intact: the Party-state, the central plan, and the political police, operating through an interlocking directorate of Party cells at every level and orchestrated by ubiquitous agitprop, the whole subordinated to the single overriding goal of building and defending "real socialism."

Eastern Europeans appropriated the cast-off Western concept of totalitarianism to designate just such a total system. For them, "totalitarian" did not mean that such regimes in fact exercised total control over the population (since this is impossible); instead, it meant that such control was their basic aspiration. It did not mean that such regimes were omnipotent in performance, but rather that they were omnicompetent in their institutional structure. In short, it was not Soviet society that was totalitarian; rather, it was the Soviet state. Thus revisionism largely directed its fire against a caricature of the totalitarian concept, indeed against a straw man. The result was to misconstrue the essence of Communism and to put an imaginary, make-believe Soviet Union in the place of the "really existing" article. And this was far worse than the totalitarian model's overestimation of the extent of the system's control over society, or of the degree of its staying power over time.

Nor is this quarrel over terminology a mere matter of labels. One of the major themes of Eastern European and Soviet dissidence after Stalin was the liberation of language from the ideological lexicon of the Party. For Solzhenitsyn in Russia, as for Adam Michnik in Poland, the first step toward the liberation of society was to "refuse to live according to the lie," to call things by their real names and not by their ideological euphemisms. Similarly, "authoritarianism," "pluralism," "developmental dictatorship," and *tutti quanti* social-science designations are grossly inadequate for the extraordinary, total phenomenon of Soviet Communism. The uniqueness of this phenomenon cries out for a separate and distinct designation, and the rude experience of the twentieth century has given us such a term. It is totalitarianism. To use any lesser, diluted name is to denature reality and to misrepresent what we are talking about.

By the same token, and again in accordance with Eastern European opinion, Sovietism must be seen as a unity from October onward, and as something radically different from anything that preceded it, whether in Russia or in the West. It is as unique in time as it is in the typology of societies. This uniqueness was borne home to the erstwhile subjects of Sovietism by the extraordinary manner of its demise. First, there was the totality of the collapse—ideological, political, economic—as if a total system could only end in total collapse. Second, there was the totality of the repudiation this collapse produced; all the institutions—Party, plan, police—all the icons, right back to Lenin and October, were explicitly deprecated and repudiated. And on all sides one heard that people wanted to return to a "normal society."

But this, of course, was tantamount to saying that for the previous seventy-odd years they had lived in an abnormal society, the institutionalized phantasmagoria of "developed socialism" that was in fact a social theater of the absurd. And this sense of the fantastic quality of the Soviet experience is perhaps the central theme of the greatest "Soviet" literature: This is obviously true of the explicit masters of the fantastic (after the manner of Gogol), such as Mikhail Bulgakov, Andrei Platonov, Abram Tertz, and Aleksandr Zinoviev; it is also true of such neoclassicists as Anna Akhmatova and Osip Mandelshtam, all of whose writings came fully into their own and into open legality at the moment of the collapse.

Seen in this perspective, it should be apparent that for the past seven decades Russia has been anything but just another modernizing country. It has been, rather, the extraordinary adventure, for the first time in Western history, of attempting to put "utopia in power."[16] The utopia, of course, was never realized, but this is not the point. For applied utopias do not simply fail and fade away; through the law of unintended consequences, they lead, rather, to the emergence of a monstrous caricature of reality—a surreality.

The outcome of the Soviet experiment, therefore, is best understood as a perverse manifestation of what Hegel called the "cunning of reason," by which he meant that historical actors are unwittingly yet purposefully led by a "logic" of events of which they themselves are unaware. So the Leninist adventure turned out to be what has been called a "mistake of Columbus": the Party set sail for socialism but instead stumbled on Sovietism, thereby landing Russia in an inverted modernity. But this unforeseen landfall did, in fact, lead to the creation of a new politics, a new economics, and (almost) a new Soviet man. And this was indeed a "world-historical" achievement, as Hegel might have put it, though not the one that his disciples Marx and Lenin anticipated.

It is only in terms of this paradox that Soviet history can be understood at its deepest level. For the former Soviet Union, though clearly a failed utopia, was neither a developed nor a modern nation. It was, rather, something sui generis, a phenomenon qualitatively different from all other forms of despotism in this or in previous centuries.

But this fact returns us to the already noted paradox that until the very end most Sovietology saw a quite different Soviet Union, one whose balance sheet was, overall, positive. So we are confronted with a final and still deeper problem: How could the Soviets get away for so long, and in full view of the outside world, with what turned out to have been from the start a world-historical fraud? And how could they deceive themselves for so long that the fantastic enterprise of Bolshevism had produced the world-historical alternative to "capitalism"? Indeed, the supreme paradox of the experiment is that never before in Western history has such a monumental failure been such an irresistible success.

Yet, the solution to all of these paradoxes is surprisingly simple. The utopia that October put in power was the ideological common property of the modern age, and the experiment was conducted not just for Russia, but for all mankind. For if Soviet Russia had only been an exercise in developing a backward country, it never would have mesmerized the world. Thus, in writing about the Soviet experience, Western observers were always indirectly commenting on their own society, and at the same time projecting Western political concerns onto Soviet reality. And this circumstance only reinforced the methodological propensity of social-science culture to homogenize Sovietism with the rest of the planet. Thus, behind the positivistic exterior of the Sovietological debate more often than not there lurked a concern for the honor of universal socialism. And this concern, no less than the developmental model, generated pressure to believe that the "experiment" would, someday, have to turn out all right.

This eternal return of utopian hope, breaking through the facade of social-science rigor, brings us back to the premise that the key to understanding the Soviet phenomenon is ideology. It is only by taking the Soviets at their ideological word, treating their socialist utopia with literal-minded seriousness, that we can grasp the tragedy to which it led.

The concrete agenda of this book, therefore, is to reassert the primacy of ideology and politics over social and economic forces in understanding the Soviet phenomenon. It is to rehabilitate history "from above" at the expense of history "from below" as the motive force of Soviet development. Finally, it is to resurrect the totalitarian perspective, but in a historical and dynamic, not a static, mode; for it was the all-encompassing pretensions of the Soviet utopia that furnished what can only be called the "genetic code" of the tragedy.

Thus the chapters that follow will be concerned in the first instance with analysis and interpretation. The necessary accompanying narrative of events is not intended to be comprehensive, but, rather, to substantiate the basic argument. The narrative, moreover, will vary in detail between the earlier and later periods of Soviet history. The events of the years 1917–1939 have been the most thoroughly staked out in Western historiography and hence will require the least retelling here. The narrative will become progressively fuller after 1939, and especially with the Brezhnev years, since were are still piecing together the basic contours of this period; and the narrative will be fullest of all for the as yet poorly structured Gorbachev finale.

A concluding methodological word: This investigation will have much to say about the "logic" of Sovietism. But lest anyone cry "determinism," it should be explained that the term is employed here in a quite ordinary sense, as when we speak of the logic of the market, or of nuclear armaments, or of contested elections—that is, the logic of a given situation as opposed to the Logic of History itself. For if we could not speak of such circumscribed logics, we could not say anything meaningful about history at all.

However, in this inquiry, a broader and more long-term (though not metaphysical) logic is also involved. It is the self-evident logic of the modern age, as that age has been defined since the Enlightenment and the French Revolution first gave men the idea that history had a secular goal, or telos—a notion generally referred to as progress. And this pattern of progress had two main aspects: First, history was leading to man's rational, scientific mastery of nature, and second, it was leading to a rational, egalitarian society. The Soviet experiment was supposed to be the culmination of this logic of progress; and this of course turned out to be an illusion. But this illusion was possible, both in the East and in the West, only because history was *in fact* in constantly accelerating movement towards greater equality and scientific prowess. It was the ideological hypostasis of this dual movement as Socialism that alone made possible the Soviet experiment.

Thus, the relevant basic concept of the present inquiry is not modernization or even totalitarianism; it is socialism. No other "model" is required to understand our story.

Part I
THE ORIGINS

1

WHY SOCIALISM?

The first man who, having enclosed a piece of land, took it into his head to say, "This is mine," and found people simple enough to believe him, was the true founder of civil society. The human race would have been spared endless crimes, wars, murders, and horrors if someone had pulled up the stakes or filled in the ditch and cried out to his fellow man, "Do not listen to this imposter! You are lost if you forget that the fruits of the earth belong to everyone, and the earth to no one!"
—*J. J. Rousseau*, Discourse on the Origin of Inequality, *1752*

The gradual development of the principle of equality is . . . a Providential fact . . . it is universal, it is durable, it constantly eludes all human interference, and all men as well as all events contribute to its progress.

Would it, then, be wise to imagine that a social movement, the causes of which lie so far back, can be checked by the efforts of a single generation? Can it be believed that democracy, after having overthrown aristocracy and the kings, will stop short before the bourgeoisie and the rich?
—*Alexis de Tocqueville*, Democracy in America, *1835*

What is Property? Property is theft.
—*P. J. Proudhon*, What Is Property? *1840*

The Russian Revolution is noteworthy not so much because it was Russian—though an ordinary "bourgeois" revolution in Russia would have been quite an event—but because it brought the world's first socialist government to power. But what does it mean to be socialist? And by what standards can we judge whether the October regime in fact produced a socialist society? Or whether any socialist government, for that matter, has ever truly merited its name?

SOCIALISM: THE HIGHEST STAGE OF DEMOCRACY

No word in the modern political vocabulary is more fraught with ambiguity or charged with emotion than "socialism." For most people, and in its broadest meaning, the term designates an alternative method to "capitalism" for organizing the economy. In this sense, socialism refers to concrete institutional arrangements and governmental programs. Yet the gamut of these organizational forms is such that the term quickly loses focus; this is clearly evident as we move from progressive taxation and "safety-net" social security to a cradle-to-the-grave welfare state, on to outright nationalization and planning of the entire economy. So perhaps a stable meaning for the antithesis capitalism–socialism can be found in the broad notion of market versus plan?

But this is not a stable focus either. For in socialist usage the market is held to be "anarchic" and the plan "rational," and these terms give a normative aura to the analysis. Further probing only expands this normative area, for socialism also means collectivism as opposed to individualism, cooperation as opposed to competition, social service as opposed to profit seeking, and altruism as opposed to greed. Thus socialism means, ultimately, a just and humane society, and its essence becomes a moral idea rather than any institutional or economic program.

But this still does not exhaust socialism's multiplicity of meanings. The word also designates a distinctive social formation, as in the antithesis "socialist society" versus "capitalist society," and both terms are seen as encompassing all human activity—political, economic, cultural, and even personal—in a single, total system. In this sense, socialism, as the just and humane system, is not just an alternative to, but is "higher" than, capitalism. So socialism also comes to mean the culmination of history, the telos of human development; in this guise it generates a theory of history, or shades off into what has been called metahistory or "historiosophy."

This confusion of meanings is still worse confounded by the variety of mutually incompatible institutional forms that have called themselves "socialist." Thus the term has been plausibly claimed by Stalinist Russia, China of the Cultural Revolution, Sweden of the Social Democratic "middle way," Labourite Britain, Israel of the Kibbutzim, the cooperative community of Brook Farm, and the Khmer Rouge.

These various socialisms, moreover, have usually challenged the legitimacy of the others, and indeed have often anathematized their rivals in shrill sectarian tones.

Still another basic confusion of meaning arises from the difference between "socialism in opposition" and "socialism in power." In the former case we have a *movement* for the organized pursuit of a more human society, as expressed through political parties, trade unions, cooperatives, or similar fraternal undertakings. In this case socialism is a moral fellowship of seekers after justice, who are set off by their calling from an indifferent or hostile world. In the case of socialism in power, however, we have an established *society*, allegedly coming at the end of history, as in the metahistorical succession of "feudalism, capitalism, socialism." But the well-known propensity of power to corrupt invariably produces a great gap between this society and the ideals of the antecedent movement. The result is that socialism in power is often denounced by socialists still in opposition as a degeneration into "state socialism" or, even worse, "state capitalism." The movement is then reborn under the banner of "socialism with a human face," and the expectation of the true socialist society is again put off to the future.

This focus on the future is the deepest cause of the ambiguity surrounding "socialism," for of all our terms designating different types of societies "socialism" alone was created before, not after, the fact of that type of society's existence. "Feudalism," "absolutism," "Old Regime," "liberalism," and "capitalism," for example, all emerged either after or simultaneously with the fact of their existence; they therefore designate something real, however imperfectly their history or reality embodies whatever principles they may claim. But the term socialism, together with its higher derivative, "communism," is unique in that it appeared almost a century before the first attempt was made, in 1917, to attain a corresponding reality. Thus socialism does not designate in the first instance an actual social formation; it designates rather an ideal alternative to all existing social formations, which are labeled for this purpose "capitalism," a term coined *after* its antithesis and designed to serve as its metahistorical foil. In sum, socialism is a utopia, in the literal meaning of that term: a "non-place" or a "no-where" viewed as an ideal "other."

The term socialism is thus unique in that it corresponds to no identifiable object in the sublunary world on whose nature all observers can agree. To be sure, there have been numerous false sightings and some temporarily convincing apparitions, but none has produced that unanimity of opinion that only empirical verification can bring. So, the full reality of socialism is reserved for the realm of faith, "the belief in things unseen, the hope in things unknown."

Thus it becomes clear that "socialism," strictly speaking, does not mean anything. First, it is meaningless, intrinsically, because its economic programs do not, and cannot, realize its moral ideal in a manner that compels recognition as true socialism. Second, it is meaningless, historically, because it has been claimed by so many mutually incompatible social formations that it loses all concrete focus. So when people profess socialism we never know just what they mean, or what they can be expected to do if they come to power. This imprecision certainly smoothed the Bolsheviks' way to total power—and eased periodic Popular Front collaboration with them.

Thus socialism is not a historical or a social-science term at all, but ultimately a messianic, indeed a quasi-magical term; in fact, it has often been claimed that the more ardent forms of socialism have something of a secular religion about them.[1] Masses of humanity could once surge through Red Square chanting "forward to the victory of socialism!" but it is quite inconceivable that shareholders should march down Wall Street mouthing such rousing slogans about capitalism. And it is an exercise in futility when champions of the free market answer Marx with "Non-Communist" or "Capitalist" Manifestos, as if faith could be vanquished by growth statistics.[2] But such is the potency of the socialist idea that most men—its foes no less than its friends—perennially mistake it for a social-science category or a putative stage of history, to the enduring confusion of what we are talking about whenever we utter "socialism."

Socialism derives its emotional charge from an equally charged and ambiguous term: "democracy." In the common usage of the late twentieth century, democracy combines three things that historically have different origins and that are not necessarily related: first, constitutional government and the rule of law; second, popular sovereignty founded on the will of the people; third, social justice understood as social equality.

The first of these, constitutional government based on a representative assembly and the rule of law through an independent judiciary, has its origin in medieval feudal institutions. To mention only the most obvious and best known instances in this development, we need simply recall that England's Magna Carta was no modern Bill of Rights but a feudal contract between the king and his barons. Likewise, the Mother of Parliaments developed as an assembly of hereditary lords with an elective Commons of equally privileged knights-of-the-shire and burgesses. In short, only gentlemen were involved, while the mass of humanity was dismissed as "peasant rogues" or "villeins" (as European villagers were once known) and excluded from public life.

It was only in the eighteenth century, in the American and French Revolutions, that this oligarchic constitutionalism began to be generalized to the whole of society. Yet even in those two revolutions, the ancient Greek word "democracy" was almost never used: Over the centuries it had come to mean "mob rule" leading to "anarchy," and absolute equality was not deemed necessary, or even feasible, in the first modern republics. Indeed, as late as 1863 the thoroughly constitutional order of the American Republic, founded on universal manhood suffrage, was still deemed compatible with chattel slavery. In short, constitutional government is far older than popular sovereignty or the equation of justice with social equality.

The latter two principles appeared only in the middle of the eighteenth century. Until that time all European societies (and non-European ones as well) rested on two other principles. The first was that legitimate authority was always superordinate authority: It came from above and was exercised through kingship or some corporate collegiality, the whole ultimately sanctioned by God or the law of nature or both. Government thus was not devised by man or society; it was simply given. The second old-regime principle was that all societies were necessarily divided into a class hierarchy of interdependent but unequal orders, whether of patricians and plebeians, of nobles and commoners, or of clergy and laity; inequality, therefore, was natural, legitimate, and inevitable.

The challenge to these immemorial ideas, though long in gestation, first became open and militant in the mid-eighteenth century. Jean-Jacques Rousseau's *Discourse on the Origin of Inequality* (1752) and *Social Contract* (1762) may be counted as the major symptoms, though not of course the cause, of this egalitarian revolution. But soon the ideas of superordinate authority and natural inequality were deemed downright scandalous. For example, it was only in this period that slavery, for the first time in recorded history, came to appear abhorrent to enlightened opinion, and that abolitionism emerged as a movement.[3]

But it was only in the American and French Revolutions that men first acted on these new principles. The American Revolution was the first political movement to enshrine popular sovereignty in practice; still, it did not explicitly advance an egalitarian agenda, for a property suffrage existed in most states until the 1820s. Then, the French Revolution carried the challenge to the Old Regime all the way by moving from popular sovereignty combined with a property suffrage to the more logical egalitarianism of universal (manhood) suffrage. Though this advance proved temporary, it nonetheless established the principle of universal suffrage as the next century's goal throughout Europe.

Why the idea of equality appeared so recently in human history is obviously a complex matter, but very plausible insights were advanced by the major thinkers of the Revolutionary Age. The number of those who contributed to the new awareness that made the egalitarian revolution possible is too large to permit even a cursory survey, but a few key names may be singled·out as epitomizing, or symbolizing, the most crucial aspects of this new world of values.

If equality among men were to become a primary moral principle and a political force, it first had to be materially possible. It was only in the late eighteenth century that this began to be true, and here the great symbolic name is Adam Smith, whose *Wealth of Nations* appeared in the same year, 1776, as the American Declaration of Independence. Until this period the productive capacity of human society had increased so slowly as to be almost imperceptible: Every increase tended to be quickly cancelled out by an even greater increase in population, which was then reined in by the scourges of war, pestilence, and famine, a pattern first analyzed by a critic of Smith, Thomas Malthus. Under such circumstances of generalized scarcity, the subordination of the penurious many to the affluent and powerful few appeared unavoidable and, hence, normal and legitimate.

What Smith did was to challenge this fatalistic view. He did not do this by proclaiming the advent of "capitalism," as some commentators today would have it, since no such word or concept existed at the time; nor did he express any real awareness of an industrial revolution occurring as he wrote, although historians now make this revolution the economic centerpiece of the period. Rather, in terms more appropriate to the age, he argued that the development of the "division of labor" had at last made it possible for mankind to enter "commercial society," the "civilized" culmination of a progression whose earlier stages had been "hunting," "pasturage," and "farming." So the natural "propensity of men to barter, truck, and exchange one thing for another" was at last unfettered, thereby making possible an accelerated "expansion of public opulence," or what would now be called "growth."[4] Although Smith had much to say about "the invisible hand" of "self-interest" working for the benefit of all, he used the word "market" sparingly and only in the limited sense of the mechanism of exchange or of a specific area of demand, not in the broader sense of the global organization of society. For him the practical task at hand was to combat the "mercantile system" of the governments and the worker guilds of his day—and, indeed, the monopolistic practices of the entrepreneurs—in order to liberate man's capacity to improve his moral and material lot.

It is this melioristic message and optimistic materialism, this belief that "opulence" could eventually be available to the larger number of men, that was the precondition for both nineteenth-century classical liberalism and nascent socialism. Both the "bourgeoisie" and the socialist spokesmen for the "proletariat"—as the commercial and laboring classes respectively came to be hypostatized after 1830—shared this fundamental optimism about the new industrial age. They differed mightily, however, in their estimates of the social conditions necessary for human liberation. For liberals it was the market, or, as the nineteenth century put it, "free trade," that was the motive force of progress. But for socialists free trade and the division of labor meant the victory of the strong over the weak: These market forces were the cause of social differentiation, inequality, exploitation, and, therefore, of dehumanization. Although Marx was the most systematic and powerful exponent of this pessimistic perception of the Smithian revolution, he did not repudiate it. For him, as for all socialists, it was the founding act of modernity. As Friedrich Engels put the matter, "Adam Smith was the Martin Luther of political economy," the liberator of mankind from the "medieval" backwardness of mercantilism.

*　　*　　*

But this material change could be effective only in conjunction with decisive cultural changes that conferred on man a new understanding of his place in nature and history. The origin of this transformation was the seventeenth-century's Scientific Revolution, which for the first time gave mankind what seemed to be infallible, or at least incontrovertible, knowledge. For the revolutionary quality of this knowledge was that while it dealt in universal and necessary laws, often mathematically expressed, it yet could still be verified empirically. Man thus appeared to have acquired absolute knowledge of the sort previously attributed only to God. So the Enlightenment of the next century brought forth the optimistic hope that the new method of the natural sciences could be extended to all human activity and all branches of knowledge to yield a universal science that would also be power—over nature, society, and man himself. And in this dynamic meliorism the Enlightenment came to view history as the triumphal march of Progress.

But this new vision could win out only by challenging the force that had hitherto dominated European culture, the revealed religion of Christianity. At first, moderate rationalists, such as John Locke, while still deferential to religion, had nonetheless relegated it to a strictly subordinate role. Later, more extreme rationalists, such as Voltaire and the Encyclopedists, or David Hume and Edward Gibbon, replaced revealed religion entirely with natural reason. Yet both moderate and radical *philosophes* understood reason to mean the empirical derivation of knowledge from sensory experience, since this seemed to be the way the new science had been built up. Concomitantly, this sensationalist empiricism transformed morality into a utilitarian calculus of physical pleasure and pain. But as Rousseau was among the first to emphasize, this is not what the "voice of conscience" tells us ethics and "virtue" are all about.

Into the philosophical breach created by the soulessness of utilitarian ethics stepped the inward-looking *Aufklärer*, the enlighteners, of still backward and pietistic Germany. The aim of the German "classical philosophers" from Kant to Hegel was not to crush religion, as the Western *philosophes* so often wished, but to synthesize the new rationalism of science with a secularized version of the old spirituality and the inwardness of religion. In Germany the aspiration of the Enlightenment therefore was to purge Christianity of superstition with the aid of science, the better to preserve its moral verities by recasting them in rational terms. The fruit of their labors was a philosophy of "religion within the bounds of reason alone," in Kant's formulation—a solution that wound up eviscerating revealed religion and divinizing human reason. Thus it is German philosophy that gave the Enlightenment view of man its most exalted and intoxicating expression, which is also the expression that, through Marx, fed most directly into nineteenth-century socialism.

Kant took the crucial step towards this end when he reformulated Christian ethics as "imperatives" of the "universal and necessary" laws of reason, which alone can command "categorically." Thus in "practical" terms the traditional Golden Rule became the rational law: "Act so as to treat man, in your own person as well as in that of any one else, always as an end, never merely as a means." Each man merited this absolute respect because each was the seat of "pure reason," and so, even in a secular world, each must still be treated "as if" he possessed an immortal soul. And on the basis of this sacral rationality, Kant, echoing Rousseau, extolled the "common man" as the beneficiary of a future "world citizenship," a possibility he believed was being realized in the French Revolution.

Hegel took the transformation of Christianity into philosophy a great step further by fusing the two into a spiralling dialectical process, in which the development of human reason was also the emerging self-consciousness of God.[5] This self-consciousness was also liberty, since understanding frees us from the necessity of blind submission to external law. Thus "World History is progress of the consciousness of freedom,"[6] and the rational soul of man is a Spirit that unfolds and grows over time towards ever greater self-consciousness and liberty.

Concretely, the "various grades in the consciousness of freedom" are these: "the Orientals knew that only *one* was free, the Greeks and Romans knew that *some* are free, while we [moderns] know that *all* men, absolutely, that is, as men, are free." Moreover, "this realization [of freedom] first arose in religion, in the innermost region of spirit." Thus for Hegel the freedom of the modern citizen has its origin in the individual immortality of the soul. Since this concept was quite foreign to the ancient world (and more will be said shortly about other limitations of ancient democracy), slavery was not a scandal to Plato and Aristotle. But it inevitably became one to the modern European mind once the concept of the immortal soul had been secularized and made into a social norm.

Although Hegel did not delineate the actual process of secularization (which is what he meant by the growth of "self-consciousness"), it is not difficult to suggest its outline. Throughout the Christian Middle Ages social inequality was not perceived as contradicting the immortal worth of each and every soul because inequality was considered to be a consequence of original sin.[7] The Fall had so corrupted human nature that the subordination of the many to the few was required both for the cohesion, indeed survival, of society, and as a purgative necessity for eventual salvation. Thus the fruits of individual immortality would come only in the next world, and in accordance with the way the soul had navigated the perils of life in this one. And it is this view, of course, that Marx, following Feuerbach, called an "inverted" consciousness and that he found "dehumanizing."

By the mid-eighteenth century the new optimism about the omnipotence of reason had weakened the hold of the doctrine of original sin, and of theology generally, over men's minds, and this was certainly one of the main causes of the egalitarian revolution of those years. Again, it was Rousseau who marked the decisive shift by declaring that evil, and with it inequality, came into the world not through some innate flaw of human nature, but through the defective constitution of society, whose existing order was founded on the usurped lordship of the strong over the weak. Evil was thus social in origin, not intrinsic to man; men's natural goodness, therefore, would permit the abolition of all inequality. And so, as Hegel argued, the Christian soul was transformed into the secular citizen.

If we should think that this excursus into metaphysics and theology is irrelevant to the genesis of Soviet socialism, we would be quite wrong. For Marx, in standing Hegel on his feet, still preserved the master's metaphysics in his own head. As Leszek Kolakowski put it in the opening sentence of *Main Currents of Marxism*, "Karl Marx was a German philosopher."[8]

This German philosophy, with its quasi-divinized idea of man, could become a major force in the modern world only if it were translated into politics; and this Marx did by grafting it onto the egalitarian tradition that came out of the French Revolution. On the import of that tradition the great commentator is Tocqueville.

The year 1789, for all its temporary failures, inaugurated the contemporary political universe. Its fallout delineated the central problems of modernity, from the management of a laissez-faire economy to the political ordering of a mass society to the fostering of social justice for all. This fallout also gave us the vocabulary of modern political discourse: Liberalism, conservatism, nationalism, socialism, and a host of other words with the then new suffix "ism" all appeared in the thirty-odd years after 1789.[9] And among these neologisms was an ancient term—democracy—which now acquired a new range of meanings.

As already noted, from Plato to America's Founding Fathers, "democracy" had carried the negative charge of mob-rule and anarchy. Although we now speak blithely of "Jeffersonian democracy," the term was not used by Jefferson himself, who only occasionally spoke of "popular government" and whose new party was called the "Republican Party." "Democracy" began to be employed in a positive sense in America only in the 1820s and 1830s when universal suffrage first became an issue of principle, and in France in the 1830s and 1840s for the same reason. Still, democracy was slow to enter official rhetoric in either country. In America, neither Jackson nor Lincoln used it—although at a nongovernmental level Walt Whitman did, and in lyrical populist tones; in both America and France until the end of the century the magic term remained "republic." (And in constitutional but monarchical Britain, of course, both "democracy" and "republic" were the property of an insignificant fringe.) Democracy acquired its present potency and range of meanings only during the First World War, when Woodrow Wilson used it to transform the hitherto narrowly national struggles of France and Britain against "autocratic" Germany into a moral-political crusade for popular government everywhere.

Among the multiple meanings of this revived Hellenic label, the most relevant for our purposes is the one conveyed by Tocqueville's *Democracy in America*. By this he meant not American constitutionalism but egalitarianism in America. And he saw egalitarianism as a Janus-headed phenomenon. Writing as he did in the 1830s when the negative meaning of the term was giving way to the positive connotations associated with universal suffrage, his concept of democracy was a hybrid mingling foreboding and anticipation. As a Frenchman coming out of the experience of 1789, he was convinced that the leveling force of egalitarianism was the prime mover of politics everywhere in the modern world. At the same time, he was deeply concerned that this irresistible force might be incompatible with the liberties, largely of aristocratic origin, which had been celebrated under the Old Regime by Montesquieu and which were then guaranteed by the class-based constitutional governments of Restoration Europe, for which liberal-oligarchic Britain was the great model.

Since the term "democracy" is Greek, we tend to assume that it means the same thing today as it did in the Athens of the fifth century B.C., and that Pericles's Funeral Oration is the source of our own political tradition.[10] Similarly, we assume that since the word "republic" is Roman, it too has a continuity of meaning, from Cicero to Madison and Condorcet. But this is only very partially true. What modern politics does have in common with the Greco-Roman past is the participation of a part of the population in public affairs through elective officers and legislative assemblies. This kind of "politics"—the word itself is obviously from the Greek *polis*—existed in no non-European societies until the twentieth century. But what modern politics possesses, and what is quite alien to its ancient predecessor, is the idea of the supreme dignity of man, the sanctity of each and every individual. This value emerged from the cultural transformations of the modern West just discussed. There were no "bills of rights" or "declarations of the rights of man" in ancient polities, and the concept of citizenship was grounded not in the mere fact of being human but in hereditary or legally granted membership in one or another class of a given polis or *res publica*. Thus Benjamin Constant, defending liberalism under the Restoration, could draw a distinction between "ancient and modern freedom," wherein the former meant the freedom of the few to participate in public affairs and the latter meant the freedom of all to be left alone by society in order to live as sovereign individuals.[11]

Accordingly, Greek democracy meant inclusion of the lowest order of free men, the *demos*, in public affairs as a measure necessary for the health of the polis as a whole, not as a natural right. Moreover, this *demos* participated in politics as a group alongside higher social groups—somewhat along the lines of an estate in the European Old Regime—not on a footing of equality with its superiors, still less on the basis of "one man one vote." The Roman republic was even more oligarchic, with the plebs quite outside the main political circuit. And it has already been noted that all ancient polities completely excluded slaves, who represented sizable portions of their populations, from citizenship. To be sure, various modern republics for a time permitted slavery; but since these republics also proclaimed the "unalienable rights of man," this anomaly could only lead to crisis and eventual abolition. And the milder form of political discrimination, a suffrage based on property, perished even more easily. But there was no abolitionism in the ancient world, and universal suffrage was never even contemplated.

It is because of this distinctively modern concept of the republic that modern democracy, in its steadily leftward movement, reached increasingly beyond constitutional government and the rule of law toward popular sovereignty and universal equality. Thus, for Tocqueville, democracy meant *"l'égalité des conditions,"*[12] the leveling of all the social gradations of the legal hierarchy of estates, or orders, that characterized the Old Regime in France and throughout Europe. But he did not have only the Old Regime in mind, for the post-Revolutionary world had its own gradations of inequality. Based on the status and power conferred by wealth, these gradations were embodied in a system of "classes," to use the new designation of the 1830s and 1840s.[13] These new forms of inequality, as well as all future possible ones, would also be challenged by which immanent, implacable logic of modernity that was equality. To recall Tocqueville's formulation: "Can it be believed that democracy, after having overthrown aristocracy and the kings, will stop short before the bourgeoisie and the rich?"

It is in this democratic impetus that lies the origin of that great movement designated by another neologism of the 1830s—"socialism." For, if one is ruthlessly logical about the idea of democracy as equality, then one inevitably arrives at the concept of socialism. So long as there are differences of wealth in society, there will be differences of power and status; and so long as there are differences in power and status, there will be exploitation of some men by others, and domination of some human beings by other human beings. But any exploitation and subordination are a denial of human dignity, a profanation of the sacred persona of Man. Inequality, therefore, is dehumanization, and thus a moral scandal that must be ended if the world is to become truly civilized.

The means to do this is the social appropriation of individual wealth, and this is the core instrumental program of integral socialism. As Marx put it in *The Communist Manifesto:* "The theory of the Communists may be summed up in the single phrase: Abolition of private property."[14] From this it follows that the fruit of private property—profit—and the means for realizing this profit—the market—must also be abolished. With this, the maximalist formula of socialism is complete: Socialism originates in a moral idea—equality—and culminates in a practical program—the end of private property and the market. Anything short of this is something less than full or integral socialism.

But this maximalist program of socialism as full noncapitalism has always proved impossible to implement without a shattering revolution. So in practice the socialist movement has usually settled for more modest goals and for evolutionary methods. And it is this, of course, that has led to the already-noted gamut of programs—from progressive taxation to a universal welfare state—that also claim the title "socialist" and that have so confused the debate about its "true" meaning. No such confusion, however, need intrude into the present book. Here "socialism" will always carry its maximal meaning of full noncapitalism. For this was the form intended by Marx and that the shattering circumstances of 1917 permitted socialism to take in Russia.

Throughout the nineteenth century, socialism had been a moral idea, a movement of opposition and protest. It was only with the Bolshevik October that socialism crossed the threshold from movement to society. It was only then that democratic forces were able to test the proposition that abolition of private property and the market would produce the moral world of equality and the full humanization of man. And the verdict in this matter was not clearly rendered until our own fin-de-siècle. So until then, the integral socialism of the Communists was the gold standard for all the lesser breeds of socialism in the West, and it turned out that the more these latter were democratic and evolutionary politically, the less they realized of the socialist economic program. They were therefore chronically as over-awed by the Soviets' bold results as they were disturbed by their brutal methods. Soviet socialism, by getting there first, thus defined the socialist discourse until the great crash of 1989–1991.

MARX AND CLASS STRUGGLE

The usual assumption no doubt is that the socialist idea played this pivotal role in the modern world because it was the class consciousness of the "proletariat" (another neologism of the 1830s and 1840s).

But this was hardly the case. The center of the industrial revolution and the new working class was Britain, whereas the homeland of nascent socialist ideology was post-Revolutionary France, or more precisely, France during the July Monarchy of 1830–1848. It is true that Robert Owen used the adjectival noun "socialist" as early as 1827, but the main English radical movement was Chartism, which stood simply for parliamentary reform and universal suffrage. It was in France that socialists and communists of various stripes were at the forefront of a Left awaiting the next revolutionary outbreak; and it was in France, under the pen of the Saint-Simonian Pierre Leroux, in 1831, that the new concern for the "social" first acquired the totalizing suffix "ism."[15]

Yet the belief that socialism is the class consciousness of industrial workers was already prevalent during the July Monarchy. The most notable expression of this is given by Marx and Engels. In a footnote that Engels later appended to a translation of *The Manifesto*, he remarked that he and Marx had taken England as "typical" of the economic development of the "bourgeoisie," and France as typical of its political development.[16] But what he did not note was that it is a non sequitur to derive the French Revolution from English industrialization, or to deduce the later politics of French socialism from the condition of the English working class in the 1840s.[17] All of which means that the socialist impetus will be found not in economic circumstances but in political circumstances, as dramatized by the French case, and that these political circumstances are far broader than the consciousness of any one class.

As Tocqueville noted, once the old-regime hierarchy of estates was levelled, the new-regime hierarchy of classes was also logically imperiled. Thus as early as 1796 there appeared the first modern movement of levelling, the *Conspiration des Egaux* of Gracchus Babeuf. This, of course, was put down, and its heritage remained submerged until the July Revolution of 1830. But the result of this overturn was that the new "bourgeois monarchy" of the "citizen king," Louis Philippe, was riven by egalitarian sentiments and expectation of another insurrection, one that would at last complete the unfinished work of 1789, which had been too timidly resumed in 1830. So the revived Left lived in anticipation of a Second Coming of 1789, and of a New Republic that, this time, would be not merely political but social as well. It is in this perfervid atmosphere that "socialism" be-

came current; that "communism" emerged as its most radically egalitarian form, continuing in the tradition of Babeuf;[18] and that
"democracy" acquired that levelling connotation which prompted
Tocqueville's reflections on the political sociology of the modern
world.

This ebullition, which was soon to overflow in the Revolution of
1848, also prompted the more elaborate reflections on modernity of
Marx and Engels. As they often put it, their system, first fully brought
together in the *German Ideology* of 1845, was a fusion of British political
economy, French revolutionary socialism, and German classical philosophy. To the resultant amalgam they gave the most radical label of
the day, communism, and they set forth their doctrine in popular,
sloganlike form in the *Manifesto* of 1848. Though almost unknown at
the time, they and their theory were fated to have a phenomenal
destiny by the end of the century. And this was so because, for all
their years in France and England, they remained German philosophers. To the prosaic and forthright British and French contributions
to democratic modernity, they adjoined cardinal features of the German speculative tradition: its logical and visionary power, its grand
historical sweep, and its covert divination of Man. It is with this
synthesis that their movement, among all of the competing socialist
sects of that age (to which they derisively affixed the label "utopian"), would emerge as the world-historical winner in the sweep-
stakes of modern radicalism.

Since we know that Marx and Engels are going to win, it is best to
discuss the nature of their system here, in the context of the 1840s and
the period of their obscurity, rather than later, in the context of their
fin-de-siècle triumph. That is, it is best to look at Marxism at its
closest to Hegel and to philosophy, rather than in its later guise of
pseudopositivism and would-be closeness to Darwin.

The system must be approached at two levels: that of its formal
tenets and that of its deep structures. The formal tenets are the most
obvious and the best known. In brief, these are: first, a sociology in
which the economic and social base determines the cultural, political,
and ideological superstructure of society; second, a theory of history in
which mankind, driven by the class struggle, progresses from slave-
holding, to feudal, to bourgeois society, towards the end of its "pre-
history" in socialism; third, a theory of economics setting forth the

"internal contradictions" of capitalism that would at last produce the socialist revolution of the proletariat.

The formal tenets of the economic theory were the most prominent aspect of Marxism in the nineteenth century, and they indeed unfold with an implacable logic. Beginning with the principle that all value is created by human labor, this theory traces the inexorable process whereby the "surplus value" of the laborer is confiscated to produce the "accumulation of capital." This capital is then invested in labor-saving machinery, which represents both a great advance of productivity and riches for the species and the beginning of the end for the "bourgeois mode of production." For competition generates the "law of the falling rate of profit," and this produces simultaneously the concentration of capital in fewer and fewer hands and the "increasing immiseration" of the proletariat. The resulting centralization of the means of production and the socialization of labor through the factory system "at last reach a point where they become incompatible with their capitalist integument. The integument is burst asunder. The knell of capitalist private property sounds. The expropriators are expropriated." And socialism emerges from the ruins.

This entire system—the sociology, the theory of history, the economics—looks like, and indeed was intended to be, an analysis of advanced industrial society. In short, the method of Marxism appears on the surface to be specific to the most developed portions of Europe, whose civilization was viewed as the culmination of history and thus the unavoidable stage through which all more backward countries would have to pass before reaching socialism. And Marx explicitly said that Europe showed to the rest of the world its future.[19]

The socialist revolution anticipated by Marxism of course did not occur first in Western Europe. Yet this does not so much invalidate Marxism as point to the deep structure behind its formal tenets. For this deep structure is relevant to conditions anywhere in the world, even in largely preindustrial societies, and in times long after the specific internal contradictions of capitalism argued by Marx have ceased to be plausible. This deep structure is defined by the principle of contradiction itself—the dialectic—which for Hegel and Marx both was the motive force driving the logic of history. And this force operated by a perpetual process of alienation and rebirth of all being.

Hegel's presentation of this vision runs as follows: In abstract logical terms, the dialectic is a cosmic drama in which all imperfect forms of being transcend themselves through the act of losing, or alienating, themselves by subordination to something outside themselves. In theological terms—and alienation was initially a theological concept—the Incarnation is the self-alienation of God, and by the same token, the raising up of man to immortality. In the natural realm, divine reason objectifies itself in servitude to the material world in order to make manifest the rational laws of all nature. And in human history, more primitive cultural forms and nations must decay and be destroyed by higher ones in order to perfect the life of mankind as a whole: So Greece had to give way to Rome, and Rome to the barbarians in order to produce the still higher Christian, and ultimately liberal, civilization of the modern West.

Thus, everywhere progress comes about only through negation, privation, and death. Alienation, therefore, is both destructive and creative, humiliating and ennobling, enslaving and liberating: In a word, it is self-enriching. Thus, Hegelian Reason harks back to the old religious notion that he who loses his soul shall find it, and that redemption comes only through sin, suffering, and privation. Or as Hegel put the matter in more secular terms in the metaphysical parable of the master and the slave: The master affirms his selfhood imperfectly and without awareness of his identity by subjugating the slave; but the slave, in laboring for the master, transforms the material world and by his creativity rises to a more genuine selfhood; and when to this self-consciousness is adjoined the freedom of the master, the slave becomes the universal consciousness of Man.

For Marx, the process of self-enriching alienation through the master–slave dialectic comes out as the class struggle; and we should recall how central this principle is to his thought: "All history," as the first page of the *Manifesto* proclaims, "has been the history of class struggles." The matter bears emphasis because the class struggle would become the cardinal article of Marxist doctrine for the Soviets. And it must be emphasized also that this struggle is not a struggle of minds and souls, as with Hegel, but a violent, physical struggle. Taking the concept of the "*lutte de classes*" from François Guizot and other French historians of the Great Revolution, Marx transformed the religious-philosophical dialectic into class warfare.

The class struggle is fueled by the cruel but necessary exploitation of some men by others; only through such dehumanization can man at last become fully Man. Thus the labor of one class is alienated to serve another class in order to create the material means for the overall progress of the species. At the same time, class resentment of this exploitation produces social revolutions propelling humanity forward from one mode of production to another. And so history implacably advances from the struggle of plebians against patricians in antiquity to that of serfs against feudal lords in the Middle Ages, on to *la lutte finale* of the proletariat against the bourgeoisie in the modern age.

Thus, for Marx the last and greatest protagonist of the drama of human progress is the proletariat.[20] But this proletariat is not simply the "working class" as that group might be defined by some British political economist. Marx's proletariat, rather, is an analogue of what Hegel called the "universal class" of rational bureaucracy, a group whose mission was to be the vehicle of Absolute philosophy in the government of the State. Marx replaces what might be called this "universal class from above" with the proletariat, a "universal class from below"; and the proletariat's mission is to humanize a society founded on the dehumanization of class inequality, a transformation it can accomplish precisely because it is the most dehumanized class in bourgeois civil society under the State. The proletariat is thus the redeemer class because it is the productive and yet the suffering class.

As Marx himself put it in 1843, before he had ever laid eyes on real proletarians at a factory bench:

> A class must be formed which has *radical chains*, a class in civil society which is not a class in civil society, a class which is the dissolution of all classes, a sphere of society which has a universal character because its sufferings are universal, and which does not claim a *particular redress* because the wrong which was done to it is not a *particular wrong* but *wrong in general*. . . . [A class,] finally, which cannot emancipate itself without emancipating itself from all the other spheres of society without, therefore, emancipating all these other spheres, which is in short, a *total loss* of humanity and which can only redeem itself by a *total redemption of humanity*. This dissolution of society, as a particular class, is the *proletariat*.

In this scheme of redemption, backward Germany—which, because of its very backwardness, was a kind of deprived, oppressed, and proletarian nation—for the young Marx had a special mission. "This emancipation is only possible *in practice* if one adopts the point of view of that theory according to which man is the highest being for man.

Germany will not be able to emancipate itself from the *Middle Ages* unless it emancipates itself from the partial victories over the Middle Ages [that is, from mere liberalism]. In Germany *no* type of enslavement can be abolished unless *all* slavery is destroyed. . . . The *emancipation of Germany* will be an *emancipation of man*." And the passage concludes with this astounding statement: "*Philosophy* is the *head* of this emancipation and the *proletariat* is its *heart*. Philosophy can only be realized by the abolition [*Aufhebung*] of the proletariat, and the proletariat can only be abolished by the realization of philosophy."[21] In other words, for Marx the proletariat is less a social group than a metaphysical entity whose essence is given by privation, and whose deprivation is at the same time the source of the cosmic strength necessary to abolish all privation.

This paradigm or core concept of Marxism obviously echoes in secular terms (once again) one of the core concepts of Christianity. What we have here is a reprise of the classic religious logic that in the final days the last shall be first and the humble shall be exalted, but it is given a new militant, indeed vengeful cast. It is the logic of "blessed are the meek and poor in spirit, for they shall inherit the earth," but with the meek now summoned to fortify and enrich their spirit to do battle in the class struggle.

This paradigm may also be transferred from the working class of the advanced industrial nations of Europe to any other group that is deprived, humiliated, offended, exploited, or victimized. It could be applied by Lenin to a "worker and peasant alliance" in "backward" Russia. Similarly, the role of proletarian nation that Marx in 1843 had assigned to "medieval" Germany could in 1917 be transferred by Lenin to the "weakest link in the capitalist chain," "semicolonial" Russia. Or, after the Second World War, the paradigm could devolve to the Third World of excolonial and underdeveloped nations, as in the thought of Frantz Fanon and Fidel Castro, or in the politics of Mao Tse-tung and Ho Chi Minh. Or, in the overdeveloped America of the late twentieth century, the paradigm could migrate from class, to race, to gender, to sexual orientation. The essence of the "universal class" of the exploited indeed seems eternal in its universality.

For its universality rests on the faculty of what Rousseau extolled as "pity," or compassionate feeling, for those who are suffering or deprived, and this "pity" is both the emotional and the moral basis of socialism. It is also the same as that "respect for human nature" and the "common man" that Kant acknowledged he derived from Rousseau and that he put at the heart of his ethical system. And the politics of compassionate egalitarianism has always had a special appeal to the sense of *noblesse oblige* among intellectuals. But, Janus-like, it could also shade off into a consuming hatred of the master. Thus, the historical contribution of Marx was to give the quest for equality a wrathful and agonistic thrust, one possible only after the French Revolution and necessary for the success of the coming emancipatory struggle—*la lutte finale* of socialism.

HIGH CAPITALISM AND FIN DE SIÈCLE

This core paradigm, or deep structure, of Marxism is most apparent in the early works of the founders, when they were still close to Hegel and living in expectation of what became the Revolution of 1848. But beginning with *The Capital* in 1867, the tone is more like that of a scientific critique of political economy, and after Marx's death in 1883, with Engels alone in charge, the tone of the movement became increasingly positivistic: Marx the German philosopher gave way to Marx "the Darwin of the social sciences," as Engels put it at his comrade's graveside. And it is in this would-be scientific guise that Marxism at last became a world-historical force.

What catapulted Marxism out of obscurity and into prominence was the Paris Commune of 1871. This fortuitous event, produced by the Franco-Prussian War, was one with which Dr. Marx's International Working Men's Association, or the First International, had nothing to do. But the established governments of Europe, horrified at the spectacle of a major capital taken over by Red insurrection, blamed Marx's organization for the outbreak—an "honor" he was only too glad to accept. And what put Marxism over the top was the repeal, in 1891, of Bismarck's Anti-Socialist Laws, which had been passed a few years after the Paris Commune to keep the specter of revolution out of Imperial Germany. This made it possible for Marxists to capture the largest working-class party in Europe, and thus eventually to dominate the Second International, which was founded in Paris in 1889 on the hundredth anniversary of the French Revolution, both to complete its task and to continue that of the Commune.

The growing success of the socialist movement, however, also carried the danger of backsliding into moderation. Yet Marxism was ready with an antidote. Marx had adopted the most radical label on the Left for his *Manifesto* in 1848; he never liked the reformist implications of another term first heard in that year—"social democracy." Still, he was stuck with it by the new German workers' party after 1863. So, to combat this party's reformist tendencies, in the "Critique of the Gotha Program" of 1875 (published only in 1891 by Engels), he returned to the term communism and made it the higher, final stage of socialism, when "society [would] inscribe on its banner: From each according to his ability, to each according to his needs." The two-stage vision of communism arising from socialism at the end of history would be continued by Lenin and the Soviets, while at the same time furnishing the labels separating dictatorial from democratic socialists in the twentieth century. Yet it should be emphasized that throughout this process of terminological refinement the basic and generic term for the collectivist Left always remained socialism.

But the growth of the Second International, and of Marxism within it, would have been impossible without the profound economic and social changes that culminated during the last decades of the nineteenth century. For this was the period of the maturity of what Arnold Toynbee, in 1895, called the "industrial revolution." Historians today would trace its beginnings to late eighteenth-century Britain and to the first inventions—from the spinning Jenny to the steam engine—that made possible machine production. By the end of that century the factory system had replaced the domestic system of cottage manufacture in the first "modern" industry, textiles. By the 1820s the steam engine had been put on rails to produce the railroad, and this modernization of transport soon necessitated bringing together the mining of coal and the smelting of iron into a third great industrial endeavor, steel metallurgy. Thus by the eve of 1848, the mill-mine-and-smokestack economy of early industrialism had fully emerged in Britain; its apotheosis is usually taken to be the Crystal Palace Exhibition of 1851, the same year in which, for the first time, about half the population of England and Wales lived in towns.

By the 1820s the new industrial order had reached Belgium; and in the 1830s and 1840s, during the Bourgeois Monarchy, it reached France. Under this impetus, the protosocialist Saint-Simon coined the term "industrialism" to designate the new system of socioeconomic organization. It was, of course, with the evils of this new industrial world that nascent socialism was concerned, and the term "pauper-ism" took its place alongside "proletariat" to designate the humili-ated and the offended of the new order. It is obviously from this world of early industrialism that Marx derived the nonmetaphysical, or em-pirical, parts of his system, in anticipation of the industrial proletariat's appearance in Germany.

This finally occurred with the German "takeoff" of the 1860s, at roughly the same time as the great American post–Civil War surge of industrialization. By the 1880s there at last existed a genuine indus-trial society throughout Western Europe and North America. In this world the issue of "pauperism," first posed in the 1840s, became the central social issue of the age. For the condition of the new mass of workers was indeed abysmal. Moreover, the contrast with the more affluent classes was made shockingly visible by the concentration of an ever-larger proportion of Europe's population in great cities. In England, Disraeli spoke of "two nations" and Marx called the "labo-rious classes" the "dangerous classes," while the Paris Commune demonstrated both the misery and the explosive potential generated by the new urban and industrial order.

Historians have debated the human costs of unbinding the modern industrial Prometheus. In the long run, it certainly improved the ma-terial lot of most of the population in the advanced countries. But in the short run, these costs were clearly great. To be sure, life in the villages of preindustrial Europe had often been a grindingly penuri-ous one; famine was frequent as late as the "hungry forties" and migration to the cities or across the ocean to America was long the chief remedy for the most deprived. Still, life in the new industrial towns often was hardly an improvement: Housing was primitive, san-itary conditions were appalling, and labor was arduous and poorly remunerated. In addition, the factory worker had lost the indepen-dence of the artisan or peasant freeholder and become a mere cog in a vast machine controlled by capital. Moreover, the working class was as yet largely ununionized, without the right to strike, and without any social-security "safety net." By the fin de siècle, the proletariat thus was indeed the most deprived, excluded, and victimized group in society.

Accordingly, its right to organize, to be heard, and to find expres-sion in political parties was therefore at the cutting edge of democratic politics; and since by the end of the century this group represented about one-third of the urban population, the "labor question" became an ever more pressing one. The Second International, accordingly, made May Day the international feast of labor, and in 1892 it adopted the "Internationale" as its hymn to replace the once revolutionary but now "bourgeois republican" anthem "The Marseillaise."

Drawing strength from a mature industrial system and a growing working class, the Second International merited its name far more than the First. By 1905, nationwide socialist parties had also appeared in Britain, France, Austria, and the lesser European states; even the United States had something of a socialist movement. To be sure, nowhere in the Western world were socialists near to being a majority (their highest tally was in Germany in 1912, when they polled one-third of the vote); still less was there any prospect of socialists coming to power. Classical liberalism, rugged individualism, laissez-faire economics, and constitutional democracy were still very much in the ascendancy throughout the Western world. Nonetheless, Marx's "specter of Communism," which in 1848 had been little more than a bogeyman, was now a fairly substantial affair. And his doctrine, made prestigious by the success of German Social Democracy, was in one or another form taken up in all branches of the International, from that of Jean Jaurès in France to that of Georgii Plekhanov in Russia.

It is the positivistic and *ouvriériste* Marxism of the Second International that would be adapted in Russia to produce, at last, the world's first Marxist revolution. In this period it is the economic and sociological tenets, the formal features of the doctrine, that came to the fore. The emphasis of Marxist parties, therefore, was on the implacable logic of history leading Europe, stage by stage, from feudal, to bourgeois, to socialist society. But the more romantic, metaphysical, and revolutionary deep structure of self-transcending alienation was never far below the surface, and crisis would bring it out.

Thus Marxism came to possess a unique winning combination of qualities: The genius of the system is to express a pseudosalvation religion as a would-be positive science, and to combine the consolations hitherto reserved for the next world with the certitude of scientific knowledge that is man's supreme intellectual achievement in this one. As Alain Besançon put it: "Moses and Saint John ... knew that they believed. ... [Marx and] Lenin believed that they knew."[22]

* * *

The potency of Marxism is reinforced by the doctrine's association with a vaguer and vaster term than socialism, one capable of bringing nonsocialists into the moral fellowship of reason and progress—the Left.[23] The division of the political world into two camps, the Left and the Right, dates of course from the French Revolution and the seating arrangements of radicals and moderates in its various assemblies; by the time of the Restoration, this bifurcation had become more or less synonymous with two other new labels, "liberals" and "conservatives." From its origins in France, where politics were dynamic and ideological, the division by the 1830s had spread eastward to Germany, where politics did not yet exist, and where it was applied to ideology alone, as in such a term as "Left Hegelian." In this extended meaning the dichotomy spread throughout Europe, coming into use last in countries where politics were more gradualistic and pragmatic: It reached Britain towards the end of the nineteenth century and the United States at the beginning of the twentieth, thereby radicalizing their existing Liberal-Conservative and Democratic-Republican divides.

The destiny of this dichotomy was that its content shifted constantly to the Left over time. At the beginning, the "Left" meant opposition to traditional kingship in favor of, at the least, a constitutional monarchy, or, on its more radical fringe, a democratic republic founded on universal suffrage; it also meant hostility towards established religion. The "Right" stood reactively for defense of "altar and throne," and later for holding the line against democracy at a property suffrage. Moreover, since the successive revolutionary shocks of 1789, 1830, and 1848 were pushing history itself to the Left, the latter camp also came to be known as the "party of movement," whereas the Right became known as the "party of resistance." Eighteen forty-eight, finally, made the "people" the spearhead of the Left, thereby bringing to the fore the notion that the political republic was not enough, and that a social republic, or "social democracy," was necessary for true human emancipation. And so socialism found its place on the left of the Left.

The year 1848 also gave this socialist Left its great symbol, the Red Flag. This banner had been used under the Old Regime as a means of reading the riot act and heralding the repression of civil disorder. But the flag's meaning was reversed on the second Bastille Day, in 1791, when the "hero of two worlds," Lafayette, raised it to put down in blood a radical protest; the symbol of seditious riot was taken up in defiance and transformed into that of liberating revolution. Although the Red Flag was rejected by the Second Republic in 1848, it remained in reserve should the softer elements of the Left ever falter or fail. And this banner would henceforth be juxtaposed with the White Flag of the Bourbons, the symbol of counterrevolution since the aristocratic terror that accompanied the Restoration in 1814.

Thus the socialist ideal continued to drive the Left leftward until the end of the century. And at the very fin de siècle, the movement acquired two new overlays: internationalism and the struggle for peace.

For a century after 1789, the Left had been patriotic and, indeed, had gloried in wars of revolutionary liberation; these sentiments, culminating in the "Springtime of the Peoples" of 1848, had still inspired the Parisian Communards as late as 1871. But the emergence of this nationalism was only the logical counterpart of democracy founded on "one man one vote." For once all the king's subjects have become equal citizens, a uniform bloc or mass is created, and kingdoms give way to nations animated by a general will. But universal suffrage also logically entails universal military service—which is one reason, along with the development of science and technology, why modern wars have generally been far bloodier than earlier ones.

At the century's close, most of Europe was organized into compact nation-states with mass conscript armies. Thus the socialist advocates of the worker-soldier became internationalists, and in their new hymn proclaimed that "tomorrow the International would be the human race." Concurrently, the former defenders of altar-and-throne discovered in the new nation a bulwark of social order and turned into patriots, even chauvinists, arrayed against "those fellows without a fatherland," as Kaiser Wilhelm II called his worker-conscripts. And so nationalism—now often combined with a new political anti-Semitism—migrated from Left to Right, and the lyricism of Mazzini and Mickiewicz gave way to the strident tones of Treitschke and Barrès.

This shift was accompanied by the emergence of the world's first peace movement. Beginning with the Enlightenment, visionaries like the Abbé de Saint-Pierre and Kant (in the wake of such religious pacifists as the Quakers) had imagined schemes for "perpetual peace." But on the whole the Europe of peoples found war as noble as had the Europe of kings. It was only in the buildup to 1914 that concern for peace became a mass cause, and that the Socialist International emerged as its principal voice. So as the European powers, driven by both greed and vainglory, scrambled to partition Africa and Asia, economic "imperialism" was denounced as the cause of war by liberals and socialists alike, and thus viewed as a rival international force.

And so, by the eve of 1914, the Left was a diffuse entity of populist, pacifist, internationalist, and usually secular forces increasingly weighted toward its internal, socialist left. And the dynamic that held this coalition together, while at the same time giving socialism the moral edge within it, was fear of the Right and the threat of reaction. "No enemies to the Left" became the golden rule of progressive politics, and "playing into the hands of the Right" the great betrayal of the cause of progress. By the First World War, this internationalist political culture would furnish the indispensable matrix for both the domestic and foreign fortunes of Bolshevism.

But where, in the nineteenth-century discourse on society, is the missing link in the conceptual chain—namely, the "capitalism" that socialism is supposed to replace? The fact is that until almost the end of the century people did not talk about capitalism at all; and when they did take up the term, the initiative came not from the "capitalists" themselves, but from socialists seeking to brand the world they hoped to negate.[24]

One will search in vain for the word capitalism in Adam Smith, David Ricardo, Jean-Baptiste Say, John Stuart Mill, or any of the other worthies of classical political economy. Indeed, one will not even find the word in Karl Marx. The term "capital" had been in use since the sixteenth century to signify the monetary and material means of production. The word "capitaliste" appears in the *Encyclopedia* of Diderot to designate the owner of capital, or an entrepreneur. But by around 1830, "capital" had come to mean the social power of money, or the "monied interest" as a political force. And this, of course, is the usage that Marx picked up and generalized into the "capitalist mode of production." He also spoke of "bourgeois society" (*moderne bürgerliche Gesellschaft*) and called "our epoch" the "epoch of the bourgeoisie" (this time using the French word, more clearly a socioeconomic term than the German *Bürgertum*).[25] But he never made the leap to the substantive "ism," which, as with all such words, has the effect of hypostatizing matters into a total system, fusing the economic, the social, the political, and the cultural realms into a single whole endowed with its own inherent "logic."

The substantive "capitalism" was first, and only occasionally, used by such socialists as Louis Blanc in the 1840s, and then only in the pejorative sense of a system working for the owners of capital. It was with this meaning that it was put into broader circulation around 1870 by such figures as Karl von Rodbertus and Karl Liebknecht. From Germany, it next made its way not to England, as we might expect, but to Russia in the 1877 program of the revolutionary organization "Land and Freedom."[26] Indeed, Russian peasant-oriented socialists had already shown themselves to be more precocious than the entire industrial West by giving Marx's *Capital* its first translation into a foreign language in 1872. All of which serves to show, once again, that the socialist and revolutionary impulse derives initially from moral and political, rather than economic, considerations.

The real emergence of "capitalism" to designate a total system dates only from the 1890s. This occurred under the combined influence of the rise of German Social Democracy and of the *Methodenstreit* (methodological debate) in German economics between the adherents of the British analytical approach and those of the native historical school. In this debate the latter took up the socialists' old polemical slogan and gave it massive structural and developmental content, with the result that by 1900, for both German liberals and socialists, modernity came to be defined as "capitalism" in the sense of an all-encompassing system.[27] Thus Werner Sombart produced his *Modern Capitalism* in 1902, and Max Weber his *Protestant Ethic and the Spirit of Capitalism* in 1904. (Yet Lenin, benefiting from the precocity of Russian radicalism, had already beaten them to the draw with *The Development of Capitalism in Russia*, which he composed in Siberia and published in 1899.) Thus it is the German tradition of global synthesis, going back to Kant and Hegel, and now turned to answering the challenge of Social Democracy, that produced the last of the great nineteenth-century "isms." The historically more advanced yet conceptually laggard French, British, and Americans would not fully naturalize this terminology until after 1917.

Yet what did this neologism mean once it had become the coin of the Western cultural realm? "Capitalism" clearly means quite a bit more than "socialism," since it refers to institutions that really existed before it came into being. Still, it does not signify anything that can be rigorously defined and clearly delineated historically. Thus, like socialism, it is a metaphysical far more than an empirical term. And like socialism, its meaning ranges from the ethical to the institutional spheres, when it does not combine and confuse the two. Morally, it carries a positive charge of dynamism, but a far stronger negative charge of individual greed and social exploitation. Institutionally, it ranges from the extreme laissez-faire policies of nineteenth-century Manchester liberalism—what its critics call "wild" or "untamed capitalism"—to a whole gamut of twentieth-century modes of state regulation in the service of the welfare state. Historically, it covers various degrees of development, from sixteenth and seventeenth century merchant and "comprador" capitalism, to the classical industrial system, to the postindustrial service-dominated economy. And sociologically, within the twentieth century, its ranges from the predominantly free market of the United States, to the more *dirigiste* and "social market" economies of the European Community, to the state-industrial corporatism of Japan.

To call all of this "capitalism," though not actually meaningless, is not very helpful in understanding how the "system" works, or how its institutions came into being. Indeed, for practical purposes it would be a blessing if we could get rid of the term capitalism, together with its polar opposite, socialism. But this is not a likely prospect, since there does exist a core reality behind the various capitalisms—a core which is precisely the mirror image of integral socialism. For all the societies that may plausibly be called capitalist accept, in some measure, the institutions of private property, profit, and the market. Yet at the same time these institutions always conflict, in some measure, with the egalitarian ideals embedded in the democratic political forms necessary to the optimal functioning of the "capitalist" economies. So the polarity of "cap-ism" and "soc-ism," to use Aleksandr Zinoviev's vocabulary, while analytically obfuscating, nonetheless retains its moral magnetism. The two, like Siamese twins, remain joined at the spine by the eternally raw issue of property.

Once all of Europe had adopted the new totalizing term "capitalism," around 1900, it immediately fell under the political rubric of the Right. For the term's predominantly negative connotation made it a liability in democratic politics, where the moral high ground is invariably occupied by the Left. Candidates rarely advertise themselves as champions of capital, whereas concern for labor and the public profession of socialist ideals is usually an admissible, and often an advantageous, stance.

And so, by 1914, a dual process of amalgamation had occurred: On the Right were aligned capitalism, unbridled individualism, nationalism, militarism, and social hierarchy; and on the Left were arrayed socialism, economic rationality, internationalism, peace, and equality. The stage was thus set for the great *Auseinandersetzung*, the world-historical clash, between capitalism and socialism that would dominate our short twentieth century.

This clash, however, did not occur in the designated world-historical place, the mature industrial West, nor according to proper historical procedures, through the dynamic of social revolution. Hegel's Cunning of Reason[28] played a perverse trick on all its historical pawns. For the world's first socialist revolution triumphed in the most backward nation of Europe, Russia; and it did so not through the logic of Russia's internal processes, but because of the "accidental," or contingent, factor of external war. And the result was the paradox of a proletarian revolution in an overwhelmingly peasant country.

This untoward outcome has often been taken to exculpate the Revolution from its obvious later shortcomings, or even to suggest that backward Russia somehow spoiled the logic of history. In other words, the problem with the Bolshevik Revolution was not integral socialism; it was Russia. But in fact there is no paradox at all; the significance of the unexpected results of October is simply that the formal tenets of the Marxist theory underlying it are wrong.

Nevertheless, October does have its logic, though not that of its authors' formal doctrine. And this logic is quite compatible with Marxism's deeper structure: the self-enriching alienation of privation and suffering, as this dynamic was expressed after 1914 in the devastation of modern, total war. Therein lies the "rational" character of the apparent paradox. For all Marxist revolutions, from that of Lenin to those of Mao and Ho Chi Minh, and from the First World War to the Second, were produced in backward countries and under the impact of war. This *is* their logic, and not an accident at all.

2

AND WHY IN RUSSIA FIRST?

These poor villages, these humble fields,
O native land of long suffering,
Land of the Russian people!

—Fedor Tiutchev, 1855

There are at the present two great nations in the world . . . the Russians
and the Americans. Both have grown up unnoticed . . . and the world
learned of their existence and their greatness at almost the same time. . . .

The American struggles against the obstacles which nature opposes to
him; the adversaries of the Russian are men. The former combats the
wilderness and savage life; the latter, civilization with all its arms. The
conquests of the American are therefore gained by the ploughshare; those
of the Russian by the sword.

The Anglo-American relies upon personal interest to accomplish his
ends, and gives free scope to the unguided strength and common sense of
the people; the Russian centers all the authority of society in a single arm.
The principal instrument of the former is freedom; of the latter, servitude.
Their starting point is different, and their courses are not the same; yet
each seems marked out by the will of Heaven to sway the destinies of half
the globe.

—Alexis de Tocqueville, Democracy in America, *1838*

The Great October Socialist Revolution, as it was once invariably called by the Kremlin, is noteworthy not just because it was socialist but also because it could have occurred in no other country but Russia. For the Empire of the Tsars was indeed the weakest link in the European "capitalist" order, as Lenin correctly perceived. But what in the pattern of Russia's development accounts for this fateful weakness? And what is the historical logic that conferred on her the improbable destiny of becoming the first nation to cross the world-historical threshold from capitalism to socialism?

One widespread view of this logic is that the despotism and the servitude of old Russia simply reproduced themselves in socialist guise in the totalitarianism of Soviet Russia. Russia's destiny, therefore, was to be essentially unchanging, and her history could be summed up as the transition from the "white to the red eagle."[1] Historically, this view has been particularly prevalent in Poland and Hungary, and among Germans of the Left. This is so for the obvious and sufficient reason that from the late eighteenth century onward Russian power has regularly and brutally intervened in that area— from the Partitions of Poland between 1772 and 1796 to the crushing of the Revolution of 1848, and on down to the "Brezhnev Doctrine" of 1968. Though he obviously could not have compared old Russia with its Soviet successor, Marx, like most 1848 Germans, was convinced that tsardom was a Byzantine-Mongol monstrosity incapable of change and eventual Europeanization.[2]

On a superficial glance at the historical record, this view would seem to have much empirical evidence in its favor. Old Russia, after all, knew a regime of serfdom verging on chattel slavery from the late sixteenth century to the peasant Emancipation of 1861, that is, longer than anywhere else in Europe, and in more brutal form. Soviet Russia, in the institution of Stalin's collective farms, developed a new and even more exploitative type of serfdom. Old Russia sent its dissidents and political prisoners to the frozen waste of Siberia; the new Russia did the same in Stalin's Gulag. Finally, the immutable political order of old Russia was autocracy, and her historical development was marked by despotic, indeed at times insane revolutions from above under Ivan the Terrible and Peter the Great. The new Soviet autocracy was brought to its perfection by the even more terrible revolution from above of Stalin. In short, Russia throughout her history has been an "Oriental despotism"; it has always been quite separate and apart from Europe or the West, "whose history is the history of freedom," as Hegel and Ranke put the matter.[3]

All of these similarities between old Russia and Soviet Russia have real bases in fact. But similarities are not the same as continuities, and still less are they causal explanations. For what is lacking in this monochrome picture is the presence of empirically documented agents of transmission taking us from Ivan and Peter to Lenin and Stalin. Moreover, the Russian people in 1917, as well as the outside world, had the overwhelming impression of a radical break in October. And this should lead us to suspect that the thesis of basic continuity in Russian history is founded on the fallacious principle of *post hoc, ergo propter hoc,* of "after this, therefore because of this." The fallacy of this causal principle, of course, does not mean that old Russia did not mold its Soviet successor in many decisive ways, but simply that the process through which this occurred was much more complex than one of direct continuity.

RUSSIA AND EUROPE

The thesis that Russia throughout her history has been an "Oriental despotism" obviously goes *pari passu* with the idea that there exists a clear and distinct contrasting entity called "Europe" or "the West." In other words, in this interpretation we are dealing with unchanging cultural essences in the metaphysical sense of that word. Indeed, most people in the modern age function automatically as if the Europe–Asia dichotomy was built into world history from the beginning. Leaving Russia aside for the moment, what are we in fact talking about when we speak of "Europe" and "the West"?[4]

The word Europe as a geographical term appeared as early as the Greeks and at first referred only to the Aegean Peninsula. Eventually, of course, it came to refer to the whole of what is now called Europe, and at the Congress of Vienna in 1815 its eastern frontier was officially fixed at the Urals. The use of the term Europe to designate a culture or a civilization, however, is of very recent vintage, dating only from the eighteenth century. And at that time it also took on the connotation that the area in question represented the most enlightened and civilized portion of mankind, and the culmination of historical development.

Yet well before the eighteenth century, the European peoples had a clear sense of their kinship and distinctiveness, as well as an exalted view of their preeminence in the world. This distinctiveness, however, was defined in religions, not in secular terms. They thus referred to their society as Christendom (*Christianitas,* or the *respublica Christiana*), a term created under the Carolingian Empire, which viewed itself as the continuation of the Roman Empire reborn as a higher, Christian entity. And this new term replaced the older word *Romanitas*, which had defined the Empire—even after Christianity under Constantine had become its dominant religion—in political, not religious, terms. To emphasize this change in values, the Carolingians started counting the years from the birth of Christ (and numbering them *anno Domini*, or A.D.) rather than from the beginning of the world, which was the Hebrew manner previously used by Christians.

To be sure, the Eastern Empire was also Christian; but there the Greek Church remained subordinate to the state, and these "Byzantines," therefore, continued to call their world *Romanitas*. Nor did they change their calendar as a sign that they lived in a new, messianic era; this revolutionary pretension was characteristic only of what the Byzantine Greeks now viewed as the "barbarian West." This division of the old world of Imperial *Romanitas* is, of course, the origin of the idea of "the West" as a civilization distinct from "the East," or "Asia," or "the Orient." And with the passage of centuries this once backward West would come to regard itself as higher than all its stagnant neighbors to the East.

What is now called Europe is the civilization that came out of Western, or Latin, Christendom during the millennium after Charlemagne, a civilization that defined itself in opposition to both Eastern Christianity and Islam. Geographically, this included the lands of the Carolingian Empire—France, the Low Countries, northern Italy, western Germany—and the British Isles. Over the next four centuries this area expanded east and north by converting the Western Slavs and the Scandinavians; it also expanded south, in a series of Crusades, by conquering the Iberian Peninsula and southern Italy. Then, in the sixteenth century, this dynamic Christendom grew in a quantum leap to take in the whole Western hemisphere; at the same time, its navigators traveled east to the Indies and Cathay, thereby for the first time achieving the unity of the planet. Thus, however unfair it may be to most of mankind, the modern world is in fact a Eurocentric creation.

In other words, Europe, or the West, is not a fixed geographical entity. Nor is it a static cultural quantity, for the initial medieval Catholic civilization received numerous overlays in the course of its expansion. To mention only the most obvious and most important: With the classical humanism of the fifteenth century, this civilization began to be secularized; and with the religious schism of the Protestant Reformation in the sixteenth century, the unity of Latin Christendom was shattered. Then, as already noted, the Scientific Revolution of the seventeenth century produced the overtly antireligious challenge of the Enlightenment in the eighteenth century. As a result, the culture of Christendom was secularized in the two meanings of that word: Religion was displaced from the center of life, and formerly religious and transcendent values were often transmuted into rationalistic and immanent ones. It is at this juncture, and because of this new secularizing culture, that in the eighteenth century the term Europe displaced the term Christendom. Add to this the fact that the eighteenth century marked the great takeoff of Europe into sustained economic growth, and we have a picture of the West as a dynamic, expanding entity, and of Europe as a "moveable feast" in which new nations were constantly able to join.

Russia, of course, joined this expanding Concert of Europe under Peter the Great at the beginning of the eighteenth century. This event was not a great shock to either party, however, because the Europe Russia joined was kindred in two respects.[5] The first was that the Enlightenment had softened the once central importance of the antagonism between Western and Eastern Christianity; consequently, the "enlightened despotism" of Peter the Great and Catherine the Great, in the eyes of most educated men of the age, made their Empire seem a genuine part of Europe. The second factor of kinship was that the social and political forms of Western old-regime absolutism were not strikingly different from what might be called the universal service state of the tsardom of Muscovy before Peter. Thus the new Imperial Russia of the eighteenth century became more or less a European-style Old Regime, or, if one prefers, a military monarchy.

Russia in this new, early modern Europe, therefore, is best understood not in terms of the antithesis "Russia and the West," but as part of a continentwide West-East continuum, or of what the Germans call the West-East cultural gradient. In this perspective, Russia is the eastern extreme of a gradation of European Old Regimes running from the more elaborate and developed to the more simple and brutal. In short, she is the backward rear guard of Europe at the bottom of the slope of the West-East cultural gradient.

This view of the matter is, indeed, a frequent perception in nations east of the Rhine, among the Germans, the Poles, and especially the

Russians; each of these nations has progressively more layers of "Western" Europe to compare its own development with, and hence, is more conscious of the gradations of development. It is this perception that is expressed, for example, in Leon Trotsky's once famous "law of combined and uneven development," by which he meant that Russia's backwardness forced her to compress or telescope stages of development that farther West were spread out over a long period and many stages.

The most sophisticated expression of this comparative cultural perspective is that given by Alexander Gerschenkron in his *Economic Backwardness in Historical Perspective*.[6] Gerschenkron was primarily concerned with economic development and the history of industrialization. His thesis is that the farther east in Europe one goes, the more agrarian and backward societies become, and, therefore, the faster the pace at which they must move to catch up with a constantly rising standard of modernity set by the western edge of the continent. Under these circumstances the only possible agent for such accelerated transformation is the state. Thus, the farther east one goes—from the France of Louis Philippe and Napoleon III, to the Prussia of the Zollverein in the 1830s, to the Russia of Finance Minister Sergei Witte in the 1890s—the greater the role of the state in forcing development. To this there is a cultural corollary, namely, that socialist ideologies from Saint-Simonism under Napoleon III to "legal Marxism" under Witte played an increasingly important role in promoting this forced development from above. It is this "model" that will be followed here. However, it will be used in an adapted and expanded form, applied to historical change generally, rather than to economic development specifically.

Modern Russia's backwardness was not just economic; it was all-encompassing, involving the economic, the social, the political, and the cultural at once. Yet this had not been the case uniformly throughout Russian history. So let us begin with the beginning and with the basics.

The Russian Empire that produced the October Revolution and the Soviet regime grew out of the Grand Principality of Muscovy, a once small nucleus in a corner of the East Slavic lands. Muscovy itself was a fragment of an earlier entity, the Grand Principality of Kiev, or, more simply, *Rus*. Kievan *Rus* had a rather typical post-Roman, European origin, and it took shape, in the ninth century, at the same time as its Frankish Carolingian contemporary farther west: It was a barbarian kingdom that achieved legitimation and promotion to civilized status by conversion to the Christianity of the Roman world, but in this case it was the Christianity of the eastern capital, Constantinople, rather than that of old Rome. In short, Kievan *Rus*, like all future European states, represented a fusion of Roman, Christian, and barbarian elements that is the foundation of the European formula—though in the case of Kiev a different group of barbarians and different variants of *Romanitas* and Christianity were involved. In other words, Kiev was a variation on the fundamental European theme.[7]

The promising development of the Kievan protostate was interrupted in the thirteenth century by the commercial decline of Constantinople and especially by the Mongol conquest of most of *Rus* itself. The result was a fractured East Slavic World. The western part of this world—what is now Belarus and a good part of Ukraine—the nobility inherited power, and their territories were eventually absorbed into the "noble republic" of the Polish-Lithuanian Commonwealth. In the north, the Republic of Novgorod continued the old commercial and municipal civilization of Kiev, but this was now oriented towards the string of Hanseatic cities from Flanders to the Baltic Sea. And in the northeast, the poorest and most backward part of the East European plain, it was the power of the prince, not that of the nobility or of the commercial municipalities, that survived from the wreckage of *Rus*.

It was in this northeastern forest zone, by the late fifteenth century, that Muscovy emerged as an autocratic power capable at last of freeing itself from the "Tatar yoke." But this new freedom did not mean an automatic return to Europe, for Muscovy, after the final schism of the Churches in the early fifteenth century, regarded the West with deep suspicion as a world given over to the "Latin heresy." This autocratic Muscovy, militarized by its two-century struggle against the Mongols, then snuffed out free Novgorod and annexed its lands; beginning in the seventeenth century, it started on the conquest of Poland-Lithuania. Finally, in the enlightened eighteenth century, Peter and Catherine completed this process by taking over the present-day Baltic states and the lion's share of Poland, thus giving the Russian Empire its basic modern form. To consecrate this result, and to assert equality with the proudest European powers, Peter took the Imperial title of old East Rome, thereby claiming for the Muscovite state the supreme dignity in the European historical tradition.

Thus the modern Russian Empire was created by the most backward, primitive, and militarized portion of the East Slavic lands, an area that generated this conquering power precisely because it was a frontier march against the steppe barbarians. In this respect the Russian experience is similar to the modern German one, in which it was a backward, militarized, and autocratic Brandenburg-Prussia that wound up absorbing the more developed western and southern portions of the German-speaking lands.

The dynamic of the political advantages of backwardness for Russian Imperial state-building must be sought in the internal development of Muscovy before Peter.[8] Situated at the northeastern extremity of the northern European forested plain, Muscovy had poorer soil, a harsher climate, and a shorter growing season than elsewhere in Europe. To mention only what is most basic: The agricultural revolution of the three-field system that occurred in far-western Europe in the twelfth century, and that reached central Europe in the fourteenth century, did not come to Muscovy until the second half of the fifteenth century; and commercial towns date only from the sixteenth century and did not become a notable factor until the nineteenth. The result of all this was that the material base of the Muscovite state (and later that of Imperial Russia) was extremely weak.

At the same time, this state confronted exceptional military problems: It was exposed to nomadic incursions from the vast open steppes to the south, and it lacked natural frontiers at any of its borders. This was the origin of the exceptional militarization of the Muscovite state and, therefore, of its society. By the sixteenth century, the service gentry, or *dvoriantsvo*, was wholly subordinated to the autocratic tsar, and the peasants were enserfed to support the gentry, while both the peasants and the small class of townsmen paid taxes to the state, and the clergy prayed for the success of the whole. Thus, in Russia the lord-peasant order of traditional Europe was organized to meet the military needs of the monarchy in what is best described as a universal service state.

What Peter the Great did was to remold this primitive set of arrangements more or less on the pattern of the military absolutisms of the rest of old-regime Europe.[9] The key to all of these early modern state formations was the need to field a large standing army. Until the early

seventeenth century, the military forces of Europe had been composed of postfeudal militias, noble levies, or mercenary units. For a
variety of reasons that need not concern us here, it was only in the
mid-seventeenth century that a regular and permanent standing
army—one in which everyone wore the king's uniform and that eventually would be quartered in his barracks—became a necessity for any
state wishing to remain competitive internationally. The great model
for this development, of course, is the France of Louis XIV, but the
Sweden of Gustavus Adolfus, and the Brandenburg-Prussia of the
Great Elector are equally apposite examples. In each case the internal
administrative and fiscal systems of the state had to be adjusted to
meet these military needs. In such a world, states that could not adapt
their structures in time—notably, the Polish-Lithuanian Commonwealth—were fated to disappear from the map of Europe.[10]

Russia under Peter made an exceptionally successful adaptation.
Louis XIV, with the great wealth of France to draw on, could field
four hundred thousand men against the combined resources of Britain, Holland, and Austria. Peter, with the far more meager resources
of Russia, could field two hundred thousand, which was quite enough
against then-declining Sweden, and twice as much as Prussia could
boast at the time.

Peter achieved this very considerable feat by revolutionary state
action from above. The crux of the Petrine reform is that backward
Muscovy, once freed of the Mongols, was confronted by the far more
serious challenge of the early modern European military revolution.
Since the Russian economy and society were too weak to meet this
challenge on their own initiative, the meager resources of the country
had to be mobilized and squeezed to the limit by brutal state action
from above. This is similar to what the Great Elector had done fifty
years earlier with the comparably meager resources of Prussia. And in
both cases the great-power status that resulted would be maintained
until the catastrophic wars of the twentieth century.

NARROWING THE GAP

The pattern of revolution from above as the response of backward
Russia to the challenge of the West would be maintained down to the
end of the Old Regime in 1917.[11] This challenge would always remain

to some degree military, insofar as modern warfare became increasingly dependent on advanced technology. But over time the challenge would evolve from a relatively simple military matter to ever more complex economic, political, and cultural ones. As the West constantly upped the ante of what it meant to be European and modern, so Russia had to develop correspondingly more complex adaptations to each new Western level of development; and as time went by, it became increasingly difficult to make these adaptations by brutal state initiative from above. More and more, the resources of society had to be mobilized by society itself, which eventually took over the task of modernization from the state.

The first of these new-type challenges was the democratic shock of the French Revolution. For once the absolutist state was no longer the major force for progress in most of the West, and when the torch of modernity had been passed to the people, the Russian autocratic state was also automatically out of date, laggard, and even reactionary, first in the eyes of the West, and ultimately in the eyes of its increasingly more educated elite. Thus, since Russia remained a serf-based society in the midst of the new Europe of the democratic idea, the whole system was increasingly placed under dangerous strains.

These strains were all the greater because the Russian Old Regime, as put together by Peter, was a very rudimentary affair. The greatest of Russian historians, Vasilii Kliuchevskii, has accurately emphasized the extreme simplicity of Russia's historical processes (as compared with those of more Western European countries), a fact that derives largely from the starkness of her class structure.[12] Until well into the nineteenth century there were, in effect, only two classes in Russia, or at least only two that mattered. There was the service gentry (*dvoriantsvo*), which constituted about 2 percent of the population; and there was the peasantry, which until the 1890s constituted roughly 95 percent of the population. The gentry possessed most of the wealth, monopolized all privileges, staffed the state bureaucracy, officered the military forces, and in addition dominated culture. The peasantry, one half of their numbers enserfed to the gentry and the other half to the state, labored to maintain the nation materially, paid taxes, and furnished the foot soldiers of the military. To be sure, other estates existed as well—the merchants and the clergy—but they were insignificant numerically and counted for even less socially.

The introduction of the post–French Revolutionary concept of democracy into such a world could only have a devastating effect. The means through which this new and radical form of Europeanization made itself felt was a group that came to be known by the mid-nineteenth century as the intelligentsia.[13]

From the time of Peter, one of the principal ways in which the Russian state modernized its society was to build an educational system. Beginning with elite universities, and only later going on to secondary gymnasia and finally to elementary schools, this system sought to absorb and transmit the advanced culture of the West. Initially this was intended, and did in fact serve, to strengthen the power of the state. But in the early nineteenth century the tiny educated elite, overwhelmingly from the gentry, began to demand the rights of political participation and personal liberty put forward by contemporary Western liberalism; this only panicked the apprehensive autocracy, which was ever mindful of Russia's long history of peasant revolts. The greatest of these, that of Pugachev as recently as 1774, was what Pushkin had in mind when he spoke of "the Russian *bunt* [anarchic riot], mindless and pitiless."[14] Indeed, at the very beginning of the century, the ultraconservative Joseph de Maistre had warned Alexander I, who continued the Imperial tradition of enlightenment from above, that the real danger to the fragile structures of the Empire was not so much the peasants themselves as an eventual *"Pougatcheff d'université."*

The first such intellectual rebels appeared in the uniforms of the Imperial guards at Alexander's death in 1825. These Decembrists, as they came to be called, attempted an armed coup against his heir with the aim of giving Russia a constitution and abolishing serfdom. After their failure, the new emperor, Nicholas I, repressed all manifestations of nascent liberalism throughout his thirty-year reign. In response, the gentry intellectuals only became more political, but in the theoretical, not the practical, domain. On the one hand, the Westernizers argued that Russia, despite Nicholas, was destined eventually to retrace Europe's path to constitutional liberty, and their model was July Monarchy France. On the other hand, the Slavophiles, like the German romantic conservatives, were fearful of the disruptive Western path, and so insisted that Russia's development must be founded on the patriarchal and communal ways of the native tradition. And well might the Slavophiles have been afraid, for the most radical Westernizers, Mikhail Bakunin and Aleksandr

Herzen, by the Revolution of 1848 were demanding the ultimate in matters democratic: socialism.

Under Russian conditions, however, this new doctrine could not have the proletariat as its universal class; only the peasantry—the people, or the *narod*—could play that role.[15] So Herzen and Bakunin advanced a new version of the socialist utopia: peasant socialism, founded on the village commune, or *obshchina*. This theory, later known as *narodnichestvo*, or Populism, asserted that the peasants were innately socialist because they had no private property: They held their lands collectively and redistributed them periodically within the commune as families changed in size. Populism asserted further that the peasants were innately revolutionary because they were chattel serfs of their gentry lords. Consequently, the democratic revolution in Russia would be simplicity itself: A peasant uprising would destroy the autocracy and the gentry, and socialism would virtually exist in the form of the village commune.

Thus backward Russia, in a single revolution, would be able to leap directly from the Old Regime to socialism and avoid the Western halfway house of bourgeois constitutionalism. And so, at the same time that Marx created the greatest social fantasy of the age for the industrial West, Russia produced an answering, though more primitive, fantasy for the rural East: Backwardness was transformed from a burden into an advantage, and the last nation of Europe came to see itself as potentially the first.

In the next reign, the radical wing of the intelligentsia got its chance to act on the Populist fantasy. In the 1860s, Alexander II carried out a liberalizing revolution from above with the Emancipation of the serfs in 1861, followed by the creation of elected organs of local self-government, the *zemstvos*, and an independent judiciary in 1864. These Great Reforms were a close analogue of the Prussian Reform of 1806–1810, which introduced that part of the French Revolution's agenda that was compatible with the preservation of aristocracy and absolute monarchy. Alexander's aim was a similar controlled modernization, and he indeed narrowed the gap with the rest of Europe more than did any sovereign since Peter. But as Tocqueville famously observed, the most dangerous time for a bad government is when it starts to reform itself. And indeed, the more impatient members of the intelligentsia were radicalized by the Great Reforms to the point where they produced a continuing revolutionary movement.

This change was effected in the sixties by the revolt of the plebian "sons" against their gentry "fathers," in Ivan Turgenev's famous dichotomy. The latter were liberals in politics and philosophical idealists and romantics in culture; or when they were socialists, like Herzen and Bakunin, they sought to fuse German philosophy with French socialism, Hegel with Saint-Simon or Proudhon. The uncouth sons, often from clerical families, adjoined to their Populism a philosophical "nihilism" that was an aggressive compound of positivism, materialism, and utilitarian ethics; in this perspective, gentry liberals were judged to be worse enemies of progress than the autocracy itself. Herzen called these commoners "the bilious ones," and they indeed represented a particularly hard-bitten and crude strain of the European Enlightenment tradition.

Their great figure was Nikolai Chernyshevskii, literary critic and social philosopher. In his worldview everything in life was subordinated to politics and the service of the people. All art had to be civic, all personal relationships had to be sacrificed to the public cause, and all energies devoted to the revolution which would bring Russia to the Crystal Palace of a rational society. He expounded this ethos in 1863 in a utopian novel, *What Is To Be Done?*, which for the next half-century would be the revolutionary breviary of the "repentant noblemen" who increasingly rallied to the people's cause.

In the same years, this cause became an active revolutionary movement. The Emancipation radicalized the Populists because of what they believed was a niggardly settlement of land for the peasants, indeed a veritable "swindle" to the profit of the gentry. Clearly, the peasants would now rise up in a socialist revolution. To further this revolt, in 1861 a group of students formed an amateur conspiracy, "Land and Freedom." They were soon arrested, along with their mentor and alleged co-conspirator, Chernyshevskii, who would spend the rest of his days in exile, a martyrdom which reinforced the message of his novel. But when a later group of radical students finally went on a "crusade to the people" in 1874 with an appeal to insurrection, the peasants totally failed to respond. So after 1878 the radicals, now grouped in the clandestine organization the "Will of the People," turned to terrorism against the government in the hope that the shock would at last ignite the popular explosion. They even condemned the emperor to death and succeeded in "executing" him in 1881. This fantasy reenactment of the French Revolution was the beginning of political terrorism (as opposed to isolated acts of assassination) as a systematic tactic in the modern world. Thus, the Populist strategy of mass insurrection from below, in conjunction with that of elite terror from above, combined in Russia to lend further legitimacy to political violence over and above the initial legitimation provided by the Western revolutionary tradition from 1789 to 1871.

Dostoevsky called these new radicals "the possessed," and all of his great fictional portraits of the 1860s and 1870s, from Raskolnikov to Stavrogin to Ivan Karamazov, are in fact case studies of the sickness inhabiting Russia's "nihilist," revolutionary intelligentsia. Too often, Dostoevsky has been read in the West primarily as a psychologist of morbidity and neurosis, or as a precursor of Nietzsche and Freud, and he is, of course, both of these things. Yet he came by these insights because he was in the first instance a critic of modernity, of the whole of European culture since the Enlightenment. He developed this critique to defend what he saw as the humble but holy values of the long-suffering Russian people, values menaced by the modern world of the West then bursting into Russia through the breach of the Great Reforms. And what first alerted him to this menace was Chernyshevskii's *What Is To Be Done?*; Dostoevsky's *Notes from the Underground* of 1864, the work in which he discovered his true vocation as a writer, was a direct answer to Chernyshevskii's visionary novel. And as Dostoevsky persevered in his attack down through the terror campaign of the Will of the People, his counter-vision became ever more clear: The self-proclaimed friends of the people, the radical intelligentsia, were in fact their potential slave-masters—as in the legend of the Grand Inquisitor.

Dostoevsky's heroes thus are studies of the dark side of enlightenment, of the potential demonism of rationalism, and of the psychopathology of noble intentions. And the burden of his fictional explorations is the somewhat Aeschylean one that the hubris of modern reason leads to moral sickness and murderous crime. Thus, the reasonable fathers begat the fanatical sons who produced the criminal terrorist Sergei Nechaev. This somber vision is a caricature no doubt, and indeed something of a libel on both the Russian liberals and the West. Yet it is a vision that the twentieth century would do much to validate, particularly once the heirs of Chernyshevskii—and by the time of the Yezhov Terror of 1937, even of Nechaev—had come to power.

Dostoevsky's portraits are also a commentary on the special fragilities of Russia's culture that made her so vulnerable to all ideological winds from the West—a situation that allowed Chernyshevskii to turn the sober utilitarianism and political economy of John Stuart Mill into the premises of the revolutionary ethos expounded in *What Is To Be Done?* Under such circumstances, poor Turgenev, the civilized incarnation of Russian reasonableness—in a lineage running from Pushkin to Chekhov—was condemned to run as a loser, vainly expostulating, in the name of the liberal fathers, with their revolutionary sons.

To put the whole matter in a single proposition: The great fragility of old-regime Russian politics is that socialism came into existence almost simultaneously with liberalism, a pattern quite unlike that of far–Western Europe, where several decades elapsed before the political stakes were raised so dramatically. And this occurred when the real issue in Russia was not a Crystal Palace of social reason, but the abolition of serfdom and, if possible, the achievement of some modest limitations on the power of the autocracy. The result was that the Great Reforms of Alexander II, instead of initiating an orderly transition to a modern political system (a process that was rarely orderly even in the West), inaugurated a revolutionary movement that would not abate during the remainder of the Old Regime.

And no other country in Europe had such a continuing revolutionary movement. To make the extreme contrast with Britain: It took Britain, even with a long prior parliamentary tradition, from 1832 to 1912 to effect the transition from an old-regime class suffrage to universal manhood suffrage, and only at the end of this period did socialism become a political force. Russia, however, had a shooting socialist movement decades before she had any suffrage at all. The political formula produced by Russian backwardness, then, is the compression or telescoping—and thus the chronic radicalization—of the stages of the modern movement towards democracy. This formula, in turn, produced a veritable cult of Revolution as the highest form of the modern political process.

The final challenge put to Russia by the rest of Europe was that of the industrial revolution. Textile manufacture had arrived by the 1840s and a railroad boom by the 1860s, but it was only through the exertions of Finance Minister Sergei Witte in the 1890s that it became possible to speak of a revolutionary industrial transformation of Russia. In this process, once again, it was state action from above, rather than social initiative from below, that was the motive force.[16] And again, as in the past, the state's motivation for forced modernization was concern for its survival among the powers of Europe. For the once mighty war machine that Peter had created and that had sufficed to defeat Napoleon was no longer competitive internationally after the Crimean War of 1854–1864. Indeed, recognition of Russia's declining military status was a major impetus to Alexander II's Great Reforms. By the 1890s, as Europe was dividing into a Triple Alliance at its center and a Triple Entente at its longitudinal extremities, rapid industrial development was a greater imperative than ever before.

Once again, modernization was compressed and telescoped, and its consequences were not entirely what had been intended. Witte's industrialization was lopsidedly oriented towards heavy industry and the most modern equipment, and large factories were located in the biggest cities. Light industry and the production of consumer goods were accordingly slighted, and the peasantry was squeezed through taxation to finance the whole undertaking without benefitting from it in any tangible way.

The results of this crash modernization were twofold and contradictory. On the one hand, Russia by 1914 had become, in terms of total output, the fifth-ranking industrial power in the world, behind the United States, Germany, Britain, and France, but ahead of Austria-Hungary, Italy, and Japan. On the other hand, in terms of per capita production, her rank was the lowest in Europe and not much above that of many Asian nations. Thus Russia could plausibly be viewed by many of her own intellectuals as a special and separate cultural entity, a "Eurasian" civilization;[17] budding revolutionaries such as Lenin, meanwhile, could see her as "semicolonial," both an exploiting European power and a country exploited by the more advanced imperialist countries of the West.

Yet another imbalance in Russia's fin-de-siècle status could be found in her fragile lord-peasant social order, which had been made even more precarious by the addition of two new elements: The first was an industrial working class. Though small in number, it was concentrated in a few large and strategic urban centers, and was therefore potentially dangerous to the established order in a way that the dispersed peasantry had never been. The second new element was an aggregate of various commercial, technical, and professional middle classes. Concentrated in the same urban centers as the workers, they constituted the most literate and "European" part of the population. Thus socialism and liberalism, hitherto both confined to the airy sphere of the intelligentsia, now each had a modern political clientele fully meriting the name "civil society," a term employed in classical European political theory.

Under such circumstances, the pressures for social participation in public affairs and for constitutional government became irresistible. Yet the autocracy, by its very nature the expression of traditional military monarchy, had no more intention of surrendering its prerogatives than did its Prussian or Austrian cousins. Indeed, because the assassination of Alexander II convinced the government that any further reform would be downright dangerous, it stubbornly dug in its heels against all change. At the same time, because the level of social tension in still autocratic Russia was much higher than in half-constitutional Prussia or Austria, the radical intelligentsia's decades-old fantasy of total, Promethean revolution as the path to true democracy remained very much alive.

Indeed, this fantasy gained renewed strength as Marxism began to compete with Populism for primacy among the intelligentsia. This occurred first because of the failure, by 1881, of Populism's two tactics: mass peasant insurrection and elite terror. Accordingly, the one-time Populist Georgii Plekhanov drew the conclusion that the peasantry was, in fact, a retrograde class and that its intellectual spokesmen were dangerous deceivers. For Russia was not an exception to the universal logic of history; her way to democratic revolution therefore must follow the Western progression from feudalism to capitalism to socialism. In the 1880s Plekhanov acclimated Marxism in Russia, and in the 1890s Witte's industrialization produced a "proletáriat" that seemed to prove him right. Thus, by 1900, a part of the socialist intelligentsia shifted its allegiance from the peasants to the workers, who were now seen as constituting the new "universal class" of the coming democratic revolution. And so Russian radicalism at last drew abreast of the ultimate in European social ideology and embraced the winning fantasy of the modern age, Marxism.[18]

But the Russian revolutionary movement did not owe its strength to the historical logic of Russia's social processes alone. It progressed as much through the catalytic impact of that great contingency of human affairs—war. Russia's first modern military defeat, in the Crimean War, triggered the Great Reforms and their ensuing revolutionary spinoff. Even Russia's "victorious" war against Turkey in 1877–1878 greatly aggravated the revolutionary crisis associated with Land and Freedom. This losing streak continued with the Russo-Japanese War of 1904–1905, in which Russia suffered the most humiliating type of defeat for the imperialist era: defeat at the hands of a non-European "yellow" power. This last war also inflamed an already acute internal crisis to produce the Revolution of 1905.

This event, although it came to be overshadowed by the Revolution of 1917, is all too often portrayed as a "workers' revolution," the "dress rehearsal" for Red October.[19] In fact, however, 1905 was a thoroughly "normal" European revolution, the kind that Marxists would characterize as "bourgeois." That is, it was a political revolution against an Old Regime, in favor of constitutional government, a legislative parliament, and the equality of all citizens before the law. There was nothing socialist about the aims of most of its participants, and the industrial workers were only one of the social elements involved. In reality, the Revolution was led by the liberal professional classes and the gentry, it was supported by virtually all the urban elements in the country, and its aims were liberal-democratic.[20] The workers, of course, played a major tactical role in the revolutionary events because of their ability to paralyze the economy and the transportation system—that is, as a force for direct action analogous to that of the Parisian plebs, the *sans-culottes*, in the liberal revolution of 1789–1793. The role of the workers was particularly evident in the October general strike, which at last brought the autocracy to its knees and compelled it to grant a legislative Duma. But at no time did this worker activism give the movement a class character or political aims that were distinctively "proletarian." And the socialist parties—the Menshevik and Bolshevik Social Democrats, or SDs, and the neo-Populist Socialist Revolutionaries, or SRs—played only a minor organizational role, one far behind that of the emerging liberal Constitutional Democrats, or Kadets.

Nonetheless, this demi-Revolution turned out to be a significant defeat for Russian liberalism, in very much the same way that the Revolution of 1848 in the Germanies was a defeat for Central European liberalism. For in both the German and the Russian cases the revolution was won by the conservatives, who, throughout the radical storm, managed to hold on to the armed forces and thus to put down the "street." In both cases, therefore, the outcome was what was called a *Scheinkonstitutionalismus*, or a pseudoconstitutionalism, in which the monarchy granted a legislative parliament but did not accept that the government be responsible to it. In Russia, this arrangement gave the Kadets in the Duma a measure of responsibility for the state of the country without their gaining any corresponding constitutional power.

Thus, the liberals continued to be overshadowed by the autocracy, and their concomitant inability to produce change in matters important to the mass of the population—above all, land reform—compromised them as an effective political force. In consequence, when social and political agitation resumed after 1912, the Kadets were poorly positioned to profit from it, and the political initiative on the Left therefore passed to the socialist parties. Once again Russian liberalism was overrun on its left by revolutionary socialism, in the pattern going back to 1861–1863. Thus, even before the Revolution of 1917 began, the liberals in effect had already lost their leading political role, and what is usually considered the initial, moderate phase of a great revolution was basically over in Russia.[21]

It is this political, economic, social, and cultural heritage that Russian history brought to the revolutionary explosion of 1917 and to the new Soviet order that emerged from it. As a preliminary to assessing the uniquely Russian contribution to the Soviet socialist mix, how may we characterize the salient traits of old-regime political culture?

The first of these traits is no doubt the weakness and fragility of Russian governmental and social structures. A crude military-bureaucratic autocracy capped a primitive two-class lord-peasant society, and the political oppressiveness of the state, in conjunction with the social oppressiveness of serfdom, created a systemic instability greater than in any other European nation. In consequence, Russian history from the late sixteenth through the eighteenth century was punctuated in a unique fashion by huge peasant revolts—those of the Time of Troubles, Stenka Razin, Bulavin, Pugachev—that far surpassed all Western jacqueries and called into question the very existence of the social order and the state. Even in the nineteenth century, when Pushkin's "mindless and pitiless" Russian *bunt* had ceased to be practiced, the specter of mass anarchy still hung over the system.

It was for this reason that the liberal socialist Aleksandr Herzen could declare that the Russian system resembled a "temporary bivouac" that could easily be swept away by a revolutionary storm. Likewise, the revolutionary socialist Petr Tkachev (who has often been seen as a precursor of Lenin) could argue in the 1870s that the fragility of Russia's structures made possible a preventive socialist revolution before the development of capitalism had diversified and solidified the country's social system.[22] To put this insight in the language of classical political theory, because the "civil society" of old-regime Russia was exceptionally weak, the state had hypertrophied, thus making the whole system uniquely vulnerable to revolutionary action.[23]

A second aspect of the Russian national heritage that made for instability was the nineteenth-century Russian intelligentsia's propensity for maximalism. All of the strictures that Edmund Burke and Tocqueville, in famous diatribes, levelled against the impractical and ideological intellectuals of eighteenth-century France apply even more strongly to the pre-Revolutionary Russian intelligentsia. This is so for two reasons. The first is that the Russian intelligentsia came into existence before the creation of the more usual intermediary classes between lords and peasants that were found farther West. Suspended in midair, without roots in social groupings with a practical role in society, to an exceptional degree the intelligentsia fell back on theory alone, and never had to confront it with the test of real politics. The second reason for this maximalism was that the Russian intelligentsia, appearing late in Europe's cultural development, inherited the whole staggering baggage of the English, French, and German intellectual traditions. And because the far-reaching implications of these traditions were quite beyond the capacity of a serf-based autocracy to accommodate smoothly, the result was an overrich ideological diet and a chronic intellectual indigestion.

We may add to all this a Russian propensity for moralism in intellectual life—a quality that has made Russia's nineteenth-century literature so great, and therefore so appealing to the more jaded Western public. This moralism expressed itself, first, in unabashed preoccupation with the Big Questions of the human condition, a mode of which Tolstoy—in the persons of his Pierre Bezukhov, Platon Karataev, Levin, or in his own well-publicized personal questing—is the unsurpassed artist. But this moralism was rarely abstract and theoretical, turned toward the transcendental Holy Grail of some universal Categorical Imperative. It was characteristically expressed in an overriding concern for the concrete application of ethics to society and politics.

Thus Russian political thought was dominated by such moral and practical questions as, Who is to blame? Who are the friends of the people? What is to be done? This propensity, however, was by no means the expression of some special religious qualities of the Russian soul, as Nicholas Berdiaev and his Western emulators would have us believe. Rather, the major source of the tendency to maximalism in Russian public life was that, until 1905, real politics as practiced in Western Europe were illegal, and this meant that all politics in Russia were automatically both *a priori* and revolutionary. So once again we are confronted with the compressing, telescoping, and inverting of general modern modes of culture that make backward Russia a radically distinctive variation on common European themes.

In consequence, Russian political parties, when they emerged on the eve of 1905, were all of an unusual type. In the West, parties had been created only once it became possible to govern through elections, and their purpose was to win the vote and then exercise power constitutionally. This, as we have seen, was how politics first became divided into a Left and a Right. In Russia, however, "parties" emerged before elections and constitutional government existed. These parties, therefore, were in effect conspiracies designed more to promote revolution than to govern constitutionally. Even the legalistic liberals—after 1905 to become the Constitutional Democrats, or Kadets—had to accept revolution as the midwife of constitutionalism. And all the parties to the left of the Kadets subordinated their commitment to a constituent assembly to social revolution. The neo-Populist Socialist Revolutionaries, or SRs, of Victor Chernov spoke in the name of the peasantry. The "moderate" Menshevik Social Democrats of Iulii Martov spoke in the name of a "mature" working class, on the model of the developed European countries. And the more impatient Bolshevik Marxists of Vladimir Ulianov-Lenin, after 1905, spoke in the name of both the workers and the peasants, or at least of the peasantry's poorer strata.

Yet this political activity was very much only "in the name of," for all Russian parties were dominated by intelligentsia. Socially, these parties differed in terms not just of their presumed clientele, but also of the quality and status of their intellectual leaders. Among the Kadets we find a high level of creative talent, cosmopolitan culture, and solid academic or social standing in such figures as Professor Pavel Miliukov or the economist Petr Struve. As we move to the left, the political intellectuals become more provincial, more marginal in social position, more purely Russian in culture, and more ideological in their programs. Thus the SR activists had their principal roots among the schoolteachers and technical specialists of the *zemstvos*. The Mensheviks drew heavily on the urban petty intelligentsia, particularly among Jews (who were by definition marginalized in Imperial Russia), and in the marginal nation of Georgia. Finally, the Bolshevik activists were recruited from a more heterogeneous, provincial, and largely Great Russian petty intelligentsia; and they had the lowest level of formal education because their radicalism all too frequently led them to drop out of, or be expelled from, the academic system—Lenin and Stalin being two cases in point.

Yet marginal social status would prove to be no bar to great destinies in the crucible of the First World War—the blacksmith's son, Mussolini, and the custom official's son, Hitler, are two examples. And since we know·that Lenin and his motley followers are going to win in Russia, it is best to discuss him and his Bolsheviks here, in the context of the Old Regime and the period of their obscurity, rather than later, in the context of their revolutionary triumph.

LENIN AND BOLSHEVISM

Lenin was the product of what was best in the Russian Imperial order: the educational system and the culture of the moralistic intelligentsia. Born in 1870, he was from a background of modest gentry and middling state officialdom in the Volga city of Simbirsk, where his father had risen to become inspector of schools.[24]

Lenin became a revolutionary by the usual path to that vocation since the 1860s: conflict between youthful idealism and state power leading to punishment and disaffection from the system. The process began when his older brother Alexander joined a successor to the Will of the People and was executed in 1887. The family was ostracized by established society and Lenin was soon expelled from the University of Kazan. Though he eventually became a lawyer (a profession he never practiced) by taking correspondence courses, he was totally alienated from the system. Living in provincial Volga cities until the age of twenty-three, he evolved from his older brother's Populism in the tradition of Chernyshevskii to the new Marxism of Plekhanov.

In the mid-nineties Lenin moved to St. Petersburg, began agitating among the workers during Russia's first major industrial strikes, and so became a professional revolutionary. In the classic formula of this new calling, arrest followed and then exile to Siberia—accompanied by much research and publication—and finally, in 1900, escape abroad, where he would remain (except for a brief return in 1905) until April 1917. In emigration Lenin was single-mindedly devoted to building a party for the eventual seizure of power. This is not to say that he was not also a deeply committed Marxist and a theoretician, for he was both, always taking immense pains to ground his programs in Marxist principles. But above all he was a practitioner of revolution and a technician of power. Thus his great task was to adapt the general worldview of Marxism to the particularities of the Russian situation.

Later, after 1917, Social Democrats alleged that the Leninist Party was not authentically Marxist, but a throwback to the conspiratorial tradition of the Will of the People and, as such, a response to the oppressive conditions of political struggle in Russia. However, all Russian parties faced the same conditions, yet only the Bolsheviks became a conspiratorial organization. The reasons for this are clarified by the contrast with the SRs. The SRs' terrorist wing, the Combat Organization, was conspiratorial, but the main party, despite its large membership, was so loosely structured that it was the least effective politically of the three socialist groups. This was not just because its constituency was the dispersed peasantry; it was even more because the SRs lacked a structured ideology. Simply put, their ideology was: Power to the people, land to the peasants, and "revolution now"— generalities that had little operational focus.

The SDs, on the other hand, derived their superior capacity for organization not only from their concentrated worker "base," but also from the rationalistic structure of their ideology. Yet this ideology, as we have seen, was a Janus-headed affair. Thus, within a shared worldview, the Mensheviks emphasized its formal tenets and the logic of history as the key to revolution, whereas the Bolsheviks assigned that role to "scientific revolutionary consciousness." And when there is only one true doctrine, the tendency is strong to believe there can be only one true party with a single "correct" line.

The result of Lenin's encounter with Marx, therefore, was the creation of the most extraordinary political institution of the modern age: the Communist Party. Marx's *Manifesto* already accorded a vanguard role to people he called "the Communists"; and he certainly ran the First International in an authoritarian and manipulative manner that can fairly be called proto-Leninist. But the relatively stable conditions of post-1848 Europe did not lend themselves to the institutionalization of such practices; so Western European Marxism became identified with mass Social Democratic parties that increasingly were concerned with winning elections rather than with making a revolution. By 1900, only Russian conditions still made it possible to bring out the "vanguardist" potential of Marxism.

In 1901 Russian Marxism began to organize around the émigré newspaper *Iskra* (The Spark) under the leadership of the elder Plekhanov and the younger Lenin and Iulii Martov. This theoretical organ sought to coordinate the scattered Marxist groups within Russia to produce a national Social Democratic Party. The Iskrists' first battle was to convince the intelligentsia that the Populist belief in a peasant revolution that would permit Russia to skip over the bourgeois phase of development was an illusion. Instead, they argued, Russia, like all other countries, must suffer the full Way of the Cross through capitalism before reaching socialism. The Russian revolution, therefore, would be in two stages, in perfect fidelity to Marxism's formal tenets: The impending first stage would be bourgeois democratic, while socialism would come only in a second stage, once capitalism had created the requisite objective conditions.

But the Iskrists also faced an enemy within Marxism itself, one known as "revisionism" in the West and "economism" in Russia, both of which subordinated the revolutionary goal of Marxism to the struggle for the immediate material betterment of the workers. This backsliding into reformism provoked Lenin into his most decisive contribution to Marxist doctrine: the theory of the vanguard party, set forth in 1902 in a pamphlet called, after the title of Chernyshevskii's revolutionary breviary, *What Is To Be Done?*[25] This theory proclaimed that the mere "spontaneity" of the workers could lead only to "trade unionism" and that the proletariat, therefore, must be informed from without by the "consciousness" of "scientific" revolutionary theory, which could only come from "educated" members of the "bourgeois intelligentsia." Thus Lenin launched the idea of his "party of a new type," a party designed to "overturn all Russia"; its defining characteristic was that it would not be a mass organization but a conspiratorial body of professional revolutionaries.

It was precisely over this organizational issue that the SDs split at their first congress in London in 1903, with Lenin insisting on centralization but Martov and Plekhanov wanting a more broadly based movement. Thus there emerged two Russian Marxist factions: Lenin's Bolsheviks, or majoritarians, and the Mensheviks, or minoritarians, so named because in the final votes of the meeting the former had a temporary edge.

For the time being, however, the two factions remained formally united in a single party whose structures were borrowed from the prestigious Social Democracy of Germany. And these structures lent themselves readily to Lenin's enterprise, for they already offered a quite new type of party organization. Most nineteenth-century parties were small and elitist affairs: Whigs and Tories, Liberals and Conservatives, Orleanists and Legitimists, Democrats and Republicans—all lacked structured organizations. Organized parties were a late-nineteenth-century invention of the socialists, and the most precocious in this matter were the German SDs. It was they who introduced party cards, regular dues, party cells, and a hierarchy of committees leading up to periodic congresses and a standing Central Committee. They did this in part because they were an embattled, adversary party—indeed a counter-society in Imperial Germany—and in part because universal suffrage made such a mass party possible.

But as Weber's pupil, Robert Michels, pointed out as early as 1911 in his classic study of the SDs, *Political Parties*, the Social Democratic mode of organization inevitably tends to bureaucracy and oligarchy, thus thwarting egalitarianism (and also braking revolutionary élan).[26] Still, in the German case, genuine elections made the bureaucratic oligarchy more or less responsive to the base. But if ever elections atrophied in such a structure, the pyramid of power would be inverted and the party would become a dictatorship under the euphemistic designation "democratic centralism," where initiative flowed from the top down. This was Rosa Luxemburg's criticism of Lenin's program during the period now under discussion. And this, of course, is precisely what happened once his party came to power. To this it may be added that a similar bureaucratic centralism was adopted by parties of the revolutionary Right after the First World War in imitation of their SD and Communist adversaries, and the Communists transmitted the same type of organization to China's Kuomintang.

Thus, in every SD Party there is a Leninist Party *in potentia*. To anticipate a bit, this circumstance goes far to explain the love-hate relationship of these *frères ennemis* of the Left and the recurrent mirage of the Popular Front as well. But is the reverse of this proposition true, namely, that in every Leninist Party there is a social democracy struggling to be reborn? Numerous reform Communists and Western revisionist historians have thought so. But the answer to this question must await examination of the actual record. For the moment, suffice it to note that the existence of a dormant SD "constitution" within Communism would play a real role in Soviet affairs.

Thus the first defining characteristic of Bolshevism to emerge was not social but organizational; Bolshevik substantive programs would always be subordinated to this political imperative.[27] And these programs quickly emerged, usually through opposition to the Mensheviks. First, by 1905 Lenin, taking half a leaf from the Populists, was advocating an alliance of workers and peasants to make the "bourgeois" revolution against autocracy that the bourgeoisie itself was too cowardly to carry out, while the Mensheviks favored supporting the Kadets to achieve political democracy and then waiting an unspecified period for conditions to mature for a socialist revolution. Second, in 1912 Lenin adopted another dubiously Marxist idea by espousing self-determination for the Empire's minority nationalities in order to generate further revolutionary pressure. Third, again in 1912, Lenin set up his faction as a separate organization claiming to be the one true Marxist party in Russia, in effect purging the Mensheviks as deviationists—a precedent that would not be forgotten in the factional fights within Bolshevism in the 1920s and the Party Purges of the 1930s.

Finally, after the outbreak of war, Lenin made his major theoretical contribution to Marxism in *Imperialism, the Highest Stage of Capitalism*. For Marx, the fatal internal contradictions of capitalism were to have worked themselves out in the industrial societies of Europe; Lenin globalized these contradictions into an antithesis between the monopolistic "finance capital" of advanced Europe and its backward "colonial and semicolonial" dependencies, which thereby became a kind of planetary proletariat or universal class. In this vision, the *fin de siècle* scramble of the European powers to divide up Asia and Africa in order to compensate for falling profits at home could only end in world war between rival imperialist camps; and out of this apocalypse would at last come the world socialist revolution. Moreover, since Russia suffered the double instability of being both an exploiting and a semicolonial country, this revolution might conceivably begin in the Tsarist Empire. The "weakest link of the capitalist chain" would thus logically become the strongest force for world revolution.

In short, at each stage of his evolution from 1902 onward, Lenin construed Marxism in a manner that progressively contravened its formal tenets and recast its official logic of history to accommodate Russian backwardness. Yet in so doing, he always remained faithful to Marxism's deeper structure, which privileged social deprivation and dehumanization as the demiurge of the class struggle. For the workers and peasants, and even the nationalities, of the tsarist Empire were in fact the most deprived and dehumanized masses in Europe, with almost literally "nothing to lose but their chains," as the finale of the *Manifesto* has it. The result of these adaptations of Marxism was an implied strategy of "revolution now"; of revolution first of all in Russia; and of revolution only under the leadership of Lenin's own party. Yet he advanced this bold program without a trace of personal ambition. Like Marx, he was simply and unquestioningly convinced that in his "scientific consciousness" he was always right, and that all his socialist rivals therefore were in fact "petty bourgeois" traitors.

As of 1914, however, the kind of maximalist radicalism represented by Lenin did not seem to be a prime contender for power in Russia. Certainly, Russian political life was strongly weighted to the Left, but this Left was a variegated one, with its center of gravity somewhere between the Kadets and the SRs. Lenin and his movement were largely unknown to most of the population. Moreover, the relative failure of the Revolution of 1905 had disabused much of the intelligentsia of its long-time dogmas of progress, materialism, and popular revolution, a change made manifest in a spectacular volume of intelligentsia self-criticism called *Vekhi* (Signposts), published in 1909. And the aesthetic culture of the Silver Age of Russian literature during these same years fostered pluralism within the intelligentsia even more.

At the "base" of society, finally, the transformations of the beginning of the century meant that the structural gap between Russia and the more advanced Western nations was constantly closing. Thus, to most of the Russian intelligentsia, whether liberal, socialist, or apolitical, Russia's future clearly lay in her complete "Europeanization." In this view, those elements of her heritage that left her with one foot in Asiatic despotism were deemed to be holdovers from the past rather than harbingers of the future.

Nor would these holdover national traits be the catalysts of the future in any simple sense of direct continuity, still less of causality. The weakness of Russian civil society and the maximalism of the intelligentsia could react with one another to produce Sovietism only when refracted through the pan-European utopia of socialism. And the path to this would-be culmination of history could be blazed in Russia only by the pan-European cataclysm of the First World War.

The result would be an astounding change in Russia's relationship to the West: In a Marxist transposition of the Populist fantasy, the most backward country of Europe suddenly became, at least in aspiration, the most advanced; the erstwhile follower became the leader; and the last among the peoples became the first. For Russia, starting from the low end of the European cultural gradient, appeared able to draw the practical conclusions from all of Europe's anterior development, and so to trump everyone else's ace.

Marx once said: "In politics, the Germans have *thought* what other nations [i.e., England and France] have *done*. Germany was their *theoretical consciousness*."[28] To this it might be added, first, that the Germans had thought quite a bit more than the English and French had ever done; and second, that the Russians then actually did what the Germans had only thought of. And so, by 1914 Russia was poised to become the practical revolutionary consciousness of the entire modern world.

Part II
THE EXPERIMENT

3

THE ROAD TO OCTOBER

1917

The moral nature of the Bolshevik Revolution was inherited from the war in which it was born.

— *Victor Chernov*

The war has reaffirmed clearly enough and in a very practical way . . . that modern capitalist society, particularly in the advanced countries, has fully matured for the transition to socialism. If, for instance, Germany can direct the economic life of 66 million people from a single, central institution . . . then the same can be done, in the interests of nine-tenths of the population, by the non-propertied masses if their struggle is directed by the class-conscious workers. . . . All propaganda for socialism must be refashioned from abstract and general to concrete and directly practical; expropriate the banks and, relying on the masses, carry out in their interests the very same thing the W.U.M.B.A. [i.e., Weapons and Ammunition Supply Department] is carrying out in Germany.

— *V. I. Lenin, December 1916*

As of the summer of 1914, two potential logics of history were contending for Russia's future, the one liberal and the other socialist. Both, however, promised a "Western" destiny for the country. So the great question about the Revolution of 1917 is this: Why, in a reversal of the usual European order of historical priorities, did the socialist logic win out, and why did the result turn out to be so despotic and "Oriental"? Or, to put the matter the other way around: Why did the liberal logic prove to be so weak—that is, did Russia ever stand a chance of avoiding Bolshevism?

It is this second formulation of the question that was at the center of historiographical concern from the time of the Revolution itself until after Stalin's death—a period when émigré Russian liberals and their Western counterparts dominated the debate about the meaning of October. It was only with Stalin's death and Khrushchev's reforms that the question of how Bolshevism itself might have taken a more liberal, "Western" course—one leading to "socialism with a human face"—came to dominate the debate. Following in the traces of this historiographical progression, the present chapter will explore the now-neglected liberal question; the question of Communism's potential for liberalization will be treated in later chapters. The purpose of the present exercise, however, is not to lament the road not taken; rather, it is to bring out more clearly why, in reality, an alternative route was followed. All historical investigation entails a component of the might-have-been, for assessing reality in terms of alternative possibilities is the way that historical actors in fact make their choices.

The essence of the liberal argument is that from the Great Reforms of Alexander II in the 1860s, down through the "constitutional experiment" under the State Duma after 1905, Russia was evolving towards a constitutional democracy on the Western model, as that model was defined by Britain and France rather than by Germany and Austria. Accordingly, the constitution of 1905–1906 was viewed as a halfway house, or an apprenticeship, on the way to full political modernity. This was to be Russia's Westernizing logic, her final realization of a common European destiny. A major corollary to this argument is that the concurrent agrarian reforms of Prime Minister Petr Stolypin, if they had had twenty or so more years to work, would have solved Russia's peasant problem and thus would have provided a social foundation for a democratic order. For these reforms were designed to break up the archaic peasant commune into individual holdings and so create a more prosperous and stable countryside—"a wager on the strong and the sober," as Stolypin put it. In this liberal view, Russia eventually fell short of her Westernizing promise because of the "accident" of the First World War. This war disorganized Russia's still immature political structures to the point where the Bolshevik Party, a throwback to the violent and conspiratorial politics of the 1870s, was able to seize power in the "October coup" of 1917. Thus Russia missed her chance for democracy and relapsed into a despotism far worse than any she had known in the past.

The liberal view raises three fundamental questions of historical interpretation. First, how good were Russia's chances for democracy under the constitutional experiment and before the shock of the First World War? Second, how good were her chances after the fall of the monarchy in February 1917, in the midst of that war? Third, in what proportions were the factors of internal social development and the impact of external war instrumental in determining the failure of democracy and the victory of Bolshevism? Only in the context of these three questions is it possible to grapple with the problems of the nature of Bolshevism itself and of the legitimacy of October.

TO THE FEBRUARY STATION

The nature and the vulnerabilities of the political edifice of pseudoconstitutionalism that emerged from 1905 have already been described. But what of the social setting in which that system operated in the years down to 1914? It is only by examining that setting that we can answer the three broad questions of interpretation just posed.

By the time of the constitutional experiment, the population of the Russian Empire had reached approximately one hundred seventy million. Of these, some 80 percent were peasants. Approximately 15 percent of the peasants had individual land holdings separate from the commune, while more than 50 percent still lived in full-fledged communes. Furthermore, the Central Russian provinces were overpopulated and their inhabitants underemployed, a situation the peasants thought could be remedied through the confiscation of lands that remained in the hands of the gentry and the state. Though this supposition was in fact false, peasant "land hunger" was nonetheless a potent force in Russian life. In short, as of 1917 Stolypin's agrarian reforms had not had the time to change the Russian countryside fundamentally, and it remained a source of major instability vis-à-vis the gentry of the country.

It was only in the late nineteenth century that Russia for the first time had a network of sizeable cities. St. Petersburg's population passed the million mark in 1897, Moscow's did the same five years later in 1902; by 1917 the population of each city had grown to somewhat more than two million. Overall, the Empire counted some ten

million to twelve million urban residents by 1914, most of them middle class, at various levels, or state functionaries of diverse rank. Industrial workers numbered from three million to three and one-half
million, and in addition there were one million employees of the
railroad system. Whether or not one calls these latter groups the proletariat is a question of politics and ideology, but as a practical matter
their material situation was marginal and their right to organize limited. The workers were therefore regarded by both the regime and the
revolutionary parties as "dangerous" elements, especially in view of
their concentration in large urban centers and along key arteries of
communication. Thus Russia's new cities added a second radical cohort to that furnished by her old villages.

These well-known basic facts are often set forth as if the October
Revolution would automatically arise from them by spontaneous social combustion. But throughout the twentieth century, situations of
comparable social instability have existed in rapidly industrializing
countries—from Brazil to South Korea—without producing Marxist
revolutions. Indeed, around 3 million "proletarians" out of a total
population of 170 million is hardly an impressive social base for so
momentous an undertaking as the world's first leap from capitalism to
socialism. Clearly, other factors must have been involved in producing
this result, and these factors were not social and economic but, rather,
political and ideological.

The first political factor is the incompleteness of the constitutional
order created in 1905. No longer a military autocracy and not yet a
constitutional democracy, this order was an inherently unstable compromise that sooner or later had to give way: Sovereignty would one
day have to devolve clearly on the people or the nation, for this had
been the momentum of representative institutions elsewhere in Europe since the seventeenth century. But in these cases the transition
had required a great deal of time and a succession of political upheavals. It took England forty-eight years—from 1640 to 1688—to dilute
absolute monarchy with a constitutional oligarchy, and then a long
nineteenth century to add universal suffrage. France required the
years 1789–1875 to move from absolute monarchy to an enduring
republic with universal suffrage. The United States is an outstanding
exception in this pattern because, as Tocqueville said, "it arrived at
the fruits of revolution without having to go through the process,"[1] or,

as the Americans said of themselves, they were "born free." Leaving aside the successful smaller nations of Northern and Western Europe, we can note that Germany, Italy, and Japan did not become stable universal-suffrage democracies until after their defeat in the Second World War.

Thus the road to constitutional democracy has been long, rocky, and tortuous for most modern nations. In this comparative perspective, and even granting that in the twentieth century everything moves faster than it did in the seventeenth, it still requires a major act of faith to believe that the Russian constitutional experiment of only twelve-years duration had reasonable prospects of attaining its democratic goal short of further revolutionary incidents.

Indeed, after 1912 both the social and the political situations in Russia were heating up once again for a new crisis that would pit the regime against society for a second time. Liberal agitation for a real constitution resumed; worker militancy revived—this time under socialist rather than liberal leadership; and the peasantry remained as sullenly alienated as it had been since the beginning of the century. Concurrently, after Stolypin's assassination in 1911, the autocracy increasingly dug in its heels against any further change. An evolutionary transformation was therefore increasingly unlikely, and extralegal action was correspondingly more probable. In short, the country was headed towards a major constitutional crisis. Given the fact that Tsar Nicholas II had no intention of accepting demotion to the status of his British cousin, he would have to be forced to either capitulate or abdicate, and the use of force would make the crisis to some degree revolutionary.

In speculating on the various scenarios for such a crisis, the key question is how big would the new revolution be. This would largely depend on whether the crisis came in peacetime or, as in 1905, during a war, and, if the latter, on what sort of war. As we know, the crisis in fact came in the midst of a uniquely devastating war. But what might a peacetime second Russian revolution have looked like? What little we can say on this subject must be extrapolated from what we know of what actually happened in 1917 and from other cases of peacetime revolution in Europe.

Yet at the outset of this brief excursus into counterfactual history, it is possible to say two things with near certainty. First, whether in peace or in war, there are only three possible outcomes to a situation such as

Russia's in 1914: Either constitutional democracy wins out in the first round; or the socialist Left seizes power; or the monarchy and the Right restore order. Second, revolution, by its very nature, puts the constitutionalists at a major disadvantage; for constitutionalism, by its nature, is incompatible with violence and extralegal means. Thus, whatever measure of extralegality proves to be necessary to bend or break the monarchy also entails the risk of developing its own momentum and getting out of hand. But this dilemma is by no means peculiar to Russia: The English Parliament in 1640, and the French Estates General in 1789, faced exactly the same dilemma, and both lost the battle for constitutionalism in the first round to a strongman. Constitutionalists, it seems, have to wait until the second round to have their day.

One reason for the failure of the "moderate" English revolution is that it was not, of course, a peacetime revolution: It was triggered by limited war with Scotland, and then radicalized by a more serious war in Ireland. But even the examples of peacetime revolutions are not encouraging. The French Revolution began in peacetime, but within two years it generated an international war that then led to civil war and general radicalization at home. The revolutions of 1848 also broke out in peacetime, and though hardly as radical as that of 1789 they nonetheless ended everywhere with the establishment of authoritarian governments. This is in large part because, in France no less than in Austria and Prussia, the peasant majority eventually supported the restoration of order, thus isolating the radical urban lower classes, a pattern which would be repeated in more drastic form in the case of the war-engendered Paris Commune in 1871.

Russia, of course, was an overwhelmingly peasant country, and her peasantry was radical—like that of France in 1789, but unlike that of France in 1848 or 1871. In any peacetime Russian revolution, the peasants would certainly have demanded and received the land, for even the Constitutional Democrats (Kadets) wanted to cede it to them with reimbursement to the gentry, and the socialists wanted to surrender it outright, as in fact happened in 1917. Still, even in peacetime such a transfer would have entailed an enormous, brusque, and probably disorderly upheaval with a corresponding potential for civil strife. Could a newly elected Constituent Assembly have managed this more smoothly than the French National Assembly of 1789 managed the Grande Peur and the night of August 4? How would a Russian Provisional Government have met an urban insurrection on the model of the Parisian June Days of 1848 or the Moscow uprising of December 1905? How would it have reacted to the inevitable new Polish insurrection and declaration of independence?

We obviously do not know. But any new government's reaction to these and other problems would have been largely conditioned by how quickly the peasantry "deradicalized" itself after receiving the land, as has always been the case for European peasantries once they have become their own masters. It is this factor in particular that would determine the fortunes of any urban insurrection, for a worker revolt in a largely agrarian country could not succeed if the peasantry supported the government. In such a case, a socialist insurrection would only push the country to the right, and the outcome might resemble that of another peacetime revolution, that of Spain in the 1930s.

But no matter how we imagine a peacetime Russian revolution, the least likely outcome would be a Red October. Social historians have argued with some plausibility that an urban insurrection was a potentiality of the strike wave of 1914, and that in all probability a peacetime crisis would have produced an actual revolution.[2] But this would not have been at all the same as a Bolshevik Party seizure of power leading to an enduring "workers' state"; nor would it have been the same as an indefinite Bolshevik exercise of power with a maximalist program of suppressing the market and nationalizing the entire economy. Any such long-term "building of socialism" was hardly in the peacetime cards. A far more likely outcome of the hot summer of 1914 would have been an abortive workers' revolt, the failure of constitutional democracy, and a national conservative regime of the sort that interwar Europe saw all too often. But such a regime, however brutal its politics may have been, would at least have preserved the market, private property, and the fundamentals of a civil society—as did Franco's Spain.

So in answer to our first question, we may conclude that it would have required a near miracle for Russia to have evolved organically and peacefully into a constitutional democracy had she been spared the shock of the First World War.[3] Yet even in the worst-case peacetime scenario of a national conservative regime, she would have fared far better than she in fact did as a result of that war.

But it would have required another near miracle for Russia and Europe to have avoided such a war. Five major powers were arrayed in two tight alliances on what is, after all, the planet's smallest continent.

Each power was armed to the hilt; all except Great Britain had mass "democratic" armies based on universal military service, a degree of social militarization never before realized in history (and one that Britain would soon have to imitate); all the powers had mobilization schedules that, once started, were almost impossible to stop; and each had equally constraining military commitments to other powers.

Just as important, however, none of the major powers knew what modern war was really like; each thought in terms of the seven-week Austro-Prussian War of 1866 or, at the worst, in terms of the six-month Franco-Prussian War of 1870–1871, during which there were, in fact, only eight weeks of active combat. Thus all the belligerents—with Russia perhaps being the most extreme example—carelessly contemplated a general European conflict without realizing its potential for destroying their domestic regimes and the whole European order. It is futile to reason about Russia's early twentieth-century social polarization in abstraction from this ever present threat, for if the incident at Sarajevo had not triggered the deluge, in all probability some slightly later incident would have done so.

As it in fact turned out, after 1914 the war radically altered the nature of the then-gathering second Russian Revolution by subordinating the logic of the country's internal processes to the "extraneous" contingency of brute events. The first characteristic to note about developments between February and October 1917 is that the course of the Second Russian Revolution was "nasty, brutish, and short." Only eight months separated the fall of the Russian Old Regime from the Bolsheviks' proclamation of the world's first socialist government, a telescoping of history without precedent in the annals of European revolutions.

The cause of this acceleration lay in an equally unprecedented occurrence in European life: the world's first "total war," as one of its prime practitioners, General Erich von Ludendorff, called it.[4] For the first time, in each of the belligerent nations of Europe and with one or another degree of success, the whole of the population was mobilized either to participate in the conflict at the front or to work to support it in the rear. Normal politics were suspended, the economy was nationalized and militarized, culture was turned to propaganda, and private life was eclipsed by public purpose. No nation's social order could survive such intrusion unaltered, and that of fragile, rickety Russia least of all. Her economy, her society, and her political system alike were radically transformed from what they had been in 1914.[5]

First of all, some eleven million Russian men were mobilized in the course of the hostilities, and eight million of these, or twice the populations of St. Petersburg and Moscow combined, as of 1917 were strung out along the roughly two-thousand-mile front from the Baltic to the Black Sea. Furthermore, as of 1917 this force had suffered some three million casualties, more in absolute terms than any other belligerent nation. And all of the survivors had become accustomed to violence as a way of life. Yet these enormous human sacrifices seemed to have been made without avail: For three years the Imperial army went from defeat to defeat, and by 1917 it had lost a significant portion of the Empire's western provinces.

The removal of so huge a mass from the labor force, moreover, contributed significantly to the disorganization of an economy that was already being undermined by other factors. First, the blockade of Russia's Baltic and Black Sea ports by the Central Powers ended her export of grain and raw materials and deprived her of major revenues; this blockade also ended the import of needed industrial equipment and consumer goods. As a result, the country was glutted with foodstuffs that the peasants had little incentive to sell because of the dearth of consumer goods, and the cities consequently began to experience severe scarcities. At the same time, the war effort monopolized transport, industry, and fuel, further diminishing supplies to the civilian population of the cities. In addition, in the face of decreased revenues, the government met the exceptional expenses of the war by printing money, thereby inaugurating this century's first great inflation, a condition aggravated by the scarcity of supply vis-à-vis demand in the economy as a whole. Finally, the Imperial government, less open to modern business interests than the governments of the other belligerent powers, was far less effective in organizing the economy for war; this, too, aggravated the country's fissiparous tendencies.

On the political front, meanwhile, the semiconstitution of 1905–1906 was virtually suspended.* In any war the executive power is always

---

* Dates for the events of 1917 given here are "Old Style," that is, according to the Julian calendar, which was used in Russia until February 1918. In the twentieth century this calendar was thirteen days behind the Gregorian calendar used in the West.

strengthened vis-à-vis the legislative and the judicial; but in Russia this process went much further than in the other belligerent countries. Because Nicholas had never really accepted the dilution of autocracy, he seized on the military emergency to rule almost without convening the Duma—and thus also without the support that the liberal opposition offered for the war effort. This policy, in conjunction with the ascendancy of Rasputin and his influence over Empress Alexandra, who in effect governed while Nicholas was away at the front, looked to the opposition like a coup d'état against the constitutional order.

The liberal opposition, therefore, mounted a quasi-countercoup by forming the Progressive Bloc in the Duma. Ranging from the Kadets to the moderate conservatives, it demanded a government that would enjoy the confidence of the nation—a concession that, in effect, would have amounted to a real constitution. Thus, a constitutional crisis unfolded in the midst of a losing war and while the economy was beginning to break down: Only with the combination of these three circumstances could the social discontent of February among the Petrograd workers become the February Revolution of 1917.

This Revolution came as a brief but devastating explosion.[6] In the last days of the month worker protests against food shortages escalated into industrial strikes, and finally into mass political demonstrations against the war and the autocracy. These disturbances became a revolution when the Petrograd garrison of peasant soldiers refused to fire on the crowds, thus depriving the government of power in its own capital. They became a victorious revolution, first, when the Progressive Bloc of the Duma abandoned the monarchy and stepped in to form a Provisional Government in an effort to stabilize the situation, and second, when this usurpation was approved by the army high command, thereby forcing Nicholas's abdication. Thus, in five days the Russian Old Regime, without putting up the slightest resistance, collapsed like a house of cards.

Although the trigger in this process was the working class of the capital, the decisive revolutionary agent was the peasant in uniform, for it was his refusal to obey that neutralized the Imperial government. It should be emphasized, however, that his motivation was not primarily social solidarity with the workers—although this factor was of course present—but revulsion against the war. Yet even this mutiny would not have sufficed to make a revolution had it not been for the constitutional crisis. For the paralysis of power at the top meant that neither a discredited state authority nor an unorganized opposition could find the will or the means to resist the eruption of the street. The result of this impotence was the unraveling of all public authority, from the police to the local administration, both of which simply melted away. It is this completeness of the February collapse that determined the impotence of the Provisional Government that succeeded the defunct Old Regime.

The new government was formed by the Progressive Bloc of the Duma and was initially dominated by the Kadets. But from the outset this government was the hostage of the workers and soldiers whose mutiny had permitted it to come to power. These forces, moreover, were immediately organized by socialist intellectuals into a Council, or Soviet, of Workers' and Soldiers' Deputies. In addition, amidst the February events this Soviet issued its famous "Order Number One" democratizing the army, a measure which had the effect of neutralizing the officer corps and thus undermining the new government's control over its armed forces. The Provisional Government was therefore no government at all, but a mere provisional administration; its ability to function was dependent on the goodwill of the Soviet, which expressed the distrust of the worker and soldier "masses" toward the "bourgeois" and "capitalist" ministry.

TO THE OCTOBER TERMINUS

This system of divided authority and institutionalized suspicion has been called a regime of "dual power." It soon became apparent that such a system was intrinsically unstable and hence would inevitably end with one of the two powers eliminating the other. Out of this situation necessarily developed the political struggle, so often portrayed in epic terms, between the "bourgeois" Provisional Government and the socialist Soviet.

The well-known story of the eight months separating February from October falls into four phases. The first extended from February to April, a time when the dominant Kadets sought to adjourn any further radical change in order to concentrate on winning the war. This prowar policy produced in April a crisis in which the Mensheviks and SRs in the Soviet forced the Provisional Government to adopt a more "democratic" and purely "defensist" military stance. But in exchange they had to enter the government alongside the Kadets, thereby abandoning the role of hard-Left opposition to the Bolsheviks. It was at this timely juncture that Lenin arrived home and, in his April Theses, converted his hitherto confused Party to a program of "down with the war," "down with the Provisional Government," and "all power to the Soviets."

The second phase extended from the April Crisis to the July Days. This period was marked by a rapid deepening of the Revolution as the new socialist Defense Minister, Aleksandr Kerenskii, quixotically attempted to mount a "democratic offensive" to demonstrate the vitality of reborn Russia and thereby bring all the belligerent powers to the negotiating table. The only beneficiaries of this policy, however, were the Bolsheviks, who went from one propaganda success to another. In early July, however, they overreached themselves with an ambiguous try for power and were half-heartedly put down by their fellow governmental socialists; consequently, Lenin had to go into hiding until October.

This setback for the Bolsheviks inaugurated a third phase extending to the end of the summer. As was only to be expected, the leftward surge of April–June produced a rightward surge in July–August. This reactive thrust sought to end dual power, suppress the Soviet, and get on with the war; and so it appropriately focused on a general, the commander in chief Lavr Kornilov. It ended with the fiasco of his equivocal try for power at the end of August—an event which demonstrated that the Russian Right was a mere bogeyman, without any real strength.

This circumstance opened the doors wide to the Left, thus yielding a fourth phase extending to October. During these autumnal months, the Provisional Government—now presided over by Kerenskii—was no more than a phantom. Lenin's Bolsheviks were therefore free to take over the nether half of the "dual power," the Soviet. Using it as a base of operations, they openly organized to cast the Provisional Government, as Leon Trotsky famously put it, into the trash can of history.

This so-called October Revolution was an "armed insurrection" carried out by the Party using the apparatus of the Petrograd Soviet.[7] Lenin insisted that the transfer of power take this militarized form rather than the political form of a vote by the forthcoming All-Russian

Congress of Soviets, the course favored by his more pragmatic colleagues Grigorii Zinoviev and Lev Kamenev. And he did so because
for him, as for Marx, the class struggle was literally class warfare,
necessarily involving physical violence. No other method could adequately demonstrate where the real power lay. In the same manner,
Lenin gave the most literal meaning to Marx's call to "expropriate the
expropriators" by urging the masses to "steal the stolen" (*grab na-
grablennoe*). But this was no violation of Marx's view of the logic of
history, for armed coercion was always integral to that logic. And so,
October set the precedent for the continuing use of coercion by the
Party through all the stages of its construction of socialism.

Lenin, from his refuge in Finland, had initiated pressure for such
an insurrection in the wake of the Kornilov affair, and by October 10
he had persuaded the Central Committee to vote 10 to 2 for such an
action "in principle." But the task of organizing the insurrection fell
to Leon Trotsky, who, in order to give the Party coup an appearance
of greater proletarian legitimacy, delayed it so that it would coincide
with the forthcoming national Congress of Soviets—against Lenin's
express commands. Trotsky also engineered the creation within the
Soviet of a Military Revolutionary Committee, which was in fact dominated by the Bolsheviks, to carry out the actual takeover of the
capital.

In other words, this "Revolution" was a minority military action, not
a mass event like the one in February. Or, to be more precise, what
occurred was an amateur police operation of the Military Revolutionary
Committee, some sailors of the Baltic Fleet, and a handful of worker
Red Guards to take over the nerve centers of the capital on the night
of October 24–25. The Petrograd "proletariat" and the city's military
garrison remained overwhelmingly neutral. Because there were no
forces to fight for the Provisional Government, the Bolsheviks had almost nothing to overthrow. As Lenin himself put it, the Party "found
power lying in the streets and simply picked it up."

Thus the gambler's strategy announced in the April Theses, and
singlemindedly pursued by Lenin thereafter, paid off in the October
seizure of power. The Bolshevik leader, hitherto unknown to most of
his countrymen and quite unknown to the outside world, suddenly
found himself the chairman of the Council of People's Commissars of
the Russian Soviet Republic, a government that was in fact his Party
in power. This new power immediately issued two dramatic decrees:

The first, "on Peace," called for a negotiated end to the war, which in effect meant Russia's unilateral withdrawal from the conflict; the second, "on Land," socialized gentry and state properties, which in effect meant endorsing the already accomplished agrarian revolution. As Lenin put it to Trotsky on the night of the takeover: "It makes the head swim."

This sense of wonder at the Bolshevik victory has lingered in the historiography ever since, where it has produced still another problem of interpretation. This problem arises from the facts, first, that the Bolshevik Party was largely Lenin's personal creation, and second, that his personal insistence on armed insurrection was the driving force leading up to the October coup. But do these circumstances mean that without him there would have been no October takeover and hence no Soviet regime?

This extreme version of the "great man" theory of history has often been advanced. Even Trotsky, though committed as a Marxist to the primacy of an objective social logic in history, comes close to holding Lenin indispensable to Bolshevik victory. Yet Trotsky might well have been more cautious, for the events of 1917—from Order Number One in February to the emergence of the Left SRs in October—show that even without Lenin there was ample room on the Russian Left for an extremist party of "revolution now." Moreover, before October it was the case that Lenin's Party, though the most hierarchical of all the competing Russian parties, was not as yet the monolithic instrument commanded at will by its leader that it later became.

Indeed, Trotsky's own historical role belies the overriding importance he attributed to Lenin; in addition, it points up the fluidity of the Party in 1917. Trotsky abandoned his independent brand of Menshevism to enter the Bolshevik ranks only in June; yet by October he was directing the Bolshevik seizure of power. He even countermanded Lenin's impatient directives in order to coordinate the Party takeover with the Congress of Soviets, so as to enhance the coup's "proletarian" appearance. Lenin, for all the impetus he gave to the coup, had nothing to do with carrying it out, since he was still in hiding when it came. Where he was more truly indispensable was in his role, over the previous fourteen years, as architect of the Party organization; yet even in this domain, by 1917, there were numerous little Lenins, such as Ivan Smigla on the Northern Front (with whom

Lenin in fact conspired against his more moderate Central Committee), who could have pursued the same maximalist policies.

More basically still, however, the maximalist strategy enunciated in the April Theses would work only in the exceptional social circumstances that the war had by 1917 created in Russia. For the central fact of that year is that once the linchpin of the hypercentralized Russian Imperial system was removed, all subordinate structures in the country began to unravel. The army, the industrial economy, the social structure of the countryside, and the administrative system of the Empire, both in the Great Russia provinces and among the border nationalities, all disintegrated to where, by the end of the year, the country no longer possessed any functioning, organized structures. The result was a generalized void of power, an interregnum in all aspects of national life. Thus, by October the wreckage of the Russian Empire was up for grabs, vulnerable to whatever force with the will and the organizational capacity to take it over.

The dynamic of national disintegration began with the army and was driven throughout the year above all by the war.[8] The policy of the Provisional Government was to prosecute the war to a victorious conclusion at the side of its democratic allies. The policy of the Soviet was to fight only for a "democratic peace without annexations or indemnities." Once discipline had seemingly been restored after the damage done by Order Number One, the liberal-socialist coalition government formed in April adopted a compromise war policy and so launched Kerenskii's "democratic" offensive in June. This self-contradictory enterprise ended in a rout, undermined army discipline once again, and fueled the Bolshevik thrust of the July Days. And that event in turn led to General Kornilov's attempt in August to restore Russia's fighting capacity by sweeping away the soviets. But this failed effort definitively discredited the army command and officer corps. After August, therefore, the army simply melted away, with the peasant soldiers trekking home to participate in the partition of the gentry's lands. Thus, all the political crises of the dual power, from April to July to August, were directly caused by the war, and by autumn, the impact of these crises on the army was such that the coercive power of the state was destroyed. The name for such a situation is anarchy—not as yet of the overt and violent sort, but a genuine absence of government nonetheless.[9]

This anarchy alone made possible the great agrarian revolution of 1917, that is, the liquidation by the peasantry of gentry land holdings, indeed, of the Russian gentry as a class. All peasant revolts in Russia had hitherto been suppressed because the predemocratic army had always remained intact.

The peasant out of uniform had played no part in the February events, but as the weakening of state authority accelerated throughout the year, these peasants progressively realized that their age-old dream of possessing all the land was at last within grasp. The Provisional Government had promised a Constituent Assembly for some future, propitious moment. This body would of course be empowered to address the land question, and everyone expected it to accede to the peasants' desires. Yet this near certainty of satisfaction did not moderate the attitude of the peasants: it simply increased their impatience. Thus during the summer they began to move against the gentry on their own and quickly discovered they could get away with this; by autumn, once state authority was vitually gone, they moved massively to expropriate everything in the countryside. This action in turn accelerated the disintegration of the army by drawing soldiers home to their villages to participate in the great partition. This revolution was not notably violent or murderous: The peasants were pursuing their economic interests, not social vengeance. But this revolution was extraordinarily thorough; by the end of the winter it had completely eliminated the century-old lord-peasant social structure of the countryside—a structure that had been intimately related to the officer-soldier hierarchy of the army. This revolution also liquidated the results of the Stolypin reform.

With all this transpiring in the Great Russian center of the Empire, the restive border nationalities were free to take control of their own affairs. For the most part, this occurred in two stages: by the summer of 1917 these regions were demanding autonomy, and by the end of the year or the beginning of the next, with the Bolsheviks in power, they were asserting their independence. Leading the way were the Grand Duchy of Finland in the north and the Ukrainian Rada (Soviet) in Kiev. (The most dissident nationality, the Poles, was already under German occupation.) By the beginning of 1918 the Baltic states and the Transcaucasian nations were equally restless. And so the Russian Empire, built through conquest and maintained by force, went the way of the army that had created it.

Thus, in the course of 1917 all of old Russia's structures—the state, the army, the Empire, the local administration, the economy, and both the urban and the rural societies—came apart simultaneously. This provides the answer to the second question posed at the beginning of the chapter: amidst such generalized collapse, there was no realistic chance of establishing a durable constitutional democracy. Any government that would have tried to intervene against this revolutionary process before its full unwinding would have been discredited. Even if the Provisional Government had found the resolve to immediately convene a Constituent Assembly, to unilaterally take Russia out of the war, and to give the land to the peasants—measures that critics later felt it should have adopted to stave off Bolshevism—this would hardly have had the desired result. For these measures were, in fact, similar to Bolshevik policy. They would have been revolutionary and disruptive in their effect, and they would have only deepened the anarchy without giving the Provisional Government the new coercive means to master it—means that came naturally to the Bolsheviks.

The sad fact of the matter is that in 1917 the impetus for disintegration was such that, once it had played itself out, only an authoritarian, coercive solution was possible for creating some new type of order. As the Kadet leader Miliukov put the matter, by the end of the summer the alternatives for Russia were either Kornilov or Lenin. But since Kornilov and the forces of traditional order that he symbolized had no power, only Lenin and the Bolsheviks were in a position to pick up the pieces and to fashion a new type of order once the social storm had spent its force.

This new type of order would be the "dictatorship of the proletariat" proclaimed after October as the vehicle for the transition from capitalism to socialism. Drawing on Marx's analysis of the Paris Commune, during the summer of 1917 in *State and Revolution* Lenin had interpreted the direct proletarian democracy of the workers' soviets as the realization of a new "commune state." As such, the soviets constituted the basis of the coming dictatorship and the new socialist state.[10] Thus, although it is only amidst a general process of national disintegration that the Russian workers' movement could have acquired "world-historical" significance, this broader process indeed received its political and ideological meaning from working-class action or, at the least, from action in the name of the working class.

It is for this reason that interpretation of the Russian Revolution, both in the East and in the West, has been overwhelmingly concerned with the working class in relation to the Bolshevik Party. This question is all the more urgent because whatever legitimacy the Soviet regime could once claim, in its own view and in that of the outside world, depended on the consubstantiality of the proletariat with the Party and, hence, on the socialist authenticity of October.

PROLETARIAT OR PARTY?

Although there has obviously been dissent from the equating of Bolshevism with the working class, there has nonetheless been a dominant tendency in the pre-1991 literature to ground October in social history and, in particular, to make it the product of "polarization" or class struggle between labor and capital. This approach goes back to 1917 itself, when it first became the dominant discourse of politics. For let us recall that in 1905 the Russian public by and large had not spoken of the "bourgeoisie" and the "proletariat," but instead had used the classical political language of liberalism and the struggle against autocracy to argue for a Constituent Assembly. The Russian political vocabulary became Marxist only towards the end of the constitutional experiment, and this process was brought to its culmination when the tensions generated by the "imperialist war" came out into the open in 1917.

This change of vocabulary had a very real effect on events in 1917. For Marxism invariably reduces politics to sociology, thereby obfuscating the purposeful use of power in public life. The Mensheviks in particular were adept at such reductionism. They argued, notably, that the Bolsheviks were rashly insurrectionary because they drew their support from workers recently out of the backward peasantry, whereas skilled workers with a genuine proletarian consciousness gravitated towards the Mensheviks themselves. This Russian Marxist manner of reducing politics to social base has mightily influenced Western writing on 1917 since the Second World War. Indeed, one of the main tasks of pre-1991 Western revisionist writing was to revise the old Menshevik opinion of the Bolshevik "base" by seeking to demonstrate that the Bolsheviks' workers, too, had a mature proletarian consciousness.[11] Even granting that this is true, what difference does it make to the political process leading to October, as well as to the political results of that event?

First of all, it is quite true that there was increasing class polarization in 1917 between the upper and the lower strata—or the *verkhi* and the *nizy*, as they were called at the time—of Russian society. The members of the *verkhi* were derisively called *burzhui*, a colloquial deformation of the French and Marxist term "bourgeois," and the *nizy* were less often designated by the old term for "people," *narod*, than by the ideological neologisms *proletarii* or *trudiashchiesia*, the "toilers." At the same time, the "masses" and their political friends were called "the democracy" as opposed to the "exploiters," who were "capitalists" or "feudal" landowners. A great deal of genuine class hatred lay behind this new vocabulary.

And, in fact, dual power appeared in Russia's factories just as it had in the army, the countryside, and the administration of the cities. Industrial dual power took the form of factory committees designed to oversee management and engineering personnel. These committees had the minimal goal of wresting classic trade union concessions from the factory owners. One such concession, the forty-hour workweek, was in fact obtained in June through strikes and other forms of labor pressure that at times were ineffectually yet threateningly answered by lockouts. In this classic type of labor struggle the workers were actively supported by the moderate (Menshevik and SR) socialist parties. And all of this, of course, further disrupted production for a war these same socialists now supported. Yet the maximal goal of the factory committees was even more disruptive; this goal was "workers' control of industry," which initially meant worker supervision of capital but in time came to mean worker takeover of the plants. In short, there was real class struggle in Russia's factories in 1917. In consequence, distrust and suspicion pervaded Russian industry as it was rapidly grinding to a halt.

The political consequences of this social revolution, however, were ambiguous. On one hand, from April to October the mood of the workers radicalized and became increasingly hostile to the "imperialist" war, the "capitalist" Provisional Government, and the "traitorous" moderate socialist parties that supported the war and the coalition with the "bourgeoisie." On the other hand, worker activism and militancy declined throughout 1917; these had reached their peak during the February Days, when the workers took real risks and payed with seventeen hundred casualties. The April crisis and the July Days produced a lesser though still respectable mobilization of workers in the streets. But popular reaction to the Kornilov incident was meager, and October was not a mass affair at all but an operation carried out by a small number of Bolshevik Party cadres and affiliated military units. Thus by October the revolutionary momentum of 1917 was winding down as the working class, along with the other components of Russian society, was disintegrating as a group and succumbing to weariness amidst a constant struggle to survive.

How, then, did this working class come to power in October? In fact, of course, it did not come to power; what came to power was a political and ideological organization, the Bolshevik Party. This raises two questions: the immediate empirical question of the nature of this Party and its relationship to the workers; and the general theoretical question of the relationship of "social base" to political power in any situation.

To begin with the first question, we must return to Lenin's call, in 1902 in *What Is To Be Done?*, for "a party of a new type," composed of full-time revolutionaries. Such a body he deemed necessary in part because of the conditions of illegality and clandestinity that weighed on all political life in Russia before 1905. But his paramount reason was that the "spontaneous trade unionism" of the workers had to be informed by the "conscious" and "scientific" revolutionary theory of the "vanguard" party. In other words, the Bolshevik Party was the vehicle for the logic of history that would lead mankind to the socialist revolution—or in practical terms the Party was a surrogate for the revolutionary intelligentsia. As for the actual workers, they participated in the Party's life only insofar as they worked for revolution and not for short-term economic gains. If the workers fell into the latter "revisionist" trap, they ceased being authentic proletarians and became part of the "petty bourgeoisie," whose natural spokesmen were the "traitorous" Mensheviks or the "renegade" German SDs. For there existed basically only two classes with two worldviews in society, the proletariat and the bourgeoisie; if any political actor, whatever his de facto class, did not have a scientific revolutionary consciousness, he was automatically a *burzhui* and an enemy. The Leninist Party thus represented a metaphysical, not an empirical, proletariat, and this primacy of ideological "consciousness" over real life was Lenin's understanding of the class struggle and the driving force of all his politics.[12]

It is this ideologically defined political organization, and not the mere empirical proletariat, that seized power in October 1917. In order to do this, however, the Party had an absolute need of real working-class support for at least as long as it took to vault into power. Its leaders also genuinely needed to believe that the Party and the real workers were in fact one, just as numerous workers sincerely believed the same thing. And it is on the basis of this misunderstanding that Lenin and the Party leadership in 1917 transformed their elite operation into a temporary mass organization.

The Bolsheviks had played no significant role in the events of 1905, despite the flurry of the Moscow December insurrection; in fact, Lenin did not even return to Russia in time for the Revolution. The Bolsheviks began to acquire a significant, though hardly a mass, following only after 1912; by the time of the strikes in the summer of 1914, they had pulled ahead of the Mensheviks among the workers. But all this was dashed by the patriotic wave that followed the outbreak of war in August. Thus the Bolsheviks—and the other revolutionary parties as well—had to build their popular base all over again after February 1917. By the late summer of that year, however, the Bolsheviks had again pulled ahead of the Mensheviks and the SRs in the cities and the northern part of the front. But given the fluid nature and the short time span of working-class political involvement, it is far-fetched to argue that the proletariat had any deep and enduring commitment to any one party organization.

Nonetheless, between April and October the Bolshevik Party became the provisional preference of the more radicalized workers. According to the Party's own estimation of its strength at the time, its membership was 23,600 at the beginning of 1917, although most of these of necessity participated clandestinely in what little Party activity there was.[13] By January 1918 membership was around 115,000, and quite possibly more; some 60 percent of the members were classified as workers, while 32 percent were "white-collar" employees or petty intelligentsia. For the first time, Lenin's Party ceased being essentially an organization of professional revolutionaries and became a body composed predominantly of workers.

This new Party, moreover, was not a disciplined army to be maneuvered at will by the leadership. The base, especially in Petrograd, was more radical and impatient than the Central Committee and exerted considerable pressure on Lenin and his colleagues; decisions were largely made through a process that involved debates and votes.

Organizationally, as already noted, the Party had the classic structure of a Social Democratic Party, with a Central Committee chosen by a Congress elected by local committees. It is these characteristics of 1917 Bolshevism that have been called "democratic."[14] But this democracy existed only for members of one class, the workers, and only for politics within the Party. And in the Leninist ideology that pervaded this organization, the rest of society and all rival political organizations—even the other socialist parties—were regarded as class enemies, as "bourgeois" or "petty-bourgeois," who therefore would have to be eliminated once the true party of the proletariat came to power. Thus, the more or less "mass" Bolshevik Party of 1917 was never democratic in the sense of being willing to share power, or to alternate in power, with other groups.

This circumstance provides the key to understanding the October overturn. From the April Theses on into the autumn, Lenin's organization built its influence through a drumbeat of agitation for the end of dual power in favor of the class-based soviets. The Bolsheviks' refrain was "bread, peace, land, all power to the soviets." This program was irresponsible and demagogic in the sense that the seizure of power by the soviets would not in fact solve the problems of bread, peace, or land, as Lenin's socialist adversaries constantly pointed out. But this program made great sense as revolutionary politics because it mobilized workers and soldiers angry with an increasingly desperate situation with the purpose of seizing power for the "toilers."

But, as we have seen, the toilers did not seize power directly.[15] That the Party did it for them is best brought out by the contrast with February. In October there was nothing like the hundreds of thousands of strikers who had faced real danger in the streets for five days in February, nor was there anything like the seventeen hundred casualties of that event. In October the streets were empty of workers, and the number of victims was around a dozen. These "ten days that shook the world," therefore, were in reality a coup d'état, and the prodigious efforts deployed to deny this obvious fact are a classic case where protesting too much is an indirect admission of something to hide.[16] Indeed, until the mid-1920s the Bolsheviks themselves called October a *perevorot*, that is, an "overturn" or coup. Nonetheless, this coup did in fact shake the world in an unprecedented and world-historical manner; for, although the empirical proletariat largely sat out Great October, the metaphysical proletariat was catapulted into power, and this political-ideological entity would prove to be far more revolutionary than all the real workers of the world united.

To be sure, the events in Petrograd were not the whole of the October Revolution: in Moscow, for example, there was a genuine struggle and a greater number of victims. And in the days that followed, local soviets under Bolshevik and Left-SR leadership took control from the *burzhui* throughout much of the country. Although this hardly amounted to the "triumphal march" of Bolshevik power of which Soviet historiography once spoke, there was in fact a national revolution of soviets in answer to the Petrograd coup.

The October Revolution may be considered national, however, only in conjunction with the peasant jacquerie of the winter of 1917–1918 which liquidated gentry landholding in the countryside and made the peasants (temporarily) their own masters. This agrarian revolution was, of course, neither commanded nor controlled by the Bolsheviks, although their agitators advocated seizure of gentry lands by the peasants.[17] Yet it was the Bolsheviks who profited most from the jacquerie politically, incorporating it into the myth of a single Great October.

This confiscation was facilitated by the left wing of the SRs, who seceded from the main SR party in October to support the Bolshevik seizure of power because they thought it meant soviet power. Thus Lenin was able to claim that his Soviet government represented a "revolutionary alliance of workers and peasants." And this was the real meaning of his Decree on Land of October 25, socializing the land in accordance with the traditional SR program. In fact, however, the decree simply appropriated a fait accompli for Bolshevik purposes, since the government could do nothing to determine the course of events in the countryside. As Lenin put it at the time, Bolshevik policy was simply "to give the peasant nag its head."

Lenin's policy of "revolutionary alliance" with the peasantry and his appropriation of the SR land program have often been cited—especially by Mensheviks and SRs—as proof that October was not a proper Marxist revolution but a throwback to the Russian Populist tradition of the 1870s. There is indeed some truth in this: Lenin did fuse the heritage of Chernyshevskii and the Populists with Marxism. But it was the Marxism that came out on top; for Lenin never intended that the land would remain "socialized," that is, in the peasants' own hands, in accordance with the real SR policy. Accordingly, in February 1918 his government nationalized all land and put legal title to it in the hands of the state. Although for the time being the Bolsheviks could not implement this measure, it did at least reveal their true aims.

Moreover, there is good Marxist authority for Lenin's limited borrowings from Populism. The founder himself, in a letter to the Populist leader Vera Zasulich in 1882, had approved of combining a peasant revolution in Russia with a proletarian revolution in the West (a document Plekhanov and Engels conspired to suppress lest it scandalize the nascent Russian Marxist movement). And it is just such a strategy Lenin thought he was following in 1917. Earlier still, in 1851, Marx had argued that his own backward Germany could telescope the bourgeois and proletarian revolutions and ride piggyback on a socialist upheaval in France; this scenario, shifted a bit to the east, is what Lenin also thought he was carrying out in 1917.

The real objection to caviling about Lenin's orthodoxy, however, is that this is an issue only for those who hold that the essence of Marxism lies in its formal tenets of lockstep succession from feudalism to capitalism to socialism. But the essence of Marxism—let us recall—lies in its deep structure of reliance on the alienation of the most deprived classes as the demiurge of revolution; and the peasantry fitted quite logically into this mold as the junior wing of the universal class. Lenin, like Marx (and later like Mao), would take the fire of revolution where he found it, and adjust the formal tenets of his theory accordingly. A similar adjustment, as we have seen, was achieved by Lenin's theory of imperialism, which made Russia the "weakest link in the capitalist chain." What Marxism is all about, after all, is changing the world, not just understanding it.

Thus, it was thanks to the peasantry that the world's first Marxist revolution occurred in the only European country it could—Russia. And this revolution occurred in the only way it could under Russian conditions—as a movement of workers *and* peasants. So all of the toilers were brought together in a synthesis under the sign of the hammer and sickle emblazoned on the internationalist red flag. Never before had *"les damnés de la terre, les forçats de la faim,"* as the new Soviet anthem, the "Internationale," put it, so truly appeared to be the universal class from below.

Still, the workers, as the progressive and technological class, had to remain the vanguard of this movement, and their alleged "armed insurrection" in Petrograd had to be the pivotal event of the world-historical transformation of Red October. And, of course, the real workers were absolutely necessary to this metaphysical event. To be sure, these workers had hardly been responsive to the Party long enough to constitute its "social base" the way trade unions, say, have been the base of socialist parties in Western Europe. Nonetheless, these workers were the indispensable springboard from which the party catapulted to power.

But this springboard alone would not have been enough: The rest of the Russian national system—the state structures, the army, the rural order—had to be in terminal crisis as well. Thus overall, October represents a conjunction of the greatest military mutiny of all time, and the greatest peasant jacquerie in history, with a simulacrum, artificially engineered, of the Paris Commune.

In reality, the comparison of this communette with the Commune of 1871 or with the Paris June Days of 1848—the two models, for all Marxists, of what a proletarian revolution should be like—is quite abusive. For these latter two events were genuine urban (if not actually "proletarian") insurrections of heroic proportions. In fact, one is tempted to adapt Marx's *mot* that history always repeats itself—first as tragedy, then as farce—to Red October, with Lenin's Petrograd "insurrection" very much in the latter genre.

Take away either of the first two elements of the October triad of mutiny–jacquerie–communette, and the "Petrograd Commune"—whether occurring under a monarchy or a republic—would have been crushed by the peasant soldier just as surely as was its Parisian predecessor by rural France. Take away the First World War, and there would have been neither the mutiny nor its social prolongation in the universal jacquerie. It is all these factors working together, not some proletarian-bourgeois polarization, that constitutes the real social history of October.

It is in this perspective that we find the answer to the third question posed at the beginning of this chapter, namely, what were the respective roles of Russia's internal social processes and the impact of the war in producing October? The answer, obviously, is that the two factors acted in combination, though not through any simple addition of the latter to the former. Although there was no lack of social tension in the brutally hierarchical society that was old Russia, these tensions were aggravated to murderous intensity by the sufferings of the war. Thus the social polarization that finally occurred was far more explosive than that of 1905–1906, a circumstance that continued into the even more exceptionally brutal Civil War that ensued. Moreover, the war destroyed the institutional restraints of state power that might have held this polarization in check.

In view of such weighty "contingencies," it is far-fetched to view October primarily as the outcome of the logic of Russia's social processes: There are times when contingency itself is structure, and the role of the Russian Revolution is one of these. And it is even more far-fetched to accept the Party's definition of itself as a proletarian organization. Both of these propositions are myths.

Nevertheless, the October myths were indispensable to the Bolsheviks' daring at the time and to their ruthless revolutionary action from above once they were in power—as well as to their international success. And these myths had sufficient empirical underpinning to appear credible as scientific facts, both to the actors involved and in much of the historiography since. Yet this overlap of Party and proletariat proved transitory. By early 1918, as we will see, the proletariat had begun to dissolve as a cohesive social group; and after the Civil War the Party was so firmly entrenched that it required no social base of any kind to remain in power. Thus the issue of the social history of Bolshevism, so obsessive for October, quickly fades into insignificance as we move into the Soviet era itself.

Moreover, even in late 1917–early 1918, when the overlap between Party and workers was greatest, it was based largely on a misunderstanding. To be sure, in October the workers wanted a government of soviets, but one that would be a coalition of all of the socialist parties. Indeed, a number of Bolshevik leaders, notably Kamenev and Zinoviev, wanted the same thing, which is why they had been reticent about October and why Lenin always somewhat distrusted them. And, for a few months in early 1918, Lenin did opportunistically accept a coalition with the Left SRs. But from the beginning, the majority of the Party leadership, and certainly the great architects of October, Lenin and Trotsky, intended only a one-party Bolshevik regime for as long as it would take to reach socialism. In their view, and in that of the Soviet state ever after, October represented a once-and-forever transmission of democratic legitimacy from people to

Party, with no need for any "bourgeois" renewal of mandate. Thus Mikhail Gorbachev, until the very end, always spoke of "the socialist choice made in October." But it is quite gratuitous to assume that the workers of Russia intended any such definitive commitment to the Party when they endorsed, or acquiesced in, the October overturn.

What we do know the workers wanted in October was "workers' control of industry" and the dispossession of the "*burzhui*," measures by which they sought to secure direct control over their social environment. But this is hardly the same as integral socialism, even though the workers did use the term "socialism" in a very general fashion. This vague socialism, moreover, could be secured by the workers' political preference for a coalition soviet government of all three socialist parties. But "building socialism" in the integral sense, not some anarcho-syndicalist "workers' control," was the true aim of the Bolsheviks. Just what, precisely, the building of socialism entailed, not even the Party leadership knew in 1917; but whatever was required clearly did not depend on the will or choice of the workers. It is significant that on October 25 there was no dramatic "Decree on Workers' Control" to accompany the "Decree on Land," for in the Leninist view the Party *was* the proletariat. Only a month later was workers' control put into law.

But the question of the proletarian nature of October goes deeper than the political and social contingencies of that event. To pose the question at all presupposes the existence of proletarian revolutions. Yet even the most cursory examination of European history shows that if October is not the genuine article, then there never has been a proletarian revolution, anywhere, anytime. The same might also be said of bourgeois revolutions. The only halfway plausible example of such an event is France in 1789; indeed, the French case furnished the model for the whole idea. Nowhere else—neither in England nor in Germany nor in the United States—did the bourgeoisie require a political revolution to come to power (if indeed "bourgeoisie in power" appropriately describes modern constitutional arrangements anywhere); nor does the French case offer us the industrial bourgeoisie at its most dynamic. Moreover, both the bourgeois revolution and the proletarian revolution represent the oddity of generalizations from a single case. Yet these obvious empirical considerations are secondary in this mode of analysis; for in discussions of the procession from the bourgeois to the proletarian revolution we are not dealing with sociology but with eschatology.

Neither the bourgeois revolution nor the proletarian revolution, then, is an empirically compelling, or even a useful, category. Indeed, it is possible to go still further and say that social classes never rule: state and governments do. Politics cannot be reduced to some social or economic base, and the state is not simply the agent of a ruling class. Politics is an "independent variable," as current sociological terminology has it, with its own logic and laws. The political sphere, of course, interacts with the social and the economic spheres, and some groups profit far more than others from any given political arrangement; but the exercise of political power also has a dynamic of its own. It is thus futile to try to organize history around the putative progression from one dominant class to another; yet such a progression is precisely what the debate over Red October presupposes. And so once again, that event turns out to be embedded in a metaphysic vaster than the brute events of Russian history.

For the myth of proletarian October is the myth of the triumph of the alienated and dehumanized masses over all their sufferings and deprivations. In this eschatological perspective, suffering is the criterion of authentic humanity, for Marx no less than for Dostoevsky. And since intense crisis makes suffering most acute, the war and the social collapse of 1917 conferred on the humiliated and offended of Russian life quintessential human status. For the suffering of 1917 was no myth, but the most cruel empirical fact. In these circumstances, the modest Russian proletariat could indeed appear in the eyes of its self-appointed leaders, and in those of many socialists throughout the world, to be the universal class and the bearer of the logic of history. Thus patent myth became a mighty empirical force, the indispensable launching pad of the whole fantastic Soviet adventure.

4

A REGIME IS BORN
War Communism, 1918–1921

The ideas of economists and political philosophers, both when they are right and when they are wrong, are more powerful than is commonly understood. Indeed the world is ruled by little else. Practical men, who believe themselves to be quite exempt from any intellectual influences, are usually the slaves of some defunct economist. Madmen in authority, who hear voices in the air, are distilling their frenzy from some academic scribbler of a few years back.

—John Maynard Keynes

To the adamantine incarnation of all the greatness and vigour of the proletariat ... to the great Communist Party—we dedicate this book [The ABC of Communism]. *We dedicate it to the Party which commands an army of a million men, dwells in the trenches, administers a vast realm, carts wood on Communist Saturdays, makes ready for the resurrection day of mankind.*

—Nikolai Bukharin and Evgenii Preobrazhenskii

Socialism = Soviet Power + Electrification

—V. I. Lenin

Dvanov thought up an invention: to convert sunlight into electricity. To do this Gopner took all the mirrors in Chevengur out of their frames, and also collected every last little piece of thick glass. From this material Dvanov and Gopner made complex prisms and reflectors, such that the light of the sun, passing through them, would be transformed and would at the end of the device become an electric current. The device had already been completed for two days, but still no electricity appeared. Everyone came by to look over Dvanov's light machine, and though it did not

work, nonetheless they decided that it was needed: the machine was po-
litically correct and necessary, in as much as it had been thought up and
built by the bodily labor of two sterling comrades.
　　　　　　　　　　　　　　　—*Andrei Platonov*, Chevengur

It was war that had made possible the Bolshevik seizure of power; and it was war that would set the parameters within which the basic institutions of the new Soviet order would be .built. The Party's "dictatorship of the proletariat" thus was born into the world as War Communism. And this rough beast would be a hybrid of military communism and militant communism, in which each component fed on, and at the same time reinforced, the other.

In October 1917 the Bolsheviks had succeeded in occupying the physical seats of power, but they were hardly in a position to actually wield power. Though it was no small feat to take over the nerve centers of a major state, such an exploit was not without precedent in European history, and the Communards of 1871 had done almost as much. The real test of the Bolshevik's mettle would be their ability to consolidate power and to build a functioning new order; and they met this test in an unprecedented outburst of revolutionary vigor between 1918 and 1921, the years of the Civil War and War Communism.

These years were the founding years of Communism as a really-existing system, the time when the matrix of Sovietism as it would endure for the next three-quarters of a century was set. Indeed, the most "creative" stage of this process was the year 1918, during which all the essential measures were taken that made the Soviet system possible. It is 1918, not 1917, that is the truly decisive year of the Russian Revolution. This is the year in which the Party of a new type showed just how new it was by creating an entire society of a new type.

The Party created this unique society by its daring responses to a succession of crises that would have overwhelmed any lesser form of political organization. Yet these responses are by no means the haphazard improvisations they may seem to be at first glance; rather, they reveal a pattern of political will directed towards the subordination of all social "spontaneity" to Party "consciousness."

THE DESCENT INTO CHAOS

The expectation of the Bolshevik leadership in October was that the Russian Revolution would trigger a revolution that would sound the death knell for capitalism across Europe. The mechanism by which this would be achieved was fraternization among the various belligerent armies: This movement, a response to the Soviet Peace Decree of October 26, would bring soviets to power everywhere. In the first months after October, Lenin, Trotsky, and others in the Bolshevik and the Left SR (Socialist Revolutionary) leaderships all firmly believed that such a revolutionary end to the imperialist war was imminent. How far down in Party ranks and in the working class this belief extended is difficult to say; but it is a fair guess that, despite relentless propaganda for the anti-imperialist view, most Russians were simply, and untheoretically, against the war regardless of the political consequences. For the people making the decisions on the Left in Russia at the time, however, October made sense only as a detonator, not as an end in itself.

A corollary to this belief was that once capitalism had collapsed, socialism would automatically appear, more or less full-blown, because it was allegedly already present "in the womb of bourgeois society," as Marx put it. Lenin had updated this proposition of Marx to take account of the innovations of the age of "finance capital" and "imperialism." In his view, the total mobilization required to wage modern war represented that rational organization of economic life that was the essence of socialism; it would therefore be enough to end the war, thereby overthrowing capitalism, and socialism would practically be there. For this reason, Lenin had the highest regard for the policies of General Erich von Ludendorff and his economic planner Walter Rathenau, policies that they themselves called *Kriegsozialismus*, or War Socialism. And to these Lenin added his belief in the "scientific" American method of Taylorism for the rational organization of work. Real socialism, therefore, would result from similar policies implemented by proletarian power. And all this would come about fairly soon, after an intermediate stage that Lenin sometimes called "state capitalism," which is essentially another term for War Socialism. The Bolshevik policy after October, therefore, was to begin the advance toward socialism in Russia by imposing state control on the existing capitalist industrial system while awaiting the European, especially the German, revolution that would make full socialism possible across the continent.

But as the months dragged on into 1918, the imperialist war did not end in revolution. It soon became apparent that Russia's tentative advance towards socialism through state capitalism would be the whole of the Bolsheviks' economic policy for the foreseeable future. In other words, whatever fuller socialism would follow from breaking the capitalist chain at its weakest, Russian link would have to be engineered by Soviet power without any input from the advanced West. So, as events moved on into the summer, the effort to engineer socialism eclipsed the previous policy of waiting for it, and state capitalism gave way to War Communism. In short, when the logic of history did not produce socialism automatically, the hand of history had to be forced by the Party; that is, socialism would have to be "built," as the Soviets would later say. And it is the aspiration to build socialism that furnished the pattern, or the logic, that governed all of the Bolsheviks' seeming improvisations in 1918.

This point bears emphasizing because the Bolsheviks' policies throughout the Civil War are too often dismissed as quasi-accidental, an aberration from the original Leninist course of waiting for objective circumstances to mature sufficiently for genuine socialism to become possible. And this premature, forced march into the New Society is explained by the cruel exigencies of the struggle for survival in the Civil War. In consequence, this period appears as a neglected poor relation in the historiography of Leninism, an embarrassment to be gotten over as rapidly as possible in chronicling the work of the Founder. This attitude, however, is a grave error, for War Communism was seminal to the whole Soviet experience. War Communism was no aberration, but the crucial episode that first revealed to the Bolsheviks who they in fact were.[1]

This process of self-discovery under fire began in the immediate aftermath of October and lasted until the autumn of the following year. It was propelled by a succession of crises that showed that all of the problems—from the war to the economy—that had plagued the Provisional Government had not disappeared but had grown worse under the disintegrative impact of Soviet power itself. Yet the new government, unlike its predecessor, did not collapse under the strain; rather, catastrophe galvanized it into ever bolder and more drastic action.

The first problem the Bolsheviks had to face was that of state power, and this they solved, after a fashion, by eliminating all rival loci of power through police measures.[2] Among Lenin's very first acts, on December 7, 1917, was to establish the Extraordinary Commission for the Struggle against Counterrevolution and Sabotage, commonly known as the Cheka, under the leadership of a Polish nobleman rallied to Bolshevism, Felix Dzerzhinskii. This arm of the proletarian dictatorship was deemed necessary to dispossess the former exploiting classes—the bourgeoisie and the gentry—and to suppress their political activities. Very soon, however, such "economic crimes" as "speculation" and "hoarding" came under the Cheka's jurisdiction. In other words, Lenin from the beginning was preparing to wage civil war against all the class enemies of Soviet power. Although the first shots in this war were actually fired by the White Volunteer Army in the region of the Don Cossacks in December, it was the Bolsheviks' presumption to exercise a monopoly of power that left opposition forces no recourse but armed resistance.

But the first major clash in the war was between the Bolsheviks and all the other political parties. Elections for the Constituent Assembly, on the basis of universal suffrage, at last took place at the end of 1917. The results were more a victory for social revolution than for constitutional democracy; the only party for whom the latter system was the first principle, the Kadets, received only 4.7 percent of the vote. But the elections were not a victory for the Bolsheviks, either; they received 24 percent of both votes and seats. The clear leader was the protean SR Party with about 40 percent of the vote, and this yielded the mainstream, or "Right," SRs 54 percent of the total delegates and the Left SRs 5.5 percent (the single SR list had been drawn up before the two groups split). The Mensheviks and Kadets had about 2 percent of the seats each.[3]

Thus, although some 85 percent of the seats went to socialists of one or another stripe, the Assembly was still not a body that would do the Bolsheviks' bidding or recognize their "Soviet" government. Lenin solved this problem by arguing, first, that the mainstream SR delegation was not representative of the base, which he held had moved to his kind of Left after the single electoral list had been drawn up. A more important argument was the teleological one that the "soviet" democracy of the toiling classes alone was "higher" than the "bourgeois" democracy of one man, one vote. Thus in the course of the elections he had outlawed the "bourgeois" Kadets. And when the Assembly met on January 6, 1918, he dispersed it with the help of sailors from the Baltic Fleet who, with the words "the guard is tired," told its chairman, the SR Victor Chernov, to decamp.

The dispersal of the Constituent Assembly is usually alleged to be the Bolsheviks' supreme crime, on a footing with the October coup, against democracy. And this is quite true. But it is not often enough noted that, realistically, this body could hardly have governed amidst the mounting disorder of the time. As Trotsky put it, with only slight exaggeration, politically the Assembly was nothing more than the pale shadow that the Provisional Government had cast before itself into the future. For the Assembly was dominated by the same parties that had been unable to master the situation when they were in power in 1917; it had no armed forces and no administrative apparatus, not even in the soviets. Nor did it have a program: the only two resolutions it adopted were simply endorsements of the Bolsheviks' decrees on peace and land. Finally, it had no constituency prepared to fight for its right to govern. Once the peasants had the land, they lost interest in politics; and the workers, for the time being, still thought that the soviets were really theirs. So no real resistance, or even outrage, answered the Assembly's demise. As for the nonbourgeois parties—the majority SRs and the Mensheviks—they continued to be technically legal, but in practice they were increasingly harassed as the Civil War progressed.

Soon Lenin dispatched his only socialist allies, the Left SRs. In January 1918, in anticipation of trouble with the Assembly and pressed by the more timorous members of his Central Committee, Lenin had accepted a coalition government with four Left SR ministers. But they resigned in March in protest against his peace with the Germans at Brest-Litovsk. From then until the demise of the Soviet state in 1991, government was strictly a one-party affair. It is difficult to believe that this swift emergence of a one-party regime was forced on Lenin and Trotsky by a civil war that had not yet begun. A one-party order was implicit from the beginning in the October overturn, in which the unilateral Bolshevik seizure of power was barely camouflaged by a facade of soviets.

Still, the Party did not govern directly. Rather, it ruled through an ostensibly normal state apparatus that bore the name "Soviet" and exercised its power through ministries given the populist label "People's Commissariats." This arrangement, which has been variously called the Party-state or the dual state, is the great Bolshevik innovation in politics. In this dual state, real power in the country was held by the Party, a self-appointed organization recruited entirely by co-optation; it was thus in effect a secret society, or what has been called a "conspiracy in power," which ruled behind the scenes through a formal state apparatus theoretically resting on the people. In this dichotomy the Party was "the power," as people later said, and the Soviet administrative network was its "apparat."

Both the Cheka and the framework of the Party-state were created during the first three months after October, before any serious challenge to Bolshevik power had emerged (the miniscule White movement that had appeared in the south was as yet no threat). These two institutions, however, were still embryonic. In the next eight months they were to attain their full stature under the impact of a cascade of calamities that by August seemed about to sweep the Bolshevik regime away entirely.

The first of these crises was occasioned by the disastrous peace of Brest-Litovsk. An armistice in November 1917 led to peace negotiations in that city between the Central Powers and the Soviet government in December. The purpose of the Bolsheviks, of course, was not to negotiate a peace with their interlocutors; it was to use the negotiations as a propaganda platform against the imperialist war and for "a democratic peace without annexations or indemnities." Thereby, they hoped to produce fraternization between the troops of the two armies, and through this to transform the imperialist war into an international class war leading to socialist revolution. In short, they were projecting into the international arena the maximalist tactics that had brought them power at home.

But this enterprise, conducted by Trotsky with the same revolutionary gusto with which he had presided over the Petrograd Soviet in October, led to fiasco at Brest-Litovsk. The soldiers of the Central Powers were not swayed; their commanders soon lost patience with Bolshevik grandstanding; and in February their armies again began to advance into Russia. But by this time Russia no longer had an army with which to resist them. The capital was hastily moved from Petrograd to Moscow so as to be farther from the front. Lenin urged the realistic course of accepting a dictated, "imperialist" peace in order to save the Soviet regime. Trotsky, Bukharin, and others romantically advocated one version or another of "revolutionary"—that is, guerrilla—war to stop the German advance and spread the Revolution westward. Lenin carried the day in the Party and in the Soviet Congress by only the narrowest of margins. But the cost to the country was enormous: The Baltic provinces, Ukraine, and southern Russia on into the Caucasus passed under German control. These territories represented a third of the European portion of the old Empire and almost half of the Empire's industrial capacity and food production. But such is the price of a separate peace in a losing war. It was because of the likelihood of similar terms that the Provisional Government had never dared to unilaterally leave the war that was destroying it.

Lenin's rationale, of course, was that since world revolution was still imminent, the concessions of Brest-Litovsk would soon be wiped out; in the meantime, the overriding consideration was to obtain a "breathing space" to consolidate socialist power, which was also the Party's power, in the only place it existed. Lenin's "realism" in this crisis of survival has been much praised by historians, including those unsympathetic to the Soviet regime. Yet his realism in this and other matters can be exaggerated: It concerned tactics, not strategy, for his realism was always predicated on the wild ideological premises of world revolution—as had been the case with his realism in October. Nonetheless, with his Brest-Litovsk breathing space, he scored his second great coup as a revolutionary leader, for eventually this new gamble did pay off with the collapse of the Central Powers at the end of the year.

In the short term, however, Brest-Litovsk created new life-threatening problems for the Soviet regime. The decision to sign an "imperialist" peace split the Left coalition of October. There was, first, a temporary schism among the Bolsheviks when Nikolai Bukharin and a group of Left Communists broke Party ranks to continue agitating for revolutionary war. More serious still, the Left SRs left the coalition formed in January and went into active opposition to undo the Brest peace. Soon they were given a more potent reason for opposition because of Bolshevik pressure on the peasants.

The form this pressure took was a momentous new Bolshevik agrarian policy—"class warfare in the village"—which will be discussed more fully below. At this point, suffice it to note that by April–May the economy of the central Russian regions—the only parts of the old Empire that remained under Bolshevik control—was beginning to come apart. Hunger was felt in the cities at the end of a long winter that had seen the populations of Petrograd and Moscow decline by about a third. The Party sought to meet this problem by proclaiming "class warfare" in the villages. This meant inciting the "poor peasants"—the functional equivalent in the villages of the "proletariat"—to extort the "surplus" grain of the "petty bourgeois kulaks"; this policy culminated on June 11 with a decree organizing "Committees of the Village Poor."[4] Although this policy brought in almost no grain, it did have the political effect of alienating the peasants from the regime and turning the Left SRs into an armed opposition.

Then, in late May and early June, what seemed like the ultimate disaster struck. Some thirty-five thousand Czech prisoners of war who had been formed into detachments of the Imperial army to fight against Austria were now strung along a line running from the Volga across Siberia to Vladivostok. Awaiting evacuation around the world to the western front in France, but fearing that they might be disarmed by the Bolsheviks, the Czech troops seized the whole trans-Siberian railroad line.

Soviet power immediately collapsed everywhere along the route. The mainstream SRs reemerged from the shadows and convened a rump Constituent Assembly in Samara on the Volga. An alternative government to that of Lenin now became a serious possibility, and the small White movement in the south suddenly acquired a genuine base. Meanwhile, the Western Allies, furious at Russia's desertion at Brest-Litovsk, now saw the possibility of reopening an eastern front. The Allies therefore told the Czechs to stay put and began to intervene themselves against the Reds. It should be noted that it is this military consideration—not economic imperialism as the Bolsheviks claimed—that motivated the Allied intervention in the Revolution.

By June Bolshevik Russia had been reduced to roughly the area of the medieval Grand Principality of Moscow. Even within this area the Bolsheviks' control was unsteady. In July the Left SRs attempted a revolt in Moscow with the aim of drawing Russia into revolutionary war with Germany, and Boris Savinkov staged an uprising in Iaroslavl on the upper Volga. Rudimentary White armies were also advancing from the Urals to the middle Volga. Then, in August, a Left SR terrorist nearly succeeded in killing Lenin. By the summer's end it looked as if the Bolshevik adventure might soon be over and the whole episode would enter history as a second, grander Paris Commune, a glorious failure that would live only as a beacon for future socialist revolutions.

THE PARTY STRIKES BACK

It was in response to this succession of crises that the embryonic Party-state which had emerged from October grew to full stature. The Bolshevik counteroffensive developed simultaneously on three main fronts. First, there was the political-administrative front of class war against all other parties. Second, there was the military front of the Civil War against the Whites. And finally, there was the economic front of War Communism narrowly defined, that is, the building of a socialist order.

Beginning in the spring of 1918, the Cheka was put to vigorous new uses, not only to combat the Whites, but to roll back a resurgence of non-Bolshevik socialist strength. As the situation deteriorated during the spring, the Party's worker "base" began to crumble, and Mensheviks and SRs once again won majorities in the soviets; in answer, those bodies were simply purged of the "petty bourgeois" elements by the Cheka, and reliable Bolsheviks were appointed in their place.[5] And as the danger to Bolshevik power increased in July and August with the Left SR revolt and the White advance on central Russia, the omnipresent network of soviets was wholly subordinated to the Party; from that time on, the soviets were purely formal institutions.

Thus by the end of the summer the commune state, celebrated by Lenin in *State and Revolution* and adumbrated in fact in 1917, had fully given way to the Party-state.[6] Then, after the August attempt on Lenin's life, the regime officially proclaimed a policy of Red Terror, which would be directed by the Cheka against all enemies of the people, of the Revolution, and of the Party. And so the "dictatorship of the proletariat" came to acquire its full, postrevolutionary meaning of an "unlimited power above all law," as Lenin liked to put the matter.

The second, or military, response to escalating catastrophe came in the immediate wake of Brest-Litovsk. It consisted of replacing the people's militia of Red Guards that had been formed in 1917 with a Red Army based on the conventional formula of conscription, discipline, and a top-down chain of command.[7] The key measure—conscription—was introduced on April 22, and Trotsky redeployed his talents from diplomacy to war as Commander in Chief of the new revolutionary institution. For the Red Army, despite the return to hierarchy and discipline, remained a revolutionary institution, not a classical army.

The experience with the Germans prior to Brest-Litovsk, and then the growth of the White movement after May, had demonstrated that an amateur, volunteer force with elected officers simply could not provide for survival. Warfare is a technical profession, and professional officers were necessary to wage it. Such officers could be drawn quickly only from the ranks of the old Imperial army, but these gentlemen could not be trusted. So Trotsky conscripted them freely and flanked them with a corps of political commissars whose role was to countersign all orders, to persuade the Red ranks to obey their new officers, and to indoctrinate everyone with a correct political attitude for class war. Thus was created another indispensable element of the nascent system: the Party monitor who would subordinate all "bourgeois" technical experts to the political purposes of socialist revolution.

Although this system of dual administration was first developed for the army, it could be applied to any function in society, to all economic and other civilian tasks. Eventually, in the mature Soviet order, Party representatives or departments would supervise industrial managers, collective farm chairmen, educators, scientists, writers—indeed, everybody and everything. This is because the mission of the Party was to realize a political and ideological vision; its vocation was not to exercise technical and professional competence in any of the activities necessary for the functioning of modern society.

This discrepancy between Party purposes and the functional needs of the society it controlled was particularly acute during the first years of Soviet power, when a hitherto underground, conspiratorial organization suddenly found itself in control of a recalcitrant state organization. If society were to function at all, the Party would have to use "bourgeois specialists" from the old order whom it could not trust politically. And the impressment of such specialists in all fields, not just the military, began immediately in 1918. In time, of course, the Party would train its own "Red specialists," in whom technical competence and political correctness would be united. But for a lengthy and indeterminate period, or until socialism had arrived, the Party monitor, commissar, or political officer was an absolute necessity.

This need for ideological control was the germ of the Party apparat's right of appointment to any functional post of importance in society, a right that defined a system later known as the *nomenklatura*. Such dual administration thus spelled the end of "civil society"—a term which in the twilight years of the regime Soviet dissidents used to designate all groups capable of self-organization independent of the state. This mode of control became the operational essence of the Party-state, the means whereby the functional, governmental, or "Soviet" bureaucracy was monitored from behind the scenes by a parallel and unaccountable Party administration that had the real power of decision.

The first great success of this new system was the creation of an effective Red Army—effective, that is, in comparison with the White forces, not with the regular armies of the First World War. All told, in the course of the Civil War some six million men were conscripted into the Red Army (obviously, rather more of them were peasants than workers). Of these, some three million deserted or disappeared back into the villages from whence they had been dragooned. According to Trotsky's own estimate, only around five hundred thousand or six hundred thousand of the total could be used as an effective fighting force. Of these, soldiers of worker background were the most disciplined and the most committed to the Revolution—the "red corpuscles" of the army, as they were called at the time. In the course of the conflict, cadets taken from this group and trained as officers began to progressively replace the holdovers from the tsarist period. In this manner the Red Army became a major source of recruitment of new men for the new regime. At the same time, the army largely absorbed the proletariat as the civilian economy ground to a halt and factories slowed production or closed altogether.

This hastily improvised, poorly structured, and socially fluid force would hardly have been a match for a regular European army—say, if the Germans had advanced once again into the country, or if the Western Allies had ever landed a serious expeditionary force. But it was enough to fend off the equally improvised, less ideologically motivated, and even more fluid White armies. And this, of course, was what counted.

Still, it would be a mistake to take too literally Bolshevik rhetoric about the Civil War being a class struggle, with the Red proletariat pitted against the bourgeois and feudal Whites. Institutionally, what made the Civil War possible was a split within the officer corps of the old Imperial army: One group of officers worked for the new Soviet state, which, in the eyes of many of them, was still a Russian state; another group fought to reestablish something resembling the traditional Russian Empire, "one and indivisible." In short, on the battlefields of the Civil War we are dealing as much with two rival state powers, or incipient state powers, as with two social classes. The Soviet Party-state, for all its ideocratic aspirations, was a state power in militant gestation, albeit a state power of a radically new type.

The acute period of the contest between these two incipient successor states to the Russian Empire lasted eighteen months, from mid-1918 to the end of 1919.[8] During this time the Soviet regime was in mortal danger on three occasions. The first, as we have seen, was the summer of 1918, when the Germans occupied the west and the south, and the Whites advanced from the east. The second was the spring of 1919, when Admiral Kolchak advanced out of Sibèria towards the new capital, Moscow. And the third occasion was the fall of that year, when General Denikin advanced from Ukraine to within two hundred kilometers of the capital, and General Yudenich moved on Petrograd from Estonia.

This is not the place to enter into the vicissitudes of the armed struggle; our concern here is with the impact of the war on the development of the Soviet Party-state. Suffice it to say that Bolshevik success was by no means foreordained. At each of the three moments of mortal danger just mentioned, if contingent events had taken a different turn—if, say, Kolchak and Denikin in 1919 had advanced on Moscow simultaneously rather than five months apart—Bolshevik military defeat, and hence political collapse, would have been as wholly conceivable as during the Czech episode of 1918. Chance, obviously, was one reason this did not occur.

And another element of contingency was that the Germans lost the war in the West. For if they had broken through to the Channel ports and Paris in the spring of 1918—as they almost succeeded in doing—they then would have been free to resume their victorious eastward advance interrupted by the peace of Brest-Litovsk, and the ragtag Red Army could hardly have stopped them. Of all the hypothetical scenarios that might have permitted Russia to avoid Bolshevism, this is perhaps the most "realistic." Yet, for obvious reasons, historians in the Western democracies have never been prone to contemplate it, even though it would have made Hitler superfluous into the bargain.

But there were structural reasons for the Bolsheviks' survival as well. First, they had the advantage of interior lines of communication radiating out from Moscow, whereas the Whites were operating on the periphery. Second, the internationalist Reds oddly enough could appear to be Russian patriots because they were not beholden to foreign interventionist powers. Third, although the peasants (now often called the "greens") had come to detest the Reds because of their requisitions of grain, they feared the Whites even more because the latter's return often brought with it the restoration of the landowners' power. As a consequence, as competing Red and White armies passed successively over their fields, the peasants had a marginal preference for the Reds and therefore revolted behind White lines.[9] It was this factor, in particular, that undid Denikin in 1919, allowing the Bolsheviks to definitively take over Ukraine and thus wrap up their victory overall.

But even more important than these specific factors was the Bolsheviks' superior capacity for organization—in building the Cheka, in structuring the Red Army around the political commissar, and in turning the Soviet state into a mere apparat of the Party. This capacity for organization derived from their ideological drive for a monopoly of power in the transcendent cause of socialism. Thus, where the Provisional Government had been unable to govern, the Bolsheviks after only eight months in power were well on their way to becoming a total government. Against the same forces of soviet fractiousness, worker indiscipline, and peasant anarchy that had destroyed the Provisional Government, the Bolsheviks fought back with every nerve of their dictatorship to bring under control the centrifugal forces their agitation of the previous year had helped unleash.

The great paradox of Communist policy, not just in Russia during 1917–1919 but throughout the world thereafter, was that it was anarchist in opposition and totalitarian in power, and it saw no contradiction between the two. Indeed, in the Bolsheviks' logic there was no contradiction: they were anarchist in order to pulverize the old, capitalist world, and dictatorial in order to build a new, socialist world. In both phases they had the right, in fact the obligation, to be totalistic in their policy because in both they were the vehicle of the logic of history and the vanguard of the universal class. In short, what explains the Bolsheviks' ruthless capacity for both disorganization and reorganization is their ideological fanaticism. And in this the Whites could never compete.

Where the Communist capacity for ideologically driven organization and state-building came through most tellingly during the Civil War was on the economic front and in those policies later baptized War Communism. It is in this area that the Party-state, its political police, and its new model army found their ultimate application; for remolding the economy would be the chief means for building socialism, and thus accomplishing the final purpose of the system. And it is on the economic programs of this period that the historiographical debate is most intense.

What is at issue is this. Even though the socialist revolution had not yet spread to the rest of Europe, in the three years of War Communism the Soviet regime went all the way (at least in intention and on paper) to full state control of the economy and the building of what its leaders then simply called Communism—without any qualifying adjective. All of this was quite contrary to proper, "orthodox" Marxism as well as to the Bolsheviks' own originally proclaimed intentions. Then, in 1921, they brusquely abandoned this course, which they now admitted had been premature and mistaken. Attributing the error to the Civil War emergency, the Bolsheviks took to calling the recent past "War" Communism; at the same time, they launched a New Economic Policy, or the NEP, based on a semimarket economy.

The great question, then, is which of these two courses was the Bolsheviks' true policy for reaching socialism. A corollary question is whether War Communism was an aberration caused by the pressure of circumstances or an ideologically driven enterprise that expressed the Bolsheviks' basic aspirations. Or was War Communism the product of both circumstance and ideology? Most historical commentary has wavered between the latter, inconclusive middle way and the assertion of the primacy of circumstances. But by and large Western historiography deals with this painful period as quickly as possible in order to focus on the allegedly more promising years of the NEP.

Yet the stakes in this matter are very high for understanding the whole of Soviet history. If the brutal practices of War Communism were the true Bolshevik policy, then it is only logical that the whole future of the regime was as bleak as it in fact turned out to be; in particular, Stalin then appears as the legitimate heir of Lenin. But if War Communism was an aberration from Leninism caused by the contingency of war, then it is possible to view most of subsequent Soviet history as an "aberration"; Stalin is expunged from the true canon, and the Soviet enterprise is presumed to have had a potential for ending up with a human face. Indeed, Gorbachev's *perestroika* was supposed to have been just such a culmination.

As noted earlier, during their first eight months in power, the Bolsheviks at times referred to their economic policy as state capitalism. Believing that it would be premature to attempt building full socialism in Russia before the European revolution, the new government nonetheless could not permit capitalism in Russia to remain unadulterated. State capitalism was the vehicle whereby the bourgeoisie was supposed to be made to serve the workers' state.

In fact, this process developed through a dialectic where events prompted drastic action and then ideology radicalized these actions still further. Thus, when the employees of the State Bank refused to provide the new government with funds, armed detachments occupied the Bank on November 7, 1917, and nationalized it. Then ideology took over and five days later all private banks were nationalized and all foreign debts repudiated. Yet these actions only earned the regime new enemies, both foreign and domestic, thereby making its economic problems still worse—and so prompting further drastic action.

This initial phase of state capitalism received its fullest expression on December 2 with the creation of a Supreme Council of the National Economy, known by its Russian abbreviation as Vesenkha. This body was charged with organizing, coordinating, and regulating the activities of the commissariats dealing with "trade and industry, food supplies, agriculture, finance, and trade unions"—in short, everything connected with the economy.[10] Very soon Vesenkha created departments, called *glavki*, to deal with the various branches of industry, from textiles to metallurgy; and by the spring a sizeable bureaucracy had emerged to issue ever more detailed decrees regulating the activities over which it had nominal control. Thus, well before Brest-Litovsk and the onset of major crisis, state control of credit and bureaucratic coordination, if not as yet planning, had been established in principle. This was, first of all, the minimum that a socialist government could be expected to do to defend the interests of the toilers against their now defeated exploiters; it was also a practical necessity to cope with an increasingly chaotic situation.

The momentum of state intervention received a mighty impetus from the crises of the spring of 1918. An exceptionally severe winter had accelerated the economic collapse that was already under way in 1917, but the process was now aggravated by the loss of Ukrainian grain, iron, and coal as a result of Brest-Litvosk. By April–May the food situation in the cities had become desperate: The peasants now had no incentive to produce for the market, where they received only increasingly worthless rubles with which, moreover, there were no consumer goods to buy.[11] Lenin therefore decreed a "crusade for bread" and a "food dictatorship," a policy to be implemented by the Supply Commissariat with the aid of the Cheka and directed against "hoarders" and "kulaks." By June, as already noted, this program had become "class warfare in the villages" waged by the "Committees of the Village Poor," or Kombedy.

With this new policy, and these new labels, Lenin's Decree on Land of October 1917 was revealed for what it had always been: an expedient to ease the Party's way to power; by the same token, the Bolsheviks' real attitude toward the peasantry at last began to emerge. Officially, of course, the regime would remain a "revolutionary alliance of workers and peasants"—what Lenin called the smychka—symbolized by the omnipresent hammer and sickle. But even in October, the peasants had been at most a very junior member of the Revolution's extended universal class. In the Bolshevik view, they were eligible for "alliance" with the workers only as an exploited, and therefore a disruptive, force. Otherwise, the Bolsheviks regarded them as a retrograde class incapable of constructive, socialist aspirations. The proletariat, as the modern and technological class, alone could be the bearer of progress.

Thus in the post-revolutionary situation, the course of the two partners in the smychka could only diverge. This was true first in practice; once the peasants had the land, they lost interest in Lenin's revolution. As they often put it in the spring of 1918, when the Party changed its name to Communist and started requisitioning grain: "we are for the Bolsheviks, but against the Communists." This was true also in the Bolsheviks' policy toward their "allies"; the Party now began to distinguish among subclasses of the peasantry, only the most oppressed of which remained within the alliance.

This new approach represents perhaps the greatest triumph of ideology over real life produced by the Bolsheviks. In the Marxist theory of history there is no meaningful place for peasants; they are an irredeemably "awkward" class, fit only for elimination if history is to reach modernity. Russian Marxists solved the problem of this awkward class by obliterating its particularities under a grid of class-struggle categories taken from their sociology of the urban world. This process began in the 1890s when the Marxists argued against the Populists that capitalism had already arrived in Russia; among its chief consequences was the destruction of the village commune through the creation of class differentiation among the peasants. Lenin's *Development of Capitalism in Russia* in 1899 was a key item in this debate.

The result of the development of capitalism, according to Lenin, was a division of the village into three classes. At the top, there was a functional equivalent of the bourgeoisie: the kulaks (from the word for "fist," the traditional term for village usurer). In the middle there was a surrogate petty bourgeoisie, the *seredniaki*, or middle peasants. And at the bottom, there was a stand-in for the proletariat, the *bedniaki*, or poor peasants, who were exploited as laborers by the kulaks. The latter, therefore, became the cutting edge of "capitalism" in rural Russia.

Although peasants, unlike Marxist theorists, rarely write books about rural sociology, we do know that all of the foregoing bears little relationship to the real though minimal social differentiations within the village, or to the peasants own view of their situation. After 1917, a kulak was no more than a muzhik with one horse and three cows who would hire a couple of poorer peasants for part of the year. The peasants, moreover, found such relationships of interdependence normal; the more enterprising peasant was in fact a model for the middle peasant mass, not a class enemy. For peasants of all levels, the real enemy was the world outside the village: the state, the city, and, after 1917, the Party.

Yet, absurd though Lenin's rural sociology is in itself, it had a major function for building what the Party called socialism; it furnished the indispensable political means that permitted the Party to exploit, and ultimately to subjugate, the village. This objective, not merely grain collection, was the real meaning of class warfare in the village, a war to be waged by the new "alliance" of the rural proletariat, the *bedniaki*, and its urban big brother, that is, the Party. Only with this ideological illusion could the Party turn on the larger, rural wing of its *smychka* and still believe, in all good conscience, that it represented the peasants' "real" interests.

Thus, by the summer of 1918, ideological, political, and police mechanisms had replaced the market in Russian agriculture. In one guise or another, crude ideo-political and, indeed, military measures would substitute for the market up to the beginning of 1921, that is, until well after the end of the Civil War. The only variations within this pattern were due to expediency. Thus, the plunder of "kulak surpluses" by the "village poor" under the guise of class warfare in the countryside proved so disruptive of production, and so alienated the peasantry politically, that early in 1919 the regime had to abandon it. But it was replaced by something just as primitive: the state requisition of grain by proletarian detachments or the Cheka, a system known as *prodrazverstka*. At times the requisition was in exchange for consumer goods, and at other times it was simply confiscated at gunpoint; but in both cases it was forced.

Yet this was not the whole of the Bolsheviks' agrarian policy. Their ultimate aim was the abolition of the "contradiction between town and country" by the introduction of "rational," large-scale mechanized production into the villages. As a first rough sketch of this agrarian future, a number of former gentry estates were transformed into state farms, or sovkhozy, where the peasants labored as salaried workers. This experiment was a complete failure at the time, but it nonetheless showed what the Bolsheviks really wanted to do with the recalcitrant peasant mass if ever they had the means to implement their ideal of rational agrarian organization. In the meantime, however, they relied on *prodrazverstka* to survive. But this policy, too, was not really a success beyond meeting the minimal needs of Party survival, for what little surplus grain there was went increasingly to the black market. Worse still, *prodrazverstka* was so disruptive of production that it was a major cause, together with drought, of the disastrous famine of 1921–1922.

Any government in Russia at the time would have been driven to some measure of coercive political action as a substitute for a market whose collapse could not be avoided; indeed, the Whites engaged in similar, though less drastic, practices in the areas they controlled. What is noteworthy about the Bolshevik action, however, is its ideological nature, a characteristic that made it systematic, all-embracing, and logically linked to the ultimate purpose of the regime—socialism. The Bolsheviks were not simply feeding their constituents at a time of desperate penury; their vulgar and often violent activity—in fact, it was not very different from theft—was raised to the level of an indispensable step towards a New World. Small matter that the inane practice of class warfare in the villages only made the supply situation worse: It fueled conviction and helped to keep the Red movement going. Thus, although War Communism was launched in the countryside in response to the peasants' withdrawal from the market, by replacing that market with the political appropriation of resources, the Bolsheviks were accomplishing what socialism was supposed to do anyway.

War Communism in industry began as a similar response to the disruptive force of worker "spontaneity." In the course of the spring of 1918, faced with the grain crisis, workers began to divert production to whatever goods could be bartered for food. Thus "workers' control of industry" often evolved from supervision of management to outright takeover of the plant, and then to local "nationalization." Since some of these plants were owned by Germans, the situation could offer the German army a pretext for further intervention. Just as threatening, this grass-roots nationalization negated Bolshevik power.

On June 12 the government decreed general nationalization by the state of all heavy industry. In the course of the next six months, the government went on to issue a flurry of decrees nationalizing light industry, wholesale trade, retail trade, the cooperatives, and ultimately every last artisan or commercial enterprise in the country, down to those that had only five employees. Thus, once again, a process that began as a response to the challenge of events acquired a totalizing ideological momentum that left the country, in principle at least, as a single state enterprise.

As might be expected, this statist overkill produced very mixed results. Although the Red Army was equipped and fed, the dwindling population of the cities was not even minimally supplied with the bare necessities. At the same time, the hypercentralization of the system, in conjunction with internecine conflict among the *glavki*, actually contributed to industrial disorganization. In addition, state control of distribution was totally ineffective: the market was not suppressed but driven underground and into illegality.

Yet, once again, small matter these side effects, for something much more important had been achieved: private property in industry and commerce had been eradicated and profit had been abolished; by these means, the bases for the "exploitation of man by man" had been overcome. Just as important, the market had received a socialist successor in the political command structure of Vesenkha. And by early 1921 this agency had created a special unit for long-term economic coordination, Gosplan, or the State Planning Commission, which for the moment had little to do but was destined to play a central role in the system. For the "rational" ordering of economic activity in terms of "real needs"—not in terms of profit and reliance on the "anarchy of the market"—was what socialism was supposed to achieve in the long run, even if there had been no civil war to fight.

But if private property, profit, and the market had been suppressed, then there was no need for money. As it happened, the momentum of events, in the form of the most extreme inflation Europe had yet seen, was doing away with money anyway. This was taken as a sign that the course of history had propelled Russia fully out of capitalism and into socialism, and so by the end of 1920 the Bolsheviks were preparing to formally abolish money.

In fact, what had occurred during the Civil War was an extraordinary primitivization of Russian life: a near collapse of industrial production and an unprecedented reversion to a natural or barter economy barely plastered over with the paper decrees of Vesenkha and its *glavki*. Perhaps the most extreme indication of this primitivization came once the war was won and the Party turned to rebuilding the economy. Trotsky then advocated that reconstruction be carried out simply by transferring to the operation of the industrial plant the methods that had brought victory in the Civil War. This "militarization of labor" (a program also defended by Bukharin) meant literally running industry like the Red Army; in fact, for a time, military units were used to reopen mines and factories and to get the railroads running again. Indeed, Lenin and most of the Party leadership for months after the end of the war believed that the methods of War Communism in general were the right ones for arriving at socialism and should be continued indefinitely. Thus, in a veritable ideological delirium, the most colossal economic collapse of the century was transmogrified into really-existing Communism, the radiant future *hic et nunc*, a vision projected in Bukharin's and Preobrazhenskii's once famous *ABC of Communism.*[12]

A FIRST-QUARTER REPORT

So what should we conclude with regard to the relative weight of circumstance and ideology in producing this bizarre result?[13] First, it should be noted that the practices of War Communism both ante-dated the conflict and continued after its conclusion. The national-ization of credit and the creation of the basic framework for state control, Vesenkha, preceded Brest-Litovsk; moreover, such measures of economic class warfare as the food dictatorship came before any serious fighting began. Even the most drastic measures of War Com-munism—the full nationalization of industry, class warfare in the vil-lages, and Committees of the Village Poor—came in the late spring of 1918, at a time of great crisis, to be sure, but not yet of serious conflict with the Whites. The sustained military emergency came in 1919, the year of Kolchak, Denikin, and Yudenich, and this of course was the time of *prodrazverstka* and the nationalization of the entire urban economy. Thus, overall, the military emergency can account for only the lesser part of War Communism, and its intensification rather than its origins. So at the very least we must opt for the inconclusive solution that both circumstance and ideology were operative—in other words, the safe middle way.

But this double-entry bookkeeping approach to historical causation is really no solution at all, for reality does not work in such compart-mentalized fashion. Rather, War Communism should be understood in the light of the key Marxist principle of the "unity of theory and practice": Ideology and action, or praxis, are two facets of the same process. There can be no practical action without a guiding concept, and ideology is always consubstantial with political life itself. It is from this Hegelo-Marxist perspective—which, after all, the actors in question took most seriously—that their policies of 1918–1921 can best be evaluated.

We are therefore profoundly mistaken to assert that during War Communism Marxism served simply as an ex post facto rationalization for actions undertaken in response to the military emergency, or to argue, as did E. H. Carr, that the Bolsheviks simply did what they had to do to stay in power. Quite true, they were obsessed with preserving power. But the real question is why they wanted it so passionately; after all, the Party of Lenin was not some tin-horn dictatorship to which power was an end in itself. The Bolsheviks required power in order to achieve their luminous goal of socialism, and the manner in which they fought to preserve that power was constantly molded by the end it was to serve. Thus, class warfare in the villages was simultaneously a way to feed the army and a means to advance toward the goal of socialism. And so, from one such emergency measure to another, the Bolsheviks convinced themselves that in the "heat of the class struggle" they were simultaneously, and dialectically, destroying capitalism and "forging the institutions" of the coming socialist order. Thus the universal collapse of the Civil War could appear, in their logic, as a great leap forward.

And all of this is quite Marxist if we see Marxism as an ideological totality rather than as a scholastic list of programmatic points. Ideology is not a set of precepts that people look up in a book and then apply. It is an all-encompassing mind-set that pervades actions and decisions that to nonideological observers appear disparate and ad hoc. Thus, one of the arguments frequently used to write off War Communism as an aberration is that no such program for socialism is explicitly set forth in Marx, who was allegedly concerned only with producing a critique of capitalism. And, to be sure, Marx did refuse to give any detailed blueprint for the future order, as was so rashly done by those socialists he branded "utopian." Nonetheless, the basic outlines of his socialism are quite clear from his negative critique of capitalism.

Above all, private property and the market would have to go; so too would money, "which came into the world dripping with blood through every pore." Whole categories of the population—from "feudal" aristocrats to "petty bourgeois" democrats, and even errant socialists—would have to be excluded from the suffrage or in some manner repressed because they were reactionaries trying to hold back the logic of history. In particular, the retrograde "division of labor between town and country" would have to be ended by eliminating the "idiocy of rural life," that is, the peasantry, that great "sack of potatoes" around the neck of mankind. Concretely, this meant that the countryside would have to be urbanized by making the peasants into laborers in agricultural factories, or collective farms.[14]

All of this is quite explicit in Marx and Engels, and many of their German and Austrian followers in the Second International made matters clearer still by talking in some detail of collective farms and centralized planning.[15] Similarly, it is of only secondary importance that Marx used the phrase "dictatorship of the proletariat," a concept so central for Lenin, a mere handful of times. Marx made clear his positive attitude toward coercion by copious encomia to "revolutions as the locomotive of history," or "violence as the midwife of history." Thus, the main lines of his program for the future are hardly in doubt: It was an all-embracing project of nationalization, collectivization, and planning, presumably to be realized by the logic of history—and revolutionary coercion was also integral to that "logic."

It is just such a total program of communization that the Bolsheviks attempted to implement under War Communism. As for the formal logic of history, they left reliance on its more lockstep aspects to the Mensheviks and the Western Social Democrats, and emphasized instead the voluntaristic and coercive power of the class struggle. Thus the Bolsheviks escalated the military communism of the Civil War emergency into a militant and millenarian communism, one that was designed to endure. And despite the strictures of Karl Kautsky and Iulii Martov, this enterprise was legitimately in the mode of Marxism's deeper structure. Lenin and his colleagues were quite right in thinking so at the time, and somewhat disingenuous in disowning their handiwork once they were forced to embark on the NEP. And they were indeed *forced*, for their utopia in action had produced such a national disaster that it threatened to destroy the Party's power. They therefore temporarily jettisoned their maximalist program in order to preserve that power, so that the Party might live to fight again another day.

Though it was derived from ideology, as a practical matter the extraordinary leap into the future that was War Communism was made possible by the equally extraordinary social revolution of the Civil War years. This revolution took the form of the nearly complete decomposition of the old social fabric. This process had begun in 1917 and steadily worsened during the Civil War years, only reaching bottom with the end of hostilities in the fall of 1920.

This outcome represented a radical departure from the pattern of previous European revolutions. In earlier revolutions, once the old order had been overthrown and the dust had settled, it turned out that some social groups had moved up in the world while others had moved down; almost all, however, were still there in the end, and thus society had remained diversified and stratified. In France after 1789, for example, the nobility and the clergy had moved down while the middle classes and the peasantry had moved up; although the structure of society had changed mightily, and the status of each group had changed greatly, none of them had been totally eliminated.

In Russia after 1917, however, the extraordinary fact is that all social groups above the "simple people," or the "toiling masses," were eliminated as cohesive bodies. The gentry, the clergy, the liberal professionals, the middle classes, or the "bourgeoisie"—all ceased to exist as organized entities. The only classes of the old Russian society that remained were those of its manual laborers, the workers and peasants. Most of the individuals in the dispossessed groups remained of course, but their group or class cohesion was destroyed. Moreover, these individuals were legally discriminated against under the new order: They were deprived of the suffrage and received reduced food rations. In short, "civil society" disappeared, and all that was left of Russian society was a largely undifferentiated mass of "toilers."

This unprecedented social levelling occurred because, unlike in earlier European revolutions, private property had been abolished. This came about in part because property had not been all that widespread before 1917, since most of the peasantry did not own their land. The abolition of private property was also facilitated by the elemental forces of social revolution in both the countryside and the cities. But, in even larger part, property disappeared as the result of deliberate Bolshevik policy.

The consequence of all this was that the masses, no less than their former masters, were deprived of any political leverage vis-à-vis the state. To be sure, the workers still had their unions, but after the summer of 1918 these organizations were subordinated to the Party. When, at the end of the Civil War, the so-called Workers' Opposition attempted to revive the unions as the organizing force in rebuilding the economy, they were decisively defeated at the Tenth Congress in 1921; control of the economy remained with the Party, and the unions were definitively transformed into its agents. The peasants still had their traditional rural commune—which was even strengthened by the agrarian revolution of 1917—where they in fact managed most of their own affairs. But in their relations with the Soviet state, the peasants' only leverage was either sullen refusal to cooperate in grain deliveries or revolt. The workers' and peasants' soviets, which nominally constituted the Soviet state, were in fact largely transmission belts of the Party's will.

Never before in European history had such a radical social levelling occurred; never before had a society been so thoroughly disarmed vis-à-vis the state. The Bolsheviks were able to achieve this extraordinary feat only because of the immaturity and fragility of prerevolutionary Russian society. Unlike most countries of Western and Central Europe, old Russia lacked the solid structures of a venerable civil society, one with a plurality of entrenched vested interests and large masses of people who had much more to lose than their chains. In particular, old Russia had too many peasants with too little stake in the system. This is a major reason why the Imperial regime had collapsed so easily, and why the Provisional Government had never been more than a phantom. This is also why the Bolsheviks could seize power so easily, and why they could impose the surreal fantasy of War Communism on the country so quickly. There were simply no structures capable of opposing them effectively—that is, of putting up a real class struggle.

It is the inveterate weakness of Russian civil society that furnishes the distinctively Russian component to the Communist amalgam. The totalitarian nature of Communism is not to be explained as the prolongation of traditional Russian authoritarianism or Oriental despotism; nor is the collectivist nature of Soviet society to be construed as the continuation of traditional Russian communal and servile social relations. It is difficult to find any such agencies of transmission from the old to the new Russia in the actual policies pursued by the Bolsheviks after 1917, but it is very easy to find the origins of these policies in the socialist purposes of the Leninist Party. What traditional Russia contributed to the Leninist project was a lack of social and cultural antibodies sufficiently strong to resist it; in other words, her contribution was much more negative than positive. This is why the world's first socialist society appeared in the European country that was putatively the least prepared to give birth to it. The socialist idea was everywhere in Europe at the time, but only in Russia was there a social void that permitted ideological politicians to get away with acting on it.

This unprecedented social void also explains another aspect of the Bolshevik feat. No society can exist as an undifferentiated egalitarian mass. Any society, no matter how democratic its ethos, requires functional differentiation—a social and economic division of labor—in order to operate, indeed to exist. And differentiation of necessity entails some measure of hierarchy, subordination, and inequality, approximately according to the level, usefulness, and rarity of skills. It is this functional and social pluralism that is the basis of civil society. It is also the basis of a theory of justice in which each component of the body social receives treatment according to its due, a theory that is in constant tension with the dominant modern view of justice as equality.

But in Russia, with the amputation of all the upper echelons of the old order, what might be called the managerial corps of the nation had disappeared. And into this void stepped the cadres of the omnicompetent Party. This was accomplished indirectly, of course, through the new mechanisms of Bolshevik dual administration. Thus, the Party-state substituted itself for the now defunct civil society, at least on paper.

The result was an enormous increase in Party membership during the Civil War. From some 115,000 members in January 1918, the Party grew to 576,000 or 775,000 in March 1921, depending on what count one believes; this averages out to a roughly sixfold increase in three years.[16] So it is clear that the Party that built the first version of Soviet socialism was a product not of industrial relations under "capitalism," nor of the proletarian ardor of 1917, but of the violence and chaos of the Civil War. And this showed in its composition: by 1921 only a minority, or 41 percent, of its members were workers; of the remainder, 28.2 percent were peasants and 30.8 percent were "employees and others," these latter usually being some sort of petty intelligentsia.

But what is more important than members' previous social condition is their motivation for joining. Adhering to the Party at this time meant risking everything on its victory. Thus the Party was in significant measure an organization of the bold and the committed: it included idealists and zealots, seekers after vengeance on the *burzhui*, and opportunists and thugs. But it was also an organization of the upwardly mobile, of the shop stewards and noncoms of the old order for whom service to the Revolution was both a cause and a career, qualities epitomized by such figures as the future Marshals Mikhail Tukhachevskii and Semën Budennyi. In addition, since the times were chaotic and survival difficult, the Party was a profitable berth for nonideological survivors, of whom the leadership expelled some two hundred thousand in 1921. And since the chief business of the Party at the time was war, it was also home for those who liked to fight or simply to plunder, such as the partisan leader Chapaev, or the protagonists of Isaak Babel's *Red Cavalry*.

But above all, the Party was a vehicle for the creation of a human being of a new type out of the social raw material of the prerevolutionary class structure. For when workers and peasants entered the Party, they acquired a new social identity. They became a special breed: Communists, Party Men, fighters imbued with a spirit that brooked allegiance to no rival authority. And here one of the most typical examples of these new men is Nikita Khrushchev, who was born in 1894 a peasant in Kursk province, became a worker at age 16, joined the Red Army when he was 20, and entered the Party soon thereafter. In fact, almost all the key leaders of the Soviet Union during the next two decades, and all the master-builders of socialism in the 1930s, cut their political teeth as commissars during the Civil War. Beginning with Stalin himself, the roster is indeed stunning: Viacheslav Molotov, Lazar Kaganovich, Klementii Voroshilov, Sergei Kirov, Valerian Kuibyshev, Sergo Ordzhonikidze, and Andrei Zhdanov.

Finally, the Party of these years was a school of high heroism as well as of rule by violence; it produced the image of the true Bolshevik as a tough, decisive warrior with a leather jacket and "Comrade Mauser" on his hip. For the Russian Civil War was one of the most brutal episodes in a century that has known only too many. To three and one-half years of world war before October, War Communism added still another three and one-half. The brutalization of the population by the First World War prepared the country for the brutality of the Civil War, and the brutality of the Civil War then brutalized the population further still. As the SR Victor Chernov put it, war "wiped out the value of human life—both of one's own and of others. It hardened people not to care about the death of millions. The right to spill blood and take away life ceased to be a tragic problem. Here was the new breed of sadists in power."[17]

Indeed, around 15 million people perished during the Civil War, some of them from the actual conflict itself, even more from epidemic and famine. But disease and famine were hardly adventitious factors; both were in large measure caused by the destruction of war—as was the case also farther west, where the worldwide influenza epidemic of 1919 carried off almost twice as many victims as the 10 million killed in the First World War itself. But during its Civil War, Russia alone reached half the figure for the rest of the planet. And to these human losses for the country must be added an emigration of around 1.5 million of the old upper classes. For the most part, these émigrés were not "White Guardists" but intelligentsia whose skills were cruelly lacking for the postwar reconstruction.

In the light of a calamity on this scale, it is farcical to make the class triumph of the "proletariat" over the "bourgeoisie" the centerpiece of the Russian Revolution, or to claim that the Revolution was the product of the "polarization" of industrial society. These almost genteel Marxist categories denature the titanic descent into chaos, barely mastered by the Party, that characterized these years.

What did in fact occur is best described by a term from earlier Russian history, *smuta*. Usually translated as the "Time of Troubles," this term was used in particular to designate the breakdown and near disappearance of the Tsardom of Muscovy between 1605 and 1613. During that period the autocratic monarchy collapsed; the Muscovite social structure, composed of hereditary boyars, the service gentry, and the enserfed peasantry, almost dissolved; and an anarchic Cossackry as well as foreign powers intervened to appropriate what was left of the country. Mutatis mutandis, what occurred between 1917 and 1921 was a similar political and social implosion, but one with a radically different outcome: not a restoration of the order that existed before the *smuta*, as in 1613, but the triumph of an absolutely new type of order—an ideocratic partocracy.

"Partocracy," a term coined by Abdurakhman Avtorkhanov, aptly characterizes the new Soviet regime because all of life was subordinated to the political imperatives of the omnicompetent Party.[18] But the Soviet regime was also an "ideocracy," to use Nicholas Berdiaev's term for a secular theocracy.[19] In a traditional theocracy, God rules not directly but through His priests; in the secular ideocracy that was Soviet Russia, the Idea of Socialism ruled indirectly, through its "vanguard Party," in a dictatorship of the proletariat that was in fact a dictatorship of the apparat. Workers and peasants do not create ideocratic partocracies; ideological politicians do.[20]

Thus, by the end of the great revolutionary *smuta* of 1917–1921, all the essential institutions of Sovietism had been either created or sketched in: the Party-state, with its monopoly of power (or "leading role," as it was later called); the dual administration of the soviets and the apparat; the universal monitor of the Cheka; and, finally though more tentatively, the central economic plan and the agricultural collective. It is difficult to believe that a system of such internal coherence and functional logic should be the passing product of military emergency. And, in actual fact, it is this model that was to furnish the main line of Soviet development from Stalin to the eve of *perestroika*. As Soviets throughout those long years were taught to believe, this fact was surely "no accident."

5

THE ROAD NOT TAKEN

NEP, 1921–1928

Footfalls echo in the memory
Down the passage which we did not take
Towards the door we never opened
Into the rose garden.

—*T. S. Eliot, "Burnt Norton"*

His [Bukharin's] biographer calls him "the last Bolshevik," a description which is true or false according to the meaning we attach to it. It is true if we mean by a Bolshevik one who accepted all the principles of the new order—the unlimited power of a single party, "unity" within the party, an ideology excluding all others, the economic dictatorship of the state—and who also believed that it was possible, within this framework, to avoid despotism by an oligarchy or an individual, to govern without the use of terror, and to preserve the values that the Bolsheviks had championed during the struggle for power: namely, government by the working people or the proletariat, free cultural development, and respect for art, science, and national traditions. But if "Bolshevik" means all this, it simply means a man incapable of drawing logical conclusions from his own premises. If, on the other hand, Bolshevik ideology is not just a matter of generalities but involves accepting the inevitable consequences of one's own principles, then Stalin was right to boast himself the most consistent of all Bolsheviks and Leninists.

–*Leszek Kolakowski,* Main Currents of Marxism

Hardly had the Bolsheviks prevailed in the Civil War when they were plunged into a new crisis of survival. On the international front it became apparent that no world revolution would come to their aid; on the internal front their worker and peasant "base," no longer afraid of the Whites, began to defect. So after three years of revolution, the Bolsheviks found themselves a beleaguered minority in a hostile country, surrounded by a hostile world.

Each year since October the Party's hopes for world revolution had surged only to be disappointed in a matter of months. The expectations of October itself had been dashed at Brest-Litovsk. The collapse of the Central Powers at the end of 1918 had produced by the following year ephemeral Bavarian and Hungarian Soviet Republics and, in answer, Lenin's Communist, or Third, International; but again the Western revolution failed to materialize. The greatest surge of hope came in 1920. After the defeat of the main White forces, and while the International was holding its first real Congress in Moscow, Soviet forces headed West "over the corpse of White Poland to world revolution." But the Polish proletariat desired no such liberation, and Marshal Pilsudski stopped the Soviets at the gates of Warsaw. Although there would be flurries of hope for a German revolution down to 1923, the defeat before Warsaw really marked the end of the Western revolutionary mirage. Thereafter, it was clear that for the foreseeable future the dictatorship of the proletariat would be locked up in a backward, peasant country. Retreat from the millenarian hopes of War Communism therefore became inevitable in every aspect of Soviet policy.

WOE TO THE VICTORS

This lowering of expectations entailed, first, retrenchment within a stable state framework. After 1922, this new state was organized as the Soviet Union, and, in territory, it was essentially the old Russian Empire shorn of some of its western borderlands. Though this situation had not been intended by the Bolsheviks, it was nonetheless accepted as a substitute for the unrealized world union of soviet republics; the new state was accordingly structured in revolutionary fashion. Thus the Soviet Union developed as another of the great Bolshevik improvisations of the founding years—that is, experimental in its details but directed overall to building Party power.

The origins of Soviet nationalities policy lay in the pre-1917 drive for power. Nationalism is, of course, not a progressive force in the Marxist canon. Yet after 1912 Lenin espoused the right to self-determination of the Empire's minorities, at least on a provisional basis, as a revolutionary force against the existing system—in the same provisional way he espoused the non-Marxist force of peasant radicalism.

After the Empire collapsed in 1917, the Bolsheviks' initial expectation had been that once the revolution became worldwide Russia would cease to exist as a separate state and become part of a broader union of socialist countries. Accordingly, the first Soviet constitution in 1918 had provided for a federation open to prospective new members, and the Bolsheviks expected the Empire's liberated minorities would be the first to join this grouping. But this scenario worked no better than the Bolshevik scenario for world revolution. The socialist Revolution of 1917 turned out to be strictly a Great Russian affair, and all the border nationalities opted for independence under "bourgeois" governments.

In the course of the Civil War, therefore, the Bolsheviks shifted to a policy of supporting proletarian self-determination as a "higher" political form than bourgeois independence (just as after the Revolution they viewed the poor peasants as a "higher" social force than the peasantry as a whole). This policy meant civil war in most of the border states, with the Russian Bolsheviks intervening on the weaker, "proletarian" side. The "Whites" won in Finland and the Baltic states, which became independent; but in Ukraine, Transcaucasia, and eventually Central Asia, the Reds triumphed, and those regions lost their independence by the early 1920s. The Soviet Union was devised to accommodate this situation, which, though far short of a world federation, was still much more than ethnic Russia. The new Union, therefore, had to pay formal homage to the principle of national self-determination for all its members by adopting a federal structure, which also entailed nominal ethnic autonomy and the official use of native languages, a set of arrangements that the Russian Empire had never known.

Later the official slogan came to be that the "constituent" republics were "national in form, but socialist in content." Concretely, this meant a policy of "*korenizatsiia*," or the "implantation" of Soviet institutions in the non-Russian cultures. Yet, this "Union" of Soviet Socialist Republics was as much a fiction as was "soviet power" within each of the "republics," for everywhere behind the ethnic facade the Party was in full control. Thus from the time it received its first,

Leninist-Stalinist constitution in 1923, the Soviet Union, created by Party conquest, was always ruled as a unitary Party-state.[1]

It would therefore be a mistake to view the Soviet Union as a simple continuation of the tsarist empire, as has often been asserted, or as a perpetuation of traditional Russian domination of its neighbors in socialist guise. Though in its own way imperial, the Soviet Union differed in major respects from its predecessor. It was a Party-empire that existed not for circumscribed Russian national purposes but for the internationalist task of building socialism. And this mission made a great practical difference in the way it treated its minority subjects. On the one hand, it raised them to the new dignity of nationhood, and on the other hand it subjected them to the even newer and more onerous servitude of mass mobilization for Party purposes—the same mixed lot that fell to the Russian workers and peasants.

Still, the Soviet state's camouflage of pseudofederalism presented the danger that minority elites would try to make their "autonomy" real. The fostering of national languages, the building of republican political institutions, including even separate Communist Parties, gave the non-Russian nationalities a framework in which to develop a genuine identity. Thus the history of this empire that dared not speak its name would be one of recurring challenges by the "periphery" to the "center," followed by an administrative reconquest of the republics by Moscow.

The Bolshevik regime's greatest problem at the close of the Civil War, however, was not the failure of world revolution or the reabsorption of the borderlands but a looming internal crisis. Within the Soviet Russian bastion itself an abyss suddenly opened beneath the Party's power: In early 1921 both components of Lenin's *smychka*, the revolutionary alliance of workers and peasants, started to defect simultaneously. In March strikes in Petrograd escalated into a revolt at the naval base at Kronstadt. This movement was driven by the conviction that, with the military emergency over, the people should take back power from the Party.[2] With the slogan "the soviets without the Communists," the new insurgents in this cradle of the Revolution sought to return to the 1917 utopia of the commune state. Although this formula could have worked no better now than it had before the Civil War curtailed it, the Party's response was nonetheless the most cynical indication yet of its real relationship to the worker "base."

The presumptuous empirical proletarians of Kronstadt were denounced as "White Guardists" and lackeys of the Entente, and were put down militarily by the metaphysical proletariat, then assembled for its Tenth Party Congress. The Congress interrupted its sessions to dispatch a cohort of delegates, led by Trotsky and including the Workers' Opposition, to storm the fortress and execute the ringleaders. But cynical is perhaps not the proper word; these battle-hardened Bolsheviks sincerely believed that any enemy they encountered was ipso facto an enemy of the people.

At the same time, the peasantry of the central provinces, now that the menace of the Whites had been removed, was stirring in revolt. Although the peasants were less committed to government by soviets than were the workers, their aims were essentially the same: to take back the confiscated Revolution and to manage their affairs through institutions of their own creation. Among these new jacqueries, the insurrection in Tambov province under the leadership of the SR peasant Aleksandr Antonov was only the most serious.[3] The Party denounced these forces as "bandits" and dispatched Marshals Tukhachevskii and Budennyi, fresh from their victories in the Civil War, to put them down. Even so, the countryside was not brought fully under Soviet control until 1924.

The shock of the worker and peasant defections brusquely disabused the Bolsheviks of the illusion that they could continue with War Communism as a quick road to socialism. It was suddenly borne in on them that their policies had brought the economy to ruin, as some Mensheviks had been claiming all along. Let us recall that by 1921 the output of mines and factories had fallen to 21 percent of the 1913 level and that agricultural production was down to about 38 percent of normal. Concurrently, the working class had almost withered away: it numbered no more than 1.2 million in 1920. As certain Mensheviks ironized, there remained only a dictatorship without the proletariat.

In short, by the Tenth Party Congress in 1921 the Soviet regime was near collapse, not in the sense that there was an organized adversary ready to overthrow it—the Red Army had eliminated any such direct threat—but in the sense that the Bolsheviks could not continue their current course without the human and material fabric of the country disintegrating beneath them. One possible solution, of course, would have been for the government to convene a new, democratically elected Constituent Assembly to pick up the pieces and make a whole new start—as was done in France in 1871 and 'Germany in 1919, after the demise of failed regimes. But the Bolsheviks were not exactly in that situation; they had suffered every kind of defeat but military, and their mandate from the logic of history seemed only to have been confirmed by victory in the Civil War. So they stayed put and brazened it out by turning their economic policy upside down, thereby saving that monopoly of power for socialism which had been their raison d'être from the start.

Accordingly, the Party's response to the crisis of 1921 was two-pronged. On the one hand it made significant concessions to the peasants and the market in order to revive production; this retreat to the market was soon baptized the New Economic Policy, or NEP, a designation that eventually would be applied to the entire decade of the twenties. Yet on the other hand the Party tightened discipline within its ranks and strengthened its political control over the country; so the period of the NEP, broadly defined, also means the building of a "monolithic" Party and the transition of leadership from Lenin to Stalin.

In fact, the NEP years saw both a struggle for power among Lenin's heirs and a contest to determine which of his two policies—economic War Communism or the NEP narrowly defined—was the true road to socialism. Of the two contests the struggle for power is the more spectacular and the better known, indeed only slightly less familiar than the drama of 1917. It will therefore be sketched only briefly here, before moving to the more complex matters of the economic dilemmas of the NEP and, finally, the deeper political processes underlying the struggle for power.

Briefly, then, the competition for Lenin's mantle opened unexpectedly only a year after he had inaugurated the new economic course. In 1922, he suffered two strokes that effectively removed him from power until his death in January 1924. "Collective leadership" by the Politburo was the immediate result, but everyone expected that a single chief was bound to emerge. The obvious successor to Lenin appeared to be the coauthor of October and the commander of the victorious Red Army, Trotsky. Precisely for this reason, a "triumvirate" of his Politburo colleagues—Zinoviev, Kamenev, and the newly appointed General Secretary of the Party, Stalin—united against him.

The ostensible issue pitting the triumvirs against Trotsky was his impatience with the NEP and consequent advocacy of rapid industrialization at home and permanent revolution abroad. These "superindustrialist" views were condemned as a "Left" deviation at the Thirteenth Party Congress in 1924, thereby removing Trotsky from the competition for power.

At this point, Stalin's fellow triumvirs became alarmed at *his* growing power as "Gensek," or director of the Party apparat. They also became alarmed at the government's increasing concessions to the peasants and the market at the urging of Bukharin, by now Stalin's political ally. So in 1925 Zinoviev and Kamenev, little realizing how well Stalin controlled the apparat, formed a new "Left Opposition," which was duly condemned at the Fourteenth Party Congress at the end of 1925. Then, in 1926, they belatedly joined forces with Trotsky to form a "United Opposition" around the usual Left criticisms of the NEP; and in November 1927 they broke Party discipline by taking to the streets on the tenth anniversary of the Revolution, and so were expelled from its ranks.

At this juncture the economic programs of the NEP (as we shall see shortly) turned sour and Stalin moved towards what had hitherto been the program of the Left. His recent ally, Bukharin, together with Bukharin's Politburo allies, Prime Minister Aleksei Rykov and trade union leader Mikhail Tomskii, objected, though unlike the Left, they did not dare to make their opposition public. In 1929, therefore, Stalin and his Politburo allies—Molotov, Voroshilov, Kirov et al.—branded the Bukharinists as a "Right deviation" and deprived them of all their posts.

Thus, the two great issues of the twenties—Who would be the new Lenin? and Which Leninist policy was the true one?—were decided in favor of Stalin and a return to War Communism. With all factions and deviations overcome, this new Lenin then went into action, making 1929 the Year of the Great Break, the beginning of the regime's second Socialist Offensive.

ECONOMIC DILEMMAS

What, however, was the nature of that New Economic Policy that had fueled the political struggles of the twenties? The first step into the new policy was the decision, taken at the Tenth Party Congress in 1921, to replace *prodrazverstka*'s forced requisitions of grain with a tax in kind, calculated as a percentage of the harvest. Even more important, the peasants received the right to sell their surplus production on the free market. Initially, such sales were authorized only at the local level, but since this proved to be an unenforceable restriction, by the end of the year the market for agricultural products became general. And with the peasantry operating through the market, the rest of the economy had to do the same. As occurred earlier under War Communism, the Bolsheviks took what they thought was a limited measure only to fall into a process with an independent momentum. This time, however, the logic they unleashed was not that of their own ultimate program but that of petty bourgeois "speculation"—in a word, "capitalism."

Soon, the logic of the market permeated the whole economy. Money came back into use, and the currency was stabilized. In 1924, therefore, the tax in kind on the peasantry was replaced by a money tax. In addition to this tax, the peasants were expected to sell to the state a percentage of their harvest at prices determined by the state— purchases known as *zagotovki*, or procurements—while the remainder could be sold on the free market. Thus, there in fact existed two parallel market systems in NEP agriculture.

Given this transformation of the largest sector of the economy— agriculture—state-owned industry, too, had to produce for the market and thus to make a profit. The same was true of retail commerce and services, which were denationalized outright. Finally, the State budget had to be balanced. So Russia made a partial return to economic orthodoxy. Lenin began to exhort his Communists "to learn to trade" and to master *khozraschet*, a term usually translated as "cost accounting" but which is more accurately rendered as "profit-and-loss business methods."

Thus by the Founder's death at the beginning of 1924, Soviet Russia had developed a novel form of mixed economy. Agriculture, services, and petty commerce were abandoned to private peasants and a new entrepreneurial class of "nepmen"; but credit and heavy industry were kept under the control of the socialist state and privileged as the "commanding heights" of the whole system, thereby guaranteeing there would be no "restoration of capitalism." Even though this compromise was quite lopsided in favor of the state, the country made a rapid recovery from the horrors of the Civil War and the disasters of War Communism. Indeed, by 1924 Russia enjoyed a genuine, if modest, prosperity for the first time since 1913.[4]

The fundamental question, then, is this: How did the NEP fit into the logic of a regime whose goal remained integral socialism? Was the NEP a betrayal of the socialist dream and a capitulation to the petty bourgeois peasantry and the nepmen speculators, as Trotsky insinuated? Or was it an "economic Brest-Litovsk," a temporary retreat necessary to give the country a "breathing space" before advancing once again towards socialism, as Lenin seemed to say? Or was it more than a Brest-Litovsk and in fact the true path of a gradual, evolutionary "growing into socialism," as Bukharin eventually argued was Lenin's meaning? A corollary to this last position, of course, is that Stalin's brutal Great Break of 1929 was not only unnecessary but a veritable betrayal of true Leninist socialism. And a corollary to this corollary is the question of the Founder's real attitude towards the two-headed legacy of War Communism and NEP that he bequeathed to the Party.

These issues were hotly debated within the Party at the time, and they have been debated in the historiography ever since. But there is a pattern in which the various positions of the 1920s recur in later political contexts. To anyone who believed that the Soviet Union of the 1930s had at last made it to socialism, no matter how flawed, the NEP was not the final word of Leninism but at best a temporary retreat. And not all such people were Stalinists; Trotsky himself shared this view, as have many socialists in the West. But to those who believed that Stalin's methods had compromised Soviet socialism per se, the NEP, if properly interpreted as a gradualist revolution in the process of transcending itself, was the true Leninist path and, therefore, the great missed opportunity of Soviet history. And not all such people were Leninists; many, such as John Kenneth Galbraith or the early Andrei Sakharov, have been social democrats or left liberals who believed that a humanely socialist Soviet Union could someday converge with a socializing West.

Thus partisans of the NEP never viewed it simply as an episode in the Soviet past; rather, they saw it as a permanent alternative to the Stalinist course, and thus as a model to which the Soviet Union might someday return. Indeed, they saw a series of such attempted returns after Stalin's death, in various quasi-market initiatives under Khrushchev and Prime Minister Aleksei Kosygin.[5] Gorbachev's *perestroika*, of course, was to have been, at last, the successful return to a neo-NEP and, therefore, the redemption of the Soviet experiment overall. There is in fact good reason to believe that Gorbachev himself thought this, and that he came to this idea in part under the influence of Western, NEP-leaning Sovietology.[6]

Thus the NEP became the touchstone of what one thought of the Soviet system and, by implication, of socialism. As the years passed after Stalin's death, it became more and more difficult to defend his record openly (though it remained possible to defend it obliquely by discussing the triumphs of industrialization, urbanization, and upward social mobility in the 1930s; but more on this later). It is for this reason that in most Western writing Stalin was eventually excluded from the canon of true Soviet history, and his policies and methods were demoted to the rank of an "aberration." In his once central place Lenin's final years and Bukharin were enshrined, and the NEP became the centerpiece of Soviet history. And so the road to Soviet socialism that was not in fact taken became the royal road of Leninism in retrospective imagination.

Of course in strictly temporal terms this is absurd. The twenty-five years of Stalin's rule clearly eclipse the eight years of the NEP; and if one adds to Stalin's side of the ledger the three years of War Communism and the eighteen of Brezhnev, while conceding bits and pieces of Khrushchev to the side of the NEP, Stalinist socialism is clearly the empirical norm of Soviet history, while it is the NEP that comes out as the "aberration," or at best as the metaphysical norm of a "real" Leninism. Further, if one takes into account the fact that the institutional impact of Stalinism was enormous and enduring, while that of the NEP was soon obliterated, the disproportion between the two columns of the historical ledger becomes overwhelming. So in approaching the ever-recurring cult of the NEP we encounter a strange inversion of Soviet reality.

In the thought of one of the principal celebrants of this cult, the NEP was (accurately) viewed as the "golden era of Marxist thought in the U.S.S.R." and, by extension, as a golden age of the Soviet experiment *tout court*, a period of "pluralism," "diversity," and "variety."[7] This view is true or false depending on what one means by it.

It is true if by golden age one means the best period in Soviet history for the well-being of the population. In these empirical terms it was clearly far better than the chaos and penury of the War Communism that preceded it, or the terror and penury of the Stalinism that followed. Indeed, the prosperity of the NEP of the mid-twenties was not only the greatest the country had known since 1913 but, for the average muzhik, it was probably greater than any he has known since. Although the difference between what constituted a satisfactory standard of living in 1913 or 1924 and what would constitute such a standard in the 1990s makes such a comparison difficult to quantify, the superior living standard of the NEP is eminently plausible with respect to the obvious availability in the earlier years of food, of consumer goods that people actually wanted, and of personal freedom. It is for this reason that the NEP long remained in legend a golden age for ordinary Russians, as in the tales of Mikhail Zoshchenko, the novels of Ilf and Petrov, the poetry of Sergei Esenin, or the satirical plays of Vladimir Maiakovskii.

But this freewheeling and hedonistic NEP is not what most eulogists of the Soviet twenties mean by golden age. In this second meaning, the time was golden because the policies of the NEP, had they been pursued, would have led to that true socialism which had eluded the regime under War Communism. The NEP thus became the "correct" course for Communist development. In order to judge the truth or falsehood of this claim, it is necessary to look more closely at the NEP's actual economic record.

From 1921 to 1924 the Russian economy went through a wild swing of disequilibrium between industrial and agricultural prices before it stabilized into a functioning system. In 1922 the new market was disrupted by a dearth of agricultural products and a glut of manufactured goods that caused the state's profits to plummet. This situation was then reversed in the "scissors crisis" of 1923, when the peasants overproduced while the factories held back, thus costing the peasants their profits and, hence, their incentive to produce for the cities. By 1924, however, the state's manipulation of credit had closed the scissors by forcing the blade of industrial prices down and that of agricultural prices up, thus stabilizing the situation. As a result the country had three "normal" years, 1924–1926. These were the years of what has been called the "High NEP"—not very long for a golden age.

Then, in the winter of 1927–1928, a new crisis hit. As the regime saw it, the problem was the opening of another, seemingly permanent scissors. And in fact the terms of trade had turned against the village: Agricultural prices fell while consumer goods became scarce as the state shifted production from light to heavy industry. In answer to this "goods famine," the peasants went on what the regime called a "production strike" by refusing to market at state-determined prices the quotas of grain the regime had set for the harvest. Instead, the peasants chose either to sell to nepmen at higher prices on the parallel free market or to produce higher-priced industrial crops for the state. Or they fed their grain to livestock and then ate the fatted calf.

What made this "procurements crisis" so dramatic to the regime was that it coincided with the beginning of the First Five-Year Plan, which had been decided on at the Fifteenth Party Congress in December 1927 and which formally started in October 1928. By the summer of that year, the situation had become so bad that rationing was introduced in the cities; by 1929 agrarian Russia, scandalously, had to import grain. In practical terms, therefore, by 1929 the NEP had "failed"—at least from the Party's point of view.

And so, once again, as in the summer of 1918 or in the spring of 1921, the Soviet regime saw itself confronted by a crisis of survival. As in 1921, this crisis did not take the form of an adversary directly threatening the regime's hold on power; the threat, rather, was that if existing policies continued unchanged the economy would collapse from under the Party. So the NEP ended as War Communism had: in a failure of Party policy that called into question the continuation of Party power. A change of direction was both imperative and urgent.

It was against this background of mounting conflict between the peasantry and the Party's Plan—a situation reminiscent, mutatis mutandis, of the Civil War emergency—that the Soviet leadership under Stalin abandoned the NEP at the end of 1929 and opted for a brusque switch to forced collectivization and crash industrialization. This decision was preceded by a debate within the Party during which Bukharin argued, against Stalin, in favor of adjusting the NEP and thus of relying on the market and the peasants for a way out of the crisis and for the financing of the Plan. This "Bukharin alternative" is the crux of the controversy over whether the NEP or Stalinism was the true Leninism.

*   *   *

But in order to assess the feasibility of Bukharin's alternative it is necessary to return to some enduring paradoxes of Soviet power. The first is that a "proletarian" regime held sway in an overwhelmingly peasant country. We now know this to be the norm in Marxist-governed countries, but at the time it seemed to be an anomaly, the world turned upside down. Lenin seemed to have inverted Marx the way Marx had inverted Hegel, for the world's first victorious proletarian Party had wound up as a kind of "superstructure" suspended in the air without the necessary industrial "base" to fulfill its socialist mission.[8]

Initially, the Western revolution was supposed to provide the economic assistance to tide Russia over the duration of this dilemma. When this support failed to materialize, the only acceptable solution was for the Party to somehow generate the appropriate industrial base beneath itself. Another solution, of course, would have been to recognize that the premises on which the Revolution had been based were false and to give up the whole enterprise of socialism in Russia. Needless to say, in the land of Andrei Platonov's Chevengur, and to the heirs of October and the victors of the Civil War, this alternative lacked appeal. Hence, one way or another, the Party was bent on conjuring up a proper industrial base. Since War Communism had proved counterproductive in this respect, after 1921 the question was whether the NEP could do the trick.

Another paradox of Soviet power is that the Revolution, contrary to Marxist theory, did not liberate dynamic productive forces; instead it set the country back economically in every respect. Not only did actual production decline drastically after 1913 and the capital stock of the country become dilapidated during seven years of war, but structurally Russia was in a far worse position for development than before the Revolution.

Under the Old Regime Russia was a part of the world market: Her currency was on the gold standard, and foreign capital was invested massively in her industrialization. Indeed, in the 1890s under Finance Minister Witte, her annual rate of industrial growth was 8 percent, the highest in the world, surpassing those of both Germany and Japan.[9] After the Revolution, however, Russia no longer had the resource of foreign investment. She had withdrawn from the world market and become an autarchic backwater in which the state exercised a jealously guarded monopoly of foreign trade. Recovery and further industrial growth, therefore, would have to be engineered entirely out of her own resources.

But Russia's internal situation had worsened because of the Revolution. A good portion of her "capitalists" and intelligentsia had emigrated, and those who remained as "bourgeois specialists" were second-class citizens under institutional suspicion as class enemies. Even more important was the changed status of the peasantry. Before the Revolution Russia was the world's leading exporter of grain, a circumstance that earned capital for her industrial development. This was possible because of large-scale production by the gentry; in addition, a taxation system that fell heavily on the peasants obliged them to work on gentry estates, and thus for export. And Stolypin's "wager on the strong" created a class of more prosperous peasants (later called "kulaks" by the Soviets) who also produced a surplus for the market.

The Revolution swept all this away, not so much through the Bolsheviks' action—they were too weak for that—as through the great jacquerie of 1917–1918.[10] This revolt liquidated the large landholdings of the gentry and forced the kulaks back into the commune, thereby eliminating the surplus-producing units of Russian agriculture. This downward levelling also acted to perpetuate the primitive character of Russian agriculture; in particular, the country still operated largely under the three-field system and most peasants used the wooden plow. The Revolution of 1917, finally, transformed the Russian countryside into an egalitarian sea of peasant households oriented towards subsistence farming. The number of these households increased from fourteen million to twenty-five million as a result of the Revolution. To be sure, new kulaks emerged during the NEP, but they came nowhere near to producing a marketable surplus comparable to what had been available before the Revolution. And whenever the terms of trade were unfavorable, the peasants, chronically suspicious of Communist power because of their experience with *prodrazverstka*, could simply withdraw from the market and distill their modest surplus into spirits. The dictatorship of the proletariat, having almost no institutional or political presence in the countryside, had little choice but to capitulate to the peasants' needs in order to keep the workers of the cities and the Red Army fed.

It is within these international and domestic constraints that the policies of the NEP would have to operate. And it is in this context that the prospects of the NEP providing the Party with a proper industrial base must be judged. Small wonder that many in the Party were skeptical of the new policy. Whereas the economic policies of War Communism had enjoyed nearly unanimous support within the Party, the NEP always encountered unease and division.

At first, in 1921–1922, the NEP was viewed by most of the Party as a harsh necessity and a forced retreat, and by some as a defeat of socialism, indeed as the failure of the Revolution. This fact merits emphasis because it has tended to be obscured by later enthusiasm for the "Bukharin alternative." As a practical matter, however, the disgruntled Party accepted the NEP because the alternative would have been a return to the dangers and turmoil of War Communism. Thus, it was fear of instability that kept the NEP ascendant during the rest of the decade.

In the meantime the Party was given a second reason for caution when Lenin suffered two strokes in 1922; after January 1923, he was effectively out of action until his death twelve months later. The Party thus lost the man who, in every crisis of its existence, had turned out to have the "right" solution. At the same time, since a struggle for the succession inevitably opened among his presumptive heirs, it was difficult to effect major changes in economic policy until this matter was settled, and that would not happen until 1927–1928.

It was the declining Lenin who first provided ideological rationalizations for a protracted NEP. He declared that War Communism was an error due to the military emergency, and that the NEP was a return to the Party's initial and correct course: the state capitalism of early 1918. Though this was not really true—the old form of state capitalism had meant tolerating big industrialists, whereas the new form meant tolerating small peasant agriculturalists—it still offered a good rationalization of harsh necessity because it presented the NEP as a transition in a logical process of advancement towards socialism. Lenin therefore stated that the NEP had been adopted "seriously and for a long time," a span he variously estimated as "not less than a decade, and probably more," yet certainly under twenty-five years.[11]

If this was vague, the substance of the transition was vaguer still. As Lenin's physical powers waned during 1922 his exhortations to the Party revealed deep bafflement about the paradoxical outcome of the Revolution. The best-known illustration of this (to be discussed later) is his so-called political testament of December 1922, which expressed his anxiety about the future leadership of the Party. Yet just as revealing are his last five articles, dictated in January 1923, which have often been treated as his economic and social "testament."[12] These ruminations addressed two fears.

Lenin grappled first with the problem of growing bureaucratization and corruption of both the Party and the state apparatus—a phenomenon he misdiagnosed as a holdover from tsarism rather than as a consequence of the new partocracy itself. In order to fight this bureaucratization, toward the end of the Civil War he had created parallel monitoring bureaucracies: the Workers' and Peasants' Inspectorate for the state, or Soviet, administration; and the Central Control Commission for the Party. This multiplication of bureaucracies did not work, of course, but Lenin's only solution by the beginning of 1923 was still more of the same: he recommended a doubling of the size of the Control Commission by the addition of honest proletarians from the factory bench.

His second fear was that the Revolution was being suffocated by "Asiatic" ignorance and old Russia's *nekulturnost* (approximately: "precivilized," uncouth, or rustic mores).[13] To remedy this, he called on the Party and the country to "study, study, study." In particular, the Bolsheviks were to study at the feet of the bourgeoisie and use its specialists "to build Communism with non-Communist hands." In other words, they were to move "to socialism through state capitalism."

As for the all-important *smychka* with the peasantry, Lenin insisted that henceforth persuasion would be the only correct approach for bringing socialism to the village. And apropos of this, he noted that Russia's once extensive network of rural cooperatives, which had been nationalized as distribution outlets during War Communism, had reemerged with the NEP; these, he now declared, provided the means to reconcile private interest with socialist purposes. But whether these new units would be consumers' or producers' cooperatives he did not say, nor did he offer any hint as to how these cooperatives might contribute to industrialization. And Lenin concluded his career with the assertion that for Russia "a system of civilized cooperators is the system of socialism"—a minimalist definition that Gorbachev was fond of repeating at the end of Sovietism's life course.

What should we make of Lenin's socioeconomic testament? The

question is more than academic, for the words of the Founder, and in particular those of his last days, would henceforth carry scriptural authority, not only in intra-Party controversies but, bizarrely, in the Western historiography as well. So much has been made, in both East and West, of the dying Leader's fragmentary pronouncements because on them depends the belief in a once and future democratic Leninism; they serve to put War Communism in parentheses and to point the Soviet experiment in the direction of Bukharin, not Stalin. In evaluating Lenin's final assessment of his Revolution, therefore, we are in fact dealing with the first of the roads not taken in Soviet history; for the widespread assumption has been that "if Lenin had lived," he surely would not have acted as Stalin did, either toward the Party or toward the peasants. As an actuarial matter this question is by no means a frivolous one. Lenin was only fifty-three years old when he died, so projecting another decade or more of active life is quite plausible.

Still, politically, the best answer to this question is that a prolonged Leninism would not have made any notable difference: The real choice was not between a longer-lived Lenin and Stalin, but between accommodating or coercing the peasants; Lenin's cooperatives were an evasion of this issue. The true significance of his final pronouncements is that their very confusion articulated this dilemma. As Lenin himself admitted, his equation of socialism with peasant cooperatives was a reversion to Robert Owen, whose once "romantic" program had now become realistic and legitimate because of the victorious class struggle in Russia.[14] For a great Marxist revolutionary, and in view of the staggering problems at hand, this "solution" was . . . pitiful.

It was, moreover, halfway incoherent: Lenin's advocacy of cooperatives was in effect negated by other, more authentically Marxist declarations he made warning against the "private principle" in the countryside. For his deepest conviction was that "petty production gives birth to capitalism and the bourgeoisie—continuously, every day, every hour, spontaneously, and on a mass scale,"[15] a view that stigmatized the village as an enemy to be eliminated. But what is most bizarre in the fetishization of Lenin's last words is the notion that the supreme achievement of the October Revolution was the discovery, only after 1921, of the virtues of cooperatives and the market—both of which Russia had possessed under the Old Regime.

If one adds to this Lenin's notion of curing Party bureaucratism with more bureaucracy, one has the impression of a leader bewildered and frustrated because the outcome of the Revolution had refuted its original premises. And even if Lenin had not been too intelligent to miss seeing this himself, certain of the Mensheviks were there to remind him of it, even claiming that his NEP simply implemented their own policy. So the ailing Leader was in a constant fury with these critics because in his heart he must have suspected that they might be right. Indeed, it is plausible to surmise that Lenin's premature physical decline was due not just to the two bullets he still had in him from 1918, or to a bad cardiovascular heredity, but to the "somatizing" of his revolutionary disappointment.

His various heirs, however, less directly responsible for leading the Revolution, would find it easier to salvage something from its disappointing results. The first of these heirs was the coauthor of October, Trotsky; his tack was to hew as closely to the original Leninism as was feasible, and hence to urge the earliest possible end to the NEP retreat.

Beginning in 1922–1923, Trotsky warned that excessive concessions to the peasantry were the real danger to Soviet power. He also called for a new "socialist offensive" of planned industrial development—to be sure, within a quasi-market framework—as a way of keeping Russia proletarian and progressive. Because he coupled this with an insistence that full socialism in Russia would still require a revolution in more-developed countries, Trotsky's overall position came to be known as "permanent revolution." This label made it easy for his rivals to claim that he wished to subordinate, even sacrifice, the Russian Revolution to world revolution; and thus they sought to discredit his position as the deviant, non-Leninist doctrine of "Trotskyism." However, the fact is that Trotsky wished to combine the two revolutions.

But this is not the point here, for there was little that Russia could do directly to foment foreign revolution (though not for want of trying, as during the Ruhr crisis in Germany in 1923, and in China in 1926). As a practical matter, the operative part of Trotsky's program was to push for planned industrialization in Russia immediately in order to roll back the NEP. This, as we have seen, was the program on which he and his later allies, Zinoviev and Kamenev, were defeated between 1924 and 1927.

The most original theorist of this dissenting Left, however, was not any of the big-name political leaders but Bukharin's erstwhile collaborator in defending War Communism, Evgenii Preobrazhenskii. In 1924 Preobrazhenskii first propounded his theory of "primitive socialist accumulation of capital" as the means by which backward Russia could industrialize. Taking his basic categories from Marx, he argued that all capital was initially accumulated through the expropriation of surplus value through the "exploitation" and "plundering" of subordinate, noncapitalist groups, such as an internal peasantry or external colonies. Russia, however, had no choice but to finance her development from domestic sources alone, that is, from the "internal colony" of the peasantry, as Preobrazhenskii once rashly called it. Moreover, he explicitly drew the parallel between financing socialism in Russia and Marx's analysis of primitive capitalist accumulation through enclosures in England.[16]

By analogy, primitive socialist accumulation in Russia would take the form of "pumping over" capital from the peasantry to the state. This would be achieved by what Preobrazhenskii called "nonequivalent exchange" between the socialist state and the private peasant producer. Preobrazhenskii, of course, did not advocate that this squeeze on the peasantry take the violent form of a new War Communism. On the contrary, like all Soviet leaders in the twenties he insisted that the transformation of the countryside must be pacific and voluntary. Thus he argued that the necessary exploitation of the village could be achieved by fiscal and financial means within a quasi-market framework. Concretely, this meant disproportionate taxation of the peasants and, especially, state action to force agricultural prices down while pushing industrial prices up. In this way the maximum of capital would be pumped over into industrial expansion, especially into heavy industry and metallurgy, now viewed by the planners as the cornerstone of modernity. For Preobrazhenskii, as for most of the Party, fostering industrial expansion had become virtually tantamount to building socialism.

Preobrazhenskii's realistic assessment of the dilemmas involved in industrializing peasant Russia also had political significance in the intra-Party struggles of the day. By emphasizing industrial expansion, the Left also made the proletariat, not Lenin's peasant cooperator, their central concern. Thus they capitalized on the scandal of persistent urban unemployment after 1921, a phenomenon caused by NEP market relations.[17] The Left's call for planning, furthermore, seemed to refuel the socialist élan of War Communism that had been broken by the NEP. At the same time, the Left's insistence on the voluntary transformation of peasant agriculture, in conjunction with its attack on the continuing bureaucratization of the Party, seemed to take full account of the warnings in Lenin's last articles. Finally, as the Left went from defeat to defeat at the hands of Stalin's apparat in Party congresses, it called ever more insistently for intra-Party democracy. After the 1930s all of this came to be taken as the fair promise that if the Left had won the struggle for power it would have built a more humane socialism than the one constructed by Stalin.

This alleged Left promise, which once appeared to many as the great missed opportunity of Soviet history, came to be known as Trotskyism. This belief was reinforced by use of Lenin's political testament, which could easily, if not quite accurately, be read as a repudiation of Stalin and an anointing of Trotsky as the true successor. Thus, from the 1930s to the 1960s Trotskyism was deemed the second and principal Communist road not taken, the ideal alternative against which real Soviet socialism would have to be measured. In its day this belief produced a Fourth International and a congeries of Trotskyite parties throughout the world. It also inspired Isaac Deutscher's great literary monument, his Marxo-Miltonic trilogy on October's coauthor and Stalin's archrival, in which Trotsky is presented as a prophet-victim, the true hero of the Soviet tragedy. And this trilogy was supplemented by an essentially positive biography of Stalin, who after all had built a species of socialism.[18] Together these works have offered the Western public what is arguably the single most influential paradigm for judging the Soviet experience.

This Trotskyite view of Sovietism begins with the premise that the isolation of the world's first socialist revolution in a backward peasant country was an "accident": Had the Western revolution materialized as it was supposed to, it would have come to Russia's rescue. Because impoverished Russia could not provide the material abundance necessary for socialism, the workers' Party was transformed into a semi-corrupt bureaucracy that appropriated the country's meager resources. Stalinism thus was reduced to sociology as the expression of this degenerate Party. So, in this view, the Revolution came to be "betrayed." But it was not destroyed—Soviet Russia remained a workers' state because the basic program of socialism had been realized: private property had been abolished. From all of this it followed that if Stalin and his henchmen were removed, the system could flourish once again and the Soviet Revolution would at last become worldwide. Trotsky, of course, did not live to see the end of Stalin and the expected fulfillment of his prophesies of true socialism's rebirth in Russia. But Deutscher did outlive Stalin, and he immediately began to prophesy that Trotsky's vision would soon be realized in the policies of Khrushchev.

Needless to say, this did not happen. Hence, in the course of time Trotskyism faded away, and the various Trotskyite parties dwindled into miniscule sects. Nonetheless, the whole Trotsky episode, as expounded by Deutscher, left an enduring intellectual residue. First, there was the idea that the failure, or "tragedy," of the Russian Revolution lay not in its Leninist premises but in Russia's backwardness; as Deutscher put it, it was "Mother Russia" that spoiled socialism, not socialism that ruined Russia. A corollary to this was that a Leninist socialism would have worked under more favorable conditions, the usual choice being in Germany. In fact, a much more likely supposition is that a Communist revolution—or, more exactly, a temporary takeover—in Germany would have led to civil war and economic destruction; indeed, this process actually began during the Communist uprisings of 1919 in Bavaria and Hungary. In such a case the only result would have been to extend the Russian disaster into Europe rather than to liberate Russia from her backwardness.

Nonetheless, one version or another of this Trotskyite perspective has dominated much of Western writing on Soviet Russia. This is especially apparent in the second great monument of Western Sovietology, E. H. Carr's multivolume *The Bolshevik Revolution*. Briefly put, the conceptual framework of this series is that the Bolsheviks were working towards the self-evidently realistic goal of socialism, but that they were constantly deflected from appropriate socialist policies by untoward Russian circumstances. Thus, they expended most of their energies doing what they had to do to stay in power, until they finally mastered their recalcitrant raw material and proceeded to the great "socialist offensive" of 1929–1930, which successfully laid the "foundations of a planned economy"[19]—all of which comes down to the Soviet story told from within a Soviet perspective, though in more sober, value-free Western language. But the question of how best to bring a country to socialism is not a historical question; it is an ideological and political one.

Yet it is precisely this question that has been the implicit premise of much of the empirical research on Soviet history, thereby generating the inverted historiography already discussed. And it is this inversion that is the essence of the Trotsky paradigm. So the theme constantly recurs that the Revolution was "betrayed"—betrayed by Russia, or by backwardness, or by Stalin . . . that is, by everything but the Revolution's own goals. The corollary to this is, of course, that if Trotsky had won, the Revolution would have worked out all right. Hence, long after Trotsky, his paradigm would return with different details, even with different "Trotskys"—for example, Bukharin or Gorbachev.

Likewise the paradigm's basic Marxism could be updated and crossbred with modernization theory or the social history methods of the Annales school. Thus, the paradigm's regnant form at the time of Communism's collapse ran as follows: Though Lenin received a socialist "mandate" from the Congress of Soviets in October, his Party was unfortunately hardened into a dictatorship by the outside world's hostility. An even greater misfortune was that peasant Russia left the workers' Party in the incongruous status of an "advanced political . . . 'superstructure' in the air." So under Stalin this superstructure coercively "rushed ahead" to build an appropriate "base" beneath itself. Inevitably, however, the new society was "contaminated" by the superstitious and servile "mentality" of the peasant mass, as well as by the authoritarian tsarist heritage, thus generating the great deformation of the Stalin cult. Nonetheless, since the new society was "industrial, urban, and educated," eventually the Party's superstructure could be softened by its developed base, and so the socialist mandate of October would at last be made good.[20] Thus were Trotsky, Deutscher, and Carr constantly recycled.

Thus also, from decade to decade the false question tirelessly returned: Why did the Soviets encounter such staggering difficulties in realizing their goal? Yet all along these very difficulties cried out that the true question was: What happens when one tries to realize the intrinsically impossible goal of building a just and humane society by concentrating all political, economic, and cultural power in one set of hands?

Another feature of the Trotsky paradigm is that it set the expectations that recurred with every change of Soviet leadership, for with each succession hope surged that the Revolution would at last be put back on track. Yet on the first such occasion, at Stalin's death, the myth of Trotsky himself fell victim to the very syndrome he had inaugurated. For Khrushchev's reformism, in conjunction with the Western New Left of the 1960s, produced a third ideal alternative to Stalinism: after a longer-lived Lenin and a victorious Trotsky, Bukharin, as the patron of the High NEP, came to point the true road not taken.

In this new perspective, Trotsky, the proponent of the militarization of labor in 1920, and of "superindustrialism" when he was leader of the Left, came to be seen as no more than a failed Stalin. Or more accurately, it gradually became clear that "Stalin was Trotsky *in actu*," as Leszek Kolakowski put it. And Kolakowski continues: "Deutscher says ... that Trotsky's life was 'the tragedy of the precursor' ... but it is not clear what he is supposed to have been the precursor of.... Trotsky was not a 'forerunner' but an offshoot of the revolution, thrown off at a tangent to the course which it had followed in 1917–1921, but which it subsequently had to abandon.... It would be more exact to call his life the tragedy of the epigone...." And this epitaph concludes: "There was never any such thing as a Trotskyist theory— only a deposed leader who tried desperately to recover his role, who could not realize that his efforts were in vain, and who would not accept responsibility for a state of affairs which he regarded as a strange degeneration, but was in fact the direct consequence of the principles that he, together with Lenin and the whole Bolshevik party, had established as the foundations of socialism."[21]

This brings us to the most plausible road not taken in Soviet history, for Bukharin's defense of the NEP *did* seem to offer a genuine economic alternative to the policies of both Trotsky and Stalin, as well as a considerable improvement upon the meager hints of Lenin about cooperatives. Bukharin was roused to this defense by Preobrazhenskii's theory of primitive socialist accumulation, which he saw, not incorrectly, as a policy containing the seeds of a return to the lethal strife of War Communism and as the end of the Leninist *smychka*.

The *smychka*, of course, was a fiction that existed only in the mind of the Party. Social classes do not form alliances any more than they rule. Only political parties form alliances, and no political party— especially the now defunct Left SRs—had ever meaningfully committed the Russian peasantry to support of Lenin's organization. Thus "preservation of the *smychka*" was now simply Bolshevik language for saying that the Party could no longer afford to attack the peasantry for fear of undermining the regime itself. And this was Bukharin's great concern in the face of what he considered to be the Left's new adventurism. Yet he also had to take account of the real problem raised by the Left, namely, how to finance industrial development in a peasant country.

In 1925, therefore, Bukharin produced the first and only general theory of the NEP. The basis of this theory was a belief that industrial growth, and thus progress towards socialism, depended on an expanding consumer market that, in turn, led to private peasant accumulation. In this way the capital for industrial expansion would be generated, and the two sectors of the economy, agriculture and industry, would move forward in tandem, in a process of "growing into socialism through exchange." At the same time, Bukharin had to recognize that this process would be protracted and slow, probably a matter of decades; it would be progress "at a snail's pace," or like "riding into socialism on a peasant nag."

Bukharin also recognized that this policy meant favoring the stronger and more productive peasants, those class enemies of the *smychka*, the kulaks. Yet he did not shrink from expanding the NEP in their direction: In 1925 he advocated giving these peasants the right to lease land for an indefinite term and to hire up to twelve laborers, practices that had previously been condemned as exploitation. He was even so bold as to summon the peasants—in the words of the bourgeois prime minister of the July Monarchy, Guizot—"to get rich," a gaffe he quickly had to retract.

The Bukharin program's principal points were these: The growing prosperity of the stronger peasants and their cooperatives would furnish capital to the state, both through their taxes and through the profits of state factories producing consumer goods for their needs; this capital would permit expansion of the socialist industrial sector, thereby making it possible to create model mechanized collective farms; these collectives would serve as magnets for the weaker peasants; thus over time the socialist sector would compete the private sector out of existence; and in this way the open and revolutionary class struggle of 1917–1921 would be transformed into peaceful market competition, and Russia would "grow into socialism" through the market. This program was virtually the official policy of the Soviet government in 1925-1926, the two years of Bukharin's alliance with Stalin.

Yet it should be emphasized that Bukharin's socialism, once achieved, would have had nothing of a mixed economy about it. His ultimate goal was the same as that of all the other Bolshevik leaders: the end of private property, profit, and the market; a fully planned economy; and a wholly collectivized agriculture. Could his program have produced such an integral socialism? Could it have worked at all? Or was it only market Chevengur for Marxist ideologues and assorted fellow travellers?

In order to answer these questions it is necessary to look more closely at the nature of the crisis that undermined the NEP after 1927. By that year the Russian economy had virtually completed its post-Revolutionary recovery and had returned to some 90 percent of pre-war agricultural production and some 75 percent of industrial production. But this was the easy part of economic reconstruction. The country had started from so low a level that progress could only be swift and growth rates correspondingly high. Moreover, the task at hand had been to put an existing industrial plant back into operation, and this had required a relatively low outlay of capital.

By 1927, however, the task was to refurbish and replace an increasingly obsolete industrial plant that had received no new investment since 1913. Such an effort would have been required no matter what kind of government ruled Russia and whether or not it aimed to build socialism. And this effort would have absorbed very large sums of capital. Since these sums could not come from abroad, as under tsarism, capital would have to be shifted increasingly from production for the domestic consumer market to investment in heavy industry. This meant that, one way or another, industrialization would be financed on the backs of the peasants—just as Preobrazhenskii had argued. It was the peasants' reluctance to produce on these terms that led to the "procurements crisis" that hit the regime at the end of 1927 and deepened each year thereafter as the Plan swung into action. Thus the structural dilemma facing the regime in 1927 was this: It had no choice but to industrialize more rapidly, yet if it did so, it would inevitably alienate the peasantry.

But why could not the Communists have done better at keeping the peasants producing? The NEP, after all, had been designed for just this purpose, and it should have been possible to adjust the policy once again to eliminate the new scissors. The reason is that the NEP in fact had never been the mixed economy it was later taken to be. It had never been more than a barely tolerated quasi-market subject to constant and minute harassment from the state.

First of all, the basic institutions of War Communism had not been dismantled after 1921. Vesenkha, with all its *glavki*, was still there, and it continued to oversee the still nationalized "commanding heights" of the economy, even though many factories now had a limited autonomy to pursue *khozraschet* by organizing themselves into production "trusts" and marketing "syndicates." The State Bank was revived and given a near monopoly of credit, which it turned up or down at the behest of the Party. And Gosplan, too, was still there. Indeed, it now began its real career: After 1923 it started issuing "control figures," or forecasts, for production and drafting increasingly detailed plans for the day when the socialist offensive would be resumed. Naturally, this organization had become a base for the Left and for Mensheviks who rallied to what was, after all, a socialist regime. And all of these institutions generated a statist momentum that continued unabated throughout the NEP.

At the same time, some 80 percent of the nonagricultural economy remained nationalized. Thus the urban private sector consisted only of small retail commerce, petty artisan manufacture, marginal institutions of credit, and a few modest factories. Above all, this private sector consisted of a great variety of middlemen, intermediaries of all sorts who operated in the interstices of the state distribution system to scrounge up scarce goods to sell at higher than state prices. These were the nepmen, stigmatized by the regime as "speculators" and often resented by the population, yet necessary if there were to be a market at all. The peasantry, of course, made up the rest of the private sector; here the alleged lord of the village was the kulak, another "exploiter" and, as such, a class enemy.

Clearly, this private sector of nepmen and kulaks, huddling in the shadow of the "commanding heights" and explicitly destined by the regime for eventual liquidation, was no match for the Party's socialist sector. Nor are we dealing here with a mixed economy in any recognizable sense of that term, whether in the mode of Social Democratic Scandinavia or state-corporate Japan.

Given these circumstances, it is hardly surprising that in NEP Russia the Party never played the economic game according to market rules. Rather, its principal method of management was, in Bolshevik jargon, "administrative," by which was meant political fiat or outright coercion. To be sure, all governments intervene to some degree in the operations of the market, but the Soviet government's interventions during the twenties were constant, ubiquitous, and above all capricious. And this was no "accident" or the result of obtuse leadership. The cause of these interventions was uniformly political, namely, to bolster Party power by combatting allegedly hostile social classes, even though this hurt the real production and distribution of goods.

Thus the nepmen were taxed, regulated, and indeed arrested for "speculation," despite the fact that they brought consumer goods to the villages when state "syndicates" could not, or that they bought up peasant grain at higher than state prices for resale in the cities when official *zagotovki* were not forthcoming.[22] Consequently, the number of nepmen steadily declined in the second half of the decade, and the role of the market in the national economy correspondingly dwindled in this supposedly mixed economy. Similarly, the productive and prosperous kulaks were overtaxed and overregulated, thus decreasing their production and disrupting state procurements.

In other words, the crisis of 1927 was not an *economic* crisis in the sense of a failure of market mechanisms or a decline of productive capacity. The peasants were able and willing to produce a surplus if they received something they wanted in exchange, but the withering of the NEP market under state pressure prevented any such equivalent exchange. For after February 1927 the Party increasingly intervened to raise industrial prices in order to reduce the pressure of peasant demand on investment, while simultaneously lowering procurement prices in order to make food cheaper for the state. The reason, of course, was the political and ideological priority accorded to planned industrialization as the base for a proletarian regime. But the result was incompatible with maintaining the NEP. As our longest-running authority has put the matter: "The [pricing] policy chosen [in 1927] was basically hostile to market forces in industry, trade, and agriculture. Either the policy would have to be amended, or the market and its manifestations would have to be destroyed."[23] In short, the problem was not the kulaks, it was the Party. Thus, the crisis of the end of the decade was *political*, and it would receive a political solution in the Great Break of 1929.

Moreover, the psychological effect of regime pressure on the market was to keep the population in constant uncertainty about what might come next. This only fostered distrust of Soviet power, especially in the villages, where suspicion was already deep owing to War Communism. Under such circumstances, the population had little incentive to accumulate anything, and still less to invest it in the regime's socialism—thus confounding the expectations of both Preobrazhenskii and Bukharin.

It was under these circumstances that in 1927 Bukharin adapted his original theory of the NEP to take account of the exigencies of the forthcoming Plan; and it is this revised theory that is known as the Bukharin alternative.[24] Leaving aside for the moment the question of its feasibility under more ideal circumstances, we may note that in the situation at the time it was largely an effort at damage control. For in essence he moved in the direction of Preobrazhenskii and the Left by agreeing that the state should use "some squeeze" in order to extract from the peasants the capital for industrialization; he insisted, however, that this should be done slowly and cautiously. And when the going got rougher still in 1928, he even allowed that "a little" coercion might be in order, but without specifying how much was "a little." His program thus represented a difference in tempo more than in substance. In other words, he resorted to a softer version of Bolshevik *administrirovanie*, not to a deepening of the NEP in the direction of the market. For the rest, he advocated that grain imports should be increased to tide the cities over the slack in *zagotovki*.

It is difficult to see how these measures could have made a substantial difference in the existing situation, for the regime was confronted with two basic facts in 1927–1928. One was that *any* pressure on the peasants would only make the procurements crisis worse—after all, the peasants had reduced marketing immediately following the "goods famine" of 1927. The second was that the regime, with its Plan already under way, could not afford a slow solution to this problem. At such a juncture, an outright wager on the market—which would have been the true logic of the NEP—would have taken an unpredictable length of time without guaranteeing any predictable quantitative results. Such a gamble was therefore far too risky to contemplate, and Bukharin never even suggested it. So as a real alternative to the soft administrative squeeze of the NEP there remained only physical coercion of the peasants in the manner of War Communism. And this was the course finally adopted by Stalin in 1929.

But this choice of route was not just Stalin's personal caprice, nor an error in judgment that could have been avoided if wiser, or softer, or more "Leninist," leaders had been at the wheel of the Party during the NEP's final days. The problem was not with the driver but with the vehicle. The Party was not a machine to be harnessed to some peasant nag and drawn for decades through the backward countryside before reaching socialism. The Party had been created to lead and to fight, to charge the class enemy and to force the hand of history. A Brest-Litovsk, whether diplomatic or economic, was only a strategem to gather strength for a new offensive. And by the end of the twenties the Party had this strength. The great "social" fact of the NEP years was the maturation of Lenin's Party into an organization of a still newer type: an authentic war machine to complete the conquest of Russia interrupted by the retreat of 1921.

POLITICAL SOLUTIONS

The key to this development was given in 1921 when, at the Tenth Party Congress, Lenin made it clear that the economic NEP would not entail a political NEP. On the contrary, discipline within the Party was tightened and the Party's control over the country was strengthened. The logic behind this was the familiar military one for Bolshevism: with the Party besieged in a hostile country and in a hostile world, any fissure in its ranks would make the dissidents "objectively" the agents of enemy forces within the country and in the camp of imperialism outside it. This, indeed, had been the lesson of Kronstadt.

Intra-Party discipline was therefore insured by banning "factions" and making expulsion the penalty for factional activity.[25] The only democracy that now remained in the Party was "democratic centralism," which meant nonfactional discussion before any major decision and then conformity with the new Party line thereafter. Thus was established the principle of the "monolithic unity of the Party." To be sure, the ban on factions was not observed in practice during the 1920s, but the constant tendency of the Party's development was towards the elimination of factions, and by 1929 they were all gone. Thus Trotsky and others who later alleged that the ban was to have been only temporary took a superficially formalistic view of the matter. In fact, such a ban followed logically from the structure of the Party as outlined in *What Is To Be Done?*; Trotsky himself had acknowledged this in 1903 when he declared that in Lenin's scheme of things "the Party apparatus is substituted for the [rank and file], the Central Committee is substituted for the Party apparatus, and finally a 'dictator' is substituted for the Central Committee."

Concurrently, Lenin tightened the screws of political control over the country. This was done in 1922 with the first two show trials in Soviet history. One was for the SRs, whom Lenin initially wanted to shoot; but on the intercession of foreign Social Democrats they were only exiled to Siberia. The other was for the Mensheviks, who—again in order to mollify Western opinion—were simply expelled to the West. Thus the last political anomalies were removed from the one-Party state.

At the same time, the Party was expanded and tightened internally. As of 1929 the Party had gone through four phases of development. Until 1917 it was an underground organization—in fact a conspiracy—of full-time revolutionaries whose goal was to come to power if the tsarist regime were ever overthrown. In 1917 it briefly became a mass party, or at least a party with a mass following, though its leadership remained committed to a conspiratorial seizure of power. During War Communism the Party became a state institution that ruled, or tried to rule, through an omnicompetent and universal Soviet bureaucracy, one that it controlled through the dual administration. But because most of its membership was preoccupied with the emergency task of war, the Party was unable to stabilize in its governing role during this period. It was only after 1921 that the Party assumed its final form as an enduring state administration, a settled Party-state.

The Party's development is reflected in the growth of its membership. Ninety percent of the Party's 600,000 to 700,000 members in 1921 had been recruited during the Civil War. Although many of these new members were zealots, many were also opportunists of dubious reliability, and almost all of them were poorly indoctrinated for the long-term purposes of the Party. By 1922 some 200,000 members had been "purged," which in those days meant they were simply expelled from the Party; by 1924 around 200,000 more were gone, leaving a total of 350,000. At the same time, extensive efforts were made to recruit new and largely proletarian members, notably in the great "levy" of worker members in 1924 in honor of the late Lenin. Additional recruitment drives brought the Party's membership to 1,090,000 in 1929, the last year of the NEP.[26] These new members were not random volunteers, as during the Civil War; rather, they had been selected and screened by the Party itself. Moreover, they were all well indoctrinated in an increasingly simplified and standardized, or catechized, version of Marxism that became known after 1924 as Marxism-Leninism. Stalin's *Questions of Leninism* is the best-known document setting forth this new creed.

Nikita Khrushchev is once again a good example of this new Party man. After serving as a junior political commissar with the Red Army throughout the Civil War, at the beginning of the NEP he received something of an education at the "Workers' Faculty" (adult crash schooling) of the Donbas branch of the Mining Institute. From there, in 1924 at the age of thirty he moved on to become the local Party secretary, thus entering full-time Party work. In 1925 he was an alternate delegate to the Fourteenth Party Congress, and in 1927 a full voting delegate to the Fifteenth Congress, both of which were occupied with destroying the Left. With a million such new men, Stalin by 1929 had a political army more solid than any Lenin ever possessed, one ready to do battle, without discussion or haggling, at the call of the new Leader.

For the internal organization of the Party had changed greatly since the days of War Communism. As the Party grew in size and became an administration, it acquired its own internal bureaucracy of full-time apparatchiki, whereas the ordinary members became transmission belts for bringing the Party's line to the various functional administrations and the population at large. This internal bureaucracy consisted of a hierarchy of Party "committees," or executive bodies, from the localities up to the All-Union Central Committee. The permanent executive organ of this body was the Politburo, which after 1921 became the real center of power in the country. But the Central Committee also needed a permanent staff to manage the new bureaucracy; this was the Secretariat, of which Lenin made Stalin the head, or General Secretary, in 1922. Stalin thus became, in effect, the personnel officer of the Party: He assigned Party workers where he deemed they were needed and was accountable only to the Politburo and the Central Committee. Under the regime of democratic central-ism, Party workers went where they were told.[27]

In practice this method of personnel management came to mean that the General Secretary could appoint the secretaries of subordi-nate local committees, who would then choose the delegates to Party congresses; in turn these delegates would reelect Stalin General Sec-retary. It was in this way that he had shouldered Trotsky out of the succession in 1924, and then disposed of his fellow triumvirs, Zi-noviev and Kamenev, in 1925–1926, and finally crushed the United Left in 1927. With the field so narrowed, by 1928–1929 it was quite easy for him to turn on Bukharin and his allies, Rykov and Tomskii, and exclude them from power as the "Right deviation." Thus by the Great Break of 1929 Stalin had become the unchallenged master of the Party. He was not yet an absolute dictator, but he had an absolute right of initiative within the Party structures.

Stalin, of course, wanted this power, just as he wanted to be Lenin's sole successor. But to explain his ascendancy essentially by personal ambition would be superficial in the extreme. Party structures had to make it possible for him to formulate his ambition, and these struc-tures cried out for personification in one Leader. A single "correct" doctrine, an embattled siege mentality, and recruitment based on cooptation from the top down—all taken together could only produce a military command organization functioning through orders from a single center. The ban on factions formalized, but did not create, this situation. It was because Stalin understood the true nature of the Party better than his rivals that he was able to eliminate them so effectively. From 1922 to 1927, while they debated high policy, he concerned himself with getting control of the Party machine. And in this endeavor he maneuvered just as Lenin had done within the Russian Social Democratic Party in his struggle against the Menshe-viks between 1903 and 1912. It was only once Stalin had control that he came out with his own policy; in the meantime he supported Bukharin's cautious course.

But bureaucratization of the Party was not the only key to Stalin's success; what put him over the top was the Party's ideocratic nature, on which he also played adroitly. For this Party was no ordinary political body but the vehicle of the logic of history, and all of Stalin's rivals believed this so deeply that they disarmed themselves before him in every crisis. As Trotsky said at the moment of his defeat in

1924: "The Party in the last analysis is always right, because the Party is the single historic instrument given to the proletariat for the solution of its fundamental problems. . . . I know that one must not be right *against* the Party. One can only be right with the Party, and through the Party, for history has created no other road for the realization of what is right."[28] With adversaries like this, Stalin hardly needed allies. And all his rivals, "Right" and "Left," Bukharin no less than Zinoviev, thought the same. So they all capitulated and recanted their errors (with the sole exception of Trotsky, who after 1929 no longer had the option of recanting because he had been cast out of the country).

Indeed, they all went on to serve the new Leader until he cut them down in the Purges. Thus Preobrazhenskii, Iurii Piatakov, and all the Left worked for the First Five-Year Plan as if it were their own. And Bukharin dutifully fell silent during the Plan's collectivization; he even penned what he considered to be the crowning achievement of both the new socialism and his own career, the Stalin Constitution of 1936, proudly exhibiting the historic pen to an émigré friend in Paris the same year.[29] For to him, as to all the others, *partiinost*, or Party spirit, meant more than any economic program or policy towards the peasants.

In the course of the 1920s, moreover, this spirit was extended from the Party itself to the population at large. The years of the NEP, as we have seen, have often been described as a period of cultural pluralism, of avant-garde art, and of audacious speculation about the hoped-for socialist future.[30] And it was indeed a period of often daring social experimentation, of radical legislation permitting easy divorce and abortion on demand, and of modernist or "progressive" educational reform.[31] It was also a time when non-Communists, if they accepted the Revolution, were welcomed by the Party as "fellow travellers" in creating the new culture. Thus, for a few years and in a few areas, there was a prolongation of the great prerevolutionary flowering of Russia's Silver Age. Yet on the whole, the movement of the decade was steadily in the opposite direction: towards ever greater ideological conformity and state control over education, culture, and the arts.

To begin with, all cultural currents deemed hostile to the Revolution were actively combatted. All politics, from Menshevism to monarchism, were proscribed. Religion became the butt of a massive campaign of persecution conducted by the League of the Militant Godless.[32] What is more, the Party engaged in a historically unprecedented effort to indoctrinate the population in a single "correct" worldview, an effort that earned for the period the appropriate title "birth of the propaganda state."[33]

In the course of this operation, Marxism was transformed from an ideological tool of political intellectuals seeking to understand their world so that they could change it—which is how Marxism was used by Lenin and Trotsky, or by Preobrazhenskii and Bukharin—into a scholastic system manipulated by the state to justify its policies of the moment. Stalin's doctrine of "socialism in one country" is transitional in this respect; it was half an analysis of Bolshevik Russia's isolation and half a means of fostering Party hope in such a bleak situation.

Thus, the vocabulary of what was now called Marxism-Leninism was standardized and ritualized into what has variously been called "wooden language" or "newspeak." All groups and individuals had their fixed labels, from greedy kulaks to traitorous petty bourgeois to imperialist sharks to valiant shock workers: The world was divided, in Manichean manner, into friends and enemies, and all current events, foreign and domestic, were refracted through the prism of the class struggle.

These new categories were then dinned into the population through the daily press, the new art of the cinema, and soon the still more ubiquitous medium of radio. As Lenin said of the first of these media: "A newspaper is a collective agitator and a collective organizer." And so the country was inundated by agitprop, both to put over the Party line of the moment and to mobilize the population for the eventual effort to achieve socialism.

Nothing on this scale, and nothing this total, had ever been seen before in the world of "culture." Nor was this new language a mere ornament or rhetorical embellishment. It was essential to the power of the regime. Language, like everything else in life, had to be made to serve the cause of socialism. Indeed language, more than anything else, had to be politicized, since it was both the means of social mobilization and the way into the consciousness of the population. The meaning of ordinary words, accordingly, had to be altered to conform to ideological precepts.

The ideocratic partocracy, therefore, was also necessarily logocratic;

and as such it was of a piece with the monopolistic structure of the now monolithic system. Without this logocratic spell, the system could not function: Trotsky and Bukharin could not have believed that it was impossible to be right against the Party; and Stalin could not have bent his opponents to follow his General Line and rush into the Great Break.

Thus politically—with the growth of the Party apparat—and culturally—with the rise of newspeak—the line of development during the NEP did not lead to liberalization, but to where matters actually wound up under Stalin in the thirties.

It is only against this political and cultural background that it is possible to answer the socialist counterfactual question of the feasibility of the "Bukharin alternative." Or, to put the matter the other way around, and in the terms of a famous essay on this central issue of Soviet history: Was Stalin really necessary?[34]

Yet whichever way the question is put, the answer can be either yes or no, depending on what one considers Bukharin's alternative to mean. If it is understood to be basically an economic program designed to make Russia a developed country—and this is what is frequently taken to be its essence—then Bukharin's formula of a state-guided yet market economy would have produced respectable results, and at far less human cost than Stalin's program. In fact, roughly comparable versions of a mixed economy have often been followed since then in such places as South Korea, Taiwan, and Brazil.

But this is not what Bukharin himself meant by the alternative that bears his name. He meant, rather, a transition to full or integral socialism, to be achieved, moreover, under the political monopoly of the Party. Nor had he really thought out the details of the transition. His strategy of "growing into socialism through the market" would have required a great deal of time, on the order of a decade or more, and grain procurements under existing NEP policies were declining by the month. Would the Party's revolutionary zeal have held up for a long transition to its goal? Bukharin's strategy, moreover, would have required two concessions that he barely hinted at: first, real peasant soviets to give the rural half of the *smychka* some measure of confidence in the Soviet state; and second, partially opening the country to foreign capital on terms permitting normal profit, in order to get Russia through the crisis into which mismanagement of the NEP had already plunged her.

But both of these concessions would have meant breaching the Party's monopoly of power, in other words, attacking the Party's very raison d'être—or, as the Party's now well-honed logocratic idiom put it, capitulating to the "kulak petty bourgeoisie" internally and to "imperialism" externally. Thus, in the crisis of 1928–1929 the men who controlled the expanded Party machine swiftly concluded that they did not have time to wait years, or even many months, for a solution to peasant "sabotage," because the realization of the Party's goal, building socialism, was already under way with the Plan. For the Party, the NEP was never an exercise in "development economics"; rather, it was simply a strategy for moving towards socialism. And once the NEP got in the way of this goal, it was time to discard it.

In this perspective, the final answer to the question of the Bukharin alternative's feasibility must be negative. Given its nature, it was wholly implausible to expect the Leninist Party to capitulate, under pressure of a crisis, to the class enemies it had been created to destroy. Similarly, it was no accident that the Party's leadership had fallen into the hands of men like Stalin and the other Civil War commissars— Molotov, Kaganovich, Voroshilov, Ordzhonikidze, Kirov, and Andreev—who now dominated the Politburo. In the crisis of the NEP, such a party and such leaders could only be expected to make a political rather than an economic decision—or more exactly, to make a political-military decision (as we must call their reversion to the coercive methods of War Communism) to carry out collectivization.

Thus, given the principle of Party hegemony Bukharin himself accepted, his alternative was too narrowly economic to prevail in a crisis of Party survival. Conversely, Stalin's option for the primacy of militarized politics was quite in accord with basic Leninism. For the essence of Leninisn had never been one or another economic program; it had always been the armed seizure and preservation of a monopoly of power for the Party as history's only vessel for achieving socialism. Mistaking Leninism for some kind of "economism," or near-Menshevism, was Bukharin's great error in the twenties, as it has been that of his votaries ever since. For a Bolshevik Party the real choice in 1929 was not between Stalin's road and Bukharin's; it was between doing approximately what Stalin did and giving up the whole Leninist enterprise.

It will no doubt be objected that this reasoning is "deterministic" and makes Stalin's choice appear inevitable or necessary. In fact, it is nothing of the sort: It is an "if-then" argument that holds that once a Leninist Party comes to power, a whole range of options is thereafter excluded, leaving only another, narrower range as possible or feasible. Thus after October the market and private property were structurally "out," and Party-state "command-administrative" methods, as they came to be called by the opposition under Gorbachev, were structurally "in." The Bukharin alternative went too far towards what October had already excluded to be the long-term road for true Bolshevism. So the Party cut the NEP short before it destroyed the Party itself, and returned to its first course of War Communism.

Still, the NEP did leave an enduring residue: It became the permanent alternative to the Party's first and basic program, an alternative that would resurface each time a bout of War Communism pushed the human and material fabric of the country to the breaking point. In this way, by 1929 Soviet history had staked out its fundamental pattern of alternating between "hard" and "soft" Communism, between full noncapitalism and forced compromise with the inveterate "class" enemy—that is, with reality. This pattern made "the Soviet historical drama a two-act play, replayed several times with different sets and characters."[35] And so it remained until the final curtain came down on the whole threadbare show after the last NEP—*perestroika*.

Yet in 1929 the Party of Lenin was still at the peak of its revolutionary vigor, so the curtain went up on the grandest act of all—the building of socialism through Stalin's Five-Year Plan. This time there would be no turning back short of the goal, no compromises with the class enemy. The last, whining opposition would be swept aside, and the now perfected Party army, led by a new "Lenin for today," would march forth under the slogan "there are no fortresses that Bolsheviks cannot storm."

6

AND THEY BUILT
SOCIALISM

1929–1935

We are going full steam ahead along the road of industrialization to socialism, leaving behind our century-old Russian backwardness. We are becoming a metallic country, an automotive country, a tractor country. When we have put the USSR in an automobile, and the muzhik on a tractor, then let the esteemed capitalists, preening themselves with their "civilization," try to overtake us. We will see then which countries can be "classified" as backward and which as advanced.

—J. V. Stalin, November 7, 1929

No, comrades,... we must not lower the tempo [of industrialization].

...To reduce the tempo would mean to fall behind; and those who fall behind are beaten.... The history of old Russia showed her constantly beaten for her backwardness. She was beaten by the Mongol Khans, she was beaten by the Turkish Beys, she was beaten by the Swedish feudal lords, she was beaten by Polish-Lithuanian Pans, she was beaten by Anglo-French capitalists, she was beaten by Japanese barons, she was beaten by all—for her backwardness. For military backwardness, for cultural backwardness, for political backwardness, for industrial backwardness, for agricultural backwardness. She was beaten because to beat her was profitable and went unpunished. You remember the words of the pre-revolutionary poet [Nekrasov]: "Thou art poor and thou art plentiful, thou art mighty and thou art helpless, Mother Russia."

...This is why Lenin said in October: "The choice is either death or catching up with and overtaking the advanced capitalist countries."

...We are fifty or a hundred years behind the advanced countries. We must run that same distance in ten years. Either we do it or they crush us.

—J. V. Stalin, February 4, 1931

177

The socialism built by Stalin's Five-Year Plans of the 1930s was the climax of the Soviet experiment. It brought to a culmination all the years of Bolshevik searching after 1917, and it created the basic institutions of the Soviet system as it would exist until the collapse of 1991. The rough sketch of the future order offered by Lenin's War Communism was now completely filled in through a new Offensive by the man of steel. In 1929, debate on the General Line ended for good: The Bolsheviks stopped talking about what they were going to do and at last did it.

THE STALIN QUESTION

Stalin's rule during this decisive decade has been called the Second Russian Revolution, and the designation is quite apt. It has also been called "primitive socialist accumulation by the methods of Tamerlane,"[1] and this is even more apt. Yet neither label really conveys the specificity of the event: The transformation of Russia during the thirties was unprecedented in scope, to the same degree as the means employed to achieve it were unique in their mixture of the insane and the criminal with—it must be admitted—the grandiose and the epic.

This poses another major problem of historical interpretation.[2] The previous chapter argued that the choice of a coercive road to socialism was no accident but the logical course for a Bolshevik Party in a crisis of survival. Yet it does not automatically follow that the extraordinarily brutal manner in which Stalin implemented that choice was equally governed by the Party's ethos. The pace at which collectivization and industrialization were forced was not the outcome of an automatic process but the result of conscious decisions. And after 1929 Stalin's power was so great that he personally made, or at least supervised, the most crucial of those decisions.

So the question of the logic of the system versus Stalin's personal role does not end with the Great Break but continues throughout the thirties, from the collectivization to the Purges. How much of the criminality of the collectivization was due to Stalin's own criminal character? How much of the madness of the Purge was due to his own possible insanity? Surely—this line of inquiry goes—neither Lenin nor Trotsky (both hard Bolsheviks who could quite conceivably have adopted a coercive policy in 1929) would have deliberately starved

the peasants or murdered revolutionary comrades. The personal paranoia and the individual sadism of Stalin the man must constitute the
decisive element that made his reign seem, in Bukharin's metaphor,
like the return of Genghis Khan.[3]

To this argumentation is often added the theme that Stalin's Second Revolution (unlike the first Revolution of 1917) was a revolution
from above, and revolution from above is the time-honored Russian
method of catching up with the advanced West.[4] Thus Stalinism
represented a reversion to the more extreme phases of Russian autocracy, as under Ivan the Terrible or Peter the Great. And at a
superficial glance this explanation seems eminently plausible. Indeed,
Stalin himself liked to compare his rough nation-building with that of
these two tsars, Peter for the Plan and Ivan for the Terror. Yet it would
be prudent to reserve judgement on this matter until Stalin's own
record has been examined, and to seek the sources of Stalinism, in the
first instance, not in remote centuries but in the actual circumstances
that produced the revolution from above. Here, in this line of inquiry,
Stalin's personality is far more germane than are the ghosts of auto-
crats past.

Even so, caution is in order on this score, too, for Stalin's lugubrious
figure, like Hitler's equally macabre one, can easily overshadow his
period and the system he represented. Thus "Stalinism" in common
parlance too often means a style of rule—an extreme personal tyranny, an exceptional despotism, or a superdictatorship—created and
sustained by the man, Stalin. But these Greek and Roman terms do
not do justice, any more than does the invocation of Genghis Khan, to
the historical particularity of the Stalin phenomenon.

So Stalinism must also be viewed as a *system* of hyperbureaucratic
and terroristic control. Yet even when this is done, the system's genesis is still too often explained not by structural factors but by the
tyrant's overweening ambition. The consequence of this is that once
the evil author of the "ism" has disappeared, the system itself may be
considered to have ended. Thus in both Western and Soviet usage, as
we have seen, Stalinism was at times held to be a completely different
phenomenon from Bolshevism and Leninism.[5] In Soviet parlance this
assessment was expressed as "the cult of personality," which meant
that an otherwise sound socialism was "distorted" by the undue and
accidental power of one leader. So the logics of backwardness, of the

monolithic Party, of primitive socialist accumulation, and of the ideo-cratic partocracy were all obscured by a logic of abstract tyranny, the "cult."

This approach might be called the "bad man" theory of history. Its appeal is to simplify a painful past by personalizing it and concentrat-ing it in a single focus of evil.* But, as just noted, the defect of this universal penchant is that it obscures the deeper system behind the man, or at least subordinates it to his continuing presence. Thus, what came before him and what came after can be viewed as a different system, and the belief arises that once the focus of evil has disap-peared this system can recover a healthy normality. Hence, the "bad man" approach to Stalinism is related to the aberration thesis. Indeed, Stalin's evil personality is at the heart of the "aberration" thesis be-cause there is no alternative way to explain how an otherwise healthy organism went awry. Stalin climbed to dictatorship because he was, as Bukharin liked to see it, "an unprincipled intriguer who subordinates everything to the preservation of his own power."[6]

Now, Stalin was a bad man, indeed a very bad man, and he grew steadily worse with age. But much more than this is needed to explain the momentous policies of his twenty-five-year reign. He had to have a context of institutions and ideas within which to work and through which to vent whatever dark drives haunted his psyche. Moreover, we must assume that there were quite a number of other individuals in Russia and in the Party who had equally harsh childhoods and cruel fathers, who were equally neurotic and thirsty for power, but who did not become politically significant figures. Psychology does not trans-late into politics unless there is first a political problem to be met. In explaining any political leader's policies we must accept, just as he does when he acts, the primacy of political motivation. Political lead-ers who use their power simply to act out their psychoses do not keep power very long, as the cases of Peter III, or Paul I, and on back to Emperor Commodus, serve to illustrate. But Stalin lasted a quarter of a century, and by any mundane standards of judgement he must be considered a world-historical success: After all, he built socialism,

---

* The personalization of history is not confined to negative phenomena. There is also a "good man" view of history, of which a striking example was the Western cult of Gorbachev, which for six years sustained the illusion that Communism was reforming itself when in fact it was collapsing. Indeed, personalization of public life is well-nigh universal—from Romulus to George Washington—because it seems to make reality easily comprehensible to everybody.

defeated fascism, and created a Soviet empire. Psychological reductionism in history works no better than socioeconomic reductionism.
One of the purposes of this chapter, therefore, is to derive Stalin's
policies from the Soviet system rather than to work the relationship
the other way around.

Still, within the political context of Communism, Stalin's personal
biography is pertinent, and the most basic facts are these: He was the
only member of Lenin's Politburo who came from "the people." His
father was an alcoholic village cobbler who became a worker in a shoe
factory, and his mother was an illiterate, pious peasant. His uncom-
pleted education in a seminary of the Orthodox Church gave him the
equipment to become a well-read autodidact in Russian, though not
in European, literature. He did not become an *intelligent*, however,
because, unlike real members of the intelligentsia, he was not interested in ideas as such, and still less in their moral implications. Nonetheless, once he became a Bolshevik he did receive a thorough
grounding in Marxist ideology. There is no reason to doubt the gen-
uineness of his commitment to Marxism, however crudely he applied
it: It furnished the basis of his worldview for the whole of his adult
life. In manner he always remained rough and plebeian, but he was
not, as many Russians believe, a social type that in his native Georgian
is called *kinto* and in Russian *shpana* (approximately "street tough" or
"street survivor"), a type that would easily turn to crime in appropriate circumstances.

Instead he became a tough-minded revolutionary, and in that capacity he acquired a "legitimate" outlet for his asocial energies. But
this can be said of many other Bolsheviks; it is also true of members
of the Combat Organization, or terrorist wing, of the Socialist Revolutionaries, many of whom later wound up in the Cheka. (The Mensheviks, by and large, tended to be more intellectual and less
comfortable with violence.) And Stalin in his early days in the Caucasus compiled a record of turning strikes and demonstrations into
physical brawls. But it was no simple stroke of bad luck that someone
of his temper became head of the Communist Party: By its conspiratorial recruitment, structure, and militant ethos, the Party brought
many such people to positions of authority. Indeed, they were all
around Stalin during his revolution from above; without such kindred
spirits this revolution would not have been possible at all.

Stalin owed his political career entirely to Lenin. In 1912 Lenin needed someone from a minority nationality to express his own new views on the revolutionary potential of nationalism, and Stalin was tapped for the job. Even more important, in the same year Lenin co-opted him into the Party's Central Committee (at the same time that he put another marginal type, the police agent Roman Malinovskii, on that body). Thus, when Stalin returned to Petrograd from Siberian exile in March 1917, he was the chief Bolshevik in town; moreover, from that time on he remained in the top leadership of the Party.

At the beginning, however, Stalin's role was to be Lenin's faithful second. Indeed, he was the only important Bolshevik not to have a major public disagreement with Lenin: Trotsky, Bukharin, Zinoviev, and most other members of the Central Committee had clashed with the "Old Man" on one or another major issue, from October to Brest-Litovsk and beyond. Yet to the public throughout 1917 Stalin was only a "gray blur," to use the expression of a Menshevik chronicler of that year, and he played no visible role in October, a glaring gap in his revolutionary record that weighed on him in later years until, once in power, he rewrote the record to make himself coauthor with Lenin of October, thus usurping Trotsky's place.[7]

In real history, however, Stalin came into his own only during the Civil War, when he served as People's Commissar for Nationalities and, above all, as a political commissar on various fronts, especially in the vital battle for Tsaritsyn (later renamed Stalingrad) in 1918, and then in the Polish War of 1920. It is in this period that he acquired a network of cronies and allies, mostly fellow commissars, who would be his special retainers within the Party and who, after 1929, would furnish his high command in the new civil war to build socialism: Molotov, Kaganovich, Voroshilov, Mikoyan, Kirov, Zhdanov, Andreev, Ordzhonikidze, and Kuibyshev, to name them once again. In assembling this clientele he was not violating the Party norms of the time; all the other Bolshevik leaders had their clients, who later formed the oppositions of the twenties. Despite this increased status, however, Stalin was still careful to appear, at least publicly, as Lenin's faithful chief lieutenant for administrative matters, and, as already noted, this is one reason why he was made General Secretary in 1922. Even then, however, he was not perceived by his colleagues as an important figure, still less as a threat; to Trotsky he appeared only as a "mediocrity."

The dying Lenin was among the first to express doubts about Stalin in his new role as "Gensek." In 1922 the two men clashed over the form of the new Soviet Union, whose constitution Stalin was then writing in a centralizing spirit while Lenin wanted a somewhat looser structure. This clash led to Lenin's political "testament," which has usually been read as proof that Stalin usurped the Old Man's "caftan" and, therefore, that Stalinism was not true Bolshevism. These dictated notes, however, are by no means so simple. Lenin took only two of his lieutenants, Trotsky and Stalin, seriously as possible successors: He rated them the "ablest leaders of the Party" and devoted the bulk of his remarks to a discussion of their characters. Zinoviev and Kamenev together were dismissed in one line, while Bukharin rated barely more, and Piatakov, hardly prominent at the time, seemed to have been thrown in only to give the impression of a genuine survey. Yet, after singling out Stalin and Trotsky, Lenin proceeded to cut both down to size. Stalin was criticized for being "too rude" and for amasing "inordinate power" as General Secretary. Lenin therefore proposed removing him from that post, though not from the top leadership, for Lenin did not intend to destroy Stalin politically, as is sometimes alleged. Lenin then evenhandedly criticized Trotsky for being drawn too much to the "administrative side of things," which in plain language meant he was too autocratic. Even more negative remarks were directed at Zinoviev and Kamenev, whose conduct in October was labeled "no accident," and at Bukharin, who was called a "poor Marxist."

Thus, in this curious document Lenin managed to denigrate all his chief lieutenants. In so doing, he may have hoped to diminish the pretensions of each one so that none could aspire to be sole leader should he die, thereby avoiding rivalries that could split the Party. Or he may have expected he was going to recover, and so sought to keep his colleagues subordinate by pointing up his own continued indispensability. But whatever his intention, the document had no practical effect because his heirs were unanimously unwilling to act on it at the time. Only later was it exhumed by the partisans of Trotsky and Bukharin to delegitimize the General Secretary—but this was after Trotsky and Lenin's widow had already declared it to be false. To be sure, the document was always an embarrassment to Stalin in the theological culture that Marxism-Leninism had become. But his real power remained intact, and by 1929 he had made himself the sole leader of an ever more tightly structured Party, in the manner already described.

So, for Stalin, in 1929 the moment had arrived for policy. During the struggle against Trotsky and the Left Opposition, Stalin's policy had been largely Bukharin's, but he had given it a more practical cast. This meant emphasizing the idea of "socialism in one country," a phrase that had already been used by Bukharin but which in 1924 Stalin made into a theoretical principle to indicate to the Party that it could finish the task of October at home and on its own. This did not mean rejecting world revolution, however, because the final overthrow of capitalism was still deemed necessary for the safety of the Soviet state. But it did mean that in the interval full socialism could be built in Russia alone. Since at the time the Party had nowhere else to build it, this was an astute rejoinder to the Left's infatuation with world revolution.

But Stalin acquired a concrete program for building socialism in Russia only in 1928–1929, and he took it from the same Left he had just crushed. Until then he had not been notably interested in problems of industrialization. Even as late as 1926 he had opposed the construction of the great Dnieprostroi Dam, saying this was like the folly of a peasant buying a gramophone when he should be using the money to repair his plow. Industrialization became central to Stalin only when it became central to the Party with the launching of the First Five-Year Plan in 1928. Even then, however, the Plan was not a product of Stalin and his group: It developed out of the general technocratic momentum of the Party in the twenties; and to the extent that it had a "factional" base, this was furnished by the Left together with various ex-Menshevik, former SR, and bourgeois specialists.

It is this Plan that was to be the vehicle for Stalin's revolution from above. After 1928 he annexed it and transformed it into a program for a Second Socialist Offensive leading to a permanent, institutionalized version of War Communism. And it is this transformed Plan that gives us the meaning of Stalinism as not just a terroristic tyranny or a hyperbureaucracy, but as a total system. Stalin would go down in history as the creator of the two great pillars of the mature Soviet order, Planning and Collectivization.

*   *   *

What was this Five-Year Plan that in its day mesmerized not only Russia but much of the outside world? It was nothing less than the first attempt in history at economic planning, and as such it marked a new stage in the development of socialism as well as a new stage in the history of economic thought and practice generally.

As a movement in opposition, classical Marxism had focused its critique of capitalism on private property and private profit, and on the evil of exploitation these institutions generated. It had also inveighed against the division of labor, the accumulation of capital through the expropriation of surplus value, and the wastefulness of competition. But it had not made a central and explicit issue of the anarchy of the market, nor of the blind irrationality of supply and demand as a means of allocating resources. To be sure, since private property, profit, and money were to be abolished under socialism, the market, too, would have to disappear, and its place would have to be taken by some sort of rational planning. But none of this was spelled out in detail or emphasized.

The logical consequences of classical Marxism began to emerge only in the German economic debates of the very end of the nineteenth century that produced the already noted awareness of capitalism as a total system. Social Democrats such as Karl Kautsky began to speculate about planning and the rational reorganization of life under socialism, a concern echoed on the Right by the "Socialists of the Chair." This concern with economic planning was then heightened by the already noted War Socialism of Ludendorff and Rathenau. And it was this Central European Left-cum-Right urge to plan that stimulated the Austrian school of economics to its laissez-faire critique of planning. In this school's view, planning was an intrinsically impossible enterprise because in any given situation the amount of necessary information and the number of variables were too great for advance calculation.[8] As Ludwig von Mises argued in 1920, against the background of Russia's War Communism, only market prices could allocate resources to where they were in fact needed.[9]

But it was the Russian experience of Marxism in power that first brought out fully the institutional implications of socialism, and not just for Russia. Nationalization under War Communism had for the first time anywhere in the modern world led to the suppression of the market, and the suppression of the market had led to the first ever intimations of planning. Conversely, the proclamation of the New

Economic Policy had made the market, not private property, appear as the central institution of capitalism. Then, in answer, the drafting of the First Five-Year Plan after 1926 had made planning the central institution of socialism.

From this time onward the antithesis capitalism–socialism would above all be the antithesis market–plan; people everywhere would henceforth speak of "market economies" and "planned economies" as the two possible ways of organizing life in this world. Thus the Soviet Five-Year Plan hardly appeared simply as a device for overcoming backwardness; it was viewed by both the planners and the outside world as the pilot project for creating an entirely new economic order.

Yet it was more than an economic project of any kind. The Plan derived ultimately from the Saint-Simonian technocratic strain in Marxism that in turn goes back to the eighteenth-century Encyclopedists who were, after all, *philosophes*. And this strain descended in a direct succession from d'Alembert to Turgot, to Condorcet, to Saint-Simon, to Comte—social engineers all—and thence to modern sociology generally. And at each stage this tradition held with an almost religious fervor that the rational, scientific ordering of human affairs could produce a new society and a new man. It was not an accident that Condorcet predicted the "absolute perfectibility of the human race," or that Saint-Simon called his technocratic doctrine the "New [secular] Christianity." In particular, by the time of Saint-Simon and Comte this tradition had adopted the belief that modern industry founded on advanced technology was the Prometheus that would transform the human condition, an idea that Marx fully shared.

And the industrial Prometheanism of Marx had its counterpart in a Russian tradition that led from Chernyshevskii's crystal palace to Vladimir Mayakovskii's futurism and Nikolai Fedorov's technological millenarianism. All of these currents of expectation attached themselves to the Plan once it was proclaimed in 1928 and so produced a groundswell of emotion within the Party and in urban society generally. At last, the radical intelligentsia felt, there would be a great breakthrough to wrest Russia from her inveterate backwardness.

This surge of enthusiasm also carried a great charge of hostility toward that bastion of backwardness—the "dark people," the benighted Russian peasants. The peasants had always occupied a central place in Russian society—where they constituted the overwhelming majority—as well as in the Russian national mythology. Ever since Peter cut his famous window through to Europe, Russia, culturally speaking, had been divided into two: the Europeanized and secular gentry and intelligentsia on the one hand, and the still Muscovite and Orthodox peasantry on the other. Depending on one's point of view, this could mean that the upper classes had become foreign and the peasants alone were the true Russians; or it could mean that the gentry and intelligentsia were the force for rationality and progress, and the peasants were a dead weight of Asiatic barbarism, superstition, and stagnation.

These two perspectives had much to do with the differences between the Slavophiles and the Westernizers when the two camps first emerged in the 1840s. Later, Dostoevsky would be an extreme example of the former view, and Lenin, as we have seen, an even more extreme representative of the latter position. But for both camps, the peasantry defined the meaning of Russia in a manner that the rural classes defined no other major European nation—even when, as in the France of 1789 (or in most of nineteenth-century Europe, for that matter) these peasants constituted 80 percent of the population. Thus, since the Plan promised to end the preponderance of the peasantry in Russian life, it also proposed a radical redefinition of the nation. In this sense it was a measure of revolutionary Westernism, the lever for the ultimate Europeanization of Russia.

The Party, of course, did not put matters in these conventionally Russian terms, but its Marxist categories expressed something similar; indeed, they added a lethal new charge, for in its formal tenets Marxism is fundamentally and aggressively antipeasant. We have already seen this in action during War Communism; it would come fully to the fore during the First Five-Year Plan.

In Marxist terms the peasants are not just inefficient producers who must somehow be brought into modernity. Rather, they are a hopelessly archaic class condemned by the logic of history to extinction, indeed to "liquidation." Now, when Marx used the word "liquidation" to describe what needed to be done to the idiocy of rural life or to hopelessly retrograde nations such as the Czechs, he did not mean physical extermination: he meant urbanization in the case of the peasants, and Germanization in the case of the Czechs, but in both cases he meant the elimination of entire groups. To be sure, Lenin had exempted the poorer stratum of the peasantry from Marx's global condemnation of the village; but he did so essentially on tactical and temporary grounds.

In Marxism, moreover, the logic of history was driven by the class war; it followed, therefore, that the peasants would be civilized and urbanized by means of an economic struggle that would culminate in their elimination. This indeed had been the fate of the English peasantry at the hands of the bourgeoisie during the emergence of capitalism, and although Marx excoriated those bourgeois exploiters, he also firmly held that their action was necessary and progressive because it was part of the logic leading to socialism.[10] Finally, Marxism held that all of the more backward nations of the world would have to follow this painful European path.

This whole mode of thinking, as we have seen, was integral to the planning debate in Russia. Thus elimination of the peasantry through class struggle was both a premise and a final implication of the Plan, whatever the actual percentage of collectivization it called for. For in effect the Plan proposed to end the "division of labor between town and country" that was the first and most basic form of human alienation for Marxists.

To be sure, these were not the terms Stalin used to urge his General Line on the Party and the country. Nonetheless, that General Line drew subliminally on the Westernizing tradition in Russian culture, and it drew quite explicitly on the Marxist view that all politics is class struggle culminating in the final resolution of history in socialism. It is only in the context of this eschatology that the mad wager of the First Five-Year Plan is comprehensible. For it cannot be emphasized enough that the Bolsheviks were not just out to develop a backward country; they were out to build socialism.

The Plan as finally adopted in April 1929 attempted to translate "scientifically" these general goals into precise quantitative targets for agriculture and industry. The methods for doing this had been several years in gestation. In 1924 Gosplan had begun to publish "control figures," or projections, for the coming year. In 1925 it started drafting actual plans for future development. In 1926, when the postwar recovery was largely completed, this planning for future industrial expansion became urgent. By 1927 expansion was already underway, so the Party at its Fifteenth Congress, at the same time that it expelled the Left, adopted the Left's program and thus charged Gosplan with drawing up a Five-Year Plan. Indeed, so universal had support for this program now become that the Plan which would go down in history as Stalin's means of building socialism was first sponsored before the Congress by Bukharin and Rykov.

The Congress also decided that the Party's goal in the countryside should not be Lenin's puny cooperatives but real collective farms. Just at this point, moreover, the "procurements crisis" hit, and this gave an added urgency to both collectivization and industrialization. In the course of 1928, urgency was fused with exhilaration within the Party at the prospect of a new Socialist Offensive that would at last put an end to the humiliations and compromises of the NEP. And this mood by early 1929 produced a Plan (whose beginning was quite unscientifically backdated to October 1, 1928) that went far beyond anything the Left had proposed in its day.

The result was a program that would have been over-optimistic even for a country whose cities were not already running short of food. The Plan was predicated on the assumption that industry and agriculture would expand in tandem, with growth in one feeding growth in the other. Within the industrial sector, moreover, both heavy and light industry were to advance together. Thus investment and consumption were to increase simultaneously: The capital stock of the country was to multiply, while at the same time people would live better, with the worker and the peasant benefiting equally. In addition, the Plan was proposed to the Party in an "initial" and an "optimal" variant, and of course the Party chose the latter. That version anticipated, for example, that by 1933 the production of iron ore would increase 233 percent, and that of steel 160 percent, while national income would go up 506 percent!

It has often been argued that the Plan as first adopted, though inflated in some of its projections, was nonetheless not unrealistic as a whole, particularly in view of the modest target of 15 percent collectivization by 1933. This view also holds that if the Plan went awry, it was because Stalin's interference denatured it.[11] But this assessment of the Plan is doubtful: The data were simply insufficient at the time to produce anything like the precision to which the Plan pretended. Then there are serious theoretical objections to projective planning for so long a period as five years, and for every aspect of the economy; in fact, during decades of trying, no Soviet-type economy has ever succeeded in producing a plan it could actually carry out. It is for reasons such as these, and in answer to both Stalin and the Austrians, that some of the more cautious Western socialists at the time came up with the hybrid alternative of market socialism—a theoretical concept yet to be realized in practice.

Thus the Plan, even before Stalin got hold of it, is best understood as a flight of technocratic utopianism born of a conjunction of the genuine development problems Russia then faced and the ideological currents just mentioned. At the beginning, Stalin and his men rode this technocratic impetus as much as they incited it. Then they stepped in and transformed the impetus into an onslaught.

What Stalin did was to take over the political management of this would-be technocratic enterprise. Concretely, this meant linking the economic Plan with a political-military campaign to end the procurements crisis through forced and total collectivization; and this in turn meant politicizing and militarizing the industrial plan by constantly accelerating its "tempos" of development. This process of transforming the Plan was carried out by Stalin and his group during the period 1928–1929. And because the process was resisted by the "Right," it became the occasion for that faction's elimination.

THE ULTIMATE CLASS STRUGGLE

> *C'est la lutte finale*
>
> —*The first line of the "Internationale," 1888*

The meaning of the Stalinist system created by the First Five-Year Plan can only be understood in terms of the succession of events, unfolding through action and reaction, that generated the new order. Despite the fact that Stalin and his men were operating in the context of a "Plan," they had no grand design, or even an approximate draft of a program, or any clear idea of how to implement it. Instead, they had only the general goal of socialism understood as planned industrialization and full collectivization. Within these parameters they improvised their concrete program, but with results they had never anticipated. So the Party unleashed the Second Russian Revolution in the same way that it had initiated War Communism and the NEP: It took a first, apparently limited, step, and the process thus initiated quickly acquired a momentum of its own; hence one crime necessitated another in order to stave off defeat of the entire Offensive.

This process began with the famous shortfall in grain procurements of December 1927. Stalin immediately responded in January 1928 with what came close to being an intra-Party coup d'état. After obtaining approval of the Politburo for a limited, emergency collection of grain, Stalin mounted a major campaign of *prodrazverstka*: he and some of his chief lieutenants—Molotov, Kaganovich, Zhdanov, Andreev—fanned out to the regions where kulaks were allegedly hoarding a surplus and extorted it from them through the methods of War Communism. Because Stalin personally worked over the Urals and Western Siberia during this campaign, this new version of *prodrazverstka* came to be known as the "Urals-Siberian method."

And the campaign worked: The peasants were cowed, the grain was collected. When Bukharin and his allies objected that this threatened the *smychka*, Stalin backed off and said it was only an emergency measure, not a new departure. A precedent had nonetheless been set, and Stalin returned to it later in 1928 and again in 1929 to back up the Plan that had just been adopted. Still, only minimal quantities of grain were collected each time. Such a method, clearly, could only be a temporary expedient, not a solution to the long-term dilemma of feeding the cities and the Red Army. Stalin therefore decided to solve the grain problem definitively by applying the Urals-Siberian method to achieve full and immediate collectivization of the entire country.

But it would be possible to act on this intention only once other fronts had been secured. First, the industrialization drive might face problems arising from bourgeois specialists turned "wreckers." As a warning to these indispensable yet dubious aides, both Russian and foreign, in the spring of 1928 some fifty engineers from the Ukrainian mining region of Shakhty were given a show trial for sabotage in the service of international capital. The prosecutor was Andrei Vyshinskii; all of the accused confessed, and five were executed. Although the Shakhty affair in fact disrupted industrialization, it nonetheless had the political effect of showing the workers that their miserable plight was due to the never-ending machinations of class enemies; accordingly, vigilance and struggle must also be unending. The affair thus created a formula that would be repeated until the grand crescendo of the Purges of 1936–1938[12]—when Vyshinskii again was prosecutor.

At the same time, the Party itself had to be secured. Although Bukharin would now accept "some squeeze" on the peasants through fiscal means and occasional emergency resort to the Urals-Siberian method, he could not be counted on to agree to forced collectivization, an attitude shared by Prime Minister Rykov and trade union chief Tomskii. It was for this reason, as we have seen, that Bukharin and his allies were branded as the "Right," and that the next year they were removed from both their Party and state posts.

This gave Stalin for the first time a Politburo composed entirely of his own men, and a Central Committee only slightly less homogeneous. It also gave him for the first time direct control of the state apparatus. To be sure, all state leaders had always been good Party men. But when Molotov replaced Rykov as Prime Minister, and when a Stalinist committee took over from the relatively independent Tomskii, these two fiefs were directly subordinated to the Leader. At the same time, the planning apparatus began to lose its quasi autonomy as Vesenkha under Kuibyshev—who was of course supported by Stalin—pressured Gosplan after early 1928 to radicalize its projections: The result was the escalation of expectations from the bold "initial" to the utopian "optimal" variant of the Plan. In consequence, ex-Menshevik planners began to feel that their prudence could be construed as sabotage and hence muted their alarm, while Stalin genuinely believed that all moderate advice was suspect as petty bourgeois and thus could safely be ignored. And so matters spiralled toward surpassing even the optimal Plan.

Finally, ideology was revised to justify the coming offensive. Stalin declared that the nearer the country got to socialism, the stronger the resistance of the class enemy became and the more intense the class struggle grew. This theory has often been ridiculed as debased Marxism (and thus still another proof that Stalin betrayed the legacy of Lenin) since the class struggle should logically abate as the victory of socialism approaches. This criticism, which goes back to the debates of the 1920s (Bukharin called Stalin's view "idiotic ignorance"), is correct in terms of Marxism's formal tenets—and this is precisely what is wrong with it. For such criticism presupposes a literal-minded acceptance of Marx's vision of the historical logic leading to socialism;

and such literal commitment to ideology can only obscure the way ideology in fact operates in history.

The dilemma confronting the Party in 1929 was that history does not in reality conform to its presumed logic, yet the Party as an ideocratic regime was irrevocably committed to following this logic nonetheless. Marx's doctrine therefore could only fall victim to the perverse cunning of Party reason. For there was no class struggle in Russia at the time, but only a struggle of the Party against the peasant nation; thus Marx's theory was made to serve as justification for a coercive Five-Year Plan designed to perfect the Party's power. Indeed, it is perhaps inherent in the real logic of history that ideologies are almost invariably debased on contact with political action; the higher the ambition of the ideology, and the more drastic the contemplated action, the more likely is the debasement in practice. By this devious route Stalin's much derided theorem in fact creatively adapted the cardinal Marxist principle of the class struggle to desperate Party policy, thereby making it the cardinal principle of the building of Soviet socialism.

For the practical meaning of Stalin's theorem was quite clear: The nearer the country got to collectivization, the more strongly the peasants could be expected to resist; and the more industrialization was forced, the more likely was the occurrence of crises that were best overcome by blaming them on the sabotage of bourgeois specialists. Since the regime was preparing to use coercion, it was only prudent for it to prepare also for strong action in response and thus for further coercion. Stalin's new ideological stance was thus intended as psychological mobilization for the coming social war.

But the decisive factor in making possible Stalin's new course was his experience with the Urals-Siberian method. The Party had tried coercion and it worked: The peasants did not fight back, and the country was not plunged into the disorder of War Communism, as timorous "Rightists" had predicted. So Stalin concluded that if the Party machine applied massive, sustained pressure, the peasants, dispersed in small units across the country, would be incapable of offering serious resistance. And it is this great miscalculation that turned the Plan's collectivization drive into a war between the regime and the peasants.

Systematic pressure began in the summer of 1929, when Stalin's chief aides secretly led Party activists in trying out mass collectivization in selected areas and by whatever means seemed appropriate. In consequence, by October 1 collective-farm, or kolkhoz, membership has increased from approximately one million to two million. Stalin then alleged that this was proof that the "middle peasants" had been won over to the cause of socialism and were entering the kolkhozes voluntarily and en masse. He could thus present the Party's revolution from above as a response to pressure from below; and he may well have believed a good part of his own propaganda.

For it is a startling fact that after his foray into the Urals-Siberian region in January 1928, Stalin never visited rural Russia again. Throughout the whole collectivization drive, in fact to the end of his days, he never inspected a Red kolkhoz; the photographs of him with smiling peasant women were purely staged affairs. Stalin saw rural Russia only through the ideological categories of kulak, middle, and poor peasant. Indeed, he hardly looked in on the new urban and industrial Russia that was the Plan's focus, and even during the supreme emergency of the Second World War his one visit to the front was a hasty, official event.

From 1928 on, Stalin ruled Russia and built socialism entirely from within the Party precincts in Central Committee headquarters on Old Square, down a side street from the Kremlin, and in the governmental compound of the Kremlin itself. By 1930 his primary base, the Secretariat, had become a veritable party within the Party; with its six departments it monitored the ordinary membership and oversaw all governmental activity. In addition, at the end of the twenties, Stalin created a personal secretariat under Aleksandr Poskrebyshev and staffed with such sinister creatures as the future head of the political police, Nikolai Ezhov. From these Muscovite fortresses he ventured forth only to his suburban villa of "Nearby" ("Blizhnii") at Kuntsevo, and in summer to equally guarded retreats in the Crimea or at Sochi on the Black Sea. Cut off from the real country, he saw it only through the eyes of Party reports and policy. Small wonder, then, that when he started the Second Offensive he really believed he could win it with a lightning stroke.

Thus, on November 7, in his address on the twelfth anniversary of the Revolution, Stalin declared that 1929 had been "the year of the Great Break" and that the country was ready to advance "full steam ahead" to socialism. And this soon meant also the goal of mass or total (*sploshnaia*) collectivization. But this revision of the Plan for agriculture necessarily entailed a revision for industry as well, so in December the Party proclaimed that the goals of the Five-Year Plan were to be achieved in four years. Stalin thus made it clear that the country was embarking on a Second Revolution.

To heighten the symbolism of the occasion, on December 21 his fiftieth birthday was celebrated with full Party pomp. He was thus transformed from Boss (*khoziain*), his strictly Party role hitherto, into Leader (*vozhd*), his national role henceforth. Thus he began his career as the "Lenin of today." The clear message was that Lenin had made the first, October Revolution, and that Stalin would now make the second and final revolution for the actual building of socialism. The Lenin cult, elaborated in the twenties as the Party's cult of itself, had already created the model of the all-wise Leader;[13] Stalin had only to step into the role. By the end of December 1929, all the elements necessary for the Soviet great leap forward had been assembled. The attack could begin.

To use the military terminology of the day, the campaign unfolded on two major "fronts," agriculture and industry. Within each of these there were numerous subfronts: the wheat front and the cotton front, for example, and the coal front and the steel front. Then there was a third great front, "culture." By this was meant the war against illiteracy, technological ignorance, and that general *nekulturnost* which had earlier so bothered Lenin, or raw Russia's overall ineptitude for modern life—characteristics that were obviously associated above all with the *muzhik*. On any of these fronts, moreover, if there was a bottleneck or other unforeseen contingency, the problem was to be met by throwing in "shock brigades"; *udarnik*, or shock worker, became one of the highest titles of honor among the working class. In similar fashion, groups of workers were called on to compete in contests of "socialist emulation," to raise production by psychological means, since material incentives could not be offered.

And if there are fronts, there must also be enemies. The principal of these, of course, was the kulak. But there were also other species of enemy: nepmen, speculators, bourgeois specialists working in Gosplan or as engineers, Right- and Left-wing deviationists still in the Party; all of these might turn into "wreckers," and all might enter into contact with foreign "imperialists." So the struggle on each front had to be conducted with appropriate class "vigilance" and in a spirit of class warfare.

The struggle on each front was, moreover, perceived as organically linked to all the others, and failure in any one was believed to threaten defeat in the whole war. It is this belief in the global or total nature of the Great Socialist Offensive that explains in part the haste and unpreparedness with which it began in January 1930. In particular, once the tempo of industrialization had been radically accelerated at the end of 1929, the Party leadership was convinced that unless the peasants were collectivized immediately, the industrial front would collapse by 1931 for want of an adequate food supply. And this circumstance made the agricultural front the chief priority as the offensive began.[14]

Accordingly, the first step of the Great Leap was to proclaim, in January 1930, the "liquidation of the kulaks as a class." Brigades of Party activists, worker battalions, Komsomol students, and detachments from the GPU (as the Cheka was now known) were dispatched to the villages. Among these groups the most famous was the Twenty-Five Thousanders, which consisted of Party workers whose zeal could make the collectivization drive appear as a spontaneous initiative of the proletariat.[15] The ostensible mission of these groups was to "ally" with the poor peasants in order to evict the kulaks from the village and win over the middle peasants for the kolkhoz. In fact, these always vague terms now lost all meaning. What really occurred was the forcible subjection of the whole village to the Party: "kulak" came to mean simply any muzhik who resisted collectivization and therefore became an "enemy." Party workers, with the aid of the more indigent peasants, summarily dispossessed these "kulaks" of their lands and livestock, and either cut them adrift in the countryside or, more often, packed them into freight cars for exile to the north; for former "kulaks" were not allowed to join the new kolkhoz. In the course of collectivization, according to Politburo figures, some five million to six million persons were "dekulakized." The tactical principle in the campaign of 1930 was to take the peasants by surprise and divide the village before resistance could be organized, and so finish the whole job before spring sowing.

Beyond this, however, there was no real plan of campaign. No adequate number of tractors or harvester-combines was ready. The form of the new kolkhozes had not even been specified by the Party. Should it be a "TOZ," or loose association of producers, whose members only pooled their tools? Or should it be an artel in which lands would be pooled and cultivated in common? Or should it be the "highest" and most socialist form of kolkhoz, the commune, where everything was pooled and the members lived communally?

Before the collectivization drive most kolkhozes were mere TOZs. Once the drive began, Party activists aimed for the artel, and even beyond it for the commune, collectivizing cows, pigs, chickens, the peasants' garden plots, and even household implements. At the same time, the village church was closed, its bell taken down, and the priest chased off. The immemorial way of life of peasant Russia was shattered with one blow. Needless to say, this operation was no longer a Plan. "Plan," along with "liquidation of the kulak," was now only a battle cry in the Party's storming of the traditional Russian village.

So matters proceeded for eight weeks, at which time it was announced that 55 percent of Russian agriculture had been collectivized. In reality, half of the collectives existed only on paper, and most of the others were weakly structured and lacking in equipment. The peasants, moreover, quite unexpectedly began to resist through the only means left to them: destruction of their property in order to avoid surrendering it to the kolkhoz. Four million horses were slaughtered, and fourteen million head of cattle were killed and eaten. The state had far too few tractors to replace the lost horses, and there were far too few peasants trained to operate what little machinery did exist. It began to dawn on the leadership that more-adequate plans for the countryside were needed lest the whole drive end in disaster for the regime.

On March 2, therefore, Stalin was forced to call a temporary halt in a famous article entitled "Dizziness from Success." Its burden was that the local comrades had misunderstood the Party's directives, thus pushing collectivization to excessive lengths, and that they should now slow down. This article is usually cited as an example of Stalin's hypocrisy: since he himself had egged the comrades on, the blame was his. In fact, matters are not so simple. Stalin and his men had indeed spurred the Party into battle, but the troops had then charged off on their own, in part out of genuine zeal and in part out of fear of being accused of "Rightism" if they were not adequately zealous.

Thus local activists were often furious with Stalin for going soft. But the real culprit in this affair was the Party's ethos itself, and in the ranks as much as in the leadership, as it had developed during the Bolsheviks' long years in power.

Stalin's retreat, however, was only temporary, merely for the duration of the sowing season. In the next three months the level of collectivization dropped to 23 percent of peasant households, as weak or paper kolkhozes were dissolved. Then in the fall of 1930 the offensive resumed more methodically, and the regime began to feel its way towards a new order in the countryside. It was decided that the artel would be the standard form of organization. In addition, it was deemed prudent to leave the individual peasant in possession of his hut, garden plot, and some domestic animals. Machinery now began to become available and was concentrated in Machine Tractor Stations, or MTSs, which were each given a political section. For the first time the Party had a genuine outpost in the countryside. At the same time, the peasants, now lacking draft animals, could neither sow nor reap without the MTS, and so the state was at last guaranteed its cut of the harvest.

These measures produced a second collectivization drive in 1931; by the end of that year the percentage of peasant households in kolkhozes had increased to 52.7, and that of crop area collectivized to 67.8. But this was achieved only at the cost of an equally ferocious but more controlled struggle than the one in 1930. Destruction of property and the slaughter of draft animals and livestock resumed, this time on a greater scale than before. Altogether, in the course of collectivization Russia's livestock population declined by about half, and in certain categories by even more. Near-chaos reigned as the old village was dismantled to form the new collective. At the same time, a major by-product of collectivization and the deportation of kulaks was the emergence of the Gulag; only a modest enterprise under Lenin, it now became a major component of the Soviet system—but of this more later.[16]

The second collectivization drive soon resulted in famine, which began after the harvest of 1932 and continued until the following autumn. Although the 1932 harvest was somewhat smaller than average, this was not the famine's cause. The cause, rather, was continuing peasant resistance to the regime's purposes and the regime's answering drive to break the peasants' will to resist once and for all.

The triggering circumstance was the opening of peasant markets in May 1932, a measure undertaken in the belief that the new kolkhoz system was sufficiently well established to supply the state's needs. But grain procurements plummeted and Party controls proved inadequate to remedy matters. As in the days of the Urals-Siberian method, Stalin believed that the peasants were concealing food and that local party officials were not ruthless enough in taking it from them. So Party pressure was drastically increased to teach the peasants a great lesson: The state simply took its procurement quota without regard to what would be left over, even though the authorities well knew that famine could result. Thus the famine of 1932–1933 in the Volga valley and Ukraine has been called a "terror famine."[17] It claimed from six to eleven million lives, depending on how the estimate is made. Even though this was one of the greatest criminal acts of the century, at the time it was largely kept secret from the outside world and even from those parts of the Soviet population not directly affected. And the famine worked. It at last brought victory to the Party in the countryside. The peasants would never again have the will to defy Soviet power.

Thus, by 1934, 71.4 percent of village households were collectivized, and by 1936, 90 percent. The 25 million peasant homesteads of Russia had become 240,000 kolkhozes. The myriad of dispersed subsistence units of muzhik Russia with which the regime had had to contend under the NEP was now concentrated into a more "rational," that is manageable, socialist organization of production.

At the same time, and parallel to the kolkhoz system, the regime created a less extensive network of sovkhozes, or state farms. These large mechanized units, in which the peasants labored as workers, were supposed to be agrarian factories. Although the sovkhozes accounted for only a modest proportion of Soviet agriculture, they were viewed as the ideal form of socialism in the countryside, an anticipation of the future in which the famous "contradiction between town and country" would at last be resolved.

Yet the material transformation of the countryside should not be exaggerated. After the new system had shaken down and its mode of organization was codified in the Kolkhoz Charter of 1935, the humble Russian village of Tiutchev was still very much there, with its unpainted log huts listing to one side, its one-room store, and its more recent one-room school. Daily life was still so traditional that by 1939 only 4.5 percent of kolkhozes had electricity. At the same time, however, there was much less to eat in the village than had been the case in 1929 or even in 1913.

What had changed in the village was its political and economic organization. The muzhik was not personally seated on a tractor, as Stalin had promised; the tractors were all in the hands of the MTS that serviced a number of kolkhozes. Thus the MTS had become the pivot of the Party's presence in the countryside, which until collectivization had not known effective Party control. The Bolshevik conquest of Russia that had not gone beyond the gates of her cities in 1921 was now completed, and the whole country was at last occupied.[18]

Yet the regime had been forced to make one significant concession to the peasantry in the form of the individual peasant plot. To be sure, this concession was made grudgingly; during the remainder of its history the Soviet regime would constantly strive to decrease the role of these plots. But it would never succeed in eliminating them, and so a small measure of private enterprise and a marginal market would continue to exist in Russia. These peasant plots, moreover, would soon produce an inordinate proportion of the country's food; in 1937, for example, around 25 percent of the food came from only 5 percent of the cultivated land.

Nonetheless, these peasant plots could not challenge the state's control over the main crop, grain; obtaining that control had been the real purpose of collectivization. After 1933 the state had a stable supply of food for which it did not have to pay, since it was no longer constrained by the market to offer the peasants any significant compensation in consumer goods. Thus once again an economic problem had been solved by political means, and *administrirovanie* had replaced the market. The only bastion of Russian civil society that had survived the Revolution, the peasantry, was eliminated as an independent and self-managing force. The class whose jacquerie alone had permitted a small band of fanatics to seize power in 1917 now became the chief victim of their fanaticism.

Thus the traditional Russian village was crushed once and for all. To be more exact, less than a century after their Emancipation in 1861, the peasants were reenserfed by the Party-state. The Party now could get on with the central business in the building of socialism: crash industrialization.

* * *

Yet, whereas Stalin's collectivization was an unrelieved disaster for the country, his industrialization drive—for all its inordinate cost, brutality, and wastefulness—was a significant historical accomplishment. It was indeed the Soviet experiment's only real achievement.

It was a source of genuine pride for much of the urban population; it was a major factor in the regime's other main achievement, its victory in the Second World War; it endowed the country with a bare-bones modernity that irreversibly transformed peasant Russia into an urban society, or at least the simulacrum of an urban society. And, finally, it was the supreme feat of Bolshevik voluntarism.

This great leap into the Crystal Palace of technological society was very much the product of the Party's war against peasant Russia. For the rush to industrialization after 1929 was accelerated by the drive to collectivize, just as the drive to collectivize had been generated by the rush to industrialize. The two processes fed on each other and evolved *pari passu*, though not in the way the Plan had anticipated. The Plan had foreseen mutual support through mutual enrichment; the interconnection between the two "fronts" was in fact through reciprocal panic leading to reciprocal intoxication.

Concretely, once the decision for full collectivization was taken in late 1929, it was considered necessary to accelerate the Plan in order to mechanize the kolkhozes. Accordingly, on December 1 the targets of the optimal Plan were "amended" upward. A few days later a congress of "shock brigades" called for completing the Five-Year Plan in four years, and this immediately became government policy (the Plan would now officially end on December 31, 1932). In fact, the Plan in its original technocratic version, which was already utopian enough, was discarded. "Plan" came to mean instead a series of crash priorities, or selected strategic objectives, in industry, to be achieved whatever the cost. By the same token, the Plan became a device for the psychological mobilization of the Party and the population, a mechanism to keep the troops advancing on the "industrial front." But beyond this there was no more of a precise order of battle on the industrial front than on the simultaneously opened agricultural front, and the initial results in the factories and foundries were almost as disastrous as those in the countryside.

The slogan of the attack was "technology decides everything," by which was meant that the mere acquisition of industrial machinery would automatically yield modern efficiency and socialist success. This simplistic approach was not just the result of Stalin's primitive understanding of Marxism; it was very much in the vein of a technological determinism prominent in Marx himself—as when the founder declared that the hand mill produces a society of feudal lords and the steam mill a society of industrial capitalists, a viewpoint continued in Lenin's dictum that "socialism equals Soviet power plus electrification." Stalin simply updated this equation by decreeing, in effect, that the blast furnace produces a socialist society. To this Marxist tradition must be added the example of America as the very model of modernity, an image that had emerged throughout Europe as a result of the First World War and that was amplified by the formulae for labor efficiency of Taylorism and later by the assembly line prodigies of Fordism. And in fact the technology of the First Five-Year Plan was that of advanced America only a few years earlier. Thus, building Marxist socialism in Russia came to be tantamount to a race "to catch up with and overtake America."

The Party therefore took as its chief strategic objective the development of heavy or capital goods industry, and it threw all of its resources into projects that would promote still further industrialization. This was all that the Plan now amounted to, for the Party made this choice without giving any thought to how its basic crash programs would relate to light industry, to the budget, to the workforce, or to the consumer population. The result was a "bacchanalia of planning"[19] from 1930 to 1933 that reeled from crisis to crisis and almost ended in collapse.

At the center of this effort was heavy metallurgy. The Offensive's chief priorities therefore were coal, iron, and steel, together with machine tools and new factories to turn out turbines, tractors, trucks, and automobiles.[20] To accommodate this effort, the bureaucracy expanded, too: Vesenkha began to diversify into specialized industrial People's Commissariats, or ministries. The first of these was that of Heavy Industry under Politburo member Ordzhonikidze, who functioned largely as political trouble-shooter, leaving technical management to his better-qualified deputy, Piatakov. The greatest single project of the Plan was the Urals-Kuzbas Combine, which linked the iron of the new Urals city of Magnitogorsk with the Kuznetsk coal basin one thousand miles away on the Chinese frontier. This project gave the Soviet Union an alternative to the pre-Revolutionary Krivoi Rog-Donbas coal-steel combine in Ukraine, which was no longer modern enough and was too vulnerably close to the western frontier.

Other high-priority projects were the Stalingrad Tractor Factory, or later the Molotov Automobile Works in Nizhnii-Novgorod (soon renamed Gorky), and the Kaganovich Metro in Moscow. At the same time, a major emphasis was placed on electrification, as exemplified by the great Dnieprostroi Dam (this was also the era of the Hoover Dam and the Tennessee Valley Authority). A lesser emphasis was placed on transportation: major projects in this sector included the Turksib Railroad across Central Asia and the Baltic-White Sea Canal, which was built with convict labor and turned out to be too shallow for use because it had been dug with hand shovels.

To finance this industrialization program, the regime sold grain abroad, even during the famine. This allowed it to import Western equipment and to hire Western engineers to build Magnitogorsk and other pilot projects. With these projects as a base, the regime then used its own resources to build factories across the country to produce the automobiles, tractors, and other heavy equipment it needed. Even so, throughout the thirties the regime remained heavily dependent on foreign models: Its ZIS-ZIL limousine, for example, was essentially a Soviet Buick; the Stalingrad tractor factory was a literal copy of the Caterpillar tractor factory; and the Gorky automobile works was the copy of a Ford plant.[21] But imitation, though a quick road to growth, had its costs: Soviet industry, although it was soon able to produce great quantities of industrial goods, was rarely able to achieve internationally competitive quality, and it almost never invented new products or technologies.

Moreover, all of this construction was carried out amidst constant crisis bordering on chaos. The first crisis occurred in the summer of 1930. The light or consumer-goods industry, deprived of investment capital, began to sag just as the labor force swelled in size with the influx of "dekulakized" peasants and other new workers into the cities. There was suddenly a dearth of consumer goods, food, housing, and urban transportation to meet the most elementary needs of the workers. Prices soared and the regime was obliged to resort to near-universal rationing to care for the burgeoning urban population. Because conditions only grew worse as the Plan progressed, "1933 [in Russia] was the culmination of the most precipitous peacetime decline in living standards known in recorded history."[22] But then it was not really peacetime in Russia.

By the fall of 1930, as consumer goods disappeared and as prices rose, it became clear that, contrary to expectations, industrial production overall was falling.[23] Since this occurred in the immediate wake of the first fiasco of collectivization, voices within the Party began to call for a slowing of the "tempos" of industrialization. Yet Stalin was no more to be turned back in the city than he had been in the village. His response combined an adamant refusal to reduce existing tempos with an effort to cope with an emerging new crisis caused by the inadequacies of the labor force.[24] For it had by now become apparent that technology would not decide everything, and that the country's dearly-bought new machinery would not work without competent workers.

In a speech he delivered in July 1931, Stalin sought to accommodate the purposes of the regime to the frailty of the "human factor." In doing so, he produced a compromise policy that was analogous to his simultaneous concession of individual plots to the peasants. Hitherto, Bolshevik wage policy had been egalitarian; Stalin now denounced "levelling" (uravnilovka) as un-Marxist and "petty-bourgeois." The true socialist policy, he declared, was to offer workers piece-rates, or payment in accordance with the quantity of goods they produced. In other words, faced with a situation of unanticipated and almost universal scarcity, Stalin resorted to unequal rewards to stimulate production. This was his carrot.

Stalin unveiled his stick when he also attacked the "fluidity of labor," or the nomadic habits of a labor force searching for some improvement in the new world of endemic scarcity. Accordingly, internal passports were introduced: each person had to be registered with the police in order to live in any given city; access to housing and rations was linked to fixed employment; and criminal penalties were introduced for absenteeism. This was the beginning of a process that by the end of the decade would bring back the nineteenth-century police device of labor books, and indeed the possibility of the Gulag, to tie workers to their jobs. Although this regimen was less severe than the neoserfdom of the kolkhoz—where peasants had no passports at all—it represented an analogous subordination of the population to the purposes of the regime.

But Stalin also looked to the future when he urged the necessity of creating what would amount to a new working class.[25] The existing labor force, especially the recently transplanted peasants, lacked the requisite "culture" for this new industrial order; and the bourgeois specialists who had this "culture" were politically unreliable—like the tsarist officers of the Red Army during the Civil War. At the start of the industrial offensive there had been two new show trials of "wreckers," that of the so-called Industrial Party of "bourgeois" engineers in 1930, and that of the Mensheviks (that is, the early planners) in 1931.[26] But the need for skilled personnel had proved to be so great that, as a stopgap solution, Stalin now called off this "spets-baiting." As for a long-term solution, he launched a massive attack on the "cultural" front by calling for technological education that would produce a socialist "worker intelligentsia." Simultaneously, reliable proletarians were to be "moved forward" by means of education into managerial positions, a process of *vydvizhenie* that would give the dictatorship of the proletariat its own class of "cadres," or technical personnel. Just as tsarist officers were phased out of the Red Army at the end of the Civil War in favor of newly educated Red Cadets, so in the industrial army the bourgeois officer corps was now to be replaced by newly trained Red managers.

In 1935 this emphasis on the "human factor" reached its culmination. At the level of the industrial rank and file, the principles of shock work and socialist emulation were now institutionalized in the Stakhanovite movement.[27] A coal miner named Stakhanov, with the aid of the authorities, created for himself artificially ideal conditions of work and thereby overfulfilled the established "norm" for coal production. He was immediately made a hero, and workers in all fields were spurred to emulate his feat. Such feats were possible because Russian productivity at the time was so low that it was feasible to raise it very quickly; they were possible also because a significant number of workers were genuinely moved by zeal for the building of socialist industry. But once these mini–leaps forward had been made, they furnished the new norms for all workers; the proletarian mass was thus "sweated" more than it had been before the Stakhanovite movement. Still, piece-rate "heroes of socialist labor" did become a kind of worker-aristocracy in the completed Stalinist system.

But Stalin was even more solicitous for the industrial officer corps, since its skills were the most essential of all for the system's success. Accordingly, the regime after 1931 fostered elite higher education, but only for promising elements of the population; once educated, these "cadres" received material and social privileges commensurate with their managerial responsibilities.

These responsibilities, however, were assigned according to lists of posts *(nomenklaturas)* controlled by Party committees at various levels; the new cadres, therefore, eventually came to be known collectively as "the *nomenklatura.*" Assignment by *nomenklatura* list had emerged as an administrative device in the twenties, but it was only after Stalin's industrialization had created a mass of new posts that this system could give rise to a veritable caste. Thus by 1935 this group had become the apex of the new social order. Stalin therefore revised the General Line by declaring that the most "precious capital of all is man," and the new slogan of the day became "cadres decide everything."

A similar revision of the original aims of the Offensive occurred in other areas as well. In 1930, as the country moved from the semi-market economy of the NEP to the allocation of resources through the Plan, the status of money once again came under question, as it had during War Communism. It was widely assumed, even by Stalin himself, that money would give way to socialist "product-exchange" between enterprises. However, it soon became apparent that money could not be abolished because product-exchange (which is in fact only barter) was too cumbersome and crude for what was becoming a very large-scale industrial network. And so to harness the alien force of money to the Plan, the government centralized all credit in the State Bank. But industrial growth was so chaotic that the planners ultimately took to financing it through the printing press. And this, in conjunction with universal scarcity, produced a sixfold increase in inflation during the period of the Plan. Inflation made planning in any meaningful sense still less possible by aggravating the difficulties of prediction and coordination. At the same time, because industrial wages did not keep up with inflation, and because the peasants were hardly paid at all, the falling value of the ruble became another means of siphoning wealth out of the population and into industrial expansion.

The result was a new variant of a socialist economy. The market was suppressed in favor of the political allocation of resources. But since money and prices were preserved, unlike at the end of War Communism, they acquired a new function, which was to transmit the political purposes of the regime to all economic actors. Thus money continued to be used, but in a fashion very different from that during the NEP. Prices and wages were not governed by supply and demand; they were set by the state. At the same time, a turnover tax was levied on all products at each stage in their production, thereby driving prices up where desired, while subsidies were used to bring prices down where desired. This did not balance supply and demand in any usual sense, but it did create a kind of equilibrium that was necessary for state purposes. Thus prices, wages, and taxes were all made to obey a political, not an economic, logic.

Thus there emerged a new formula for organizing production and distribution, that of a marketless money economy. This formula was not identical to that of the original War Communism. Under War Communism there was a bureaucratically centralized economy (at least on paper), but no Plan and virtually no money. In the Stalinist system there was a Plan and money. This new system obviously could not be meshed with the world economy, so the ruble remained non-convertible in order to keep external market forces out. In the short run this insulation provided the advantage of enhancing state control over internal economic developments. In the long run it isolated the Soviet Union from the stimulus of external developments, and so turned out to be one of the causes of the system's ultimate decline.

There was still another difference between the Stalinist system and original War Communism, a difference that also constituted an anomaly in the new order. In fact, a market did continue to exist under planning. First, there was the legal kolkhoz market. Second, there was the illegal black market, or what later came to be known as the "shadow economy." This "second economy," as it was also called, was of large, if unknown, proportions. In part exchange was conducted with money, and in part goods were paid for by political favors. But regardless of the form of payment, the legal, planned economy could not function without this dark double. Both factory managers and ordinary consumers needed it just to survive. Driving these indispensable economic energies underground and into illegality weakened the whole fabric of the system. And this factor, too, would eventually erode the Stalinist command economy.

Thus, on still another front the Bolsheviks had improvised their way into a solution of sorts to an unanticipated problem. And the solution they devised once again offered a short-term advantage at the cost of preparing a long-term structural disaster.

*   *   *

By 1933 Stalin's great leap forward had been completed in agricul- .
ture, industry, and the organization of finance. A second and more
realistic—though hardly "scientific"—Five-Year Plan had begun, and
the country knew three years of growth between 1934 and 1936. Thus
by mid-decade the results of the Second Revolution had been stabilized, and a new Soviet system had emerged on the ruins of the NEP.
But what was the overall structure of this system? And what was the
dynamic driving it?

First of all, the regime had achieved its priority economic objectives. All the heavy industrial projects mentioned earlier, and then
some, were completed, if not according to plan, at least in very short
order. Moreover, the balance of the Russian economy was irreversibly
shifted from agriculture to industry, and from country to city. Some
thirty million peasants were uprooted and transferred to the city in the
course of the thirties: This was the largest and most rapid leap in
urbanization in history.

Such a massive rural exodus, of course, cannot be explained by the
lure of Russia's raw new industrial cities. Rather, it was engineered by
the regime through the *trudoden*, or labor-day, system of measuring
and rewarding the work of kolkhozniki. The work units required from
each household deliberately received such low remuneration that they
would be supplied basically by women, children, and oldsters. This
system obviously was a major cause of the low productivity of collective agriculture. At the same time, however, it virtually forced able-
bodied men off the land to work in industry, and this was its rationale
in the eyes of the regime. Indeed, this economic compulsion was
often supplemented by contracts passed between kolkhozes and factories for the transfer of live souls. And once in the new cities, these
ex-muzhiks were summarily educated, "cultivated," and indoctrinated in the principles of Marxism-Leninism.

The economic result of all of this was that by the end of the decade
the Soviet Union had a "modern" industrial economy that for the first
time made Russia autarkic. The system's earlier dependence on foreign prototypes, blueprints, and experts had ended; it now produced
the full panoply of basic industrial products, from steel mills to machine tools to turbines, from coal to oil, from tractors to tanks, and
from automobiles to airplanes, entirely with its own resources. This
achievement put the Soviet Union in a unique category with the

United States: Both were much more self-sufficient than any European power or Japan. And for Russia this was no small matter as the international situation grew more perilous in the thirties.

Indeed, from the beginning national defense had been one motive for industrialization, as was evident in Stalin's famous remark in 1931 that Russia should never allow herself to be beaten again. But defense was not the primary motive at the outset of industrialization; that motive clearly was to put an industrial and proletarian "base" under the existing "superstructure" of the Party, and thereby to make the Party viable within the country as the vehicle for building socialism. Thus, in the inverted Soviet world, the first purpose of industrialization was to bring Russian reality into line with Marxist sociological postulates.

In 1929–1932 the Nazi threat did not exist, and Japan's occupation of Manchuria in 1931 was hardly a major menace to Soviet Russia. Nor was the constant preoccupation with international security an expression of nationalism; it signified, rather, a concern to defend the Revolution and its Party-state against encircling world capitalism. This was revealed most notably by the imagined war scare of 1927 and by Stalin's declaration in 1928 that the stabilization of international capitalism had ended and that the Soviet Union should be on guard against the totally improbable menace of an Anglo-French imperialistic assault. Thus, the influence of the international situation on the Soviets' crash industrialization can be attributed not to any specific or, at the time, realistic threat, but to the Soviets' ideologically induced paranoia about the "capitalist" world.

This abiding fear was given substance only in 1936–1937 when Hitler entered the Rhineland and Japan entered China proper. These developments at last gave the Soviet industrial plant a telos more practical than socialism. For Soviet industrialization, when it acquired its definitive formula in the mid-decade, amounted basically to this: Contrary to the declared goals of the regime, it was the opposite of a system of production to create abundance for the eventual satisfaction of the needs of the population; it was a system of general squeeze of the population to produce capital goods for the creation of industrial power, in order to produce ever more capital goods with which to produce still further industrial might, and ultimately to produce armaments. This was the dynamic driving the mature Soviet system.

Thus the concentration on heavy industry that had initially been intended to create a base for diversified economic expansion became an end in itself. The production of military power at last gave the system its true purpose and final cause, and the regime's command-administrative structures effortlessly lent themselves to this purpose. Beginning in 1937 the emphasis of Soviet industry shifted increasingly to military production; this emphasis would remain basic to the system until its collapse in the late 1980s.

A concomitant of these developments was Stalin's new, highly stratified society. This reality, of course, could not be acknowledged. The new order was officially designated "socialist" in 1936, and it was held to be founded on three nonantagonistic classes—the workers, the peasants, and the "intelligentsia" (that is, the new managers)—which, taken together, constituted "the people." In fact, however, rewards and power were doled out strictly in accordance with one's usefulness and political loyalty to the regime. And, insofar as it was humanly possible, everything was run by command from the top down.

Stalin himself, using imagery appropriate to the new industrial Russia, liked to compare his system to a "machine and its cogs."[28] But his preferred imagery was military, and he likened the Party in particular to an "army":

> If we have in mind its leading strata, there are about 3,000 to 4,000 first rank leaders whom I would call our Party's corps of generals.
>
> Then there are about 30,000 to 40,000 middle rank leaders who are our Party's corps of officers.
>
> Then there are about 100,000 to 150,000 of the lower rank Party command staff who are, so to speak, our Party's non-commissioned officers.[29]

But this imagery only took one step further Lenin's principle of 1917 that Ludendorff's War Socialism could easily be turned into War Communism, just as it further developed Trotsky's program of 1920 for the "militarization of labor." Even the NEP, with its "commanding heights," continued this military spirit.

Thus it is only appropriate that after the Second World War the mature Stalin system came to be called by American Sovietologists a "command economy." This label is a translation of the German word *Befehlswirtschaft*, a term coined by refugees from Nazism to designate Hitler's Four-Year Plan—an idea the Führer derived as much from the Soviet experience as from the memory of his old commander and sometime political ally, Ludendorff.[30] In the late 1980s the Russian democratic opposition to Communism adopted the American Soviet-ologists' term and conflated it with the old Soviet euphemism for coercion, *administrirovanie*, to yield the label "administrative-command system." For these democrats needed such a circumlocu-tion as a stand-in for "totalitarianism" until the latter term ceased to be taboo with the collapse of the system. Yet whatever term was used—in Ludendorff's and Lenin's time, through Stalin's and be-yond—the Soviet system was always a militarized political economy, both in its organizational structure and in its products. This is how it began under War Communism, and this is how it stormed through to victory in the Second Socialist Offensive.

SOME MID-COURSE EVALUATIONS

But what of the Stalin revolution as an undertaking in development economics, or as a pilot project of modernization under conditions of backwardness? To be sure, the question cannot be disentangled from the political circumstances of the day, in particular from the circum-stance that after 1937 the menace of Hitler increasingly deflected the Soviet economic effort towards unproductive military ends. Even so, the fact remains that Stalin's Russia, through an extraordinary boot-strap operation, became a major industrial power, and this industrial might helped make possible the politically productive result of her survival in the Second World War.

Thus, at the time, and indeed until the 1980s, the answer to the question of the Stalinist system's economic performance would have been one or another variant of "very good indeed." The early 1930s, after all, were the years of the Great Depression, when eleven million were unemployed in the United States and six million in Germany, and when America's gross national product (GNP) averaged an annual decline of 8 percent. While the blast furnaces of Magnitogorsk were being fired up, those of Pittsburgh and the Ruhr were being damp-ened down. Stalin was building socialism while Hitler's Brown Shirts and Storm Troopers were building fascism. The anarchy of the mar-ket seemed to be destroying the West, while the rationality of the Plan was creating a new world in the East.

This continued to be the perspective of many in the West through-out the war and the period of postwar reconstruction. Not only did the war bring together a Popular Front coalition of democrats and Communists against fascism, but Soviet industrial planning seemed to explain the wartime victory and to make superfluous any Marshall Plan for Eastern Europe's reconstruction. Thus, during the long trauma that extended from the Great Depression through the postwar reconstruction, a rough correlation emerged in the Western liberal consciousness between unregulated capitalism, economic crisis, and war on one hand, and planning, growth, and peace on the other—twin constellations already adumbrated on the eve of 1914.

A prime expression of this mentality was *The Great Transformation*, by the Austrian economist Karl Polanyi. Published in 1944, this work condemned the market as "unnatural" and as the chief source of the modern world's ills. Immediately after the war, socialists came to power in Britain, and France initiated her own form of "indicative" planning; shortly thereafter West Germany was to describe its economic miracle as a "social market." Against this background the Soviet performance could easily earn respect and, in many quarters, indulgence.

In the thirties the Soviets gave out per annum growth figures for the whole economy of some 16 percent to 20 percent, which would make their performance the best in the world until then. At the time, Western methods of calculation were not sufficiently refined, and Western economists were not sufficiently interested in Russia, to produce serious efforts at verifying the Soviet performance. But the consensus of journalistic reporting—the predecessor of academic Sovietology—was that Russia must surely be credited with uniquely spectacular achievements. And after the war, when academic Sovietologists began calculating the GNP in the Western scientific manner, they came up with annual growth rates for industry of 12 percent to 14 percent for the period 1929–1940 (though much lower figures were calculated for agriculture and per capita income). The major effort at recalculating Stalin's overall economic performance held that total output in 1955 was 3.5 times that of 1928; this translated into an average annual growth rate of between 4.7 percent and 6.7 percent (the average for the thirties alone, of course, was even higher because the war lowered the overall percentage).[31] Although all of these calculations were lower than the official figures given by the Soviets, they still added up to one of the great economic performances in history, and these calculations would be repeated in countless textbooks and journalistic accounts during the next four decades.

Then, during *perestroika*, Russian economists entered the debate with a devastating critique of Soviet statistics dating back to the 1930s. As a result, the average rate of growth of Soviet national income for the years 1928–1940 shrank to 3.4 percent in the estimate of the insider Nikolai Shmelev, or to no more than 5 percent in the estimates of outsiders.[32] At the same time, Western specialists largely fell silent; the only answer most would give after Communism's fall was that Soviet data were so defective, and the task of conceptualization so daunting, that it is simply not possible to determine the true rate of growth in the 1930s. Indeed, the leading economic history of the USSR gives no growth figures at all for the whole of the Soviet story. So we are back with the journalistic assessment of the thirties that Soviet industrial growth under Stalin was very good indeed.

It is true that we do not know the exact measurements of the Soviet performance in classic GNP terms. But we do have a pretty good idea of its general contours from the way the system ended. The critique of earlier, inflated figures has demonstrated that Soviet economic growth was never of world-historical magnitude. Witte, who in the 1890s achieved 8 percent annual growth in industry with far milder market methods, probably did as well as Stalin. And Meiji Japan, with 6 percent annual growth for its entire economy, did better, not to mention postwar Japan's world record of 16 percent to 18 percent for its economy as a whole—or even Deng Xiaoping's China at 10 percent to 12 percent in the 1980s.

But growth rates are hardly the only measure of economic success; the cost of Stalin's industrialization must also be taken into account. If, as he claimed, people are the most precious capital of all, then the six million to eleven million victims of collectivization represent an exorbitant waste of national resources. As regards less precious capital, one must add the livestock losses of collectivization. The result of this "investment," moreover, was not a more productive agriculture; it was, rather, the creation of a chronically disfunctional agrarian economy. In 1939 the rural standard of living was far below that of 1929, indeed, below that of 1913; and most of the urban population lived only marginally better.

Nor would conditions improve until after Stalin's death, when Khrushchev and Brezhnev sought to return the kolkhoz system to its original aim of increasing agricultural productivity. But even then con-

ditions never improved significantly, despite enormous new investment in the countryside. Structurally, the kolkhoz was hopeless
because collective labor gave no one an incentive to produce. Thus
Russia, which before 1914 had been a major grain-exporting country,
was regularly obliged to import food in the 1970s and 1980s (whereas
both India and China were able to export it). And the human cost of the
system continued to be high. The Russian peasantry had become, and
would remain, a demoralized, listless, and largely alcoholic work force
suspicious of state power and unwilling to take any initiative on its own.

The degradation of what had once been seen as Russia's quintessential class would become a central theme of Russian literature, from
Sholokhov's *Virgin Soil Upturned* in 1932, to Solzhenitsyn's *The House
of Matryona* in 1963, to the works of the "Village Writers" in the
1970s. The implied message of these authors was that collectivization,
over and above its character as an economic blunder of the first order,
was a crime of the same magnitude, one that indelibly tainted a whole
system built on peasant bones.

The capital for Soviet industrialization had indeed been "pumped
over" from the peasantry, as Preobrazhenskii had foreseen. But this
method of financing in fact turned out to be an ineffective formula for
modernization because of its excessively ideological premises. It is
incorrect to view the Soviet method as analogous to the primitive
accumulation of capital through dispossession of the peasantry in early
modern England, for that was not how capital had been accumulated
there.[33] No serious economic historian would argue today that capitalism was founded on anything so simple as the expropriation of
peasant land, or that it drew its labor force primarily from a peasantry
thus made landless. And aside from the English case, it has never
really been argued that capital was accumulated in this manner. The
sources of capital formation in the West were in fact varied and complex. But Marxism required a neat and compelling historical logic of
exploitation, and it found it in the mechanism of expropriation
through enclosure. The financing of socialist industrialization through
expropriation of the muzhik also needed a simple, driving logic. Thus
the primitive accumulation of capital that never occurred in England
was actually carried out in an unprecedentedly brutal manner in Russia under Stalin. The result was the sterile institution of the kolkhoz
that would remain ever after an impediment rather than a stimulus to
growth.

To be sure, in any developed country the traditional peasantry has to give way to the forces of urbanization. Schematically, this process begins with the peasants migrating to the cities and becoming workers; in a second phase the countryside is mechanized and the peasants are transformed into farmers. This leads to a progressive diminution of the differences between town and country (more or less as the Marxist formula holds), with the end result being the overwhelming preponderance of the city as the rural populations of advanced countries drop to 5 percent or lower. Thus the peasant winds up being phased out everywhere.

The real question, however, is the way this is achieved. Under "capitalism" this occurred over decades and largely through the pressure of the market (though the European Community also consciously promoted it with the Meinhold Plan in the 1960s and 1970s). The outcome was a situation in which something less than 5 percent of the population was able to feed the home population almost sinfully well while also exporting great quantities of foodstuffs. In Soviet Russia the displacement of the peasant occurred over a decade (as Stalin said it should) and through destructive state action. But there the results were a perennially disastrous organization of agriculture and an enduring wound to the national psyche. Hence "modernization" is hardly an appropriate term for what Stalin wrought: We are dealing rather with the ultimate in ideocratic and partocratic revolution. In the short term this revolution permitted a great spurt of basic industrialization, yet for the long term it left behind a structurally crippled society and economy.

It has been argued that this occurred only because Stalin went too fast. If he had adhered to the Plan's original goal of 15 percent collectivization in five years—so this reasoning goes—the peasants would have been won over gradually, and socialized agriculture would have proved more productive than the old isolated peasant households. There is no reason other than a priori faith to believe that this is so. Long experience indicates that large-scale mechanized agriculture is superior only for certain crops and under certain climatic and geographic conditions; it is not the universally valid formula that the Plan assumed it was.

Likewise, the cult of the collective farm as a superior social form derives not from economic considerations but from ideological ones.

More precisely, it derives from a conflation of the socialist commitment to the moral superiority of collective over individual labor with
an idealized image of the large-scale, mechanized American prairie
farm (which the Bolsheviks failed to note was usually a family farm).
It is for this reason that the least successful of all Soviet institutions
became the most cherished in official Soviet mythology. Extolled as
the acme of socialist labor—and compared to a real factory, it was
indeed a more collective enterprise—the kolkhoz was proclaimed the
bedrock of the Soviet order. Stalin erected a temple to this institution
in the form of a giant Agricultural Exposition that for decades was
presented as an object of mandatory admiration to all who visited
Moscow. Thus canonized, the kolkhoz simply could not be given up,
even in the face of mounting evidence of its inefficiency, because to
do so would be to repudiate the whole system.

The kolkhoz (as well as the sovkhoz) did not fail because it was
introduced too rapidly and through coercion. Rather, the cause of the
failure lies in the institution's purpose, which was to transform Russia's peasant farms into agrarian factories. By its very nature the
kolkhoz was a projection of the urban-industrial Marxist perspective
onto the peasant world. Moreover, Soviet Marxists, because of their
hostility to peasant backwardness, never wanted to understand the
rural world; they were only interested in changing it. And this abysmal
ignorance also contributed mightily to the catastrophe of 1930–1933.

Yet there were those at the time who tried to warn of the dangers
of collectivization. For example, the SR economist Andrei Chaianov
argued that the natural productive unit for the peasant was not some
vast *kollektiv* but the household, which grouped two or three generations of an extended family. The high productivity of the individual
family plot throughout Soviet history bears this out. Chaianov also
argued that the natural form of association for the peasants was the
classical producers' cooperative, which the peasants controlled themselves and in which each household preserved its economic identity.
Indeed, before the Revolution peasant Russia, with the aid of the SR
intelligentsia, had created one of the largest cooperative movements
in Europe.

Furthermore, even though some of the poorer peasants could be
incited by the Party to pillage the kulaks, by and large the peasantry
rejected the Party's division of the village into three antagonistic
classes. Instead, almost all peasants shared a sense of village solidarity

vis-à-vis the outside world of the city and the state. Thus, most of the peasants viewed the kulaks as community leaders, not exploiters.

Given this village solidarity, what the peasants did not want and would not accept was a collective farm organized by the Communist Party. All of their experiences with the Party—the outright violence of War Communism, the manipulative pricing of the NEP—had been negative. And the Party's ceaseless warnings against the kulaks throughout the twenties sounded to peasant ears like a threat to the whole village. The peasants saw the campaign for collectivization that built up after 1927 as a prelude to institutionalized *prodrazverstka*.

In view of this ingrained mentality, the Communists' expectation of voluntary collectivization was completely utopian. Engels and Kautsky in the 1890s, in anticipating collective agriculture, had insisted that it must be voluntary. After 1921 Lenin, Trotsky, Bukharin, and even Stalin had all sworn the same thing. Yet none of the Bolshevik leaders ever faced openly the question of what they would do if the peasants refused collectivization and the Party therefore had to choose between coercion and capitulation. Even when Stalin in fact chose coercion, he did not admit this publicly. Instead, coercion was camouflaged as a class war waged by the proletariat and the poorer peasants against the kulak, who was striving to restore "capitalism." Without this ideological camouflage, plus a great dose of ignorance, the Party could hardly have carried out coercion on such a colossal scale. Besides, Stalin and his troops really believed their campaign was a class war, for the Party had talked in no other terms from the time it came to power.

These considerations now make it possible to address the questions of interpretation posed at the beginning of this chapter. First there is the matter of autocratic continuity and periodic revolution from above in Russian history. The phenomenon, of course, is undeniable; but the real problem is how we explain it, and how we relate one episode of revolution to another. And on this score analogy is too often confused with cause, as if some metaphysical essence were operating from Ivan to Peter to Stalin.[34] Nor does Stalin's own penchant for this type of thinking prove much. His self-comparisons with Peter and Ivan served to illustrate and justify what he had already decided to do for other reasons; they were hardly his inspiration when he set out to do it. At that point his ideological references were Marxism and socialism and, especially, Lenin the Leader.

Thus it is very easy to establish empirically the sources of Stalin's policies in the Bolshevik tradition; but it is extremely difficult, if not impossible, to find empirical transmission belts leading to those policies from Ivan or Peter. The most that one can say in support of a traditional Russian input into Stalinism is that roughly analogous situations of backwardness produced roughly analogous responses. But this is a far cry from saying that the earlier responses caused the later one, or that the later response in some mysterious manner reincarnated the earlier ones. The nature of Russia's industrial backwardness in the 1930s is as different from that of her military backwardness in the eighteenth or the sixteenth century as are the politics of ideocratic partocracy from those of divine-right absolutism.

Moreover, the intensification of autocracy has hardly been the only theme in Russian history. In particular, from Peter's time to 1917 Russia was moving steadily in the opposite direction, towards a more pluralistic and "European" order. The process of the "unbinding" *(raskreposhchenie)* of the Russian universal service order proceeded from the gentry's emancipation from compulsory state service in 1762 to the peasant's emancipation from serfdom in 1861, and from local self-government through the *zemstvos* and a largely independent judiciary in 1864 to the legislative Duma of 1905—in short, to the creation of a civil society.

Furthermore, if we move from loose analogies to a closer look at actual comparisons, it should be clear that revolution from above on Stalin's titanic scale has no precedent in Russia, or anywhere else for that matter. Both Ivan the Terrible and Peter the Great worked with a universal service state.[35] A country with no natural frontiers, with a poor agricultural base, and with only a minuscule urban population was constrained to general mobilization of both its material and human resources in order to survive as an independent entity, and later in order to expand. This meant that the peasants were enserfed to the gentry in order to permit the latter to serve in the armies of the autocratic tsar, while the gentry's possession of its lands and serfs was conditional on that same service. Russia's was the harshest system of universal service anywhere in Europe, though it was not without partial parallels farther West, particularly in Prussia.

Peter the Great tightened the requirements of state service for all social classes, from the gentry to the serfs, in order to give Russia for the first time a standing army on the Western model. But he did not substantially alter the basic structure of the system; rather, he gave the form of a European ancien régime to the already existing Muscovite service state. He could do this because the difference between the militarized systems of Russian autocracy and of Western absolutism was not all that great at the time. But he in no way replaced the old Russian order with a new one of his own devising. The revolutionary aspect of his rule lay in cultural Westernization rather than in social and political reorganization.

Ivan the Terrible's policies, to be sure, were more socially destructive than Peter's. The old hereditary boyar aristocracy was effectively broken as a cohesive group and replaced by the service gentry; Ivan's "political police," the *oprichnina*, acquired a separate territorial realm-within-a-realm where autocratic caprice was the supreme law; and the whole Muscovite system was put under such strain that soon after Ivan's death it collapsed in the great *smuta* of 1605-1613. Although we can surmise that Ivan's policies were due to the pressure of the unsuccessful Livonian war with Poland and Sweden, we do not really know his motives; but it is not very likely that they add up to a "modernizing" response to the European challenge, as was clearly the case with Peter's. The ultimate result of Ivan's policies, moreover, was not revolutionary, for the Muscovite order restored by the Romanovs after the *smuta* was fundamentally the same as that which had existed before Ivan.

Stalin's revolution from above, in contrast, cannot be situated in any continuum with the social order that preceded it, whether under the NEP or the Old Regime. But just as important the radical ideological envelope of Stalinism: in reality it is ideology that explains both the total scope and the inordinate cost of Stalin's revolution. Peter and Ivan, on the other hand, in their justifications of autocracy, used only the most conventional arguments of the European tradition: either the Christian duty of submission to divinely ordained power or the imperatives of natural law. Thus, even though Stalin, like Peter (though not like Ivan), was responding to the pressures of economic backwardness and military lag, his overall ambition to bring history to its culmination with the new world of socialism is quite incommensurate with his predecessor's limited, purely national projects.

Similarly, a secondary role must be assigned to Stalin's personality in explaining his system. Before 1929 the worst that could be said about his character was what Lenin had said—that Stalin was "too rude" for state responsibilities—though Lenin deemed such rudeness quite acceptable among Bolsheviks. To be sure, the overall record of Stalin's career shows him to be cruel to the point of sadism, and suspicious to the point of paranoia. Still, this was not apparent at the start of his Great Offensive. It is thus best to assume that his character was not a constant, but that it evolved under the pressure of the unprecedented risks of the Offensive.

In 1932, in the midst of that Offensive, Stalin's wife committed suicide after a violent argument that apparently concerned his policies toward the peasants. Even though he was hardly a sensitive man, this must have produced some effect on him, and for the worse. And the carnage of the collectivization no doubt hardened him even more. Later, he told Winston Churchill that the ordeal had been as frightful as the war.[36] We may also assume that for one so deep in crime as was Stalin by the time of the terror famine, any further crime could only come more easily. As with a drug, ever larger doses of crime could only produce a lesser effect, and murder could degenerate into mere habit. Thus, although Stalin's criminality did not simply derive from his character, his criminal character may have increasingly derived from his crimes.

But more important than history or psychology is the institutional setting in which Stalin operated, a setting that bred both cruelty and paranoia. The Party, as its agitprop ceaselessly proclaimed, was in a class war to the death. It was surrounded by enemies without and within: international capital, petty bourgeois kulaks, bourgeois wreckers, and deviationists within the Party. Stalin no doubt personally aggravated this mood of universal struggle and suspicion, but he by no means created it; it derived, rather, from the Party's whole heritage. This was a Party with which his "rude" character meshed only too readily.

To discover the impetus behind the Great Break, therefore, we must return to what had been the driving force of Communism since it first discovered its vocation in the militant and military frenzy of 1918. What fueled Bolshevism's Second Offensive was what had fueled the first: the vocation of the Party itself as the military-political vehicle for bringing humanity into socialism. The Party had no other reason for existing. By 1929, after twelve years of vainly waiting for socialism to appear, the time had come to force the hand of history and to build the future by an act of will. The alternative was not Bukharin's "growing into socialism"; the alternative was the withering away of the Party's ideological momentum in an interminable effort to wait out the muzhik. And with the dissipation of ideology, the Party's will to monopolize power would have eroded as well.

So the second episode of War Communism was launched, but it unfolded with a much greater sweep and intensity than the first. And the tone of the operation was quite different: Whereas 1918 had seen a hot hysteria, unpremeditated and unrehearsed, 1930 saw a colder hysteria, prepared and channeled to a high degree. This was because the tasks to be accomplished in 1930 were more complicated than those in 1918, and the Party-army was now more numerous, disciplined, and stronger. Let us recall the sequence of causation leading to this Second Offensive.

The Revolution and War Communism made Russia much more backward than she had been before 1917. Thus, when the market was reborn after 1921, the peasants became the arbiters of the country's economic destiny. By 1926 the regime had no choice but to increase investment in industry, if only to renovate an obsolete and decaying plant; but the Party at the same time wished to build socialism to give itself a worker and urban "base." Yet the Party's ideological distrust of both the market and kulak "capitalism" led it to set prices too low to keep the peasants producing. Thus in 1927 foodstuffs became scarce in the cities just as industrial expansion was taking off. The solution of raising state prices and relying on the market for the rest was rejected, since this would have made the Party and its industrial program hostage to uncontrollable, "anarchic," and "capitalist" forces. Therefore, it was decided to take the peasants' grain by coercion through immediate and full collectivization. Once this choice had been made, it also became necessary to accelerate industrial expansion to the maximum. And these two decisions together meant suppressing the market as well as all social classes that lived off it, from the kulaks to the nepmen.

But this amounted to a total "solution" to all problems at once through the total subordination of the whole of society to the Party-state. Thus one step inexorably led to another, all the way to the creation of a new, totalitarian order. There is no overall logic of Russian history leading to this result; but there *is* such a logic of Bolshevism—realizable should circumstances permit the Party to act out fully its Marxist fantasy. In 1918–1921 the circumstances of economic breakdown cut the process of Bolshevik self-realization short. In 1929–1933 the circumstances of a stronger Party and an economy in reasonable health (at least at the start) permitted the Party to take the Marxist logic to its resolution.

This does not mean, however, that the Party consciously desired or even anticipated what it found when it reached that culmination. Instead, as in 1918, it improvised its way into discovering what its true program was. Soviet socialism was built not out of any genuine plan but as if driven by Hegel's "cunning of reason"—that is, the outcome of the Offensive was determined by the logic of the system itself, a logic leading the Party in ways not fully apparent to its leaders. Thus Stalin and his men moved by a process of trial and error, and from one crisis to another, to arrive at the unproductive kolkhoz system and the military-industrial complex they had created by 1935. And when they got there, of course, they had no choice but to proclaim that these were the "socialist" results they had aimed at all along.

In fact, for a time they were not sure they would reach this "socialism" at all. Stalin knew at the start that his Offensive was a high-risk gamble that put the survival of the system at stake. To be sure, Lenin had gambled everything in October and again at Brest-Litovsk, but at that time there was much less to lose than in 1929 when a Soviet state existed. And, indeed, by 1931–1932 it looked as though Stalin would lose his gamble, for the early blunders in both agriculture and industry had thrown the country into such chaos that it seemed, once again, as if the whole system might collapse. It was only in 1933, after the fall harvest had been brought in and such industrial projects as Magnitogorsk had at last begun producing, that Stalin won his gamble. It was only in January 1934, at the Seventeenth Party Congress, that the Party could draw its first confident breath since January 1930 and proclaim the "victory" of its Offensive.

Thus another crisis of survival was surmounted. And it was surmounted because, at the height of the danger, the Party in a visceral reflex had closed ranks behind the Leader. Preobrazhenskii and most of his colleagues on the Left rallied to Stalin because he was implementing, however crudely, their platform, and because they could not bear to be left out of the building of socialism. One of them, Iurii Piatakov, not only became Sergo Ordzhonikidze's deputy but was indeed the real brains behind the industrialization drive. Bukharin and most of the Right, despite their declared commitment to the peasant and the market, did the same because they too could not bear being left out of the Great Offensive, no matter how botched its execution and how uncouth its leader. It is noteworthy that not one prominent Bolshevik resigned from the Party or publicly protested its crimes. Only Trotsky, who by now had been expelled from the country, openly campaigned against Stalin's "mistakes"—but as distortions of his, Trotsky's, correct policies.

Yet what really brought the Party through the crisis were not these holdovers but the likes of Nikita Khrushchev and their simpler faith. In 1928, during the Shakhty affair, Khrushchev was active against "wreckers" in his home region of the Donbas; shortly thereafter he moved to Kiev to become head of the Organization Department of the Ukrainian Party. In 1929 an Industrial Academy (in effect, a school for adult education) opened in Moscow to train Party cadres of working-class background to assume responsibilities in the now revolutionary economy, and Khrushchev became one of its first students. There he participated in expelling a group of fellow students as "Right deviationists." In 1931, on the recommendation of the former General Secretary of the Ukrainian Party, Kaganovich, he became a Party district secretary in Moscow and helped clean out the supporters of his Rightist predecessor, Riutin (of whom more shortly).

In 1934, at the age of 39, Khrushchev was rewarded by election to the Central Committee at the Congress of Victors. Soon thereafter he succeeded Kaganovich (who had been promoted to higher things) as Moscow Party chief and thus took over supervision of the construction of the Moscow Metro. It is upwardly mobile worker-peasants turned Party-workers like Khrushchev that Stalin called the "salt of the earth." Like the Leader himself, they could quite sincerely see themselves as the proletariat in power; and they could feel just as sincerely that they had an inherent right to exercise their class dictatorship for the building of socialism and the betterment of all mankind.

*　　*　　*

But was the result of their efforts really "socialism?" It was clearly not "capitalism," but is that enough to qualify it as true "socialism?" Socialist opinion outside Russian was divided over this question at the time, and it has bedeviled all discussion of socialism ever since. With Stalin's achievement the discourse of world socialism entered a wholly new phase.

From the 1830s to the First Five-Year Plan, socialism was a state that lay in the future; with Stalin's victory for the first time it could be alleged that socialism actually existed in the present. It had passed from the status of a prospective utopia to that of a palpable reality, and from the status of a movement to a society. Or at least the Soviet regime claimed that this had occurred. From that time onward, therefore, any socialist had to define his position in terms not just of the Soviet "experiment" but of the Soviet "achievement." But what are the criteria for deciding Soviet socialism's ontological status?

The Soviet Union had indubitably arrived at noncapitalism. It had suppressed private property, profit, and the market, and this is clearly the instrumental program of integral socialism. But most of the positive moral benefits that were supposed to result from this program had not appeared; on the contrary, a large number of unanticipated negative consequences could be observed. There was no growth of material abundance, but rather an increase of penury. There was no advance of human freedom, but instead a regression into servitude. There was no triumph of equality, but rather a new stratification of the population as a function of the Party's purposes. There was no end of the exploitation of man by man; indeed, to this was added the exploitation of everybody by the Party-state.

In short, the Party had built socialism, and it turned out not to be socialism. Or, to be more precise, the Party had realized the instrumental program of socialism, but socialism's moral program still remained in the future. Indeed, the new present was arguably worse, in terms of socialist morality, than the old capitalist past.

There are several ways of coping with this unexpectedly contradictory outcome. One is to deny that any contradiction existed at all, and to claim that the moral consequences of socialism did in reality follow from the practical program. This is the course that was adopted by the Soviet regime, and it is difficult to see how it could have done otherwise without admitting that it had failed and that the system was a fraud.

Another solution is to say that the central objective of the Soviet Revolution was realization of the instrumental program of non-capitalism—namely, the end of private property—and that since this had been achieved, the Soviet order was a real, if incomplete, socialism. This is the course taken by Trotsky, Bukharin, and a multitude of later commentators, both in Russia and abroad, from Roy Medvedev and Gorbachev to any number of Western authorities. This solution, of course, embraces the already mentioned aberration thesis; the bad-man theory of history; and/or the heavy heritage of Russian autocracy, bureaucracy, and backwardness. And until 1991 it entailed the belief that in the fullness of time the moral program of socialism would be added to the instrumental one. It is this hopeful and consoling *via media* that has been far and away the most popular solution to the Soviet conundrum, both in the East and in the West.

But there is a third solution, which is to say that the instrumental program of socialism leads quite logically to the perversion of its moral program. In other words, the failure of integral socialism stems not from its having been tried out first in the wrong place, Russia, but from the socialist idea per se. And the reason for this failure is that socialism as full noncapitalism is intrinsically impossible. For the suppression of private property, profit, and the market is tantamount to the suppression of civil society and all individual autonomy. And although this can be approximated for a time, it requires an inordinate application of force that cannot be sustained indefinitely.

As a practical matter, therefore, socialism leads not to an assault on the specific abuses of "capitalism" but to an assault on reality *tout court*. It becomes, in effect, an effort to suppress the real world, and this is something that cannot succeed in the long run. But for a protracted period this effort *can* succeed in creating a surreal world, one defined by the paradox that inefficiency, poverty, and brutality can be officially presented as the *summum bonum* of society, and one where society is unable to challenge this fraud.

It is this resolution of the Soviet conundrum that East European dissidents adopted when they were first able to speak up after Stalin's death. And it is on this solution that the majority of the people of Eastern Europe acted in 1989–1991 when they concluded that the system could not be reformed but had to be abolished, and that the basic social realities of private property, profit, and the market had to be restored if ever the East was to make an exit from the failed surreality of "really-existing" socialism.

But it would take a half-century for all of this to become clear. In the meantime the regime's greatest successes were still before it. In 1934–1935 Stalin gave his country a new breathing spell, a mini-NEP—but only in the psychological sphere. With a second and more sober Five-Year Plan under way, rationing could now come to an end. The Leader therefore proclaimed in a new slogan that "life has become better, life has become more joyous." But this was only a respite before he moved to complete his work through the Great Purges.

7

PURGE AND CONSOLIDATION

1935–1939

We [Bolsheviks] are not like other people. We are a party of people who make the impossible possible. . . . And if the Party demands it, if it is necessary or important for the Party, we will be able by an act of will to expel from our brains in twenty-four hours ideas that we have held for years. . . . Yes, I will see black where I thought I saw white, or may still see it, because for me there is no life outside the Party or apart from agreement with it.

The specter of revolution is haunting the world. . . . And do you really think I'm not going to be part of it? Do you really think that in this great world-wide transformation, in which our Party will play the decisive role, I will remain on the sidelines?

–Iurii Piatakov, 1928

We exist in a land grown unreal and strange;
Ten steps away no one hears the talk we exchange.
But when chances for half-conversations appear,
We will never omit the Kremlin mountaineer.

Each thick finger, a fattened worm, gesticulates
And his words strike you like they were many-pound weights
His full cockroach mustache hints a laughter benigning,
And the shafts of his boots: always spotlessly shining.

–Osip Mandelshtam, 1934

In the first half of the 1930s Stalin had dug a great "foundation pit" (in Andrei Platonov's phrase) in the body of old Russia, and in it he implanted the rude material base of the mature Soviet system. And now in the second half of the decade, through the new class struggle of the purges, he forged that superstructure of values and culture indispensable for making the system function. Indeed, he sought to fashion a special breed of man—a "new Soviet man," *Homo Sovieticus*—appropriate to the new civilization the Party had built. And so at the end of all the travails of the thirties, the Soviet system at last would come to realize its maximum totalitarian potential.

The centerpiece of this process of consolidation was of course the purge, or the Great Terror of 1936–1939. This episode remained ever after in the national consciousness as the peak of Stalinist crime and the most fantastic of Stalinist exploits. It was remembered in particular by the Soviet elites, its principal victims, as a time of mythic dread. As was the case with collectivization and the Gulag, the real nature and the full extent of the purges were largely concealed at the time. Yet the effort to pierce the secret of the purges would become the entering wedge for the future unmasking of the Stalinist achievement as a whole.

Thus in the debate over Sovietism, interpretation of the purges focuses familiar problems in a new and sharper way. To that majority of commentators for whom the great divide in Communism runs between Leninism and Stalinism, forced collectivization is of course the watershed event; nonetheless, it is the Great Terror that clinches the majority's case, because it was only then that Stalin turned against Bolshevism itself and destroyed the Party of Lenin. Indeed, for those committed to the virtue of Lenin's Revolution, the purge of "good Communists" counts as a rather worse crime than the extermination of the kulaks; hence, 1937 has received distinctly more attention than has dekulakization.

Thus the purges are the crux of the "bad man" and the "aberration" theories of Soviet history, for they seem to place the blame for this aberration squarely on Stalin's character. If ever there was a case for the decisive role of Stalin's lust for power or his insanity or both, this is it. And if such a case can be made for so crucial an episode, then it rubs off on all the rest of Stalin's record and effectively removes him from the canon of Soviet socialism. On the other hand, if Stalin's actions after 1936 can be shown to be politically functional within the Communist system, then his place in the logic of real Sovietism is secure and the system itself is the "bad man" of our drama. For by 1939 his work of system-building had been completed, and its essentials would remain in place until the grand collapse of 1989–1991.

But the purges can serve to found still another interpretation: they may be seen as a great divide within Stalinism, between the early, constructive years of building socialism and the later, destructive period of decimating the Party.[1] In this perspective the major part of Stalin's work is authentically socialist and progressive, and only the lesser part, the "cult," must be excised from the canon. This was the view that Khrushchev put forth in his "secret speech" in 1956.[2] And this was still the perspective put forth by Gorbachev for the seventieth anniversary of the Revolution in 1987. Indeed, a similar selectiveness in evaluating Stalin's record has been common in Western historiography, in particular among those who believed that the partisans of the "Bukharin alternative" surrendered too much of the Soviet achievement.[3]

This balancing act was necessary while the Soviet regime existed. The foundation pit of the system had indeed been dug during Stalin's first years in power and therefore could not be accounted criminal if Soviet socialism were to be reformed rather than replaced. With the regime's collapse, however, the motivation to believe in a creative phase of Stalinism by all logic should now disappear. But we should not count on such an outcome, for the need to salvage something of Stalinism will endure so long as belief exists in the instrumental program of integral socialism—namely, the end of private property, which was achieved for the first time in history under Stalin.

Yet if the purges were the centerpiece in the consolidation of mature Sovietism, they were by no means the whole process. During the same period, all cultural activity was brought under the direct control of the Party-state and subordinated to the political commands of the regime. Thus the struggle on the "cultural front" against illiteracy that began in 1929 culminated in the nationalization, or "stateization," of thought and art, thereby carrying the totalizing logic of the system to its final extreme.[4] It is only in the context of this new culture that the purges can be adequately understood. In fact, the cultural change preceded, and prepared the way for, the purge that brought the "new Soviet man" onto the scene.

SOVIET CULTURE

The politicization of Soviet culture started well before Stalin and indeed without any Party initiative. Beginning in 1917 and continuing through the Civil War, there was a great outpouring of utopian and millenarian expectation in circles far wider than the Party. This movement ranged from intellectual aesthetes such as the poets Aleksandr Blok, who saw the Revolution as the earthly realization of the word of Christ and his Apostles, and Vladimir Mayakovskii, who saw it as the advent of futurist civilization, to simple workers and even peasants, who saw it as a liberation of their humanity and creative potential. The most important manifestation of the populist form of millenarianism was the organization "Proletarskaia kúltura," or "Proletarian Culture," commonly known as Proletkult.[5] Its guiding principle was the plausibly Marxist idea that a proletarian state should have a proletarian culture, one that was radically distinct from its bourgeois predecessor. The mission of Proletkult was to encourage workers to produce this new culture out of their own experience. By 1920 Proletkult had some seven hundred thousand members, or a bit more than the Party. Lenin could only view this organization as a rival, since its mass appeal and subjectivist ideology implied that proletarian spontaneity did not need to be guided by Party consciousness. At the end of the Civil War, therefore, he subordinated it to the Party and thus killed it as a movement.

It was only during the NEP that the Party itself turned to the problem of culture in a socialist state. All the Bolshevik leaders were—and indeed, as Marxists, had to be—in agreement that eventually the new society would require a new culture. Yet most of them also felt that this result could not be artificially produced, as Proletkult had tried to do, but would emerge naturally as society changed; in the meantime, society needed to go to the school of bourgeois culture.

It is this attitude, as we have seen, that led to the relative cultural vitality of the twenties. Nonproletarian writers and artists, provided they were not hostile to the Revolution, were therefore allowed to function as "fellow travellers," in Trotsky's famous phrase, in the same way that other bourgeois specialists were tolerated. Similarly, modernist experimentation was permitted in education, for example, with the appropriation of the theories of John Dewey. More generally, the twenties were a period of utopian thinking about the future collectivist and technologically perfect human condition. The regime did nothing to discourage these "revolutionary dreams,"[6] even though they were not directly in the Party line, because they created an atmosphere favorable to radical social transformation. There was no formal Party line in the arts, and both Trotsky and Bukharin actively defended this situation (while Stalin simply said nothing). In short, there existed a cultural NEP in the form of a circumscribed and truncated marketplace of ideas.

Compared to the situation under Stalin, this cultural NEP was clearly the most creative period of Soviet intellectual life. Compared to the situation under the Old Regime, however, it just as clearly marked a regression: It was ambiguous in its very nature, and at the same time it contained the seeds of the Stalinist culture that would destroy it.

We have seen one aspect of this Stalinist prelude with the birth of the propaganda state and the creation of its logocratic idiom in the course of the twenties. Just as important were the new cultural institutions of the period and the ideologization of the key areas of intellectual life. For the cultural NEP, like its economic counterpart, lived in the shadow of the Party's commanding heights.

A Red Academy was created to compete against the official Academy of Sciences, and an Institute of Red Professors was formed to train cadres to take over the "bourgeois" university. Bukharin actively supported both of these enterprises. Bourgeois philosophy was abolished, some of its leading practitioners were exiled, and dialectical materialism became the only permitted school. Bourgeois law was also proscribed, and the Russian legal profession, one of the main bases of Russian liberalism before 1917, was dismantled. Economics also became basically Marxist, as was evident in the debates over the Plan—though in this instance the result was not a regression, since the exceptional circumstances governing Russian development provided a stimulus for innovative thinking. History, although not directly subjected to Party control, was in fact dominated by the Marxist school of Mikhail Pokrovskii. On the other hand, the natural sciences were largely left alone, since they did not offer a potential for ideological competition with the regime.

Before 1930, however, very little of this mobilization on the ideological front was directly controlled by the state. It was the work, rather, of self-appointed Marxist groups with a mission to supplant bourgeois culture in one or another field. The great prototype of this phenomenon, of course, was Proletkult.

In the universities, the Pokrovskii "school" of the twenties was a similar endeavor.[7] Pokrovskii was a professionally trained historian, a pupil, along with Miliukov, of the great Vasilii Kliuchevskii. He was also a convinced Marxist who explained Russian history as the mechanistic product of the evolution of the means of production and the class struggle. Although he had a genuine concern for documentation, he and his school nonetheless believed that their approach alone revealed the truth; in consequence, bourgeois historians in the universities who would not accept this approach were removed from their positions. Thus an ad hoc group of ideological zealots established a monopoly around an intellectual orthodoxy.

A similar process occurred in philosophy. Here the leader was Abram Deborin, another professionally trained academic with genuine Marxist convictions. In the twenties, the great issue in Soviet philosophy was the struggle between the "mechanists" and the "dialecticians," and Deborin was the leader of the second group. The "mechanists" held that the scientific worldview was merely the sum total of all the concrete sciences and therefore sought to keep philosophy out of the practice of science, whereas the "dialecticians," following the metaphysical tack of Engels and Plekhanov, wished to show that dialectics was a universal science embracing both society and nature. By the end of the decade Deborin and his allies had won and established their intellectual and personal hegemony in philosophy.[8]

But perhaps the most notable example of ideological vigilantism was that of the Russian Association of Proletarian Writers, or RAPP, which was founded in 1928 and led by the literary critic Leopold Averbakh.[9] Developing in more doctrinaire fashion earlier seeds of militant leftism, RAPP's program was that literature should obey an explicit "social command." It thus followed that literature must also be dominated by proletarians, or at least by Marxists, and in fact the members of RAPP were Party activists, not workers. Consequently, bourgeois fellow travellers should be shoved aside, and the new "proletarian" writers should inherit their leadership and rewards. RAPP came on the scene at the time of the Shakhty trial and the launching of the First Five-Year Plan; celebration of the Plan in the spirit of class war, therefore, became the focus of its activities. As a sign of changing times, the conformist pressure this drive generated contributed to Maiakovskii's suicide in 1930.

The conjoined efforts of Pokrovskii, Deborin, and Averbakh were part of a general movement of militant leftism, especially among Komsomols and shock workers, during the launching of the First Five-Year Plan between 1928 and 1931. This movement has sometimes been called the Cultural Revolution (as if it were a kind of Soviet anticipation of Maoism).[10] But basically it has been presented as if it were the source of Stalin's Great Offensive—an approach that would make his First Five-Year Plan a revolution from below, at least at the start, rather than from above. In short, the idea of Cultural Revolution, understood as a distinct period of Soviet history, is still another way to solve the Stalin problem: It makes his Offensive appear to be democratic in origin, and hence a genuinely socialist achievement.

But the leftist surge of 1928-1931 is hardly so simple. Militant leftism had been endemic to Soviet life since the Left Communism of Bukharin and the beginnings of Proletkult in 1918. The high NEP had put a damper on its expression, but the buildup to the Plan in 1928, together with the expansion of the Party and the growth of indoctrination, rekindled the still-live embers. Indeed, at the beginning of the Shakhty affair, before the GPU (the successor to the Cheka) took it over, there was genuine worker suspicion of engineers of bourgeois origin. Stalin and the leadership then stimulated these radical energies during 1928-1931 for the assault on the peasantry and the drive for industrialization. Thus, though the Offensive was in no sense produced by a surge of leftism, it first stimulated and then utilized this surge for its own purposes. But when leftism got out of hand, it was immediately reined in with a monitory denunciation on the model of "dizziness from success." Perhaps the last gasp of Soviet leftism was the initial phase of the Stakhanovite movement; henceforth, all enthusiasm from below was channeled by action from above.

A similar taming and "statization" of militant leftism occurred on the cultural front, and this process began with the implementation of the Plan. Culture, too, was now absorbed into the General Line and soon was centrally planned. Between 1930 and 1932 each of the sensitive fields just discussed was annexed by the regime and directly subordinated to its immediate political purposes. And in each case Stalin personally initiated the change. Yet in no instance was he acting out of personal caprice; there is a pattern, indeed a logic, running through all the cultural changes of the thirties.

The first field to be "nationalized" was philosophy, as if in homage to Marx's theory of the proletariat as the active agent of that science.[11] In December 1930, at the height of the crisis of industrialization,

Stalin gave an interview to the Party executive of the Institute of Red Professors in which he denounced Deborinism as "Menshevising idealism." The executive then passed a resolution condemning this idealism as semi-Trotskyism and denouncing "mechanism" as the ideological basis of the Right deviation. The first result of this abstruse maneuver was that there now existed a single orthodoxy of dialectical materialism that was associated not with the Menshevik Plekhanov but with Marx, Engels, and Lenin—and, of course, with Stalin after the new Leader's intervention. A new apostolic succession of the four great figures of world socialism was thereby established. A second result was that this new orthodoxy, and the succession of its true prophets, could be used to measure political deviations with the intent of condemning them. Henceforth such deviations were not to be treated as disagreements within Communism, but as non-Marxist and hence anti-Soviet and traitorous movements fit only to be destroyed. A third result was that ambitious younger philosophers now had an authorized standard by which to condemn the Deborinites and take over their academic positions. And a final result was that the Party-state had a rigorous ideological criterion for determining the loyalty of its personnel.

Nonetheless, Deborinism did not perish utterly. Its crude dialectical materialism was simply made cruder and standardized in catechetical form; and in this recycled guise, especially as Stalin himself repeated it in a famous chapter of his *Short Course* of 1938, it would live on until the end of the Soviet regime. Thus the lot of Deborin and of other militant leftists at the end of the twenties was to furnish the ideological weapons for their own undoing, and to supply the basic ingredients of the emerging Stalinist culture.[12]

The same fate befell the discipline of history the following year, in 1931. This time the turn was announced in a letter of Stalin to the editors of the journal *Proletarian Revolution* and concerned Party history. The journal had printed an article analyzing certain mistakes of Lenin in dealing with the Second International. Stalin replied that Lenin had never made mistakes, thereby laying down the rule that there was a single correct view of Party history, of Lenin's role in it, and, by implication, of his—Stalin's—position as Lenin's successor. The new orthodoxy came to be that Lenin and his Party had always been right; that Stalin had been Lenin's closest collaborator in building the Party and in leading the October Revolution; and that Stalin was now completing that Revolution by building socialism. By the same token, Trotskyism and other deviations were not a part of Party history at all but alien enemy manifestations similar to Menshevism and all the other forms of Social Democracy that Lenin had combatted earlier.

The next step in the taming of history was to combine Party and prerevolutionary Russian history, and this meant the elimination of the Pokrovskii school. Pokrovskii had presented the old-regime Russian state in completely negative but quite Marxist terms as the agent of the ruling classes in exploiting the Russian people. He left no positive heroes or glorious deeds in Russia's past. By 1934, however, as the new order was nearing completion, such disparagement of the national past came to be viewed by the leadership as demoralizing to the citizens of the new state. This was so because the glory of Russia was to have created the world's first socialist society; that is, the Old Regime was to be viewed not as a Russian past but as the past of a radically new entity, the Soviet Union. Pokrovskii's views were accordingly denounced as "abstract sociological schemes," and the Party called for concrete names, dates, and events to make the teaching of Russian history more vivid for students in the new mass system of education. In particular, the new history was to emphasize the creation of a centralized Russian state as a progressive development; Peter the Great and Ivan the Terrible, therefore, became heroes insofar as they had been mighty state-builders.

This partial rehabilitation of the Russian past coincided with the reintroduction of insignia for military rank, of uniforms and discipline in the schools, and of traditional family values in legislation regarding such matters as divorce and abortion. All of this taken together has sometimes been regarded as a "great retreat" from revolutionary utopianism and a return to Russian nationalism."[13] As such, it has been seen by some as still another aspect of Stalin's betrayal of the Revolution and of socialist internationalism. In short, together with the NEP, these changes are one of the two candidates for the role of Soviet "Thermidor," that is, the end of the true Revolution.

In fact, however, there never was a Soviet Thermidor; the Russian Jacobins remained in power permanently. Moreover, nationalism is a very misleading term for what was involved in the overthrow of Pokrovskii and, more broadly, in the great retreat. The rehabilitation of Russian national symbols was both highly selective and wholly subordinated to Soviet purposes. All that was rehabilitated was forceful leadership in the building of a centralized state; and this had indeed been a component of traditional Russian nationalism. But the other two staples of Russian national sentiment, Orthodoxy and the cultural specificity of peasant Russia, remained proscribed. Moreover, the old Russian state was presented as no more than a precursor of the very new and different Soviet state, which was a socialist and multinational Party-state. In addition, the revolutionary movement under the Old Regime continued to be emphasized as an even more progressive force than the autocracy, since it eventually produced Lenin and October. This "social movement," more than Ivan and Peter, was indeed the true national accomplishment of Russia: It demonstrated Russia's superiority to the West in matters revolutionary, and thereby made her the progressive leader of all mankind. This situation is in fact best characterized by the official formula proclaimed in 1934: All the "constituent" Soviet republics were "national in form and socialist in content."

What the regime sought in post-Pokrovksii historiography was a Soviet patriotism that would glorify the new socialist order and inspire pride and loyalty in the freshly educated worker population. A specifically Russian nationalism was only one component of this patriotism. In fact, what occurred was an annexation and exploitation of Russian national sentiment in order to lend strength to the Soviet Union's still artificial and fragile Soviet socialist amalgam. In short, what emerged in the mid-thirties was the state patriotism of socialism in one country. The fact that Stalin was a non-Russian and therefore may have been personally inclined to emphasize Russianness by way of compensation probably facilitated this development. But the principal motive for this patriotism was the need to justify to the population the unanticipated fact that the creation of a centralized state had been among the chief results of the Great Socialist Offensive.

Moreover, the new historiography, like Pokrovskii's, was founded on historical materialism. Although it gave new emphasis to the heroes of the pre-October revolutionary movement and to an occasional autocrat, Soviet historical writing continued to rest on the old sociological model of the base and the superstructure in conjunction with the class struggle, but this model was now made still cruder and more mechanistic. So Pokrovskii's basic approach, like Deborin's dialectical materialism, lived on in the new Stalinist culture. The culmination of all this came in 1938 with the publication of Stalin's *History of the All-Union Communist Party* (*Bolsheviks*)—better known as the *Short Course*—in its day one of the great best-sellers of the twentieth century, not just in Russia but around the world.

This document pulled the whole new Soviet culture together. It set forth a triumphal and sacred history of developments, from the Emancipation of the serfs in 1861 to the codification of socialism in the Stalin Constitution of 1936; and it catalogued all the enemies of the people's cause, from the Populists and the Mensheviks to the Trotskyites. And in chapter 4, section 2, "On Dialectical and Historical Materialism," it gave Stalin's own exposition of the fundamentals of Marxism-Leninism. Here at last was a compendium of the major "intellectual" developments of the thirties, and the answer to all significant questions of life and thought. This was the authoritative canon of high Sovietism, and the intellectual straitjacket around all cultural life until well after Stalin's death. Despite a number of later emendations, the basic tenets of the *Short Course* would not be repudiated as long as the Soviet regime lasted.

An analogous process of consolidation and nationalization occurred on the literary front. As the Plan went into high gear, expounding its meaning could not be left to the freelance ideologues of RAPP. In 1932 that organization was dissolved and a new, state-sponsored Union of Writers was created in its stead, with the proletarian realist Maxim Gorky as honorary godfather and the Politburo member Andrei Zhdanov as principal ideologue.[14] In 1934 the Union held its first congress; various fellow travellers recanted their errors and Zhdanov proclaimed the doctrine of socialist realism. Henceforth, writers were to be, in Stalin's words, "engineers of human souls." Specifically, this meant that they should write in the accessible manner of nineteenth-century realism, unlike the abstruse "formalists" and modernists of the twenties. At the same time, however, they should not mirror reality mechanically, but instead should offer heroic, idealized models of socialist devotion and achievement. Subjects, moreover, should be taken from the immediate, practical tasks set by the Party line, and from the lives of workers and activists attempting to carry it out. Thus socialist realism in fact meant Party-minded idealism, and the initial leftist idea of proletarian art became the direct "social command" of the Party-state. Yet again the leftist impetus survived its apparent defeat, for the basic notion of aesthetics as transposed politics was still present, though in cruder form, in the completed Stalinist culture.

Once this formula had been worked out for literature, it was easy to apply it in all the arts. By 1936 there was a Union of Cinematographers, and then a Composers' Union and a Union of Artists; and the doctrine of socialist realism was adapted to the activity of each of these Unions. Each had a monopoly in its field; all were under the dispensation of the *nomenklatura* and in fact governed by Party men. At the same time, this "creative intelligentsia," like other types of cadres, was richly rewarded and integrated into the elite. And, of course, creative figures who could not live by the social command risked penalties at times as severe as the Gulag, as in the cases of Osip Mandelshtam and Isaak Babel.

In this manner all the "soft" forms of culture were assimilated into the Party line. But even the "hard" forms of culture—the natural sciences, whose subject matter and methodology traditionally epitomized an objectivity immune to any social influence—now began to be ideologized.

The principal case was genetics, and the leader of the campaign was Trofim Lysenko.[15] A self-taught biologist, he argued against the Mendelian theory of inherited biological characteristics in favor of a neo-Lamarckian position that he called Michurinism, after an earlier Russian scientist. This new genetics held that biological characteristics were acquired and therefore could be changed by manipulating the environment. Lysenko accordingly denounced Mendelianism as reactionary and extolled Michurinism as complementary to the Marxist thesis of the malleability of human nature through change in the social environment. All of this was linked to the transformation of society through the Five-Year Plans, and in particular to the hope of breeding new varieties of crops to remedy the ever-disastrous performance of collective agriculture. Lysenko performed inconclusive experiments to prove his theories, but despite this relative failure he caught the attention of Stalin, another self-educated man of the people who was vulnerable to the promise of a miraculous improvement in kolkhoz production. By the end of the decade the Mendelians had been largely purged from Soviet biology, and Lysenkoism had established an hegemony that would last into the Khrushchev era.

The hardest of the hard disciplines, physics and chemistry, however, by and large escaped direct subordination to the Party line.[16]

Certain aspects of theoretical physics—most notably Einstein's theories of relativity and, later, cybernetics—were condemned as forms of idealism. And dialectical materialism was declared to be in principle the theoretical basis of all natural phenomena. But as a practical matter physics and chemistry were largely left alone, at least in part because Soviet physicists were aware of the military potential of the atom. During the Second World War the physicists told Stalin frankly that ideology must be kept out of their discipline, and Stalin, in this practical matter of power, agreed. As a result, after the war the Soviet Union would produce nuclear weapons with a rapidity that astounded the West.

Thus, by 1938 and the publication of the *Short Course*, virtually the whole of Russian culture had been nationalized as well as ideologized in two senses. First, all branches of creative activity had been given a Marxist-Leninist methodological and philosophical underpinning; second, activity in each branch had been made subject to the direct administrative commands of the Party.

The Soviet totalitarian system thereby at last became complete: Every aspect of life, from economics to culture, had been made political; and everywhere the politics expressed the ideological purposes of the Party-state. The whole of Soviet life was now directed towards one end: the building and defense of socialism. Everything was evaluated in terms of its relation to this supreme goal, and everything that did not contribute to achieving this goal was ipso facto a hostile element to be purged from the system. The formula of ideocratic partocracy had now been carried to its logical conclusion.

Such, at least, was the formal structure of the system. But the question remains as to how far in practice the regime was able to mold the population to its purposes. Obviously, the Party's control was not so total that an order from the Kremlin could command the entire country at will. Even though a structured civil society no longer existed in Russia, there nonetheless existed elements of group cohesion in the population that constituted a kind of shadow society beneath the formal structures of the regime.

And this shadow society always found covert ways to resist or evade the pretensions of the state, thereby restricting the state's freedom of maneuver and forcing it to partially reshape its policies. A prime example is the peasant resistance that extracted from Stalin the concession of the family plot and the kolkhoz market. A still more important example is the "shadow economy" of illegal yet indispensable private entrepreneurship that paralled the Plan from Stalin to the collapse of the system. Other examples may be found in the initial phase of the Stakhanovite movement, in concessions to the Russian national tradition, and in the increasing privileges of cadres. Indeed, the whole process by which the regime under Stalin was obliged to improvise its way to a bastard version of its original goals is an illustration of the enduring recalcitrance of the shadow society. And it is one of the merits of social history revisionism to have brought out this interaction of state and "society" as a major thread of Soviet development.

Nonetheless, such interaction hardly amounted to "negotiations," as some would have it, or to an equal ability for society to act, for the entire population operated in a context where politics, the economy, and culture had all been collapsed into a "mono-organizational" Party-state. It is this structural factor that made the system totalitarian; that in practice the regime fell short of total control of society hardly alters this basic reality. Total state control of any society is impossible; but a total state framework of social organization *can* be achieved with a totalizing ideology buttressed by terror.

Moreover, even in practice the presence of the Party-state was overwhelming. For the concession of the family plot to the peasants was derisory in comparison to the regime's appropriation of the whole village, just as the workers' ability to ration their efforts was powerless to alter the hegemony of the Plan. And if we trouble to look upward from the bare social facts, we see that there weighed upon peasants, workers, and cadres alike the mind-numbing obligation to subscribe, or at least to render lip-service, to socialism as the supreme meaning of life. It is thus quite abusive to call the Soviet social tug-of-war "pluralism" or incipient "democracy" in any sense that is applicable to societies without an ideological state apparatus. For it is the ideological pretension of the Soviet system that defined its sociological uniqueness. The result was a pervasiveness of state purposes in all of life that was without historical precedent.

This triumph of ideocratic partocracy was accompanied by the maturation of the personal cult of Stalin. Beginning with the Congress of the Victors in 1934, he was habitually referred to only with the most extravagant epithets, from genius to coryphaeus of the arts and sciences, from the greatest friend of children to the father of the peoples and the leader of the world proletariat, and so forth. The celebration of his sixtieth birthday in 1939 was a veritable apotheosis. And, as we have seen, he *did* personally make the crucial decisions, both in the economic revolution of the decade and in the nationalization of culture. Therefore, the temptation is great to conclude that all of these enterprises were conducted to enhance his personal power, and that a regime that culminated in the cult of his person was basically his personal creation.

A more plausible view, however, is that Stalin in the era of the cult was an expression of the system rather than its creator. For all of his interventions on the cultural front presupposed an existing system and a ready-made ideology. In each sector the NEP had already created a "union" or "society" of specialists—whether proletarian writers or Marxist historians—and each such group had developed a Marxist justification for subordinating its discipline to the immediate tasks of the Party and for eliminating nonconformists. Stalin's appropriation of these enterprises, therefore, was hardly a quantum leap: He simply subordinated the lot of them to the ideological department of the Central Committee and to his personal will. Hence all culture was centralized under a single state agency, a circumstance that made everything cruder than before and more dangerous for the unorthodox, but one that also represented a logical growth rather than some imaginary betrayal.

Thus Stalin did with the NEP culture what he had done with the Trotskyite-Menshevik NEP Plan: He annexed it and transformed it by subordinating it to the actual rather than the prospective task of building integral socialism. The same occurred with all the other forms of militant leftism and the "revolutionary dreams" of the twenties. But since building socialism in practice turned out to be far more brutal than even the most brutal theoretical anticipations of class warfare had imagined, the resulting Stalinist culture was a comparably brutal affair.

Something analogous may be said of the cult of Stalin itself. Stalin no doubt enjoyed the adulation without being entirely taken in by it, so some role must be accorded to his personality in the creation of the cult. But the cult also served a major function within the system. The hypothesis has often been advanced that the backward Russian peasant had always had a sacred father-figure in the tsar, and that the Stalin cult therefore offered the people a kind of "icon" for their primitive emotions."[17] In this view, the cult has nothing especially socialist or *partiinyi* about it; it is rather a prolongation of the autocratic and Orthodox burden of Russian backwardness. Given what Stalin had done to the peasants, however, to insist on their need to deify him is, to say the least, bizarre. It is very clear, moreover, that the cult emerged from the Party, not from the people.

The Stalin cult, as already noted, had its origin in the Lenin cult of the NEP, and that cult, too, originated in the Party, not in the people.[18] To be sure, Lenin himself, as his widow averred, would not have wanted any such veneration, since he had always shunned it in his lifetime. But this is beside the point: He could no more control the uses made of his person than he could those made of his political legacy. Yet this does not mean that the Lenin cult does not follow logically from that legacy, which made "the Party [in Trotsky's words] the single historical instrument given to the proletariat." Thus, the Lenin cult, with its mummy, its mausoleum, and its Marxist-Leninist orthodoxy, was the Party's cult of itself: The Leader who had always been right was the necessary talisman for the Party that would always be right. As Maiakovskii put it, "Lenin lived, Lenin lives, Lenin will live!"

Stalin, the Lenin of his day and the new incarnation of the Party's infallibility and immortality, inevitably adapted this cult to his own leadership. Indeed, given his real pivotal position, it would have been impolitic for him not to have done so. But when a "leader cult" is applied to a living person, it is magnified by that very fact. And when the Leader leads the population from one wrenching revolutionary break to another, the focus on the quasi-magical powers of his person is further enhanced. In a situation of constant crisis, the hero theory of politics is a natural recourse even for a nontotalitarian society—as the careers of any number of American chief executives, or of Churchill and de Gaulle, attest. But when the society is totalitarian, the alleged hero is inflated to superhuman, quasi-divine proportions. So Stalin, who had almost no direct contact with the people of his country, was transformed by the omnipresence of his image in plaster, paint, or celluloid into a charismatic icon for the masses.

Yet in such a system this patent absurdity is in fact functional: The Leader becomes the incarnate ideological linchpin holding the whole ideocratic phantasmagoria together. Thus by 1939, when the main part of his domestic work was done, Stalin had become the supreme cog in his own machine. For such a total leader was the product of the logic of such a total system, and the poor Russian muzhik had precious little to do with it. And without such a system, the mere man Stalin could never have gotten away with anything so absurd as Stalinism.

THE GREAT TERROR

Nor could Stalin have gotten away with the Great Terror without the support of a total system. Once again, of course, he was the prime mover, and so the temptation is great to make him the whole story. Yet once again a broader process was at work, and its wellspring was in the system itself. But in this case it is much more difficult to discover the steps in that process, for the Soviet leadership covered its tracks too well to make it possible to reconstruct even the basic narrative. The essential outlines of the collectivization eventually came to be known; the purges will no doubt always remain something of a mystery. Anyone who approaches them, therefore, must engage in an unusual degree of conjecture; and where proof is impossible, plausibility will have to suffice. This is the method employed here.

It would be too much to say that the purges were a "rational" political undertaking in the usual sense of that term. They did nonetheless have a rationale in the nature of the mature Soviet system and in the circumstances of the day. In a broad sense this rationale lay in the fact, already alluded to, that the mid-thirties marked the watershed between the socialist utopia *in potentia* and its realization *in actu*: The instrumental program of integral socialism had indeed been carried out, but its consequences were a travesty of the expected moral results. This unacceptable fact somehow had to be negated or denied.

The origin of the purges thus lies in the trauma of the First Five-Year Plan, and in particular in the disaster of collectivization. As Pasternak put the matter in *Doctor Zhivago*:

> Collectivization was an erroneous and unsuccessful measure and it was impossible to admit the error. To conceal the failure people had to be cured, by every means of terrorism, of the habit of thinking and judging for themselves, and forced to see what didn't exist, to assert the very

opposite of what their eyes told them. From this came the unprecedented cruelty of the *Ezhovshchina*, the proclamation of a constitution that was not meant to be applied, and the introduction of elections not founded on the elective principle.[19]

Existing reality therefore had to be denied through the creation of a new culture, or a surreality, and the population had to be terrorized into accepting this culture as the truth about the new socialism. This is the basic logic that connects the Plan to the Purge.

But this process worked itself out through three more specific problems, each with its own logic, that confronted the system in the years between the end of the first Plan in 1932 and the start of the first purge trial in 1936. The first of these problems was the still insecure position of Stalin, who was not yet absolute dictator. The second was the unstable state of the Party in a society that had just been turned upside down by the Second Revolution. And the third was an international situation that suddenly became dangerous just when the Second Revolution was completed.

These three problems converged in 1936 to produce the first of the three spectacular show trials that riveted the world's attention and that have ever since been at the center of speculation about the purge phenomenon. But these trials were directed at the has-beens of the old oppositions, at individuals who were no longer credible enough to aspire to displace Stalin. Far more important than this public melodrama was the enormous and invisible purge-in-depth that swept through the Party, the managerial cadres, the officer corps, the cultural elite, and the security police itself in 1937 and 1938. This purge-in-depth was carried out not against the old oppositionists but against good Stalin men, the Leader's faithful comrades in the building of socialism. Thus the Great Terror in fact amounted to a gigantic coup d'état carried out by Stalin and the top leadership against most of the key personnel of the system they were leading. It was indeed Stalin's Second Revolution from above.

The first factor leading to this coup d'état grew out of the circumstance that Stalin's General Line had come near to disaster in 1932–1933. Although the Party closed ranks during the emergency, Stalin's errors were widely criticized in private, especially by members of the old oppositions. Sympathizers of Trotsky who were still in the Party regularly sent him damning material for publication in his *Bulletin of the Opposition* in Paris; it seems that in 1932 there even existed a small, organized, though hardly terrorist, group in Moscow that maintained contact with Trotsky's son.[20] More threatening still, in the same year a group of "Rightists" associated with Mikhail Riutin produced a platform calling for a halt to crash industrialization and collectivization and for the removal of Stalin. It also seems that such sentiments were shared on the Left and indeed among some who had hitherto been Stalin's adherents.[21]

This was treason to the cause and to the Leader just at the most dangerous moment in the battle. Stalin reacted by having the eighteen signers of the Riutin platform expelled from the Party; but it seems he wished to go further and have Riutin executed. With this demand, however, he came up against a major Party taboo: The Bolsheviks, ever mindful of the French revolutionary precedent, were determined that their Revolution would not devour its children, for lethal strife among the leaders could end by destroying the whole movement. The Politburo therefore refused to permit the death penalty, and it seems that Kirov was the sanction's chief opponent. But this defeat rankled Stalin, so he determined that he must break that taboo if ever he were to govern the Party. However, since he could not impose his will at that moment, he retreated and bided his time, as he had done on a number of occasions in conflicts with earlier oppositions.

It seems that there was further challenge to Stalin's authority—at the Seventeenth Party Congress in 1934.[22] Although the Congress heaped the most lavish public praise on its General Secretary, there was an undercurrent of criticism of his leadership during the recent Offensive. It seems also that some of the critics hoped that Kirov might be a suitable and more moderate successor: He was the leader of the second most important Party organization in the country, that of Leningrad; he had not been compromised by a central role in carrying out collectivization; he was more an ally of Stalin than a toady such as Molotov; and he was no sly Caucasian, but a hearty down-to-earth Russian. It also appears that Kirov received more votes than Stalin for election to the new Central Committee.

But there is absolutely no evidence that there was a Kirov program, or that he saw himself as an opposition leader or possible successor to Stalin. On the contrary, he had been a Stalin man since he took over the Leningrad leadership from Zinoviev in 1926, and all of his speeches of the period were thoroughly hardline. It is understandable nonetheless that Stalin should take umbrage at Kirov's popularity and at the wishful thinking that probably surrounded this younger man. This is all the more likely since Stalin could not help but know that his blunders during the Great Offensive were so great that in any normal political system they would have been cause for removing him from power. And the Communist system still retained enough vestiges of Social Democratic constitutionalism to make such action technically possible.

But does all of this mean that Stalin was the author of Kirov's assassination on December 1, 1934? If Stalin wanted a purge, he first needed an emergency to justify the exercise of special powers; and for an emergency he needed an atrocity to demonstrate that the country was in danger. The previous year the Reichstag fire (which at the time everyone erroneously believed had been set by the Nazis) had furnished Hitler just such an occasion, and this fact could hardly have escaped Stalin's attention. Was Kirov's murder Stalin's Reichstag fire?

The mystery of this "murder of the century," as it has been called, will probably never be solved. Khrushchev strongly hinted at Stalin's guilt in his secret speech to the Twentieth Party Congress in 1956, and there is much circumstantial evidence in favor of this hypothesis. The ease with which the assassin, Leonid Nikolaev, gained access to Kirov's office, and the mysterious accidents that befell key players in the drama immediately after the assassination, indicate that the crime was the work of the NKVD (as the political police had been called since 1934). Just as suspicious is the rapidity of Stalin's reaction. Within twelve hours he had issued a special decree establishing expeditious procedures for punishing terrorist acts and reached Leningrad by special train to interrogate Nikolaev personally. Still, there is no direct evidence of Stalin's involvement, and there are persuasive arguments against it. He would hardly wish to set a precedent for the assassination of Communist leaders, or to have risked a botched attempt on Kirov's life.

In any event, with Kirov's death Stalin had "proof" that opposition to the Party logically led to crime. Thus moral responsibility for Kirov's death was soon attributed in 1935 to Zinoviev and Kamenev, and from them the "plot" expanded in concentric circles. These two leaders were tried for direct responsibility in 1936; Piatakov and Radek were incriminated in a second trial in 1937; and finally

Bukharin, Rykov, and the NKVD chief Genrikh Yagoda became the villains of a final trial in 1938. These Party leaders were now branded "enemies of the people," a label used also for all the lesser victims of the purge-in-depth. Moreover, the theoretical justification for their elimination was the same that Stalin had employed in launching the revolution of the First Five-Year Plan. Once again, it was proclaimed that the closer the country drew to socialism, the more bitter the resistance of its enemies became and therefore the more intense must be the class struggle against them. This was the ultimate debasement of the cardinal principle of Marxism, for no semblance of a social class was involved in the purge; there was only a struggle of the leadership against the bulk of the Party.

But accusations of treason in the Party would acquire full potency only in conjunction with another process leading to the great coup d'état. This second line of development derives from changes in the Party's makeup in the course of the Second Revolution.[23]

Stalin had begun his Offensive with a Party of slightly more than one million members, most of whom were well indoctrinated and committed to the General Line. Between 1930 and 1933, however, the Party more than doubled in number, with the overwhelming majority of the new recruits coming from the working class and the poorer peasantry—the most rapid and plebeian expansion since War Communism. And, as under War Communism, these recruits were poorly screened, hastily indoctrinated, and only loosely integrated into the Party's hierarchical structures. The structures themselves, moreover, were strained to the limit by the expansion of the Party's role. A whole new Party network had to be created in the recently conquered countryside and in the newly built industrial centers. In addition, Party men now had to be more than political agitators and administrators: Since the Party's main responsibility had become the economy, they had to have technical competence, whether for industry or agriculture, not just Red credentials. And, despite a great effort on the cultural front, not enough new Red specialists had as yet been trained. Nor could all of the new members even be counted on to be adequately orthodox, for forming Leninists also took time.

This expanded Party, moreover, was put under great strain by the near-chaos that reigned in society as a whole during 1930–1933. For although the regime sought to fashion a monolithic order, its revolution from above had in fact created a society later described by the

Soviet novelist Vasilii Grossman as a world that was *Forever Flowing*.[24] In answer, Stalin in his "six points speech" in 1931 sought to mobilize the Party against the "fluidity of labor," or the vast migrations of the population set off by the upheaval of the Plan. But the Party, too, was fluid, for some of the flotsam of a society in upheaval had infiltrated its ranks. Thus by 1933 Stalin had an acute problem of ill-trained and unreliable cadres on his hands, and this problem lay at the heart of the system—within the Party itself.

His response was a purge, a "cleansing" of the Party similar to what occurred at the end of the Civil War. In 1933 some 400,000 of the incompetent, the unmotivated, and the "class-alien" were expelled.[25] But the Party machine still did not seem adequately reliable, so in 1935 a "verification" of Party documents eliminated nearly 200,000 more members; and the next year a similar number was weeded out through an "exchange" of Party documents. Thus by the end of 1936—that is, before the purge-in-depth had really begun—Party membership was down to only 1,450,000, which signified a drop of 750,000 in four years. And in 1937, the first year of the purge-in-depth, 500,000 more members disappeared from the Party's books. This time, however, they were not simply expelled; they were more often than not shot or sent to the Gulag. Nonetheless, there was a logic that linked the purge as cleansing and the purge as bloodletting, and this continuity was provided by a drive to renew cadres and to staff the Party with submissively reliable members. In short, Stalin was striving for the ideal hierarchical army, that machine of obedient cogs of which he spoke in these same years.

Stalin knew very well he could get away with this coup, for, as one cynic put it, he had 500,000 new jobs to give away each year. This is the number of members he purged in 1937, and by the end of 1938, 450,000 new men had taken their place in the first increase of Party membership since 1932. And in each of the next two full years before the war, some 500,000 more were added, for a total of 1,500,000 new members since the great divide of the blood purge, 1937. In short, given the fact that some of the new men were also purged, more than half of the Party membership at the outbreak of war had been recruited after the purge.

These new men were "thirty-something" products of the Second Revolution of the thirties, Stalin's upwardly mobile yuppies, so to speak. Almost all of them were graduates of one or another technical or engineering school created during the first Plan—metallurgy was the favored field.[26] Yet these institutions were made increasingly professional in the mid-thirties as Stalin became more conscious of the crucial importance of "man as the most precious capital." First, "democratic" class origin ceased to be a criterion for admission to higher education, and, as a stopgap, bourgeois specialists were once again welcome in technical jobs. Then, as the technical schools became capable of large-scale production of genuinely competent cadres, these new specialists assumed managerial command and were taken into the Party in the upsurge of enrollment that began in 1938. The officer corps of the armed forces was rejuvenated by a process similar to the one that replenished the managerial corps of industry.

Thus the purges gave Stalin a Party composed for the most part of people who had been formed after the Great Offensive; these people were products of the new socialist system, of its institutions and its culture. Although there was doubtless no master plan at the beginning of the coup—just as there was none in 1929 for the economic revolution—by early 1937 Stalin and his men clearly intended the sweeping results they in fact achieved. These results, moreover, are quite consonant with the totalizing thrust of the nationalization of culture that culminated at the same time. Seen in this context, the purges are a part of the process of *Gleichschaltung*, the bringing into line, of all aspects of Soviet life in the second half of the thirties.

It is this exchange of cadres, and the concomitant replacement of the old Party by a new one, that is the heart of the great coup d'état. The coup's pivotal moment was 1937, the year in which Party membership reached its nadir. At this point the "cleansing" of Party lists suddenly turned into an annihilation of anti-Party "enemies." That year would therefore remain ever after a time of legendary horror for the nation's elite, and mark the great divide in Stalinist and Soviet history.

There is little doubt that this renovation of the Party was in fact the central purpose of the coup. The real questions are: Why did Stalin feel he needed a coup? By what steps did he carry it out? And why did it begin only in 1936, two years after the pretext for the whole operation—Kirov's assassination?

A part of the reason for the delay was that Stalin no doubt continued to encounter resistance in the Politburo and the Central Committee to his desire to crush all old oppositionists and new waverers, and this resistance could only have increased his anger as well as his determination to have his way eventually. It is also quite possible that Ordzhonikidze, Kuibyshev, and others had taken up the earlier role of Kirov in urging moderation. At least this is a reasonable inference from Stalin's known hostility toward them during their last days, as well as from the later, and documented, case of Pavel Postyshev, who in 1937 openly clashed with Stalin in the Central Committee regarding a prospective purge victim.

Stalin's fury must have been all the greater since these objections came not from old oppositionists but from good Stalinists of long standing. Contrary to what Deutscher and others have argued, Stalin could not have been very concerned about the prospect of a coalition of the old Left and Right oppositions replacing him in a crisis.[27] These figures no longer had an adequate base in the Party for such action. If there were to be any threat to his power it could only come from Stalinists who wished to replace a failing Boss but keep his system, which they had helped to build and in which they had the support and political authority to lead. The old oppositionists were prominent only in the show trials, and this circumstance has obscured the much more important fact that, once Stalin at last got his purge, its victims were overwhelmingly his own men.

But Stalin's frustration with the Party was aggravated by still a third problem that took a sharp turn for the worse in 1936. For this was the year when the international situation, so long an object of quasi-paranoid concern to the regime, at last became genuinely dangerous.[28] By 1934 Hitler, whom the Soviets had until then discounted as a German Kornilov, had consolidated his power internally; in 1936 he reintroduced universal military service and reoccupied the Rhineland. At the same time, Japan advanced from Manchuria into China proper, while she simultaneously tested Soviet strength along the Amur River. From this time onward, the Soviet Union had to take seriously the possibility of war in the near future. And war, especially if it went badly, could only too easily trigger a fatal domestic crisis, as every Soviet citizen remembered from the experience of 1914–1917.

But 1936 also brought the Soviet Union a new kind of foreign danger: The international scene suddenly polarized over the issue of fascism, and Russia as an ideological power was automatically thrust into the middle of this maelstrom. In France a Right-wing attack on the republic in 1934 had produced the first Popular Front of liberals, socialists, and Communists against fascism. The next year the formula of the Popular Front became the policy of the Comintern, but more to defend the Soviet state against Hitler than to promote revolution in the West. In 1936, however, the Popular Front phenomenon got out of hand, at least from the Soviets' point of view. In France a Popular Front victory in the May elections triggered in June a wave of sit-down strikes (at the time a novel phenomenon) that for a while appeared insurrectionary. The next month the Spanish Popular Front was confronted by the revolt of General Franco; this began a three-year Civil War in which he was aided by Germany and Italy. The French events made it possible for Trotsky to speak of a new revolution, and the Spanish events presented Trotskyites and other militant Leftists with an actual revolutionary war.[29] The radical surge unleashed by the First World War and broken in the early twenties now seemed to resume; permanent revolution appeared once again to be on the march, and this time against a new mutant of the "highest form of capitalism"—fascism.

The emergence of this new force had a major and enduring impact on the Soviet Union's position in the world. Henceforth the world's first workers' state could present itself, and was often perceived by others, as the polar opposite of fascism and hence as the world's only unwavering antifascist force. For the Left generally, fascism stood for absolute evil, and so Communism *ex contrario* was cast in the role of the indispensable guardian of good. Thus, from the mid-thirties onward the old principle of "no enemies to the Left" was given a new, more radical meaning. Liberals seemed summoned by history to the perilous policy of allying with the antiliberal Left against the new ultra-Right.

Indeed, the concept of generic fascism as the new face of imperialism was a Communist creation. (The fascist powers themselves did not think that they constituted a common movement until they formed political alliances after 1937.) Fascism as a generic term was first put forward by the Comintern in 1922 on Mussolini's accession to power, and was soon elaborated into a general theory whereby political fascism was seen as a front for "finance capital." It was thus ready-made to explain Hitler's seizure of power, and thereafter to characterize any anti-Communist force as a species of fascism, as when Communists in the early thirties labeled Social Democrats "social fascists." On the basis of this generic theory of fascism, militant antifascism became the central theme of Communist agitation throughout the world. Thus, after 1935 the antifascist Popular Front was the Soviet Union's principal trump in international affairs and the means of spreading Communist influence far beyond the working class.

But since this influence was sought by Stalin to further Soviet security rather than to promote foreign revolution, from 1935 onward the "struggle against fascism" was always coupled with the "struggle for peace." Consequently, Stalin was not prepared to do much in a concrete way to combat fascism, for any support of revolution in the West would alienate the bourgeois powers—France and England—that he might need against Hitler. Just as important, any significant Soviet involvement in the antifascist struggle abroad would endanger the still-shaky Soviet state. Hence for Stalin, Spain was not so much an opportunity as a danger. Soviet involvement in Spanish affairs was directed less at supporting the republic than at preventing it from falling into socialist revolution; and the NKVD liquidated the Trotskyites in Spain as ruthlessly as it did those in Russia.

Under such circumstances the anti-imperialist and antifascist traditions of the Party came to appear perilous to the Soviet Party-state, which was then in the process of consolidation through purge. Yet these traditions had been the strident staple of Party rhetoric ever since 1928, when Stalin inaugurated the militant Leftist policy of "class against class" in international affairs as the pendant to his class warfare at home. This rhetoric, moreover, corresponded to the deeper sentiments of many members of the Party, who remained, after all, emotionally on the Left. A literal interpretation of the Popular Front as antifascist revolutionism appealed not only to residual Trotskyites within the Party; it was also voiced by such figures as Bukharin and Marshal Tukhachevskii. On this issue the internal Soviet division between "Right" and "Left" ceased to hold. In an international crisis such unthinking Leftist sentiment within the Party might push the Soviet state towards dangerous foreign entanglements. It would be better, therefore, to eliminate such tendencies before the world situation got any worse, and to have only one center of authority in foreign as in domestic matters—as well as new men unencumbered by outmoded Leftist slogans to obey this authority. It is probably no accident that the purge finally began in the internationally pivotal summer of 1936.

* * *

Still, the coup d'état had to take off from a specific issue, namely, the persistence of inadequately punished opposition within the Party; this was a matter that had not ceased to fester in Stalin's mind since the Riutin affair in 1932 (and perhaps since the creation of a small Trotskyite group the same year). Another reason why Stalin may have returned to the matter at this time is that Hitler had already given an example of a successful blood purge when, in June 1934, he liquidated Ernst Roehm and his SA troops in the Night of the Long Knives. According to a well-placed NKVD defector, Stalin commented on this action with admiration in a Politburo meeting. Stalin also asserted that Hitler's coup had moved Nazism from its revolutionary to its state-building phase, and he declared that it was time the Soviet Revolution made the same transition.[30] So to cap off the process of Soviet state-building, Stalin once again moved to break the Party taboo against the death penalty within its ranks.

Stalin chose as his first victims Zinoviev and Kamenev, the most vulnerable of the old oppositionists. These two had already been expelled from the Party and had recanted; indeed, they had been in and out of jail so many times that they were thoroughly discredited as political figures. The formula for the trial—confessions leading to death sentences—went back to the Shakhty affair (and indeed to the trial of the Socialist Revolutionaries in 1922); even the prosecutor, Andrei Vyshinskii, was the same. So in August 1936 Stalin put Zinoviev, Kamenev, and fourteen others in the dock and accused them of having formed a "Trotskyite-Zinovievite terrorist center" that murdered Kirov and conspired to assassinate Stalin and most of the Politburo, all with the alleged purpose of restoring capitalism with the aid of German and Japanese fascists.

The trial, however, was botched. It seems that Yagoda, the head of the NKVD and the trial's organizer, carried out his distasteful orders with reluctance. Evidence concerning meetings in the West between oppositionists and Trotsky's son was palpably false, and this was immediately pointed out in the Western press. Although the "guilty" of course confessed and were duly condemned to death, the pedagogical effect of the performance was nonetheless spoiled. Stalin therefore proceeded to create a more submisive NKVD to organize new trials. On September 25 he and Zhdanov, while on vacation at Sochi on the Black Sea, sent a telegram to the Politburo saying it was urgent to replace Yagoda with a member of Stalin's personal secretariat, Nikolai Ezhov. The reason they gave for this change was that the political police was "four years behind" in "unmasking the Trotskyite-Zinovievite bloc"—a time span that clearly took matters back to the Riutin affair in 1932. It is this action that turned the purge into a coup d'état. The coup then unfolded with stunning rapidity between the September 1936 trial of Zinoviev and Kamenev and the execution of the Soviet marshals in June 1937.

The first step was to bring the NKVD under Stalin's direct control. That agency, of course, had never been an independent body, but under a succession of directors, from Dzerzhinskii to Yagoda, it had enjoyed a relative professional autonomy and sense of corporate identity. This situation ended with Ezhov's appointment: The "organs," as the security apparatus was called, grew greatly in size, and their chief mission now was to serve as Stalin's weapon against the Party. Stalin thus expanded his sphere of personal control from the Party, which he had conquered in the 1920s, to the government, which he had taken over in 1930, to the universal monitoring system, the political police.

The second step was to repair the damage done by the August 1936 trial. This was done by staging new, foolproof trials of remaining old oppositionists. Many of the defendants, including the former Leftist Iurii Piatakov as well as Bukharin and Rykov, had been implicated in testimony at the first trial. But it seems there was again resistance within the Central Committee, where these three sat, to a clean sweep of old oppositionists. This attitude expressed both a concern for the Party's stability and a sense of corporate identity its cadres had by now acquired. The result was a compromise: Stalin backed off from accusing the two Rightists, but in January 1937 he tried and condemned to death Piatakov and fifteen other members of a "Trotskyite Center" on the usual accusations, from assassinating Kirov to restoring capitalism with fascist connivance.

At the same time a new crime was charged: industrial wrecking, which meant that through Piatakov, who had been the brains of Soviet industrialization, the whole managerial corps of the country was threatened. But this brought Stalin into conflict with some of his own closest supporters, most notably Piatakov's superior, Ordzhonikidze, who apparently objected that this extension of the purge imperiled the whole system. This conflict led to a violet quarrel and Ordzhonikidze's suicide (or murder?) in January of 1937. And this event convinced Stalin that the coup had to go all the way and clean out every potential pocket of resistance to his absolute, centralized rule.

The coup culminated in a protracted meeting of the Central Committee in February–March 1937.[31] In stormy debates, Stalin, Ezhov, and Molotov faced down the advocates of moderation, most of whom were apparently connected with the new heavy industry, and obtained at last the heads of Bukharin and Rykov, who were arrested during the session (their erstwhile colleague, Tomskii, had committed suicide after being implicated in the August 1936 trial). In March of 1938, Bukharin, Rykov, and the deposed NKVD chief Yagoda, together with eighteen others, were tried for the usual universal conspiracy as an "Anti-Soviet Bloc of Rights and Trotskyites." Although this was the most famous of the trials—given the personalities of the defendants—by the time it occurred it was an epilogue rather than the centerpiece of the coup.

The real culmination of the coup came in June of 1937. After Stalin had unleashed the NKVD on the Party between the August 1936 trial and the February–March plenum, there remained only one institution that might possibly act against him: the army. Indeed, his attack on the Party and the industrial managers for the first time gave the armed forces a possible motive for deposing a leader who they might well feel now endangered the whole system—as Ordzhonikidze had felt earlier—and at a time when the international situation was heating up. Even a less suspicious person than Stalin would have reason to protect himself on his military flank. The army, moreover, though covered by the *nomenklatura* system, possessed, like the political police, a tradition of relative autonomy and a professional esprit de corps going back to the Civil War. In addition, it was led by a number of living heroes of that epic, the most prominent of whom was Marshal Tukhachevskii.

Given the potential power of this group, Stalin wasted no time in contriving a show trial for these (to him) potentially dangerous men, who might well not have cooperated anyway in such a farce. Tukhachevskii and six other marshals and generals were summarily tried in camera and immediately shot. The public learned about this coup only when the group's "treason" was revealed in a terse public announcement. But why did these well-armed men submit so easily? The question is especially pertinent in view of the fact that they had some warning of what was coming; for Stalin had demoted a number of them in the previous weeks, a piecemeal degradation they had seen him practice on Piatakov, Yagoda, and so many others. The only answer can be that they were not just military heroes, but also— indeed, above all—Party men, and like their erstwhile commander Trotsky, Piatakov, and so many others, they knew that no one could be right against the Party. So the last area of semiautonomy in the system, the military, was suppressed without it emitting so much as a whimper.

All power in the Soviet Union now culminated in a single man: Stalin had become "dictator" in the perverted modern meaning of that venerable Roman and republican word. The February–March Central Committee plenum and the trial of senior military officers had effectively broken the back of all actual or potential resistance to Stalin. The coup had now been completed at the highest levels; from this time and until Stalin's death the vestiges of Party constitution- alism ceased to operate. The way was thus open for the coup-in- depth, that great sweep of personnel, at all levels of the Party, towards which Stalin had been groping since 1932. Every effort to thwart this desire—whether it was Kirov's, Yagoda's, Kuibyshev's, or Ordzhoni- kidze's—had only succeeded in stoking Stalin's passion. After March 1937, therefore, and until the end of 1938, the Great Terror of the *Ezhovshchina* unfolded without let or hindrance.

Stalin oversaw the operation at the highest level and often signed, together with other Politburo members, lists of people to be elimi- nated. But Ezhov and his NKVD staff actually carried out the purge, and they enjoyed pretty much carte blanche in determining its mo- mentum and extent. Very soon the operation acquired a dynamic of its own and became a self-propelling mechanism: Each forced confession led to the incrimination of new "conspirators" whose confessions in turn incriminated still others, and so on in an exponential progression. As those accused in this manner were arrested in their various places of work some of their remaining colleagues would denounce others in order to demonstrate their own vigilance or to move into their col- leagues' jobs. Thus new arrests led to new confessions and then to new denunciations in ever widening circles of panic fear. And after this process had gone on for more than a year, it acquired a momen- tum that even Stalin found difficult to brake.

Between March 1937 and early 1939, the coup-in-depth engulfed the overwhelming majority of Central Committee members, almost all former delegates to the Congress of Victors in 1934, the upper echelons of the officer corps, and most provincial and local Party secretaries, together with their staffs and very often their families. The victims either were shot without public trial or disappeared into the Gulag. And since the Party now directly managed all sections of society—from the economy and the ministries to the arts—a major part of the country's professional cadres also disappeared. Thus it turned out that by 1939 Stalin had in effect given himself a new Party and a new corps of cadres in every field of national activity. This consolidation of the system was the ultimate rationale of the Great Purge, however irrational it was otherwise. Stalin now had the personnel of the socialism he had built.

The outstanding characteristic of this new revolution was that almost all of the new men brought to the fore after 1937 were products of the system created after 1930. There were now very few pre-Stalin holdovers, or "former people"—whether old bourgeois, Old Bolsheviks (that is, Party members since before the Revolution), old oppositionists, or old militant Leftists—left in positions of responsibility. The new cadres were the upwardly mobile of the Second Revolution, the *vydvizhentsy* of the Five-Year Plans, people who had little adult memory of the world that existed before built socialism, people who were formed and educated under the new system, pupils of the cultural world of dialectical materialism and socialist realism, devoted followers of the great Leader, people who owed everything to the architect of all this, Comrade Stalin. And these were the people who, after their Leader departed this world, would manage the system until it crumbled in the late 1980s.

All of these people were quite directly the beneficiaries of the purges, as another glance at the continuing ascension of Nikita Khrushchev reveals.[32] Though he owed the beginning of his career at the center to Kaganovich, who first brought him from Kiev to Moscow, once in the capital Khrushchev owed his subsequent rise within the Party directly to Stalin. After becoming Moscow Party chairman in 1934, he functioned essentially as Stalin's deputy for the administration of the city, which obviously was not governed in the same way that other urban centers were. He also supported the Boss at the February–March 1937 plenum that launched the *Ezhovshchina*, and he later organized street demonstrations against the crimes of Marshal Tukh-achevskii.

But Khrushchev's grand career began only in 1938 and as a result of the extraordinary purge in Ukraine. The Ukrainian Party had always been a semiautonomous fief, almost a principality, within the All-Union Communist system, somewhat like the army. Although Ukraine had in fact been conquered by the Bolsheviks, and its government—whose first leader was Piatakov—had been imposed by the Party, in time the local apparat became responsive to Ukrainian national sentiment and interests. Moscow therefore periodically dispatched new personnel to bring things back under the center's control, yet after each such occasion Ukraine relapsed into its old errors. In the twenties Kaganovich was such a satrap; in the thirties it was Pavel Postyshev who played that role. Although he was a ruthless centralizer, Postyshev nonetheless spoke for moderating the purge at the February–March 1937 plenum. And this was his undoing, as well as the undoing of the whole Ukrainian Party and government.

Khrushchev, Molotov, Ezhov, and a trainload of NKVD troops were dispatched to Kiev to prune the local apparat, but the Ukrainian leadership refused to cooperate. Moscow therefore decided on a clean sweep of all Ukrainian structures: By 1938 the Party and state apparats of Ukraine at all levels, as well as the cultural elite, had been replaced not once but twice or thrice. In January of that year Khrushchev was appointed first secretary of the "Ukrainian" Party, with the mission of building an entirely new structure. At the same time, he was elected to Postyshev's old seat as a candidate member of the Politburo, and the next year he became a full member. He thus became a leader of the second, younger Stalinist group, which also included Zhdanov, the cultural tsar since 1934, and Lavrentii Beria, the future police tsar.

But behind this group, and as a result of its efforts in carrying out the Boss's behests, there was still another Stalinist generation on the rise after 1937. Khrushchev needed new men for his new Ukrainian Party, and one of them was Leonid Brezhnev.[33] Like Khrushchev, Brezhnev came from a Great Russian family that had been transplanted to Ukraine at the end of the Old Regime to work in industry. Born in 1906, Brezhnev was the son of a worker in the steel town of Kamenskoe on the Dnieper River. An apolitical adolescent at the time of the Revolution and the Civil War, he received something of a

secondary education in the local gymnasium. By the beginning of the
NEP the local steel mill where his family had worked had closed. He
moved back to the family's province of origin in Russia, Kursk, where
in 1923, at age seventeen, he joined the Komsomol and entered a
vocational school to become a surveyor. After occupying a number of
posts in rural Russia, by 1931 he had returned to Kamenskoe, where
he studied at the newly founded Metallurgical Institute while working nights at the reopened steel plant, now named for Dzerzhinskii. In
short, he was one of Stalin's *vydvizhentsy* and an aspiring member of
the new Soviet worker intelligentsia. At the same time, now twenty-
five years of age, he entered the Party and was put in charge of the
Komsomol organization of his Institute. In those days Party activists in
Ukraine were regularly sent to the villages to impose collectivization,
and in all probability Brezhnev was among them.

Having graduated from the Institute as an engineer in 1934, Brezhnev was made director of the local vocational school in 1936. Then, in
1937, the purge swept through Ukraine. In May of that year Brezhnev
moved into the vacant job of vice chairman of the city soviet of what
had recently been rebaptized Dneprodzerzhinsk. The next year the
new Ukrainian First Secretary, Khrushchev, needed sixteen hundred
Party members to fill empty posts in the republic's apparat, so Brezhnev was named head of the Ideology Department in the provincial
Party committee of the much larger city of Dnepropetrovsk. In this
post his responsibility was to root out all manifestations of the
Trotskyite-Bukharinite-fascist conspiracy and, of course, any elements of "Ukrainian bourgeois nationalism." Thus a wholly Stalinist
generation emerged from the purges to continue the work of the
dwindling number of older Stalinists, from the aged cohort of Molotov
to that of the younger Khrushchev, all of whose careers antedated the
Great Leap.

As one authority put it, this new group of junior Stalinists may
appropriately be called the "Brezhnev generation."[34] In it we also
find Andrei Gromyko, Aleksei Kosygin, Mikhail Suslov, Iurii
Andropov, and Konstantin Chernenko—that is, the men who would
rule Russia for some thirty years after Khrushchev and until the advent of Gorbachev. The humble origins and spectacular rise of this
group have been described as a triumph of upward social mobility,
and, as everyone knows, upward mobility is a democratic phenomenon. Since Stalin's "cultural revolution" from below can also be given

a democratic aura, his revolutionary modernization comes out looking progressive overall. Thus the Soviet experience has been summed up as "terror, progress, and social mobility."[35] And, indeed, there was a rough social democracy involved in the rise of all those sons of toil who made it to the top of the *nomenklatura* as a result of Stalin's policies, and who stayed there for thirty stagnant years. But this cheery assessment rests on a very partial view of the 1930s, one that sees only Stalin's efforts at industrialization, urbanization, and education, and that virtually ignores the collectivization and mass purging, as well as the adulteration of culture, that the Soviet manner of modernization necessarily entailed. That variant of the modernization theory that focuses on social mobility thus comes down to another attempt at solving the Stalin problem. By isolating one quite real aspect of the record, *vydvizhenie*, and amputating all the rest, we get a sanitized Stalin who fits comfortably into a canon of progress. But this stratagem does not work, for the rise of the Brezhnev generation coincides far too uncomfortably with the great downward mobility of the Gulag.

The twenty-five years after 1929 were also the great age of the Soviet labor camp system, still another product of collectivization and the purges. Ever since Solzhenitsyn's *Gulag Archipelago*, it has been common knowledge that the concentration camp system began not under Stalin but under Lenin in 1918 with various outposts along the White Sea. The system continued to grow during the twenties, receiving in particular many religious dissenters. But it became a gigantic operation only with the deportation of the kulaks after 1930. At the same time, it acquired major economic significance as forced labor was used to develop natural resources—from timber and coal to diamonds and gold—in inhospitable northern and other Siberian regions, where wage labor was considered too expensive by the regime. In addition, the inmates of the camps, the *zeks*, were employed on some of Stalin's pet projects, such as the White Sea or Moscow-Volga canals. *Zeks* could even be found working behind barbed wire on certain projects right in Moscow. The Gulag system, moreover, was a regular part of the Plan from 1930 onward.

The Gulag grew constantly throughout the Stalin years. Its second great levy, of course, was furnished by the purges. A third came from the "bougeois nationalist" elements in the western territories annexed in 1939–1940. A fourth infusion resulted from the Second

World War itself: laggard soldiers, military personnel who had been critical of the regime (Solzhenitsyn is only the most famous case), and a number of minority nationalities. A fifth came from the victory in war: Soviets who had collaborated with the enemy in occupied territories or who had been taken prisoner and hence were classified as deserters. Other waves followed in the postwar years, for mortality rates were high in the camps, and new recruits were constantly needed.

How many *zeks* were there in the camps? How many died there? How many were executed during the purges? Firm figures are as impossible to come by in these areas as are Soviet economic growth rates during the same period. There were obviously no official data on the subject at the time, and the now open Soviet archives have so far only been sampled. Thus the estimates that we have were derived from the accounts of former camp inmates and extrapolations from census figures. And both of these sources are sufficiently imprecise as to leave considerable latitude for legitimate debate and disagreement—to which must be added a subliminal political tendency to argue the figures up or down depending on one's evaluation of the Soviet regime overall.

Nonetheless, over the decades a fair consensus has emerged as to the order of magnitude involved. In the 1930s the outside world by and large knew nothing about the scope of the purges or the existence of the Gulag. After the Second World War, when the first accounts by *zeks* appeared in the West,[36] it was for a long time a delicate matter to give them credence, because to do so implied equating the Soviet Union with Nazi Germany. It was only after Khrushchev hinted at the sweep of the purges in his "secret speech" of 1956, and then acknowledged the existence of the camps by authorizing the publication of Solzhenitsyn's *One Day in the Life of Ivan Denisovich* in 1962, that it was no longer possible for anyone to deny the basic facts. The debate then came to turn on the extent of the purges and the size of the Gulag. Yet it was only after 1968, with Robert Conquest's *The Great Terror* (1968) and especially Solzhenitsyn's *The Gulag Archipelago* (1973–1975), that it became indisputable that both phenomena were not incidental but central. Even so, as late as the 1980s there continued to be significant foot-dragging in the West and renewed assertions that the whole matter of Soviet terror had been vastly overblown. Indeed, one of the more extreme revisionists advanced the absurd claim that the purges had only killed "thousands" and imprisoned "many thousands."[37]

With *glasnost* and the collapse of the Soviet regime the opinion of Russian scholars and of political figures close to the subject essentially confirmed the gloomier Western estimates. Nonetheless, it is still difficult, and may be forever impossible, to give firm and precise figures. The initial difficulty in giving a realistic estimate of the scale of the purges lies in defining what one considers a purge loss.

First, there is the clear-cut category of executions. These were often summarily ordered by special councils, special tribunals, and wholly extra-legal "troikas" composed of the local Party First Secretary, an NKVD officer, and the district prosecutor. In addition, there were mass executions involving thousands of victims, such as the Katyn Forest massacre of Polish officers in 1940 or the slaughter of Soviet civilians at Kuropaty near Minsk in 1939.

Second, there is the more elastic category of deaths from the conditions in prison and camps, and the related matter of the number of those incarcerated in both institutions. There were different levels of punishment, ranging from hard-labor camps in the arctic or the Kolyma valley (which were often engaged in mining or cutting lumber for the Plan), to the deportation to Central Asia of whole nationalities, such as the Chechen-Ingush, to the milder forms of exile to unenclosed "settlements" in Siberia that were at times inflicted on kulaks. There is also the question of the longevity, and consequently of the inmate turnover, of the camp population—and its variations from year to year. Pending serious examination of what archival evidence remains of the camp system, our most telling testimony about its nature is literary, such as Solzhenitsyn's *Gulag* or Varlam Shalamov's *Tales of the Kolyma*. There are no physical remains of the Gulag, or camps that have been preserved as memorials to the dead. The entire system was bulldozed into the ground under Khrushchev.

Finally, there is the still more difficult question of the deficit in births arising as a byproduct of deaths due to executions and the camp system. And this question raises the matter of the demographic pool from which the purged population was drawn. The census of 1937, the first since 1926, revealed a deficit from anticipated population growth of six million, a shortfall obviously caused by the collectivization and the purges. In response, Stalin suppressed the census, had the census takers shot, and ordered a new census made in 1939 which yielded more "satisfactory" but clearly falsified results. Even though the 1937 census has now been published, the task of reconstructing the demographic history of the period remains a difficult one.

Yet despite the tangled and inadequate nature of this body of evidence, the picture that emerges of the Stalin era in Russia is the grimmest of any period or country in this century. In global terms, the demographic deficit for the years 1926–1939 is probably fifteen million, mostly in the villages. The demographic deficit for the years 1939–1950 (a period which includes the parallel catastrophe of the Second World War) is probably fifty-five million, one-half of it a shortfall in births and one-half an excess of deaths. In computing the total loss in population one must also include one or two million émigrés during the war.

To turn to actual deaths in the camps, Conquest gives the figure of eight million *zeks* as of 1938; taking this as the average camp population for each of the years between 1936 and 1950, and assuming that at least 10 percent of the camp population died each year, he estimates that there was a total of some twelve million deaths in this period. To this must be added around a million executions at the height of the Terror in 1937–1939. Finally, if we add the lower estimate for the victims of collectivization, six million, we get a grand total approaching twenty million deaths from political causes for all of Stalin's reign. Economist Alec Nove, in his more cautious computations, arrives at comparable estimations of the cost of Stalinism. And the figure of twenty million is now the most widely accepted in Russia.[38]

This figure is twice the number of all losses in the First World War, and approximately the same as the Soviet losses in the Second World War. As such it is the largest single harvest of terror in history. And to this human horror must be added the material fact that the Gulag was a monumentally wasteful economic enterprise, even worse than collectivization: The eight million *zeks* of 1938 represented 9 percent of the Soviet adult population.

It was in this peak year of the Gulag, 1938, that the dangers of the terror began to become apparent to the regime. Accordingly, Ezhov was given a deputy, Lavrentii Beria, and the purge was slowed down. In particular, Beria cushioned the wastefulness of the Gulag by introducing the institution of the *sharashka*, or elite camp, where highly qualified personnel worked on research projects for the military. Ezhov was soon moved to the Commissariat of Water Transport, and then disappeared the following year when Beria took over completely. There was never any trial, or even public condemnation, of Ezhov, but the change of NKVD chiefs was a signal that the Great Terror was over.

This does not mean, however, that all terror ceased. Rather, under Beria it was routinized, along with the Gulag, as an integral part of the system. Before 1936 the Soviet Union had been a society with a lurking police threat, but it had not been a police state in the sense of a ubiquitous police presence. Nor had it been a thoroughly terrorized society, which is one of the reasons why Stalin could get away with the purges: The Party and the population simply could not believe that anything like the *Ezhovshchina* was possible, and so they were taken completely unaware. After 1937, however, the Soviet Union was a terrorized police state. Although no publicity was given to the full power of the NKVD, and the Gulag was not mentioned at all, everyone was aware of the role of these institutions and so behaved with appropriate caution. The country had been taught a mighty lesson, and from this time onward the Soviet Union was ruled in large measure by fear.

THE CUNNING OF UNREASON

So when we survey the whole scene of Stalinist purge and consolidation—from the nationalization of culture to the show trials, from the replacement of Party cadres and the coup against Ukraine to the Siberian camps—what plausible generalizations can be made about the deeper causes of this upheaval? And, again, what were the relative roles of Stalin the individual and of the system's overall dynamics in this process?

Although Stalin was clearly the initiator of each event in the upheaval, this does not mean that he was the *diabolus ex machina* of the drama, an agent external to the system who deflected it from its natural course. Nor were there signs before 1937 that he was losing control either of himself or of the situation. Only in 1937–1938 did his suspiciousness seem to cross the border into the pathological, as in his public declarations that no one could be trusted, or that those most zealous in unmasking enemies of the people might in fact be only covering up their own treason. Yet even in this paroxysm of suspicion he never attacked the hard core of long-time stalwarts at the top of the Party who were necessary to the carrying out of his coup against the Party as a whole. His old Politburo cronies, Molotov, Kaganovich, and Voroshilov, or, at the next level, newer men like Zhdanov, Khrushchev, or Beria, seem to have had little to fear.[39] The only figures in this top group whom Stalin touched were men who actively resisted the coup, such as Ordzhonikidze, or possibly the head of Gosplan, Valerian Kuibyshev, whose death in 1935 was suspiciously convenient. In 1938, however, Stalin approached the threshold of real danger to his own command structure when he purged five second-rank Politburo members, principally in connection with the Ukrainian matter. This step, in conjunction with the runaway decimations among industrial managers and the military, at last caused him to turn back, perhaps prodded by his chief lieutenants, and to stabilize the terror by replacing Ezhov with Beria.

Moreover, by this time the coup had achieved its political objectives. For, to repeat, there were political objectives that made perverse sense in the surreal world the Soviet Union had now become. The overall objective has already been mentioned, namely, to give the Party the personnel of the socialism it had built. To be sure, the vast majority of the purge victims—from Ordzhonikidze and Piatakov to innumerable local Party secretaries and members of the officer corps—were loyal Stalinists who would have continued to serve the Leader and his policies indefinitely. To replace them en masse was not only unnecessary to make the system function better in practical terms, it was indeed downright harmful, especially in view of the looming possibility of war. But all these men, despite years of indoctrination, were not yet passive cogs of the system; they had supported it out of conviction as it was being built, and they retained a vestigial capacity for critical thought and talking back—the example of Postyshev is a case in point. In short, they were not yet the "new Soviet men" that the mature system required and that the nationalization of culture had been intended to produce. Stalin, after all, put the finishing touches on the *Short Course* at the same time he put Bukharin in the dock.

And this circumstance explains another political objective of the purge: In cases where the power of the new culture proved insufficient, it would be backed up by institutionalized terror and rule through fear. But to explain this tactic we do not need to have recourse to the unique nature of Sovietism or, still less, to Stalin's psyche. A deliberate policy of social control by terror has been all too frequently a "rational" goal in twentieth-century politics. The Soviet system simply carried this to its ultimate extreme.

A more uniquely Soviet aspect of the Great Terror is revealed by two mysteries in the manner of its unfolding. The first is that all of the victims of the purge were required to confess to crimes that they had not committed and that their NKVD interrogators knew they had not committed. The second is that none of the indubitably sane people at any level of the system attempted to resist the whole fantastic charade.

There is no mystery as to how people were made to confess: They either succumbed to torture or to threats against their families. Nor is there any mystery as to why the regime used these means to bring the accused in the three show trials to repeat their confessions in public. These confessions were necessary to educate the population about the universal plot of traitors and wreckers, and so to stimulate a national campaign of vigilance. Much more intriguing and important is the fact that many tens, and probably hundreds, of thousands of "enemies" were made to sign confessions behind the closed doors of NKVD prisons, confessions that were never made public and whose authors were quietly shot or shipped off to the Gulag. Untold man-hours were expended on activity without pedagogical value for the population, when the NKVD could have forged the documents or simply shot these "enemies" without a confession.

The mystery of this apparent absurdity may be clarified by a comparison with the practices of the Nazis, who had no need of recantations but simply crushed their enemies by brute force. Both the Soviet and the Nazi regimes in fact rested on force, but each applied it quite differently. The Nazi concentration camps were by and large for non-Germans, and the regime's aggression was directed against other nations. Soviet camps were above all for Soviet citizens, and the regime made war first of all against domestic "class enemies." The Nazis' ideology was a relatively simple ideology of will and force; therefore they could openly proclaim their aggressive and punitive intentions. The Soviets' more complex ideology made ample allowance for the violence of class struggle but nonetheless formally subordinated this to the promotion of rational progress and humanity; therefore they could not publicly admit that their rule rested basically on force. It was thus necessary for the Soviets to make their "enemies" confess to criminal actions and thereby recognize their elimination as just and deserved. By the same token, the motivation of these enemies was viciously debased. Nazi camps did not bother with confessions.

This was the message of Vyshinskii's rhetoric against "mad dogs" in the show trials, and of the incessant warnings of the Soviet press against the great plot to "restore capitalism." But the same language was used by the NKVD's interrogators behind closed doors, where both they and their victims knew it was fraudulent. The absurdity of this exercise, however, should not lead us to dismiss it as meaningless. Its political purpose was to compromise the population in the ideological aims of the regime.[40] So the victims of the Second Revolution were forced to become accomplices in their own undoing, thereby both absolving the regime of its crimes and celebrating the victory of its policies. And, although this charade was not made public, it became generally known within the Party and among the Soviet elite that such confirmation of the great plot's existence was required of all. People did not have to believe in the plot, but they did have to pretend they believed.

This phenomenon, moreover, is related to other Soviet practices. Its most general form is the institution of "self-criticism," a ritual whereby delinquent comrades were made to confess their errors and to subscribe to the "correct" line before a Party meeting. Or it is similar to village meetings during collectivization, when peasants had to denounce the "kulak danger" as if such a danger really existed for the peasantry. Finally, the purge confession is analogous to the practice of holding regular and meaningless elections under the Stalin Constitution, elections in which 99 percent of the population voted for the "list of Party and non-Party candidates." In terms of rational politics all of this is senseless. But in the ideocratic world of built socialism, it made an odd sort of sense. After 1937 Stalin may have been somewhat mad—the system, however, most certainly was.

The second major mystery of the purges is why no one in the Party attempted to resist. There had, of course, been resistance to the Stalin revolution outside the Party: The so-called kulaks had fought back, but more in despair than out of any hope of victory; and workers had often assassinated Stakhanovites as, in effect, "scabs" who forced work norms upwards. But in a decade of terror from above, the only act of violence against a leader of the regime was Nikolaev's assassination of Kirov. The helplessness of the population at large, however, is easily explained by the fact that the regime's monopoly of military and police power was such that no elements in society stood a chance against it. And in this the Russian case is not unique: It was equally impossible in other totalitarian states to organize resistance. What is less understandable is why the Party, the police, and the military, each having access to means of struggle, submitted so meekly and indeed cooperated in their own destruction.

The reason is that they were paralyzed by the nature of the system and by the momentum it had acquired over the years. They were all prisoners of the logic that Piatakov, echoing Trotsky, boasted was his: "If the Party demands it . . . I will see black where I thought I saw white . . . because for me there is no life outside the Party." By the late 1930s this mentality had deprived them of all capacity to organize or act collectively. To this must be added the fact that these same Party, police, and military personnel had for years engaged in systematic violence against the population and therefore were without moral defense for objecting when violence was turned against them.

Moreover, they had all condoned a succession of political purges that had progressively narrowed the range of dissent to zero. First the monarchists and liberals had been proscribed, then the Mensheviks and SRs, and then the Trotskyites and Bukharinites; and with the disappearance of each group, it became easier to eliminate the next. Thus at the end of the process there was no reason why Stalinist Bolsheviks should not also be purged if the only remaining authority in the Party, the Leader, declared that they, too, had now become an "anti-Party" force. The purges therefore are the end point of the logic that began with Lenin's condemnation of all non-Bolshevik politics as "petty-bourgeois," that is, the politics of a class enemy fit only to be destroyed.

But this culmination does not mean that the security police had now replaced the Party as the heart of the system, as Stalin's heirs later asserted to explain why they failed to resist at the time.[41] Stalin now used the police to rule the Party, just as he had always used the Party to rule the country. But he did all of this as the embodiment of the Party, not as the mere head of the police. For the latter task he had the expendable Ezhov or the servile Beria. Stalin had to keep the Party supreme because it was the embodiment of the ideological purpose of the regime, and therefore the basis of its legitimacy.

Otherwise, why should he bother to write a chapter on dialectical materialism and force it on all the schools of the country? Such a country could not be delivered over to the unbridled control of the police as if it were the Paraguay of General Stroessner. It had been born, and therefore had to remain as long as it survived, an ideocratic partocracy.

The purges and the institutionalization of terror thus completed the Party's pulverization of civil society and the near-atomization of the population. Vis-à-vis the Party-state there now existed only a palid shadow society and a mass of isolated individuals afraid to associate among themselves and constrained even from thinking of doing so by the new culture of socialism triumphant. Mandelshtam was one of the first to describe this new world: "We exist in a land grown unreal and strange, / Ten steps away no one hears the talk we exchange."

The population adapted to this new situation by developing a two-tiered consciousness, or a permanently schizophrenic vision. This was particularly true of the intelligentsia, though the workers were also affected, while the peasants were probably touched least of all. In general terms, the young accepted the myths of the regime at face value, and their elders usually would not take the risk of disabusing them. As people grew older, however, they realized more fully the gap between the myth and the reality, yet they knew that this could not be acknowledged openly. So as public, social persons they subscribed to the official view of the world, spoke its wooden language, and even half-believed it. But as private, individual persons they used normal logic and human language, while never wholly repudiating the official worldview. It was only at the price of this psychological compartmentalization or, in Orwell's term, doublethink that personal sanity could be preserved amidst a system now at the triumphant pinnacle of delirium.

Nonetheless, this very triumph had created the conditions for the system's ultimate undoing. After the purges, the gap between reality and the ideal was even greater than it had been when socialism was first achieved in the mid-decade. This gap could now be bridged only by permanent terror in the service of a surreal conspiracy theory. Concomitantly, the ideocratic legitimacy of the Party had been wholly absorbed into the person of the Leader. The whole edifice was a unique and extraordinary achievement. But it was also a very fragile one.

*　　*　　*

For the reduction of the ideological purpose of the regime to these crude and simple expressions was beginning to destroy the basis on which the regime rested. The ultimate consequence of the extraordinary transformations of high Stalinism was that their source, the Socialist Myth, had now been transformed into the Soviet Lie, to use a term that was first brought to public attention by Solzhenitsyn but that had long been current throughout Eastern Europe. For Soviet socialism as actually realized was a fraud in terms of the Myth's own standards. So long as the living embodiment of the Myth-Lie remained in power, the whole astounding structure would hold together. But his very triumph as Leader would also leave an inordinately heavy bill for his Party and, even more, for his people to pay over the ensuing decades.

Part III
THE EMPIRE

8

THE FORTUNES OF WAR

1939–1953

*And when war broke out, its real horrors, the real danger and the threat
of real death were a blessing compared with the inhuman reign of fiction;
they brought relief, because they limited the power of the evil spell cast by
the dead letter [of ideology].*

*People, not only . . . in the camps, but decidedly everyone, in the rear
and at the front, breathed more freely, from the depth of their lungs, and
enthusiastically, with a feeling of true happiness threw themselves into the
brazier of the terrible struggle, mortal and yet liberating.*

*The war was a special link in the chain of the revolutionary decades.
It marked the end of the action of the causes arising directly from the
nature of the [October] overturn.*

—*Boris Pasternak,* Doctor Zhivago

At the outbreak of war in 1939 the Soviet Union was only one of seven
major powers; at the end of the war in 1945 she was one of the world's
two superpowers. Before the war she had no friends or allies, and was
indeed a pariah in international affairs; after the war she was the
leader of a Eurasian "socialist camp" arrayed against the "imperialist"
forces led by the United States. Before the war the Soviet system had
appeared as a rather poor bet for longevity because of the great crisis
of the purges; after the war this system appeared as the great alternative model to capitalism because it could now be credited with the
victory over fascism. The First World War had brought Communism
into being; the Second World War made Communism a genuine global
force and launched it on its grand career.

The Second World War thus changed the focus of Soviet history.
As Pasternak noted, it marked the end of the chain of causation
inaugurated by October and leading, through the vicissitudes of the

NEP and the Five-Year Plan, to Stalin's consolidation of the new order on the eve of hostilities. With the system built, the Soviet Union became an essentially conservative enterprise internally. But externally, victory in the war brought new opportunities for radicalism; so the focus of the Soviet enterprise moved to the international arena. For Sovietism, the era of the experiment was over; the era of the empire was about to begin.

The first fruit of external success was a great gain in internal viability. Before the war the regime's only legitimacy was its alleged mandate from the logic of history; after the war the regime derived a far more real legitimacy from its role as organizer of the national victory. It was only during the war that, for the first time, the regime and the people had a task and a purpose in common. Until then the regime had done things *to* the population; now the population and the regime did things together. To be sure, this new legitimacy would diminish as the war receded into history. Still, the bond it created gave the regime an additional forty-five years of life, something its virtues as a system alone probably would not have afforded it.

In the immediate postwar years, the Soviet Union went from one new success to another. The whole eastern half of the continent fell under its sway; and all of the region's "people's democracies" adopted their elder brother's socialist system, while a similar regime was created in North Korea. In 1949 Communism came to power in China, and there now existed a great Red bloc extending from the Elbe to the Pacific. At the same time, there were powerful Communist insurgencies in Vietnam, Malaya, and the Philippines. When Stalin celebrated his seventieth birthday in 1949 with greater pomp than ever before, he indeed appeared as the "father of the peoples" to about a third of humanity; and it seemed as if the worldwide triumph of Communism was at last possible, perhaps even imminent. The next year, with the outbreak of the Korean War, there were grounds for fear that Stalin, now protected by the atom bomb, might seek this triumph by military means.

In retrospect, of course, it is clear that during the years 1945–1953 Moscow's strength, as well as the cohesiveness of the Communist bloc, was greatly exaggerated by the outside world. Nonetheless, this period was in fact an awesome high-point of Communist power, a time when the movement seemed at last to have a chance of realizing the hopes that had brought it to power in October. And this success, like October itself, was due less to any social dynamic than to the fortunes of war, to the brute logic of military might and the contingency of events.

The war was also the supreme test of the merits of the system. Stalin and the Soviet leadership were well aware that their regime owed its existence to Russia's defeat in the First World War. As hope of international revolution faded, they also understood that their principal goal must be to prepare for and win the next such test, which both their ideology and their common sense told them was sure to come. Indeed, as we have seen, the building of socialism had quickly shaded into state building for international survival; in a less rational manner, the purges had also been intended to serve the purpose of state-consolidation for a military emergency. As of 1939, the great question was whether this jerry-built socialism would be any better than tsarism at holding the national fort.

Socialism obviously did hold the fort, and even did a great deal more than that. In the ensuing decades, therefore, Soviet leaders attributed this victory to the merits of their system, and so concluded that it required no fundamental change. Still, the question of the system's wartime performance will always remain a live one, for the Soviet Union almost lost the war before she at last began to win it. And this returns us to the more fundamental question: How much was this reversal of fortunes due to the system, and how much was it due to such factors as geography, Russian patriotism, or simply chance?

THE GREAT PATRIOTIC WAR

Stalin had never been sanguine about the system's capacity to compete in modern, mechanized warfare. Indeed, it was in part to create such capacity that he made his two revolutions from above. For he believed from the beginning of his career that the new Soviet Russia lacked the means to be a significant factor in international affairs; this is one reason why he inclined to the cautious policy of "socialism in one country." And in this he was right: The Revolution had been as much a disaster for Russia's status as a great power as for her economic development.

Stalin therefore saw his historical mission to be the restoration of Russia's great-power competitiveness through a regime of forced economic development. His socialism was in no way in contradiction with this ambition, for he held socialism to be a more effective means of economic development than capitalism. At the same time, he thought the militant revolutionism associated with Trotskyism had to be reined in because it could be dangerous to the security of the Communist state. It was only in the mid-1930s, and under the pressure of growing international crisis, that Stalin pulled all of these strands of thought together into a system that he would follow for the rest of his reign. Until then, Stalin had been as little concerned with international affairs as he had been with economic matters before 1928. By 1939, however, he had taken over the management of foreign policy, just as he would take over management of the war in 1941. Thus the last areas of national life came under his direct control. And so at this point, as Pasternak noted, Stalin finally closed the chain of causation begun in October.

In the immediate wake of October, the Bolsheviks thought that the only foreign policy they would need would be the promotion of international revolution.[1] When this policy failed as a means of defense at Brest-Litovsk, they had to settle down and organize a state. The international mission of this state, however, remained revolution; and by 1919 this mission had received institutional expression in the form of the Communist, or Third, International (Comintern), an organization that mirrored the centralized structures of the Bolshevik Party itself. The great adventures of this institution were the Polish War of 1920 and the hoped-for German revolution in Europe, and helping Chiang Kai-shek to build the Kuomintang in Asia. The European half of this offensive failed completely; the Asian half brought more to Chiang than to Communism.

The result was a "NEP" in international affairs. In 1922 the Soviet Union first entered into normal relations with a foreign power through the Rapallo Agreement with Germany; this pact established trade and clandestine military cooperation between the two "out" powers of Europe. The next year the Ruhr crisis produced the last possibility of revolution in Germany, but the Communists proved unable to exploit it. The Soviet Union, therefore, had to recognize that world capitalism had "stabilized" itself for an indefinite future.

From this time onward, as has often been remarked, the Soviet Union had a dual character in international affairs: It was both a state

among states and the center of an international revolutionary movement.[2] But since there were no prospects for actual revolution, it was
inevitable that the interests of the Soviet state should take precedence over those of the Comintern. Yet the continued existence of
this revolutionary movement compromised the Soviet state in its dealings with other states, thereby both hindering trade and creating diplomatic isolation. In 1926 Chiang Kai-shek crushed his Communist
allies; in 1927 Britain broke off diplomatic relations over Soviet support to British unions during the general strike, thus provoking the
"war scare" of that year. In short, as of 1928 the Comintern had only
compromised the security of the Soviet state without successfully
promoting revolution.

Stalin therefore abandoned the international NEP and embarked
on a policy of ultraleftism. He declared that the stabilization of capitalism was over and summoned the Communist movement, both at
home and abroad, to brace for crisis and struggle. This led to the most
bizarre, destructive, and abstractly ideological phase in the history of
Soviet foreign policy. Social democrats were declared to be the objective allies of fascism, and foreign Communist parties everywhere
were instructed to make the struggle against these "social fascists"
their first priority. This stance was in part a reflection of the old
Bolshevik belief that moderate socialists, such as the Mensheviks,
were more dangerous than outright reactionaries. It was even more a
projection into international affairs of the militant leftism of the First
Five-Year Plan. On both counts, however, this policy showed appalling ignorance of foreign conditions, and it would in fact do great harm
to the interests of the Soviet state.

For this was the period when the Great Depression created a new
sort of revolutionary situation in Germany. Throughout the twenties
European Communist parties everywhere had been politically insignificant; the first mass Communist Party now appeared in Germany.
But at the same time, Nazism also became a mass movement. The
new policy of the Comintern, however, pitted the German Party
against the Social Democrats—indeed the Party often found itself in
tactical alliance with the Nazis—in order to destroy the Weimar Republic. In the event that the Nazis came to power, or so the theory
went, they would not be able to maintain themselves for long, but
would instead radicalize the masses for Communism, as Kornilov had
done in Russia. Although it is difficult to believe that Stalin would

have actually wished an independent Communist regime to come to power in Germany, this seems to have been the rationale of his bizarre policy. But there is another possible explanation, namely, that his policy had no rationale, and that his ultraleftism was simply a mindless reflection of the "class struggle" he was then waging at home.

It has often been argued that Hitler's rise to power could have been avoided if the Communists had allied with the Socialists, and perhaps also with the center, to save the Republic.[3] In short, a German Popular Front could have changed the course of history, and Stalin's obtuseness alone prevented this. But more was involved than Stalin's shortsightedness. A Popular Front is a form of class collaboration of the sort that had always been anathema in the Leninist tradition. The brief period of Comintern moderation in the mid-twenties was an aberration in the Soviet tradition, and Stalin's ultraleftism after 1928 was a return to the Leninist norm. It would take the shock of Hitler's consolidation of power to drive home in Moscow the point that the Leninist tradition in this respect might be dangerous to the Leninist state.

Moreover, if a German Popular Front had come to power in 1933, it very probably would not have been able to govern. All Popular Fronts are unstable and transitory arrangements: because Communist parties are not constitutional parties, whereas socialist parties are, the two partners invariably come into conflict, and one or the other is forced out. Thus a German Popular Front in all likelihood would have lasted as long as the Communists mistakenly thought Hitler would— that is, just long enough to create a major crisis. Furthermore, the specter of Communists in, or even near to, power would have terrified the center and strengthened the Right, which, after all, could count on the army in a crisis. So a German Popular Front could well have ended in the Nazis coming to power anyway. It is simply not realistic to have expected that a Leninist Party would disinterestedly help save the "bourgeois" Republic from Nazism and then step aside and let the Socialists run things. This had been the Menshevik attitude towards the Provisional Government in 1917, and it should hardly be surprising that the Comintern did not adopt it in 1933. In any event, the Comintern's policy in Germany in fact helped Hitler come to power, and thus for the first time the Soviet Union was confronted with a genuine "imperialist" danger. And this shock at last sobered the Soviet leadership and taught it to subordinate its leftism to realpolitik.

The occasion for putting this change of approach into practice came with the next challenge of a European far Right to a "bourgeois" republic. As already noted,[4] the French Popular Front was formed in reaction to the events of February 6, 1934, and in 1935 the Comintern had adopted a policy of supporting such coalitions everywhere. The purpose of this new Comintern line, however, was not to seize power abroad but to further Soviet state security by supporting "bourgeois" governments willing to pursue a policy of "collective security" against fascism. Accordingly, the Soviet Union entered the League of Nations in 1934, signed a military alliance with France in 1935, and convened no congresses of the International after the latter year. And in 1936, once the French Popular Front had come to power under Léon Blum, the policy of the Communists was to moderate insofar as possible working-class militancy in order not to hinder French rearmament. But the clearest case in which a Popular Front was used in the interests of Soviet security to stifle foreign revolution was of course that of Spain, where the policy was even enforced by an imported NKVD.

From this time onward, the international revolutionary movement lost all autonomy and became a weapon of the Soviet Union in defense of its state interests. European (though not Asian) Communist parties were controlled directly by Moscow, and they obeyed orders as scrupulously as provincial Party committees in Russia did. But what is extraordinary is that they did this freely, without the pressure of punishment, and out of blind ideological commitment. Foreign Communists genuinely accepted the equation of their national working-class interests with those of the world's only workers' state, whose survival was the guarantee of their own ultimate victory. Thus the spell of the "cult" was worldwide and did not require coercion in order to flourish. And so the expanding international Communist movement of the 1930s was integrated into the state-building phase that the Russian Revolution had by then reached. No other power had at its disposal an international weapon of this sort.

But the Popular Front and collective security with bourgeois states were only one possible line of defense for the Soviet Union. The other was a policy of agreement with the state most dangerous to Russia —Germany—and Stalin clearly had this option in mind throughout the 1930s, even while his official policy was collective security. Like all other Bolshevik leaders, including Trotsky, Stalin had no moral or ideological preference for the democracies over the fascist powers. Both were "imperialists" mortally hostile to the Soviet Union, and someday, therefore, conflict with both was inevitable. The only question was which imperialist camp was more dangerous at any given moment; consequently, alignment with one or the other was no more than a question of expediency.

Within this ideological context Stalin's overriding concern was to avoid the supreme test of war for as long as possible. However, since he was realistically aware that war in Europe was unavoidable, his practical aim was to keep out of it if at all possible and, if he had to participate, to keep it off Soviet soil. For he was constantly apprehensive about the weaknesses of his new Soviet state: the deficiencies of its industry, the hatred of the peasantry for the kolkhoz, and the restiveness of the border nationalities.

Of the two possible diplomatic solutions to this problem, Stalin preferred alignment with Germany; because of her geographic proximity, she presented the greater danger, and the lesson of Brest-Litovsk had not been forgotten. Another reason was that peace with Germany would preclude a two-front conflict if Japan attacked Siberia. Finally, Stalin feared that the Anglo-French imperialists, wily and unreliable as they were, might try to maneuver the Soviet Union into conflict with Hitler. So, throughout the years of collective security, Stalin put out feelers to Berlin. And if nothing came of this, it was because Hitler, engrossed in consolidating his positions in the West, was not interested.

He became interested only in 1939, when he needed Soviet neutrality for his campaign against Poland. This quickly led to the famously infamous Molotov-Ribbentrop Pact of August 23 and the beginning of the Second World War a few days later. This pact has been denounced as Stalin's most cynical betrayal of the Left. It has also been defended as a reasonable measure of self-defense, one that was provoked, moreover, by the Western powers' pusillanimity at Munich: Stalin believed that Britain and France could not be trusted to fight for Poland, and that he would be left to confront Hitler alone. To accuse Stalin of cynicism in this matter, however, is naive: Ever since Brest-Litovsk it had been Communist doctrine that defense of the Soviet state automatically equalled defense of the world socialist movement. The real question is whether Stalin made a sensible decision in terms of the defense of the Soviet state; and the best answer is that he did not.

It is first of all not true that he was driven into a deal with Hitler by the Allies' deviousness. While Britain and France were sufficiently clumsy in negotiating with Moscow to make it possible to accuse them ex post facto of duplicity, in fact they had no choice but to seek Soviet help in pressuring Hitler. The real sticking point was Poland's understandable unwillingness to accept Soviet troops on her soil for fear they would never leave; hence the Allies could offer Stalin nothing he really wanted. He therefore used his negotiations with them to pressure concessions out of Hitler, who was now in a great hurry and thus in a poor bargaining position. And Hitler could, and did, offer Russia not only noninvolvement in the war but also a glacis of territory in Eastern Poland, the Baltic states, and ultimately Bessarabia and Finland—in other words, roughly the western frontiers of the old Russian Empire. So Stalin turned down the Allies and gave Hitler the green light to move into Poland on September 1.[5]

The wisdom of this decision can be judged only by comparing it with the alternatives. If Stalin had struck an agreement with Britain and France, would Hitler have plunged into Poland knowing he might then be attacked in the West and would soon confront the Soviet lines in the East? In 1939 Germany was not even remotely prepared for such a conflict on two fronts, and indeed Hitler thought he could bluff the Allies into backing down from their guarantees to Poland. Yet even if Stalin did not wish to join the Allies' side, he still did not have to join Hitler's. He could have remained neutral, and this in itself would have cast a great cloud over the viability of Hitler's Polish adventure. And if Hitler had plunged ahead anyway—which for this gambler is conceivable, though it would also have been foolhardy—and Stalin had confronted him, the correlation of forces would have been much more favorable to the Soviet Union in 1939 than in 1941.

If Stalin did not seriously consider these options, it was because he wished above all to stave off for as long as possible the evil day of entering the war, and also because he thought that war in the meantime would develop like the premechanized war of 1914–1918. That is, he expected a protracted stalemate in the West that would free him to rearm; after which he would be the arbiter of the situation. And this of course was his great miscalculation. For the effect of the August 1939 Pact was to free Hitler from a war on two fronts like the one that had defeated Imperial Germany, and this alone made possible Hitler's stunning expansion over the whole continent during the next two years. To be sure, Stalin was not the only player who failed to anticipate the sudden French collapse of June 1940 that was the key to Hitler's aggrandizement. Even so, it should have been apparent that the surest way to contain Hitler was the vise of the two-front option.[6]

Having thrown this trump away, Stalin was left with an increasingly weak hand. First, although before 1939 Russia had no common frontier with Germany, his new glacis deprived him of the buffer zone of an independent Poland that had previously made a German surprise attack impossible. Second, once Hitler had conquered the whole continent, its resources and population could be put to work for his war effort. Third, Stalin's agreement in August 1939 to supply Germany with such strategic raw materials as oil, various nonferrous metals, and foodstuffs also contributed to Hitler's Western conquests. And, since Stalin scrupulously continued these deliveries after the fall of France as, in effect, protection money, this meant he was helping Hitler prepare his attack on the Soviet Union. As a result, in June 1941 Germany was an immeasurably more formidable adversary than she would have been in 1939.

At the same time, Stalin used the breathing space provided by the Pact to make his own situation still worse. The defenses on the old frontier were dismantled before the defenses on the new frontier could be completed. Soviet socialist institutions were introduced into the annexed territories, thereby wholly alienating their populations. But above all, Stalin's Winter War against Finland in 1939–1940 revealed that the Soviet armed forces were gravely defective in leadership, morale, and equipment. Emboldened by these developments, in the summer of 1940 Hitler decided to attack in the East, and by the end of the year his plans were ready. The invasion, scheduled for mid-May 1941, actually began on June 22.

In the first five months of this war the Soviet Union escaped defeat only by a hair's breadth; indeed, it was not until the Battle of Stalingrad a year later that defeat was no longer a serious possibility. Although the whole war was a calamity for the peoples of the Soviet Union—one far beyond anything experienced by the Allied populations in the West—the first eighteen months were the most devastating part of the ordeal. The stunning reverses of this period raise the related questions of Stalin's responsibility for the disaster and of the role played by the structural deficiencies of the system he had built. Indeed, perhaps no other part of Stalin's record has aroused as much passionate commentary in the former Soviet Union as has his conduct of the war; for the near destruction of the nation, and the millions of losses incurred, touched everyone in the country.

The bad gamble of the Molotov-Ribbentrop Pact must be counted as the first of Stalin's errors leading to near defeat. Even worse was his conduct of operations in 1941. Despite numerous and very precise warnings from Soviet intelligence, as well as from the British and the Americans, that Hitler would attack in May or June, Stalin refused to take precautionary measures for fear of "provoking" Hitler. Soviet preparations for war were scheduled to be completed only in 1942, and Stalin, his will apparently paralyzed by his dependence on Hitler, refused to believe that his gamble would not hold for another year. Even when German troops crossed the frontier, Stalin's orders were not to return their fire, again for fear of provoking a greater attack. As a result, almost all Soviet fighter planes were destroyed on the ground in the first day. Stalin himself was so shaken by the failure of his policies that he apparently fell into a state of shock. It was left to Molotov to announce the news of the attack to the population by radio; Stalin did not speak or, it would seem, resume active command until two weeks later.

When he did take control, his orders were that Soviet forces, no matter how endangered they might be, should only attack or stand their ground but never retreat. Given the speed of the German advance, this directive was an absurdity. The only result was that time and again Soviet forces were surrounded and captured, sometimes in packets of 600,000 men. All told, in the first seven months of the war 3.9 million Soviet troops were taken prisoner, that is, somewhat more than the number of Germans deployed in Russia.[7] But Stalin's orders were not the only cause of this catastrophe. The overcentralized command structure of the Soviet army, which reflected the overcentralization of the system as a whole, led to an incapacity for local initiative at all levels of the hierarchy: Army and divisional commanders were afraid to make decisions on their own even in the direst emergencies.

Moreover, Soviet troops had also been molded by the system, and they clearly felt no ardor for its defense or fear of capture by the more "cultured" Germans. Although it would be too much to equate the inaction of the troops with desertion, they could not have been taken prisoner in such numbers had they had any strong motivation to fight. This indeed was Stalin's assessment of their conduct. To Moscow, throughout the four years of conflict there was no such thing as a legitimate Soviet prisoner in enemy hands: All were regarded as deserters and hence subject to execution if they were recovered. There is no more telling measure of the regime's lack of confidence in the viability of its own handiwork than this view of Soviets captured by the enemy. And the sad fact is that this lack of confidence was well founded, for never in modern European military history had an army in the field lost such a high proportion of its men with so little resistance.

Even clearer signs of collapse appeared among the civilian population. As the Germans advanced into the Baltic states, Bielorussia, and Ukraine, civilians often welcomed them as liberators. Accustomed to discounting Soviet propaganda, they had not believed their government's descriptions of Nazi brutality and so expected more "cultured" behavior from the Germans than from their own rulers. In particular, they hoped for the dissolution of the kolkhozes and the reopening of the churches, and in these border regions they hoped for national liberation as well. But similar reaction greeted the Germans' penetration into Great Russia. Thus the system, both military and civilian, continued to unravel for five months, until the first successful Soviet counteroffensive stopped the Germans in December at the very gates of Moscow.

Stalin's worst fears about the solidity of the socialism he had built seemed to have been confirmed. And if the Soviet Union had been a country the size of France, or even several times the size of France, the Soviet experiment would in fact have ended in 1941. So the first reason why the system survived Stalin's mistakes was that the Soviet Union's huge size and enormous population made it possible for the country to sustain losses that would have destroyed any other European state. It was only at this exorbitant cost that the system bought the time that was necessary for Hitler to make the mistakes that would eventually turn the tide.

The second factor that helped the Soviet Union out of its near disaster was the errors of its adversary. Hitler's invasion of Russia was not in itself or a priori a fatal mistake: Despite her vast area, Russia had been decisively beaten before, most recently by Germany itself in

1918; and with modern mechanized means such a feat would have been easier in 1941 than in the past. But any campaign against Russia would have required a careful adaptation of means to ends, and Hitler's goal of subjugating the entire East to create a lebensraum for Germany went beyond the means he could feasibly deploy.

First, it turned out that he started a month too late to finish the task of cracking Russia in 1941. The invasion had been scheduled to start in mid-May, but it was delayed until late June when Hitler decided to take Yugoslavia and bail out Mussolini in Greece. So the Germans reached Moscow just as the onset of winter halted their blitzkrieg, and this permitted the Russians to bring up fresh forces for a counteroffensive that saved the city. Thus, for the first time it was demonstrated that the Germans could be beaten. Not only did the counteroffensive boost Russian morale, it also forced Hitler to put off his next campaigns until the following spring. But in symbolic and practical terms, what was most important was the fact that Moscow had been preserved; for losing the capital of so centralized and yet so ramshackle a system would quite probably have caused the whole edifice to crumble.

At least one other Nazi error contributed to this outcome. The German generals had wanted to concentrate their attack on the central front leading to Moscow. But Hitler—swelled with hubris after his brilliant victories in the West and the Balkans, where his judgment had indeed often been better than that of his commanders—overruled his generals and ordered an advance on all fronts, from Leningrad in the north to Ukraine in the south. And this dispersal of German resources made certain that Moscow would not be taken in the first campaign.

The second campaign, that of 1942, was marked by even greater errors. Again disregarding his generals, Hitler as supreme commander bypassed Moscow and pressed his offensive in the direction of Ukraine, the Volga, and the Caucasus; the aim this time was to split the country and gain control of the food and oil of the southern regions. After making a wide and swift advance, by the fall the Germans had bogged down once again, this time at Stalingrad on the Volga. Although the city was not of major strategic significance, it became a symbolic test for both sides. Hitler refused to retreat even when it became clear that he could not cross the Volga, so the Soviets encircled the city and forced the surrender of the German armies. Although this defeat did not entirely destroy the Germans' capacity to attack, it signified the end of their ability to defeat the Russians.

Protected by this new security, Stalin was now able to mobilize his country's resources for eventual victory. The next year the Germans mounted their last great tank offensive at Kursk, and once this attack had been thrown back the Soviets commenced an inexorable westward advance.

But Hitler's greatest error stemmed from the ideological nature of the Nazi enterprise. Although it was possible for him to have won the war in the East, he could not have done this by military means alone. He would have had to mobilize the discontent of the Soviet population, but this was precluded by the very nature of his regime. All the Slavic populations were to be treated as *Untermenschen* and forced to work for their new masters. Thus the kolkhoz was kept as a convenient means for the Germans to obtain food from the territories they occupied. Nor were the pagan Nazis interested in reopening churches. And above all, the Germans were hostile to any eastern nationalisms, whether Ukrainian or Russian, and no matter how anti-Soviet they were.[8]

It is no exaggeration to say that in the first calamitous months of the war much of the Soviet population was neutral towards the two sides: people simply did not believe their government's claims of Nazi brutality.[9] But when Soviet forces in their first offensives recaptured territory from the Germans, the worst of these claims were confirmed, and the population concluded "better our beasts than theirs." By 1942 this had become the general opinion, and the population actively rallied to the Soviet side. This surge of sentiment, drawing on residual Russian rather than Soviet patriotism, was no doubt the decisive factor in producing the victory over Hitler, for no amount of space can save a people that will not fight. But it took until the Battle of Stalingrad for this patriotism to become effective; in the meantime the military initiative remained with Hitler, while Russia accumulated the staggering losses already described.

Hitler's final mistake overlaps with one of the most poignant indications of the underlying weakness of the Soviet system: the movement of Soviet resistance to Stalin led by General Andrei Vlasov.[10] Vlasov's career was the epitome of Sovietism. A peasant by birth, he had served in the Civil War and later had become one of the new "Red commanders." His father had been "dekulakized" but, as in the case of Gorbachev's father and so many others, this did not affect his son's loyalty, and Vlasov became a Party member around 1930. He was one of the heroes of the Battle of Moscow in 1941. But he had the bad luck to be captured in the summer of 1942, when his army was surrounded by the Germans and simply abandoned by Stalin. Thus Vlasov had lived through the worst of the system—collectivization, the purge of the army, the incompetent conduct of the war. When some German officers, wishing to play the card of Soviet resistance to Stalin, approached him to head a Russian National Committee, Vlasov agreed. But Hitler could not bring himself to accept an ally so Soviet and so Slavic. The Vlasov movement, therefore, was not allowed to mobilize and arm the vast reservoir of some two million Soviet prisoners then in German hands. It remained militarily insignificant until almost the end of the war, and at the same time it was hopelessly compromised in a political sense by its association with Nazism. In fact, the Vlasov movement was anti-Soviet without being pro-Nazi, and its aim at the end was to join with the advancing Western Allies. The Allies, however, had little choice but to turn Vlasov—and soon thereafter the two million plus Soviet prisoners in the West—over to Stalin. Vlasov, of course, was shot; the prisoners were either executed or sent to the Gulag.

This tragic episode highlights like no other the intractable dilemmas of the Second World War. The struggle had two conflicting aspects. On the one hand, on the Eastern front it was a confrontation between two ideological powers, and in each the ideology inflamed the struggle and yet impeded its conduct. Hitler's racial theories deprived him of the anti-Soviet support that alone could have brought him victory. Stalin's ideology of class war had so alienated a part of his population that many Soviets failed to resist his adversary, thereby almost ensuring his defeat. On the other hand, globally, the Second World War was fought as a Popular Front, an international coalition of democrats and Communists against fascism. This coalition displayed the weakness of all Popular Fronts: It was an alliance against a common enemy but without a common purpose. It therefore could end only in the moral ambiguity exemplified by the Vlasov affair; that is, with the Hobson's choice of furthering the interests of Hitler or those of Stalin. Only Finland was able to fight through the whole war as Hitler's ally and yet come out of it not as Stalin's captive but as a nation in good standing on the democratic side.

By the end of the Battle of Stalingrad in early 1943, Hitler had made enough mistakes to set the Soviet Union on the path to victory. Russia enjoyed a distinct advantage over Germany in manpower, natural resources, and, of course, space. What was required to bring these advantages into play was time, and that had been purchased at inordinate cost.

But other factors contributed to the victory. First, Stalin and his commanders learned from their mistakes. The Soviet-German war was extraordinary in that, among other things, the supreme commanders on both sides were amateurs: Hitler was a mere corporal in the First World War, and Stalin was a "defeatist" political exile in Siberia at the same time. Hitler displayed real brilliance in his western campaigns; Stalin was a bungler at the start. By 1943, however, Stalin had become competent at his latest trade, while Hitler had gone into decline. In particular, Stalin at last came to trust his generals: he reduced the role of the political commissars and learned to delegate operational authority. The results were a methodical marshaling of the Soviet Union's natural advantages and a cautious advance between 1943 and 1945, westward towards Poland and Berlin and southwestward into the Danube valley. The Soviet performance was never a brilliant one, but it was the decisive factor in defeating Hitler. The Second World War in Europe was, after all, won in the East. By the time the Allies landed in Italy in 1943, and in France in 1944, Nazism's fate had been basically sealed; it is doubtful that the Allied invasions by themselves could have succeeded in defeating Hitler.

Just as important, the Soviet regime became more responsive to the population. The early slogans about fighting for socialism were dropped, and Stalin appealed instead to Russian patriotism, invoking the military heroes of the Old Regime from Aleksandr Nevskii's time to the War of 1812. Indeed, the Soviet regime did not call the new conflict an anti-imperialist war but instead gave it the 1812 title "Great Patriotic War." And in truth it was far more a Russian than an All-Union war: Since the western border republics had no love for Russia and, moreover, were occupied for most of the war's duration, the brunt of the fighting and most of the sacrifice were borne by the Russian heartland. In recognition of this fact, in 1943 Stalin permitted the election of a new Orthodox patriarch and used the Church to give moral meaning to the war effort. As he frankly admitted to one Western diplomat, "the population won't fight for us Communists, but they will fight for Mother Russia."[11]

Concessions were also made to ameliorate the population's daily life. In order to keep the country fed, the regime closed its eyes to a great enlargement of the peasants' individual plots at the expense of the kolkhoz. Even on the collectively tilled lands, many kolkhozes introduced the *zveno*, or "link" system, in which families took on the responsibility for food production, both for the state and for private sale. But this of course meant expansion of the market, and again the regime expediently closed its eyes. At the same time, the disruption of normal administration led to the creation of local defense committees; operating under a three-member directorate chosen from the Party, the soviet, and the NKVD, these committees were charged with mobilizing volunteers for combat as well as production. The regular Plan was scrapped as industry was turned entirely towards meeting military needs, and factory workers were encouraged to provide their own food by cultivating nearby vacant fields. In short, amidst the turmoil and uncertainty of the time, the rigid structures of life developed during the thirties were generally relaxed, and the population found a new place for exercising independent initiative. Russia was once again becoming "fluid." It would be too much to say that this amounted to a new NEP, but it did represent a significant erosion of the system. In the short term, this furthered the war effort; in the long term, it presented a threat to the very nature of the system.[12]

But what was the contribution of the system itself to the victory? The answer must be that it was considerable, and this for the good reason that the system was essentially a political-military mode of social organization that was now operating in its natural element. Immediately after the invasion, the country was placed under a State Committee for Defense—composed of Stalin and his familiar group—which now focused the instrumentalities of the Party, police, army, and economy on the immediate tasks of war. One of its chief accomplishments during the first months was to organize the evacuation of some fifteen hundred factories, together with their workers, eastward to the Volga, the Urals, and Siberia. Altogether, about ten million people were transferred in this way during the war, and by the end of the conflict more than half of Soviet metal was produced in the east, compared with only a fifth on the eve of the war. By 1943 this extraordinary industrial redeployment had put Russia's production of planes, tanks, and artillery far above Germany's. The Party's ability to mobilize and rapidly concentrate great masses of men and materiel at strategic points and under crisis conditions was clearly a major factor in the Soviet victory.

This does not mean, however, that the system was decisive, as Stalin claimed after the war and as his successors believed down into the 1970s (a belief that blunted their timid resolve to reform). Geography and chance alone gave the system time enough to work; but the system became truly effective only with Stalingrad, when it was supported by the patriotic commitment and formidable tenacity of the population. Nor was the Soviet effort at national mobilization a unique wartime exploit. The American mobilization of some fifteen million men together with their materiel—a mobilization, moreover, which started from zero—and their projection across two oceans, was a considerably more impressive feat of "modernity."

At the same time, the system continued to expend much energy on its classic repressive functions. At the beginning of the war all private radio receivers were confiscated, and the public henceforth got its information only from public loudspeakers. The NKVD never stopped arresting and deporting to the Gulag "defeatists" and other suspect elements behind the lines; later, real or alleged collaborators were apprehended as the occupied areas were liberated. In these tasks the NKVD was seconded by a new military counterintelligence organization, SMERSH (the acronym of the Russian words for "death to spies"), and Aleksandr Solzhenitsyn was only the most famous victim of its vigilance. In crisis situations, SMERSH battalions would position themselves behind Soviet troops with orders to shoot, thereby making it more dangerous to retreat than to advance.

The system also acquired new repressive functions. One of these was to remake the ethnic map of the Soviet Union through the deportation of whole nationalities, allegedly in the interest of security.[13] The Volga Germans were the first group to go; even though they had been in Russia for almost two centuries and were thoroughly loyal, they were deported to Central Asia in 1941. In 1944, after the German retreat from the North Caucasus and the Crimea, the Chechen-Ingush, the Crimean Tatars, and other small nationalities were also dispatched to Central Asia. Although only a few individuals had in fact welcomed the Germans as liberators, all members of these nationalities were deported in freight cars, with enormous losses of life. In effect, these operations applied the principle of the purge to the nationalities; their purpose was to achieve ethnically homogeneous populations in sensitive areas, thereby eradicating any putative source of disloyalty. As such, the deportations were related to the ethnic purging of Jews and Slavs that was carried out by Hitler in Eastern Europe after 1939. Stalin also engaged in similar ethnic engineering in the Baltic states, where a high proportion of the native population was deported and Russian immigration was promoted in the hope of making the annexations irreversible. Finally, in Poland, after Hitler had ˙already "simplified" the country's ethnic composition by exterminating its Jewish component, Stalin finished the job by displacing Poles from the east to the former German lands along the Oder-Neisse line, thereby giving Ukraine, Belorussia, and Poland a homogeneous character they had never before possessed. And all of this was as much a product of the organizational capacity of the Party-state as was the evacuation of factories with their workers to the Urals.

Yet however we evaluate the weight of the system's merits in producing the triumph of 1945, there can be no doubt that this victory immeasurably strengthened the system itself. It made Communism at last impregnable at home by elevating it to the status of a global political force. At the same time, it endowed the cult of Stalin with a new aura, not only in the eyes of the Leader's subjects, but also from the perspective of what was now in truth a world Communist movement. The seven years that remained for Stalin to rule would thus witness that movement at the height of its success and at the acme of its unity. But these years were also the time when Communism and its Leader appeared most ominous to the rest of the world. Hence, the last years of Stalin were also the first years of the Cold War and indeed the time when the Cold War seemed most likely to become hot.

THE COLD WAR

Externally the Patriotic War brought the Soviet Union an empire, but internally it set her back almost to where she had been a decade earlier. Thus, if the Soviet Union after 1945 appeared ominously strong to the outside world, to its leaders it looked much too vulnerable for comfort or for any relaxation of effort by the population.

Despite the success in moving industry east of the Urals, the economy overall was devastated. The results of the Second and Third Five-Year Plans were largely undone. Agricultural production had declined by about one-half, and steel production, which was to have been twenty-three million tons in 1941, was now down to ten million tons. At the same time, the old administrative structures in the western, recently occupied parts of the country had been dismantled. The Soviet population—whether the troops who had been beyond Soviet borders or the civilians in the occupied zone—had been exposed to a relatively higher foreign living standard and freer alien ideas. The work of the thirties, therefore, had to be in large part redone.

And this was the essence of Stalin's policy during his last years: he simply restored everything the war had partially undone—in politics, in the economy, and in culture. Yet the tone and style of this rebuilding of socialism were distinctly new. The thirties, for all their horror, had been an adventure; the late forties were a plodding restoration. There was no longer a trace of the militant leftism and the grim novelty of the first Five-Year Plans. The postwar years were a time of lead, not of steel; they were gray, not Red. Internally the last years of Stalin were the ice age of Sovietism, just as they were the high point of the Cold War externally.

Politically the war and postwar period marked the emergence of a mass Party appropriate to the new imperial tasks of the regime.[14] During the war the Party had expanded from some 2.5 million members to 4 million (or from 3,400,000 to 5,760,000 if candidate members are included). This unprecedented expansion was carried out to give the Party a mass base in the all-important armed forces. After the war, however, as after earlier periods of rapid expansion in a time of crisis, large if unknown numbers of these hastily enrolled and minimally indoctrinated recruits were weeded out, though by and large not with the extreme methods of the *Ezhovshchina*. From 1947 onward, Party members were replaced only slowly, and they were selected much more carefully, as in the earlier periods of consolidation after 1921 and 1933. The result by the eve of Stalin's death was a Party of 6 million members (6,880,000 with candidates), not all that much larger than it had been at the end of the war.

This greatly expanded Party, like the Party of the late thirties, was composed almost entirely of new Soviet men. It was even more clearly a Party of cadres; most members were from the managerial, technical, military, and administrative elites of the mature Soviet system, and there was only a decreasing number of workers and peasants. The Party had become, in short, the corporate organization of the *nomenklatura*. This huge Party, to be sure, was not in any sense an autonomous corporate entity. It was, rather, the instrument of government of the Leader who commanded it, Comrade Stalin; and throughout these years it was subject to pruning by Beria's security organs. Still, a major mutation of the Party had occurred. Although the Party continued to have important administrative and ideological (that is, propaganda) functions, it was increasingly employed in the management of the economy. But the professional skills required for that task now necessitated a relative stability of cadres. And this need for stability would progressively limit the top leadership's freedom of political maneuver and of purge.

In the economy, the industrial system of the thirties was restored with the launching of a new Five-Year Plan, the fourth, in 1946. It continued the old emphasis on heavy industry, especially metallurgy, over light industry and consumer goods for the population. And the rate of growth of industry was comparable to that of the thirties; that is, it was the highest the Soviet system would ever reach. Thus by 1950 the country had surpassed the prewar production of its great staples: coal, iron, and steel, as well as oil and electricity. But the system continued to be oriented towards military needs. Although large-scale demobilization took place, and the massive production of conventional weapons was correspondingly curtailed, the Soviet system acquired a new priority sector: atomic weapons, missiles, and the exploration of space. Investment in this new sector was enormous, and progress was rapid: The Soviet Union had its first rudimentary atomic bomb by 1949 and its first hydrogen bomb prototype by 1953.

And, as in the thirties, all of this was achieved at the expense of the peasantry. Nikolai Voznesenskii, the head of Gosplan and the talented director of the Soviet economy during the war, wished to continue and expand the wartime policy of concessions to the peasantry. This would have meant an increased role for the peasants' individual plots and the market, including giving the peasants access to the state retail network. In particular, he wished to make the "link" system the basic mode of exploiting the kolkhoz's collective fields. But all of this would have meant a significant return toward a new NEP, and so in 1950 the various wartime concessions were rolled back and a drive to strengthen the kolkhoz was commenced. The "link" was condemned, lands appropriated by the peasants during the war were taken back, and the Machine Tractor Station (MTS) with its Party organization was restored as the master of agricultural production. Even more, Khrushchev launched a campaign for a revolutionary transformation of the countryside through the construction of "agrovilles," or rural factory-cities. Although in practice matters did not go this far, there was a great consolidation of kolkhozes; their number was reduced from 250,000 to 97,000, while some were converted into sovkhozes, or state farms, an operation that was made possible by the fact that industry was now producing three times as many tractors as in 1940. At the same time, Voznesenskii was purged and shot in an episode known as the "Leningrad Affair," although it is not clear that his fall was occasioned by his views on agriculture. Still, this was the first time since the late thirties that a Politburo member had met such a fate, and it served as a warning against any rethinking of the Soviet economy.

The consequence of these policies was that everyone, but especially the peasants, continued to live badly. In 1946 there was again a famine because the state took the peasants' food reserves in Ukraine to meet its procurement quotas. In 1947 food rationing was ended (that is, sooner after the war than in any other European country), but prices were raised at the same time. In the same year there was a currency reform, with most rubles held in cash converted at a rate of ten to one. This amounted to the confiscation of savings accumulated during the war by "speculators" on the black market and, especially, by peasants. In other words, it was still another blow to the nascent NEP of the period. After this stabilization, the government was able to reduce food prices every year from 1948 to 1954, and this policy left an enduring legacy of popular belief in regular progress under Stalin. In fact, real urban wages by 1952 were only roughly what they had been in 1928, and that was not much better than what they had been in 1913. And the situation was much worse in the countryside. The 1952 grain harvest was still lower than the one in 1940; in other words, it was no better than the 1929 harvest, which in turn was inferior to that of 1913. A similarly dismal picture obtained with respect to urban housing; already a casualty of the planning of the 1930s, housing was further neglected in the postwar reconstruction, when the urban population was again expanding rapidly. All of this was part of the price that Stalin's Party-state imposed on the population to maintain the country's new status of superpower.

The final price included an unprecedented stagnation in culture. The war had also brought a measure of relaxation in culture, as writers produced a fairly realistic and definitely patriotic literature that the population genuinely desired. The creative intelligentsia had hoped this relaxation would continue after the war, just as the peasants had hoped for a relaxation of the kolkhoz system. But immediately after the war, the regime, in the person of Zhdanov, served notice that order would be restored in the arts. In 1946 the poet Anna Akhmatova and the satirist Mikhail Zoshchenko were condemned as decadent and foreign. Soon these condemnations were expanded into a campaign of crude cultural nationalism and xenophobia directed against the West. Russian and Soviet priority was claimed for an improbable variety of inventions and discoveries, from the radio to the rocket. Acknowledging Western influences on anything Soviet—even Hegel's influence on Marx—was denounced. And "kowtowing to the West" was blamed on "cosmopolitanism," which was in large part a code word for "Jewish influence." Zionism, moreover, was held to be a Trojan horse for the United States' designs on the world. Thus the whole postwar cultural campaign was part of the Soviet Union's struggle against its new great enemy, "American imperialism," which had become the successor to the Trotskyite-Bukharinite-fascist enemy of yore.

The Soviet system always needed a conspiracy of internal and external foes. With the kulaks and the deviationists gone, to achieve the necessary effect of unending struggle the regime now used the "anti-cosmopolitan" campaign to tap a certain traditional Russian anti-Semitism and to transform wartime patriotism into militant xenophobia. Thus the political purpose of the *Zhdanovshchina* was to isolate a shaken and still fragile society from all disturbing foreign influences, and at the same time to frighten the population into accepting the sacrifices necessary to rebuild the structures of Soviet power. The *Zhdanovshchina* was also an effort to give the system a sense of self-sufficiency and combativeness for the new international tests ahead. And it was intended to provide the six million members of the Party, the cadres of the postwar imperial system, with the conviction of superiority appropriate to the system's new grandeur.

For Soviet Communism had now entered the third and final phase of its history. The initial revolutionary phase had been superseded by the state-building phase with the First Five-Year Plan, and after 1945 this second phase culminated in an imperial stage that would last until the end of the system. The "Internationale" was now replaced by a new anthem celebrating Soviet might: "An indestructible union of free republics has been forged for eternity by Great Russia." Uniforms for diplomats were reintroduced, and ranks, epaulettes, and decorations appeared for the military, all in imitation of the Old Regime. People's commissariats now became ministries, as befitted the administration of a mature state. But above all, the Soviet Union acquired control of, or influence over, enormous territories beyond its old borders.

This process began in 1939 with the Molotov-Ribbentrop Pact. One of the reasons why Stalin entered into this agreement was that he very much wanted the territories he eventually gained from Finland, the Baltic states, Poland, and Bessarabia, territories that for the most part had once belonged to the Russian Empire. Even in the desperate early days of the war he firmly maintained his claim to these lands. When he made an agreement with the Polish government-in-exile in London at the end of 1941, he pointedly refused to accept a return to the Soviet-Polish frontier of 1939. And as the fortunes of war improved, he pressed this matter with increasing belligerence even though it increasingly eroded the indispensable Grand Alliance. In 1943 the Germans discovered a mass grave of Polish officers in the Katyn Forest near Smolensk, and claimed that they had been murdered by the Soviets in 1940. The Polish government in London demanded an international Red Cross investigation. Stalin indignantly denied 'the charges and broke off relations with the London Poles, after which he formed a "Union of Polish Patriots" in Russia. At the end of the year, at the Teheran Conference of the Big Three, Britain and the United States began to abandon their Polish ally when they conceded its eastern territories to Stalin in exchange for eventual compensation from Germany in the west.

The next year the abandonment of the London Poles was completed.[15] In 1944 the Soviet army entered ethnic Poland and Stalin installed *his* Poles as the new government in Lublin. On August 1, after the Red Army had reached the Vistula, the Home Army of the London Poles launched an insurrection to liberate Warsaw before the Soviets arrived. But the Soviets sat on the other side of the river and, letting the Germans do their work for them, watched as the Polish resistance was crushed and the capital was destroyed. The following February, at Yalta, the Western Allies had to accept the new status quo in Poland; they agreed to recognize the Lublin government with the token addition of a couple of representatives of the London Poles and with a promise of democratic elections after the war.

Later, in many quarters in the West, Yalta became the symbol of the West's naive surrender of Eastern Europe to Stalin. This is a great oversimplification. Although the wartime Popular Front had engendered in the West considerable naive trust in Stalin's democratic intentions, Poland's fate was in fact decided by military factors over which the Western Allies had no control. The Allies got what few concessions they could from Stalin in the low-odds hope that he might actually keep his promises. Indeed, the fact that these paper promises existed later made it possible for the West to argue the illegitimacy of the Soviet presence in Eastern Europe.

That the promises were not kept derived from the simple fact that Stalin, true to his form since 1939, would not trust any political arrangement that he did not control directly, and this made Soviet intervention in Polish affairs inevitable. For Poland, astride the invasion corridor from Berlin to Moscow, was too important geopolitically for its status to be left to chance. Yet any Polish government that would emerge from the free elections agreed to at Yalta would be anti-Soviet; and even if it accepted the kind of imposed alliance that applied to Finland, it would still not be a foolproof element in the Soviet security system. So Stalin would settle for nothing less than a Polish government controlled by Communists, and this he achieved by rigging the election of 1947. Even his great compensatory gift to the Poles was a means of tying them permanently to Russia; for the incorporation into Poland of the former German provinces, with the approval of Britain and America, meant that henceforth Poland would always need a Russian alliance against possible German revanchism. Thus, between 1939 and 1947, in the crucial Polish case, the formula for the future Soviet empire was worked out. And this same crucial case also generated the conflicts of interest and the mutual suspicions that dissolved the Grand Alliance into the Cold War.

How far did Stalin intend to go in 1945? And was Soviet expansionism in Eastern Europe the root cause of the Cold War? Or could his appetites, and therefore international tensions, have been moderated by a more understanding response to his fears on the part of the West? Answers to these questions have ranged from Churchill's alarmed diagnosis in his "iron curtain" speech of 1946 that Soviet aggressiveness was innate, to a Solomonic attribution of equal blame to East and West, to contorted "revisionist" arguments that Stalin was simply defending himself against American nuclear blackmail. While the Cold War was on, these various positions were not just varieties of historical interpretation; they were also arguments for greater or lesser military preparedness and diplomatic firmness towards the Soviet Union. Now that the Cold War is over, the political passion has gone out of these debates and a more realistic assessment of the record ought to be possible.

Briefly, in the crucial years of the Cold War's gestation, 1946–1948, Stalin did not know how far he was going to go. But it was no accident that he eventually went as far as he did, and once he had reached the famous line of the iron curtain, an enduring period of cold hostilities was inevitable.[16] In other words, the basic cause of the Cold War lay not in any mistakes or misunderstandings on either side, but, quite tritely, in the structural incompatibility between Communist and constitutional democratic polities. The Cold War was inevitable given the simple existence of the Soviet Union, and it therefore automatically ended when the Soviet Union collapsed. By the same token, the tension of the Cold War years did not derive from some inveterate Russian expansionism, for Russia is still there but is contracting. Rather, the Cold War derived from specifically Soviet socialist methods of organizing power and the projection of these methods into the international arena.

Having said this, it must be added that Soviet expansion was accelerated and hardened during 1946–1948 by Western efforts to contain it. The basic fact of the situation was Soviet conquest of most of the continent up to the Elbe and the Adriatic. This was in part the inevitable result of Hitler's defeat, and in part the product of deliberate Soviet policy. Already in 1940 Stalin was coming into conflict with Hitler over the Balkans, which had not been covered by the Pact; and in 1944, rather than advancing directly on Berlin, Stalin took a long detour through the Balkans to Budapest and Vienna, with the clear aim of staking out an enormous Soviet sphere of influence—and also of thwarting Churchill's designs on the area. But this does not mean that he aimed at that time to introduce the Soviet system into this zone, as he had done in the Baltic and Polish territories acquired in 1939. Rather, he was playing his power politics by ear, as is indicated by his leniency towards Finland when she sued for peace in

1944. A Karelo-Finnish Soviet Socialist Republic had been created as a base for absorbing the whole of Finland, but Stalin abandoned this project in return for slices of territory protecting Leningrad and Murmansk because he did not wish to rile the Allies while the war was not yet won, and while he was pressing them hard on the more important matter of Poland. Even after the war had been won, he still proceeded with relative caution in order to gain as much as possible through diplomacy in the most important matter of all, Germany.

Of course, as in Poland, Popular Front coalitions were installed in Romania, Hungary, and Bulgaria, with the key ministries of interior and defense in Communist hands; and socialist parties were pressured into merging with the local Communists to produce "United Workers' Parties." A Popular Front with Communist predominance came to power through genuine elections in Czechoslovakia, while a monochrome Communist regime under Tito gained power through military victory in Yugoslavia. Thus by late 1946–1947 the chronically unstable formula of the Popular Front had set the stage throughout Eastern Europe for full Communist takeovers through the application of what Matias Rakosi of Hungary called "salami tactics" to the more moderate members of the Fronts.

Still, the cleaver would not fall until Stalin became convinced not only that diplomacy would not get him Germany but that the Western "imperialists" were acting to undermine his hard-won Eastern sphere of influence. Although a third of Germany was under Soviet occupation, this beachhead could not be expanded into a regime of People's Democracy for the country as a whole. The Potsdam Conference of July 1945 had stipulated that Germany would be governed as a unit; the Western allies, however, would not agree to a Popular Front, as they had been forced to do in the case of Poland, because this would only extend Soviet influence westward to the Ruhr and the Rhine. The only alternative that was acceptable to the Soviets was a permanently neutral and demilitarized Germany. But since this option could not be effectively enforced if their troops were withdrawn, by 1947 they fell back on governing their zone as a separate unit, a policy that at least kept them permanently on the Elbe. The Allies answered by consolidating their three zones to form what would soon become the Federal Republic.

Once wartime cooperation had collapsed in this manner over Germany, the West began to mobilize to defend what it now considered to be its menaced positions. The first step came in early 1947 with the Truman Doctrine, under which the United States took over the British role of containing the Soviets in Greece and along the Turkish frontier. But the main Western counterthrust was the Marshall Plan—unveiled in June 1947 and applied in 1948—whereby the United States undertook to rehabilitate the economies of Western Europe in order to end the social instability that could make the region vulnerable to Communism. Marshall Plan aid was at first offered to the countries of Eastern Europe, including the Soviet Union, an offer made in part sincerely and in part as a ruse. For a short time Stalin seemed hesitant about accepting the aid; but after the Czechs announced their acceptance, Moscow quickly concluded that American aid would result in the capitalist subversion of its zone—as indeed it would have. So the Soviet Union and what were now its "satellites" vociferously denounced the Marshall Plan, and Europe as a whole was divided into two antithetical socioeconomic zones.

Thus the Grand Alliance foundered—first in Poland, then in Germany, and then throughout Europe—because of the intrinsic incompatibility of the Soviet and Western modes of organizing society. There was simply no middle ground between the two: One mode required a multiparty system and a market, whereas the other required a single Party and a command economy. To govern Germany as a unit, either the Allies would have had to Sovietize their zones, or the Soviets would have had to refrain from Sovietizing theirs. Accordingly, the matter was decided the way sixteenth-century religious wars were: by military lines óf demarcation on the basis of, to paraphrase, *cuius regio, eius societas*. Germany was partitioned, and soon the whole of Europe was divided as well: behind the Soviet lines there was socialism, and on the far side there was what the Soviets called "capitalism" and the West called "democracy."

This extraordinary division of Europe after 1945 has often been explained as a resurgence of traditional Russian imperialism in socialist guise. To clinch this argument, the parallel is at times drawn between the revolutionary messianism of Moscow, seat of the Third International, and the religious claims of "Moscow the Third Rome" (after Rome itself and Constantinople) of old Muscovy. In this view, moreover, Russian imperialism is explained as the projection outward of Russian despotism at home. Thus Stalin's imperial career after 1945 appears as the logical counterpart of his role as domestic autocrat in the lineage of Ivan and Peter.

Yet linear continuity between old Russia and the Soviet Union works no better for international than for internal affairs. To be sure, old Russia expanded mightily, but she did so in the traditional manner of a European great power. Thus, the Grand Duchy of Moscow grew over four centuries to become a huge empire stretching from the Baltic to the Pacific—but little Britain expanded during the same period to rule a quarter of the world's land surface, while France did her best to compete around the globe. And there was as much messianism in Britain's idealization of empire as the "white man's burden," or in France's conceit that empire spread liberty, equality, and fraternity, as there was in Russia's pan-Slav drive to Constantinople and the Straits.

In fact, however, in all of these cases of expansion ideology was secondary to geopolitical interest. Thus Russia, like all other European powers, went only as far as her military force and her economic power could take her. And this meant that, unlike the more dynamic Western states, she could not project her power overseas but was able only to absorb contiguous areas around the rim of Eurasia from Poland to the Caucasus to Turkistan to Manchuria. Moreover, nowhere did old Russia seek to impose a new system other than her autocratic-military control.

The Soviet Union, however, had not only the traditional means of Russian power at her disposal; she also had the weapon of the socialist idea. Thus, under Stalin the Soviets imposed their system wherever their arms reached. And beyond this reach, the Soviet Union adjoined to the socialist idea the antifascist reflex, thereby projecting Soviet power worldwide through Popular Fronts and the "struggle for peace." To anticipate a bit, under Stalin's successors the Soviets' ideological stance yielded the proxy power of "wars of national liberation" against European colonialism and American imperialism. Thus the Soviet Union could manipulate the labor unions of Western countries; she could find clients in East Asia, the Middle East, Africa, and Latin America; and she could mobilize intellectuals the world over. But it is difficult to see tsarist Russia establishing beachheads in Cuba or Angola, or recruiting admirers of her social system among the intelligentsia of the West. Stalin one derisively asked, "How many divisions has the pope?" His cynicism regarding spiritual power was disingenuous, for he himself commanded legions of ideological warriors. It is this ideologized battle order of politics that yielded the unprecedented division of Europe after 1945 and the resulting Cold War. Thus the Popular Fronts that had existed on both sides of the iron curtain dissolved in 1947–1948. In France and Italy, coalition governments of Christian Democrats, Socialists, and Communists had emerged from the resistance; and in both countries the Communists constituted the largest group, with over a third of the electorate. Moscow indeed had a larger base to work with in these countries than in most of Eastern Europe. Yet it would have been too dangerous to exploit this resource by taking power, in part because the Soviets were too weak at home to offer any direct assistance, and in part because of the probable American reaction. So as the Grand Alliance crumbled, the Communist parties in both countries did not go beyond strident "anti-imperialist" agitation. But this was frightening enough to cause their partners to force them out of the government in both countries in early 1947. The Communists then launched a wave of quasi-insurrectionary strikes to protest against the Marshall Plan and American "war-mongering" and "fascism." The purpose of this was no doubt to create a "diversion": Western governments were kept off balance at home while the Soviet Union consolidated its gains in the East.

In short, Stalin was continuing his 1930s policy of utilizing a very real foreign revolutionary movement to further the interests of the Soviet state. And this meant, once again, stoking those revolutionary fires while at the same time insuring that they would not lead to an open conflagration. This technique was supplemented by a new "peace movement" that was now centered on atomic weapons and directed against American and Western European rearmament. For as long as the Cold War and the Soviet Union would endure, "anti-fascism" and "the struggle for peace," combined with a lingering moral aura of the Popular Front, would be among the more potent weapons in the Soviet arsenal.

During these same years the formula of the Popular Front broke down in the People's Democracies in favor of the Left. Installed in 1945 under Communist leadership, these regimes did not consolidate their control over national affairs until 1947. A major reason for this was that, with the exception of Yugoslavia and Czechoslovakia, East European countries did not have enough Communists to form a government: in 1945 there were only 10,000 Party members in Poland, and 1,000 in Romania. (It is extraordinary that such an all-encompassing tyranny as that of Ceausescu could be created out of this miniscule Romanian nucleus—but then, in Russia itself, there were only 120,000 Bolsheviks when they took over in October 1917.) A coalition with other parties was therefore a practical necessity for managing affairs while the Party, with the help of Soviet advisors, acquired and trained its own cadres. Caution was also advisable because almost everywhere the national sentiment was anti-Soviet, and the new governments were viewed as occupation regimes.

But when the "threat" of the Marshall Plan appeared in 1947, tempting not only Czechoslovakia but also Poland, Communist hegemony was immediately made absolute. In Poland, after rigged elections, the Socialists were finally merged with the Communists into a single party. The most dramatic case, however, was that of Czechoslovakia. In February 1948 twelve non-Communist ministers resigned in protest against their Communist colleagues' creeping takeover of the administration; their hope was to provoke elections that they could quite reasonably expect to win. The Communists, aided by the left Social Democrats, thereupon ended the Popular Front and took over completely. It should be pointed out that this coup was entirely a Czechoslovak operation, for there were no Soviet troops in the country at the time. And, even though indirect pressure was exerted on the Czechoslovaks by the mere proximity of the Soviet Union, it would nonetheless have been a major matter for Stalin to intervene if a non-Communist government had been formed. Czechoslovakia became Communist through the perilous dynamic of the Popular Front.

Any Popular Front is an inherently unstable and transitional alignment. This is so because a Popular Front is composed of two incompatible political elements—adherents of constitutional democracy on the one hand, and aspirants to Leninist dictatorship on the other. The two are held together, at least temporarily, by the conviction that they are both on the "Left" in the sense of being opposed to a "Right" that seeks to replace constitutional government with an authoritarian regime. But this is a marriage of convenience, not a genuine union. A Popular Front is beset, moreover, by other ambiguities. Its liberal or Christian Democratic members do not want socialism, only welfare reformism; and its Socialist and Communist members, though they both say they want socialism, in fact mean very different things by it: The former aspires only to a comprehensive welfare state, while the latter desires integral socialism on the Soviet model.

Hence, neither the Communist nor the non-Communist component of such a Front can deal honestly with its "partner." Each must try to use the other for its own ends. The liberals and the Socialists seek Communist support to get through a difficult pass and to achieve certain social reforms, as in France in 1936; the Communists use their temporary allies to climb to full power, as in Czechoslovakia in 1948. Yet the two sides are not really symmetrical. The liberals, especially the Socialists and certain Christian Democrats, are perpetually vulnerable to the mystique of the unity of the Left. The Communists have no such illusions, for they have known since Lenin that they are the one true Left; they can therefore behave more ruthlessly and cynically than their softer colleagues—as they did in each of the People's Democracies after 1945. And these ambiguities apply equally to international affairs, as in the negotiations among the Big Three over Poland, or in the Western debates about Soviet intentions during the buildup to the Cold War in 1946–1948.

Given the internal contradictions of any Popular Front, therefore, this kind of alliance can only end fairly quickly and in one of two fashions. Either the non-Communists become alarmed at the Communists' strength and force them out of the government, as in France and Italy in 1947; or the Communists use that strength to force out their erstwhile allies, as in the Prague Coup of the following year. But a Popular Front can never end with the establishment of an enduring "democratic socialism," that mixture of a planned economy with a humane constitutionalism that has variously been known as "the third way," "convergence," or "socialism with a human face." Yet the illusion that this outcome was possible would endure for as long as Communism itself, despite all empirical evidence to the contrary.

And that evidence continued to grow after the Popular Front's failure of 1948. The next Popular Front was tried in Chile between 1970 and 1973; it ended when the Christian Democrats, unwilling to rein in their one-time ally Salvador Allende as he moved towards a Castro-like socialism, were overrun on their right by General Pinochet. Another Popular Front appeared in Portugal in 1975; after a great leftward lunge under the leadership of a military revolutionary council and the Communist Party, the experiment was ended by the Socialists and the liberals. The final appearance of the Popular Front syndrome occurred in the late 1970s, in the form of Eurocommunist overtures to Socialists and Christian Democrats. These initiatives culminated in the very modest Popular Front coalition of François Mitterrand in 1981–1984; it ended when the Socialists backed off from their commitment to the "transition from capitalism to socialism" and then dropped their compromising colleagues from the cabinet.

Thus the Popular Front formula that had been created in France a half-century earlier ended in that same country and so faded from political history for lack of a credibly progressive Communism. But the mystique of the united Left that reached its high point of practical effectiveness in Eastern and Western Europe in the years 1945–1948 surely has not disappeared along with Communism. It is too organic a part of modern politics not to reappear eventually, albeit in new political guises.

The culmination of the Cold War, and with it the polarization of the planet into a "socialist camp" and a "free world," occurred in 1948–1950. In 1948, as the Communists were taking over in Prague, the Western allies were creating a unified West Germany with a new, strong Deutsche mark. This the Soviets construed as a prelude to eventual German rearmament; in the summer they answered with a blockade of Berlin that was designed not so much to take the city as to disrupt the whole German operation of the Allies. This effort failed, and in 1949 the German Federal Republic was formally established. In response, that same year the Soviets promoted their zone of occupation to the status of "the first workers' and peasants' state on German soil" under the name German Democratic Republic. And also in 1949, the North Atlantic Treaty Organization (NATO) was formed, though it did not initially include West Germany.

In the same period, the Soviets completed their consolidation of the Eastern "bloc." Already in 1947 they had created a successor to the Comintern under the name Communist Information Bureau, or Cominform. Since 1945 the Communist movement in Europe had grown enormously; mass Parties now existed for the first time in France and Italy, and six Parties were in power in the East. The purpose of the Cominform was to coordinate the struggle of these Parties against imperialism and cosmopolitanism—or, as the organization's newssheet put it, "for a lasting peace, for a people's democracy."

This effort at centralized direction, however, soon provoked a conflict with the only genuinely independent new Communist regime, that of Yugoslavia.[17] The regime's charismatic leader, Tito, though devoted to Stalin and the Soviet model of socialism, had made his revolution on his own, and in the euphoria of victory he now wished to create a Balkan federation with Albania and Bulgaria. Stalin vetoed this ambitious initiative because he wanted no rival centers of power in the new Communist empire. After an acrimonious correspondence between the two leaders, in the summer of 1948 the Cominform publicly condemned Tito in the hope of arousing the Yugoslav Communists to oust him. A prolonged campaign of vilification failed to achieve this, however, because the Yugoslav Party was, so to speak, an autocephalous organization with its own apparat taking orders from its own center.

Thus, only three years after the first Communist regimes outside the Soviet Union had come to power, it became apparent that their centralized Leninist structures offered the possibility of creating rival poles of power to the original Leninist system. This demonstrated that the world socialist system would remain unified only if it were directly controlled from Moscow. Although this situation was disturbing to Stalin, Soviet prestige in the world Communist movement nonetheless remained overwhelming. As a consequence, the Yugoslav defection was not answered with military intervention, and Tito was treated as an outcast heretic who would eventually wither away in provincial isolation.

Still, by the summer of 1948 Communism had developed its first heresy since Trotskyism, and Stalin reacted—as might be expected of such a leader in such a system—with a purge of everything he did control. During the next year Eastern Europe was *gleichgeschaltet* with Soviet conditions. Party leaders suspected of Titoism, nationalism, or any proclivity for insubordination to Moscow were replaced. In Warsaw Wladislaw Gomulka, who had spent the war in Poland as a partisan, was jailed; his place was taken by a "Muscovite," Boleslaw Bierut, while the Polish-born Soviet marshal Konstantin Rokossovski was made minister of defense. In Hungary matters were more dramatic. The foreign minister, Laszlo Rajk, a veteran of the Spanish War, was given a 1937-style show trial. Accused of conspiring on behalf of Tito, Zionism, and American intelligence, Rajk confessed all of these sins and was executed. In Bulgaria the former first secretary, Traicho Kostov, was also tried and executed. Somewhat later, in 1952, Prague was the scene of a similar show trial for Rudolf Slansky; this episode had the same anti-Semitic accent that was then so prominent in the Soviet Union.

Collectivization, which until then had been proceeding only slowly so as not to arouse peasant resistance, was now precipitously pushed to completion in Eastern Europe; this campaign eventually succeeded everywhere except in Poland. In addition, ambitious Five-Year Plans were launched, with the inevitable emphasis on metallurgy—as at Nowa Huta, the Polish equivalent of Magnitogorsk. The churches were also persecuted, and their leaders often given show trials, as was the case with Cardinal Mindszenty in Hungary. Moreover, all contacts with the West were severed, and culture was planned according to the canons of Andrei Zhdanov. The "fraternal" Parties of the East were well on their way to becoming lesser replicas of Big Brother. By 1950 the Soviet empire had indeed become a "bloc."

At the same time, "the international workers' movement," as Communism still called itself, gathered in even greater gains in the East when the Chinese Party at last came to power in October of 1949. This, however, was not of Moscow's doing but an unexpected and not entirely welcome gift of Mao Zedong and his comrades.[18]

At the end of the war Stalin had clearly not expected a Chinese Communist victory. After the Soviets had destroyed the Japanese army in Manchuria, his first concern had been to secure his interests in that area by taking over the Chinese Eastern Railroad leading to Vladivostok and the warm-water ports of Dairen and Port Arthur. To secure his title to all of this, in August 1945 Stalin signed a Treaty of Friendship and Alliance with Chiang Kai-shek, in which he promised not to intervene in the Chinese civil war. This promise he did not keep. From the Soviet base in Manchuria Stalin supplied the Chinese Communists with captured Japanese equipment; and the next year it was the Communists, not the Nationalists, who took over Manchuria at the end of the Soviet occupation. This does not mean, however, that Stalin expected Mao to conquer all of China. Rather, he seems to have believed that America would never tolerate such an outcome, and that Mao, therefore, would wind up controlling a Communist zone in north China that would be dependent on Soviet support and protection. Stalin's expectations for China were probably similar to what he had actually achieved in Korea; there he had occupied his allotted half of the peninsula and had established a Communist regime that was at first hardly more independent than its analogues in Eastern Europe.

By 1949, however, the Chinese Party had unexpectedly expanded its "zone" to cover the whole of continental China, and this created a situation for which Eastern Europe could in no way offer a precedent. The relationship between the two Communist giants would have to be one of partnership without being one of equality. Sentiments on both sides, moreover, were mixed. Although Mao genuinely admired both the Soviet Union and the personal accomplishments of Stalin, and took both as his model, he was nonetheless resentful of the fact that Soviet support during the Chinese Communists' decades of struggle had been so niggardly, especially in the last crucial years. And Stalin was genuinely satisfied with the enormous boost to Communist power and prestige—as well as to his personal position as supreme Communist leader—that the Chinese Revolution had provided, but he was nonetheless concerned by the emergence of a center of revolutionary authority that Moscow did not control directly. Yet both Party leaders were also aware that the myth, indeed the reality, of world Communist unity was indispensable to the strength of each, and to the progress of the movement as a whole.

Accordingly, Stalin was much more careful in his dealings with Mao than he had been in those with Tito. When Mao came to Moscow at the end of 1949—right after taking power—to help celebrate Stalin's seventieth birthday, Stalin agreed to give up his 1945 gains in Manchuria and to provide China with economic and military assistance. Although the aid was by no means generous, it meant that China would follow the Soviet model of development, which the Chinese genuinely believed in anyway. Mao, for his part, was studiously deferential to Stalin's superior status but also insistent on Chinese dignity. In short, even at the start of the new Soviet-Chinese relationship, there were intimations of tension that could worsen if circumstances changed. Relations remained relatively smooth while Stalin lived because it was inconceivable to both sides that Communism could fragment and yet prosper, and this meant that all Communists would have to defer to Stalin. Tito was as much a heretic to Mao as he was to Stalin.

In retrospect it is clear that the Chinese Revolution was the apogee of Communist success: A political and a moral, if not an organizational, unity among regimes did in fact exist, extending from the Elbe to the China Seas, and the forward momentum of Communist gain seemed to be unstoppable. This was now an acute worry to the West. And the victory of Communism throughout Eurasia does seem to have become Stalin's objective, for another product of the Chinese Revolution was his decision to round off his previous gains in Korea. This overconfident decision produced the first armed conflict between Communist and Western forces.[19]

One of the guests at Stalin's seventieth anniversary was Kim Il Sung of North Korea. By this time both Soviet and American occupation troops had been withdrawn from the peninsula. Kim therefore suggested to Stalin that a military advance from the north would produce a revolution in the south and thus a wholly Communist Korea, a scenario that could be presented as a civil war. Stalin accepted this proposal and agreed to supply North Korea with up-to-date armaments. He seems to have calculated that if the Americans had abandoned the whole of China to Communism the previous year, they would not intervene for something so insignificant as South Korea. It seems that Mao Zedong was also consulted, and given his scorn for "the Paper Tiger," he did not object.

The great question is, once again, how far did Stalin intend to go with this adventure? Our best conjecture is that this time he hoped to go quite far. He had just been frustrated in Europe over the Berlin blockade. At the same time, however, events in China opened the prospect of revolutionary gains throughout East Asia. Therefore, it would be logical for him to seek new fortunes in the Pacific theater. And indeed both Stalin and Mao recognized Ho Chi Minh's provisional government in 1948; at the same time, there was a Communist insurgency in Malaya and an attempted Communist coup in Indonesia. It is conceivable that under these circumstances the usually cautious Stalin would have suddenly become receptive to the much more militant ideas of Mao, and to have opted for a general Communist advance in Asia. In particular, there was a surge of Communist activism in Japan against the American occupation government; and the design for a Communist Korea could have been, in Stalin's mind, a prelude to a neutralist, or even a Red, regime in Tokyo, an eventuality that would both discomfort the Americans and outflank the Chinese. As fantastic as these perspectives might seem, we should remember that Stalin was now, perhaps, deranged; for he was clearly contemplating equally fantastic things at home. So the Korean adventure is quite probably a sign that Stalin was now out for maximum imperial advantage throughout Eurasia. As the French saying goes, appetite comes with eating. It is clear that in Stalin's last years his international ambition had grown while his fear of the "imperialists" had diminished.

But whatever the full story behind the Korean adventure may be, the decision for war turned out to be a major miscalculation. All remaining doubts in the West about Communism's aggressive intentions vanished, and although the Korean War was blamed more on Mao than on Stalin, Communism everywhere was now viewed as an imminently threatening force. The United States intervened in Korea under a mandate from the United Nations, and although the war ended in a stalemate, it was now clear that America would not hold back from military action against Communism. In the West, German rearmament became inevitable, and NATO began to acquire a genuine military capability. The United States undertook a systematic buildup of both conventional and nuclear armaments, and the Soviet Union did the same. The Korean War thus marks the culmination and the most dangerous moment of the first Cold War, that of Marshal Stalin. And in its midst he made his exit from history.

EXIT THE RED KHAN

Stalin's last four years brought yet another crisis to the regime. The institutions and practices he had developed over the previous two decades now began to work against the functioning of the system itself. And in this final attempt at revolution from above, a case can be made that his paranoia had become dementia.[20]

In the postwar years Stalin governed by balancing one clique of retainers against another. Such elders as Molotov and Kaganovich, who had entered the Politburo in the 1920s, began to lose influence to men who attained that rank after 1939. Among the latter, at the end of the war Georgii Malenkov was ascendant. In 1946–1947, however, he was eclipsed by Zhdanov and his retainers from Leningrad, including the talented economist Nikolai Voznesenskii, also a Politburo member, who had managed the Soviet economy during the war. Upon Zhdanov's early but probably natural death in 1948, Malenkov returned to the front rank in alliance with Beria, and in 1949–1950 the two engineered the purge and execution of Voznesenskii and other Zhdanov allies in the Leningrad Affair. As this was the first purge of a Politburo member in a decade, it thus marked the beginning of the new crisis. Also in 1949, Molotov, Voroshilov, and Mikoyan were demoted from their ministerial positions; Molotov's wife was arrested and exiled; and Stalin took to saying that Molotov and Voroshilov had been British spies since 1918. At the same time, another younger contender, Khrushchev, was brought from Kiev to Moscow to counterbalance Malenkov.

With such festivities accompanying his seventieth anniversary, it is clear that Stalin was preparing another great changing of the guard within the Party. But this time he was not aiming first at the mass of cadres; he was preparing to attack the nucleus of close aides with which he had engineered the Great Purge. Possibly he believed his assistants had grown ineffective and had lost the requisite Bolshevik vigilance through too long a tenure in power. Possibly he had no reason for turning against them other than senescent paranoia and the fear that they must be living only for his death, or even conspiring to hasten it. In any event, attacking the core leadership of the system was an even greater sign of mental deterioration than voicing suspicions about Molotov's espionage.

His close aides, for their part, now believed that this situation could not go on for much longer. They therefore urged him to call a Party Congress—none had met since 1938—in order to reactivate the Party's constitution. Stalin took them up on this device, but as a means for launching his new purge. At the Nineteenth Party Congress at the end of 1952, his policy was to enlarge the Central Committee and double the size of the Politburo, now renamed Presidium, and thus submerge both generations of the old guard in a group of newcomers beholden to him alone. This was the technique of the Great Purge of the thirties applied to the beneficiaries of that purge. But it was now applied in a Party of entrenched *nomenklatura* cadres who could not be overturned without bringing disaster to the regime; and it was directed against an old guard whose members, unlike Ordzhonikidze or Postyshev, knew how the mature Stalinist mechanism worked and, therefore, might attempt to defend themselves.

The next stage of the intended purge was the Doctors' Plot of January 1953. A number of Kremlin physicians, most of them with

Jewish names, were arrested for the murder of Zhdanov and for other anti-Soviet crimes. Here was the atrocity that could serve, as had Kirov's murder, as the pretext for an ever-widening purge of "traitors" working for American imperialism, Zionism, and the destruction of international Communism. And a purge of this scope, in the tense situation created by the Korean War and the impending rearmament of Germany, would inevitably have the function—much like that of the purge of 1937—of national psychological mobilization for a major international crisis, even possibly a Third World War—who knows?[21]

In the midst of this hysterical and dangerous situation, Stalin had a stroke, and on March 5 he died. He could have been assisted on his way by a frightened entourage. Or his physical and mental health could have given way—he was 73 years old—under the strain of this new enterprise. In any event, his heirs immediately annulled the decisions of the Nineteenth Congress by resuming their old Politburo positions, and they declared the Doctors' Plot a police fabrication. The Stalin era thus ended as its work was about to be undetermined by Stalin himself.

So ended the central episode of Soviet history. Stalin died exactly twenty-five years after he had first started to remold Russia by launching the Urals-Siberian method. His was the longest tenure in office of any major twentieth-century leader except Mao Zedong. Stalin's was also the most momentous exercise of power of any leader, including Mao, because Stalin created the model of Communist society that other Communist leaders imitated or, on occasion, tried to correct. Lenin's impact, both on Russia and on the world, was by comparison significantly weaker. For Lenin's Revolution, although it created the Party and sketched the first version of the new society in War Communism, ended in failure when it had to abandon both its international ambitions and its internal socialism in 1921. And if the moderate NEP had continued as Bukharin wished, at best Russia would have bogged down in a slow-growth quasi Social Democracy that would have been a model to no one, and that could not have aspired to a major international role. It was Stalin's revolution from above that created a radical new model and oriented the system towards building international power. Thus it was through Stalin's action that Lenin's failed Revolution was revived and projected across a third of the planet.

That the resulting Stalinist system was not one that Lenin himself had explicitly envisioned, or, even more, one that Marx had anticipated, does not make that system any less Marxist-Leninist. Ideologies are not blueprints that adherents can apply point by point so that we can then say neatly that a given system has betrayed or fulfilled its origins. Ideologies are worldviews that orient political conduct towards general goals and within broad parameters. In the case of Marxism, the goal was "socialism"—in the sense of noncapitalism—and the parameters were history's inexorable progression towards this goal through the "class struggle" waged by the universal class of the exploited against its "bourgeois" exploiters. Leninism accepted all of this and added to it the parameter that history would realize its socialist purpose through the dictatorship of the Party standing in for the proletariat.

Ideologies, moreover, like all human purposes, are subject to Hegel's Cunning of Reason; that is, all human actions inevitably serve ends of which the actors themselves are not aware. Stalin is best understood as the vehicle of such a perverse process in the barbarous way he built Marx's socialism through the instrumentality of Lenin's Party. Yet that the result was both monstrous and absurd does not mean that Stalin betrayed either Marx or Lenin. It means, rather, that the Marxist-Leninist enterprise was inherently impossible; that any attempt to realize it would therefore have to rest on the massive application of force; and that such an application could only produce a preposterous surreality. This is the meaning of a whole body of Soviet satirical literature about Sovietism, from Evgenii Zamiatin's *We* in 1920, through Andrei Platonov's *Foundation Pit* in 1934, down to Aleksandr Zinoviev's *Yawning Heights* in 1974. And this, indeed, is the Cunning of Unreason that drove the whole Soviet adventure.

To put the matter another way, Marx's utopia of integral socialism could never result automatically from the logic of history, and so history had to be forced by the Leninist Party. Without the Leninist seizure of power, capitalism would have been suppressed nowhere, and the Second International Marxism would have withered away in a succession of welfare states. The proof of this lies in what actually happened throughout Europe after the Second World War: non-Communist Marxism invariably went to Canossa at Bad Godesberg. Similarly, without the Stalinist revolution from above, Leninism would never have achieved integral socialism, but instead would have dwindled away in a quasi-market, "petty bourgeois" NEP. In short, the only practical way to realize the Marxist purpose was through Leninism; and the only practical way to complete the Leninist project was through Stalinism.

The alternative to this road was to abandon the whole dream of Marxist socialism. But given the overwhelming drive towards integral socialism in the twentieth century, there was little chance that the dream would be abandoned before men had first tried to realize it somewhere. It was Russia's bad luck that it was tried out there first. And it was her supreme bad luck that it was actually carried through by so bad a man as Stalin, a misfortune that was compounded by his longevity. For after twenty-five years of the Stalinist regime, Russia and all of the other Communist systems were so deeply enthralled to the Lie that it would take them another four decades to find a way out.

9

REFORM COMMUNISM I

Khrushchev's Moscow Spring, 1953–1964

> *The most dangerous time for a bad government is when it starts to reform itself.*
> —*Alexis de Tocqueville, anent Turgot and Louis XVI*

> *We were scared—really scared. We were afraid the thaw might unleash a flood, which we wouldn't be able to control and which could drown us. How could it drown us? It could have overflowed the banks of the Soviet riverbed and formed a tidal wave which would have washed away all the barriers and retaining walls of our society.*
> —*Nikita Khrushchev, anent the changing of the guard in 1953*

Mavakovskii's words about Lenin's eternal presence in Soviet life are even more applicable to Stalin after 1953: Although he no longer lived physically, he still lived, and would continue to live, both morally and politically, until the end of the system in 1991. It is also no exaggeration to say that the remaining four decades of Soviet history would be dominated by one overriding problem: How to bury Stalin. All three of his principal successors as General Secretary—Khrushchev, Brezhnev, and Gorbachev—were primarily concerned with the problems engendered by his legacy. All of their policies were devised either to amend and reform it, or to protect and preserve it; or, more exactly, these policies oscillated between the one and the other concern. But whichever tack was followed, the problems of the system were only aggravated. Thus all three leaders departed the scene in failure and bequeathed a legacy of new crisis.

So Soviet history after Stalin marks the resumption, after the long period of apparent stability during his reign, of that alternation between War Communism and the NEP, or between "hard" and "soft" Leninism, that had characterized the first twelve years after October. The drama in two acts constantly repeated would now continue, with a muted replay of the NEP for a decade under Khrushchev, then a routinized War Communism or neo-Stalinism for eighteen years under Brezhnev, and finally a brief but runaway NEP for six years under Gorbachev. Yet these seemingly eternal returns to the basic moments of Sovietism could not really be repetitions of the first cycle, which was completed before 1929.

The routinized neo-Stalinism of Brezhnev was a pallid replica of the original: the real article could occur only once in the system's history because Stalinism was generated by the very moment of building socialism. Only this process of revolutionary breakthrough could justify coercion on a Stalinist scale, for Stalinism was not just coercive terror, as is too often assumed: it was terror to achieve the socialist breakthrough. Similarly, a "NEP" after Stalin's institutionalized quarter century of War Communism could not be the same as a NEP after the improvised and ephemeral first version of War Communism. Lenin's War Communism had collapsed in failure, leaving only a skeleton of institutions for the Party's future use; Stalin's War Communism was a "success" in the sense that it created a mountainous and resistant mass of institutions that was consecrated, moreover, by military victory and international power, and that was sacralized by the "cult." Thus Stalinism was the peak towards which Soviet history had been building since October, and from which it would slowly descend in the four decades after 1953.

The neo-NEPs of this second, descending cycle, therefore, are best given the separate designation "Reform Communism." And Reform Communism is to be understood as an effort to humanize and liberalize the Stalinist legacy without abandoning its integral socialist nature, that is to say, planning, collective property, and the leading role of the Party. The founding father of Reform Communism, Khrushchev, called his program a return to "true Leninist principles." His adversaries called it "revisionism," perhaps the worst sin in the original Leninist vocabulary. His adherents replied that these nostalgic Stalinists were "dogmatists." Another classic name for Reform Communism is the Czech slogan of 1968, "socialism with a human face."

Still another name is Marshal Tito's "socialist self-management." Deng Xiaping called his version the "four modernizations." But perhaps the most famous name for Reform Communism is Gorbachev's *"perestroika."* As these examples indicate, the phenomenon is not unique to Soviet Russia but occurs in all Communist systems once socialism has been built. As these examples also indicate, the emphasis in each case is somewhat different, depending on the nation's background and the stage of Communism at which the reform effort is attempted. Nonetheless, all of these attempts have certain characteristics in common.

These characteristics are dictated by the nature of the Stalinist order against which Reform Communism is directed. This nature may be summarized as the unity of life in one center of authority. There is one leader, one true teaching, one "correct" line of policy, and one all-embracing institution, the Party, operating through its subinstitutions: the Plan, the police, and the military. And this unitary socialist world is seen as being in constant struggle with the external capitalist enemy. This, at least, is the theory and the aspiration of the system; and during Stalin's last years it was not far from the reality in Russia, Eastern Europe, China, and, slightly later, in Cuba and Vietnam. Reform Communism developed its program by attempting to soften this system without destroying the moral and functional unity necessary to socialist society.[1]

The first element in the generic program of Reform Communism is an effort to tell a part of the truth about the Stalinist or Maoist past, to attenuate the Lie and revive critical thought in order to improve the workings of the system; and this inevitably means some measure of general cultural and intellectual liberalization. The second element is an effort at economic decentralization in order to promote greater efficiency and the material well-being of the population. The third element is related to the second: it consists of devising incentives for individuals and enterprises to work, produce, and make a profit while still not abandoning the Plan in favor of the market. And the final element is international détente, the relaxation of those tensions that maintain Communist systems in a permanent state of siege and internal mobilization. The first country to try the program of Reform Communism was that of the system's origin, Russia; and given the primacy of the Soviet model for the legitimation of Communisms everywhere, the crisis of the system in Russia could only mean the spread of Reform Communism throughout the whole international movement.

DE-STALINIZATION

The first term to emerge for Reform Communism was "de-Stalinization," for the whole movement began with the dismantling of the machinery of the late Leader's personal dictatorship. Immediately after his death the old Politburo, now called the Presidium, was restored to its pre-1937 authority, and the semiconstitution of the Party was reactivated under the name "collective leadership." Within this ruling group power at first seemed to pass to a triumvirate of Molotov, Beria, and Malenkov; and the latter, as Stalin's designated heir at the Nineteenth Party Congress, became head of the government. Khrushchev, underestimated by his colleagues, received what they thought was the secondary post of First Secretary of the Party, a position that Stalin had subordinated to his role as prime minister at the end of his career. All members of the ruling group understood that the situation was fraught with danger and that concessions to the population were therefore imperative; even Beria became an advocate of liberalization.

To his colleagues, however, Beria and his police were the principal obstacles to any such liberalization. He clearly aspired to take power on his own, and he had, in the security organs, the means to do so. An even bigger liability for Beria was the fact that after 1937 Stalin had ruled the Party through the police; so the first step in any reform of the system was to subordinate the police to the Party once again. Accordingly, Khrushchev took the initiative in organizing his colleagues for Beria's overthrow. Beria was arrested at a Politburo meeting in June, with the aid of Marshal Zhukov, the hero of the battles of Moscow and Berlin; he was tried in secret and executed in December. This would be the last time the death penalty was used against a major figure for political reasons. At the same time, the Ministry of State Security was downgraded to a Committee of State Security, or KGB, and subordinated to the Council of Ministers. This was a signal to the *nomenklatura* and to the population at large that the mass terror had ended and that the Party was now supreme in the country.

But reform, of course, could not stop with this act of self-defense by the oligarchy; the end of the terror awakened expectations throughout the country that soon acquired a momentum of their own. The intellectuals, whose expectations of liberalization after the war had been dashed by the *Zhdanovshchina*, now timidly voiced hopes for a general relaxation of the system, a "thaw," to quote the title of a mediocre novel by Ilia Ehrenburg. Less visibly at the time but more importantly, the death of Stalin, and especially the fall of Beria, undermined the old order in the Gulag. The camps were shaken by revolts so severe that they had to be put down by the army.[2] The leadership soon realized that the Gulag had become too costly politically and economically to preserve; it would have to be liquidated and its several million inmates released. At the same time, the relatives of the *zeks* who were dead as well as of those who were alive deluged the government with demands for rehabilitation.

It is against this background that Khrushchev moved to attack Stalin directly in his "secret speech" at the Twentieth Party Congress in 1956.[3] He had a number of motives. One, no doubt, was his personal ambition to become supreme leader. In 1955 Khrushchev had already forced Malenkov's resignation as prime minister and his replacement by his own ally, Nikolai Bulganin. An attack on Stalin would discredit and possibly eliminate such old-guard Stalinists as Molotov and Kaganovich, and thereby consolidate his own hold over the Party. Another possible motive, as Khrushchev's admirers assert, was a basic human decency and his genuine revulsion at the crimes Stalin had committed.[4] Still another was the harsh necessity born of the fact that, with several million *zeks* returning home, the truth would soon out; it was thus best to anticipate this development, and to do so on the Party's own terms.

But there was yet another motive, perhaps the most fundamental, though it is by no means incompatible with the first three. For all his years as Stalin's pliant instrument, Khrushchev had remained a true believer in the Leninism of his youth, in that ideological commitment to socialism as the "radiant future" that Stalin had attempted to replace, through the purges, with blind obedience to his own "cult" in the present. One reason for this attitude was Khrushchev's generational position within the leadership. Unlike Molotov and Kaganovich, he was not old enough to have become one of Stalin's henchmen during the Civil War, and thus a general during the Great Offensive; and unlike Brezhnev, he was not young enough to be entirely a product of the Stalinist system. Nor was he a pure apparatchik of the

Party's central Secretariat, as was his near contemporary, Malenkov. He had been, as we have seen, only a Party foot soldier during the Civil War and no more than a lieutenant in the Great Offensive. Moreover, most of his career had been spent with the Party troops in the field, largely away from Moscow and close to the practical problems of workers and peasants.

For Khrushchev's generation the mystique of the Revolution was always very real, although this fact did not render him any less adept than other Leninists at the raw manipulation of power. How he reconciled his commitment to the ideals of the Revolution with his close service to Stalin at the height of the purges, both in Moscow and in Ukraine, we do not know. He claimed for himself a large measure of ignorance of the true state of affairs; yet, although he was less directly involved than Molotov or Kaganovich, he could not have helped but know the basic truth. He probably got through those years by resorting to the usual Bolshevik principle "you can't be right against the Party," but at the time Stalin *was* the Party—and Stalin was a very dangerous man. In any event, once Stalin was gone, Khrushchev's aim was to purge the Party of Stalinist *peregiby*, or "distortions," and return it to its true Leninist principles.

Thus, in his own way, Khrushchev wanted to be the "Lenin of his day" (although he did not use that slogan), the leader who would at last permit the system to realize its human and economic potential. His ambition was to prepare the transition from the "socialism" that had already been achieved to the full "communism" that had been the scenario for the life history of the proletarian dictatorship ever since Marx's *Critique of the Gotha Program*. By the same token, he wanted to release the system's creative potential in order to demonstrate definitively its superiority over "capitalism." It is this uplifting prospect, and not some dire threat, that Khrushchev had in mind when he boasted to his alarmed American hosts in 1959—"we will bury you"—and when he promised them that their "grandchildren will live under Communism." And it is for these reasons that he wanted to get rid of the Stalinist old guard and become the sole supreme leader.

It is with this mix of motives that Khrushchev forced the hands of his Politburo colleagues and used the first post-Stalin Congress to launch de-Stalinization. This was no doubt the most important thing Khrushchev ever did; and the results were as mixed as his motives.

On the one hand, the Soviet populations were given nearly a decade of forward movement and hope, and the best period the country had known since the NEP, or that it would know until *glasnost*. On the other hand, since the cult of Stalin was so central to both the internal system and the world Communist movement, Khrushchev's attack on the departed leader began to unravel the threads of myth that held the whole structure together.

But the speech only began this process, for it by no means made a clean breast of the past: Khrushchev denounced only some of Stalin's crimes, and at that, only those committed against the Party and only after 1936. Nonetheless, the head of Soviet power had now admitted that criminal activity had existed at the heart of Soviety power, so this fact could no longer be dismissed as a bourgeois calumny. The contents of the speech became widely known throughout the country, and it was published in full abroad—all of which Khrushchev would have been naive not to expect. There had been no such bombshell out of Moscow since the Molotov-Ribbentrop Pact. Many of the faithful, both at home and abroad, were shaken in their faith; others of the faithful, as well as the moral heirs of the Popular Front, concluded that Stalin had been only an "aberration," and that the Soviet Union might be beginning a transition to social democracy. True, four months later, under pressure of both Soviet Stalinists and foreign Communist leaders, the Central Committee published a resolution attempting to limit the damage: Stalin was declared a great "theorist and organizer," the author of the "victory of socialism," whose record was marred only by certain abuses of power due to flaws in his character. Still, the "cult" could not really be restored; and the deleterious consequences of this immediately made themselves felt at the system's weakest link, Eastern Europe.[5]

The reasons for this are not far to seek. Stalinism in Eastern Europe was less than a decade, not twenty-five years, old; the workers still remembered a more pluralistic order—and in some countries, social democracy—and in places the peasants were not yet fully collectivized. But perhaps most important of all, Communism was experienced as an illegitimate foreign imposition. Indeed, trouble had begun immediately after Stalin's death: In 1953 there were riots in Pilsen in Czechoslovakia, and there was a genuine workers' insurrection—triggered by the raising of factory production norms—in East Berlin that had to be put down by Soviet tanks. The secret speech brought Eastern European instability to its climax.

The crisis began in the largest and most restive satellite, Poland.[6] The spark was a labor revolt in Poznan in June that was again put down by tanks. Discontent soon became national, and Gomulka, who had been released from prison in 1954, now emerged as the reform candidate to head the Party. This prospect so alarmed Moscow that Khrushchev, flanked by the old guardists Molotov and Kaganovich, flew into Warsaw in October to head it off—if necessary with Rokossovski's army. But Gomulka threatened to defend Warsaw by arms rather than back down, so it was the Soviets who gave way. Rokossovski was removed, and Khrushchev accepted the principle of "different roads to socialism" in exchange for Gomulka's pledge of loyalty to proletarian internationalism. In practice, Poland's "national Communism" meant full home rule, the end to collectivization, and broad autonomy for the Catholic Church. In return, home rule was to be exercised only under the leading role of the Party and in strict fidelity to the Soviet alliance. And so the Polish situation was stabilized for a decade in one of the few cases of a half-way successful Reform Communism. But the Polish October helped trigger a tragic outcome to a similar crisis in Hungary.

The forces of worker, intelligentsia, and national dissatisfaction in Hungary were roughly the same as in Poland, but there was no Gomulka who could represent and at the same time restrain them, and thereby gain the confidence of the Soviets.[7] When the Hungarian thaw began, the hated General Secretary Rakosi opted for repression, contrary to Khrushchev's own policy. Moscow then intervened and replaced Rakosi with the almost equally hard-line Ernö Gerö, a move that only radicalized the situation further. Moscow then put in its reserve Reform Communist, Imre Nagy, but too late, for now the Polish example had triggered large street demonstrations demanding the end of Russian occupation. Under this pressure, Nagy created a coalition government with non-Communist parties, thereby abandoning the leading role of *the* Party; and he ended by demanding the withdrawal of Soviet troops and taking Hungary out of the Warsaw Pact.

Nagy thus violated the two principles on which the Communist system in Eastern Europe rested. Moscow accordingly had no alternative but to intervene if it were to remain Moscow. And although this intervention was obviously not Khrushchev's first choice of policy, once he had made it he did not hesitate to crush Budapest with tanks, and later to execute Nagy—quite in the tradition of Lenin's action at Kronstadt. Khrushchev also summarily installed a new government under a leader recently imprisoned by Rakosi, Janos Kadar. His mission was, first, to restore Communist control and, next, to reform the system within the limits of the two cardinal principles Nagy had violated. In time, Kadar's efforts would lead to an even more successful and temporarily stable Reform Communism (it was to last until 1989) than the one in Poland.

But in neither case had a genuinely viable order been created, since the survival of both regimes depended on a degree of submission to the Soviets and to the local Party that deprived them of national legitimacy. Under Stalin the Soviet empire in Eastern Europe had been fragile because it rested on a level of coercion and centralized control that could not be maintained indefinitely, as the "October Revolutions" of 1956 demonstrated. After these explosions and the recognition of "different roads to socialism," the East European empire still remained fragile because it now depended on the willing collaboration of the local populations; yet they accorded this only because they feared Moscow's reprisals if they did not—a situation that could last only so long as Moscow retained the capacity to compel collaboration. Thus, on balance, the cohesion of the bloc had been weakened by the reforms of 1956. At the same time, the opponents of reform in the Soviet Union had been given a great argument against Khrushchev's policies at home—and against his person.

Within the Soviet Union the secret speech provoked nothing so explosive as what happened in Eastern Europe, but it did produce the beginnings of dissidence among the intellectuals. In 1956 historians such as E. N. Burdzhalov, in a series of articles, went beyond Khrushchev's circumspect reexamination of the Soviet past and began to fundamentally undo the work of the *Short Course*, beginning with 1917; Burdzhalov thereupon was fired. Even more important, Boris Pasternak in *Doctor Zhivago* undertook a reevaluation of the Revolution that came close to being a condemnation.[8] When the manuscript was turned down by the Soviet review *Novyi mir*, Pasternak had it published abroad in 1957, thereby inaugurating the great tradition of *samizdat*. Translated into all major languages, it instantly became a worldwide best-seller, and in 1958 Pasternak was awarded the Nobel Prize. The scandal in Moscow was immense; Pasternak was forced to decline the prize, and most of his colleagues in the Writers' Union were forced to condemn him. Still, it had been demonstrated that the thaw could get out of hand in Russia, just as it had in Eastern Europe.

There was yet another negative consequence of the secret speech: the beginning of the rift with China and the consequent decline of the "international workers' movement."[9] It was only Stalin's personal authority that had held the world Communist movement together; and his world-historical success made any challenge to his leadership inconceivable to all Communist chiefs except Tito. But deferring to the likes of Malenkov and Khrushchev was quite another matter, especially for the Chinese, whose own leader, Mao, was now the senior hero of the international movement. In the post-Stalin situation, therefore, the Chinese wished to be treated as equals and partners. Hence they were outraged by Khrushchev's taking so important a step as the desacralization of Communism's central icon, Stalin, without consulting them. In addition, the Chinese had their more practical grievances against the Soviets, especially over Manchuria, going back to Stalin's time. They therefore took the defense of Stalin against Khrushchev's "revisionism" as a means for asserting their independence, indeed their ideological superiority, vis à-vis the Soviets. This was not yet an open break, but it was already a disruptive tug-of-war.

The sins of the new Moscow leadership were aggravated by another of Khrushchev's innovations: his overtures to the archrevisionist, Tito.[10] In 1955 Khrushchev went to Belgrade and in effect apologized to the Yugoslavs in the hope of bringing them back into the "socialist camp"; this may be counted an internationalist reflection of his naive Leninism. The Yugoslavs, of course, were not about to rejoin the camp, but they used the Soviet recognition that theirs was indeed a "socialist country" as a sign of approval of their ongoing experiment in workers' "self-management."

In fact, Tito was now engaged in devising his own brand of Reform Communism.[11] Like the Chinese, the Yugoslavs had launched their socialism by taking over the ready-made Stalin model. By the early 1950s, however, in order to justify their break with Moscow, they began to elaborate an alternative model of society that Tito on occasion called "real socialism"—an expression Brezhnev used years later in a diametrically opposite meaning. For the Yugoslavs, this slogan meant that Moscow's brand of socialism was not the genuine article; so Tito proposed to devolve power from the centralized Party-state to popular organs of self-management—an echo of the soviets and the "commune state" of the original Russian Revolution. Concretely, this more democratic Yugoslav socialism meant: first, the abandonment of the collective farm for ordinary cooperatives; second, elected workers' councils for the management of industry; and third, a federal structure for the country's six ethnically based republics. The only centralized element of the old system that was retained was the Party (now rebaptized League of Communists) together with its army.

But this was quite enough to insure that the democratic elements of the reform would fail. To anticipate a bit, although the peasants largely went their own way, the workers' councils soon fell back under the control of the Party, and federalism divided the economy into uncoordinated segments without bringing genuine autonomy to the six regional republics. The result was local rather than central Party control over the economy, a lagging rate of development, and increasing dependence on the West—tourism and the export of *Ostarbeiter*— for whatever prosperity the country enjoyed. And federalism worked only so long as the charismatic and despotic marshal was there to hold his realm together. Although this turned out to be a very long time because he lived until 1980, it was not long enough for Yugoslav Reform Communism to transform itself into a constitutionalist order or a genuine market economy or a real federation. For Tito's radical Reform Communism, no less than Khrushchev's more hesitant version, failed to break the mold of the Party-state; and when the end came, it did so as a crash, not a transition.

Moreover, in the 1950s Khrushchev's effort at a rapprochement with Tito brought the Soviet reform few advantages. True, in 1956 Tito gave his advance approval to Khrushchev's crushing of the Hungarian secession as necessary for the defense of socialism, though he later criticized the severity of the repression. But he would never rejoin the "camp," and instead became one of the founders, with Nehru, Nasser, and Sukarno, of the "nonaligned movement," which was designed to be a third force in international affairs between NATO and the Soviet bloc. And although this force was more nonaligned in favor of the East than of the West, the Yugoslav regime because of its independence and its self-management socialism none-theless set a bad example for the Soviets' East European satellites. Finally, Yugoslavia remained a major source of friction between the Soviets and the Chinese: At international Communist gatherings in the fifties, the Chinese would attack Yugoslav "revisionism" as a way of criticizing Khrushchev, and the Soviets would attack China's ally and Tito's enemy, Albania, as a way of castigating Chinese "dogma-tism." All of this simply eroded international Communism still fur-ther.

But the most important bone of contention between Khrushchev and the Chinese, and his most important foreign policy initiative *tout court*, was the policy of "peaceful coexistence" with the West, and in par-ticular with the United States.[12] This new policy arose because of the post-Stalin need to promote internal stability by improving the pop-ulation's living standard and because of genuine fear of international instability after the Korean misadventure. And both of these concerns were linked to the problem of how to wage the "international class war" in the new age of nuclear weapons.

Accordingly, the Soviets at last agreed to an armistice in Korea as well as to a state treaty ending the four-power occupation of Austria, and they put out feelers for a reunited but neutralized Germany. This détente culminated in the first postwar summit between Soviet and Western leaders when Khrushchev and Bulganin met at Geneva in 1955 with Eisenhower and the prime ministers of Britain and France. Although the "spirit of Geneva" was touted at the time as marking the end of the Cold War, this meeting in fact inaugurated a long and stormy relationship between the two superpowers that would soon come to center around their rivalry in nuclear arma-ments.

But détente with the United States was, of course, even more of an anathema to the Chinese than the Soviet rapprochement with Tito, for the Americans were the direct adversary of the Chinese in the Taiwan Straits. Therefore, in attempting to solve his problems with the West, Khrushchev was further undermining the cohesion of in-ternational Communism. The monolithic heritage he had received from his predecessor was thus being fissured externally as rapidly as it was eroding internally. Nor was there any lack of Stalinists in the Soviet high command to take alarm at Khrushchev's innovations and so to attempt a restoration of the old order. And this led to the first great crisis of the Khrushchev years: In June 1957 a majority of his Politburo colleagues tried to depose him.

The main grievance was the secret speech and the Polish and Hungarian explosions the speech had provoked. Additionally, the wooing of Tito, the growing tension with the Chinese, and détente with the Americans were cause for concern to the old guard. And Khrushchev's impending plans for internal economic reform—of which more shortly—were perceived as equally dangerous. The Politburo attack on Khrushchev was led by Molotov, Malenkov, and Kaganovich. They were eventually joined by Bulganin, Voroshilov, and two of the chief economic planners, Maksim Saburov and Mikhail Pervukhin. But Khrushchev refused to bow to this majority and step down. He insisted that he was responsible only to the Central Committee that had elected him and all his adversaries; and he succeeded in prolonging the meeting for a sufficient number of days to bring his supporters to Moscow from the provinces, an effort in which he was aided by Marshal Zhukov's air force. Thus Khrushchev won, while his critics were condemned as "the Anti-Party Group." But it is significant that most of the group remained members of the Presidium and would stay there for a few years more. Khrushchev was not strong enough to purge them outright; nor would the Party now accept the summary dismissal of prominent leaders, because if Khrushchev could get away with that, he could then purge anyone else, as his predecessor had been able to do. It is with this far less than iron control over the machinery of the Party that Khrushchev embarked on his great internal reforms.

KHRUSHCHEV'S "NEW DEAL"

Khrushchev's domestic reforms would be upsetting to the old Soviet order all along the line, for his attack on Stalin the man was part of an effort to de-Stalinize and remold the whole Soviet system—agriculture, industry, international relations, and the functioning of the Party itself. This is not to say that Khrushchev had a grand design for reform; he clearly did much of what he did in response to crises and the actions of his opponents. But he was also not simply improvising his way from one bold program to another, as has often been alleged.

There was a pattern and a general' direction to his experiments.[13] Although this direction has often been described as "populist," Khrushchev's populism was of a very special kind, for it was to be realized only with and through the Party.

In Khrushchev's version of Leninism, the mission of the Party and of the socialist system was to improve the material existence of the simple people, the workers and peasants in whose name the Party ruled; it was in carrying out this task that socialism would show its superiority over capitalism. Stalin had not only committed crimes, he had diverted the Party from its true path and had plunged the people into poverty. And Khrushchev, through his extensive experience with the daily life of the population—whether in Moscow, on the kolkhozes of Ukraine, or in the army on the Ukrainian front—was well acquainted with the wretched conditions in which it lived. In this he was unlike Stalin who, as we have seen, almost never left the Kremlin or his nearby dacha. Khrushchev, of course, was well aware of this contrast and had clearly resolved to be a different type of leader. For Khrushchev, socialism meant material abundance for the people; for him, at last providing that abundance should be the system's primary task. This meant that the traditional Soviet priority of heavy industry over light, and of producer over consumer goods, must be reversed. And this in turn entailed a decrease in military production, and hence a policy of reducing tensions with the West. It is this package of interrelated measures that Khrushchev consistently pursued through all the vicissitudes of his eleven years in power.

It was Malenkov, however, who had first publicly proposed this reversal of priorities in 1953, and Khrushchev at that time had opposed him. The reason for this, however, was politics, not principle: The military and the planners were alarmed by Malenkov's initiative, so Khrushchev allied with them to dispose of a rival; and then, somewhat as Stalin had done with Trotsky, he adopted his rival's program.

But unlike Stalin, Khrushchev began with the most depressed area of the Soviet economy, agriculture.[14] For Stalin the kolkhoz had been essentially a means for extorting a food supply from the peasants without payment; Khrushchev aimed to transform the kolkhoz into a geniune economic institution oriented towards steadily rising productivity. In 1953 he gave the first frank governmental assessment since collectivization of conditions in the village, pointing out that the livestock population had fallen below its level of 1929 and was even smaller than it had been before the Revolution. He followed this with material concessions: Taxes were decreased on private plots and the family cow, prices for compulsory deliveries to the state were increased, the production of tractors was expanded, and chemical fertilizers were introduced.

But all of this would take time to produce significant results, and Khrushchev wanted a quick improvement in living standards. So in 1954 he launched an old-style Bolshevik offensive to open to grain cultivation some thirty-five million hectares of "virgin lands" in northern Kazakhstan and southern Russian Siberia.[15] It was Khrushchev's longtime protégé, Brezhnev, who directed the campaign in the field, and this assignment would be the latter's last stepping-stone before moving to the Central Committee in Moscow. Komsomol activists were dispatched from the cities to organize sovkhozes in the semiarid steppes of the virgin lands; some three hundred thousand people would eventually settle there, and by 1956 an expanse equivalent to the total cultivated area in Canada was in production. And the campaign worked for a time: on average, a third of the Soviet Union's annual grain harvest came from the virgin lands by the end of the decade. But the program was also extremely wasteful: drought made production chancy, and soil erosion took an ever increasing toll.

The success of the virgin lands made possible the second prong of Khrushchev's agricultural campaign. Soviet livestock herds, and consequently meat production, were low, in part because of lack of fodder. The new grain supply from Siberia made it possible to devote more land in European Russia to producing fodder, and Khrushchev chose corn because of its high yield per acre. In 1955 corn production was introduced by decree throughout European Russia, though with only meager results, since most of this area was too far north for cultivating such a crop. Yet Khrushchev pressed on. In 1957 he launched a new campaign to catch up with the United States in the production of "meat, milk, and butter," which meant nothing less than tripling the output of these products within three to four years—an impossible goal. At the same time, he lent support to the quack Lysenko, who now reached the height of his influence.

The culmination of Khrushchev's agricultural experiments was a vast reorganization of the collective farming system in 1957–1958. In spirit this reform was consistent with his earlier infatuation with agrovilles and the Marxist goal of ultimately abolishing the "contradiction between town and country." To this end kolkhozes were pressured to amalgamate, and their total number dropped from 125,000 in 1950 to 69,000 by 1958. At the same time, there was a drive to transform kolkhozes into sovkhozes, and the latter doubled their acreage during these years. These changes, of course, ran counter to Khrushchev's earlier measures regarding the peasants' family plots; but they were very much in the traditional Bolshevik spirit of large, mechanized collectives as the proper organization for agriculture, and were thus the logical expression of Khrushchev's Party populism. In fact, towards the end of his reign he cut back the size of the family plots.

Khrushchev's final agricultural reform, however, ran counter to all previous policy: in 1958 the Machine Tractor Stations (MTS), hitherto the cornerstone of Party control in the countryside, were abolished and their machines sold to the kolkhozes. The purpose of this radical reversal was to give the enlarged kolkhozes and sovkhozes the means to become the modern socialist units of production they were supposed to be in theory. In fact, however, the cost of purchasing the machines and the problem of maintaining them were a new burden on the kolkhozes; the skilled personnel of the MTS did not wish to be downgraded to the status of kolkhoz workers, so many of them did not relocate with their machines. The result of the reform, therefore, was disappointing: The enlarged kolkhozes were more easily controlled by the Party, but they could not use their machinery any more efficiently than their predecessors had used theirs under the old system.

So what was the effect of Khrushchev's exertions in the countryside? The plight of Soviet agriculture was at last well publicized, and improving it would henceforth be a major concern of the regime. The concrete results of this concern, however, were modest. To be sure, up until 1958 matters did improve notably: Peasant incomes rose, and both the peasants and the city dwellers came to enjoy a higher standard of consumption. But after 1958 agricultural production levelled off and then declined. And by 1963, following a disastrous harvest, the Soviet Union for the first time had to import grain from the United States, while the talk of corn as the key to catching up with America in meat, milk, and butter was a thing of the past. So what went wrong?

First of all, Khrushchev's impulsiveness and impatience hampered his reforms: one reorganization followed another so rapidly that the kolkhozes wound up in a state of disorganization. Another problem was that Khrushchev too often wagered everything on a single solution, whether it was corn, ploughing under clover, or opening virgin lands. His activism created yet another problem in that the peasants were now more closely supervised by the kolkhoz administration; in particular, they were more involved in collective labor than they had been during the years of Stalinist neglect, so the yield of their individual plots correspondingly declined. But the main defect of Khrushchev's reforms was that they were all introduced by decree from above and implemented through the storm tactics of Party activists: peasant initiative was suspect, and the kolkhozniki were expected to respond to orders, not to incentives.

In short, Khrushchev's improved and enlarged collective farms were only another manifestation of the usual Communist formula of attempting to solve economic problems by political means. Moreover, his campaign to transform the kolkhoz into an economic institution simply politicized the countryside further, since this effort came entirely from the Party, not from the people that Khrushchev thought, no doubt sincerely, he was working for. And yet the value of increasing popular initiative was by now self-evident: the perennial success of the family plots, as well as the achievements of the link system during the war, showed that only the incentive of individual profit could improve agricultural production. But this was unsocialist, and thus for that true-believing Leninist, Khrushchev, it was also retrograde and unacceptable. So the kolkhoz continued as a sacrosanct Soviet institution, and a new and more boastful Agricultural Exhibition was erected to its glory in Moscow.

Khrushchev was similarly energetic and radical in his industrial policy.[16] Here, however, he had to tread with greater caution because of the intimate links between industry and the military. Malenkov had been overthrown, after all, by an alliance of the military, the planners, and Khrushchev himself, for giving preference to consumer production over heavy industry. And Khrushchev was personally beholden to the military, and in particular to Marshal Zhukov, for its aid in disposing of Beria and, even more, for saving the situation during the Anti-Party crisis of 1957. Indeed, as a reward Zhukov had been made an alternate member of the Presidium, the first time any military leader had been so honored. Nonetheless, the "metal-eaters," as Khrushchev called the bosses of heavy industry, had to be dethroned from their predominance if the consumer needs of the population were at last to be met; and this, of course, meant reducing the size of the armed forces and spending less on their equipment. Khrushchev resolved this dilemma by appeasing the military with nuclear and ballistic weapons (which are less expensive than conventional armaments), and this in turn enabled him to shift investment from heavy to light industry. At the same time, to obviate any possibility of Bonapartism, Marshal Zhukov was removed from the Politburo and retired while on a visit to Albania.

But there were other potential opponents of any reversal of Soviet industrial priorities, and these were the professional planners. In the quarter century since Stalin had begun the Soviet industrial buildup, the national plant and its planning apparatus had grown enormously in size and in complexity. In effect, Stalin's system had been a war economy with one priority: the complex of coal, iron, steel, machine tools, and heavy machinery. The whole enterprise had been launched in 1930 by one agency, Vesenkha. But by 1932 this agency had been broken into three specialized industrial ministries and by the end of the decade there were twenty. The war and the postwar reconstruction entailed further bureaucratic expansion, especially for military needs, to where by 1948 there were thirty-two industrial ministries.

This Leviathan continued to grow under Khrushchev, in part to keep up with Western technological developments, as in electronics, of which television was only the most visible example, and in part to reequip agriculture and meet other consumer needs, such as clothing and household goods. In particular, Khrushchev launched a huge program of prefabricated housing to make up for one of the worst lacks of the Stalin years, for such consumer concessions to the population had become imperative for the system's stability. And this multiplication of priorities created more industrial and other economic ministries, to where by the late 1950s they numbered around forty, a growth which created a more complicated task of resource allocation, coordination, and planning. Nonetheless, the planning apparatus, with its now huge corps of professionals, remained devoted to the old overriding priority of heavy metallurgy.

In 1957, therefore, Khrushchev decided to limber up the system by abolishing most of the central ministries and dispersing their functions to some 150 regional economic councils, or sovnarkhozes. Only armaments, chemicals, and electricity were to remain under central control. This breakup of ministerial empires alienated entrenched *nomenklatura* interests at the center and in the higher echelons of the system, but it found support in the regional Party ranks where Khrushchev had always had his basic clientele. This reform also generated much administrative confusion, for the central Plan remained, yet the means for coordinating the activities of the local councils were now deficient.

Still, Khrushchev pressed on with his innovations, for he, and the system, were now riding very high indeed. In 1957 the Soviet Union astonished the world with the first Sputnik, a feat that not only advertised the progress of her technology but also demonstrated her prowess in ballistic missiles. And Soviet space exploits continued, with an unmanned landing on the moon in 1959 and the first man in space, Iurii Gagarin, in 1961. Khrushchev's belief in the intrinsic superiority of the Soviet system was only reinforced by these achievements, and that superiority even began to appear as a real possibility to many in the West.

His personal power also increased.[17] In 1958 he removed Bulganin, who had sided with the Anti-Party Group, as prime minister and assumed that post himself, thus combining, as had Stalin, the roles of Party chief and government head. He also scrapped the then current Sixth Five-Year Plan and replaced it with a grandiose Seven-Year Plan. To approve this departure from Soviet practice, in 1959 he resorted to the equally radical measure of convening a Party Congress, the Twenty-first, two years early, the first such "extraordinary" Congress in Soviet history. And in the same year, he capped a series of forays abroad—which had taken him to India, China, Yugoslavia, and Western Europe—by a visit to the United States and another summit meeting with Eisenhower at Camp David. The contrast between this tireless world travelling and the reclusive habits of his predecessor sparked the world's imagination and seemed to demonstrate the sincerity of the Soviet Union's commitment to peaceful coexistence. The "spirit of Camp David" took up the torch from the "spirit of Geneva," and the Cold War appeared to be winding down.

But the years 1957–1960 turned out to be the climax of Khrushchev's minirevolution from above. Thereafter, the increase in performance he had managed to squeeze out of the system began to decline. He met a series of international reverses. And his tireless campaigns of internal reorganization generated widespread opposition within the Party.

At the beginning of the sixties the failure of Khrushchev's agricultural program was compounded by the disintegration of his industrial reorganization. It turned out that the sovnarkhozes could not operate effectively, either within their own designated regions or in coordinating activity with other regions, without constant reference to the center. A tractor factory in one region needed steel and equipment produced by factories in another, and both regions required credits and supplies from the center. A national Gosplan continued to conduct prospective planning, while republican Gosplans were charged with implementation of the all-Union plans. In order to insure coordination between these levels and among the regions, a creeping recentralization soon emerged in the form of special state committees with approximately the same functions as the old ministries and the same personnel. In 1963 a great merger of sovnarkhozes reduced their number by half, and all of them were placed under a supercoordinating agency with the old Bolshevik name Supreme Economic Council. Thus Khrushchev's industrial reform was virtually undone. In the meantime, production had been disorganized and the Soviet rate of economic growth began a decline that would continue until the collapse of 1991.

The sovnarkhozes failed not because Khrushchev had concocted them in his usual impetuous way—although this was indeed a part of the problem—but because they went against the grain of the system. In the absence of a market to allocate resources, this task inevitably becomes the function of a directive plan; that is, one where production decisions are made administratively according to political, not economic, criteria. But a directive plan has to direct, otherwise everything collapses in confusion. In other words, directive planning must be centralized to function at all, and dividing up its activities into zones or layers destroys the necessary chain of allocative command. It is like granting decisional autonomy to the divisions of an army in the midst of a campaign; and the Soviet-style directive plan, as we have seen, is in essence an institutionalized war economy. The Soviet system, therefore, spontaneously recentralized itself in self-defense against Khrushchev's sovnarkhozes.

This does not mean, however, that he was not attacking real deficiencies inherent in a command economy. The first of these stems from the fact that in any productive process the number of decisions to be made is too large for advance calculation or central direction. Any such plan, therefore, is by its very nature woefully incomplete, and it must consequently be corrected by constant inputs from below. In a normal, or market, economy these inputs are furnished by real prices, not by the political prices of a Soviet-type system. Failing such real prices, decentralization becomes the principal means for correcting the rigidity of the plan. But decentralization, too, is only an administrative or political, not an economic, device. It thus only continues, or simply transposes to another level, the problem it was supposed to correct. And most Soviet economic reforms over the post-Stalin decades were essentially pseudosolutions of this sort.

Another deficiency of directive planning is an inbuilt tendency to stagnation. The Plan requires central, monopolistic ministries, and these tend to become self-perpetuating empires. The Plan, moreover, is made up of projections from past experience, as quantified in statistics, which are then recycled into "control figures" which serve as targets for future production. Thus each year the Plan tends to produce what it did before, only multiplied somewhat, and the emphasis is correspondingly on quantity, not quality. In such a world new products or designs are disruptive because their introduction causes delays in the upward march of Plan percentages as well as losses of rewards.

As a result of this spirit of routine, the primitive Stalinist planning mechanisms designed for heavy metallurgy almost never produced technological innovations or developed new products. And when, in the postwar years, such innovations and products were introduced from the West, the planning system had increasing difficulty in adapting; this became painfully evident as the industrial cutting-edge advanced from chemicals and plastics to electronics, and then to computers. Each time a new product or technology was introduced, a new ministry would be created, a crash "campaign" would be launched, and in a few years the system would more or less catch up with the West—but by then the frontier of technological progress would have moved forward once again. Only in the area of armaments, especially nuclear and ballistic, were the political methods of the Soviet economy genuinely effective and internationally competitive. For the rest, the farther one got from the military sector, the worse the economic performance became.

The crisis of the late Khrushchev years was thus "systemic." It was due to the institutional rigidity and the inherent conservatism of the planning system, in conjunction with the constantly expanding demands made on that system after the Second World War. Accordingly, the once impressive Soviet rate of growth declined steadily after 1958, and although the Soviet Union was still generally considered to be the "world's second-largest economy," this status was increasingly called into doubt. So Khrushchev plowed on with new political programs for solving his economic problems.

Ever since the virgin lands program, the thrust of Khrushchev's reform efforts had been to put economic considerations ahead of political ones, and to favor consumer interests over the "metal-eaters' " pursuit of growth for growth's sake.[18] These attitudes together constitute Khrushchev's version of the NEP—to be sure, a NEP without a market and in a post-Stalin context, but a NEP in revisionist spirit nonetheless. And "revisionism" was the opprobrious epithet applied to Khrushchev's policies by his adversaries in Peking and, *sotto voce*, in Moscow. For this policy was not only a reversal of accepted Stalinist priorites; it was also a challenge to the habits and convictions of the by now enormous and well-entrencned managerial and planning bureaucracies.

By 1961, therefore, Khrushchev's reforms in both agriculture and industry were encountering increasing resistance from the Party apparat. Indeed, this resistance had its roots in the affair of the Anti-Party Group of June 1957. One of the factors leading to that abortive coup had been Khrushchev's move two months earlier to introduce sovnarkhozes, but the final provocation in the eyes of the Group had been Khrushchev's campaign to "overtake the United States in meat, milk, and butter" in the ridiculous span of four years. Somewhat later, the apparatchiki were riled by his campaigns to generalize the growing of corn for fodder and to plow under the clover once favored by Stalin. But the hostility of the orthodox was brought to a peak by the abolition of the MTS—as much a fetish in socialist agriculture as metallurgy was in socialist industry—together with the switch to a Seven-Year Plan. This hostility was all the more threatening because, although Khrushchev had defeated the Group, he had not crushed it, for he had been unable to expel its members from the Party. In his view, therefore, the main impediment to reform was the still Stalinist cast of the Party. So at the regularly scheduled Twenty-second Party Congress in the fall of 1961 he sought to advance his economic programs by a political revolution in the Party and by launching a second de-Stalinization campaign.

The initial purpose of the Congress was to approve a new Party Program, only the third since 1903 and the first since 1919. Because the two previous documents had been the work of Lenin, the Congress marked a symbolically important moment for the Party, and Khrushchev resolved to make the most of it. His program was intended to guide the country to the end of the "dictatorship of the proletariat" and thus to effect the "transition to communism." Khrushchev initially wanted a detailed blueprint for the future, even spelling out the "withering away of the state" and its replacement by the Party—at last the "Party of all the people"—as the sole institution of society's self-management. But he was compelled by his colleagues to drop these utopian goals, and this only increased his impatience with what he considered their obstructionism.

Even so, the slogan of the Congress proclaimed that "the present generation of Soviet people will live under Communism," and the new Party Program rashly promised that this boast would be realized, "in the main," by 1980. The Program also included projections of a 10 percent annual growth rate over the next two decades, and on this basis it predicted that the Soviet Union would overtake the United States—whose per annum rate of growth was a mere 2.5 percent—by 1970. And in the West, such heavyweight newspapers as the *New York Times* and *Le Monde* took these claims seriously, if not exactly literally. In fact, Khrushchev had in mind something more modest than these figures seemed to suggest. The communist society of "from each according to his abilities, to each according to his needs" was not some visionary crystalline city; prosaically, it meant that housing and such services as transportation and utilities would be free. It was a utopia of full social security and egalitarianism for the common man; but it also implied a static level of needs that did not require an expanding economy once the modern industrial base had been "built." Because Khrushchev believed the Soviet system had essentially acquired this base, he could quite sincerely claim that full communism was nigh and that his country already deserved to be called "paradise." And this naive expectation of what the "radiant future" would mean in concrete terms was very widespread among his simpler compatriots.

But the entrenched apparat was barring the way to this future, and so the practical business of the Congress was to devise means to break the cadres' resistance. Accordingly, Khrushchev pushed through a revision of Party statutes limiting members of the Central Committee or its Presidium to three five-year terms; at the regional and local levels, the new rule limited officials to three two-year terms. Although exceptions were allowed for unusually qualified leaders, these new rules, if applied, would have ended the virtual life tenure that all apparatchiki had enjoyed since Stalin's death. The Party figures most threatened were the middle-level provincial leaders who had hitherto been Khrushchev's main base of support; although they dutifully voted for the new statutes, as the First Secretary demanded, their reaction was in fact hostile. And this outcome highlighted another structural dilemma of the system: A term limit was the only way to make the apparat accountable to anyone but the apparatchiki themselves, yet at the same time it set up an inevitable conflict between the apparat and its supreme leader, whose term, moreover, was not limited.

In the fall of 1962 Khrushchev compounded this potential for conflict by splitting the Party hierarchy in two, making one half responsible for agriculture and the other half for industry. The rationale for this change was to make Party officials ride herd on factories and kolkhozes to increase productivity, and at the same time make these officials directly responsible for failures. Thus every province and district now had two hierarchies of officials, and each hierarchy had overlapping jurisdictions and clashing functions, since industrial and agricultural operations in any given area could not be neatly separated. Party functionaries, moreover, had for decades been concerned primarily with political and ideological work. Their role in economic production had been that of general supervisor, troubleshooter in a crisis, and regime policeman; they had been the eyes and the ears of the system in the enterprises, and the advocates of the enterprises to the system. Now, however, they were being asked to assume a direct role in production, one for which they were not qualified and which they resented. In their view, the Party had been stood on its head, and politics had been improperly subordinated to economics. And in truth the reform did result in a further confusion in the operation of the system and a further decline in production.

So the structural dilemma of the system had once again been highlighted. In order to solve an economic problem Khrushchev had resorted to a political solution, for under Soviet conditions the economic and the political were inextricably intertwined. Yet, in fact, he had only produced another self-defeating pseudoreform, for economic forces could not be liberated by a purely administrative restructuring; they could be liberated only if they were freed from political control *tout court*. But this was impossible because it would deprive the Party of its raison d'être, and this neither Khrushchev nor the apparat were prepared to contemplate.

Khrushchev's shake-up of Party structures was accompanied by a second de-Stalinization campaign, which began at the Twenty-second Party Congress and unfolded throughout 1962. The attack on Stalin at the Twentieth Congress had had its greatest impact on the international Communist movement and on the outside world in general. The new campaign would have its most profound impact within the Soviet Union, where it changed the cultural atmosphere irrevocably.

At the Twenty-second Congress, Khrushchev departed from the prepared scenario and again launched into a vehement attack on Stalin's crimes. But this time he made the attack in public and over national radio, and he was seconded by a succession of like-minded orators. The Congress then voted to remove Stalin's body from the Lenin Mausoleum; it was buried beside the Kremlin wall under a load of concrete. Stalin's statues came down across the Soviet Union and his name disappeared from institutions and cities, including even the sacred site of Stalingrad, which became tritely Volgograd.

All this astounded the country but did not change the habits of the Party, so the next year Khrushchev enlisted the help of the liberal intelligentsia for an even bolder campaign. *Pravda* published a poem of Yevgenii Yevtushenko, "The Heirs of Stalin," aimed at all the still-living lesser despots of the apparat and calling for a vigilant guard over the new "gravestone slab" beside the Kremlin wall. In the nascent shadow politics of Soviet life, this was a major declaration.

Far more important, however, in November 1962 *Novyi mir* published the novella of a recently returned but still unknown *zek*, Aleksandr Solzhenitsyn's *One Day in the Life of Ivan Denisovich*, the first depiction of life in the Gulag.[19] It immediately became known that "He Himself" had authorized it, and that it was intended to be the signal "not just for a campaign, but for a policy." In fact, Khrushchev got a great deal more than he had bargained for. His aim was the limited one of shaking up the Party and purging the system by having it come to terms with its past. The aim of Solzhenitsyn's intelligentsia sponsors was the vaster one of liberating culture from Party control and definitively demolishing the Stalinist Lie. Ever since the thaw of

1953, and especially after the coup of *Doctor Zhivago*, Soviet writers had been growing bolder in what they put on paper about the Stalin era. The problem was to get it into print. So *Novyi mir*'s editor, Aleksandr Tvardovskii, seizing the occasion of the second de-Stalinization drive, selected Solzhenitsyn's novella as the most likely vehicle for a breakthrough; he managed to transmit it to Khrushchev's personal secretary, who read it to the leader at odd moments. Its populistic tone (the hero was a simple worker) struck a responsive chord, and Khrushchev enthusiastically distributed it to the Presidium for approval. With this imprimatur in his pocket, Tvardovskii went ahead with what turned out to be the second great bombshell of the Khrushchev era.

For the story went beyond an attack on Stalin to an implicit attack on the system as such. The camps were for the first time mentioned publicly in the Soviet Union, and thus their existence—which many people in the West still denied—was certified by the regime itself. Even more, whereas the secret speech had addressed only Stalin's crimes against the Party, *Ivan Denisovich* shifted the focus to the sufferings of the people; and this led the population to conclude that de-Stalinization should now become a general process of liberating society. A whole literature of de-Stalinization began to emerge. Anna Akhmatova for the first time dared to write down her poem on 1937, "Requiem," and younger writers, such as Andrei Amalrik, began to produce. To be sure, most of this output did not get into print. But in "pre-Gutenberg" fashion, as Akhmatova said, it did get distributed as *samizdat;* and quite often it was published "over there" in the West as *tamizdat,* and then read back to Russia by radio.

So by the end of Khrushchev's reign a culture of dissidence was born. For the first time since the 1920s critical public opinion and an embryonic civil society existed in Russia. For the moment, the members of this new critical intelligentsia had no thought of opposing, still less of attempting to end, the regime. They all kept strictly within the limits of Reform Communism, even one as embittered as Solzhenitsyn. All that they wanted was the "truth" about the past. Yet it was inevitable that this prosaic, empirical truth—if pushed far enough—would demolish that Lie which was the system as a whole. The guardians of orthodoxy, such as the Central Committee's secretary for ideology, Mikhail Suslov, immediately understood this and undertook to whip up a backlash. A month after the publication of *Ivan Deniso-*

vich, Khrushchev was inveigled into visiting an exhibition of abstract painting, which caused him to explode with a barrage of expletives and to comment that "a donkey could do better with its tail." And so the rollback began: Solzhenitsyn got to publish only two more stories in Russia, and the Gulag ceased to be a subject for literature. Nonetheless, the damage to the system's credibility could no more be undone than could the damage to the "cult" after the Twentieth Congress. With the great thaw following the Twenty-second Congress, and with his restructuring of the Party, Khrushchev had inadvertently begun the long process of subverting Communism by attempting to reform it.

RIDING FOR A FALL

Khrushchev achieved similarly contradictory results through his adventures in foreign policy. He inherited a seemingly unified international Communist movement arrayed against American "imperialism," and he left a divided movement with his own Soviet state humiliated by the rival superpower. The seemingly irresistible forward momentum of Communism during the last years of Stalin had bogged down in a global war of positions that would last for the next quarter century. The Cold War that had appeared to be drawing to a close early in Khrushchev's reign was still very much an ongoing affair by its end.

The central concern of Soviet foreign policy under Khrushchev was essentially what it had been under Stalin: international security that would permit the Soviet state to develop its global power. And Khrushchev's method of pursuing this end also showed similarities to Stalin's: an intimidatingly militant bluster with a tendency to get out of control.

A part of the bluster was a new forward policy in the Third World, an area Stalin had never penetrated. Khrushchev, taking advantage of postwar decolonization, became active in India, the Near East, and Africa; he financed Nehru's steelworks at Bhilai, built Nasser's Aswan Dam, and supported Patrice Lumumba in the Congo. All of this disturbed the West greatly, for it seemed to give Communism a renewed and extended momentum. And in fact it did serve to enhance the prestige of the Soviet Union as a power, and of socialism as a model of society. Still, it cost a great deal of money and brought Moscow no concrete economic gain.

But the primary objects of international concern to Khrushchev were the United States, Germany, and China, because a threat to Soviet security could come only from these quarters.[20] The three concerns, moreover, were interrelated, and all were linked to the problem of nuclear weapons. In brief, the chief aim of Soviet policy was to achieve nuclear parity with the United States while keeping China and Germany nonnuclear and weak. The Germans could acquire nuclear weapons only if the Americans permitted it, so the way to keep Germany weak was by some sort of deal with Washington. But keeping the Chinese nonnuclear was much trickier because they were an ally under threat from American imperialism. A deal with Washington would alienate this ally, and too active a defense of the ally would preclude a deal with Washington. So Khrushchev eventually fell between these two stools, thereby producing his, and international Communism's, first major defeat.

The root of this problem was China's very existence as a huge country bordering the Soviet Union; that fact made it a natural rival, not a natural ally. Thus the alliance between the two countries was above all the product of ideology and a shared need for the socialist mystique as a legitimizing force. But the myth of the "unshakable unity of the socialist camp" was no small matter, for Communism, like the ancient Church, must be catholic if it is to be deemed true. Its universality is the first proof of its "scientific foundation," and its unity is the main guarantee that it will prove invincible and its conquests irrevocable. Any fragmenting of the international movement, therefore, threatens its credibility and its hold on power everywhere. The defection of Tito and the creation of a rival form of Communism had been bad enough; a repetition of this on the scale of China would be a disaster. Yet circumstances inexorably pushed Khrushchev into such a fatal schism.

The first circumstance was that China was too big not to demand equality with the Soviet Union in directing the international movement, while the Soviet Union would be diminished if it abandoned paramount leadership. The second circumstance was that China in the 1950s was embroiled in a deep conflict with the United States, which was still protecting the nationalist regime in Taiwan. In the name of Communist solidarity, the Chinese demanded all-out Soviet support, including even nuclear weapons, in defying the United States and taking the island, while the Soviets held back evasively. On the one hand, the Soviets needed the Chinese alliance and the unity of the bloc to strengthen their own position in dealing with the United States. On the other hand, the Soviets were afraid that Chinese militancy might draw them into war with the United States—especially since Mao had taken to making blithe declarations about the acceptability of losing three hundred million of his people in a nuclear conflict, because China could still build socialism with the three hundred million that would remain. Soviet leaders continued this balancing act until 1959, when at last they flatly refused to help China build a bomb and wound down their aid for civilian nuclear energy.

Concurrently, the Chinese abandoned the Soviet model of building socialism, which they had hitherto followed, and embarked on a frenetic quest for their own "separate road to socialism" with the Great Leap Forward of 1958. This program was reminiscent of Stalin's revolution from above of 1929, or of Lenin's War Communism of 1918. But it purported to go beyond any Soviet precedent and to skip over mere socialism—where workers are rewarded unequally—into the full Communism of absolute equality. This was to be achieved by a return to the guerrilla ethos of the Chinese Civil War, but it would now be applied to the creation of gigantic "people's communes" and to the production of steel in backyard peasant foundries. With this Great Leap, China was supposed to become a mighty industrial power capable of defying the Americans on its own, and the whole campaign unfolded at the height of the crisis in the Taiwan Straits. This program was also to serve as a model and a magnet for all colonial Third World countries, including Vietnam, which had engaged in a "war of national liberation" against France. China's new course was thus directed against both Western imperialism and Soviet leadership of the world Communist movement.

Although China's program ended in disaster and had to be abandoned—some thirty million people perished from famine—it left an important political legacy. Henceforth China was the militant force in world Communism, and Mao the senior revolutionary leader, whereas the Soviet Union under Khrushchev (and later under Brezhnev) was the "rich man's" or the "white man's" pseudosocialism, chronically inclined to compromise with imperialism. Thus another model of socialism, alongside Tito's self-management, now competed with the original Soviet version. And these two heretical models held real attraction for countries and "people's movements" throughout the Third World, from Southeast Asia to Africa. The resulting tension between the two Communist giants was so great that in 1962 Khrushchev withdrew all Soviet advisors and credits from China, and from this time onward practical collaboration between the two powers ceased.

Still, the need of each party to define itself in terms of the socialist camp kept the dispute largely concealed from the eyes of the "imperialists" for some time longer; and this circumstance had a lot to do with prompting American intervention in the second Vietnam War. But the myth of the socialist camp also led both the Soviet Union and China to believe that unity would someday be restored once the other side recanted—perhaps after the fall of Khrushchev for the Chinese, or of Mao for the Soviets. So the actual break was followed by a long ideological wrangle over "dogmatism" and "revisionism," "capitalist roaders" and "neo-Stalinists," or over the errors of Khrushchev's new Party Program of 1961, or of Tito's New Program of 1957. It was not until 1964 that the Chinese openly denounced the Soviet Union as being no longer a socialist country but in fact an "imperialist" power. After this, Moscow's recurrent efforts to convene a world congress of Communist parties would prove futile. But it was not until President Nixon's visit to China in 1972 that the myth of a socialist camp finally died.

In terms of real international power, the Soviets lost little from this break: the support of six hundred million Chinese in the "Sino-Soviet bloc" during the 1950s had always provided more the appearance than the reality of strength. Still, in a system whose legitimacy derived from a single irresistible ideology, this schism represented a loss of credibility that would eventually translate into a loss of power. And this loss would be felt first at home. The break with China, coming in the wake of de-Stalinization, diminished still further the regime's claim that it held the one true teaching for preparing the way to the "radiant future" of full communism. And the open conflict of Chinese and Soviet interests—which led to a brief armed clash on the Amur River in 1969—undermined the Leninist proposition that only imperialism spawned war, whereas socialism bred peace.

In a sense Khrushchev "lost China" because he hoped to gain security vis-à-vis the United States and Germany.[21] His problem with the

United States was that throughout this period it was in a position of superiority with regard to nuclear armaments, and he wished to find some means of achieving a semblance of parity. His problem with Germany was that it had been rearmed and taken into NATO, and he wished to prevent this process from reaching the nuclear level. The way to solve both problems was through an accommodation with Washington. But Khrushchev's method of seeking such accommodation involved a large measure of bluster and bluff, which in fact worked dangerously against his desired end.

The Soviet nuclear and ballistic missile programs, like everything else in the mature system, had been launched under Stalin. His heirs, however, were largely unacquainted with either program and thus had to develop a strategy on their own.[22] Their problem was twofold. First, their production of bombs and warheads after the thermonuclear breakthrough of 1953 was well below that of the United States. Second, the Soviet Union could not produce a fleet of long-range bombers comparable to those of the American Strategic Air Command to deliver nuclear weapons. Khrushchev's solution to both problems has been called "strategic deception." Spectacular tests of super-bombs were conducted in the atmosphere to give the impression of possessing a huge arsenal. At the same time, Soviet successes with Sputnik and other missile launchings were exploited to give the impression of an intercontinental ballistic missile (ICBM) capability sufficient to counteract America's superiority in long-range bombers. Both of these deceptions depended on secrecy, since until late in the 1950s the United States had no adequate means of aerial detection of Soviet military installations. So Khrushchev used the appearance of strength to attempt to intimidate Washington into a global deal for mutual security.

The essence of the deal was that Moscow would keep China non-nuclear if the Americans would accept a neutral and nonnuclear Germany as well as military parity with the Soviet Union. This, of course, was never stated in so many words, but was telegraphed by political pressure and diplomatic maneuver. Through rocket rattling and bomb testing during 1956-1958, Khrushchev sought and achieved his invitation to the United States in 1959 and the scheduling of a four-power summit in Paris in 1960, both as a prelude to a settlement of the German problem. To give further impetus to this process, in 1958 he gave Washington what sounded like an ultimatum over Berlin: a German peace treaty was to be signed within six months or Moscow would make one separately with East Germany, thereby turning over access routes to Berlin to the new state. The purpose of this, however, was not so much to squeeze the allies out of Berlin as to create a bargaining chip for getting them to abandon the rearming of West Germany. When this threat did not produce the desired results, Khrushchev went to Camp David anyway (and then immediately rushed to Peking to appease his irate Chinese allies), but the Berlin issue remained as a goad to the West, even after the construction of the Wall in 1961.

This balancing act seemed to be working well enough until 1960, when the deception was found out and intimidation led to major crisis. In the late 1950s overflights by the American U-2 spy plane had revealed that the Soviets did not have the ICBM capability suggested by their testing and boasting. Then, in 1960, a U-2 was shot down over Sverdlovsk, and when President Eisenhower refused to apologize, Khrushchev abruptly cancelled the already assembled Paris summit to cover his position both at home and in Peking. In 1961 he stepped up the pressure again over Berlin at a meeting in Vienna with President Kennedy, who had just been weakened internationally by the fiasco of the Bay of Pigs invasion of Cuba, a pressure increased still further by the construction of the Berlin Wall later that year.

All of this culminated in the ultimate measure of intimidation, the placement of Soviet missiles and nuclear warheads in Cuba in 1962. This move was not undertaken primarily to defend Cuba against another American-sponsored invasion, as Khrushchev later alleged. It was, rather, a wild wager, a desperate effort to solve all of the Soviet Union's foreign problems on the cheap. It was, first, a quick way to make up for the Soviets' lack of ICBMs: By moving medium- and intermediate-range missiles to the United States' doorstep, Khrushchev hoped to achieve strategic parity through geographic proximity. Second, it was a way to appease the Soviet military, whose effectives and budgets had been cut back in favor of Khrushchev's domestic programs for consumers. And third, it was a way to force America to accept at last the Soviet position on Berlin and Germany, perhaps by using the missiles in Cuba as an actual bargaining chip. Finally, it was a way to show the Chinese that Russia had not gone soft on imperialism and that they therefore did not need a bomb of their own.

To achieve any or all of these objectives, however, Khrushchev would have had to dramatically reveal the presence of the Soviet missiles at the moment of his own choosing and then initiate summit negotiations on his demands. And this was no doubt his intention. But an American U-2 found him out before he had fully set up shop on Cuba, as indeed he should have known was likely before he started. The island was then "quarantined" by American forces; his bluff was called; and he had to back down, having gained no more than verbal concessions from Kennedy. Thus ended the gravest crisis of the whole postwar period.

Paradoxically, it occurred at a moment when the Cold War was generally on the wane. Negotiations for a nuclear test ban had already begun in 1959, and the treaty outlawing testing in the atmosphere was signed shortly after the crisis, in 1963, thereby inaugurating the long process of arms limitation and negotiations that would continue until 1990. The year 1963 also saw the first American grain sale to the Soviets, thus beginning another long-term process. Still, the Cuban missile crisis, though an exception, was not a fluke due solely to the impetuous personality of Khrushchev. It was also the expression of a fundamental weakness in the Soviets' international position: because their system did not really provide the resources for their superpower status, the temptation was always present to make up for this weakness by some rash expedient. Khrushchev's Cuban gamble was only the most spectacular case of this. Korea had been an earlier example. And there would be other instances later.

Another paradox of the 1962 missile crisis is that it was perceived as a crisis only in the West. The Soviet population did not know that anything was going on until it was over, and even then most did not realize how dangerous the moment had been. This is because the regime presented the population with a picture of the world in which the Soviet Union, although assailed by imperialism, was nonetheless invincible. The Cold War and the arms race were presented as threats unilaterally directed by the West against the Soviet Union, while the "struggle for peace" was claimed as the defining characteristic of Soviet policy. In this atmosphere, ending the Cold War and curtailing the arms race were never a widespread concern among the Soviet population, even though these causes were a major issue to important groups in the West. The Soviet population's concerns were overwhelmingly domestic—from improving living standards to curtailing repression. There was no "peace movement" in the Soviet Union, and this circumstance gave Khrushchev a completely free hand for a bold foreign policy. Thus he could leap into Cuba accountable to no one but the Party leadership.

But in the eyes of his colleagues, even though Kennedy let him save as much face as possible, Khrushchev's credibility as leader was now seriously damaged. Moreover, the defeat in Cuba occurred at the same time as his "error" in authorizing the publication of *Ivan Denisovich* and his decision to split the Party in two. These three events of the autumn of 1962, taken together, constitute the first reasons for Khrushchev's removal from power in October 1964.

An even more fundamental cause of his demise lies in the changed nature of the Party-state in the post-Stalin period. The Party itself was different from what it had been eleven years earlier, and its relationship to the leader was different as well.[23]

At Stalin's death the Party numbered 6.9 million and, as we have seen, was well on its way to becoming a *nomenklatura* Party, one dominated by the managerial elite of a now imperial state. The new corporate nature of the Party was still obscured, however, by that organization's complete subordination to Stalin and by the tutelage of the security police. By the time of Khrushchev's fall, the Party numbered 11,750,000 and had fully become a *nomenklatura* Party, the corporate organization of the managerial elite. At the same time, with Beria's fall, it was emancipated from police tutelage and, as it turned out, from its leader as well. Yet it took a decade for this to become apparent.

During his prime years at the end of the 1950s, Khrushchev tried to rejuvenate the Party just as he tried to shake up everything else. And in this domain, too, his policy was populist, another reflection of his paleo-Leninism. Of the 4.5 million new members taken in between 1956 and 1964, an increasing percentage were workers and, to a lesser degree, peasants at the time of their enrollment; the two categories together accounted for about 50 percent—a clear reversal of the growing trend of the last years of Stalin to recruit from the "intelligentsia," that is, the managerial class.

This evolution was of a piece with Khrushchev's education policy. Once Stalin had put his system in place, he restricted access to higher education by imposing tuition, thereby regulating the flow of new cadres into managerial and apparat positions; this, of course, tended to make the cadres into a caste. Khrushchev sought to democratize education by abolishing tuition for higher education and by making the basic ten-year school universal. And he attempted to bring the reformed system even closer to the people by adding two years to the basic curriculum and requiring all students in the higher classes to work half-time in the economy, thereby hopefully preventing the separation of a professional intelligentsia from the masses. As such, this reform was a part of Khrushchev's "transition to communism" and "the state of all the people." This scheme, however, went against the grain of an increasingly specialized and stratified labor force: the reform irritated the upwardly mobile families of cadres who wished their children to remain full-time in school, while the insertion of part-time workers into the economy disorganized production. Nor did the reform slow down the growth of social differentiation in the country.

The upshot was that Khrushchev's greatly expanded Party was even more an organization of the managerial elite than Stalin's Party. Members who entered as workers quickly moved up to minor managerial positions. And a constantly increasing number of members had higher education. Just as important, only around 4 percent of the working class were in the Party, whereas 25 percent of those classified as intelligentsia were members. And anyone who aspired to a position of responsibility in the system had to join the Party in his or her early thirties at the latest. Thus, overall, the Party by the end of Khrushchev's reign had become the unfettered corporate organization of the *nomenklatura* establishment.

And this establishment, especially its inner core of full-time Party apparatchiki, did not like to be thrown into one campaign after another, reorganized and then again reorganized. It wanted stability and the quiet enjoyment of its power and perquisites.

Nor was it any longer very afraid. Since the execution of Beria and his chief aides, no prominent figure had paid the supreme penalty for political reasons. The members of the Anti-Party Group—which, after all, had attempted a coup d'état—were only demoted to lesser jobs, and Khrushchev was not even able to expel Molotov and company from the Party until 1960. He was thus clearly being resisted by his colleagues, for whom de-Stalinization meant first of all protection of the Party against the power of *any* First Secretary. And Khrushchev's failure to eliminate the Group was a patent sign of weakness that almost guaranteed it would not be too dangerous for some future grouping to try a coup again.

Moreover, Khrushchev, for all his activism as First Secretary, was only a Boss, not a Leader, or *vozhd*. He never attained the charismatic stature of the supreme Communist chiefs—Lenin, Stalin, Mao, Ho, Tito, or Castro—a stature conferred only by major revolutionary accomplishment. And at seventy years of age, he appeared increasingly as an anachronistic throwback to a simpler era of the Party.

Thus in October 1964 his colleagues in the Presidium, acting as the supreme guardians of the *nomenklatura* Party, organized a successful coup and retired him. They left no possibility of summoning his one-time provincial supporters in the Central Committee, whom he had alienated anyway by dividing the Party. And since he no longer possessed the police power to terrorize his colleagues, he had no choice but to capitulate. Officially, he retired for reasons of health. After his fall, he was accused of "voluntarism," "subjectivism," and "hare-brained schemes," by which was meant the cascade of reform policies discussed above. And so ended the first great cycle of Reform Communism in the Soviet Union's painful descent from its Stalinist peak.

10

AND THE BILL CAME DUE

Brezhnev and *Nomenklatura* Communism, 1964–1982

Obviously we have already reached that dead-end where the notion of power is linked neither to a doctrine, nor to the personality of a leader, nor to a tradition, but only to power as such. . . .

    Naturally the only aim of such a regime, at least in domestic affairs, must be self-preservation. . . . The regime neither wants to restore Stalinism, nor to persecute the representatives of the intelligentsia, nor to give fraternal aid to those who do not ask for it. It wants only that everything remains as before: that the authorities are recognized, that the intelligentsia shuts up, and that the system not be shaken by any dangerous or unexpected reforms. The regime does not attack, it defends itself. Its motto is: don't touch us, and we won't touch you.

—Andrei Amalrik, Will the Soviet Union Survive Until 1984? *1969*

The twenty years after Khrushchev's fall seemed to bring the Soviet Union to the apogee of its success and to a level of international power surpassing even that attained by Stalin after 1945. The new leader, Brezhnev, at last realized Khrushchev's ambition of attaining genuine nuclear parity with the United States; he intervened at will throughout the Third World; and for good measure he ringed the continents with his submarines. In truth, the Soviet Union now bestrode the world as a superpower. Indeed, by the 1970s, as the West reeled under the impact of the Vietnam disaster, Watergate, and the collapse of the shah's Iran, it seemed as if the "correlation of forces," as the Soviets were wont to put it, was shifting definitively "in favor of socialism." To be sure, most people in the East and in the West progressively realized that the Soviets' economic performance was hardly as good as it had appeared likely to become under Khrushchev. Still, the chances seemed real that the Soviet Union could use its international political strength and freedom from internal crises to outlast the West and so emerge the victor in the "competition between the two systems," or at least the master of Eurasia.

In reality, however, these twenty years were a time of gathering crisis. Gorbachev later called it the "period of stagnation," as if to imply that the system could be set moving again, but the terms "decline" and "disintegration" were really more appropriate. This was not just because the country was ruled by an increasingly decrepit gerontocracy that lacked both the will and the strength for reform; although this senescence was a part of the problem, it was no accident but a logical consequence of the *nomenklatura* system. In fact, the deeper cause of "stagnation" was to be found in the basic structures of the Soviet system itself: Each of these structures—the economy, the administration, the ideology, the "bloc" of people's democracies—was beginning to decay. The ensemble of institutions put together in the 1930s and 1940s had yielded its maximum potential by the 1960s, and each institution now began to decompose just as the post-Khrushchev leadership moved to prop them up. The bill for the costly successes of Soviet socialism's heroic age was at last coming due. And, logically enough, the total system created by Lenin and Stalin was slowly entering into total crisis.

REFORM FLICKERS OUT

At the time of Khrushchev's fall, it seemed as if the only significant problem facing the Soviet Union was the usual succession crisis. Khrushchev's personal rule was followed by a new collective leadership in the pattern of the two Soviet successions since the death of Lenin. Yet the pattern this time was significantly modified: There was no struggle for power ending in the emergence of a supreme chief, and the new leadership would remain essentially collective until it passed from the scene in the mid-1980s.

For Khrushchev had irrevocably amended the old Stalin "constitution." By bringing Stalin's terror to a halt, he had made his Politburo colleagues safe from the political police, but their safety had then become the source of his own vulnerability: He had given away his only leverage against the apparat, and thus the safeguard of his own power. By the same token, he had given the apparatchiki not only physical security but also, and inadvertently, life tenure in their positions. Thus, when Khrushchev was deposed, the *nomenklatura* as a collective entity became the new supreme chief of the system.

Accordingly, leading careerists of the system divided the principal posts among themselves. Leonid Brezhnev, Khrushchev's longtime protégé, became the new First Secretary. Thus the ensuing eighteen years are usually called "the Brezhnev era"; and Brezhnev can indeed stand as an appropriate symbol for his whole Stalin-bred generation. The post of prime minister was given to Aleksei Kosygin, who is often classified as a "technocrat." But that is certainly a misnomer, for this former textile engineer had worked only in the Party apparat during the previous twenty years. And Kosygin's career was not unlike that of most apparatchiki of the Brezhnev generation: Their *cursus honorum* included a somewhat rudimentary "higher" technical training during the early to mid-1930s, and then a transfer from factory management to full-time Party work in the wake of the purges. Some went on to Stalin's Central Committee Secretariat, and a few to Khrushchev's Presidium. Another member of this generation who was also a protégé of Khrushchev, Nikolai Podgornyi, became the nominal head of state. But there is no point in distinguishing too finely among these figures; they are like their fellows Kirichenko and Kirilenko under Khrushchev, or, as Gogol might have said, Ivan Ivanovich Bobchinskii and Ivan Ivanovich Dobchinskii.

Still, one apparatchik deserves special mention. This is the slightly older Mikhail Suslov, the chief ideologist and éminence grise of the Brezhnev era.[1] He is of interest because his career epitomizes the life cycle of the Soviet system. Born into a family of poor peasants, he became a Komsomol activist in the local committee of the village poor in 1918, at the age of sixteen. During the NEP, he worked his way up through a "Workers' Faculty" and the Red Economics Institute to become a professor in the Industrial Institute during the First Five-Year Plan. In the wake of the purges he became Party secretary in the southern province of Stavropol; and in 1944 he supervised the Sovietization of Lithuania. In 1947 this exemplary survivor was rewarded for his services with a Central Committee post under Zhdanov, from where he moved to Stalin's Presidium in 1952.

Under Khrushchev, in the interest of Party reform, Suslov first distinguished himself as the new leader's chief supporter against the "Anti-Party Group." Then, in the interest of Party stability, he became the chief critic of Khrushchev's excesses; and this moved him to organize the palace coup of 1964. But in all these roles he was forever the quintessential Party man, and this led him to become the chief instigator of the soft Stalinism of the Brezhnev years.

The new collective leadership of Brezhnev, Kosygin, and Suslov made its program clear when it proclaimed the principle of "stability of cadres." This principle was soon given concrete meaning by the abrogation of Khrushchev's Party statutes providing for rotation of cadres in office and for time limits on tenure. The restoration continued with the recision of the Party's division into two parts and with the suppression of Khrushchev's educational reform. Next, in conjunction with a new economic reform, the sovnarkhozes were abolished and replaced by central ministries. Thus, within a year the status quo ante Khrushchev was wholly restored but for one major exception: there was no Leader, not even much of a Boss.

In the 1960s Brezhnev was clearly only *primus inter pares*, and this remained essentially true even in the 1970s, despite his growing public prominence in both foreign and domestic affairs.[2] He travelled abroad to meet with foreign heads of state, and during the period of détente he resumed summitry with Presidents Nixon, Ford, and Carter. Domestically, in 1966 he made the neo-Stalinist gestures of resuming the title General Secretary and renaming the Presidium the Politburo. In 1977 he deposed Podgornyi as president and assumed that title as well, just as Stalin had done. He made himself a marshal of the armed forces, covered his chest with medals, and published his complete (allegedly theoretical) works—all traditional attributes of a Soviet Leader. Yet these were but the trappings and the suits of *vozhdizm*, a reflection of the inevitable tendency of collective leadership in a Party-state to bring forth—at least symbolically—a single head. In fact, he was never as active a Boss as Khrushchev had been; government in practice was by consensus, and this time collegial leadership remained a political reality. For Brezhnev had learned very well from Khrushchev's fall that the old slogan "cadres decide everything" had acquired a new meaning: In the absence of terror, the General Secretary was now ultimately accountable to them, and not the other way around, as under Stalin. Thus the Brezhnev-Kosygin-Suslov years became the great age of *nomenklatura* Communism.

So the peregrinations of Hegel's idea of Reason in History had come full circle. To the founder of modern dialectics, the rational bureaucracy was the "universal" class leading mankind to its fulfillment. Marx had given this universal role to the most deprived and dehumanized class, the proletariat.[3] Lenin had substituted the Party for the proletariat, and he legitimated the resulting dictatorship by proclaiming it the expression of the Logic of History. Under Brezhnev's "developed" and "really existing" socialism, the Party dictatorship became the domination of the new class of the *nomenklatura*. Thus the universal class was once again a bureaucracy claiming to rule in the name of Reason in History.

The new leaders by no means intended their quest for stability to end in "stagnation." Initially they wanted to be cautious reformers; and if they abandoned this course, it was because, unlike Khrushchev, they soon learned through experience that reform was too dangerous to continue. Their initial program was in three parts: first, to end de-Stalinization and eliminate intellectual dissent in order to restore stability; second, to pursue a more moderate course of economic reform in order to provide for the country's long-term strength and the consumer's welfare; and third, to proceed more slowly and less provocatively with the quest for international parity with the United States. Thus, they hoped to pursue the goals of Khrushchev's Reform Communism without the turbulence and uncertainty of his methods. And they made modest headway for a few years, until the much bolder Reform Communism of the Prague Spring of 1968 so frightened them that it ended all reform in the Soviet Union until the late 1980s.

The end of de-Stalinization and the attack on dissidence was signalled by the arrest in 1965 of two writers who had published their texts abroad, Andrei Siniavskii and Iurii Daniel, and by their trial the following year. Under Stalin, many Soviet writers had of course perished without a public trial, but this was the first time any had been incriminated for the content of their works. Both were convicted and sentenced to several years in Siberia as a warning to all others to abandon *samizdat*. But this strategem did not work; instead it sparked a small but organized current of defiance. What under Khrushchev had been an anti-Stalinist explosion mingling indignation and hope—first in 1957 and then in 1962—now became a continuing movement to which the name dissidence was soon applied.

There are several reasons why the dissident movement emerged at this time. Khrushchev's fall had not only ended public probing of the Stalinist past, it had also produced an orthodox counterattack that actually sought to rehabilitate Stalin. Indeed, the Siniavskii-Daniel trial, coming on the eve of the first Party Congress of the new leadership, was widely interpreted as a prelude to active re-Stalinization.[4] So dissidence was in the first instance a movement of self-defense against this possibility, which remained a live concern until the ninetieth anniversary of Stalin's birth in 1969. But dissidence was also a sign of a deepening disillusionment with the reformability of the system. The somewhat facile optimism of the Khrushchev years now gave way to the realization that reform would not fall from on high, but would at best come about through a long, slow process of pressure and struggle. Still, as yet the discourse of dissent was only of reform, not of breaking out of the system entirely. Lastly, dissidence could emerge because the regime was no longer willing to resort to the brutal terror of the past. This was not because the system was becoming liberal, or mutating from totalitarianism into mere authoritarianism; the change came about for the pragmatic reason that extreme terror was destructive of the system itself. Hence, the regime now conducted repression by softer, less direct, and more gradual methods, usually with a coating of "socialist legality," as in the Siniavskii-Daniel trial.

It is therefore a mistake to talk of the Brezhnev period as a new Stalinism. Brezhnev the man—even doubled with Suslov—was no Stalin, and if he had attempted a revolution from above and mass terror, he could not have gotten away with it in the circumstances of the 1960s. As has already been noted, Stalinism can occur only once in the life cycle of a Communist regime, and that once is the pivotal moment of the building of socialism. Only that supreme task can fuel the fanaticism and stimulate the violence of real Stalinism. But once socialism is built, the primary task of the regime becomes the "defense of its conquests"; Stalinism, or more accurately the Stalin system, becomes routinized and stabilized as "developed socialism." The once hot ideology of class struggle and combat becomes a cold ideology of orthodox incantation.[5] And consequently Soviet leadership passes from the revolutionaries to the guardians. It is only this "soft" Stalinism that was practiced under the gray guardianship of Brezhnev, Kosygin, and Suslov.

*   *   *

Another reason why their totalitarianism was more muted was the state of the economy. It was now too huge and too complex to be run with the brutal methods employed in the 1930s, or even with the stringencies imposed during the postwar reconstruction. Moreover, it was no longer possible to defer some measure of consumer satisfaction, and that meant the performance of agriculture had to be improved. Khrushchev had already shown the way on this score, and there was no going back. Indeed, the new leadership felt it was necessary to improve on Khrushchev's economic record in the interests of both the system's stability and the development of its military strength as a superpower. In economics, therefore, there was at first no refreeze, but rather an extension of the reform effort.

This was especially marked in agriculture. Although Khrushchev's restless "campaigning" was called off, his most important programs were intensified. Investment in the chemical industry was expanded, and the production of artificial fertilizers was increased. Prices paid to kolkhozniks for grain and livestock were raised. Restrictions on the private plot were eased. Above all, during the Brezhnev years investment in agriculture increased enormously; it eventually accounted for a quarter of the budget, at which time the Soviet Union was devoting a greater proportion of national resources to agriculture than any other country. The once neglected countryside had at long last become a top priority of the regime. And production did improve notably, indeed at a faster rate than in most Western countries.[6] All the same, agriculture remained a crisis area: each bad harvest was a national drama, and the country regularly had to import grain, especially to feed its livestock.

One reason for this relative failure was that Soviet agriculture had been so depressed that even rapid growth could not raise the level of production very much. In addition, the incomes of both the urban and the rural populations had risen, and demand had therefore significantly increased. Moreover, a large proportion of the population still worked in agriculture, thus making for a low level of productivity and increasing overall costs: The Soviet Union's urban population surpassed the rural population for the first time only in 1961, and the latter still accounted for 30 percent of the total population in 1985. Even so, there was always a shortage of labor at harvest time, and millions of city dwellers and soldiers had to be mobilized to bring in the crops.

It is clear that the basic cause of the agricultural failure was organizational: The whole enterprise—the massive investments, the generalized use of chemical fertilizers, the harvest campaigns—continued to be managed from above and from the center. Thus, the regime pressed on with its policy of transforming kolkhozes into sovkhozes, and by the 1980s the latter accounted for more than half of the cultivated area of the country. At the same time, the few timid yet quite successful experiments conducted with the "link system" were suppressed by the professional kolkhoz managers. In short, the regime had amplified the usual command-administrative methods and obtained the usual counterproductive results, yet it was impossible to advocate any other policy.

Consequently, by the end of the Brezhnev era the food supply was declining in relation to demand; and agriculture, which under Stalin had been a source of (forced) accumulation of capital for investment in industry, had become a net burden on the rest of the economy.[7] It was now clear that even with a reversal of the classic Stalinist economic priorities, collectivized agriculture could not be made productive; and the cost of this impasse could only undermine the system as a whole. The resulting impoverishment was the final fate of the junior partner in Lenin's revolutionary *smychka*, the alliance of workers and peasants.

The senior partner in the *smychka*, the workers, reached a similar impasse under Brezhnev, as did the whole industrial sector. Here the turning point was the failure of the Kosygin economic reform of 1965. But this was more than just another dismal episode of Brezhnevism, for it marked the defeat of the central program of the entire Reform Communist enterprise.

Economic reform in a centralized economy can take only one direction—towards decentralization and the market. Indeed, this had been the direction taken by all reform efforts since Stalin created the command economy in the 1930s. The first, timid intimations of moving in such a direction came during discussions of the "link system" after the Second World War. The open acknowledgment by a Communist government that decentralization might be the objective of reform came when Tito proclaimed his policy of "self-management" in the early 1950s, and then when he introduced his Draft Program in 1957. This direction received theoretical sophistication at the hands of the old market-socialist Oskar Lange, who had been ignored when he returned to Poland in 1945 to participate in building socialism in his homeland, but who met with better results during the Polish October of 1956. And Khrushchev's thaw brought this line of thought into the discussion in Russia: in the 1960s the Russian tradition of academic economics, which had been one of the most creative in the world in the 1920s, began to timidly revive, not only as a theoretical and mathematical discipline, but also as a school of thought with practical implications.[8]

These implications were first spelled out in 1962 in an article by Professor Yevsei Liberman that appeared in *Pravda* under the title "Plan, Profit, Premium." What quickly became known as "Libermanism" advocated according greater autonomy to enterprises and permitting them to work for a profit, which in turn would provide investment capital as well as material incentives for labor and management. Moreover, since industry was to operate on the basis of Lenin's *khozraschet*, or profit and loss, enterprises would be allowed to go bankrupt. If implemented, Libermanism would have turned the Stalinist system on its head: production goals would not have been expressed only in physical units of quantity and tonnage, but would also have taken into account quality and cost; and management decisions would not have been commanded from above, but would have come as responses to the market forces of supply and demand. The pseudocompetitive techniques and moral-ideological incentives of "socialist emulation," "shock work," and "Stakhanovism" would have been replaced by the less socialist but more effective incentives of profit and gain.

These ideas received the support of the major representatives of the renascent discipline of Soviet economics—V. C. Nemchinov, L. V. Kanterovich, and V. V. Novozhilov. Indeed, they developed Libermanism much further: they advocated reorganizing the economy on more rational and scientific lines by introducing the insights of cybernetics and systems analysis (hitherto denounced as "bourgeois"), and by computerizing the Plan to make it more flexible. And they even intimated that these changes would require reform of the Party-state.

Khrushchev and his colleagues were interested in this new thinking, though they certainly did not realize its subversive potential for the system. Indeed, it was Khrushchev who had sponsored Liberman's article, and, just before his fall, he introduced the latter's methods into two textile factories. Two days after Khrushchev was deposed, Kosygin extended the experiment to other enterprises, where it met with considerable success. The next year another reform economist, Abel Aganbegyan (who would later play a significant role under Gorbachev), sounded the alarm to the Central Committee. In a confidential report, he detailed the decline of the Soviet economy relative to that of the United States and attributed this decline to overcentralization and an inordinate defense burden.[9] It was to arrest this decline yet at the same time maintain the defense establishment that Kosygin launched his 1965 reform.

The first step in this reform, as noted earlier, was to abolish the sovnarkhozes and to replace them by central ministries. The second step was to expand the managerial autonomy of enterprises, which were accordingly supposed to operate on the basis of profitability. Enterprises now received from their ministries a reduced number of specific targets, or "indicators" (eight instead of forty), and sales volume replaced gross output as the principal criterion of success. At the same time, material incentives—in the form of bonuses or premiums paid to both management and workers—were linked to profits by a complicated system. Yet enterprises could not set their own prices in accordance with demand or social need; prices were set by a new organization, Goskomtsen, according to the old criteria of meeting "needs" determined by the Plan, not by the market. But without the freedom to charge their own prices, the enterprises' profitability became a marginal criterion of their success. In addition, funds were not forthcoming to provide increased bonuses as incentive to the workers. Similarly, the return to central ministries tended to negate the new autonomy of the enterprises.

These built-in contradictions were one reason the reform ground to a halt after 1968. Another was the Prague Spring of that same year, the most substantial experiment in Reform Communism ever attempted (but more on this later). One of its principal features was an economic reform similar to, but bolder than, Kosygin's. And one of the lessons the Soviets drew from the Czech reform was that economic liberalization could all too easily escalate into political liberalization that would threaten the very foundations of the regime. Thus the Czech experience threw a great scare into Soviet officials at all levels: at the top, Kosygin was discouraged from pressing his program, and lower apparatchiki spontaneously cut it back.

But even in the absence of a Prague Spring, the structure of the system doomed Kosygin's program to failure. Managers used their autonomy to meet the targets of the Plan rather than to risk innovations in production; ministries were only too willing to adjust the indicators accordingly; and both, having been raised in the command culture of Stalinist economics, preferred to stick to familiar routines. Thus a silent conspiracy of bureaucrats slowly eviscerated the reform, and production continued to decline and quality to deteriorate. But at the same time, the bureaucracy expanded: Gosplan and Goskomtsen were joined by Gosnab (in charge of material-technical supply) and GKNT (in charge of scientific and technological inputs), while the number of industrial ministries increased from forty-five in 1965 to more than seventy in 1985.

Yet despite the concurrent expansion of the Soviet industrial plant and its bureaucratic superstructure, the rates of growth of both national product and worker productivity continued to decline. Although the exact figures are in dispute, the general trend is not.

At the time, the world had to choose between the official Soviet figures and the somewhat lower estimates of the Central Intelligence Agency (CIA), and there was a general consensus, even among many Soviet economists, that the latter were closer to the truth. By the late 1980s, however, it became clear that the CIA figures were only somewhat less inflated than the official Soviet ones. There are two reasons why the CIA's estimates were so far off the mark: first, the Soviet statistics the CIA had to work with were often "cooked" to exaggerate performance for the benefit of the Plan and for the purpose of obtaining bonuses; and second, and even more important, the Western method of evaluating Soviet gross national product (GNP)—a measurement not used by the Soviets themselves—was fundamentally flawed.

The flaw lay in the incommensurability of a command economy and a market economy, and therefore in the techniques for comparing performance in the one with performance in the other. Contrary to widespread opinion, GNP is not a fact but a concept; more precisely, it is a measurement, and there can be no measurement without theoretical premises. Thus any estimate of the size of the Soviet GNP is a reflection of the theory upon which it is based. And it is here, in the realm of theory, that a major problem arises. All of our theories concerning economic output are derived from Western experience and data, and the principal data are prices. But Soviet prices have no economic logic; their "logic" is a political or a "command" logic—the logic of the Plan, not of the market. Hence, a "cost adjustment factor" is required to convert Soviet "prices" into data that can be fed into the measurement models of advanced Western econometrics.

These models, developed largely in the two Cambridges in the 1930s and 1940s, were meant to handle the problems created by the Great Depression. They were then transmogrified in the 1960s for the purpose of analyzing the rival Soviet system in putatively sober and scientific academic fashion, and thereafter they were used by the CIA to monitor the rival's evolution through the decades of the Cold War.

By the 1970s the CIA's estimate that the size of the Soviet economy was some 60 percent of the American was generally accepted; this was a figure that could be construed as the indicator of a threat or of a promise, depending upon one's point of view. The CIA's evaluation, as well as earlier and even more optimistic estimates, was roundly criticized by émigré Soviet economists (such as Naum Jasny in the 1950s and 1960s, and Igor Birman in the 1980s) on several grounds. These economists argued that Soviet statistics were political, not economic; that the Plan, because it did not take account of costs, was inordinately wasteful of capital; and that Western estimates were grossly inflated because they did not take into consideration the low quality of the entire Soviet national product.[10] At the time, these critics were generally dismissed as sour émigrés. But when *glasnost* at last permitted Soviet economists—for example, Nikolai Shmelev, Gavriil Popov, Stanislav Shatalin, and Yegor Gaidar—to speak out in the late eighties, they amply confirmed the pessimistic, or more accurately realistic, verdict of their émigré compatriots on the estimates of the CIA and Western academia. In fact, these Russian economists now advise reducing the CIA's figures by about 2 percent to get an approximate idea of the truth.

So what figures can we now put on the Soviet economic performance under Brezhnev, or under Stalin in the 1930s, after he broke with "bourgeois" statistics? We still do not know, and we probably never will, for the surreal operations of the Soviet political economy by their very nature cannot be translated into "normal" economic terms. It is no more of an accident that such an "economy" did not generate real statistics than that it did not employ real prices: its bookkeeping was the political accounting of the Plan; and the Plan was driven by ideological will, not by the goad of profit and loss, however much the regime may have exhorted its managers to submit to the discipline of *khozraschet*, whether in the days of Lenin, Kosygin, or Gorbachev.

Still, the old CIA figures can give a rough indication of trend, and the trend is steadily downward.

Average Annual Rate of Growth

Year	Actual GNP
1966–1970	5.1%
1971–1975	3.0%
1976–1980	2.3%
1981–1990	NA

Thus, with the appropriate deduction of 2 percent suggested by the Russian economists, by 1979–1980 the Soviet Union had probably entered the zone of negative growth.[11]

But this was not all that was wrong. Even more threatening was the fact that the Soviet economy in the 1960s and 1970s missed the great turn from extensive to intensive development that other industrialized societies had made earlier. The great Soviet economic successes of the 1930s, the 1940s, and even the 1950s had been achieved by the methods of an institutionalized war economy that used great quantities of men and capital in large-scale projects. It had also expended these resources with wanton wastefulness—the Gulag was only the worst example. Such extravagance had been possible, first, because the great population explosion of the late nineteenth and early twentieth centuries had made Russia by far the most populous nation in Europe; hence the Soviet experiment had a demographic reservoir on which Stalin's extensive methods of development, in particular his terror famine, could draw without counting. Stalin's extravagant use of resources had been possible, second, because the country's vast Eurasian expanse—one sixth of the world's land surface, as the Soviet government constantly boasted—offered, or seemed to offer, inexhaustible reserves of raw materials: virgin lands could be plowed without heed to soil erosion, and rivers could be dammed or diverted in pseudo-Promethean engineering projects.

But by the 1970s both the human and natural resources of the country had become seriously depleted.[12] After the decimation of the peasantry under Stalin, the chronic housing shortage in the Soviet cities led urban families to restrict their size drastically; the country's labor force shrank correspondingly, especially in the Slavic heartland. At the same time, the "storm and conquer" methods of Bolshevik industrialization were beginning to exhaust once abundant material reserves, and in their place ecological disaster areas had appeared, such as the shrinking Aral Sea and the dying Lake Baikal. And the decline of the labor force and the depletion of natural resources made all economic operations more costly.

The time had clearly come for a transition from the extensive methods of development adequate for the Homeric age of building socialism to the more intensive methods appropriate to a genuinely mature industrial system—methods based on the husbanding of scarce resources, the cultivation of human skills, and a more refined technology. And some leaders of the regime, such as Kosygin himself and later Andropov, were aware of this. Kosygin initially advocated "scientific" and "rational" methods of management, rather than crash "campaigns," as the key to further growth; and later the regime claimed it was engaged in a "scientific-technological revolution." But all to no avail.

By the 1970s and 1980s the technological gap between the Soviet Union and the West was growing; even more ominous was the fact that the rate at which the gap was widening was increasing by the year.[13] The only sector of the Soviet economy that was not declining in competitive capacity was the military, but even it could not maintain its position for long if the rest of the system was becoming obsolete. Yet the transition to intensive methods was one that the central Plan proved quite unable to make.

To put the long-term dilemma of the system another way, in the 1930s the Soviets had built a crude but serviceable version of a Pittsburgh-Detroit or a Ruhr-Lorraine economy, and directed it primarily towards military uses. After the war they rebuilt this plant—when it was no longer at the avant-garde of world industrial practices—and imposed on it the new mission of nuclear and ballistic development. Finally, after Stalin's death, they multiplied this model several times over while more advanced countries were phasing out their Garys, Birminghams, and Essens, and utilizing instead such sources of cheap high-quality steel as South Korea; and back in the highly developed countries, the technological frontier moved on to Silicon Valley.

To be sure, the Soviets did match Livermore and Los Alamos. But for the rest, the West and East Asia challenged them with revolutions in plastics and chemicals, then in electronics, then in household durables, and finally in the world of computers—challenges that the Soviets could only clumsily incorporate into the Leviathan machinery of the Plan. At the same time, the quality of Soviet goods (except those for the military) steadily deteriorated, as did the national infrastructure and the capital stock, from railroads to factories to housing; by the 1980s much of the country was literally crumbling into ruin. And this descent from stagnation to deterioration was a direct result of the logic of the Plan once a certain level of industrial development had been achieved. For in the final analysis, planning implies not only a static level of supply and demand but also a static technology, and such conditions can never exist in the real world. In the dynamic world of reality things either go up or they go down, but they never remain stationary. Yet the whole Soviet system was predicated on attaining "socialism" and then staying there, as if that were the end of history.

Another cause of the decline was the sorry condition of the group that was supposed to be the Soviet system's social base, and for whose welfare that system was supposed to exist, the working class. Its plight was all the more central because during the Brezhnev years workers for the first time became the majority of the Soviet population. In 1929, at the beginning of industrialization, the working class was only slightly larger than in 1917, that is, around 2 or 3 percent of the population. Even at the end of the 1930s, the decade of revolutionary urbanization, peasants still accounted for 66 percent of the population. It was only in 1961 that the urban population surpassed the rural population. The balance continued to shift under Brezhnev; by 1982 some 70 percent of the Soviet people were urban dwellers, and of course the majority of these were workers. And it was the pressure of this constantly expanding urban population that forced the regimes of Khrushchev and Brezhnev to devote ever more resources to consumer needs and the improvement of agriculture.

The regime, of course, never ceased to proclaim that the worker was supreme in the system and that his "socialist labor" was the source of the system's strength. As a pseudo-legitimation of the sacrifices of the population, the myth of the workers' state was indeed central to the functioning of the system. This myth was undoubtedly a potent means of psychological mobilization during the crash phases of building socialism, and it is clear that a part of the working class took pride in the prestige accorded to an elite among its members. Nonetheless, a more tangible down payment on the "radiant future" was necessary for the rank and file to keep the myth alive, and this was never adequately forthcoming.

As we have seen, once the egalitarian policies of early Bolshevism were abandoned by Stalin in 1931, the labor force was driven by a combination of special rewards for the few Stakhanovite achievers and the pressure of piece-rates for the rank and file. To these measures were added, in the course of the decade, the police pressure of the labor book, the *propiska* (residence permit), and criminal penalties for absenteeism; finally, in 1940, the regime resorted to labor mobilization on the job. This draconian regimen was softened after the war; in particular, the use of criminal penalties was reduced, and prices were decreased on goods that benefited urban workers most, for Stalin had a preference for them over other social groups. Still, the general poverty of the times was such that the workers enjoyed only the most rudimentary social services, and piece-rates remained the norm.

In the relaxation after Stalin's death it was more imperative to make concessions to the workers than to the other groups in the population. In 1956 the laws regarding labor mobilization on the job and criminal penalties for delinquency were withdrawn. The same year, a minimum wage was established and modest retirement pensions were introduced. (In 1964 retirement pensions were even extended to the kolkhoz peasantry.) Also in the 1950s and 1960s, the workweek was shortened to five days, maternity leave was extended, and other social security measures were introduced. Under Brezhnev this policy of building a rudimentary welfare state was continued, and indeed somewhat strengthened, to where some in the West took it as a primary sign of the "maturing" of the system, of its evolution from a totalitarian to a merely authoritarian order.

It would perhaps be more appropriate, however, to view these changes as a form of protection money the *nomenklatura* paid to the workers to keep the system stable and safe. For in the unavoidable relaxation of state pressure under Khrushchev, the workers had become restive and potentially dangerous. For the first time since the 1920s, there were wildcat strikes and even riots verging on revolt. The first major incident appears to have occurred in 1959 at Temirtau, a new industrial town in the virgin lands. But the high point of this agitation came in 1962, the year in which the flattening out of Khrushchev's "mini-boom" led him to raise prices on meat, dairy products, and vodka. This action provoked a string of often violent disturbances extending from the Moscow region to the docks of Odessa. The most serious disturbance occurred in the southern city of Novocherkassk, where a strike, gravely mishandled by the authorities, ended in violence and repression by KGB troops (at least seventy people were killed). After two Politburo members were sent to restore order, the workers were first calmed by the rushing of fresh supplies into the stores, but then their leaders were arrested and shipped off to Siberia. The outside world did not learn about this incident until the publication of Solzhenitsyn's *Gulag Archipelago* in 1975.[14]

Although there were no more disturbances of this magnitude, significant industrial incidents continued down into the 1980s because of worker dissatisfaction with pay, housing, food shortages, and labor norms. Each time the authorities' reaction was the same: They kept the matter secret so it could not set an example for other cities, they bought off the mass with a short spurt of supplies, and they arrested the leaders of the disturbance. But more substantial concessions were also necessary. Although piece-rates were not completely abandoned in favor of time-rates, pressure on workers to produce was in fact lessened, and wage differentials between the highest- and lowest-paid workers were gradually reduced. The result of these policies was labor peace—but also a stagnation of worker productivity.

One reason why Soviet industry had surged under Stalin was an initially very low level of productivity per worker; hence it was relatively easy to raise productivity rapidly with the goad of piece-rates. After this initial rise in productivity, however, subtler incentives would have been required to achieve further progress. But this step was precluded by the rigidity of the Plan and the general scarcity of goods. Thus, by the early 1970s the system had resigned itself to a labor force with low productivity and high security of employment, or what has been called "unemployment on the job." The mentality of this apathetic labor force came to be summarized in the joke, soon heard around the world, about the Soviet worker who declared: "I'll pretend to work so long as they pretend to pay me."

The situation was far from being a joking matter, however. During Brezhnev's last years the working population was actually in a state of biological decline: In a case that was without precedent in the history of developed countries, the life expectancy of males fell from sixty-eight to sixty-four years, while the rate of infant mortality increased from 3 to 7 percent. One major cause of these adverse trends was alcoholism: always a problem in Russia, it now became rampant, increasingly affecting younger members of the population as well as women. Sales of spirits accounted for 15 percent of state revenues. The cost of this "gain," however, was even lower worker productivity and social demoralization.

There was one sector of the Soviet economy during the Brezhnev era that, after its fashion, was dynamic and growing: the "shadow" or "second" economy.[15] The history of this institutionalized black market, of course, can be traced to the earliest years of Soviet power, when the parallel market and its "bagmen" were indispensable to feeding the country during the disastrous years of the Civil War. During the permanent scarcity of the Stalin years, the shadow economy had been a constant, though it was also obviously a dangerous recourse. It was only under Khrushchev that a more or less stable and semitolerated second economy emerged as the indispensable complement to the Plan: people were now less afraid, and the state could not satisfy the consumer needs that its own policies had sharpened. So moonlighting, work "on the left," embezzlement, and "speculation" thrived, as did "parasites," or people without an official occupation who allegedly lived off of these activities. So swift was this growth that Khrushchev introduced the death penalty for some of these practices; that it was actually applied on occasion showed just how widespread and insolent this commerce had become.

But the shadow economy became a veritable pillar of the system under Brezhnev. It operated in two broad areas, or what might be called retail and wholesale trade. In its retail capacity the second economy catered to the consumer needs of the population by offering goods in short supply, the so-called *defitsitnyi* items. It thus provided services—from dress making to car repairs to medical attention—that the state system did not provide, and it furnished imported articles— from jeans to luxury items to sophisticated technology—that were coveted for their superior quality or their foreign chic. In its second or wholesale function the shadow economy acted as a support system for the official economy, or as a reserve of entrepreneurial ingenuity to supplement the rigidities of the Plan. Thus, it provided state enterprises with everything from raw materials to spare parts on those all-too-numerous occasions when an enterprise could not get necessary items from official suppliers fast enough to meet its plan. Shadow entrepreneurs would frequently siphon off or embezzle goods from one agency of the official system to sell to another. And at times the shadow economy even graduated into parallel manufacturing of household goods and industrial equipment.

In this way the second economy often generated veritable "mafias," a word adopted into current Russian under Brezhnev. These mafias sometimes even overlapped with the Party hierarchy to create a symbiosis wherein entrepreneurs received political protection in exchange for material goods and services. For in a world where the economic system was in the first instance a political one, political power became a prime source of wealth. Indeed, in some of the border republics the mafia virtually took over the local Party, or more accurately, the local Party largely turned itself into a mafia. Perhaps the most famous case was that of Georgia under First Secretary and alternate Politburo member Vasilii Mzhavanadze, who was finally driven from power by the republic's interior minister, Edvard Shevardnadze. But an even more picturesque example was provided by Rafik Adulov, a Party secretary in Uzbekistan, who kept a harem and had a torture chamber for his critics, while the Uzbek republic Party boss inflated the cotton production figures for which Moscow paid him. But corruption could also be found at the very top of the system—in the "Dnepropetrovsk mafia" of Brezhnev's own cronies and kin—a fact that was partially known to the population and thus diminished the regime's credibility even further.

Nor were these failings due to accident any more than were the failings of Soviet agriculture due to bad weather. "Mafiazation" of the apparat became a major problem under Brezhnev because of his policy of "stability of cadres," which in turn derived from the long-term evolution of the Party as an institution; and these same causes produced the new phenomenon of gerontocracy, which was so visible at the top of the Soviet hierarchy yet also prevalent at every level.

Criminal behavior had an economic logic as well, one that derived from the very nature of directive planning. The Soviet experiment, which under Brezhnev passed the half-century mark, had by then demonstrated that it was impossible to suppress the market: despite all efforts it kept coming back, whether illegally with the "bagmen" under Lenin's War Communism or legally during his NEP, or under Stalin with the family plot and the kolkhoz market. Yet the experiment had also demonstrated that it *was* possible to drive the market underground indefinitely and thereby make it criminal, both as a matter of law and as a matter of actual social behavior. But since this underground market was created by, and responded to, genuine social needs, not crass "speculation," it to some degree involved the whole population; thus everyone was criminalized in some measure, for everyone had to have a little "racket" or "deal" in order to survive. There is also corruption in the West, of course, but there it is optional; one does not have to engage in it to survive. In the former Soviet Union it was mandatory just in order to get by. So everyone was always guilty of something, and an indispensable activity was stigmatized and stunted.

How large was the second economy? No reputable economist has ever attempted to put a figure on it, although evidence of its existence was everywhere; but this unavoidable uncertainty is only an aggravated case of our uncertainty about the Soviet economy as a whole. Quantitatively, the most one can say of the parallel economy is that it was quite considerable; but the important thing is that, qualitatively, it was indispensable to the functioning of the overall system. It was not a deficiency or a product of abuses that could be corrected by better policies or more stringent discipline, as the regime maintained. It was the unavoidable consequence of an artificial state economic monopoly, as well as the indispensable means for permitting that monopoly itself to carry on. The result of making these indispensable functions a matter for the police was not only to hobble the economy, both official and underground, but to undermine public morality and the sense of law among the population. And this was another cost of the Plan's "rationality."

THE BURDEN OF GLOBAL POWER

The defects of the system's economy are only highlighted by the one sector where it was internationally competitive, military production.

As we have seen, the mode of organization of the Soviet economy in all sectors was military, but actual production for military purposes became its chief function only after 1937. To be sure, given international circumstances from then until 1945, this was only understandable. In the postwar period, however, circumstances were quite different, and the centrality of military power to the system acquired a more enduring, institutionalized character. For the Soviet Union was now not directly menaced by a nearby adversary but engaged in long-term maneuvering for "positions of strength" in Europe and East Asia vis-à-vis the "camp of imperialism." And the mode of conflict had also changed, since the Cold War was not a contest actually to be fought but one constantly to be prepared for. The resulting four decades of permanent military-technological mobilization during peacetime is probably a unique phenomenon in the history of international conflict. The burden of this conflict, of course, also fell on the American "side," but in the Soviet Union the Cold War effort consumed a far larger proportion of national resources. And this was especially true during the Brezhnev years.

After 1945 the Soviet Union demobilized almost as much as the United States. Soviet remobilization began only as a result of the Korean War, and then in the late 1950s, as already indicated, Khrushchev cut the military again while he attempted to catch up quickly with the United States in missile strength. It was only in the 1960s, after the dangerous Cuban episode, that the Soviet Union settled down for the long haul of a systematic arms buildup to match or surpass American military strength across the board. This meant, first, a permanent increase of ground forces to something over four million men. Under the direction of Admiral Sergei Gorshkov, it also meant the creation of a world-class navy—and especially a submarine fleet—capable of operating in all the oceans of the planet. It meant, finally, nuclear and ballistic parity with the United States. And by 1969 the Soviet Union had at last reached that long-coveted status: For the first time, it was truly a coequal superpower.

Because the regime's ambition was to maintain this rank at all costs, and if possible to turn it into superiority, the arms race proceeded to its culmination during the Brezhnev and Andropov years. The Soviet Union during this period has been described as a state that did not *have* a military-industrial complex but *was* a military-industrial complex. But it would be more accurate to say that it was a Party-military-industrial complex, for the military was not in charge, and the reasons for the arms buildup did not derive from strategic considerations per se but from the Party's political perception of a world divided into two hostile camps. And only the Party's capacity for total social mobilization could produce a military-industrial complex of the huge dimensions achieved under Brezhnev.

During this period the CIA estimated that the Soviet military absorbed some 15 percent of the USSR's GNP, whereas in the United States military expenditure averaged 5 percent. But in 1990 Foreign Minister Shevardnadze claimed that the true Soviet figure had been 25 percent, and other Soviet estimates of the *glasnost* era went as high as 40 percent.[16] Although Shevardnadze was surely closer to the mark than the CIA had been, we still do not know how large a percentage of Soviet GNP went to the military because the Soviets themselves never really knew. Indeed, there is reason to believe that they used the CIA's figures to calculate their own GNP, and therefore erroneously believed they had a wider margin for military expenditure than they actually possessed. At the same time, an inordinate proportion of the labor force was involved to some extent in work for the military: it was at least 25 percent, and Aganbegyan and other Soviet economists claim it was as high as 30 or 40 percent, whereas in the United States and other Western countries the corresponding figure was below 5 percent.[17] In any event, the proportion of human and material resources taken up by the sterile activity of Soviet "defense" was absolutely crushing, and it precluded any kind of economic revival for the country at large.

Furthermore, the military had at its disposal the most-advanced technology, the highest-quality equipment, and many of the sharpest minds in the country because these were allocated to it by political fiat. The military was also what might be called a "demand side" entity: unlike the civilian population, it was a consumer that could refuse products it found inferior, and thus force a revision of the Plan in its favor. It required this right because its products—again unlike those of the civilian sector—had to be competitive internationally, whether on the battlefields of the Middle East or in the arms markets of the Third World. And for a quarter century, in a prodigious display of technological and organizational prowess, the Soviet military was indeed one of the two largest and most powerful ensembles of armed forces in the history of the world. In a sense, this was the supreme achievement of the Party-state, the only kind of task such a system could excel at. But it was also an achievement that was beyond the system's real economic capacity, and thus it could not be sustained for long. And more than any other single factor, it was the regime's attempt to sustain its superpower status that would trigger the collapse of 1989-1991.

Almost as ruinous as this military effort was the foreign policy it served. After Khrushchev's adventure in Cuba, the Brezhnev-Kosygin government adopted a more cautious foreign policy. But the regime's primary aim was the same as Khrushchev's: to achieve an accommodation with the United States that would allow the Soviet Union to build up its strength at home. Yet efforts toward this end were constantly disrupted by the regime's secondary aim, which was to profit from Third World revolutionary and national liberation movements and thereby enhance Soviet power and prestige at the expense of the United States. This, after all, was Moscow's vocation, both as a world revolutionary leader and as a superpower. Foregoing favorable opportunities abroad would have automatically diminished Soviet power throughout the world and reduced the need for social and ideological mobilization at home. The unending struggle against "imperialism" was, as ever, indispensable for maintaining the internal equilibrium of the Party-state.

Most of the Soviet Union's foreign adventures in the Brezhnev years were proxy adventures. The first major area of activity was the Middle East. The Soviet Union had been involved there since 1948, when she was the first major power to recognize Israel, an action undertaken essentially to undermine British "imperialism." But almost immediately thereafter, Stalin took up the cause of "anti-Zionism," in part because he viewed the Soviet Jewish population's surprising enthusiasm for Israel as tantamount to disloyalty to the USSR, and in part because it was a means of stimulating hostility towards Israel's new patron, the United States. Later, Khrushchev extended this policy to include active support of the Arabs; he made the Soviet Union the patron and military supplier of Egypt and Syria, and later of Iraq and Libya, a policy that Brezhnev continued. Its aim, however, was not to produce an Arab victory over Israel, but to mobilize the area against Britain and France and then the United States. Moscow first focused this costly policy on Egypt. When Anwar Sadat expelled all Soviet advisors from Egypt in 1972 and soon thereafter turned to the Americans for funding and military supplies, the Soviet focus then shifted to the "revolutionary" Arab dictatorships.

The second major area of Soviet activity was Southeast Asia. In 1954 the first, or French, Vietnam War ended with the country being partitioned into a North and a South. According to the Geneva agreements of that year, national elections were to be held to unify Vietnam, but until the early 1960s it was generally assumed in the West that the country would in fact remain divided, like Korea or Germany. North Vietnam, however, fully intended to take over the South, with or without elections. After it proved impossible to organize elections, Hanoi—with the active encouragement of China—began to organize a South Vietnamese "liberation front." The United States then moved to defend South Vietnam. Because China was too weak to counter such an adversary, in 1965 Hanoi turned to the other superpower for equipment. Moscow willingly complied, both to outflank the Chinese and to undermine its American rival.

The result was the most profitable foreign policy adventure of the Brezhnev years. The United States, fearful of drawing in the Chinese, as in Korea, and wishing to avoid a direct clash with the Soviets, fought a relatively limited war. This strategy had the double disadvantage of being terribly destructive and yet woefully inadequate either to deter the North or to crush the Vietcong. The conflict therefore dragged on until the end of the decade; it divided opinion and eroded anti-Communist resolve in the United States, and, as the Soviets perceived it, shifted the "correlation of forces" in their favor. At the same time, Washington needed Moscow's help in getting Hanoi to accept negotiations for a face-saving end to the conflict, and this need strengthened the Soviet Union's international position.

Moscow eventually did help produce the negotiations that permitted the United States to withdraw from the area in 1973 yet left a Northern military presence in the South; hence the conflict could resume at any time on terms more favorable to the North. And this is just what occurred in 1975. Although the Soviets did not instigate the North's conquest of the South, they did nothing to restrain their ally, and the whole operation was possible only because the Soviets had supplied the North with heavy equipment. Thus, in terms of what Brezhnev called the "class struggle between the two systems," the Vietnam War was a great, if vicarious, Soviet victory.

During the same years, the Soviet Union's other great adversary, China, was effectively eliminated from great-power competition. The process that produced this outcome began with events in Indonesia, which at the beginning of the 1960s had the largest Communist Party in the world after those of the Soviet Union and China. President Sukarno withdrew his country from the United Nations as a preliminary to setting up a new Third World international organization with China, whose entry into the UN was barred by the United States. Sukarno and the Indonesian Communists then attempted an internal coup to establish a "progressive" dictatorship. This backfired, and the Indonesian military completely liquidated the Communist movement, killing at least one hundred thousand people in the process. Moscow did not even lodge a protest with the new Indonesian regime of General Suharto; the massacre, after all, was only a defeat for China.

China's next defeat was self-inflicted and took the form of the great convulsion of the Cultural Revolution of 1966–1969. This episode, comparable in its self-destructive fury only to Stalin's purges, largely discredited China as a rival revolutionary model and weakened her as an economy and an aspiring global power. Then, in 1972, with Nixon's visit to China, Mao did what he had earlier anathematized Khrushchev for doing: he entered into a rapprochement with the United States. Finally, Mao's death in 1976 led to new turbulence under the Gang of Four, and thus to further international discredit. Although Deng Xiaoping's "revisionism" at the end of the decade brought this turmoil to a close, it also ended the Chinese revolutionary myth in the eyes of the Third World. Thus Moscow at last recovered the leadership of the "international proletarian movement."

In consequence, newly united Vietnam wound up as Moscow's ally and an active foe of China. This turn of events greatly increased the Soviet Union's prestige, if not its actual power, in the Third World and in the eyes of its own population. But there was also a negative side to this victory: the international Communist movement, having been rent by so many schisms and defections, was no longer very credible as a revolutionary force. In fact, by 1970 the series of authentic revolutionary flare-ups ignited by the Second World War had largely ended, and "international" Communism consisted essentially of the Soviet Union's ability to project military power around the world. Still, this was quite enough to make the 1970s the high point of Soviet global influence and strength. Never had world predominance, or even outright victory, seemed nearer to attainment. It is this perception of the "correlation of forces" between the "two camps" that was the context for détente in the 1970s.

With the winding down of the Vietnam War after 1969, it became possible to seriously resume negotiations with the Americans and return to the détente that had followed in the wake of the Cuban crisis and the Test Ban Treaty of 1963. Negotiations led to the first major arms control agreement since the invention of nuclear weapons—the SALT I Treaty of 1972—which limited antiballistic missile (ABM) deployments and established very high ceilings on ICBMs. Arguably, this agreement only formalized what the two sides were intending to do anyway, but it at least kept the rivalry within the bounds of diplomacy. In the same spirit, during President Nixon's visit to Moscow in 1972, the two sides agreed on "Basic Principles" of "peaceful coexistence" in which each country pledged to refrain from taking "unilateral advantage at the expense of the other." Finally, détente meant economic bonds: Washington was to accord Moscow most-favored-nation trade status, and foreign investment in the Soviet Union was to be encouraged.[18]

On the Western side, the idea behind these policies was to reassure the Soviets and moderate their behavior by fostering a congruence of interests between East and West. If the Soviet Union, so the reasoning went, was tied into the international system by mutually advantageous arms control agreements and into the world economy by trade, she would then have a stake of self-interest in cooperating with the United States and Western Europe on other issues. As Henry Kissinger put the matter: "Over time, trade and investment may leaven the autarchic tendencies of the Soviet system, and by gradual association of the Soviet economy with the world economy, foster a degree of interdependence that adds an element of stability to the political equation."[19] A similar rationale underlay the contemporary *Ostpolitik* of West German Chancellor Willy Brandt: by reducing tension and building trust, the policy was intended to mellow and reform the East European regimes, and in particular that of East Germany.

Consequently, throughout the 1970s Western business invested extensively in the East, and especially in Poland under Gomulka's more moderate successor, Edward Gierek. But the result was not to produce progress towards a convergence of economic interests with the West; it was to bolster for another decade an already discredited

Polish regime by financing a temporary false prosperity. Similarly, SPD support for Walter Ulbricht and Erich Honecker did permit East German dissidents to emigrate to the West in exchange for money, but it did not soften East Germany's internal structures; indeed, this policy contributed to the illusion that East Germany was a genuinely successful Communist economy and the tenth-largest industrial power in the world. So no congruence of interests developed in either of these cases; rather, what emerged in both countries was a form of economic dependence on the West without a corresponding political realignment. But this was only to be expected of systems where economic policy derives from political concerns, and not the other way around as both Kissinger and Brandt assumed.

On the Soviet side, therefore, the wager of détente and *Ostpolitik* had a very different meaning from that in the West. It was, to be sure, a means for obviating the danger of nuclear conflict. But it was also a means for palliating the East's relative economic decline and growing technological lag without incurring any political dependency.

In this regard, the great pioneer project was the Italian-financed Fiat automobile works constructed at Togliatti, on the Volga, in 1966. In the 1970s the American-financed truck factory on the Kama, and the Pepsi Cola factories paid for with Stolichnaia vodka, were only the best-known examples of continuing foreign investment; but the Soviet Union also made significant acquisitions of computer and advanced electronic technology. All of this was financed by the bonanza of "petrodollars" that came Moscow's way after OPEC's oil embargo of 1973, for the Soviet Union was the largest producer of petroleum in the world. And petrodollars also paid for the grain imports that were necessary to make up for the deficiencies of Soviet agriculture. Thus, at a time when the Soviet economy was declining, the regime was nonetheless able to remain politically competitive with the West by entering into a parasitical economic relationship with it.

Furthermore, all of this occurred when the West's fortunes were at their lowest ebb since the Second World War. The petroleum shock of 1973 ended the quarter-century prosperity of the postwar period, the greatest economic expansion in world history. The American defeat in Vietnam and the Watergate scandal simultaneously shook the West's political position. To Moscow, which had never ceased believing that the internal contradictions of capitalism would one day destroy it, these events appeared, not implausibly, as the beginnings of fundamental crisis. So détente became a means for Moscow to contribute to this crisis by inducing the West to relax its vigilance in the "ideological struggle between the two systems." As such, détente was akin to the peace offensives to which the Soviets periodically resorted as an ideological means of undermining the adversary. For Brezhnev's "relaxation of tensions" (which the West translated as détente), like Khrushchev's "peaceful coexistence," did not mean that international relations had become any less a form of the "class struggle" that would end only with the victory of socialism. Nor were these ideological themes mere vestiges of revolutionary rhetoric that was not to be taken seriously in a nuclear age, as some in the West supposed. So long as the Stalin-bred generation of Brezhnev, Kosygin, and Suslov remained in charge, the belief in the "international class struggle" was a real guide to policy. And its concrete aim was to expel the United States from Eurasia.

In sum, for the West détente was a gradual way to transcend the Cold War; for the East it was a gradual way to win it. Both sides had made a bet, but, as it turned out, events followed the expectations of neither. In the first half of the 1970s, the West's scenario seemed to be coming about; in the second half of the decade, the East's scenario seemed close to realization. But in the early 1980s, the Cold War returned in full force.

In the 1950s and early 1960s, under Khrushchev, the Soviets had been tough to the point of truculence because the camp of socialism could not submit to the American pretension of negotiating "from positions of strength." In the 1960s and early 1970s, under Brezhnev, they had built up their strength to the level of that of the United States and could therefore accept the negotiations leading to SALT I and détente. As the 1970s progressed, however, the "correlation of forces" seemed to shift in favor of the Soviets, so toward the end of that decade they themselves took to acting "from positions of strength." The shift began with the fall of South Vietnam and the signing of the Helsinki agreements in 1975.

The Helsinki Conference on Security and Cooperation in Europe was the high point of détente and the occasion on which the Soviets' achieved their long-standing ambition of formal recognition of existing boundaries in Europe—that is, in the absence of a German peace treaty, acceptance by the West of the Soviets' postwar gains and of the inviolability of their "bloc." To be sure, they had to accept "basket three," which committed them to respect human rights. They considered this pledge a mere formality, but it was one the East bloc dissidents would soon use to advance their cause by forming "Helsinki Watch Groups." But this was a minor annoyance as against the great gain of international legitimation of their external empire.

At the same time, and in the wake of the American disaster in Vietnam, the Soviets embarked on a new career of expansion in the Third World. Khrushchev had already tried his luck with postcolonial power politics in Egypt, India, Indonesia, the Congo, and, in a slightly different category, Cuba; but his means, except in Cuba, had been diplomatic support and economic aid. Under Brezhnev, the means of penetration became military might, first in the form of Cuban proxies in Africa and then in the form of Soviet troops, as in Afghanistan. The process started in 1974 with the collapse of the Portuguese empire, which led to a civil war in Angola; here the Soviet client defeated the American one with the help of Cuban troops in 1976. The process continued to unfold the next year in Ethiopia, where the American client Haile Selassie was defeated, again with Cuban help, by the Soviet-supported revolutionary Derg. And shortly thereafter, the Soviets crossed the Red Sea into Yemen.

But this "arc of crisis," as these changes were called in Washington, soon extended into Afghanistan, and just at the moment of the anti-Western Iranian revolution. In 1978 a Soviet-leaning and neutralist regime in Kabul was overthrown—it seems on local initiative—by a faction of Afghan Communists. They were soon supplanted by a more radical faction that proceeded to "build socialism" with a vengeance; this policy fueled a national resistance that threatened to overthrow Communism entirely. Faced with the possibility of a "reversal of a conquest of socialism," Moscow intervened with its own troops in December 1979 to install a more moderate Communist leader, Babrak Karmal. It seems that the decision to intervene was not taken by the full Politburo but by only four men—Brezhnev, Gromyko, Marshal Dmitri Ustinov, and Andropov. It also seems that they, or at least Andropov, a former minister to Budapest, thought in terms of the Hungarian precedent, with Karmal in the role of a new Kadar. In short, the Afghan intervention was not dictated by geopolitical considerations, such as advancing a salient toward Middle East oil, as the West thought at the time, but by a senescent ideological concern for the inviolability of the frontiers of socialism.

The result was the end of détente. SALT II, which had been

solemnly sealed with a kiss by Carter and Brezhnev only a few months earlier in Vienna, was never submitted for ratification. Concurrently, the United States began a major across-the-board arms buildup that would continue through the first Reagan administration. In that same year, the international atmosphere was further soured when the overthrow of Somoza in Nicaragua led to the triumph of the Sandinistas, who were supported by both Castro and Moscow. It seemed that Nicaragua would now become a second Cuba on the American continent and also endanger neighboring El Salvador.

But the most serious new source of tension was the deployment against Western Europe, beginning in 1978, of an improved intermediate-range ballistic missile, the SS-20.[20] The introduction of this missile—it had a longer range than its predecessor and carried multiple warheads—was interpreted as an effort to intimidate the Western Europeans and hence break up NATO by driving a wedge between the United States and its allies. NATO's response to the SS-20 was a plan to deploy American Pershing II and cruise missiles in Western Europe; both of these weapons would be capable of reaching the major urban centers of European Russia.

By 1981 and the beginning of Reagan's presidency, the so-called Euromissile issue had become a major test of strength. The Soviets had stolen a march by having already begun the deployment of their SS-20s, while the deployment of the Pershings and the cruise was as yet only a threat. A failure to deploy the new American weapons would have been a defeat for the West, whereas a failure to block their deployment would have been a defeat for Moscow. A great contest of wills therefore ensued, for nothing less than the global balance of power, and in particular the fate of Eurasia, depended on the outcome of the Euromissiles issue. The conflict culminated in 1983 when the West German Bundestag approved deployment of the Pershings, and the Soviets, in answer, walked out of the INF (intermediate-range nuclear forces) negotiations they had been engaged in with the United States. And so matters remained stalemated until 1985.

Although this conflict was indeed the supreme battle between the two camps, it is less certain that it constituted a "new" Cold War, as is sometimes alleged. Rather, the clash of the early eighties continued the basic pattern of Soviet-Western relations dating back to 1948, a pattern interrupted for only a brief time by détente. For the Cold War was not the product of rash policies or misunderstandings based on mutual ignorance that could be overcome by "confidence-building measures," as the philosophy of détente had it. It was, rather, the product of the genuine incompatibility of the interests and structures of the two "camps," as standard Soviet doctrine had it. In this perspective, the three or four years of détente were a kind of diplomatic NEP designed to build Soviet strength for a new offensive, and the ten years of renewed Soviet pressure after 1975 were a return to the system's norm.

But this return, which turned out to be the system's last international hurrah, was also a caricature of the Leninist revolutionary impulse. For the world's premier socialist state, and a superpower to boot, to be rummaging in the Third World wreckage of European "imperialism" for such prizes as Angola and Afghanistan would be farcical were it not also so tragic. Marxist revolution is condemned to be permanent if it is to remain revolutionary, and therefore the so-called second Cold War represented the final cul-de-sac of the revolutionary necessity of constant advance to preserve the movement's vigor. Thus, in each of these Third World cases, the Soviets intervened to defend a Marxist regime they could not abandon without forfeiting their own revolutionary credibility. But the manner in which they intervened in each case was so cynical, and the gain so derisory, that this credibility was forfeited anyway; thus, the system as a whole was undermined rather than strengthened.

This slide into crisis of the early eighties was due not only to this atavistic ideological reflex, but also to the inertia of the military-industrial complex that the Soviet system had by now become. For under Brezhnev the relationship of the Party to the military had changed significantly because the system had assumed the mission of waging an endless Cold War for an increasingly improbable future victory. This changed relationship also reflected the fact that the system had come to be dominated by the *nomenklatura*, not by the Leader, thereby giving the military greater leeway for pressing its demands.

This is not to say that the military had become an "interest group" in the Western sense, and that "institutional pluralism" now characterized the system, with the Party playing the role of referee among the various groups—a perspective widely held in the West during the Brezhnev era.[21] The military continued to function as one face of the Party through the interlocking directorate of the *nomenklatura* system.

But within that system its weight with the strictly political leadership had increased notably since the time of Stalin or Khrushchev.

Thus in 1965 Brezhnev's crony, Marshal Andrei Grechko, became minister of defense and, more importantly, a member of the Politburo. From this time onward, and for the first time in Soviet history, the head of the Soviet military would belong to the supreme decision-making body. In 1974 Grechko was succeeded by a political marshal, Dmitri Ustinov, who turned out to be an even more ardent spokesman for military interests. Thus for the twenty years 1965–1985 the Soviet military budget grew at a faster rate than that of the American military budget. And, more and more, this growth impelled the system to put its power to some "purpose" in increasingly sterile yet provocative Third World adventures, and, finally, to deploy the SS-20s against the heart of the First World.

INTERNAL ARTERIOSCLEROSIS

The progressive melding of the Party with the military occurred *pari passu* with the Party's blending with the police. Khrushchev had greatly reduced the KGB's size and diminished its political importance by, among other things, never giving its director a seat on the Politburo. But in 1967, after the Siniavskii-Daniel trial, the KGB received a new chief and a new status when the collective leadership installed Iurii Andropov as the agency's director. A protégé of Suslov without a KGB background, Andropov was taken from the foreign section of the Central Committee and given the job of refurbishing the police organization; in 1969 he became a full member of the Politburo and one of the most influential figures of the regime.[22]

Under Andropov, the KGB was significantly expanded; better educated agents were recruited; and a grand new annex was built off Dzerzhinskii Square in central Moscow. Operating in a more sophisticated fashion than Beria had, Andropov modernized the organization's operations and oversaw a propaganda campaign that restored its prestige. Intelligence-gathering abroad became more extensive and efficient, and at home all open dissidence was slowly but effectively suppressed. At the same time, the KGB's relationship to the Party changed. Stalin had used the NKVD to govern the Party; Brezhnev and Andropov used the KGB to govern society in tandem with the

Party (this, of course, also involved the KGB in some surveillance of the Party itself). And the Party and the KGB together functioned with the military in a kind of tripolar interlocking directorate. This was the organizational formula of "developed" or "mature" socialism, the final incarnation of the *nomenklatura* Party-state.

A principal reason for the KGB's new prominence was the persistent problem of the *inakomyshliasachie*, "those-who-think-differently," the dissidents. For the Siniavskii-Daniel trial had not achieved its purpose of silencing the critical intelligentsia; it had only stimulated them to develop new techniques of struggle; other dissidents reproduced and distributed a transcript of the trial that was eventually published abroad.[23] The editors of this document were arrested in 1967, and their trials, in turn, produced new documents and further international publicity. But dissidence also appeared among the privileged servants of the regime. In 1968 Andrei Sakharov published his letter to the leadership, "On Progress, Freedom, and Peaceful Coexistence," in which he urged both the end of censorship and the democratization of public life. In his view, these steps would eventually lead to the end of the Cold War through a "convergence" of the socialist economic forms of the East with the liberal political forms of the West.[24] In that same year, the independent Marxist historian Roy Medvedev produced *Let History Judge* in *samizdat;* in this detailed "unmasking" of the Stalin era, he called for a return to an allegedly democratic Leninist socialism.[25] Because Medvedev was rather less of a dissident than were the others, he was allowed to function openly throughout the Brezhnev era.

In their different ways Sakharov and Medvedev were advancing from below versions of that Reform Communism that had hitherto come only from above. Moreover, their positions paralleled closely those actually being put into effect during the Prague Spring. But the crushing of the Czech reform movement marked the end of Soviet Reform Communism from above for the foreseeable future, and it therefore produced a narrowing of the range of opinion permitted to critics from below. In 1969 Tvardovskii was removed as editor of *Novyi mir,* and this leading liberal Soviet publication lapsed into drabness.

Despite these setbacks, dissidence continued. In 1970, from within the establishment itself, Sakharov and Medvedev, together with the physicist Valentin Turchin, released an open letter to the leadership

explaining how the country's newly recognized economic and technological backwardness was a result of the lack of intellectual freedom
and the stifling of creative thought.[26] On the level of overt dissidence,
such figures as Vladimir Bukovskii adopted the tactic of holding the
Soviet government to the democratic letter of its paper constitution.[27]
And, after the Helsinki Accords of 1975, this approach led to the creation of Helsinki Watch Groups in the various republics of the Union.
In addition, throughout the Brezhnev era an underground network
published a *Chronicle of Current Events*—a low-key, strictly factual cat-
alog of the regime's documentable violations of its own laws.[28]

Yet Solzhenitsyn remained the most vocal dissident, despite his
inability to publish in Russia after 1963. Two of his novels on the
Stalin era were published abroad in the late 1960s, and then, in 1974–
1976, he produced *The Gulag Archipelago*. When the KGB discovered
this manuscript, Solzhenitsyn immediately had its first volume published abroad, and for this defiance he was forthwith forced aboard a
plane and into foreign exile. This incident marked the end of the
regime's semitoleration of dissent.

But the repression was more subtle than it had been under Stalin:
The principal figures were, like Solzhenitsyn, summarily exiled; others were consigned to psychiatric "hospitals"; some were incarcerated
in labor camps such as Perm 43; many more were simply deprived of
their jobs, or lost their housing, or found that their children were
barred from higher education. In the late 1970s, cultural leaders of the
non-Russian nationalities were systematically exiled from the Caucasus, Ukraine, and the Baltic states. By the end of the decade the only
prominent dissident left was Sakharov. But in 1980, after criticizing
the invasion of Afghanistan, he was exiled to the city of Gorky, presumably because his knowledge of nuclear secrets prevented the regime from sending him abroad. With this action the KGB effectively
closed down the dissident movement; the consequences of Khrushchev's "hare-brained" thaw had at last been liquidated.

But the regime had also destroyed many of the talents that alone
could give it a future, for until very late almost all of these dissidents
remained within the loyal bounds of Reform Communism. Only a
very few believed that the system was incapable of reform and thus
had to be replaced, a view that Andrei Amalrik expounded in 1969 in
Will the Soviet Union Survive Until 1984?[29] And although Solzhenitsyn
no longer believed after the early 1970s that the system as such was

reformable, even he hoped for no more than a partition of functions between the state and society, with political power remaining with the former and freedom of expression going to the latter.[30] Sakharov until his exile, and perhaps even for a time under *perestroika*, thought in terms of extensive liberalization and democratization of the system, not of its supersession. And Medvedev, of course, wanted only a return to Bukharin and the NEP. To be sure, had these last three programs been applied, they would have been as disruptive of the Soviet system as the 1968 reform was of Czechoslovakia's. But the important fact is that most Soviet dissidents did not realize this or have any clear idea of how advanced the crisis of the system was, even as late as the end of the 1970s.

This was even more true of the numerous semicritical intellectuals who remained loyal to the system in the hope of improving it from within. These individuals were members of a much larger group known in official Soviet parlance as the "intelligentsia," a term that simply meant people who had been trained for one or another kind of technical or professional activity. Since the 1930s, Russia had undergone an educational revolution, in part to spread "enlightenment" and in part to form the cadres of the new industrial society. But most of these people were conformist in their thinking. Quite different were the intellectuals of the specialized institutes of the Soviet Academy of Sciences, whether they worked in the natural sciences, as Sakharov and Turchin did, or in the newer social sciences, as did Nemchinov or Aganbegyan.

The Academy's network of institutes had grown considerably in the 1960s and 1970s.[31] In Moscow the most prominent examples were the Institute of the World Economy and International Relations, the Institute of the USA and Canada, and the Central Economic-Mathematical Institute. Very often researchers from these institutes would work as "*referents*," drafting position papers in various sections of the Central Committee Secretariat. Andropov, when he was in the Central Committee, collected some of the best and the brightest of these institute men, and many of them later became prominent during *perestroika*, including Gorbachev's speechwriter, Georgii Shakhnazarov, and the editor Fedor Burlatskii. In 1965, in the Siberian city of Novosibirsk, a virtual second Academy—bolder and more innovative than the first—was created. People working in these institutes or in the Central Committee obviously could not become dissidents and still retain their posts. But they were in contact with dissident culture and shared many of its criticisms of the system.[32]

Similarly, legal Soviet literature was influenced by *samizdat* writers, from Pasternak to Solzhenitsyn.[33] As a result, the canons of socialist realism, without ever being formally repudiated, were slowly eroded in the 1960s and 1970s, if only to permit official literature to compete with its illegal rival. The heroic themes of the days of building socialism were abandoned, and a literature that addressed in some measure the disappointments and discontents of the present was allowed to appear. In particular, there emerged a "village literature" celebrating the virtues, and bemoaning the fate, of old peasant Russia—a literature that was indirectly critical of Soviet slash-and-burn methods of development, and even of industrial civilization in general. These literary changes eventually shaded off into political activism when village writers took to agitating against pollution, as in the particular case of Lake Baikal. This agitation in turn had relevance for some of the critiques of Soviet planning that were heard in the Academy's institutes. And this culture of piecemeal criticism implied a critique of the system taken as a whole, an implication that the critics themselves were not wholly aware of. Slowly, without fanfare, the basic myths of the system were being undermined and awareness of the Lie was coming closer to the surface of consciousness.

It is from all of these sources—the Academy's institutes, the Writers' and Cinematographers' Unions, and indeed the Central Committee staff—that a shadow dissidence within the regime's structures emerged under Brezhnev, Suslov, and Andropov. As the decade of the seventies progressed, it became customary in such circles to divide the intelligentsia into the "Giordano Brunos" and the "Galileos." The former were the overt dissidents who boldly spoke out and came to a bad end for their pains, whereas the latter were the closet critics who publicly subscribed to official slogans yet privately worked for a new thaw—the labels implying that the second course, though less heroic, was more effective. In fact, however, under Brezhnev the most the Galileos could claim was that they were occasionally able to prevent the worst—to get an imprudent writer out of trouble, or to expose a particularly egregious bit of corruption—but they were rarely able to mold policy. They would get their real chance only with Gorbachev's *perestroika*.

*   *   *

The old Soviet order at its end weighed on the country with an exceptional massiveness. The eleven-million-member Party that Khrushchev had bequeathed to his successors had by Brezhnev's death become a nineteen-million-member Party.[34] The latter figure represented about 6 percent of a population of almost 300 million, and a much higher percentage of the working-age population. A respectable proportion of these members came from the working class and the kolkhoz peasantry. But the great majority, around 70 percent, were drawn from the managerial cadres in the economy, the military, and the intellectual professions; and this group, because of its numbers and its skills, constituted the center of gravity of the Party. Because most within the senior cohort of these cadres were originally from "the people," all-Party gatherings retained a somewhat plebeian tone until the end of the regime. But by then it had become more meaningless than ever to speak of the Party as an organization of workers and peasants, since most of the younger recruits were largely from the "intelligentsia." But "social base" is not a relevant criterion for characterizing the mature Party: the important facts are that the Party included everyone in the country who held a position of responsibility, and that anyone who aspired to such a position had to join.

Such a Party could not be an organization of zealots or committed ideologues. Nonetheless, its members were well-indoctrinated. All of them had to pay dues and attend cell meetings to discuss the latest Party directive, and they all had to keep up with the Party press in order to explain the current line to others. Thus, for most members a degree of "Party-mindedness" (*partiinost*) had become, if not a matter of conviction, at least an ingrained habit. They were all influenced by their constant immersion in the Party's special "wooden language." Indeed, the Party's logocratic "newspeak," the language of the Lie, as Solzhenitsyn called it, was a major force in holding the whole system together. Thus the regime, until almost the end of the 1980s, employed tens of thousands of "agitators" and spent billions of rubles to din the now almost lifeless categories of the Leninist 1920s into the minds of the population, and above all into its "avant-garde," the Party.

Thus the system's agitprop continued to reduce reality to "class positions," universal "struggle," and the great dichotomy of "socialism" versus "imperialism." Aleksandr Zinoviev, an academic consultant to the Central Committee who went from shadow to overt dissidence in the late 1970s, has been the great analyst of the surreal language of the Party, satirizing Khrushchev's "radiant future" as well as Brezhnev's equally phantom "real socialism." Nonetheless, he has also recognized the inescapable character of the "powerful magnetic field of ideological influence."[35]

At least this was the situation on one level, where no one dared question the ideology in public. But on another level Party members went about their careers in a pragmatic, self-interested fashion, and this circumstance undercut their public ideological stance. Still, in this mass Party, with its members influenced by *samizdat* literature and the growing professionalization of life, the ideological veneer of thought was wearing increasingly thin. The belief that there was a single "correct" position for nineteen million people and on all questions was on the point of appearing implausible—all the more so because the Party intellectuals had read Aleksandr Zinoviev and Solzhenitsyn, and even Conquest.

The erosion of the mass Party's cohesion was furthered by changes in the organization's structural relation to society. In the 1930s and 1940s the country lived in a permanent state of emergency, first because of the internal war to build socialism and then because of the external war against Germany. Under such circumstances it made a certain "sense" for a military-type Party to mobilize coercively all of society's resources from above, and so Stalin's one- to two-million-member Party vigorously exercised its role as leader. But after the victory of 1945, the country settled down to a long process of patterned growth without war or serious threat of war. Under any other system these circumstances would have meant a return to normality, but the Party, by its very nature, was unable to accomplish such a transformation: its whole raison d'être was to command and lead in order to preserve its monopoly of power. Thus it continued to impose its nature on society rather than bend itself to the changing needs of society. But it did so now not by a violent wrench but by routine and inertia.

Hence, from the 1950s to the early 1980s the Party continued to monitor and manage all of society's activities; and since these activities constantly increased in number and complexity, the Party constantly grew in size—and cumbersomeness—in order to stay on top of everything. The result was an unprecedented bureaucratic hypertrophy. As already noted, to the forty-five industrial ministries in the

1960s were added twenty-five in other fields, for a total of seventy economic ministries by the 1980s; and more and more of central Moscow's buildings, old and new, were taken over by government staffs.[36] In the countryside the collective farms and state farms spawned some three million additional bureaucrats. The policy-making organ for the whole system, the Central Committee Secretariat on Old Square, grew in physical size and in the number of effectives, just like the KGB down the street. Party committees existed in all large enterprises, and every institution had its Party cell. Political officers responsible to the Central Committee monitored the military, and the KGB's agents, who were also Party members, monitored everybody. And so all positions of responsibility came to be filled by Party members, whose ranks now counted nineteen million.

Thus the Party, in one or another of its guises, became directly involved in every functional activity in society, and this was a new development. The Party, of course, had always led and commanded in all essential matters, but in the 1960s and 1970s it took to actually directing most things itself. The system of dual administration invented by Lenin was now pushed to its ultimate limit. In recognition of this new state of affairs, in 1977 Brezhnev replaced the Stalin Constitution of 1936 with a new fundamental document in which the principal innovation was Article VI. This provision formally recognized for the first time that the "leading and governing role" in society was exercised by the Party.

But, of course, a Party of such size cannot lead unless it is itself led. The great mass of Party members who held functional positions in society received their directives from the full-time Party workers of the apparat—or, in Orwell's terminology, the Inner Party governed the Outer Party, while the latter acted as the system's representative in the workplaces of society. Although some measure of privilege and prestige accrued to all Party members, real power and significant perquisites were reserved for the full-time apparat; and this group, together with the key governmental, economic, and military cadres, formed the *nomenklatura*.

As we have seen, the *nomenklatura* dates back to the 1930s, but the world became aware of it only in 1980 through Mikhail Voslenskii's book of the same name.[37] According to his figures, this group numbered about three quarters of a million people; together with their families, it perhaps totaled nearly three million. While other estimates are even higher, this was still a small group to wield so much power without accountability in such a huge country. Despite the Party's imposing "leading and governing role" under Brezhnev, it was in fact becoming a fragile mastodon. With the force of ideology on the wane, the Outer Party of competent professionals was less and less awed by the Inner Party of often incompetent ideological administrators. The population at large no longer expected a "radiant future" and increasingly resented the perquisites and corruption of the *nomenklatura*. And people of skill, competence, and ambition were increasingly frustrated by the omnipresent representatives and the ubiquitous agitprop of a self-appointed organization whose only function was to exercise its "leading role." And, in fact, the mass Party of *nomenklatura* Communism commanded everything yet produced nothing, and so lived like a parasite on the body of the nation. But by the same token, it was destroying the very substance on which it fed.

THE WEAKEST LINK: THE EXTERNAL EMPIRE

While the Inner Empire of Sovietism was approaching a dead end, the External Empire was moving beyond Reform Communism towards an actual exit from the system. Indeed, the most significant events of the Brezhnev era took place not in the Soviet Union itself but in Eastern Europe—first in Czechoslovakia in 1968, and then in Poland in 1980–1981. These events were all the more important because, with China in secession, the East European satellites were the most palpable indication that the "world socialist system" was still a coherent force.

The Prague Spring of 1968 was the most far-reaching attempt at Reform Communism of the post-Stalin era, and for this reason its failure was the most revealing regarding the inner contradictions of any such effort. The Czechoslovak reform began as a belated attempt at the sort of de-Stalinization that had occurred elsewhere under Khrushchev. The local Party leader, Antonin Novotny, had managed to defer de-Stalinization for a decade, thereby only aggravating frustration within the Party and the country. To unfreeze this situation, in late 1967 Brezhnev gave him a shove from office, and the Czech reformers installed Alexander Dubcek. These reformers, unlike Khrushchev in 1956, had a well-prepared and wide-ranging program;

in addition, they were operating in a country ready and eager for thoroughgoing change.

Drawing on the Yugoslav experience, as well as on Western literature about modernization, the Czech reformers, like all of their East European predecessors, sought a "separate road to socialism"; in the Czech's case, this meant a road adapted to the advanced nature of their society.[38] Their aspirations were set forth in the Party's Action Program of April 1968 and later summarized in the slogan "socialism with a human face." Since the class struggle leading to socialism had already been won, the reformers argued, the various interests in society should be allowed to organize their own institutions and even to compete politically. And indeed in the next months independent voluntary associations and protopolitical parties appeared. But this emerging social pluralism also required a "socialist rule of law," and especially the end of censorship, since freedom was a prerequisite of the cultural and scientific creativity required by a developed economy. At the same time, however, the reformers reaffirmed the principle of the "leading role of the Party" without facing the problem of how that role could be reconciled with freedom of expression and association. And this, of course, would do the experiment in.

Almost as unorthodox as its political program was the Party's economic program, the work of Ota Sik. A bolder version of the Kosygin reforms, it called for a significant measure of managerial autonomy, the use of profit as an integral component or "indicator" of the Plan, and provision for the possibility that inefficient units might go bankrupt. Workers' councils were to be elected and given a share in plant management, a measure reminiscent of the Yugoslav reforms and of "workers' control" in Russia during 1917. The program thus combined an industrial NEP with a form of anarcho-syndicalism, as well as cultural pluralism, the latter viewed as a stimulus to economic development.

It was long taken as axiomatic that this program was both promising and practical, and that if followed it would at last have led to the famous "third way" between capitalism and socialism. That the reform movement was cut off by Soviet intervention after only eight months thus has been considered a tragedy. No doubt the Prague Spring was the great lyrical moment of hope during the post-Stalin decades: in both the East and the West, many saw it at the time as the belated payoff of Soviet-style modernization and a sign that the Cold

War might end with some sort of convergence of capitalism and Communism. And the event was indeed tragic.

The tragedy, however, lay not in some missed opportunity but in the intrinsic impossibility of realizing the Prague version of Reform Communism. A part of the problem was the content of the program itself: the move towards profit and real prices was counteracted by the continued subordination of these "indicators" to a directive Plan, while freedom of speech and association were subject to the Party's insistence on its leading role. Yet the Czech leaders, like other Reform Communists before them, were quite unaware that any such contradictions existed; and this unawareness was a consequence of the reformers' psychology.

In order to take any action, the reformers had to believe that reform was possible and that the system, therefore, was malleable. They were encouraged in this belief in part by Reform Communism's relative youth in 1968: Khrushchev's fall did not appear to mark the end of change because the impetus of his thaw was still present in the policies of Kosygin and in the activities of a loyal yet critical Soviet intelligentsia. Moreover, the Czech reformers' optimism was reinforced by their own ideological presuppositions.

Starting from the premise that the system was the "highest" possible form of social organization, the reformers could not conceive of abandoning it. Yet empirically, they knew that the system in its existing state largely negated its own ideals. Since by definition this defect could not be the fault of the highest system, it had to be an accident due to an adventitious force called "Stalinism." The solution, therefore, was to purge the highest system of this alien body by devising policies that would return it to something called "true Leninism" or "socialism with a human face." But in resorting to these circumlocutory variations on Communist principles, the Prague reformers were in fact acknowledging the validity of the claims of the system they aspired to change; they thus remained prisoners of its logic even as they were implementing measures that contradicted that logic.

The tragedy of their dilemma was as follows: Had they been more lucid, either they would have been unable to act at all, in which case they would have given up in despair, or they would have had to attempt a revolution, in which case they would have gone down to defeat. Therefore, they had to take it on faith that the third way did

exist, half-fooling themselves into believing that they were not destroying the system and hoping they could fool Moscow into believing the
same thing. But Moscow at the time was recovering from its own
illusions of a post-Stalinist spring; thus Dubcek and his colleagues
sleepwalked to their doom at the hands of the "Brezhnev doctrine."

What precipitated the crisis was the fact that the system in Czechoslovakia was well on its way to unravelling by the summer of 1968. In
June a group of intellectuals issued a proclamation—the "2000
words"—calling on the people to take the process of liberalization
into their own hands and away from the Party. By August the Party
itself had issued new statutes democratizing its internal structure:
Elections were to be by secret ballot, and a limitation was placed on
the number of years leaders could hold office; moreover, groups within
the Party were allowed to organize as factions in violation of the rule
on Party unity that Lenin had set in 1921. Since these statutes had
been published in anticipation of a Party Congress the following
month, they seemed to Brezhnev and his colleagues to presage the
system's self-liquidation. East Germany's Walter Ulbricht and Poland's Gomulka, mindful of the fragility of their own regimes, were
even more vehement in their denunciation of this impending "counterrevolution."

And all of these First Secretaries were correct in their diagnosis: In
a mere eight months the contagion of liberalization had spread with
extraordinary rapidity from the reform wing of the Party to the intellectuals, and finally to the workers; the whole nation wanted a new
order that it could still call Communist but in which the Party would
in fact be superfluous. And if the Party's control collapsed in Prague,
how long could it be maintained in Warsaw and Berlin? Or, eventually, even in Moscow?

Still, an intervention in Prague would be more difficult than the
one in Budapest in 1956, when an outright revolt had made it relatively easy for the Soviets to justify the use of force. But a Communist
government was still in control in Prague, and it continued to proclaim
its fidelity to the Warsaw Pact. Hence, the intervention of August 21
was not a unilateral Soviet action but the nominal undertaking of the
"fraternal" Warsaw Pact in response to an appeal from loyal Czech
Communists. Although militarily the operation was a masterpiece of
organization, politically it was a failure: not only did the Czech leadership refuse to legitimate it, but the Czech opposition could not

produce a Kadar to take Dubcek's place. So, in the surreal conclusion to the drama, the leadership was abducted to Moscow, forced to rescind its program, and then restored to nominal power, while all concerned kept up the pretense of comradely communion in socialist values.

Behind this facade, the Soviets and their orthodox Czech allies proceeded with what they called the "normalization" of the situation. Brezhnev answered the Prague reformers' presumption to create "socialism with a human face" by recycling Tito's old slogan to declare that the Czechs already enjoyed "really existing socialism"; and this designation was henceforth canonical in all of the fraternal countries. Concretely, this meant the liquidation of all vestiges of the Spring and the purge of a third of the national Party. By early 1969, normalization was sufficiently advanced to replace Dubcek with a would-be Czechoslovak Kadar, Gustav Husak, who, like his Hungarian predecessor, had been imprisoned under Stalin; Husak would remain in power until 1988. As for Dubcek, until the very collapse of the system in 1989, he believed that the intervention had been an avoidable error and that an improved Communism remained the real answer to the country's problems.

For the Soviets and their allies, however, the intervention was a matter of basic principle, embodied in what soon became known as the "Brezhnev doctrine." This doctrine held that although the Czechs had a right to choose their own road to socialism, their misguided policies in fact threatened the existence of socialism at home and in all "fraternal" countries. Thus, the intervention was not an exercise of raw power—as it appeared to the West—but a legitimate measure of self-defense. In essence, the doctrine asserted that socialism was indivisible and that the criterion of socialism's "real existence" was the "leading role of the Party." For the international solidarity of socialist Party-states was vital for the survival of ideocratic partocracy everywhere. Solidarity was vital first for a metaphysical reason: in a movement where legitimacy derived from the logic of history, the "conquests of socialism," once made, had to be "irreversible" or the system would be unmasked as a pseudoscientific fraud. And socialist solidarity was also necessary for a practical reason: to keep the Communist populations everywhere afraid and therefore passive; for if one captive nation demonstrated that escape was in fact possible, then others would also find the courage to escape.

But the Czechoslovak leadership misunderstood another aspect of the system as well. Remembering the mistake of the Hungarians in withdrawing from the Warsaw Pact, the Czechs had insisted on their own loyalty to that organization, as if Moscow were not far more threatened by their "counterrevolutionary" example than by diminution of its military glacis. That Moscow's primary concern was ideological is borne out by considering Romania under Nicolae Ceausescu. In the year of the Prague Spring, Romania not only broke with Moscow's foreign policy by courting leaders as diverse as Mao and de Gaulle, she in effect also ceased to participate in the Warsaw Pact by, among other things, refusing to join it in the Czechoslovak intervention. Yet at the same time, Ceausescu enforced the most orthodox Communist order at home and so never suffered anything more than frowns from Moscow.

And Brezhnev was not mistaken in considering the Czechoslovaks the more dangerous deviationists. Since by definition there could never be anything better or higher than "real socialism," the most serious attempt ever at Reform Communism in the External Empire had to be ended by surgical intervention. By the same token, the impetus of Khrushchev's de-Stalinization was at last halted in the country that East Europeans now called Big Brother, and the age of full Brezhnevite "stagnation" began.

The year 1968 also marked the beginning of a new phase in the decomposition of Communism in the two East European countries that were at the center of the upheaval of 1956, Hungary and Poland. The former quietly embarked on a radical economic reform of Communism; the latter, in a spectacular way, became the first country to go beyond Reform Communism and pose a political challenge to the Party-state.

In Hungary, after a decade of repression Kadar inaugurated the New Economic Mechanism, which sought to reconcile the population with the regime by giving the former a modicum of material prosperity.[39] Even bolder than Tito's self-management, Kadar's policy was the farthest advance towards the market of any made by a Communist regime since the days of the Soviet NEP. In certain sectors of agriculture, in small-scale consumer production, and in some services and areas of retail trade, cooperative endeavors were allowed and given significant latitude in setting their prices. In the mid-1970s these semiprivate sectors were reined in under pressure from Moscow, but in the early 1980s they were again allowed to expand in order to reduce the kinds of discontent that in Poland had produced Solidarity. Also during the latter period, a measure of freedom—including the opportunity to travel abroad—was accorded to the intellectuals in the hope of reconciling the population to an unavoidable regime. The overall result of Kadarism was a growing, if modest, prosperity and the longest period of stability in Eastern Europe—and thus also the confidence of Moscow in the local leadership. At the same time, however, Kadar's low-key, creeping reformism was eroding the foundations of the system; no one dared to draw any bold conclusions from this fact, for everyone had learned the terrible lesson of 1956.

In Poland, however, although the nation's efforts to emancipate itself met with recurrent defeats after 1956, there was never an all-out disaster, and this emboldened the population after each repression to return to the attack.[40] Indeed, Gomulka's Reform Communism had at first appeared as a victory, and it eventually provoked an outburst of social creativity: workers' councils were created in the factories, and a revisionist, "humanist" Marxism emerged among the intellectuals, Kolakowski being only the most prominent example. But Gomulka turned out to be no more than an orthodox Communist with national trimmings: the workers' councils were soon neutered and the intellectuals increasingly harassed.

The first result of Gomulka's new policies was an open clash in March 1968 between the regime and its police on the one hand, and the intellectuals on the other. This episode, which was tinged with official anti-Semitism, spelled the end of revisionist Marxism in Poland: henceforth, the intellectuals would no longer try to amend Stalinism through a return to the young Marx and Gyorgy Lukacs, but would seek a philosophy of change completely outside the orbit of the system. The second result of Gomulka's reversion to classical Communist style was the Gdansk workers' strike and riots of December 1970, during which Lech Walesa discovered his vocation; like the events of Novocherkassk in 1962, these events were triggered by precipitate price rises. Although the riots were suppressed by force, the workers nonetheless achieved a measure of victory: Gomulka was replaced as Party leader by Edward Gierek, who had to promise a policy of catering to their needs.

Thus, as of 1970 both the intellectuals and the workers, and of course the Church, had morally defected from the system. So had some 70 percent of the peasantry, for Poland alone among Communist countries had largely escaped collectivization. Together, these groups comprised a renascent "civil society" openly opposed to the "power," to use the terminology of the day. And in the second half of the decade this society developed a protopolitical organization and a philosophy of action suited to the special conditions of Communism.

This development was triggered by Gierek's debased version of Reform Communism. One part of this program was a greater freedom for intellectuals, including travel abroad, a freedom that only accelerated the transition from revisionist Marxism to the cultural diversity of the West. Still more important, Gierek, profiting from détente and *Ostpolitik*, borrowed heavily from the West to build a "second Poland" of new industry that would provide the consumer goods needed to keep the population quiet. But when he could no longer pay for this expansion, he had to raise domestic prices; this led to strikes at Radom and the Ursus factory in Warsaw, which he then had to repress. This incident provoked the creation of a movement of dissident intellectuals on behalf of the arrested strikers—the Committee for Workers' Defense, or KOR—whose most prominent figures were Adam Michnik and Jaczek Kuron.[41]

In effect, KOR amounted to a protorevolutionary alliance of intellectuals and workers, for it united the two forces that had moved, and been defeated, separately in 1968 and 1970. This time, however, the regime was forced to release the arrested workers through KOR's tactic of generating social pressure by taking the matter to the regime's courts. From this success, KOR developed a general philosophy of "revolution" adapted to the peculiar conditions of struggle under Communism: reform within the system was abandoned as an illusion (the Czechoslovak pitfall), yet direct action against the system was eschewed as suicidal (the Hungarian pitfall). Instead, KOR urged that all opposition should take the form of a "social movement," or the "self-organization" of society, in order to stake out a sphere of autonomy vis-à-vis the regime. Concretely, this sphere meant such entities as the "flying university" of independent study groups for the intelligentsïa, the *samizdat* publishing house Nowa, a few embryonic unofficial trade unions, and of course the Church. By this method, it was hoped, the regime would over time be hollowed out to where it had to leave society largely to its own devices.

In Poland itself, the process of hollowing-out the system received a great impetus in 1978 when John Paul II, a Pole, was elected pope. The impact of this event, and the fragility of the system, became apparent when the next year the regime felt it would be imprudent to refuse John Paul permission to visit his native country. The visit proved to be the first occasion when the population discovered it had the capacity to mobilize itself, and by the millions, to greet the pontiff.

This renascence of civil society became openly revolutionary in 1980 with the formation of Solidarity.[42] The upheaval began with a new strike in Gdansk that quickly took up KOR's methods. When the usual Communist tactic of isolating the trouble spot failed to keep the country from learning what had occurred, the strike spread to other areas and became too big to be repressed. The regime therefore had to negotiate with the strikers, and to their amazement, after two weeks it agreed to recognize an independent trade union with a right to strike. This was the first time such recognition had been granted in any Communist country.

This outcome delegitimized what was supposed to be a workers' state. Kuron was right to claim that Solidarity, with its ten million members, represented the largest "proletarian revolution" in history, one that quite dwarfed the Bolshevik Revolution of 1917, whose motive force, after all, had been the peasantry. Yet Solidarity was much more than a trade union: it represented the self-organization of civil society, indeed of the nation, against the regime, but in a manner that fell short of open confrontation with the authorities. Solidarity therefore referred to itself as a "self-limiting revolution."

Specifically, Solidarity came to demand the "Finlandization" of Poland and a "self-governing republic." This meant that the Soviets would retain control of Poland's military and foreign policy while society would manage its principal internal affairs, leaving the Party only to reign but not rule, like the Queen of England. In fact, however, this Red queen would retain quite a bit of power: although Solidarity wanted independent trade unions and a market-oriented economy, its Program of October 1981 did not dare advocate the privatization of state industry, for this would have frightened the Soviets too much. Hence, Solidarity went well beyond Reform Communism but was still obliged to settle for something of a halfway house.

Yet it would be a mistake to think that Solidarity had fixed goals of any kind. Its existence was one long gamble: At the beginning, the organization played for time simply in order to exist; later, it played to expand the limits of the permissible and yet continue to exist. For it never had any illusions that the Party had accepted its right to be there, or that a policy of "partnership" was anything more than a tactic for either side. Its oft-repeated motto was, "What we are doing is impossible and at the same time necessary." So the members of Solidarity, deliberately closing their eyes to the obvious dangers, kept this existential wager going for sixteen unprecedented months in the hope that if they could hold out long enough, their adversary might actually accept power sharing. Although their gamble did not pay off in this way, it did yield a great return nonetheless: by the time the inevitable crackdown came, Solidarity had hollowed out Poland's Communist system beyond any possibility of repair. And this feat, rather than any particular social conquest, was Solidarity's major and original achievement.

In arriving at this result the Poles were inadvertently aided by the exceptional indecisiveness of the Soviets. At the beginning, in August 1980, the suddenness of Solidarity's eruption and the size of the movement ruled out armed repression by either Warsaw or Moscow: Although neither had any intention of tolerating Solidarity permanently, they also had no choice but to play for time. The Soviets first mobilized for intervention in December but then backed off. In February 1981 their presumptive Kadar, the minister of defense, General Wojciech Jaruzelski, was given the additional title of First Secretary, and methodical preparations for a crackdown were begun. The Soviets at last seemed ready to intervene in March, and then once more in September, but still matters did not go beyond a war of nerves. As a prelude to the actual assault, in October Jaruzelski became prime minister while keeping all of his previous titles.

Why matters dragged on for this long a time is still not clear. Perhaps the size of the country—and of Solidarity—made the operation much more daunting than had been the case in Hungary or Czechoslovakia. Possibly another reason was that the Soviets were now bogged down in Afghanistan. In any event, it was only after much debate that Jaruzelski and the Soviets finally agreed that the least costly course for the two regimes would be a "state of siege" imposed by Polish forces alone. So on December 13, 1981, this self-occupation was carried out with an efficiency the system had never displayed with the economy.

On the surface, this outcome looked like a replay of the Hungarian and Czechoslovak denouements, as almost all Western observers declared at the time; in reality, however, the result was far less decisive. The fact that Moscow had hesitated—and Solidarity had survived—for sixteen months demonstrated that the system could in fact be rolled back. The further fact that at the moment of showdown Moscow, for the first time, had not dared to do the deed itself also indicated a loss of vitality. And all of this was noted throughout Eastern Europe.

Poland, moreover, was not "normalized": Jaruzelski, who indeed wanted to be the Kadar of his decade, kept up repression for only a year and then moved to the second phase of his operation, a new Reform Communism. At the same time, Solidarity, though driven underground, remained very much alive throughout the eighties; and it viewed Jaruzelski's reforms not as a solution but as a prelude to someday achieving a "normal society." Thus the first phase of Solidarity, in 1980–1981, ended not in a disaster but only in a setback, like all the other Polish brushes with the system since 1956. And this outcome would provide the basis for the grand denouement of 1989.

By Brezhnev's death in 1982, the balance sheet of the Soviet External Empire in Eastern Europe was palpably negative. Soviet armed forces or their proxies had been obliged to suppress "counterrevolution" in Berlin, Budapest, Prague, and Warsaw. Although these interventions had appeared aggressive and threatening to the West, they were in fact defensive and conservative, albeit costly, efforts to hold on to the gains of the Second World War. At the same time, Yugoslavia and Romania had seceded from the bloc. The Warsaw Pact, far from being an adjunct to Soviet security or a shield against an attack that no one was contemplating, had become still another burden on the Soviet system.

The economies of Eastern Europe, moreover, were stagnating almost as badly as the economy of the Soviet Union, and all were far behind the increasingly prosperous (West) European Community. Finally, despite the repression, the entire region was softening up, whether through regime policy in Hungary and Poland or via the reach of West German and Austrian television in East Germany and Czechoslovakia. After almost four decades of socialism, there was no longer any illusion among the local populations that the system offered them a genuine future. They knew they were simply captive nations; and the system lived essentially off the capital of fear accumulated since 1945. But with Solidarity, even this fear had begun to ebb. It was now an open question whether Moscow would have the capacity to intervene the next time an effort at Reform Communism spun out of control.

Still, none of the Soviet Union's external problems—from Solidarity to Afghanistan—would be capable of shaking the system unless there were first a crisis at home. And there were numerous latent elements of crisis in the Soviet Union at the start of the 1980s—from the stagnation of the economy to the sclerosis of the Party to geopolitical overextension. Yet none of these elements could emerge into the open or congeal into general crisis without a precipitating shock. And this shock could originate only at the top, for the structure of the system was such that all initiative had to come from on high. Indeed, every shift of Soviet policy—from War Communism to the NEP to Khrushchev's de-Stalinization—had come as a revolution from above.

However, the Brezhnev generation—the final fruit of Stalin's social promotion through purge at the end of the 1930s—in its geriatric decline was quite incapable of any such initiative. Hence, after the exertions of defending the conquests of socialism in Afghanistan and Poland, it simply coasted into further decline. Because the system was so centralized, there would be no way out of this predicament until the gerontocrats had physically passed from the scene. This circumstance resulted in a three-year interregnum during which, one by one, they were interred beside the Kremlin wall. And this macabre process was the final element of crisis that produced the ultimate in Reform Communism, Gorbachev's *perestroika*.

Part IV
THE END

11

REFORM COMMUNISM II
Gorbachev and *Perestroika*, 1982–1988

The most widespread ideology in [Soviet] society [is]. . . the ideology of reformism. *It is founded on the idea that progressive changes and partial reforms, the replacement of an old bureaucratic elite by a new one that is more intellectual and endowed with good sense, will produce a sort of* humanization of socialism, *and that in the place of a system that is stagnant and devoid of liberty will appear a dynamic and liberal system. In other words, this theory is founded on the idea that* reason will triumph *and that* all will be well; *this is why [this theory] is so popular in intellectual milieux and in general among those who do not live too badly at present. . . . The same naive point of view explains all the hopes of the Americans with respect to the USSR. . . .*

*[But] it would be more accurate to consider the process of the in*cremental increase of liberty *as, in fact, the process of the decrepitude of the regime.*

—Andrei Amalrik, 1969

After the eighteen years of soft Stalinism under Brezhnev, Kosygin, and Suslov, the structural defects of the Soviet system once again brought Reform Communism to the fore. It fell to Mikhail Gorbachev to initiate this new round of activism from above; and while he was in power, most observers, in the East as well as in the West, saw him as a man of destiny—indeed a "miracle"—on whom both the start of the movement and its outcome depended. But to personify the complexities of history in the "good man" Gorbachev is just as simplistic as personifying them in the "bad man" Stalin. The last General Secretary, like the first, must be situated in his context.

To be sure, given the nature of Soviet institutions, the impulse for

change could have come only from the top. But this does not make
Gorbachev's *perestroika*, or "restructuring," any less an expression of
the long-term logic of the system: the oscillation between hard and
soft Communism, between War Communism and the NEP, was periodically necessary to permit the country to recoup its strength for the
next round of socialist exertion. Yet on this occasion, quite unexpectedly, the reprise of Act II of the recurring drama brought the curtain
down for good on what was by now a threadbare show.

Indeed, nothing about Communism astonished the world as much
as the manner of its exit from history. Gorbachev inherited a superpower and a nineteen-million-member Party, each bristling with a
militancy that had frightened the outside world for decades. Yet after
six years in power—the same span of time it took Lenin to launch the
Soviet state—Gorbachev saw both the Party and the Union dissolve
beneath him. They disappeared, moreover, without offering the
slightest resistance, still less without giving rise to the convulsions one
might expect from such imposing forces. The reasons for the extraordinary fragility of the Soviet system at its end will no doubt constitute
the central question in the future historiography of *perestroika*.

One cause of this fragility was that the second attempt at Reform
Communism, despite surface appearances, could only be significantly
different from the first, precisely because the structures the second
sought to reform had been undermined by the preceding effort. The
flaccid *nomenklatura* Communism of Brezhnev and Co. was not
the terroristic Communism of Stalin, and the multitudinous Party of
the last days was not the zealous band that had built socialism. Nor
was the generation that would carry out the new reform the same as
that which had attempted the first. The leaders of the Khrushchev
reform had been molded by the Stalin system: they were both terrified by it and wedded to its accomplishments; and some of these same
men, sobered by the risks of reform, then became the Brezhnev generation. But the leaders of the Gorbachev reform had been molded by
the Khrushchev thaw while they were in their hopeful twenties; and
when retrenchment became necessary, they retired to nothing more
terrifying than soft berths in the Central Committee or in the institutes of the Academy of Sciences.

Thus, both the object of reform and the perspective of the reformers were more mellow the second time around. This time the contest
would be between the crisis-wracked system nurtured by the valetu-

dinarian beneficiaries of Stalin's great social promotion of the thirties and the "men of the sixties," the *shestidesiatniki*, who themselves were now nearing sixty. At least this is the way the new reform started out—until the contest developed a momentum of its own that went far beyond the aspirations of any group raised within the seraglio of the Inner Party.

"ACCELERATION"

The first moves leading to the new era were made in the penumbra of the old. Behind the Brezhnev regime's facade of immobility there was much questioning, even anxiety, about the state of the system. These concerns partially emerged during the two-year interregnum between Brezhnev's death in 1982 and Gorbachev's election as General Secretary in 1985, an interval when that post was successively occupied by Iurii Andropov and Konstantin Chernenko. Although outwardly a continuation of the Brezhnev era, this period was indispensable—given the constraints of the system—both for disposing of the gerontocracy and for providing the psychological shock necessary to make "restructuring" at last appear imperative.

The leaders of the old guard began to disappear around 1980: Kosygin died in 1979, Suslov in 1982, and Brezhnev himself a few months later that year. A contest for the succession then developed between the secondary figures of this group, represented by Chernenko, and the "reform party," led by Andropov. With the support of the military, Andropov was promoted quickly from the KGB to Suslov's post in the Central Committee in order to position him better to succeed Brezhnev. When Brezhnev died a few months later, Andropov, at age sixty-eight, duly took over. But, in a compromise, his rival, Chernenko, was left in the second Party position, thereby indicating that the contest between would-be reformers and the old guard was far from concluded.[1]

There existed at this time among the Soviet elite a minor cult of Andropov as a man of vision, a view that presented his short reign, therefore, as another lost opportunity in the battle against Soviet decline. But it is most doubtful that Andropov, a pure product of the Stalin era and a protégé of Suslov, for all his awareness of the system's deficiencies, had in mind any very radical remedies; and this is what

his brief empirical record bears out. He saw only a "crisis of performance, not a crisis of the system."[2] Thus, he proceeded to study the
problems of the system by commissioning confidential reports from
advisors among the intelligentsia whom he had cultivated over the
years, but he also indicated the limits of innovation by cracking down
on the demidissident Roy Medvedev, the sole (somewhat) critical
figure still at large. For the rest, he initiated only the most classic type
of Soviet reform: He used the police to reduce corruption and to
tighten labor discipline, two policies that, as usual, produced short-
term success without affecting fundamental causes.

Yet Andropov was responsible for two initiatives that went beyond
these measures. First, his appeal to academic intellectuals yielded the
Novosibirsk Report, which was written in 1983 by the sociologist Tatiana Zaslavskaia, a colleague of Aganbegyan in the Siberian branch of
the Academy.[3] Advancing radical criticisms in orthodox language,
Zaslavskaia argued that Soviet central planning had become obsolete—indeed a fetter on production—and that Soviet society, far from
being the harmonious unity depicted in official propaganda, was riven
by conflicts between the rulers and the ruled, and hobbled by alienation, apathy, and lack of motivation among the working class. This
analysis pointed to a crisis of the system, not just of its performance.
And the implied remedy was, of course, decentralization, incentives,
and the stimulation of individual initiative throughout the system.
This document, leaked to the Western press in the once putatively
fatal year 1984, first alerted the world to the impending end of Soviet
stability. It recapitulated many of the diagnoses of the economists of
the 1960s and adumbrated much of what would soon become *perestroika*.

Andropov's second important initiative was to treat Mikhail Gorbachev as his designated successor. Gorbachev had been brought to
Moscow in 1978, at age forty-seven, to head the Agricultural Department of the Central Committee Secretariat. In 1981, largely at Andropov's urging, he became the youngest member of the Politburo.
(Andropov's flair for reformist talent, however, was not infallible, for
he also promoted to that rank such hidebound apparatchiki as Geidar
Aliev and Grigorii Romanov.) During this period Gorbachev became
acquainted with the intellectuals whom Andropov had gathered
around himself throughout his career, and most of these would later
become part of the brain trust of *perestroika*. In particular, he was

involved in the consultations that produced the *Novosibirsk Report*. And Gorbachev travelled abroad to display the reformist face of Soviet policy. In 1983 he toured Canada, where he first met Aleksandr Yakovlev, another Central Committee modernizer who was then ambassador to Ottawa and in the tenth year of diplomatic exile for his liberalism. The next year, after Andropov's death, and now as heir presumptive, he made what was virtually a state visit to London, where Prime Minister Margaret Thatcher declared him to be a Soviet leader the West "could do business with."

But Andropov died too soon for Gorbachev to become his immediate successor. In what was yet another compromise, the seventy-three-year-old Chernenko got the job, and Gorbachev rose to the number two position. The next year, 1985, when the succession opened again, the candidate of the Brezhnevites was the seventy-two-year-old Viktor Grishin, the rather corrupt boss of the Moscow Party. But this time the old guard divided. Elders Andrei Gromyko and Mikhail Solomentsev threw their weight to Gorbachev, as did KGB chief Viktor Chebrikov, and they had the support of influential Central Committee chiefs who were not on the Politburo, such as Yegor Ligachev. This, together with scheduling the ballot before a couple of Grishin supporters could get back to Moscow, put Gorbachev over by one vote, if the matter was indeed settled by a formal vote. In any event, even if Grishin had squeaked in, a generational change of leadership could not have been deferred for long, for too many people at the top now felt that failure to change had become downright dangerous.

What manner of man was the new General Secretary?[4] It has often been alleged that if the Soviet system were really totalitarian it could not have produced so refreshingly bold a leader. And the radical change of style he brought to Soviet affairs did seem to be living proof that the system possessed the inner resources for genuine reform. In fact, however, Gorbachev, even in his boldness, was very much a product of the system—much more talented than its average leader, to be sure, but a Soviet leader nonetheless. As for the supposed incapacity of totalitarianism to bring forth dynamic personalities, it was not by turning individuals into automatons that the system worked. It worked, rather, by setting structural bounds and mental horizons for all those who led it, and Gorbachev operated largely within these parameters. Indeed, his rise to the top was no fluke but the result of a reflex of self-preservation of the system on the part of the existing oligarchy. And it is no more miraculous that such a dynamo came out of Brezhnevite stagnation than that Stalin emerged from Lenin's Politburo, or Khrushchev from Stalin's Presidium.

Gorbachev's road to the top was the classic *cursus honorum* of the Soviet apparatchik, only faster. He was born in 1931 in the midst of collectivization and famine in the grain-rich region of Stavropol in the North Caucasus. Both of his grandfathers were dekulakized, but his father nonetheless became a Party member, a Red Army soldier, and a good kolkhoznik. Gorbachev himself moved up in the world by receiving a secondary education, working in a Machine Tractor Station, and heading the local Komsomol organization. The latter job made him a candidate member of the Party at the precocious age of eighteen, whereupon he obtained the rare privilege of attending Moscow State University. There he studied law, a discipline that at the time was useful only for a career in Party and administrative affairs.

In Gorbachev's third year at Moscow State, Stalin died and the thaw began. Gorbachev lived during this period in the old dormitory on Stromynka Street, then a place of intellectual questing and questioning of the system. There was also a touch of cosmopolitanism: one of his classmates was a Czech student, Zdenek Mlynar, with whom Gorbachev kept up contact into the 1960s and who would be one of the authors of the Action Program of 1968.[5] In other words, Gorbachev was in close contact with proponents of Reform Communism from the impressionable age of twenty-two. And in 1956 he would even be a delegate at the pivotal Twentieth Party Congress.

But to get to that Congress, he first had to go back to Stavropol and work his way up the hierarchy of the apparat. The royal road to a Party career was to begin with Komsomol administration, in which Gorbachev had already been engaged in his home province during adolescence and then during his years at the University. Back in Stavropol, he quickly moved up the ladder to First Secretary of the Komsomol, then to First Secretary of the city, and in 1970, at only thirty-nine, to First Secretary of the region. One reason for this rapid advancement was that he always enjoyed powerful sponsors, in particular Fedor Kulakov, the former Stavropol First Secretary who had gone on to head the Agricultural Department of the Central Committee and was a Politburo member. Under his aegis Gorbachev also acquired practical experience and national notoriety as an innovator in agriculture. The Stavropol region, moreover, was home to the resort where Party leaders from Moscow went for a cure, and the regional First Secretary, of course, was obligated to tend to their needs. In this way, Gorbachev met the whole high command; he frequently saw Kosygin and, even more important, Andropov and Suslov, the latter himself a former Stavropol First Secretary. When Kulakov died in 1978, therefore, Gorbachev was appointed to his position on the Central Committee. The next year he became a candidate member of the Politburo, and the following year a full member. It was the perfect Party career in fast forward. And at age forty-nine he was the youngest member, and thus putatively the eventual leader, of the establishment reform party.

In 1985, when he finally became leader, what program of reform did Gorbachev have in mind? Since he obviously could not announce his full intentions in advance and still become leader, the answer was not clear at the time and is not completely clear even now. After his fall, Gorbachev took to declaring that *perestroika* had in fact developed the way he had intended it to—with the exception of the Soviet Union's dissolution, of course. In other words, he maintained that his aims from the beginning had been to replace "totalitarianism" with "democracy" and to "liberate" Eastern Europe. And there are numerous observers, both in the East and in the West, who credit him with these accomplishments. But all of Gorbachev's later statements on this subject may be doubted a priori, for if true they would mean that he had been a secret conspirator against the Party and the state of which he was in charge. Nor do these statements fit with the limited empirical evidence we possess.

What we do know is that he was deeply concerned about the future of the system and about the country's continued status as a superpower. And he stated publicly that he believed "radical" measures were needed "if the Soviet Union were to enter the next century in a manner worthy of a great power."[6] He also felt that the whole Soviet way of life had become stifling, debilitating, and demeaning for the population. As he revealed in late 1990, he and another Caucasian reform Communist, Edvard Shevardnadze, had agreed in a confidential conversation in 1984 that "everything is rotten" and that "it's no longer possible to live this way"—an evaluation not infrequently heard among the Soviet elite from the late 1970s onward. But the most revealing statement of his initial intentions is a speech he delivered in December 1984.[7]

Gorbachev began by recognizing that the economy was in sharp decline and thus imperilling the Soviet Union's superpower status. He declared that the remedy was a rapid transition to "intensive" economic development, "increased labor productivity," and a "break-through . . . of scientific-technical progress." These objectives could be achieved by "modernizing the machine tool industry" (a standard Soviet shibboleth) and by some unspecified use of such economic levers as "prices, profit, credit, and others," and, of course, by decentralization of economic management. But he went beyond this fairly standard reassertion of Libermanism to suggest "improvements of the Soviet political system"; these could take the form of "participation" of workers in management by means of elected soviets, or councils, a proposal reminiscent of the Czechoslovak and other East European reforms. And he also called for *"glasnost,"* or "publicity" of information, about the ills afflicting the system, for only such "openness" could counteract "bureaucratic distortions" and unleash the creative intelligence of the population. Finally, he called for the "rule of law" in order to revivify the Party and advance the cause of "socialist self-government by the people."

In short, this program of restructuring, which approximates quite closely the future agenda of *perestroika*, is largely a recapitulation of familiar reformist themes sounded elsewhere in the Soviet bloc. And measures along these lines were pretty much the common property of the "shadow dissidents"—"the children of the Twentieth Party Congress," as Yevtushenko called them—or of the Galileos of the Central Committee, as they called themselves, the people with whom Gorbachev had consulted under Andropov in the preparation of such confidential assessments as the *Novosibirsk Report.* But this does not mean that his outline program constituted a grand design for action that was present at the beginning of *perestroika*. The speech set forth only general goals, and it gave no more than the sparsest of hints of how these might be achieved; its language on all points was vague, and it said nothing about the central problem—power and the role of the Party—in any future transformation. Thus, it is best read as a reflection of one facet of Gorbachev's thinking, as an indication of his higher hopes, and not as a concrete program for reform. This concrete program emerged pragmatically, in ad hoc fashion, as the General Secretary grappled with the realities he confronted.

*   *   *

Gorbachev began with a mixture of boldness in international affairs and prudence in domestic ones. The reason for these contrasting courses was that prompt liberation from international competition was necessary to address the crucial, and more intractable, internal problems of the economy. However, this did not mean indifference to, still less abandonment of, the Soviet Union's superpower status: throughout his career, Gorbachev always insisted on his country's dignity as a great state. What was involved in *perestroika*, rather, was a change of priorities: a revived Soviet economy was the indispensable precondition for maintaining superpower status.

Thus the Soviet Union needed a "breathing space" from international competition in order to recoup internally before returning to the contest with capitalism. For it would be a mistake to think that Gorbachev had ceased thinking in terms of the ultimate superiority of socialism, and thus of the ideological polarity between the two camps. The competition between them, however, in his view now had to assume more muted and less dangerous forms than it had taken in the recent past; and socialism had to modernize its structures and improve its performance greatly if it were to realize its true potential. Although Gorbachev would gradually be obliged to shed these illusions of competitiveness—he would never abandon the socialist idea itself—at the beginning he sought to perfect the Soviet heritage, not to transcend it.

His first move, therefore, was a kind of Brest-Litovsk that took the form of a nearly unilateral withdrawal from the Cold War in order to turn all energies to reform on the home front, for Gorbachev took his Leninism seriously.[8] He frequently asserted his admiration for the Founder's audacity, and at the beginning of his general secretaryship he promoted Mikhail Shatrov's plays extolling the Lenin years. Just as Lenin at Brest-Litovsk had saved the Soviet state in its first crisis of survival, Gorbachev would now save it in a new crisis by a similar display of audacity. Moreover, like all General Secretaries, he had to be the "Lenin of his day": There was no other deity left in the Soviet pantheon, and no other symbol of dynamism and daring with which to move the sluggish system. And Gorbachev, like anyone else at the pinnacle of power, was ambitious and, as events would show, not a little vain.

His return to Brest-Litovsk meant, first, withdrawing from nuclear competition with the United States by giving up the SS-20s, and, second, withdrawing from all Third World adventures, beginning with

Afghanistan.[9] Not only was such retrenchment a necessary prelimi- nary to internal reform, but foreign policy was the area where the General Secretary, as the Soviet executive, could most easily initiate policy. Accordingly, almost his first official act was to indicate his eagerness for a summit with President Reagan and to announce a unilateral seven-month moratorium on deployment of the SS-20s. There had been no Soviet-American summit since the signing of SALT II in 1979, and in the interim the so-called second Cold War had taken place: the Afghan invasion, the suppression of Solidarity in 1981 (which occasioned resumed jamming of Western radio by Mos- cow, a practice abandoned after 1982), the shooting down of KAL 007 in 1983, and the suspension of nuclear arms negotiations the same year. Moreover, Reagan in his first term had become a figure of mythic aggressiveness to the Soviets. After the soothing practices of détente, Moscow was confronted with an unprecedented American military buildup that culminated in the Strategic Defense Initiative (SDI) of 1983 and was accompanied by alarming rhetoric about the "Evil Em- pire." It is fair to say that under Andropov many in the Soviet lead- ership believed the United States actually sought war, a belief that reinforced all of the old doctrines about imperialism.[10] To lower the temperature, therefore, Chernenko had toned down vociferation about the American "Hitler" and had resumed arms negotiations.

But it remained for Gorbachev to grapple seriously with the un- derlying problems of superpower competition. For the Soviets, the first of these was their declining economy, which left them with no possibility of matching the American defense buildup, and in partic- ular the technological leap of SDI. Whether the latter would have provided the United States with a practical defense against Soviet ballistic missiles is not the central question. More important is the geopolitical point that SDI posed a technological and economic chal- lenge the Soviets could neither ignore nor match. Hence, the only way to defuse the challenge was through negotiation, and so Gor- bachev made winding down the Cold War his first priority. Many in the West would undoubtedly dispute this version of the turn towards ending that conflict, but former Soviet military personnel and political analysts generally agree that the Soviet Union's inability to keep up its half of the arms race, in particular with regard to SDI, was a principal factor in triggering *perestroika*. This conclusion is reinforced by the somewhat enigmatic firing in 1984 of Marshal Nikolai Ogarkov, the Soviet minister of defense under Chernenko, who it seems was arguing that the comparative decline of Soviet technology threatened the country's superpower status, and that the military, therefore, should receive a greater say in economic policy.[11] Ogorkov thus identified the geopolitical danger of the existing situation but advanced a remedy that menaced Party supremacy, and so provoked a rebuff to the military as such.

Gorbachev reduced the role of the military still further by not naming the new minister of defense, Marshal Sergei Sokolov, a full member of the Politburo; for the first time in two decades the military was without a seat on that body. At the same time, in July 1985, Gorbachev removed Gromyko as foreign minister and appointed in his place Shevardnadze, who also became a full Politburo member. Since Shevardnadze had no qualifications for the job other than his personal closeness to the General Secretary, this also was a clear signal that Gorbachev was personally taking charge of foreign relations and would make détente the cornerstone of his policy.

But for this gamble to work, Gorbachev needed an American president *he* could do business with, and it turned out that the Reagan of the second term was ready to make a deal. As one specialist put it: "A simple and straightforward man, Reagan took the principle of 'negotiation from strength' literally: once one had built strength, one negotiated."[12] As it turned out, Reagan, too, was something of a gambler and was willing to take a chance with the new man in Moscow; he even had a visionary side, as expressed not only in a scheme such as SDI but also in his willingness to share that program with the Soviet Union and to do away with all nuclear weapons. So Gorbachev was soon able to show results from his risky overture to Washington, and thus to disarm his orthodox critics at home.

The first summit took place in Geneva at the end of 1985. Although it led to no concrete results, it did create a new mood for negotiations and produced a promise of mutual visits by the two leaders. But Gorbachev was in a hurry. So in October 1986, without seriously consulting with the military or the Politburo, he requested an interim minisummit on neutral ground in Reykjavik, Iceland. Once there he raised the hitherto unheard-of prospect of eliminating all nuclear weapons and ballistic missiles, and he found an American president who was receptive to this goal. Gorbachev also accepted Reagan's long-standing "zero option" proposal for eliminating all intermediate-range missiles in Europe. But there were conditions attached to this acceptance, the most important one being that SDI research would be confined to laboratories and none of its components would be tested in space. This Reagan would not accept, so this most bizarre of summits ended without an agreement. Still, a principle had been dramatically asserted by both sides: Future arms agreements could not be like the largely cosmetic accords of the past, but would have to produce sweeping reductions if they were to be worthwhile at all. And it was in this spirit that the twenty-five-years-long process of arms control negotiations was concluded in the next three years.

The crucial turning point was the INF Treaty of 1987. By banning all intermediate-range missiles in Europe up to the Urals, the treaty basically endorsed the zero option Reagan had first put forward in 1981. In other words, Gorbachev bowed out of the Cold War essentially on the West's terms, and without obtaining any concessions on SDI. No doubt one reason he did so was that by 1987 (as will be explained shortly) the internal difficulties of *perestroika* had become acute. And he could get away with doing so because the military had become increasingly discredited. Not only were Soviet forces losing the Afghan war, but in May 1987 a West German teenager piloted a single-engine Cessna airplane through all of the Soviets' western radar and landed on Red Square! Gorbachev took advantage of this fiasco to fire the military high command and appoint his own man, the insignificant General Dmitrii Yazov, as defense minister.

Over and above these circumstantial reasons for agreeing to exclude intermediate-range missiles from Europe, Gorbachev was moved by common sense to make a fundamental revision in the Soviet view of world affairs. Hitherto, this view had been that nuclear armaments made no difference to the Marxist-Leninist doctrine that international relations were a form of class war; nuclear war therefore was both thinkable and winnable. Khrushchev toned this down with his "peaceful coexistence," but he did not abandon the doctrine of inevitable conflict leading to socialist victory. Gorbachev at last drew the realistic conclusion that nuclear war was neither thinkable nor winnable, a position that was the essence of his "new thinking" in international affairs.

But this position necessitated abandoning the central Marxist principle of class struggle, in international and in all human affairs. This Gorbachev did in deed when he visited Washington at the end of

1987 for the signing of the INF Treaty. And this he did in words before the United Nations in December of 1988, when he declared his government's commitment to "universal human values" (Marx had castigated such thinking as the "universal brotherhood swindle"). Yet by implictly renouncing the primacy of class struggle, Gorbachev inadvertently undermined the ideocratic foundations of the regime, a consequence later reinforced by his talk of bringing the Soviet Union into a "common European home." These renunciations would soon send shock waves through the old Soviet home, but in the meantime they made Gorbachev an international hero and cult figure. And these renunciations were indeed his greatest historical accomplishment.

Renunciation continued in a similar mixture of national weakness and new-found principle when, in 1988, Gorbachev announced the withdrawal of Soviet troops from Afghanistan and promised its completion by February 1989. For the first time, the Soviet Union was giving up territory that had once been won for socialism. Also in 1988, Gorbachev and Shevardnadze began liquidating the Soviet and Cuban commitments in Angola and Ethiopia. The following year, they started cutting back aid to the Nicaraguan Sandinistas, and even to Castro's Cuba. In February 1989, the last Soviet troops left Afghanistan exactly as promised. At the same time, the Soviets' client, Vietnam, was persuaded to withdraw from Cambodia. Thus by 1990 all of the Soviet commitments of the Brezhnev era had been liquidated. Yet by that date the calculated and "calibrated" retrenchment of the new Brest-Litovsk had long since become a rout.

Indeed, at the end of this process no one other than the Third World countries directly concerned was much interested in the details, for after the initial international breakthrough of 1986–1987 the drama of *perestroika* was played out largely on the domestic front. In fact, the Soviet population had always been most interested in how *perestroika* would affect their daily lives. Ending the Cold War had been primarily a Western preoccupation, and this is why Gorbachev's external constituency viewed him as a giant. His internal constituency, however, was preoccupied chiefly with the use he made of his breathing space at home, and here his status was always more modest.

The great internal priority was of course economic revival. But given the all-encompassing nature of the Soviet system, reviving the economy would require a general restructuring of Soviet life. Gorbachev

began speaking of such a new departure at his first Central Committee plenum in April 1985, and for several years thereafter Soviet
officials spoke of life as being divided into pre- and post-April periods.
The term *perestroika* itself appeared shortly after April, and at first it
was used largely to refer to economic matters. But by the next year, in
response to the logic of the Soviet structures, it had acquired the
broader connotation just mentioned; and by 1987, along with "new
thinking" in foreign policy, it had become a veritable mantra of the
new era, designating first a "radical," then a "revolutionary," transformation of all institutions, indeed of peoples' inner beings.

Because *perestroika* had multiple and vague meanings, it is difficult
to know just what results Gorbachev intended, or even what his operative policy was at any given moment. In fact, other than achieving
a modernized but still Leninist socialism, he was largely improvising
his operative policy as events and the resistance of the system obliged
him to move from one problem to another. The result was a considerable degree of confusion, even contradiction, in the record of *perestroika*.

In the core area of economics Gorbachev's basic goals, as they
emerged at last by 1988, were a variation on the usual program of
Reform Communism: softening the Plan through decentralization,
providing material incentives to encourage plant and individual initiative, and introducing an approximation of real prices.[13] To this he
added the aim of creating a small private, or "cooperative," sector in
services. In short, Gorbachev's economic program was distinctly
bolder than Kosygin's, and even more ambitious than the Czech program of 1968, but it hardly broke the mold of traditional Communist
"statism." Appropriately, the symbol of *perestroika*'s economic ambition became Lenin's NEP, and Gorbachev and his advisors often
referred to this precedent to legitimize their own enterprise. Of
course, they could not really return to the NEP, for there no longer
existed an independent peasantry that could be persuaded to produce
abundance simply by instituting a free market for their products. But
the NEP could be evoked as the spirit of a more liberal alternative to
the Stalinist order that in 1985 still remained essentially intact.

Still, it would be a mistake to view Gorbachev's program as "market socialism," as some observers have. First, it is not clear what a
market socialism would look like, for there has never been a case of
a really existing market socialism in history: such a system has never

been more than an idea and an aspiration, somewhat like the elusive "third way." Even more important, under *perestroika* there was never any question of creating a real market, not even to the limited extent of the market that existed under the NEP. Still less did Gorbachev contemplate giving up "socialist property," whether in industry or in agriculture. Industry would remain nationalized, as would most retail commerce; and nothing more than long-term leases and variations on the "link" system were ever contemplated for the collectivized peasantry. In sum, Gorbachev's economic program, though radical in the Soviet context, was hardly revolutionary; if revolution were to emerge from *perestroika*, it would have to come as a result of the political side effects of the economic reform.

Gorbachev's relatively moderate economic reform was tempered even more by the gradual and prudent way in which it was introduced, as well as by the application of more-traditional measures that actually contradicted it. Early on, Gorbachev's "modernizing" economic advisors—such as Aganbegyan, now returned from semiexile in Novosibirsk, and Leonid Abalkin—began working up measures to implement the long-term program just outlined. Since these measures would not be ready until 1987 or 1988, Gorbachev decided to hoist the economy in the meantime to a level where it could profit from the intended liberalization. This decision produced the first phase of *perestroika*—*uskorenie*, or an "acceleration" of the industrial process—which in effect continued Andropov's program. But this attempt at acceleration led to the application of traditional command measures that in fact made the situation worse.

Concretely, acceleration meant an ambitious and costly program of machine-tool production and industrial reequipment that was launched in 1985 as if such a program in itself constituted a "scientific-technical revolution." At the same time, a system of "*gospriemka*," or quality control, was instituted: state inspectors were empowered to accept or reject goods as they came off the assembly line in order to goad both management and workers into working more efficiently—a disciplinary measure reminiscent of Andropov. In the same tradition was Gorbachev's campaign against "unearned income"—that is, against all of the shadow activity that was necessary to the functioning of the economy and that the forthcoming creation of cooperatives was supposed to regularize. In agriculture, allegedly Gorbachev's specialty, a number of ministries were regrouped into a single giant

organization, Gosagroprom—a completely counterproductive centralization. Finally, Gorbachev, apparently at the urging of Yegor
Ligachev, launched an anti-alcohol drive that cut the number of outlets, shortened their hours, and tore up vineyards in the south, thereby
ruining a profitable industry. The principal results of this campaign
were a great increase in the private production of moonshine (which
made sugar so scarce it had to be rationed) and a correspondingly
drastic drop in state revenues. Indeed, this loss of income, together
with the costs of the industrial reequipment program, aggravated a
budget deficit that in a few years would reach crisis proportions. So by
the end of 1986, although the forced methods of acceleration had
produced a slight spurt of growth,[14] nothing had been done to restructure the economy. And in the meantime a new problem for
perestroika had emerged in the form of resistance from the apparat.

Immediately after his election, Gorbachev departed from Brezhnev's
policy of "stability of cadres." He reverted to the activism of his more
remote predecessors in order to recruit personnel suited to his intended new policies, and he focused first on replacing people at the
top. Rivals such as Grishin and Romanov, and holdovers from the past
such as Gromyko, were removed from the Politburo and replaced by
Andropov men: Ligachev, the Secretariat's chief of ideology and chief
of personnel; Nikolai Ryzhkov, an engineer and industrial manager,
who also became prime minister; Viktor Chebrikov, head of the KGB;
and others of similar background and moderately reformist inclina-
tion. But these were not Gorbachev men—they had made it to the top
on their own, and were allies, not partisans. In addition to Shevardnadze, Gorbachev's only other real ideological supporter was Yakovlev; he was brought back from Canada in 1983 to head the social-
science and international affairs think tank IMEMO (Institute of the
World Economy and International Relations), then was moved to the
Secretariat's propaganda department in 1985, and was finally added to
the Politburo in June 1987. And at the June plenum of the previous
year, Boris Yeltsin, who had recently replaced Grishin as Moscow
Party boss in order to clean out the corruption in that major fief,
became a candidate member of the Politburo. But this was hardly a
homogeneous group of liege men, or even of like-minded reformers;
and Gorbachev would never have a high command united behind
perestroika, at least insofar as he had defined that term for himself.

Matters were even worse for the General Secretary within the Party as a whole. An activist leader, Gorbachev had immediately exercised his prerogative of naming provincial and local First Secretaries throughout the country, and by mid-1986 he had replaced one third of them.[15] But because it was Ligachev, the Secretariat's chief of personnel and thus the number two man in the hierarchy, who did much of the actual appointing, the new men turned out to be younger though still very orthodox apparatchiki. Gorbachev also tried to shake up the Party at the first Congress he presided over as General Secretary in February 1986. Khrushchev's now embarrassing Program of 1961 was replaced by a new document that said nothing about the transition to full Communism but promised only an improved standard of living by the year 2000. To attain this new goal, Gorbachev for the first time called for "radical economic reform," but beyond exhortations to promote "acceleration" he gave no idea of how this reform was to be achieved. In regard to restructuring the Party, Gorbachev obtained a new Central Committee, 43 percent of whose members were elected for the first time. This change, together with the replacement of regional secretaries, represented the greatest turnover in Party personnel in a quarter century. But then nothing happened: the apparat plodded on as before, paying only lip service to the idea of economic reform.

GLASNOST

His political offensive thwarted, Gorbachev in 1986 embarked on a second subpolicy of *perestroika—glasnost*.[16] This word, usually translated as "openness" or "publicity," is in fact a bureaucratic term dating back to Alexander II and signifying officially encouraged notoriety regarding matters the government wishes to see discussed in a critical but constructive fashion. Gorbachev had desired the opening of the system before he came to power; he now made it a priority in order to stimulate the sluggish Party with the sting of criticism. But this policy was soon pushed to unintended lengths by circumstances, the first of which was the Chernobyl disaster in April 1986. This calamity revealed not only that the state of Soviet industry was far worse than the government had suspected, but that the official policy of secrecy perpetuated, indeed aggravated, these disastrous conditions as well as the criminal negligence surrounding them. After initially attempting to cover up the accident, the government therefore admitted a part of the truth, but the indignation of society pressed the government to go further.

The second new radicalizing circumstance was the attitude of the intelligentsia. As the group that had been the most stifled under Brezhnev, Suslov, and Andropov, and at the same time the group whose talents were most necessary to limber the system up, the intelligentsia at first was wary of both Gorbachev's commitment to reform and his staying power if he tried to engage in it. In the wake of Chernobyl, some of the bolder intellectuals, particularly those in the Cinematographers' Union, pressed Gorbachev in closed meetings to take a clearer stand, and they even started to take verbal risks of their own. In mid-1986 Gorbachev answered by appointing liberal editors to some of the major Moscow periodicals. These men, and in particular Vitalii Korotich of *Ogonek*, then took the bit of *glasnost* in their teeth and ran with it farther than Gorbachev had intended; but Gorbachev had no way to rein them in without undermining his reputation as a reformer. Thus, month by month the area of criticism expanded; for this was the last chance at freedom for these men of the 1960s, and they were determined to make the most of it.

Still, apprehension remained that this new thaw would end like its predecessor, and so a clearer signal of reformist intentions was awaited from Gorbachev before the intelligentsia would commit itself to his cause. And the only convincing signal could be the liberation of Sakharov. Accordingly, in December 1986 Gorbachev had a telephone installed in Sakharov's apartment in Gorky so that the General Secretary could call the exile personally and invite him back to Moscow. But Sakharov was a figure whose criticism of the system had already gone beyond the bounds of mere reform; his support of *perestroika*, therefore, was a tactical alliance, not an enlistment in Gorbachev's cause. Thus the tone of *glasnost* sharpened with his return; but, instead of stimulating the Party apparatchiki, it frightened them.

The great subject of *glasnost*, of course, now became what Gorbachev called "the blank spots" of Soviet history, or Stalinism. The beginning of 1987 was marked by two events that, for the first time in more than twenty years, reopened the Stalin question. The first was the release of a film, *Repentance*, made in 1984 by a protégé of Shevardnadze, the Georgian director Tengiz Abuladze. The film portrayed the Stalin era in a phantasmagoric and surrealistic idiom that was also brutally realistic. The second event was the publication of a (mediocre) novel by Anatolii Rybakov, *Children of the Arbat*. Written in the old-fashioned style of socialist realism, the novel at least raised, though it hardly probed, a few of the painful questions by offering a personal portrait of Stalin. At the same time, a number of memoirs and interpretive articles about Soviet history appeared in the "thick journals" of the periodical press.

The great question was, of course, how far would all of this go? For *glasnost* was not just an effort to set the record straight; it was also, as de-Stalinization had been under Khrushchev, an effort to come to terms with the present. However, it also opened the question of the legitimacy of the regime itself; for the system had a criminal past, and to raise the question of its dark origins—even if only to correct abuses—could easily turn into a denunciation of the system itself. Gorbachev and his liberal advisors obviously thought they could walk the fine line between criticism and demolition. Those who stood outside the system, the former Brunos who had once been imprisoned, such as Sergei Grigoriants, wanted to unmask the system completely, and so they founded an uncensored journal, *Glasnost*, for this purpose; Sakharov, though more prudent, was not too far from this position. But others who in 1985 had been reformers now took fright and sought to stem, if not actually stop, the threatening flood of *glasnost*. And so in the course of 1987, both society and the Party divided into camps.

At the level of the Politburo and the Secretariat there now emerged a Left of Shevardnadze, Yakovlev, and Yeltsin; a Right around the number two of the regime, Ligachev, who spoke for the Party apparat; and a center around Ryzhkov, who spoke for the government apparat and was associated with the military-industrial complex. In this alignment Gorbachev was closest to the Left, but he nonetheless was compelled to accommodate the other two groups at least some of the time and on some of the issues. Although the degree of *glasnost* was the central issue in this division, the latter was also intimately related to the question of how far and how fast the leadership would be able to purge and restructure the apparats of both the Party and the state.

For in the course of his *glasnost* campaign of 1986, Gorbachev discovered that the instrument of his reform, the Party, was in fact the principal cause of the trouble he wished to correct. In addition, he discovered that he had overestimated his real power as General Secretary. A provincial politician who had moved to Moscow only in 1978 and who lacked the long experience of his predecessors with the workings of the machine at its center, Gorbachev seems to not have realized how incrusted the Muscovite bureaucracy had become, and how unresponsive the local bureaucracies were to commands from the top. So he set about *perestroika* with the activism of Khrushchev, as if forgetting that the intervening twenty years had produced the lethargic monster of the *nomenklatura* Party. The result was that throughout his first two years he issued commands and replaced key personnel, yet nothing changed.

One young reformer summed up 1987 in a play on Leninist language: "At the Twenty-seventh Party Congress we decided *shto delat,* or what is to be done, and the answer was radical economic reform; at the June plenum we decided *kak delat,* or how to do it, and the answer was *khozraschet,* or prices for profit; and at the next plenum, in the fall, we were to decide *s kem delat,* or whom to do it with—and also *komu delat,* or whom to stick it to—but we could never get that fall plenum to meet." And this aborted scenario was indeed Gorbachev's first strategy for *perestroika*: he would use the existing Party, of which he was, after all, the Boss, as the instrument for economic restructuring.[17] When in the fall of 1986 he discovered that the existing Party could not be used in this way, he first bombarded it with *glasnost.* And when this did not work, he decided to raise the Party's rank and file against the apparat by introducing contested elections. This led to the third great subpolicy of *perestroika*, "democratization."

Gorbachev launched his drive for democratization in January 1987, when he was at last able to convene the plenum on personnel matters that he had had to postpone three times the previous fall. Still frustrated in his desire to make personnel changes, he counterattacked with scathing criticism of the Party as an institution; and, in an unprecedented move, he appealed to the country over the heads of the Central Committee by having his main speech televised. Declaring "we need democracy like air," he proposed changes in the Party statutes even more radical than those that had led to Khrushchev's downfall: multiple candidacies for contested elections, and term limits of five to fifteen years for all Party posts except a handful at the very top. The plenum, however, refused to act on these proposals, and so the battle was continued into the next meeting in June. In the meantime, the first major articles attacking the status quo appeared in the press: Vasilii Seliunin demolished Soviet economic statistics, and Nikolai Shmelev attacked central planning and advocated a measure of marketization.[18]

The June 1987 plenum marked the first breakthrough to real institutional change of the Gorbachev era. After two years of preparation, Gorbachev's economic experts were at last ready to present something more than "acceleration." Their work was endorsed by the plenum in a draft Law on State Enterprises (soon after voted as law by the Supreme Soviet), which sought to free industry from the direct control of Gosplan and the central ministries by providing for "self-management" and "self-financing." This meant that enterprises would henceforth operate on the basis of contracts passed both with the state and among themselves; profits could be used as the enterprises saw fit, whether for increased wages or investment; pricing policy was to be "rationalized," and credits were to be made available for new ventures; and the whole program was to be implemented beginning January 1, 1988, in a "step by step" and "calibrated" fashion. Still, neither the Plan nor the ministries were abolished; the reform thus remained a hybrid, like all its predecessors, though a much bolder one than any in the past. And innumerable details of implementation remained to be worked out in practice, a circumstance that could only produce a protracted struggle within both the state and the Party apparats. Nonetheless, a major shock had been administered to the stagnant system, and a return to its previous state was now impossible. And in this way Gorbachev hoped to progressively remove the Party from direct supervision of the economy.

During this same period, other laws authorized small cooperative and even individual "work activities" in the service sector for the first time since the NEP. This action amounted to the legalization of private enterprise, even though such activity still had to be labeled collective or cooperative. Some of the private enterprises were former units of the second economy that now came out into the open, while others were genuinely new ventures; some were tributary to one or another mafia; and almost all were dependent on state enterprises for raw materials and outlets. The population was often hostile to the cooperatives because their prices were higher than those charged by state enterprises, and this fact invited the charge of "speculation." By the time the cooperative movement received legal status in May 1988, it was still a very small affair, accounting for approximately 2 percent of economic activity. Nonetheless, once again the old system had been given a shock, and a space for individual initiative had been created that would prove increasingly difficult to control.

A third aspect of economic *perestroika* was the creation, beginning in 1987, of joint ventures between Soviet institutions and foreign entrepreneurs. In reality such ventures were not entirely new: Major joint projects, such as the Fiat automobile works and the Kama truck factory, had been undertaken during the Brezhnev era; and in the 1920s, and especially during the First Five-Year Plan, important contracts had been passed between the Soviet government and foreign enterprises. But all of these activities had been closely controlled by the government, and the autarkic nature of the economy had in no way been breached. The new joint ventures, however, were different: the foreign partner, though limited to minority participation, was granted greater initiative in management and better profit incentives than ever before in Soviet history; and Soviet institutions, even individuals, were allowed much greater freedom to enter into ventures independently of the state. The result was a genuine, though at the time modest, breach of national autarky, and thus a real movement towards the Soviet Union's integration into the world market.

Taken together, the new freedom for state enterprises, the cooperatives, and the joint ventures constituted the boldest program of economic reform since Stalin first built socialism. Still, they fell well short of a return to the NEP, for there was no national market, no real prices, and no free peasantry; moreover, 90 percent of the economy remained nationalized and directly managed by state organs under the Party's supervision. The great question, therefore, was whether the conflicting elements of this hybrid system could be made to mesh, or whether they would tear the whole structure apart.

The final breakthrough of the June plenum was political: Gorbachev obtained approval for a special Party Conference to be convened the following year. He had put forth this idea at the January plenum, but it had been turned down because the Central Committee feared that such a gathering (in effect an interim Party Congress) would be the occasion for those sweeping personnel changes in the Central Committee and its Secretariat that Gorbachev had been seeking for months. He won approval for his Conference in June by promising that the gathering would not be used for such a purge. Still, his purpose remained a renewed Party, and he sought to achieve this end by mobilizing the base to elect *perestroika*-minded delegates to the Conference. And once that body had convened, the General Secretary would see what he could get it to approve. But the decision to schedule the Conference resulted in an intensified polarization of the Party and a year-long campaign to control the composition of the gathering.

In the fall of 1987 the pressure came primarily from Ligachev and the orthodox, who were now increasingly labeled "conservatives": or the "Right." The great bone of contention was the speech the General Secretary would deliver in November on the occasion of the seventieth anniversary of the Revolution. The liberal intelligentsia wanted a clean break with the Stalinist heritage and a frank evaluation of seventy years of Soviet history, while the conservatives wished to keep frankness to a minimum and to present a positive balance sheet of the regime's past. Faced with these pressures, Gorbachev adopted the tactic he would henceforth employ regularly: throughout the fall he tacked back and forth between Right and Left, depending on their relative strength at any given moment, thereby constantly occupying the pivotal middle ground and thus making himself permanently indispensable to both camps. Since the conservatives were exerting the greater pressure at the time, the draft of the anniversary speech leaned in the direction of prudence, and this tilt provoked the first great crisis of the *perestroika* era.

At the October plenum devoted to consideration of the speech, Boris Yeltsin—always the most impatient of the reformers—openly attacked Ligachev and the apparat as the main obstacles to meaningful change. Gorbachev had no choice but to rebuff such a bold assault, and so the meeting ended in a crushing defeat for Yeltsin.[19] But this denouement automatically pushed Gorbachev towards the conservatives. The next month, at a meeting of the Moscow Party Committee attended by Gorbachev, Yeltsin was subjected to an old-style heresy trial and dismissed from his Party posts. All reformers were dismayed that so much of the past still survived in the Party's spirit and procedures. As Yeltsin was reviled in the Party press during the ensuing months, in the eyes of the people he appeared a martyr at the hands of the apparat, while Gorbachev's commitment to reform correspondingly seemed to be wavering. And indeed the anniversary speech was a great disappointment: breaking no new ground, it only deplored Stalin's excesses while defending his services in building socialism.

And so the seesaw contest continued into the spring of 1988. In March, Ligachev and the conservatives attempted a coup of sorts with the publication of a letter by a Leningrad chemistry teacher named Nina Andreeva. Titled "I Cannot Compromise My Principles," it attacked *perestroika* as foreign and subversive, and with anti-Semitic overtones it defended the old ways as both Leninist and national. How far Ligachev intended to go with this campaign is not clear. He could have been out to unseat Gorbachev—the precedent of Khrushchev was on everyone's mind during these years—but at the very least he was seeking to determine the outcome of the elections for the Party Conference.[20] The liberal intelligentsia, frightened at the prospect that *glasnost* might soon be ended, rallied to Gorbachev's *perestroika*. Together with Yakovlev, Gorbachev gave the intelligentsia the leadership it needed by publishing an official refutation of Nina Andreeva's positions. And against this polarized background the Conference delegates were elected in June.

The elections resulted in an overall victory for the apparat conservatives; not only did they win a majority of delegates, but many of the more prominent reformers, such as Shmelev and Zaslavskaia, suffered conspicuous defeats. Under such circumstances there was no possibility of making significant changes in the Party. But Gorbachev, using the General Secretary's power of initiative and control of the agenda, nonetheless engineered a major countercoup against the Conference majority. On his initiative the proceedings were partially televised, and this served to show the country the apparat at its worst. Then, at the end of the debates, Gorbachev, having prepared his "theses" in advance, railroaded them through the Conference without discussion and with few dissenting voices—a tactic made possible by the established habit at Party Congresses of endorsing the leadership's position.

These theses provided for a radical new phase of democratization. For Gorbachev had been convinced by the elections of Conference delegates that his efforts to democratize the Party from below had failed. He now sought to create a parallel power base outside the Party by reviving the soviets, or administrative councils, which since 1917 had been the nominal power in the Soviet state. The cornerstone of his new plan was a Congress of People's Deputies: Its 2,500 members, chosen by secret ballot from among multiple candidates, would meet only for short periods a few times each year. This body would elect a chairman of its Presidium—Gorbachev himself, of course—who would function as head of state, or quasi president. The Congress would also elect a Supreme Soviet of 542 members that would function as the standing legislature of the country. In addition, there would eventually be contested elections for all of the republican, provincial, and local soviets, as well as for their respective executive officers. Although the soviets were the main subject of the theses, the Party was not forgotten: it, too, was again summoned to hold contested elections and to limit tenure in Party offices to two or at the most three five-year terms.

Both the soviets and the Party, moreover, were to transform the Soviet Union into a "socialist state based on the rule of law," to use the usual cumbersome translation of *sotsialisticheskoe pravovoe gosudarstvo*. But what Gorbachev and his theorists, such as Boris Kurashvili, meant is best rendered as a socialist *Rechtstaat*, to use the most familiar term for what Montesquieu had called an *état de droit* as opposed to an arbitrary despotism. There were two motives for this redefinition of the system: Gorbachev and the reformers genuinely believed that the rule of law was necessary for human dignity, and thus for making the Soviet Union a civilized member of the international community; they also believed that it was necessary to promote efficiency in government and responsibility among the citizens. But the great question was whether the Party-state, which had always been above the law, was capable of such a transformation, or whether the attempt to subject it to law would simply tear it apart.

When provincial First Secretaries were briefed on these truly revolutionary proposals in a confidential meeting before the Conference, they objected that Gorbachev's scheme would give too much power to non-Party bodies, particularly in their own provincial bailiwicks. So in the final draft of his theses Gorbachev stipulated that the First Secretary of any given region would also have to stand for election as chairman of the corresponding soviet, just as he himself would stand for election as "president." Later, however, when the First Secretaries saw that the elections were intended to be real, and therefore dangerous, they switched back to a separation of Party and soviet functions. But in any event the apparat was caught, because either way, it would be subject to popular control and public accountability in a manner unknown since 1918. And this indeed was the whole point of the operation: Gorbachev wished to rejuvenate the Party and renew its cadres by making it answerable to the country for its performance.

In the wake of the Conference, Gorbachev proceeded to attack the apparat directly. During September 1988, in circumstances that still remain mysterious, he carried out a veritable coup d'état against the summit of the apparat, the Secretariat and the Politburo conservatives. The Moscow military district was secretly put on alert, and an emergency plenum was called for the last day of the month. Shevardnadze, who clearly had no advance notice of this meeting, was summoned back from the United Nations in New York where he had just arrived. The plenum lasted a mere hour, and when it was over Ligachev had been shunted aside to a lesser post in the Secretariat, though he remained on the Politburo. His ally, Chebrikov, was also shunted aside and replaced as head of the KGB by Vladimir Kriuchkov, though Chebrikov, too, remained on the Politburo. Gromyko and three other Brezhnev holdovers were retired from that body. Even more important, the staff of the Secretariat was cut back by some 40 percent, thereby significantly limiting the apparat's ability to monitor the state and economic bureaucracies. The next day the Supreme Soviet, on command, accepted Gromyko's resignation as chairman or "president" of its Presidium and elected Gorbachev to that post—the first time he acquired an office outside the Party hierarchy.

This September coup thus took the Party out of direct management of the country with a vengeance, but it did so very much in the Party's traditional autocratic and arbitrary manner. The coup was ambiguous in still another way, for Gorbachev was dismantling his old apparatus of government before he had created a new one in the form of a revived system of soviets. And this left *perestroika* suspended between two worlds in politics just as it was in economics. With democratization having become a form of warfare waged by the General Secretary against his own Party, Gorbachev had clearly decided "to go for broke," as one well-placed reformer put it at the time.

Why should Gorbachev, initially so prudent in domestic matters, now deal with those problems with the same recklessness he had shown with his foreign policy in 1986 at Reykjavik? A part of the answer must be his mounting anger with the apparat after two years of struggling with its obstructionism. Another part of the answer is his thoroughly Communist concept of his role as leader. As the head of the Party of Lenin, he had to be the Lenin of his day in the Party's latest struggle, the struggle against "stagnation." And in this role he had to be thoroughly revolutionary. Yet his revolutionary Leninism also had to be a modernized and internationally respectable one. Thus the post of Party leader had to be combined with that of a democratically and legally elected "president." Such thinking, never explicitly spelled out, was clearly implicit in the way Gorbachev implemented his program of "democratization": he always balanced his own ambiguous, indeed conflicting, roles as head of both the Party and the Soviet systems, constantly inciting the latter system against the former—but never too much. As one Soviet political scientist put it, Gorbachev never could make up his mind whether he was Luther or the Pope.[21]

And what, concretely, did he expect to accomplish with this unusual arrangement? He was not out to introduce Western-style democracy or even "market socialism," as was often assumed at the time and which he later claimed were his goals. He sought, rather, to mobilize all of the supporters of *perestroika* through renovated soviets that would remain very much under his personal leadership; and *perestroika*, of course, meant his own program for a modernized, more humane, and more efficient socialism, pretty much as this program had been revealed by 1988.

These *perestroika* loyalists would come largely from the Party and presumably be its younger and better-educated members, but they would also come from the forward-looking non-Party cadres; and the two groups together would form "popular fronts" for the forthcoming soviet elections. As Gorbachev defined the elections in January 1989, they would not be "some kind of spontaneous process," but rather "a highly important mass campaign, the success of which can be ensured by a high degree of organization and responsibility," avoiding such "negative phenomena" as "manifestations of group selfishness, arrogance, and political careerism." He concluded that "Party organizations must take clear-cut, principled positions on all these questions."[22] In other words, the new Congress of People's Deputies was to be in essence a more open, parallel Party, or a common front for national renewal. But to achieve this degree of restructuring the old

Party had to be sidelined, indeed partially dismantled; and given the nature of the Party-state, this could only be a dangerous operation.

At the time, various Soviet commentators and foreign diplomats pointed out the similarities between this strategy and Stalin's purges —although the means were different, both leaders sought similar political results. Stalin had used a parallel power base, an enlarged and perfected NKVD, to dismantle the old Party and give himself a new one, and this is just what Gorbachev was attempting to accomplish with his revived soviets. There is still another precedent for Gorbachev's strategy, namely Mao Zedong's Cultural Revolution: in this fantastic operation, the head of the Party, who had lost control of his apparat and yet retained his aura as Leader, raised up youthful Red Guards and army units to destroy that Party in order to create a new one devoted to permanent revolution. Again, the methods and the goal are quite different from those of Gorbachev, but the structure of the political action is close. Indeed, Khrushchev's de-Stalinization, in the context of its time as revolutionary as Gorbachev's democratization, was initiated as a kind of coup d'état by the Boss against the majority of the leadership. All of which is to say that Gorbachev, for all his desire to modernize and Westernize Communism, was still a Party chief operating in terms of the dynamic of a system that can change only by revolution from above.

REVOLUTION FROM BELOW

By the end of 1988 Gorbachev's revolution from above had triggered another revolution—one from the side, so to speak, among the intelligentsia. This revolution in turn started a revolution from below, in society at large. And both of these revolutions were the unintended fruits of *glasnost*.

Once the issue of de-Stalinization had been reopened in early 1987, the intelligentsia pressed forward, first in the thick journals and ultimately on television, with a reexamination of the whole Soviet past as the indispensable prelude to changing things in the present. This process made 1987–1988 the great period of *glasnost*: a cascade of revelations went far beyond what had occurred during Khrushchev's thaw and permanently changed the national consciousness. The fact that Gorbachev's anniversary speech of November 1987 had hedged

· on all of the important issues turned out to have no deterrent effect: editors pressed the censors, and authors pressed the editors, and the public pressed both, and as a consequence one taboo after another fell. *Samizdat* came out into the open, and *tamizdat* came home. Such forbidden classics as *Doctor Zhivago* at last appeared legally, as did the works of such émigré writers as Vladimir Nabokov.

The first area to be opened was the high Stalinism of the 1930s. Andrei Platonov's *Foundation Pit* (on the building of socialism) and his *Chevengur* (on War Communism) at last saw the light of day. Anna Akhmatova's "Requiem" was finally published, as were Varlam Shalamov's *Tales of the Kolyma*. Vasilii Grossman's *Life and Fate*, which in 1961 Suslov had said could not be published in less than two hundred to three hundred years, presented Hitler and Stalin as kindred figures.[23] The purge trials of the 1930s were officially declared to be fraudulent, and all of the opposition figures of that time—with the exception of Trotsky—were rehabilitated. Some of Bukharin's works were reprinted; and published for the first time was the testament-letter, dictated to his wife on the eve of his arrest, which affirmed his fidelity to the principles of the Revolution. (This document, however, undercut the myth surrounding Bukharin by revealing that he had no disagreement with the Party line during the "seven years" after 1930, that is, throughout the period of high Stalinism.[24]) Western Sovietology was also enlisted to help fill the blank spots: Steven Cohen's biography of Bukharin appeared in translation, as did Robert Conquest's *Great Terror*.

Stalin's terror, of course, raised the question of the nature of his system as a whole. This meant, first, collectivization, and Boris Mozhaiev's *Muzhiki i Baby* (*Peasant Men and Women*) gave a reasonably accurate picture of the horrors of that event.[25] But collectivization in turn raised the question of Stalin's forced industrialization, and thus of his general method of government. On this subject Aleksandr Bek's novel *Novoe Naznachenie* (*The New Assignment*), published years earlier in the West and in 1987 in Russia, was of special importance: The story of a Stalinist industrial manager, it became the subject of an essay by Gavriil Popov, later the first post-Communist mayor of Moscow, in which he analyzed Stalinism as the "administrative-command system."[26] The term "administrative" was the old Soviet euphemism for "coercive and dictatorial," and, as already noted, "command" was adapted from the Western term "command economy"; and the compound adjective "administrative-command" was a substitute for "totalitarian," a term that could not be used openly in Russia until 1990.[27] Popov's cumbersome neologism immediately became the generally accepted designation of both original Stalinism and its prolongation into the present.

But if this was the nature of the system, then the next topics to be explored were the origin of the system and the alternatives to Stalinism. For the purpose of the historical inquest of *glasnost* was not just to set the record straight: it was an effort to discover where things went wrong in the past so that they might be set aright in the present. As a part of this process, Khrushchev, for twenty-five years a nonperson, was rehabilitated.[28] But much more important was the inquiry into the location of the original sin of the system. Vasilii Seliunin opened this subject in early 1988 with an article titled "Origins," which saw the source of the trouble in part in the Russian authoritarian tradition, but even more in the utopianism of maximalist socialism; Seliunin even went so far as to raise the delicate question of Lenin's doctrinaire hostility to the "bourgeois" forces of the market as a contributory factor in the problem.[29] Aleksandr Tsipko was even more emphatic in blaming Marx and Marxist hostility to the market: Marxism made an authoritarian method of economic development almost unavoidable.[30] In response to Tsipko, Igor Kliamkin contended that it was Russian backwardness and the autocratic tradition of Ivan the Terrible and Peter the Great that had produced Stalinism, thus discounting the Bukharin alternative—but without justifying Stalin, whose policies were in effect explained as a crude form of modernization.[31]

And so by the eve of the Congress of People's Deputies the whole of Soviet history from War Communism to Brezhnev had been opened up for reevaluation, and the basic modes of explanation of the tragedy had at least been suggested. Certain taboos, however, still remained. First, except for Seliunin's hints, Lenin remained untouchable. Similarly, the positive role of the Party could not be questioned, even though most of its leaders after Lenin were officially recognized as having been basically in error. Nor could the fundamental soundness of the socialist order be questioned, even though certain merits of the market were now acknowledged. Finally, it was still not possible to publish authors who openly violated these taboos; and this meant that Solzhenitsyn remained forbidden until 1990. Still, the process of demystification had gone so far that it was only a matter of time and circumstances before the last taboos would fall.

Thus *glasnost*, which had been intended to revivify the system, had in fact undermined it by discrediting the myths that sustained it. What had begun as a limited process of filling in factual blank spots of the Stalin era had led to a flood of candor in which not only were the myths of the long decades of Stalin and Brezhnev swept away, but the very foundations of Sovietism—the economic theories of Marx and even the political practices of Lenin—were discredited. By 1988 Marxism-Leninism was a shambles, and the historian Iurii Afanasiev, one of the most radical of all the reformers, openly denounced it as an obstacle to clear thinking that had to be discarded if the country were to be restructured in any meaningful way.[32]

And so in two years a whiff of *glasnost* had demolished the ideological work of seven decades. The "wooden language" forged in the 1920s, the socialist realism of the 1930s, the image of reality as endless class war—all simply faded away, and people reverted to the use of normal speech in discussing their real problems. For each new revelation about past crimes and present disasters did less to stimulate the people to new efforts on behalf of *perestroika* than to desacralize the system as such in their eyes; it did so all the more thoroughly since the Myth had expired some time in the 1970s, especially among the young. Accordingly, the realistic half of doublethink drove out the ideological half, and the repressed awareness of the Lie poured out into the open in a flood. This loss of legitimacy would prove fatal to the system, for its surreal structures were such that they could not survive exposure to the truth. Thus, a regime born of ideology started to collapse once that ideology was extinct. Or, as a Russian proverb has it: A dead fish rots from the head.

This ideological explanation is not in contradiction with the thesis that the crisis of Communism began with the economic decline of the late 1970s. Although this decline was all too real, it did not by itself bring down the regime. In a normal system, economic crisis simply leads to new strategies of development; it does not necessarily imply changing to another kind of system. In the ideocratic Soviet world, however, the economic decline acted to destroy an indispensable myth of the system, namely that socialism in the long run is superior to capitalism as a mode of production. During the Great Depression of the 1930s, and then in the fifteen or so years of reconstruction following the Second World War, it was not prima facie obvious that Soviet socialism would not someday perform better than capitalism. By 1985, however, after forty years of peace had permitted a Soviet recovery, no illusion was possible about the real trend of the economic "correlation of forces." So long as the Soviet Union had remained cut off from the West, this decline could be concealed. But when, in the 1960s and 1970s, members of the elite could visit the West, ideological illusions began to crumble; and when, under *glasnost*, something approximating the truth was finally broadcast to the population at large, these illusions collapsed completely. Thus the economic failure· produced much more than a material crisis; it called into question the totality of Sovietism and implied that change to another kind of system was in order. All promises of a "radiant future" under the existing system were discredited; the system's present failure, in conjunction with its criminal past, added up to "seventy years on the road to nowhere," as one increasingly heard by the beginning of 1989.

So why did the regime take the risk of *glasnost* when its leaders knew full well that twenty years earlier Brezhnev had crushed the Prague Spring precisely because the Czechoslovaks had moved to abolish censorship? They did so in part because they had no choice if they were to shake up the command-administrative system in order to revive the economy and preserve the country's superpower status: it was impossible to have a dynamic economy with a passive and ignorant population. Furthermore, they believed the system had become so "rotten" that a rapid shock was necessary: as Yakovlev put it in a confidential speech to Party cadres in early 1989: "We probably have no more than two or three years to prove that Leninist socialism can work."[33] They took the risk of *glasnost* also because, as the dissident Sergei Grigoriants observed, these apparatchiki were simply uninformed regarding the society they ruled: as Gorbachev was to admit in 1990, "When we started, we did not understand the depth of the problems we faced."[34] And so the last would-be "Lenin of today" stumbled into a career of fin-de-régime sorcerer's apprentice.

The intelligentsia's revolution from the side soon became a people's revolution from below. The years 1987–1988 saw a proliferation of self-organized "informal" associations, the *neformaly*.[35] Independent of the Party, they were created to address one or another social problem, usually on a local or regional basis, in areas where the Party had been remiss or was actively at fault. Very often their origin was in threats to the ecology, such as the pollution of Lake Baikal or the nuclear power plants of the Baltic states; at times their point of departure was a concern for preserving historical monuments, such as the Leningrad hotel where the poet Esenin had committed suicide, or certain medieval churches threatened by the construction of a hotel in Moscow. But since these groups had to pressure the Party, they soon moved on to politics: By early 1987 clubs in support of *perestroika* had appeared, and many of these put the term "democratic *perestroika*" in their name to emphasize that, though they wished to work within the system, they would also push reform farther than the regime intended. By late 1987 these clubs had formed an All-Union Federation of Socialist Clubs.

But other activists concluded that the system was hopelessly "totalitarian," that *perestroika* was just another Party fraud, and that the only solution was a transition to a constitutional democratic order. And in May 1988, these activists formed what they called a political party, the Democratic Union. Their program, of course, was not active revolution, since that would be hopeless; rather, they sought to use the revived soviet system to further the principles of the February Revolution over those of October, and thus to prepare the way for the gradual liquidation of the system. As young men from this group held forth before the crowds that by the summer of 1988 regularly gathered on Pushkin Square in Moscow or before the Kazan Cathedral in Leningrad, amazed observers regarded them as marginal cranks. Although they and their kindred spirit, Grigoriants, were periodically roughed up by the KGB, within a year their opinions were secretly shared by establishment liberals, and within three years Yeltsin would be elected president of Russia on the equivalent of their program.

Taken together, the various kinds of "informals" were by 1988 known as "civil society," a term imported in that year from Poland, where the phenomenon of a social force independent of the Party-state went back to KOR and Solidarity. This was the first time a similar social force had existed in Russia since the last civil society, that of the independent peasantry, was crushed in 1930. There was, however, a reverse side to this renascence of social autonomy. A few antidemocratic social movements appeared as well, notably Pamiat, or Memory. It had grown out of the movement to preserve Moscow's old churches, but it developed into a stridently authoritarian, nationalistic, and anti-Semitic organization. Although it received much attention abroad, its importance in Russia was not great: in the elections of the next two years, at both the national and local levels, it failed to place a single candidate in office, whereas organizations growing out of the democratic *neformaly* saw thousands of their candidates victorious and under Yeltsin took over the government.

As the elections to the Congress of People's Deputies approached in early 1989, the *neformaly* entered into contracts with reformist groups in the Party to create Popular Fronts. In accordance with Gorbachev's new strategy after the Nineteenth Conference, these Fronts were intended to mobilize dynamic elements in society behind *perestroika*. But the dynamism that was generated quickly went beyond the bounds of what Gorbachev understood as *perestroika*. And this was especially true among the minority nationalities, where by the end of 1988 the situation had become explosive.

THE REVOLT OF THE NATIONALITIES

For the minority nationalities were another aspect of Soviet reality with which Gorbachev was unacquainted.[36] All of his predecessors, from Stalin onward, had had direct experience of ruling in the border areas and understood the mixture of force and tact necessary to keep them quiet. Gorbachev, however, lacking such experience, seems to have believed the official position developed under Brezhnev, namely that the nationalities had been fused into a genuine "Soviet people" committed to the "Union" as the vehicle for their economic development and international security. All they needed, therefore, was a little "restructuring," as that term was understood by the "center." In reality, however, the national republics were suffering from structural stagnation and institutional rigidities of the same sort that Gorbachev had run up against in the Party, compounded by ethnic grievances. And this problem, quite unexpectedly for the leadership, quickly became one of the three major factors—alongside economic failure and the eclipse of ideology—instrumental to bringing the system down. To explain this major problem a brief glance backward is necessary.

As noted, following the original Bolshevik conquest of the border areas during the Civil War and the early 1920s, the "center" in 1922 had created a "federal" Soviet Union that was in fact a unitary state.[37] Its unitary character, however, was camouflaged by an elaborate institutionalization of nationality, defined in ethnic-linguistic terms, on a territorial basis.[38] Each "constituent" republic except Russia, as well as various "associated" republics within the larger ones, received its own political and cultural institutions staffed predominantly by newly formed native elites operating, of course, under the close supervision of the Party. The purpose of this was to appease local nationalism by dignifying it, and at the same time to co-opt it for the purposes of building socialism. In other words, Soviet nationality policy was another aspect of the all-out mobilization of the population for state-building and extensive economic growth. And, with the aid of repression to eliminate any autonomous national sentiment, this worked about as well as the rest of the system during its decades of expansion under Stalin and Khrushchev. For example, Uzbekistan produced cotton for the entire Union, Azerbaijan produced oil, and Moldavia and Georgia contributed wines and spirits, while Russia supplied the steel.

But there were always more problems on the "periphery" than in the "center." After the original military conquest of the border areas, Moscow periodically had to undertake a political "reconquest" via administrative purge because of the reappearance of nationalist forces, now within the local Party itself. In the especially sensitive case of Ukraine—the only republic whose defection by itself could destroy the Union—Stalin carried out such purges at least twice, and Khrushchev and Brezhnev once each.[39] Even more, Soviet policy all along was inadvertently creating nationalisms where they had not existed before.

Most of the Soviet republics were not historic nations, and very few had ever known independent statehood. Georgia and Armenia were ancient national entities that had enjoyed various periods of independence. The three Baltic states grew out of submerged peasantries that had developed national consciousness only at the end of the nineteenth century, and had first become independent between the two World Wars. But Ukraine, within its post–Second World War boundaries, had never existed as a national unit or achieved effective independence; Ukrainian national feeling, though very real, had its strongest base in old Galicia and weakened progressively as one moved east to Kharkov and the Donbas or south to Odessa and the Crimea. And Soviet Belorussia was even less of a reality than Ukraine, while none of the Muslim republics had ever been nations until the

Soviets carved them out of old Turkestan. Yet after decades of territorially based ethnicity, these entities were all on their way to becoming national communities with their own elites and institutionalized vested interests.

Furthermore, they were all aggrieved national communities. Given the divide-and-rule frontiers Stalin had imposed, almost all of these republics had minorities of their citizens in other republics, and minorities of neighboring ethnic groups within their own borders. Almost all had large numbers of Russians settled in their midst as a result of industrialization; for these migrations were part of a deliberate policy of diluting territorial homogeneity in order to create a single Soviet people to go with the unitary economy and the unitary Party. Yet, despite the recurrent appearance of national cultural protest, this multinational empire remained stable as long as the economy was able to support a strong central state. So Brezhnev could easily repress overt border nationalism in the late seventies by arresting all the leading national dissidents of the Baltic states, Ukraine, and the Caucasus.

Still, stagnation was undermining the republics just as it was eating, away at the rest of the system, and for the same reasons. Brezhnev's policy of "stability of cadres" had provided each republic and region with a power structure as resistant to central initiative as was the Party apparat as a whole. Particularly in the Muslim republics, this policy had led to the virtual takeover of the Party by ethnic chieftains who controlled their regions as if they were satrapies, and who bribed Moscow into connivance. At the same time, the ecological depredations caused by Soviet-style industrialization were seen by the populations of the republics as the evil fruits of domination by the center: Chernobyl, in particular, accelerated the development of Ukrainian and Belorussian separatist sentiment; and the local apparats easily found it in their interests to espouse this sentiment against Moscow. Moreover, the decline of the economy made resources scarcer and therefore increased competition for them, both among the republics and between the republics and the center. The consequence of this accumulation of grievances was a growing movement for local control as the only appropriate "restructuring" for the national republics. And glasnost for the first time made it possible to talk about all of this without undue fear of reprisal.

The tragedy of Soviet nationality policy was that it encouraged the development of national identity while at the same time giving the energies thereby generated only a fraudulent outlet. Nothing was done to give these semi-nations any real control over their affairs, or to prepare the way for genuine federal relationships. As a consequence, when the demand for effective autonomy was at last raised, it could only take the form of a head-on clash of interests between the center and the periphery. The national discontents that came to the surface as a result of *perestroika* did not represent simply the resurgence of traditional nationalisms long submerged by Soviet rule, as has often been alleged; they were, rather, a new force stimulated if not created by Soviet power and then hobbled to the point of exasperation by Soviet control. As with everything else in the Soviet system, the rigidity of the state's unitary structure ruled out an evolutionary transition. Thus the Union could not be preserved if anything else in the system were to be reformed.

Gorbachev inadvertently stumbled into this deteriorating situation in December 1986.[40] As a part of his initial attack on the apparat in general, he replaced the corrupt but native First Secretary of Kazakhstan, who was also a Politburo member, with an honest but imported Russian. The answer was a riot verging on revolt in protest against this loss of autonomy and of representation at the highest level in Moscow. As a result, Gorbachev in effect had to back down by appointing a Kazakh Second Secretary; moreover, under *glasnost*, the publicity given to the fact that there had been a riot followed by a retreat showed other nationalities that they, too, might press their demands.

At the beginning of the next year *perestroika* was struck by a "moral Chernobyl," as one Soviet leader put it, in the form of Nagornyi Karabakh,* an Armenian enclave in Azerbaijan. This region, whose population was 80 percent Armenian, had been assigned by Stalin to Azerbaijan in 1923, because at the time he had more need to propitiate Turkish than Armenian opinion. With the coming of "restructuring," however, the Armenians of the region sought to redress this long-standing grievance by petitioning for a change in status. When the petition was rejected, crowds took to the streets in demonstrations, both in the region's capital, Stepanakert, and in the capital of the Armenian republic, Erivan; their slogan was "Karabakh is the test of *perestroika*." In February 1988, these demonstrations led to armed clashes with Azerbaijani in Nagornyi Karabakh, and these clashes prompted a pogrom against Armenians in Sumgait, near the Azerbai-

---

* The Western press has stubbornly and incorrectly referred to this enclave by the adjectival form Nagorno-Karabakh. The correct noun is used here.

jani capital of Baku. Crowds of up to a million then protested the
pogrom on Lenin Square in Erivan under the leadership of the "Karabakh Committee," and the Armenian Party in effect went over to the
national movement in an inversion of the regime's intended formula
for such Popular Fronts.

After this first explosion, Moscow, unwilling to contemplate any
border changes for fear of producing a chain reaction in other republics, played for time in the uninformed hope that passions would cool
and the problem would go away. Various schemes for giving Karabakh
a limited special status were tried and failed. The only result was that
the Armenians, hitherto traditionally reconciled to Soviet tutelage
because of their need for Moscow's protection against the Turks, now
became anti-Soviet and bent on independence. Although Armenia
was policed by Soviet troops, in fact a regime of "dual power" had
come into existence.

At the same time, the Armenian efforts to retrieve Nagornyi Karabakh had led to the emergence of a nationally minded Popular Front
in Azerbaijan. At first the Front was directed only against Azerbaijan's
neighbors, but, as Moscow appeared to waver on the status of the
disputed territory, it was turned against the "Russians" as well. Because neither Caucasian republic could obtain satisfaction from the
center, both took matters into their own hands; and, during the course
of 1989, they became locked in a low-grade war. Azerbaijan imposed
a rail blockade on Armenia, and nationals of each republic deserted
from the Soviet army with their weapons—and occasionally even with
helicopters. As if this were not enough in the way of disintegration of
central authority, mothers in Russia took to demonstrating against the
Soviet army's risking their "boys" to keep order among the "wild
mountaineers."

Finally, during 1989, ethnic conflict spread to the rest of the moun-
tain area. A movement for the secession from Georgia of the Abkha-
zian Associated Republic (created by Stalin in order to produce a
smaller and less viable Georgia) led, under *perestroika*, to an upsurge
of Georgian nationalism. But the resulting Georgian Popular Front
soon transferred its animus from the Abkhazians to their alleged spon-
sor, the Soviet center; and by April 1989 emotional crowds were
demonstrating in Tbilisi for what was becoming their real aim, independence. The local authorities took fright, and with the probable
connivance of the center, used the army against the crowds: On April

9, some one hundred persons were killed in the first bloodshed of the *perestroika* years. Although a semblance of order was thereby restored, in fact another zone of dual power had been created. Thus, in the course of 1988–1989 all three Caucasian republics had gone far beyond *perestroika* and towards the breakup of the Union.

During these same two years another movement of national liberation opened up in the three Baltic states, though here this occurred in a scrupulously legalistic and nonviolent manner. Once again, the legacy of Stalin came home to haunt his heirs. The Balts' tactic was to argue that the secret protocols to the Molotov-Ribbentrop Pact of 1939, which had awarded their republics to the Soviet Union, had never been legal; as a consequence they were only reclaiming, by stages, an independence still recognized under international law. In April 1988, therefore, liberal intellectuals in Estonia formed a Popular Front with certain elements of the Party to work for republic "sovereignty"; this marked the first appearance of that slogan in the lexicon of informal *perestroika*. When the Party Conference in June failed to pay any attention to its demands, the Estonian Party lost the initiative to its non-Party allies; and in November a radicalized Estonian Parliament implemented its demand for sovereignty by voting to give republic laws precedence over Soviet laws.

This nonviolent nullification of Union authority was even harder for Gorbachev to deal with than was Nagornyi Karabakh: he could not use force if *perestroika* were to remain credible, yet he could not let Estonia get away with its insolence if central authority were to remain real. But even before the Estonians had taken this step, the Latvians and Lithuanians had also formed their own Popular Fronts (in Lithuania, it was called Sajudis) to press for sovereignty. Moreover, by early 1989 all three Fronts were openly demanding formal denunciation of the 1939 Pact, which was also a way of saying that sovereignty in fact meant independence. In addition, this Baltic agitation was already beginning to find an echo in Lvov, or Lviv, in western Ukraine, which had also become Soviet because of the Pact.

Thus in early 1989, just when Gorbachev's greatest reform—democratization of the soviets—was about to take effect, his previous reform, *glasnost*, had already delegitimized much of the system the new reform was intended to salvage. Democratization would now permit a nascent civil society to organize and to move from mere reform to creeping revolution against the system.

12

FROM *PERESTROIKA* TO COLLAPSE

1989–1991

*For what you [the Athenians] hold is, to speak somewhat plainly, a
tyranny; to take it perhaps was wrong, but to let it go is unsafe.*
    —Pericles, according to Thucydides, anent the Athenian empire

Gorbachev doesn't know what he's ruling over.
                                                    —Sergei Grigoriants, 1988

It was against the background of crisis creeping in from the borderlands that the elections to the Congress of People's Deputies took
place in March 1989—the first real elections in Russia since 1918.
These elections, and even more the first meeting of the Congress
itself in June, marked the decisive turning point of the Gorbachev era,
the moment of transition from the restructuring of Communism to its
active disintegration. Indeed, June 1989 was the great turning point
for Communism throughout the world: the Polish elections of that
month started the collapse of the system throughout Eastern Europe,
and the Tiananmen Square massacre in Beijing demonstrated the
limits of "within-system" reform of Communism even under conditions of economic prosperity. By the end of 1989, after the fall of the
Berlin Wall and the collapse of all the Eastern European regimes, it
was becoming clear that the only alternatives for the system were
either peaceful self-liquidation or a costly but still temporary holding
operation.

445

DEMOCRATIZATION

The first shock of 1989 was the Soviet elections in the spring. They had been organized under the slogan—resurrected from 1917 and intended only rhetorically—"all power to the soviets," but the surprise for Gorbachev was that the liberals took this slogan literally and sought to wrest real power from the Party, and from Gorbachev. And they did this despite the fact that the electoral system had been constructed to yield a Congress safely devoted to the General Secretary's concept of Popular Fronts loyal to *perestroika*. Although the Congress and its Supreme Soviet formally had both constituent and legislative powers, in fact they resembled a two-tier consultative assembly designed less to govern than to provide input into the government's policy making.

The elections were conducted not on the basis of universal suffrage but by a complicated system, reminiscent of an Old Regime, intended to blunt the effect of democracy. This made it easy to criticize the new system as a mere camouflage of the continuing totalitarian nature of the regime; and the "Gorbachev Constitution" was so criticized at the time by Soviet liberals. Still, it should be pointed out that these were the first elections of any kind in Russia since 1918, and that an immediate leap from totalitarianism into full-fledged universal suffrage democracy could have been dangerously destabilizing. Moreover, all other European countries that had moved to political democracy in the century before 1915 had done so by stages. This, it seems, was the reasoning of Gorbachev and his aides: "democratization," like economic liberalization, would have to proceed in a "step by step," calibrated fashion, so as to not frighten the apparat into open opposition and to involve the people gradually in the new ways. And all of this was quite defensible.

The real flaw of the new political system lay elsewhere. As with economic reform, Gorbachev had no clear idea of the *terminus ad quem* of his political reform, for his goal was not democracy any more than it was the market: it was, rather, an unspecified measure of popular participation and the rule of law in combination with the continuing hegemony of the (putatively regenerated) Party. But real democracy has no more need for such a Party than does a market. Thus Gorbachev's bold initiative was in fact the ultimate version of the recurring "internal contradictions" of Reform Communism.

In the Gorbachev Constitution there were, first of all, two assemblies, not one. The larger Congress (apparently modelled on the Ecclesia, the Athenian popular Assembly) was directly elected by the population and various "social organizations." Composed of 2,250 members, it was too large to be a deliberative body. It was, therefore, to meet only two or three times a year for short periods, and its main function was to elect the real governmental organs: the chairman of its Presidium (the "president") and the actual legislature, a bicameral Supreme Soviet of 542 members that would meet throughout the year (the equivalent of the Athenian Boulé, or small Council). With this indirect election of the legislature, and with the president, or his deputy, actually presiding over both bodies, there was little chance of significant opposition to the government's will.

The second restraint on spontaneous democracy was the electoral process itself. Seven hundred fifty Congress deputies were elected by such "social organizations" as the Party, the Komsomol, and the Academy of Sciences; it was assumed that the Party would in fact select all of these deputies. And for the one hundred seats reserved for the Party, exactly one hundred candidates were nominated, including Gorbachev and most senior officials; this meant that no member of the leadership had to risk competitive election even within the Party. The remaining two thirds of the deputies were elected in territorial or national districts; but even in these constituencies the local Party secretary more often than not selected a deputy or stood for election himself. Thus, 85 percent of the elected deputies were Party members. Furthermore, there was a rigorous preselection of candidates through a series of "filters," as these obstacles were called. First, a candidate had to be put forth by a number of citizens; second, his or her nomination had to be approved at a meeting of no fewer than five hundred residents of the district, and the authorities could easily stack such a gathering; finally, the candidacy had to be formally registered by an electoral commission, where again the Party could intervene. As a result, 384 districts had only one name—invariably that of a Party official—on their ballot.

Nonetheless, there were means of challenging the system. The first of these was national television. Most of the people who had been writing the great articles of *glasnost* during the two previous years had, in late 1988, formed a political club, the Moscow Tribune, and many of these individuals were now candidates. Well before the elections they had been regularly interviewed on the educational program *Encounters in Ostankeno*; once the campaign started, they began to appear on the more popular and lively late-night show *View*. And then there were more direct forms of agitation: when the filters of the Academy worked so well that Sakharov failed to be nominated, there was such an outcry that the Party intervened again to put him on the ballot. In large cities with a sizeable educated population, liberal elements mounted well-organized campaigns for their own candidates and against those of the apparat; in Leningrad, the group "Elections 89" passed out leaflets at subway stations, borrowed government vehicles to use as sound trucks, and orchestrated the defeat of the local First Secretary and alternate Politburo member, who was running unopposed, by persuading a majority to cross his name off the ballot. And similar tactics produced similar upsets in such major centers as Sverdlovsk, Vladivostok, Volgograd, Minsk, Kiev, and Lvov. In the Baltic states, of course, the results were even more radical: the Popular Fronts took two thirds of the seats, while official candidates survived only if they had a Front's approval. (In the Caucasian republics growing public disorder prevented normal elections—and hence any radical breakthrough—while citizens of the Central Asian republics voted as the Party bosses told them to.)

But the most momentous upset occurred in Moscow. There, in a special city-wide constituency, Boris Yeltsin received some five million votes, or 90 percent of the total, against the official candidate, a factory director (the city's First Secretary did not dare to stand). Yeltsin, moreover, had campaigned against Party privilege and power and in favor of direct election of the new president and the creation of a multiparty system; none of the other liberals had been so explicit in stating their real aims.

The overall result of the election was that Gorbachev obtained a large majority willing to follow his lead without question—but the liberals took about three hundred seats. Although most of these liberals were formally Party members, they were not from the apparat, and besides, Party membership now meant much less than before. Furthermore, between the opening of the campaign in February and the final runoffs in May, the revolution of the borderlands at last reached the central Slavic areas. The larger cities had become politicized, though provincial centers and the countryside would remain largely under the control of the apparat until the end of the regime, and even after.

Perestroika, previously the business of only the Party leadership, now became a matter for society at large. People for the first time felt they could actually do something about their lot, and the most important thing they wanted to do was to reject the hegemony of the Party. This, not the size of the formal majority, was the true significance of the election, and especially of Yeltsin's triumph.

Nonetheless, caution was still very much in order. The apparat had fought hard at every "filter." In April there were other scares comparable to the Andreeva letter of a year earlier. As was mentioned in the previous chapter, the army fired on nationalist demonstrators in Tbilisi, apparently with Politburo connivance; and in that same week tanks were seen in the streets of Riga. Moreover, an ominously restrictive revision of the legal code was in preparation. Were Ligachev and the conservatives preparing a crackdown to annul the results of the elections? Might Gorbachev himself be having second thoughts about what he had permitted? So the Congress met at the end of May in an atmosphere in which hope was tempered by foreboding.

After some hesitation, Gorbachev decided that the proceedings would be televised live and nationally. In accordance with the strategy of the Popular Front, his agenda for the Congress called for his report to be followed immediately by the election of the president and the Supreme Soviet. But the liberals had bolder ideas: 1989 was the two-hundredth anniversary of the French Revolution, and some of the deputies, only half-jokingly, spoke of the Congress as the Estates General, and of the new Supreme Soviet as the Duma. Such comparisons aside, they did in fact want power sharing with Gorbachev and not just a consultative role. Accordingly, their agenda called for his report to be followed by a thorough debate, and only after this discussion would the Congress elect the president and the Supreme Soviet—an arrangement that implied Gorbachev's dependence on the newly elected "deputies of the people." But just before the Congress convened, Gorbachev and his chief aide, Anatolii Lukianov, met confidentially with the Moscow Group, as the liberals then were called, and "worked them over" to squelch this dissident scenario.

So the Congress followed Gorbachev's script, but not without a running war of criticism from the more militant liberals. Gorbachev was duly elected president, and the Congress chose a Supreme Soviet so traditional that it contained not a single Moscow liberal. (This was so embarrassing that one deputy was prevailed on to resign in order to make room for Yeltsin.) Afanasiev indignantly called the new parliament a "Stalinist-Brezhnevite" body and denounced the "aggressively submissive majority" of the Congress, and word soon spread in the corridors that a "declaration" from the defeated liberal minority would soon be forthcoming. As the days went by, speaker after speaker attacked one or another vice of the system: the inefficiency of the economy; the widespread poverty of the country; the corruption of the Party; the scandal of hospitals without running hot water and health care without medicines; the inadequacies of education; the misconduct of the army in Afghanistan and Georgia; and finally, in one astounding outburst, the role of the KGB as an "underground empire" exercising "comprehensive control over society."[1]

Still, no general declaration was produced by the dissidents, and the presumption was that any request to read such a document would be refused by the chair, that is, by Gorbachev. Then, on the last day, one young deputy pronounced the word "declaration" and was indeed promptly cut off. He turned out to have been a decoy, however, as Sakharov, who had already spoken eight times, immediately asked for the floor once again. Gorbachev was afraid of what Sakharov might say, but he was even more afraid of the consequences of turning him down, so he granted the persistent "Andrei Dmitrievich" five minutes, and Sakharov proceeded to read something he called a "Decree on Power." (He used the ceremonially revolutionary word "decree" because Lenin had used it in his "Decrees," on Land and Peace, in October 1917.) The substance of Sakharov's "Decree" was that Article 6 of the Constitution, establishing the "leading and guiding role of the Party," should be abrogated, and that all power should pass to the soviets and their Congress, from which the Party had seized it in 1917. Here the nub of the problem of "reforming" the system—the question of power—was at last named, and in front of the whole country. Gorbachev cut off the microphone before Sakharov had finished, but the television camera remained on. Henceforth there would be no avoiding the problem Sakharov had brought out into the open.[2]

When the twelve days of the Congress were finished, the Soviet Union was a new country. The work of desacralizing the system, begun by *glasnost*, was now completed. Millions of people had heard their private thoughts uttered in public; individuals saw that the evils they had observed in their own little corner of the system were common to the whole Union. And everyone now knew it was possible to say the boldest things without fear of retribution. So intense was the public's interest in the Congress that industrial production dropped 20 percent during the televised coverage of the proceedings. As one liberal deputy summed it up: "The main achievement [of the Congress] was the demystification of Soviet power."[3]

But the country was also left with a great feeling of incompleteness: As another deputy put it, "so many facts, and no conclusions."[4] And indeed the government offered no program for change, while at the same time the situation in the country was visibly deteriorating. During the Congress there had been two disasters: in Siberia, butane gas had leaked from a pipeline, and through an act of "criminal negligence" it caught fire from a passing train, producing an explosion that killed some 450 persons; almost simultaneously, in the Fergana Valley of Uzbekistan a pogrom against the Meskhetian Turkic minority claimed dozens of victims. The two incidents together dramatized the fragility of both the Soviet industrial achievement and the multinational Union. At the same time, living standards for everyone were now visibly declining. The country seemed caught in drift, and the government mired in impotence.

In July the population started taking matters into its own hands. The miners of the Kuznetsk Basin went on strike for higher wages, food and . . . soap. Soon the movement spread to the Donbas and the mines of Vorkuta in the north, where a political demand was added: abrogation of Article 6 and the end of the Party's leading role. Gorbachev and the government hastily took up the miners' cause and acceded to their economic demands; he had, after all, summoned the people to become involved in *perestroika*, and the government, moreover, had no reserves of coal. In addition, the railroad workers were threatening to strike, and that dire eventuality had to be headed off at all costs.

Meanwhile, back in Moscow some two hundred fifty liberal deputies, who had come to know each other only as a result of the Congress, formed a caucus called the Inter-Regional Group. Its principal leaders were Sakharov, Yeltsin, Afanasiev, and Popov. Their aim was to achieve what the first session of the Congress had failed to accomplish: a transfer of real power from Gorbachev to the Supreme Soviet. To this end they sought to form an alliance with the newly awakened workers as well as with the sovereignty movement among the national minorities, particularly the Balts. Their concrete program was to end the Party's leading role and to introduce a multiparty system, private property, and a market economy. To implement this program, they were expecting to take power through the local soviet elections scheduled for the coming year. *Glasnost* was not yet so complete that these aims could be stated in print, but the members of the group talked about them freely in private.

In the western borderlands, however, radicalism was now openly expressed: on August 23, the fiftieth anniversary of the Molotov-Ribbentrop Pact, a human chain of a million people was formed across the three Baltic states from Tallinn to Vilnius. Ukraine, too, was now mobilized for action around the organization Rukh, which in January 1990 imitated the demonstration in the Baltic states with a human chain of its own from Lvov through Kiev and on to Poltava. By the end of the summer something approximating "dual power" existed throughout much of the country. As one leader of Rukh summed up the post-Congress situation: "The country now stands at a crossroads. From here, we either go the Chinese way or the Polish-Hungarian way."[5]

The impetus of *perestroika* had contributed to a crisis of Leninist systems everywhere, and the vicissitudes of Reform Communism abroad reacted in turn on the Soviet center. In point of time the first foreign impact came from China, not because of any current Soviet connection with Chinese affairs, but because change in so huge a socialist system could only provide a challenge for the original model. It was China that had inaugurated the second great round of Reform Communism with Deng Xiaoping's economic liberalization of 1978. Down to 1989, China's great success had contributed to the pressure on the Soviets to reform; after the Tiananmen Square massacre, China became a cautionary example of the pitfalls of reform; and in both phases, the Chinese path pointed the way to the future for the erstwhile "elder brother" for the first time in their relationship.

The change began with Mao Zedong's death in 1975. Internally, this event made it possible to liquidate the hard Communism of the Great Helmsman and to launch the soft Communism of Deng, a combination of authoritarian government with market freedom. Externally, Mao's departure ended the intense animosity that had characterized Sino-Soviet relations since the split in 1963. Although important regional conflicts of interest remained, the old feud for leadership of international socialism gradually lost its meaning for both sides.

Therefore, after Gorbachev came to power, he normalized relations with the Chinese as a fraternal "socialist" state. Because Gorbachev needed this rapprochement more than the Chinese did, he had to proceed, as in his rapprochement with the West, by making all of the concessions. Thus the Soviets had to agree to withdraw from Afghanistan, reduce their forces on the Sino-Soviet border, and force their ally Vietnam to evacuate Cambodia. It was this *Ostpolitik* that finally brought Gorbachev to Beijing in May 1989, on the very eve of the Soviet Congress of People's Deputies. Although this new policy netted him nothing, the timing of his visit served to highlight an aspect of the Chinese situation most relevant to the situation at home and in Eastern Europe.

Gorbachev arrived in Beijing just as the Chinese version of Reform Communism was reaching its great crisis. The Students for Democracy were already occupying Tiananmen Square, and the example of *perestroika* was a contributory factor in emboldening them to act. But for the Soviet bloc the deeper meaning of the Chinese crisis lay elsewhere. Whereas Gorbachev had begun his reform with politics, Deng Xiaoping had pursued the opposite course by starting his reform with economics. Yet by 1989 both had arrived at an impasse because one kind of reform without the other destabilized the system as a whole. Indeed, Gorbachev told his hosts that economic reform without a correspondingly thorough political change would not work, and under the circumstances this amounted to advice not to crack down on the students. Yet in the total system of the Party-state the reverse was just as true, as the Soviet Union would discover in 1991. And this raises a question much debated in Russia at the end of *perestroika:* would Gorbachev have done better to put economic reform ahead of political democratization? In reality he did not have that choice, as a brief comparison of Soviet and Chinese conditions readily reveals.

When Deng Xiaoping began his reform in 1979, 80 percent of China's population was rural. Hence, by merely relaxing the commune system and letting the peasants produce freely, most of the population could experience a great expansion of prosperity, and the economy as a whole could show a surge of growth rates of some 10 to 15 percent annually over a decade. By contrast, in the Soviet Union the devastating consequences of collectivization and the huge agrarian bureaucracy precluded any such rapid economic upturn. More-over, Stalin had been a "success," in the sense of creating a mammoth industrial plant and building a superpower; Mao had been a failure as a state-builder with his wild Leap Forward and his inane Cultural Revolution. Gorbachev thus had to liquidate much of what his coun-try regarded as its glory; Deng only had to overcome policies that most in his country wanted to be rid of. Gorbachev therefore had to proceed slowly and indirectly by restructuring his country's administrative structures through "democratization"; Deng could leave his political system, together with its relatively small state industrial sector, in place, while "giving the peasant nag its head" (to quote Lenin) in agriculture and artisan production.

In short, after the failed Stalinism of Mao, China could return to the NEP formula of the Party-state plus the market; Russia could not, because her Stalinism had successfully destroyed the peasant civil society that was the precondition for that formula. Gorbachev there-fore first had to soften up the Stalinist system by political reform before marketization could proceed very far. And when matters reached an impasse, as they did in the wake of the Congress, he could not resort to repression if *perestroika* were to remain credible. But when economic liberalization in China produced its political counter-part, Deng's reform made repression all too feasible, for repression would not entail an undue cost in terms of economic development.

THE WEAKEST LINK SNAPS: 1989

If China served as a cautionary example for the fortunes of *perestroika*, Eastern Europe determined the outcome of the whole adventure. The People's Democracies, the sometime pride of the Stalinist em-pire, had always been the weakest link in the Communist chain—to paraphrase Lenin's characterization of Russia's place in capitalism. In 1989, however, they became the point of fatal crisis for the entire Soviet system. For the first time the "conquests of socialism" proved to be "reversible," and on a massive scale; and if they could be reversed in so huge an area, there was no reason why they could not be reversed anywhere.

The chain reaction of events leading from the Polish elections of June, through the collapse of the Berlin Wall in November, to the fall of Ceausescu in December is the most stunning episode in the disintegration of Communism. Releasing the pent-up frustrations of forty years, six regimes collapsed in the space of seven months, and each crisis matured more rapidly than its predecessor. As Timothy Garton Ash summed up this *annus mirabilis:* what in Poland had taken ten years, in Hungary took ten months, in East Germany ten weeks, and in Czechoslovakia ten days.[6]

On one level this grand implosion is very simple to explain: the East European regimes, born of conquest, had never been legitimate; hence, at the first opportunity their populations threw them off, each nation emboldened by the success of a predecessor. But on another level there is quite a bit to explain, for everything depended on getting that first opportunity, which in turn depended on the intentions of Moscow and the status of the Brezhnev Doctrine. And for four years of *perestroika* the situation was too ambiguous for the East Europeans to risk any bold action.

After it was all over it was not infrequently heard in the West that Gorbachev had "liberated" Eastern Europe; indeed, he himself was saying this as early as 1990, and he put it even more strongly after his retirement. But since a political leader does not normally liberate countries from his own government, this view requires qualification. Gorbachev and his aides did in fact have in mind a policy of major restructuring for Eastern Europe that would have certainly liberalized the area, but this by no means signifies that they intended to sacrifice the gains of the Second World War or to dissolve the Warsaw Pact. Rather, their original design was inflated through improvisations in response to the pressure of events to the point where they suddenly lost control of the situation. And the resulting inadvertent revolution was of a piece with its original but slower-moving counterpart in the Soviet Union itself.[7]

Gorbachev's original design for Eastern Europe was an updated version of the standard Soviet doctrine of separate paths to socialism.[8] This meant that the fraternal countries should be actively encouraged to "make their *perestroika*" roughly along the lines of the Soviet effort, though with a large degree of autonomy. By 1987–1988 this design had been expanded under the influence of Gorbachev's and Yakovlev's ideology of a modernized socialism founded on "universal human values" and integration of the Soviet world into a "common European home." In this new perspective the People's Democracies were to play a bridging role between Russia and the West, between socialism and capitalism, as a kind of third way of modern development. This vision did not mean that socialism was superseded as the supreme value; the intention, rather, was to bring out socialism's potential under contemporary conditions. Besides, the whole program, if it can be called that, had not been carefully thought out, and the spur to Gorbachev's policy lay largely in practical political concerns.

These concerns related to the different paths the fraternal parties were in fact following. Although every socialist country had the right · to its own separate path, from Moscow's point of view some paths were clearly better than others. From Gorbachev's perspective, Jaruzelski's Poland and Kadar's Hungary were basically on the right track of Reform Communism. Jaruzelski had spared Moscow the cost and the onus of intervention, and once he had suppressed Solidarity, beginning in 1984 he pursued a policy of political moderation, releasing his political prisoners, avoiding unnecessary conflict with the Church, and attempting to liberalize the economy. Kadar, although tired out as an individual after thirty years in power, had nonetheless created the most liberalized socialist economy, which indeed had served as a partial model for *perestroika*. However, the other People's Democracies—East Germany, Czechoslovakia, Romania, and Bulgaria—appeared to Gorbachev as a "gang of four" Stalinist-Brezhnevite regimes even more in need of restructuring than his own.

The duality of East European politics, moreover, overlapped with the political division in the Soviet Union, where the liberals favored Hungary and Poland while the conservatives favored the other four. East Germany and Czechoslovakia were the great economic success stories of the socialist camp (East Germany, wondrously, was counted a world-class economic success even in the West); they were therefore used by Soviet conservatives to argue that *perestroika* was unnecessary and that the country could overcome its crisis by perfecting its traditional centralized model of management. As a consequence, Gorbachev had to push the recalcitrant four ever more urgently to abandon that model and to "restructure" themselves. It was the need to answer his domestic critics by discrediting the gang of four, and by permitting ever bolder experimentation in Poland and Hungary, that explains in large part the rashness of his East European policy.

Furthermore, both contending groups in Moscow had their allies in the fraternal Parties, and Gorbachev actively sought to replace the

East European old guard with his own, younger men. The old guard, for its part, considered Gorbachev an adventurer who would not last, and they therefore stonewalled his *perestroika;* Honecker and Husak even forbade Soviet reformist publications in their bailiwicks. At the same time, reformist elements within the East European Parties, as well as dissidents who wanted to be done with the system entirely, took up the cause of *perestroika* and "Gorby," some out of real conviction, but most opportunistically. And everyone waited to see whether, in a crisis, Gorbachev was "for real" or whether he would revert to previous Muscovite form.

In all probability, until 1989 Gorbachev believed that there would be no crisis, that change in Eastern Europe would occur in "calibrated" fashion just as it was supposed to at home, and that no hard choices would be necessary. In reality, however, he had forfeited the option of coercion when he embarked on his "new thinking" and "universal human values" in foreign policy. The sympathy of the West, necessary for the revival of the Soviet system, precluded any recourse to the Brezhnev Doctrine. As Poland's Adam Michnik put the matter in 1988, "Gorbachev is the prisoner of his foreign policy successes."[9] Yet despite tantalizing hints from such secondary Soviet officials as academician Oleg Bogomolov and Foreign Ministry spokesman Gennadii Gerasimov that the Brezhnev Doctrine was defunct, its demise was never made explicit. Thus, the East European crisis developed after 1987–1988 with the various oppositions testing the waters as they proceeded.

Beginning in 1986, Gorbachev visited virtually all of the East European capitals to urge change. In 1987 Husak was replaced as First Secretary by Milos Jakes, but the situation in Czechoslovakia remained unchanged. In May 1988 Kadar was at last replaced by the hardly more adventurous Karoly Grosz, but this change did eventually lead to the unfreezing of the Hungarian situation. For Grosz was soon challenged by a radical reformist group under the leadership of Imre Pozsgay, and Moscow, with extraordinary insouciance, permitted the Hungarian reform to radicalize. Between January and June of the next year, the Hungarian Party made one unprecedented concession after another: The rights of assembly and of association were granted, the Party's leading role was abandoned and the Party changed its name to "Socialist," the barbed wire "wall" at the Austrian frontier was dismantled, the leaders of the 1956 revolution were rehabilitated, and Grosz was hemmed in by a four-man Presidium dominated by radical reformers. All this was undertaken in the expectation of making the Party modern and acceptable to the people. It was also done with Moscow's approval, or at least without calling forth any objections, no doubt because it seemed to be a contribution to the building of a "common European home." And as of the summer of 1989, this restructuring appeared to be a success—a fine example of advanced perestroika.[10]

But the most important change in Eastern Europe occurred in Poland, for there the stimulus for transformation came not from within the Party but from society. In 1988 continuing economic decline provoked the first strikes since 1980–1981. Although Solidarity was still illegal, its members were deeply involved in these actions. The regime realized it could not cope with the economic crisis without Solidarity's cooperation, and the union's leadership seized on this circumstance to pressure the Party into a deal for power sharing. Walesa put his prestige on the line by persuading the workers to end their strike in return for "round-table" negotiations with the regime for an "anticrisis pact," even though the radical wing of Solidarity rejected this approach as a sellout of the union. At the same time, the civilian Party accused the ruling generals of betraying the system, and Jaruzelski and his closest colleagues had to threaten to resign in order to bring the Central Committee around. At the beginning of 1989 the round table met under the sponsorship of the Church, and a deal was struck.[11]

Solidarity was legalized and elections were scheduled for June. Two thirds of the seats in the Sejm were reserved for the Party and its two longtime satellites, the Peasant Party and the Democrats; Solidarity was permitted to put up candidates for one third of the seats. A Senate of a hundred seats was created, and Solidarity was allowed to contest all of them. Jaruzelski was to be elected president by the Sejm. Freer, democratic elections were to take place in four years. Thus the Party was guaranteed control of the government until then, and in the interval Solidarity would be expected to keep the workers quiet and to share responsibility for the inevitable pain of overcoming the economic crisis. Solidarity, for its part, acquired the status of a recognized opposition and the possibility of training to assume full power in four years.

But nothing worked out as planned. The regime thought it would win the elections easily because of its tight organization and control of the media, whereas Solidarity, just emerging from the underground, was organizationally weak and had only one newspaper, *Gazeta Wyborcza* (*Electoral Gazette*), founded for the occasion. When the returns came in on June 4, however, the Party had clearly lost power in the country. Solidarity won 99 of the 100 Senate seats and most of the contests it had been allowed to enter for the Sejm. Even more important, the Party failed to win half of its reserved seats because voters crossed off its candidates' names, thus depriving them of the necessary majority; it received its quota only in runoffs, where Solidarity mobilized to help it along. Although only 60 percent of the electorate voted, most of the abstentions were due to the refusal of the radical wing of Solidarity to take part in what it considered a Communist farce.

As a result of this upset, both sides were in a quandary. The regime had lost all semblance of legitimacy, yet Solidarity could not take power because it was unprepared to govern and because of Moscow's expected resistance. So both sides at first pretended to observe the round-table agreement. Jaruzelski was elected president, but by only one vote, and that on a deliberate miscount. Still, the Sejm could not bring itself to endorse a Communist prime minister, and stalemate ensured. After two months, Walesa succeeded in prying the Democrats and the Peasants from the Party because their members were fearful of losing their positions and perquisites. With this alliance, Solidarity now had a parliamentary majority, and it proposed to resolve the crisis on the basis of "your [Communist] president, our [Solidarity] prime minister."

But this would be a momentous change, and consequently Moscow had to be consulted. In late August Gorbachev telephoned Poland's new civilian Party chief and urged acceptance of the coalition, or at least indicated that Moscow would do nothing to oppose it. At last it had been made clear that the Brezhnev Doctrine was (almost) dead. In September the first-ever post-Communist government anywhere came to power under the Social Catholic Tadeusz Mazowiecki, though a Communist minority still controlled the key ministries of defense and interior. Given the historical particularities of the Polish case, Moscow probably reasoned that this was the best way to safeguard Soviet interests in that strategic area, and that even a coalition with non-Communists was therefore an acceptable variant of *perestroika*.

But of course the system's unraveling did not stop with this compromise anymore than it had with the round-table agreements. Politically, the Poles were fairly cautious over the next year and a half: They eliminated the secret police, the Communist ministers, the *nomenklatura* apparat, and eventually Jaruzelski himself, but only by steps. Yet economically, the Solidarity-led government was radical from the start. On the initiative of the new minister of finance, Leszek Balcerowicz, it adopted the first program of genuine economic transformation in the Communist world: a clean break with the socialist past through a "shock therapy" transition to the market and private property, a violation of the two great taboos of the system. At last the economic conclusions were drawn from the disintegration of the Party-state, and this was something that had surely not been cleared with Moscow, where such ideas could still not be discussed. Elaborated in the fall of 1989, the Polish program of price liberalization and monetary reform was begun as a "big bang" on January 1, 1990. Together with the dismantling of the Party-state, this economic program revealed for the first time what the "exit from Communism" meant concretely, and the Polish example became the pilot for that process elsewhere.

By the fall of 1989, that progress was in full swing throughout the rest of Eastern Europe. The next step was taken by Hungary. In September, Budapest opened its frontier with Austria, an action that had the quite intended effect of permitting thousands of East German "vacationers" to leave their country for West Germany. The declared purpose of this action was to demonstrate to the Hungarian population as well as to the West German government, whose aid Hungary needed, that the regime had indeed reformed. But since this move was in clear violation of Hungary's treaty with East Germany, the question arises whether the move had also been suggested by Moscow as a way of undermining the East German regime, the most openly defiant of the "gang of four." In any event, East Germans now began to pour into West German embassies in Prague and Warsaw, and the ensuing exodus threw East Germany into open crisis, with massive demonstrations for reform taking place throughout the country.

On September 7, Gorbachev, the indefatigable traveller, arrived in Berlin for the fortieth anniversary of the founding of the East German state, where he was greeted with cries of "Gorby" and "Freedom."

His only public criticism of Honecker was the remark "life punishes those who delay," but it is clear that for some time he had desired to replace the East German First Secretary with one of the local reform candidates waiting in the wings. Gorbachev finally got his wish the following month. On October 16, Honecker's order to use force against a demonstration of some 150,000 people in Leipzig was countermanded by his deputy, Egon Krenz, who two days later moved into the top Party post. Under these parlous conditions, Krenz and a new prime minister, Hans Modrow, attempted a *perestroika* with the support of the local popular front, Neues Forum, many of whose members wanted only a reformed socialism, not an exit from Communism. But this belated effort fizzled pitifully, for after October 16 it was clear that neither Berlin nor Moscow would use force against the population, and without force the population would no longer obey. Accordingly, when in a further gesture of conciliation the regime on November 9 opened the Wall simply to allow free passage, the Berliners responded by tearing it down. And that event marked the end of the regime: the Reform Communist government gave way to a coalition, and when elections were finally held, the Party lost and its state soon disappeared.

The shock of the East German revolution sealed the fate of Communism throughout the rest of the erstwhile bloc. In October 1989, the Hungarian Communists were repaid for their earlier daring when they overreached themselves by abandoning Leninism in favor of "democratic socialism." They renamed their party "Socialist" and called for the reenrollment of all members in the new organization. As a result, only thirty thousand out of seven hundred thousand members chose to remain in the Party, which was thus forced to schedule elections it was sure to lose for the following year. In November the Czechoslovaks, whose leaders had been vainly prodded by Moscow to change direction since August, at last took things into their own hands. Having witnessed the ease with which the East German regime was liquidated, they dispatched their own Party-state with even less effort in the Velvet Revolution.

There thus remained only the hard-core regimes of the Balkans. In Bulgaria, Zhivkov was replaced in November by what was in effect a Soviet-directed palace revolution; there then ensued the usual progression from a Reform Communist government to a coalition to elections. In this case the Communists won the elections only to lose power somewhat later. In Romania, the worst regime of the area met the worst fate, an actual violent revolution, in December. Romania's was also the most mysterious of the East European upheavals. Ignited by the example of events in neighboring countries as conveyed through Hungarian television, the Romanian revolution was in all probability taken over by Party loyalists who basically wanted to remove Ceausescu in order to save what they could of their positions. And it is also possible that they were encouraged to do this by Moscow, for it is well known that Gorbachev had an extreme antipathy for Ceausescu and his totally unreconstructed socialism. In any event, with all the other Communisms in the area gone, the worst exemplar of all could hardly hope to survive for long.[12]

Even Communisms outside the Soviet orbit were undermined by this debacle. The first Reform Communism, that of the original dissident of the system, Yugoslavia, also began to unravel. After Tito's death in 1980, the revised system he had bequeathed held together reasonably well for another decade. Then in 1990, in the immediate wake of the collapse of Soviet Eastern Europe, suddenly and without any crisis in internal Yugoslav conditions, the same post-Communist agenda as elsewhere became urgent: democracy, marketization, and privatization. But here the outcome was far more dire than elsewhere, and nationalism as such was only part of the problem. A major aspect of the tragedy was the exploitation of Serbian nationalism by the dying Party-state and its army in order to salvage its positions where it could. The result was a kind of national Bolshevism—to use a term from German politics of the 1920s—not without parallels with post-Ceausescu Romania or certain of the more backward ex-Soviet republics. Finally, the regime in little Albania also collapsed, and for no other reason than that the model on which it was based had disappeared.

But the most intriguing aspect of this Grand Implosion is its relationship to the master model. Moscow had clearly prodded all of its satellites in one way or another on the way to reform, but just as clearly it had not desired the result. Indeed, even when the External Empire was well on its way to collapse, Gorbachev failed to realize what was happening. As late as the German October revolution, he, as well as such "little Gorbachevs" as Pozsgay and Krenz, viewed what was unfolding as the forward march of *perestroika;* even the elimination of Ceausescu was greeted as a blow struck for Reform Communism.

Indeed, until well into the autumn of 1989 the various oppositions, from Solidarity to the Czech Civic Forum, were still worrying about where the "red line" of danger might be. It was only after the new year that it began to sink in on both sides of the barricades that an enormous shift in the balance of power had occurred; but by then it was too late for Moscow to do anything about it.

In fact, during the course of 1989 there was never a time when the Soviet Union could have done anything about it. As we have seen, Moscow was already unable to maintain public order in the Caucasus. It is therefore hardly surprising that intervention on the scale required in the two crucial countries, Poland and East Germany, was now beyond the Soviets' military and economic resources. Although Moscow had three hundred thousand troops already on the spot, they had been demoralized by *perestroika;* at home, draftees were refusing to report to duty and the treasury was bare. Politically and psychologically, intervention was even less feasible because it would have alienated the now indispensable West, destroyed support for *perestroika* at home, and thrown Gorbachev onto the not-too-tender mercies of his military and the conservatives. So Gorbachev "liberated" Eastern Europe not knowing that this was what he was doing, and because he did not have the means to do otherwise.

His whole policy had been based on the mistaken belief that the East Europeans would eagerly respond to a genuine reformed socialism if it were offered to them, and that there were many lesser Gorbachevs out there to do just that. He woefully underestimated the people's loathing of Communism and the power of national sentiment in the External Empire, just as he underestimated these same forces within the Internal Empire. But once his calculations had proved themselves mistaken, he put the best face possible on the resulting collapse. He made a creative adaptation to defeat by taking credit for the collapse as a liberation in order to salvage the cause of *perestroika* at home and to keep the esteem of the West.

THE SUPERSTRUCTURE DISSOLVES: 1990

With the new year of 1990, the boomerang of Eastern European liberation came back across the Soviet frontier to aggravate a by-now rapidly maturing internal crisis. The crisis was approaching in four interrelated forms. First, the drive for republic sovereignty was moving toward the disintegration of the Union; second, the attempt at economic reform was degenerating into the collapse of the economy; third, Soviet democratization was turning into the dismantling of Party power; and fourth and finally, Russian President Yeltsin was beginning to eclipse Soviet President Gorbachev.

The structure of action during the last two years of the regime may be summarized as follows. During the first nine months of 1990, the country was driven leftward under the propulsion of these four forces, and by early fall it seemed as if the "transition to democracy and the market" (as reformers were now saying) was imminent and Gorbachev would accept it. Then, in September, the inevitable reaction to such sweeping change emerged, Gorbachev changed sides, and the conservative trend deepened throughout the winter and into the spring of 1991. This reaction, in turn, provoked a mobilization of the "democrats" which led to Yeltsin's election as president by universal suffrage in July 1991. Finally, in a desperate effort to head off this renewed threat from the left, the old guard in August staged a putsch, nominally against Gorbachev but in fact against Yeltsin and the forces of radical change he represented. The ludicrous failure of the plotters at last demonstrated that the system had lost the strength to coerce, or even to fight for its survival. And so, the whole structure simply collapsed, the Party in August, the Union in December.

The first overt move toward this outcome occurred in Lithuania at the beginning of 1990. In order to avoid losing all support in the republic, the Lithuanian Communist Party had seceded from the Soviet Party the previous December. This was an unheard-of action, for the monolithic nature of the Soviet Party was both the guarantee of its monopoly of power and the only real bond that held the Union together. Accordingly, Gorbachev determined to resist in the Baltic states what he had just conceded in Eastern Europe, and in January he arrived in Vilnius for discussions with the Lithuanian leadership. Some 250,000 people came to the capital from across the republic to demonstrate support for independence. For three days Gorbachev was seen on Soviet television pleading with the crowds: it was in the tiny republic's self-interest, he claimed, to remain integrated with the Soviet economy. But this utilitarian argument swayed no one.

The Lithuanians pressed on, and in February the national liberation movement, Sajudis, won the local soviet elections hands-down.

The new Supreme Soviet, or Sejm, then elected Sajudis's leader, Vytautas Landsbergis, president, and on March 11 it declared the country independent. Although Moscow threateningly paraded some armored vehicles around Vilnius, it did not dare use force as it had in the Caucasus, but resorted instead to an economic blockade. In addition, since the Soviet constitution nominally recognized the right of secession, Gorbachev had the Union Supreme Soviet vote a law stipulating a complex five-year process for exercising that right, a procedure that in effect nullified it.

That such legalistic obstructionism was now a hopeless anachronism was demonstrated even more forcefully in Azerbaijan, again in January 1990. Thousands of Azerbaijani demonstrated on the border with Iran, even tearing up frontier barriers. Riots against Soviet power, led by the Popular Front, broke out in Baku. Moscow brought in troops to restore order, but it then appeared to draw back to let the situation deteriorate. Further violence was probably organized by the KGB—and perhaps with the complicity of officials at the highest levels in Moscow—to provide a pretext for an all-out showdown with the Popular Front.[13] On January 15, Baku was retaken from the Front in an action that cost at least sixty lives. This was the second bloody incident of the *perestroika* years. It also marked the end of any possibility of keeping Azerbaijan in the Union. Simultaneously, Moldavia for the first time began to show its disaffection as crowds demonstrated for reunion with Romania, something unthinkable before the fall of Ceaucescu the previous month.

Thus, all along the frontiers of the European part of the Union, the idea that there existed a new "Soviet people" was exposed as an illusion. The process that had begun with the explosion of Karabakh in February 1988 was completed with the defection of Lithuania and the suppression of Baku in January 1990. Gorbachev's effort to square the circle of the competing claims of "a strong center and strong republics," as he put it, had ended in failure.

The immediate effect of these border defections on the center was to provoke a political crisis at the top of the system. Once it became apparent that the revolution in Eastern Europe would not stop at the frontier, Gorbachev's position was for the first time seriously threatened. At a Central Committee plenum in January, he was subjected to such a storm of criticism for the recent disasters that his position "hung by a hair." He was sent to Vilnius while the plenum was underway, after that body had issued to him what amounted to an ultimatum: Either end the sedition or step down in favor of someone willing to use stronger means. It seems that he survived only by offering his resignation on the dare the plenum would not accept it in the midst of so dangerous a crisis. But whatever the details of this still somewhat mysterious meeting, it is clear that by February the whole course of *perestroika* was being rethought.[14]

The first change was the abandonment of the Party's leading role. What Gorbachev had adamantly refused to contemplate all through 1989 he now urged on a reluctant Central Committee at a continued plenum in February. With Popular Fronts proliferating within the Union, the leading role was already a fiction; and with the Parties of Eastern Europe having already abandoned their claims to hegemony in favor of a tenuous participation in power through coalitions, the Soviets' Article 6 had become an embarrassing anachronism. It was thus time to modernize the system further by explicitly abandoning the command methods of the past in favor of a "humane, democratic socialism," as Gorbachev's new slogan put it. This in effect meant jettisoning yet more ideological ballast in order to preserve the Party's practical positions; for abandoning the leading role in favor of a nominal multiparty system would still leave *the* Party with an overwhelming preponderance of institutionalized power. Moreover, such a change was in line with Gorbachev's policy of removing the Party from the direct management of public affairs and, by so doing, revitalizing the Party itself. Still, at the start of *perestroika* Gorbachev had never contemplated anything so bold as his current move, and in making it he was improvising in response to the unfolding imperatives of crisis.

In late February–March these imperatives continued to accumulate. In the long-awaited elections to local and regional soviets, the liberals, now calling themselves "democrats," made the breakthrough to power sharing that they had been working toward since the Congress of People's Deputies the previous year. At the beginning of the year the Inter-Regional Group, the Popular Fronts, and various "informals" had coalesced to form Democratic Russia. As a broad "movement," not a political party, Democratic Russia sought first to organize the local election campaigns of the entire opposition and then, using the new soviets as a base, to gradually transfer power from the Party to society. In short, its goal was to dismantle "totalitarianism," as the democrats now openly called the system. And Sajudis and the other national Popular Fronts were also out do this, and to achieve independence as well.

Yet even in the era of *glasnost* such aims could not be broadcast on television or appear in most of the press, which was still owned by the Party and still subject to censorship. Nonetheless, everyone knew that these were in fact the stakes in the elections, and both the Party and the democrats were correspondingly tense. Rumors of a crackdown were rife, so the "democrats" mobilized for the first street demonstrations in the Russian republic. On February 4, approximately three hundred thousand people marched to the Kremlin to pressure the Central Committee meeting that was to debate Article 6. Addressing the demonstrators, Afanasiev called for a new "February Revolution," by which he meant a pacific return from the Leninist principles of October to the constitutionalist principles of February. Bolder members of the crowd carried placards summoning the apparatchiki to "remember Romania." So tension continued to mount. The liberals called for another mass demonstration on February 25, with some of their leaders advancing the aim of compelling the regime to enter into Polish-style "round-table" negotiations for a transfer of power. By now Gorbachev himself felt threatened because the new demonstration would also be directed against his own plans for a stronger presidency. The authorities therefore attempted to frighten the population with televised warnings of "provocations," and the crowds on the second march were in fact smaller than those on the first.

Yet a few days later, in the local elections, the democrats won clear majorities in Moscow, Leningrad, Sverdlovsk, and the other larger cities of the Russian Federation. The political hold of the Party apparat was broken in all of these centers (though it survived substantially intact throughout the provinces). An even greater victory was scored by the Baltic Popular Fronts, and particularly by Sajudis, and its electoral success became the basis for Lithuania's declaration of independence. The nationalists of the Caucasus achieved comparable victories, and Rukh did well in Ukraine, although there the Party won a majority of the vote.

In the Union-level elections of 1989, the liberal opposition had gained a public platform and a minority parliamentary caucus. In the local elections of 1990, this opposition gained an institutional base for political action. Altogether, about a third of the Union now passed into the hands of people who had gone beyond Gorbachev's policy of restructuring the old system to a policy of dismantling it in favor of a new one. Popov became mayor of Moscow and Anatolii Sobchak of Leningrad. Yeltsin scored another triumph when he won an 80 percent majority in his election as a deputy to the Russian Supreme Soviet from Sverdlovsk. And everywhere that the democrats were in power they began a tug-of-war with the apparat over control of administrative staffs, municipal and Party property, tax revenues, the press, and television.

These changes also meant a change of policy at the top. In mid-March the Congress of People's Deputies implemented Gorbachev's new policy of legalizing political parties and at the same time created the post of executive president. Designed to be more powerful than the existing post of chairman of the Congress, the executive presidency would confer on Gorbachev a putative democratic legitimacy as a counterweight to the newly powerful opposition forces in the soviets. It would also give him increased international prestige as the would-be equal of such executives as George Bush and François Mitterrand. In addition, it would give him a stronger power base independent of the ever hostile Central Committee. Finally, it would shield him from the next Party Congress—whose scheduled date had now been moved up to late June—just in case there were another attempt to remove him from Party office like that of January, or like the coup that felled Khrushchev.

The only problem was how to organize the presidential election. The liberals preferred a direct vote by the people, and many commentators would later argue that it was a mistake for Gorbachev not to take that route: he was then still popular, and a direct though unopposed election would have given him a greatly enhanced legitimacy. But this was by no means certain: voters in the 1989 elections had been inclined to vote "no" against unopposed Party figures, and had voters shown the same tendency in a presidential election, it could have led to an embarrassingly close call, or possibly even worse. By 1990 direct unopposed election was clearly a risk Gorbachev could not take, even though polls indicated that direct election was preferred by 84 percent of the public. So Gorbachev's supporters advanced the counterargument that the crisis was too grave to delay giving the country an executive. Although Gorbachev took the safe route of unopposed election by the Soviet Congress, he gained the necessary two-thirds majority by only forty-nine votes. It is fair to say that this tenuous new dignity was taken more seriously abroad than at home.

For new challenges were immediately forthcoming from the recently empowered democrats. On May 1, Mayor Popov authorized a spontaneous demonstration as a part of the parade through Red Square, and Gorbachev was heckled off the reviewing stand atop Lenin's Mausoleum. Far more serious, Yeltsin, taking a leaf from his rival's book, posed his candidacy for "chairman" of the Presidium of the new Supreme Soviet of the Russian Federation, a post that in effect would make him president of the republic. Correctly sensing a threat, Gorbachev put his prestige on the line to oppose Yeltsin before the Russian parliament. That body, elected in February at the same time as the municipal soviets, was distinctly more conservative than the new governments of the big cities; it had only a minority of democrats, a goodly portion of Party-minded provincials and apparatchiki, and a sizeable "marsh," or swing group, in between. The contest at the end of May was accordingly close: Yeltsin won only on the third try, and by a mere four votes.

Still, he had won despite Gorbachev's open opposition, and this made him virtually a coequal national leader: Yeltsin had added a major institutional power base to his already unique status as the country's most popular political figure. And using this base, he took a leaf from the Lithuanians' book and persuaded the parliament on June 8 to vote a Russian declaration of sovereignty as a means for transferring power from the center to his and all the other republics. The boomerang had now come all the way home, for with Russia in a state of semisecession, the Union as a whole was fatally undermined; and in the ensuing weeks all the other republics voted similar declarations in what horrified apparatchiki called a "parade of sovereignties." And well might they have been horrified, for the sovereignty movement immediately generated a "war of laws" as all the republics asserted the right to nullify Soviet statutes with their own legislation. The prize was the same as in the local battles begun in the spring between the soviets and the apparat: control of property, mineral rights, tax revenues, and administrative jurisdictions. By the end of the summer all the old structures were dissolving, with the democrats pitted against the apparatchiki, and the center against the republics for possession of the rubble.

In the midst of this process—which Louis XV would have called a deluge—Gorbachev scored his last political victory at the Twenty-eighth Party Congress in early July. The purpose of the Congress was that elusive reform of the apparat which Gorbachev had pursued since he came to power, a task more urgent than ever now that the Party had lost its leading role and had acquired political competition from the revived soviets. The elections of delegates to the Congress were to be conducted in the new democratic manner, but Gorbachev, mistakenly believing that the base would follow his lead against the apparat, did not intervene actively enough, and so the apparatchiki themselves wound up providing the majority of delegates. With the democratic soviets already threatening him on the left, he was now menaced by a militantly conservative Congress on his right.

In June this right-wing menace took the form of a newly created Russian Communist Party. Of all the republics, Russia alone had never had a separate Party, because the enormous size of such an organization would have automatically made it a rival to the central, All-Union Party. This deprivation had constituted a suppressed grievance for years, all the more so since the supposedly imperial nation also had none of the other attributes of republic "sovereignty"—a separate Academy of Sciences, for example—accorded to lesser members of the Union. The Russian republic, moreover, had a lower standard of living than the border nations, in part because of its poorer soil and northern location, and in part because of the defective organization of the supply system. The Russian delegates already elected to the Union Congress seized on these grievances to found a separate Party, and Gorbachev went along with this initiative because such a Party would be a counterweight to Yeltsin's Russian Parliament. But the new Russian Party turned out to be rabidly conservative, and it elected an archfoe of *perestroika*, one Ivan Polozkov, as its First Secretary. And since the Russian delegates constituted about half of the Union Congress, there was fear that Gorbachev would be in danger when it met.

What occurred, however, was another virtuoso performance by Gorbachev: he balanced the Right against the Left, playing on each one's fear of the other to make himself appear indispensable to both, and thus became the near-unanimous choice of all to continue as General Secretary. On the one hand, he lectured the apparatchiki on the need to reform if they wished to preserve the Party's leading position in the

country; on the other hand, he emphasized his own reformist intentions in order to keep the democrats within the Party, or at least
within the circle of his personal leadership as president. "Consolidation," or unity, was his watchword, and with this theme he turned the
conservative Congress around, receiving three-quarters of its votes on
a secret ballot; for the apparatchiki feared above all a split that would
destroy the Party, and with it their own positions.

At the same time, the old Politburo was replaced by an expanded
body that included the First Secretaries of all fifteen republics; this
unwieldy arrangement meant that Gorbachev now had undivided executive authority within the Party. Accordingly, the Secretariat, already reduced in 1988, was now shrunk to almost skeletal proportions.
With these two changes the central institutions of Party government
forged by Stalin were in effect destroyed. In their place the president–
General Secretary governed with a kind of "personal politburo," the
Presidential Council (which was created in March and to which he
appointed a discordant group of figures from both the Right and the
Left), and with a Federation Council composed of the presidents of
the now rambunctious republics. But these improvised bodies constituted less a government than a permanent balancing act of a now
isolated leader amidst the accelerating deluge. For this Congress of
the last chance turned out to be the last Congress *tout court:* while it
was taking place, the Party's membership began a terminal hemor-
rhage.

The loss of Party members began with the Russian Party Congress.
The strident orthodoxy of that assemblage convinced reformist members that they had no choice but to leave; but the process gained its
full momentum when, at the Union Congress, Yeltsin resigned his
membership on national television and then walked out. Before taking this action he had warned the gathering that if the Party did not
heed the popular will for reform, it would lose its property and prerogatives and might even face trial for its misdeeds. The pretext for
his resignation was that continued membership in a single Party was
incompatible with his obligations as "president" of all of Russia. The
deeper reason was his now mature conviction that the Party was incapable of real reform, which could be pursued only outside of, and
ultimately against, it. And other leading reformers, such as Popov and
Sobchak, immediately followed suit. In short, this moment marked

the end of *perestroika* and the beginning of a genuine exit from Communism.

In this transition Boris Yeltsin, hitherto often dismissed by Moscow intellectuals and foreign statesmen alike as a "maverick populist," indeed a "buffoon," at last came into his own. For he now appeared to most of his compatriots as a genuinely charismatic figure; and his leadership from the summer of 1990 onward played an increasingly catalytic role in the outcome of the last act of the Soviet drama.

A part of Yeltsin's success was due to the fact that he had never been a classic apparatchik.[15] Though like Gorbachev he was the son of dekulakized peasants, he had not made his career entirely in the apparat by moving up through Komsomol administration to full-time Party work. Rather, he had been trained as an engineer at the Polytechnic Institute in Sverdlovsk, and then worked in that capacity in the great Urals Machinery Plant (Uralmash) before becoming a manager at age thirty-two. He had joined the Party two years earlier principally because membership was a necessity even for a nonpolitical career under "real socialism." He became Party First Secretary in Sverdlovsk in 1976 largely because, under Soviet circumstances, political power was inextricably linked to the possibility of producing those economic and social results that interested him most. In his earlier years he was a true-believer in the system and thought those results could be achieved through it; his experience of the Brezhnev era, however, convinced him, like so many others of his generation, that the system thwarted all practical improvement. He thus became an ardent convert to *perestroika,* and that was why Gorbachev made him head of the Moscow city apparat in 1986, with the sad result that we have seen.

Yeltsin's political destruction at the hands of the apparat in the fall of 1987 was apparently the crucial episode in his mature life. He became convinced that the system could not be reformed, a sentiment that was reinforced when he was vilified for the next year and a half in the Party press, with no opportunity for reply. This ordeal also made him, along with Sakharov, one of just two prominent democratic leaders who had been victims of the system; that he had suffered at its hands helped to guarantee, in the eyes of many people, the honesty of his convictions. He evidently resolved to pursue as his life's mission both his personal "political rehabilitation" and the "liberation" of Russia from the Party. With his election in 1989 as Moscow deputy-at-large by 90 percent of the vote, he began his long march to become, first, "chairman" of the Russian parliament, then patron of Russian sovereignty, and ultimately, in 1991, Russia's first democratically elected executive. It is difficult to see how any other Russian democratic leader could have managed such a feat.

And these experiences also made it possible for him, as it was not for Gorbachev, to jettison the Party, Lenin, socialism, and all of the other shibboleths of the system. For this is what his actions in 1990 amounted to, even though his public rhetoric had to be more cautious. Thus, as the months passed he pushed his radicalism to its logical conclusion by demanding the marketization and privatization of the economy. And so by the end of the summer of 1990, Yeltsin had put together the bases of Russia's post-*perestroika*, indeed post-Soviet, program. It was compounded of the principles of republic sovereignty, or the local control of resources and power; of a separate Russian presidency (whose occupant would soon be democratically elected); and, as we shall see shortly in greater detail, of an unambiguous transition to the market and private property. In bringing these three principles together, Yeltsin was of course exercising leadership to force the pace of change. But even more, he was articulating a consensus that was now emerging from the rush of events. And in no area were events moving faster or more ominously than in the economy, which was now on the verge of collapse.

This crisis, like the related crises of the nationalities and of the political system, suddenly assumed overwhelming proportions in the winter and spring of 1989-1990. The origin of the crisis was first of all internal: the scarcity of goods became extreme, exchange degenerated into barter, and the country broke up into local economic units. Here was the most fundamental crisis of all, for without the staff of life everything else would collapse. At the same time, the East European crash dramatized that this failure was one of the system per se, a problem that only a change of system, not a mere reform, could solve. So it suddenly became possible to advocate publicly the previously taboo ideas of private property and the market; and by March–April 1990 the government was actively preparing plans for a Soviet version of the Polish model of radical economic transition.

But more was involved than a change of economic policy. What occurred in the spring of 1990 was a revolution of consciousness, and not just in the former Soviet bloc but throughout the world. There was suddenly a general consensus that the market, private property, and democracy formed an organic whole; that one could not have the rule of law, human rights, constitutional government, and political pluralism without a material "base" for civil society in personal property and freedom of economic choice. This package suddenly came to define the only possible form of a feasible society—or what people in Eastern Europe now called a "normal" society—as opposed to the abnormal ideological world of scarcity, servitude, and structural inefficiency.

But this revolution of consciousness also meant the end of socialism, or at least integral socialism as it had been understood and practiced since 1917. This socialism had always been in essence noncapitalism, or the negation of private property, profit, and the market. So the advocacy of returning to these principles in essence meant that "restoration of capitalism" which had always been the ultimate crime in Soviet accusations of the class enemy. With Soviet acceptance of the necessity of a market economy, therefore, the demolition of the ideological basis of the system was complete. And so history moved to the "Right."

Accordingly, in the spring of 1990 censorship gradually collapsed, and then was legally abolished in June. For if one could talk about the market, one could talk about anything: Solzhenitsyn's *Gulag* was at last published in the summer; and by the end of the year Mikhail Soloukhin violated the ultimate taboo with a pamphlet called "Reading Lenin," in which the Founder was reduced to human and fallible size.[16] The term "totalitarian" was now openly used in print, and at times was even pronounced by Gorbachev himself. To be sure, television and the informational press still belonged to the regime, and the democrats, in what was called "demi-*samizdat*," had to resort to the subterfuge of taking over professional journals to publish their political programs. Nonetheless, the Lie was all but dead.

THE BASE CRUMBLES: 1990

The Soviet economic breakdown came in three stages. The first occurred under Brezhnev, whose stagnation aggravated the structural defects of the command-administrative system. A Soviet-type economy, as Igor Birman and Janos Kornai have argued, is by its very structure an economy of shortages.[17] Under Brezhnev, as we have seen, an increasingly complex productive system encased in an increasingly cumbersome administrative apparatus had, by the end of the 1970s, led to declining production, deteriorating quality, and a growing technological lag—and hence also to scarcity for both enterprises and consumers. The situation was further aggravated by the exhaustion of cheap natural resources and by an incentive system that gave no one any motive to work. And it is this decline that had triggered *perestroika*.

Gorbachev's remedies made a bad situation still worse, and they did so in two stages. In the first, or authoritarian, phase of economic *perestroika*, from 1985 to mid-1987, the emphasis on investment in machine tools and heavy industry increased consumer shortages; "state acceptance," or quality control, of goods also reduced production; and the anti-alcohol campaign wiped out profitable businesses. All of this, moreover, cost great sums of money, which brought to the surface for the first time the problem of the budget deficit.

Socialist economics had always treated money as something unimportant, a mere matter of tokens to facilitate exchange. So the fact that there had been a deficit since the mid-1970s, that is, roughly since the economic slowdown began, received so little attention that Andropov never told Gorbachev about it. It was only in October 1988 that the government admitted the deficit existed, and even then it did not show any great concern. Yet by then the deficit, which before Gorbachev had been around 2 to 3 percent of the GNP, had risen, as a result of his policies, to about 11 percent. And the remedy that was adopted was the usual one for desperate governments: the resort to the printing press. But this remedy, in conjunction with the growing shortages, contributed to another phenomenon unknown since the first Five-Year Plan, inflation; and inflation led to the increasing use of the dollar as a parallel currency. None of this had been anticipated because none of this was supposed to occur in socialist economies, so Gorbachev's economic reform developed without any attention to its monetary base.

These fiscal and monetary imbalances came to magnify the destabilizing effect of the second, or liberal, phase of economic *perestroika*, from mid-1987 to 1989, which even without these imbalances would have been destabilizing enough. To begin with, the new cooperatives relieved some shortages but also increased purchasing power, which in turn accelerated inflationary pressure; at the same time, the cooperatives interacted with the state sector to undercut the Plan. But the most disruptive factor of all was the program of self-management and self-financing introduced by the Law on State Enterprises. The overall effect of this program was to destroy the vertical chain of command by which the Plan had previously been carried out, without creating the channels for horizontal exchange among producers, distributors, and consumers that were necessary for a market economy.

The first disruption caused by this law arose from the fact that it was applied in two stages: enterprises producing 50 percent of the national output went over to the new system on January 1, 1988, and the other 50 percent only the following year, thus making the economy a disjointed two-track affair. But in the first stage of the reform, the enterprises did not really strike out on their own. Under the new system, 70 percent of their production was to be devoted to filling state orders, or *goszakazy* (in effect, this was the old Plan), and the rest of their output would be for other customers; these percentages were supposed to shift annually in favor of the second category. In fact, through 1989, enterprises allotted 90 percent of their effort to state orders—in part because these offered a sure market, in part because supplies still came from the central Gosnab, and in part because Gosplan and the ministries, in their own interests, encouraged this. In addition, enterprises often used their new freedom to produce modified versions of their old products but with a large markup; and since for a year managers were elected by the workers, factory directors granted large wage increases in order to compete for skilled labor in a tight market. Thus shortages, inflation, and the deficit all increased.

At the same time, the administrative apparatus of the command system was drastically cut, an effort that paralleled the concurrent pruning of the Party apparat. Between 1986 and 1989 the staffs of the ministries, of Gosplan, and of Gosnab were reduced by almost 50 percent, which meant that, willy-nilly, the enterprises were increasingly left to their own devices and to the mercies of the market. The only trouble was that there were no market institutions into which they could integrate themselves.

A market in an industrial society cannot be created by simple fiat, as was possible in the peasant-dominated societies of Russia in 1921 or China in 1979: then it had been sufficient for the state to stop interfering with the peasants' production and to let them take their goods to town in order for prosperity to return overnight. An industrial market requires complex wholesale and retail distribution networks, well-developed credit facilities, and a body of law covering everything from contracts to labor relations; it also requires disciplined habits of work, positive attitudes towards profit, and a willingness to take calculated risks. And it takes time to build such institutions and to nurture such attitudes. But the Soviet regime had actively discouraged all such developments; thus, by 1989, when the central administrative-command apparatus was half-dismantled, the state enterprises stepped out into a void.

This void, moreover, was ruled by shortages—of industrial supplies the center no longer provided, of consumer goods for the labor force, and of food for the cities. And all of these shortages occurred at the same time that the currency was rapidly losing its value. By 1990 the result of all this was a transition to rationing on a local basis, barter in place of the Plan, and the breakdown of the country into (would-be) self-sufficient regional units. Each enterprise and each locality increasingly hoarded whatever commodities it controlled. Stores in Moscow and Leningrad demanded to see residence permits before they would sell to customers; other localities introduced ration coupons; factories bartered their products for fuel, raw materials, or consumer goods needed by their employees; kolkhozes refused to part with their produce for rubles and held out for hard goods instead. At the same time, the breakdown of the center's administrative system made it impossible to coerce kolkhozniks, workers, managers, or city soviets into keeping the system functioning. Indeed, the disintegration—the "cellularization," as the experts say—of the economy was simply another aspect of the systemic decomposition known in politics as the sovereignty movement, and this in turn was a facet of the transfer of power from the hemorrhaging Party apparat to the soviets. Symbolically, the year of the last Party Congress was also the final year of the last Five-Year Plan. The system had always been of a piece, and it was only logical that all of its parts should disintegrate in unison.

This generalized collapse led to the first serious effort to go beyond the half-measures of *perestroika* and to effect not a graft of market methods onto the Plan, but rather a real transition to a market-driven economy. First, the government once again revised its strategy of economic reform. The previous year, after the First Congress of People's Deputies, Prime Minister Ryzhkov had made Leonid Abalkin, a more open-minded figure than Aganbegyan, his first deputy; and the expectation was that the government would at last act with a boldness commensurate with the crisis. But Abalkin's economic plan was watered down by the more cautious Ryzkhov, by early 1990 it was already an anachronism, so Gorbachev turned to the still more liberal-minded economist Nikolai Petrakov. Yet as a sign of the government's persisting hesitation, the talk was now of a "regulated market economy," in other words, not of the real thing. Still, in March–April experts of the government's Reform Commission were feverishly drafting decrees, and expectations were high for a breakthrough. Then Gorbachev drew back, and the only practical result of all this activity was an inept one-time price rise on bread, introduced by Ryzkhov in late May as a prelude to an ever-so-gradual transition to the market. Goods of all kinds disappeared from the stores and panic buying swept the country.

The initiative then passed to bolder hands. At the beginning of 1990, within Abalkin's Commission, a team of younger economists led by Grigorii Yavlinskii produced a plan for shock-therapy marketization and privatization—only to be turned down by Gorbachev's Presidential Council. But, after Russia's declaration of sovereignty in June, Yeltsin aggressively took up this plan and appointed Yavlinskii a deputy prime minister of Russia. Faced with this pressure, Gorbachev made up with Yeltsin in early August and the two agreed to seek a common economic program. Accordingly, Gorbachev appointed a new commission chaired by the liberal economist Stanislav Shatalin, but in fact propelled by Yavlinskii, to devise a real transition to the market. The outcome was the so-called 500-Day Plan, which both Gorbachev and Yeltsin endorsed with fanfare at the end of August: it now seemed as if the country at last had a united leadership committed to genuine transformation of the system. And Yeltsin's and Gorbachev's reconciliation seemed all the more complete in that they agreed to cooperate in devising a new constitutional structure for the now battered Union; such a structure would also be directly relevant to economic reform, given the republics' new pretensions to control their own resources.

In fact, the 500-Day Plan was as much a political as an economic document, for its provisions could hardly be implemented in the time allotted. If such a short time-frame was set, it was to give the country a sense of momentum; and the economic provisions were not intended to be comprehensive but to stake out the general direction of movement. The most important of these provisions were, first, the stabilization of the situation by massive sale of government assets to soak up the monetary overhang, and second, the rapid introduction of the market in conjunction with large-scale privatization. But perhaps the plan's most controversial proposal was to delegate to the republics the power of taxation as well as control over their natural resources, hard currency proceeds from trade, and the administration of agricultural privatization and price reform.[18] In effect, the 500-Day Plan would dissolve not only the Five-Year Plan and the Party but the Soviet state itself. And this is just the direction in which the leftward surge of 1990 had been heading all along.

Then in the early fall of 1990, this leftward momentum was broken. For while Shatalin and Yavlinskii had been drafting their plan in one dacha, in a neighboring dacha Ryzkhov and Abalkin had been drafting another; and Gorbachev put the two (incompatible) documents before the Supreme Soviet in September. Although the Ryzkhov-Abalkin plan indeed provided for a transition to the market, it proposed taking five years, not five hundred days, to get there; and it delegated no powers to the republics. Gorbachev at first called for a "synthesis" of these two plans and he brought back Aganbegyan to produce it—in effect to square a circle, as Gorbachev well knew. He then turned down the resulting compromise and retreated still further by persuading the Supreme Soviet to give him three weeks to synthesize what were now three plans. In October, all that was actually approved were a few generalities from the Shatalin plan and airy platitudes about "deep reforms." With this scuttling of the 500-Day Plan *perestroika* was in fact dead, although this would not become apparent until several months later. Gorbachev now found himself increasingly defending the status quo.

At the time, Gorbachev's October backtracking appeared to many as yet another of his tactical retreats designed to buy off the Right before moving forward again. Most democrats still hoped for a "Left-center coalition" as a solution to the deepening crisis. In fact, for the first time they had encountered the real Gorbachev. The 500-Day Plan, if implemented, would have dismantled the system, and that was just what Yeltsin and the plan's sponsors desired. But Gorbachev, as ever preoccupied with politics—the Party Congress, the Union Treaty, and German reunification—realized the Shatalin plan's revolutionary implications only belatedly, and so sabotaged it while appearing to put it into effect.

For when the chips were down, he could not accept the abandonment of "socialist property," the sovereignty of the market, or a real devolution of power within the Union. Nor, it must be added, could he accept the diminution of his own "presidential" power. In short, for all his rhetoric about revolutionary change, Gorbachev had never been anything more than a Reform Communist, albeit of a very advanced sort. Or more exactly, he was a Reform Communist who had never understood the structural limitations on reform imposed by the nature of the system. So he rashly pushed restructuring to the point where he had irreparably "destructured" the system and then drew back when it was too late to stop the forces he had conjured up. So, like the sorcerer's apprentice, he would spend the rest of his time in power trying to ride the deluge he had unleashed.

REACTION AND COLLAPSE: SEPTEMBER 1990–DECEMBER 1991

Thus the last year of the Gorbachev era—from the October retreat of 1990 to the August putsch of 1991—is essentially a long epilogue to *perestroika* and to the Soviet phenomenon itself. Having broken with the economic plans of the democrats, Gorbachev was forced to rely increasingly on the old establishment, which was now in a mood of militant reaction against the radical breakthrough of the summer. And this, in turn, could only further radicalize the democrats, and thereby set the stage for the showdown test of strength that would culminate in the putsch.

If Gorbachev's October retreat was at bottom a matter of conviction, this conviction was reinforced by pragmatic calculations of power.[19] For, though the democrats were now carried forward by the strength of public opinion, the real power in the country remained with the Party apparat, the KGB, the army, and the military-industrial complex, which controlled nearly half of the country's economy and employed probably one third of its work force. And these centers of power made it increasingly clear to Gorbachev that if he did not halt the democrats, they would do so in his place. So to keep his place he went along.

In September, mysterious army maneuvers around Moscow had been widely interpreted as a warning to Gorbachev to change course. In October, tense meetings with leaders of the military-industrial complex, and pressure from Vasilii Starodubtsev's new "Peasant Union," which represented some three million kolkhoz bureaucrats, helped persuade Gorbachev to bury the 500-Day Plan. In November, stormy sessions with more than one thousand army officers convinced him that the conservatives were nearing the boiling point. Accordingly, in early December he replaced the liberal interior minister Vadim Bakatin with the former KGB general Boris Pugo. Later in December, the tepid reformer Ryzhkov was eased out as prime minister, to be replaced in January by the die-hard, old-line economist Valentin Pavlov. In a final personnel change, in December Gorbachev forced a reluctant Congress of People's Deputies to elect the incompetent Gennadii Yanaiev as vice president. At the same time, state radio and television were placed under a conservative official responsible to Gorbachev alone; in January the program *View* was closed down, and Gorbachev sought to repeal the law on press freedom of the previous year. It was in the midst of these changes, in late December, that Shevardnadze dramatically resigned with an enigmatic warning against the "onset of dictatorship." And, indeed, Starodubtsev, Pugo, Pavlov, and Yanaiev would all show up among the leaders of the August coup.

In mid-January 1991, what was by now a creeping coup d'état went into action with bloody military attacks against the communications facilities in Lithuania and Latvia. The intention behind these actions seems to have been to put down these troublesome secessionist republics as a prelude to cracking down in the center, for in February soldiers were assigned to patrolling the streets of Moscow. At the same time, using almost Stalinist language, Pavlov claimed that Western economic aid was part of a plot to destroy Soviet socialism; meanwhile, KGB chief Kriuchkov accused the CIA of conspiring to subvert the Communist system through agitation for the market. Simultaneously, Pavlov confiscated all bills larger than fifty rubles, ostensibly to reduce the monetary overhang, and Gorbachev gave the KGB full powers to fight "economic crime" by searching all business offices, including joint ventures; it is quite likely that these were an inept prelude to a program of rigid state economic controls designed to accompany the police actions already in progress. Then, unaccountably, all of this activity stopped, as if its perpetrators did not dare to follow through.

Nonetheless, the conservatives' activity had sufficed to produce a new mobilization of the democrats: over a hundred thousand demonstrators protested in Moscow's streets against the bloodshed in the Baltic states, and Yeltsin, no doubt thinking he would be the old guard's next target, called for Gorbachev's resignation and even for a "declaration of war" by the democrats against the president. And indeed he *was* the next target, for in March the Communist plurality in the Russian parliament attempted to impeach Yeltsin as chairman. This strategy was thwarted, however, when he successfully called for a massive demonstration of his supporters on March 28 in direct defiance of a ban by Gorbachev, a ban backed up by fifty thousand troops. Several hundred thousand people assembled nonetheless, and the day ended without violence in a political victory for the democrats. And by this time the sparring extended well beyond Moscow: strikers in the Siberian coal fields and the Bielorussian factories expressed support for Yeltsin and called for Gorbachev's resignation, while the latter reacted by denouncing the "Bolshevik" street tactics of his opponents.

But the most important result of the March crisis was the creation of a Russian presidency whose occupant would be chosen by universal suffrage. And this development was intimately linked with another process transpiring that spring, namely Gorbachev's quest for a new Union Treaty. From the eruption of Nagornyi Karabakh in 1988 until Lithuania's declaration of independence in early 1990, Gorbachev had treated the nationalities as a secondary problem. But he was at last frightened into action by the "parade of sovereignties" of the summer of 1990, and from that time onward saving the Union was his primary preoccupation, far ahead of economic reform.

By November 1990 he had the draft of a new Union Treaty to replace the founding document of 1922. It proposed changing the country's name to Union of Sovereign Soviet Republics but essentially retained most of the real power at the center. Since this was not acceptable to the republics, he tried to undercut them by organizing a referendum for March 17, 1991. It asked voters to approve the preservation of the Union as a "renewed federation of equal Soviet republics"—language so vague it would be difficult to say no. In response to this would-be clever move, Yeltsin made a genuinely clever one: he persuaded the Russian parliament to append to Gorbachev's referendum its own separate question on the establishment of a popularly elected Russian president. Gorbachev's referendum was approved by 70 percent of the Soviet voters, whereas Yeltsin's referendum received the approval of 85 percent of Russian voters. Faced with this pressure, the Russian Congress of People's Deputies set the presidential election for June 12.

After the March victory of Yeltsin and his democrats against the second phase of the creeping coup d'état, Gorbachev in April had to double back to the Left. Still in pursuit of a new Union Treaty, he entered into secret negotiations with the leaders of the nine republics that had not declared their intention of seceding, negotiations in which Yeltsin and his colleagues held the strong hand. These discussions were roughly the Soviet equivalent of the Polish "round table," a parallel the democrats explicitly drew.

The resulting "9-plus-1" agreement, although formally a compromise, gave far more to the 9 than to the 1. Gorbachev obtained a call for "work discipline" to stabilize the economy, and the end of the strikes that had recently supported Yeltsin. But the 9 obtained implicit acceptance of the Baltic and the Caucasian republics' right to secede, which was also the guarantee of real sovereignty for those that remained; this was spelled out by the transfer of significant economic and administrative power to all member republics, and by the promise of a new constitution and genuinely democratic elections throughout the Union by 1992. In addition, Russia received ownership of all mines on its territory; a separate KGB; and an independent television, which at last broke the government's monopoly of the most important of the media.

The next month the democrats consolidated their victory when Yeltsin, after stumping Russia with an overtly anti-Communist program, won the June 12 elections hands down. He did so on the first round with 57 percent of the vote against two Communist candidates, the conservative Ryzhkov and the liberal Bakatin, who had been fielded to split the vote and force Yeltsin into a run-off, while the far-right candidate Vladimir Zhirinovskii received 7 percent. The revolutionary import of the election was driven home symbolically by a municipal vote to change the name of Leningrad back to St. Petersburg. The outcome of June 12 meant that it was merely a question of time before the Communists, now clearly in the minority, would lose power. Thus they launched their third coup attempt of the year.

In late June Pavlov went before the Supreme Soviet and demanded that the decree powers normally held by the president be transferred to himself. At the same time, Yazov, Kriuchkov, and Pugo told a closed session of the legislature that the country faced an imminent disaster, and they clearly implied that Gorbachev was responsible. Though this was insubordination verging on sedition, Gorbachev came up with nothing more forceful in response than to appear before parliament to harangue the deputies into refusing Pavlov's demands. But no one was arrested or even fired. Gorbachev had clearly lost control of the situation and of his own government; even worse, he did not seem to know it. And so he sleepwalked into the final showdown of August.

Along the way, and under continuing pressure from Yeltsin, Gorbachev in late July agreed to expand the promises of the 9-plus-1 agreement into a draft of a radically decentralizing Union Treaty. This document conceded to the republics the authority to collect taxes and to retain a portion thereof, turning over only a share to the center. Thus Gorbachev's quest for a new Treaty, undertaken to save the Union, wound up providing for its near dissolution; and he scheduled the signing of this document for August 20. He then departed to London for a summit of the seven leaders of the major industrial states, the G-7, in the hope of promoting a "grand bargain," or Marshall plan, whereby Western aid would secure a stable Russia. His position was weakened further when he came back empty-handed.[20]

On his return home he made his last attempt to save the situation by seeking to transform the Party into a quasi-social-democratic organization. In a final bravura performance—he always spoke well—Gorbachev persuaded a meeting of the Central Committee to endorse a new Party platform that jettisoned Marxism-Leninism in favor of a vague "humane and democratic socialism," as if such a deathbed conversion of the Party by verbal formula would make a difference to the country. This was the tactic of the Hungarian and the other East European Parties in 1989, and it worked no better now than it had then.

*   *   *

It is these concessions of July that provoked the final coup attempt in August. Although its beginning date, August 19, was no doubt determined by the fact that the new Union Treaty was to have been signed on the 20th, its real motivation was to stave off the defeat of the system that had been looming since the June elections, indeed since the 500-Day Plan of the summer of 1990. As such, it was a belated act of desperation, ineptly carried out after three previous and hesitant attempts, by people who no longer believed they stood a real chance.

The "general staff" of the coup had been in place for months: to the names already mentioned it is only necessary to add Oleg Baklanov of the Defense Council, that is, the military-industrial complex, and Valerii Boldin, the chief of Gorbachev's personal cabinet. In short, the coup was not an action of some adventitious "coup plotters"; it was an action of the Soviet government itself, and was carried out in defense of the existing Communist establishment. Its initial aim was to force Gorbachev to declare a state of emergency and to "restore order" by putting down Yeltsin and the democrats. Its leaders probably believed that Gorbachev, faced with the dangers to the state of repudiating their initiative, would join them. Moreover, the option of a state of emergency had been under consideration in the government for a long time and could hardly come as a surprise to Gorbachev. Nonetheless, when he was confronted by the conspirators with the emergency decree to be signed, he backed off with the answer that the matter should be referred to the Supreme Soviet. So they decided to depose him in favor of his vice president and to declare the emergency themselves. But the move had been inadequately prepared. The army and the KGB did not dutifully follow orders as the government expected; thus Yeltsin and the democrats had time to organize a resistance that in three days produced the collapse of the conspirators' will, and with it the collapse of the regime. Thus the August putsch was, mutatis mutandis, analogous to General Kornilov's failed action in 1917: it demonstrated that the Right had no force, and so permitted the Left to rush forward in revolutionary fashion to destroy the old order.

And there was preparation and a real political will on the side of Yeltsin and the democrats. Gorbachev had not been entirely wrong in comparing them earlier to the Bolsheviks, for in response to the governmental "junta" the democrats mounted what was in effect a countercoup to insure that the system did collapse completely. Alerted by their near-brush with doom during the winter, and enlightened about their adversaries' mode of operation by their own past as Party members, they had prepared in advance for just such a contingency as the one they encountered in August: all they did not know was the date.

Their strategy was, first, to act scrupulously within the framework of the new Soviet *Rechtstaat*, claiming to work only for the defense of the constitution and the restoration of the legitimate authority of Gorbachev. Their more basic strategy, however, was to use their power base in the Russian republic—its new KGB, the army units that had supported Yeltsin in the elections, and its Council of Ministers together with related staff—to turn the Russian Federation's "White House" into a command post for thwarting the putschists—that is, the Soviet government. Once this strategy had succeeded, on the second day of the coup, they exploited the crisis in order to dismantle the Party-state, which had been their real aim all along.

And they succeeded because they had popular support where it counted. To be sure, Yeltsin's appeal on the first day to the Moscow population for a general strike failed. But this was largely because with tanks in the streets people believed that the Soviet government had already won—as it always had in the past—and Party members anxiously started paying up back dues. Yet once Yeltsin's resistance had demonstrated the coup's failure, the real feelings of the populations of the capital and St. Petersburg burst out in the open in a euphoric rush to liberation. Although these sentiments were most marked in the large urban centers that since 1989 had voted for the democrats (the provinces remained largely passive), there can be no doubt that the politically active elements of the population supported Yeltsin's countercoup. The Dzerzhinskii monument was toppled, the Lenin statues started coming down, the red flag was replaced by the tricolor of the Provisional Government of 1917, and the Central Committee headquarters on Old Square was sequestered by the government of the Russian Federation. Thus Yeltsin and the democrats, in ostensibly defending the existing Soviet order, in fact subverted it; in the guise of preserving political continuity they made a revolution.

Gorbachev's behavior upon his return to Moscow completed the task of discrediting the system, and his person. First, he did not go immediately to thank his saviors at the White House, but instead telephoned his fellow heads of state in the West to inform them of his deliverance. Second, he did not go to the Russian parliament, but instead called a press conference where he talked not of the country but only of his personal ordeal during the coup. Finally, he failed to notice that the country had changed completely during the three days of the coup, and instead asserted that the Communist Party remained indispensable to the further progress of *perestroika*. So when he at last visited Yeltsin and the parliament, he was met with hostile cries that the Party was "a criminal enterprise"; Yeltsin made him read the minutes of his Council of Ministers approving the coup; and the Russian president then ostentatiously signed a decree—obviously prepared in advance—suspending the Party throughout Russia. These televised proceedings went over badly with the Western public, which still thought that Gorbachev was in charge and that after what the West misjudged as a "failed coup" (not a revolution) *perestroika* would proceed as before. But in Russia the televised confrontation played very well, for the population was genuinely indignant that Gorbachev's *perestroika* had brought the country so low and that he failed so completely to understand what had happened.

Thus, although nominally restored to power, Gorbachev was in fact now only a figurehead, indeed something of a hostage, whom Yeltsin and the democrats then used to give a legal basis to the liquidation of the main institutions of the system. First, he was told to appoint Yeltsin candidates to the posts of minister of defense and head of the KGB, and control of the economy was taken from him and put under the Russian prime minister. When realization that the country had fundamentally changed at last sunk in, Gorbachev dissolved the Central Committee and resigned as General Secretary. Next, he was employed as president to engineer the self-liquidation of the Union's Supreme Soviet and the Congress of Peoples' Deputies—thus demolishing his own major reform. At the same time, all the republics that had not yet done so declared their independence, thus in fact dissolving the Union. The final blow to the system came in late October, when Yeltsin, by decree, transformed his suspension of the Communist Party into a permanent ban and confiscated all of the Party's property.

There remained only two major matters to be cleared up before this revolution would be complete: first, there was the still formal existence of a Soviet state, the titular possessor of an enormous nuclear arsenal and the signatory of numerous international obligations. Second, there was the persistent illusion of that state's "president" that he still governed, an illusion even more strongly held in foreign capitals.

On the surface it would seem plausible to preserve the political framework of the Union in some form in order to provide a unified economic space, to serve as a buffer among the nationalities, and to execute existing international treaties. But to argue in this way, as many have, is to forget that the Union was in fact a fraud, an agency not of its members but of the Party, a structure entirely imposed from above and as such an instrument of oppression to almost all its non-Russian and many of its Russian inhabitants. With the Party gone, there was no force—neither the army, nor the ruble, nor the *lingua franca* of the Russian language—capable of holding the Union together. Realistically accepting this fact, Yeltsin and the democrats not only refrained from resisting secession but indeed facilitated the dismantling of the Union and even accepted the radical decentralization of the Russian Federation itself. The rationale behind this seemingly risky strategy was that it was first necessary to destroy the old state structures so that later the Russian Federation, and possibly some confederal successor to the Union, might reconstitute themselves from below in authentically democratic fashion.

After the August Revolution, therefore, there was no longer any point in seeking a new Union Treaty. Still, Gorbachev kept trying, in part because he was genuinely committed to the Union, both as a matter of utility and as a matter of national grandeur, but in part also because he needed something to be president of. And this anachronistic persistence, which was also a potential political threat to the democrats, in fact only helped to doom the Union, since by November it had become clear that this rival executive would not retire so long as there existed a shadow of the old state.

But what finally sealed the Union's fate was the radical economic choice of Yeltsin's government. He returned to the goals of the 500-Day Plan—marketization and privatization—if not to its actual provisions for achieving them. After some hesitation, in late October he opted for a still more radical policy of "shock-therapy" price liberalization and appointed Yegor Gaidar prime minister to carry it out. And, as was the case with the 500-Day Plan, this policy entailed far-reaching republic sovereignty as a means of diffusing economic power to promote economic initiative. In the wake of the August

Revolution and after Gaidar's appointment, however, the Russian Federation was moving far more rapidly toward a liberal economy than were the other republics, which indeed had no program of reform at all. Moreover, the Russian Federation had dismantled the Party-state much more thoroughly than had most of the other republics, where the old Party apparat and economic *nomenklatura* were still in power, though now under national flags. Since meshing Russian shock therapy with these republics' conservatism would have only hobbled reform, Gaidar's "Young Turks" became determined to cut free from the Union.

The coup de grâce came in December, when Ukraine confirmed its parliament's earlier declaration of independence in a referendum, thereby in effect ending the Union. So at Yeltsin's instigation the three Slavic republics—Russia, Ukraine, and Belorus—formally declared the Union to be defunct and replaced it, following an old idea of Sakharov's, with a loose Commonwealth of Independent States. As an intended by-product of this change, Gorbachev was left with no choice but to retire.

Thus, by December 25, 1991, when the red flag came down over the Kremlin for the last time and Gorbachev read his farewell address over television, none of the key Soviet institutions remained. The process that had begun with the collapse of Leninism in Eastern Europe in 1989 was now completed with Leninism's collapse in the mother country. As one Russian commentator put it, the Soviet Union had suffered the structural equivalent of defeat in a major war.[21]

In fact, the Soviet catastrophe was worse, for it was self-inflicted. The Russian Imperial regime, which by 1914 was already in an advanced state of decay, nonetheless still had to undergo three years of bloody war before it fell apart in February 1917. And the only other comparable collapses in this century, those of the Axis and of Japan in 1945, were produced by crushing military defeat. But that an ostensibly advanced industrial nation and superpower should collapse without any large-scale military defeat, after forty-five years of peace, and essentially from internal causes, is unheard of in modern history.

13

THE PERVERSE LOGIC
OF UTOPIA

In my beginning is my end.

—*T. S. Eliot, "East Coker"*

What is primarily at issue is not the applicability of the totalitarian model to Stalin's Russia. . . . What is at issue is socialism. For some, it is a matter of moral urgency to link the victims of Stalinist terror to socialism; for others, it is no less urgent to detach the terror from the socialist cause and show it to be an aberration . . . [and thereby to] uphold the honor of Soviet socialism. . . .

—Russian Review, *introducing a debate on Stalinism in 1986*

Amidst the rubble left over from seventy-four years of the Soviet socialist experiment, what has become of our classical categories for explaining that greatest of all utopian adventures of the modern age? Have any new questions emerged from the unprecedented manner of its demise? And what does the collapse portend for the future, above all of Russia and the other former Communist countries, but also of socialism as such? Leaving these last two questions for a speculative epilogue, we will begin with interpretations of the past.

THE ROOTS OF FRAGILITY

A few new questions have indeed emerged, but on closer examination most lead back to the old debates around the reformability of the Soviet system. These new questions, of course, no longer raise that issue primarily in terms of the legitimacy of October, the NEP alternative, or the "necessity" of Stalin. Instead they focus, though now in the past tense, on the great question debated during *perestroika* itself: could Gorbachev's reforms have succeeded? But this, of course, is just another formulation of the implicit central question about Sovietism since Khrushchev: can a Leninist system transform itself into a social democracy and/or a semimarket socialism?

One might think that the great crash of 1989–1991 would have settled these questions once and for all with the conclusion that Communism was irreformable, since it in fact failed to reform itself. But no: the objection is raised that because something did not happen, this does not mean it could never have happened. And as a matter of abstract logic, this is true. But we are not dealing with abstract logic. We are dealing with concrete historical events, and the cascade of Communist collapses in 1989–1991 ought surely to tell us something about the logic of that particular system.

Yet this fact has been slow to sink in. We thus hear once again of promising alternatives in Soviet history, and breathe the sweet scent of nostalgia for all the roads not taken, from the NEP onward. In its new guise, this nostalgia takes the form that the Soviet collapse was produced by accidents and errors of the last years of the regime, and hence that it represented a contingency that might have been averted.[1] Another way of putting this proposition is that the Soviet collapse of 1991 was not a revolutionary break, as Yeltsin and the democrats claim, but a "transition to democracy and the market," and thus the "evolutionary" fulfillment of. Reform Communism and *perestroika*. Indeed, after August this was the position of Gorbachev himself. And all of this, of course, raises again the issue of predetermination versus freedom in the unfolding of the experiment.

There is indeed something to this evolutionary perspective—but only if we restrict ourselves to the proximate causes of the collapse. And these causes have been examined in detail in the preceding two chapters. To recapitulate: The most fundamental cause was the economic decline and its repercussions for the Soviet Union's superpower status. It is this crisis of performance that moved Gorbachev to launch *perestroika* in the first place; and this restructuring soon led him to attack the Party, and so run what turned out to be the suicidal risks of *glasnost* and then of democratization. Finally, the economic decline discredited the claims of the ideology, and *glasnost* made it possible to proclaim this fact, thereby delegitimizing the system and, ultimately, depriving it of the will to coerce. And this circumstance in turn made possible the revolt of the minority nationalities and the collapse of the people's democracies. Finally, we may include in the chain of causation various tactical errors of Gorbachev, such as pushing democratization faster than economic liberalization, or, at the end, surrounding himself with conservative enemies of his own reforms.

But explanation of the Soviet collapse by these proximate causes, together with the evolutionary perspective in which they are usually inserted, is, like so much of the old Sovietology, both a mode of analysis and a political statement. As already noted, this approach is a continuation of the expectations aroused by *perestroika*—indeed the last gasp of what Amalrik called the "ideology of reformism," prolonged beyond the life of what was supposed to have been reformed. Or perhaps it is not quite the last gasp, for the evolutionary argument returned in the immediate post-Communist period to condemn Yeltsin's shock-therapy conversion to the market and urge retention of as much as possible of the "accomplishments" of Soviet socialism: state ownership, a strong "industrial policy" of residual planning, and a broad social safety net; and at times such communal solidarity was also represented as the authentic Russian tradition, somewhat as old-regime Populists had argued.

In the post-Soviet context, this return of the ghost of Reform Communism has usually gone by the reassuring names "centrism" and "gradualism," by which is meant a reasonable median course between a discredited Communism and an imported ideology of unregulated capitalism. In short, we have been offered a post-Communist version of the famous "third way" that has been with us since the 1930s and that was also associated with the Western cult of "Gorby." Not surprisingly, therefore, many of the former votaries of *perestroika* in both Russia and the West have become proponents of "centrism," and erstwhile Gorbophiles have made a comeback as Yeltsinophobes.[2] Indeed, it is amazing how little Communism's fall did to change the basic structure of the debate about Communism's meaning.

It is therefore all the more necessary to emphasize that the proximate "causes" of Communism's collapse are not discrete or adventitious phenomena, a rearrangement of which could have permitted *perestroika* to salvage the system. Rather, they are parts of a pattern arising from the nature of that system itself. Thus, the post-1991 questions about the putative promise of *perestroika* turn out to be in the same category as earlier questions about the reformability of Communism—that is, they are false questions. The real new questions concern the sources of the extraordinary fragility of Communism at its end. For the collapse of 1989–1991 was truly amazing: Indeed, nothing about Communism ever astounded the world so much as the manner of its exit from history. One of the world's two superpowers imploded without its guardians offering any serious resistance to the debacle. The most militant political movement of the modern age, which in its time had made a career of armed insurrections and minority coups d'état, at the end proved capable only of the pitiful farce of August 1991.

The explanation of this terminal fragility lies in those long-term "systemic" flaws of the Soviet system that have been the subject of all the preceding chapters. So to recapitulate again: The Soviet system had its deepest origins in, and drew its justification from, the moral idea of socialism as the fullness of human equality. This moral idea necessarily leads to an instrumental program for the suppression of the prime sources of inequality: private property, profit, and the market, an ensemble of institutions called capitalism. This program was supposed to emerge by itself from the logic of history (which is also the logic of democracy). In fact, however, history refused to cooperate in producing the requisite instrumental program, and so the latter had to be implemented coercively through a new and unique political instrument: the Party.

Thus, the enduring formula of Sovietism is maximalist or integral socialism as the alleged culmination of the logic of history in conjunction with the dictatorship of the Party substituting for history's allegedly annointed vehicle, the universal class of the proletariat. This formula has been abbreviated in these pages to "ideocratic partocracy." It is building socialism with this blunt instrument, not development or modernization, that the Soviet experiment was all about. But such an enterprise is intrinsically impossible, for the primitive military means of the partocracy by their very nature cannot realize the combined ideological ends of an efficient economy and a just, egalitarian society. Under such circumstances, the building of Soviet socialism could proceed only as a mixture of ideological illusion and raw coercion. And this meant that the whole "experiment" unfolded in perverse fashion from its beginnings, that is, from the first Bolshevik attempt to coerce history by the October coup of 1917 and the ensuing effort of 1918 to build Communism by military means. From this "original sin" flowed all of the succeeding acts of coercion, starting with the revolution from above of 1929–1933, continuing with the purges, and culminating with the postwar restoration of the system.

It is necessary to emphasize, however, that this argument is in no way a deterministic one. So to recapitulate one final time: The "logic" of Soviet history that has been developed in these pages amounts to an "if-then" argument.[3] In other words, once a given event in the life of a nation has occurred, certain avenues of development are thereby foreclosed, and only another, narrower range of possibilities remains open. Thus Russia in 1917 could have evolved into a constitutional democracy (an option that includes a "soft" socialist welfare state, as in the West), or a national authoritarianism, or a Communist dictatorship. But once the "socialist choice" (as Gorbachev used to say) was made, only a very narrow range of options remained possible—that is, possible without abandoning the system. This confining circumstance has been called in these pages Communism's "genetic code." Specifically, this means that given the Bolsheviks' goal of integral socialism in conjunction with the dictatorship of the Party, the Soviet regime could accept only those programs that both suppressed "capitalism" and preserved the Party's monopoly of power, for anything else would have annulled the famous "national choice made in October."

In practice this course meant permanent revolution from above. But since such a regimen, if pursued too relentlessly, would also have menaced the regime by destroying the country, it had to be tempered by periodic retreats to some form of NEP, thus producing a pattern of alternation between "hard" and "soft" Communism. But soft Communism could not be permitted to triumph either, for it too would have destroyed the regime. Thus Bukharin and the NEP were never the real alternative to Stalinism. The real options for a system founded on the Leninist choice were either doing, and then adamantly defending, approximately what Stalin did, or abandoning the whole system; and this latter outcome is just where Gorbachev's neo-Bukharinism led in 1989–1991. Bukharin and the NEP were never more than the eternal—and indispensably comforting—illusion of achieving that contradiction in terms: democratic Communism, or "socialism with a human face."

Yet a "permanent" revolution from above cannot be sustained indefinitely. After an initial burst of economic expansion under Stalin, Communism therefore yielded progressively diminishing returns. At the same time, the brutal results of the instrumental program increasingly belied the original moral inspiration. Thus, no sooner had socialism been built in the 1930s than the Myth on which it was founded was transformed into the Lie. Then, with creeping economic decline and the moral failure of the regime during the long years after Stalin, the credibility of the ideology evaporated; and without the prop of ideology, the Party's will to coerce eroded. By the time of Gorbachev, this erosion permitted a nascent civil society to challenge the Party's hegemony. So when the apparat's inevitable attempt to roll back reform was made in August 1991, it was defeated ignominiously, and the whole decrepit structure collapsed in three days. For it had always been only a question of time before the internal contradictions of the impossible undertaking of "building socialism" worked themselves out to a total discrediting—and hence to the brusque implosion—of the system. If in the end Communism collapsed like a house of cards, it was because it had always been a house of cards.

In sum, there is no such thing as socialism, and the Soviet Union built it. Thus, when a disastrously noncompetitive economic performance at last made this paradox apparent, the institutionalized fantasy of "really existing" Marxism vanished into thin air. The "surreality" of Sovietism suddenly ceased, and Russia awoke as from a bad dream amidst the rubble of a now septagenarian disaster.[4] And the rest of the world awoke with her from the morbid fascination with October that has dominated our short twentieth century.

Still, there *was* something incomplete about the August revolution in 1991. It is perhaps no accident that the terms "failed coup" or "putsch" were not immediately replaced by the more appropriate "August Revolution," or that Yeltsin's revolutionary marketization and privatization were persistently referred to as "reform," as if he were some Gorbachev II. To be sure, 1991 was a less sharp break than 1917 or 1789, but then there are only two such tectonic dates in modern history. So where does August 1991 fall on the revolutionary Richter scale?

One can argue, on the side of evolution, that violence was minimal, that most of the old actors were still there after the deluge, many of them in their old jobs, and that the essential changes in mentalities and, partially, in institutions had occurred in 1989 and 1990, not in the wake of August. All true, as far as it goes. But if we go a bit farther, we see that in 1991 the Communist Party was destroyed and a super-power was dismembered; "socialism" was renounced by the world's first socialist society in favor of the "restoration of capitalism"; and the most enduring fantasy of the twentieth century, the pseudoreligion-cum-pseudoscience of Marxism-Leninism, simply evaporated. Nor could any of these things have occurred as a gradual process and without the August shock: a test of strength between the forces of the old order and those of the new was imperative to effect the "transition."

In normal parlance, all of this qualifies as "revolution." After all, the basic components of the Soviet system—the Party, the Plan, the political police, and the Union—were not transformed; they were abolished, and in the short span of three months after August. To argue that this destruction was in reality an evolution is a bit like arguing that because Louis XVI had summoned the Estates General and then remained on a diminished throne until 1792, the events of 1789 represented an evolutionary rather than a revolutionary exit from absolutism and Louis therefore should be congratulated for "liberat-ing" France, as Gorbachev has been for liberating Russia. (In fact, Louis was so congratulated during the first two ambiguous years after the fall of the Bastille; it seems that the true significance of world-historical dates is always slow to sink in.)

Still, the revolutionary exit from Communism of 1989–1991 was revolution with a major difference. Although the word "revolution" has no single or fixed meaning,[5] it usually implies a breakthrough of already-formed and vital forces against an outworn shell of power. In England in 1640 and 1688 such a force was a venerable Parliament; in British North America in 1776 it was thirteen already self-governing colonies; in France a few years later it was a dynamic Third Estate that could plausibly assert that it was, in the words of the abbé Sieyès, the whole nation. And in all three cases these forces were supported by men of substance and property. But in the Communist case, al-though the old shell of power was indeed hollow, there were no preexisting structured forces—whether political, economic, or social—ready to take over: after the Soviet deluge there was only a void.

Thus, the August anti-Soviet revolution was a revolution not by breakthrough but by implosion. And the force that took over from the

Communist regime was a relatively unstructured "civil society" of former dissidents, ideological democrats, and moral leaders. To revert to Marxist terminology, they constituted a superstructure without a base: they were quite lacking in material power or property of their own because these were still controlled by the old *nomenklatura*—real socialism had done its work of social pulverization only too well. And this insubstantiality of civil society was also true of the equally weak ethnic-territorial units of the former "republics." Though the program of the democrats throughout the former Soviet Union had been to build a "normal" society of multiparty democracy and a market economy, the result of the implosion was to leave them with only paltry means for doing so. Thus the legacy of seventy-four years of Communist "development" was not "modernization" but generalized institutional rubble.

THE CUNNING OF UTOPIA

And this perverse outcome has very much to do with the perverse logic of integral socialism itself.[6] But this aspect of the Soviet disaster is seldom explored because of the emotional charge emanating from the socialist idea. The problem is this: Since socialism set out to realize the "noble dream" of human equality and fraternity, how could it have produced such palpably bad results in Soviet practice? One way to solve this problem, as we have seen, is to blame the bad results on Russian backwardness or on the failure of the Western revolution to come to Bolshevism's rescue or on the heritage of Ivan the Terrible, and by these means to exonerate socialism itself for another try. Another "solution" is to say that Soviet Communism was not genuine socialism, for the authentic article is by definition democratic.[7]

Not to put too fine a point on it, all such approaches are patent evasions, and the awful truth must as last be faced. For if we look closely at what basic socialism means, the obvious answer to the false paradox of good ends and bad results is that the Soviet experiment turned totalitarian not *despite* its being socialist but *because* it was socialist. Indeed, socialism—in the integral or maximalist sense of Marx and of the Second International—is the ideal formula for totalitarianism. For the suppression of "capitalism"—in the form of private property, profit, and the market—means the extermination of civil society and the statization of all aspects of life; and, since such an unnatural order cannot come into existence by itself, integral socialism also means institutionalized coercion by the Party.

To put the matter in its simplest terms, full socialist nationalization, by concentrating all political and economic power in one set of hands, leads inevitably to monstrous crimes against the individual and the people at large. Although Stalin represented the apogee of this development, the Leninist law of primitive socialist accumulation of power obtained to the end of the regime; and the idea that under Stalin's successors the Party-state bureaucracy, local Party "prefects," and professional "interest groups" provided a functional equivalent to a normal society with multiple loci of power is simply social-science double-think.

Seen in this institutional context, the initial "noble dream" of socialism only makes matters worse because it has the perverse effect of legitimizing and thus amplifying the coercive concentration of power. Yet this cruel paradox really should not be too hard to grasp, or to require once again rephrasing as Hegel's Cunning of Reason: it is no more than the standard folk wisdom about that infernal road which is paved with good intentions.

Socialist good intentions, moreover, helped make Soviet totalitarianism quite the most long-lived and the worst of the whole twentieth-century lot. Nazism lasted a mere twelve years, and Italian fascism only twenty-two. To be sure, the difference in longevity between the red and the black-brown dictatorships is in part due to accident, since the latter were cut short by defeat in war. But this "accident" in fact had its structural causes, which were rooted in the very different natures of the two types of totalitarianism. For the central European dictatorships were built precisely to continue the conflict that had been interrupted in 1918 on what they considered to be unacceptable terms.

Thus neither the German nor the Italian regime could afford a devastating internal revolution such as Stalin's and yet be ready for its intended war of revanche; and in Hitler's case this war had to begin around the time he was fifty, in 1939, so he would have time to finish it. Therefore, neither of these regimes created internal structures anywhere near so total as those of the Soviet Union: industry was not nationalized, and the market was not suppressed but only subjected to "command" and regulation by the state. And, although society was cowed by the state's known capacity for ruthlessness, active terror was practiced against no more than a small part of the population. Thus Hitler purged what he considered to be such unnational elements as Jews, Communists, and Social Democrats; the rest of society was simply *gleichgeschaltet*, or brought into line, and indoctrinated for impending war. (To be sure, had he won the war he would have revolutionized Germany internally, but this was not his first priority.) Mussolini made Italy into what he fondly thought was a "total" order, though in fact it paled beside Moscow's performance (and beside Hitler's, too). And, needless to insist, the Soviet collectivization, terror, and Gulag took at least twice the number of victims as did Hitler's camps. This at least is the self-evident score for the two types of totalitarianism if we make the comparison empirically.

But of course we rarely do so because of the very different ideological envelopes surrounding the two types of system and the different ways we react to these ideologies. A primary difference between the two types of system is that neither of the Western totalitarianisms produced such a fantastic yet plausible intellectual psychedelic as Marxism-Leninism. For the two Western totalitarianisms appealed to intuition and the visceral forces that derived from Romantic nationalism in conjunction with social Darwinism, where Soviet totalitarianism drew on the structured, rationalistic categories of the Enlightenment as transmitted by the German dialectical tradition. But, as Dostoevsky pointed out apropos of Lenin's hero, Chernyshevskii, enlightenment does not bring only light. It wears a dual face, and its dark side is all the darker for sharing the universal pretensions of its luminous counterpart.

And the pretension to universality reveals the most crucial distinction between the two types of totalitarianism. The nationalistic totalitarianisms were by their nature exclusive: they could not appeal beyond the boundaries of their respective countries, and indeed made all other countries into potential enemies. Although both Mussolini and Hitler formed alliances with similar national-authoritarian regimes, ultimately "nationalists of the world unite" is not a feasible slogan. The appeal of Enlightenment-derived Soviet socialism, however, was by its nature inclusive, and hence directed to all mankind; for the ideals of reason and egalitarian democracy have nothing specifically Russian about them, but are universal in their reach and application. And since much of the Left and Center of the outside world shares these ideals, foreign opinion has always been more indulgent toward Soviet totalitarianism than toward its rivals.

Yet the Soviets' firm anchor on the Left did not prevent them from also playing on nationalist sentiments, at least for home consumption, while beguiling the outside world with their "proletarian internationalism." Thus, the Soviet regime wound up with its own kind of national socialism; in this one respect, at least, it was similar to the totalitarianism of the revolutionary Right. Indeed, it surpassed the Right's performance as a system of national mobilization, for under Stalin it fused glorification of the Motherland with the consolidation of socialism. And this is one reason why, after 1991, Sovietism's heirs could plausibly be called the "red-browns."

This convergence of Sovietism with the revolutionary Right was possible because the latter had precious little to do with the traditional antirevolutionary Right, whether descended from the Old Regime or from modern "capitalism"—if indeed "Right" is at all the proper term for these new national revolutionaries. Fascism was a radical, levelling, demotic, and usually pagan movement, and hence fundamentally hostile to the old conservative, elitist, and usually clerical Right. Thus fascism not illogically appropriated the Left's name for the ultimate in democratic levelling, socialism. It is surely no accident that Mussolini had been a leader of the Italian Socialist Party, and that Hitler adapted to his purposes some of the mobilization techniques and the socialist label of his Communist and Social Democratic rivals for mass support.

Nor is this conjunction of the national and the social revolutions of the twentieth century, despite our habit of viewing them as polar opposites, really surprising, since it should be remembered that modern nationalism, like socialism, is a direct product of egalitarian democracy. For when the French Revolution refounded politics on the basis of popular sovereignty, it transformed the hierarchical old-regime world of "estates" and "orders" into a uniform mass of equal citizens, and thereby created the populist nation-state. And in this unitary community the logical counterpart of universal suffrage was universal military service: whereas under the Old Regime armies were composed of noble officers and mercenary soldiers, and wars were limited, in the democratic republic armies were for the first time raised by *levée en masse*, and warfare was on its way to becoming total.

It is this second, military, facet of modern democracy that made possible the mass citizen armies and the extraordinary carnage of the First World War. (The progress of military technology was only secondary in this development.) And it is this second facet of democracy that the national revolutionaries of central Europe put at the center of their enterprise, since their aim was to resume and win that war. Indeed, it is the military facet of mass democracy that engendered the two contending types of modern totalitarianism. So our short twentieth century produced twin degenerations of egalitarian democracy, and they logically met in the common worship of struggle and force and in a shared contempt for the rule of law.

But the two totalitarianisms construed the cult of struggle in different ways. The national struggle of fascism was a Darwinian contest in which survival went to the fittest; it therefore frankly exalted brute force and the right of victors to totally dominate the vanquished. The social class struggle of Communism, on the other hand, though also a war for total victory, was supposed to produce the abolition of all classes, the full humanization of man, and the unity of the species under socialism. But the dictatorship of the proletariat transformed the Communist cult of force from a means into an end, and "real" socialism thus came to signify not human emancipation but the perpetuation of Party power. And thus the quest for Socialist utopia ended in Soviet tragedy.

It is wisdom as old as Aristotle that tragedy consists not in the triumph of blatant evil but in the perversion of the good. The highest social good of the modern age has been democracy in the multiple meanings described in these pages. One perversion of this good has been divisive and aggressive nationalism. But this is a crude and obvious departure from the core democratic principle of the absolute worth, indeed the sanctity, of all human beings, of Kant's rational individuals hypostatized as ends and not means, of Hegel's slaves-become-souls-become-citizens.

The perversion of internationalist socialism, however, is a more subtle affair. Socialism was conceived as the *summum bonum* of egalitarian democracy, yet its Soviet application yielded the most thorough and durable of modern totalitarianisms. What is more, its profession of humane intentions obscured its real nature for decades in the eyes of much of mankind: The Soviet perversion of the dem-

ocratic good, therefore, took the supremely cruel form of the dehumanization of man in the name of the eventual humanization of
humanity. So the Soviet socialist tragedy was played out for seventy-
four years under the sign of the paradox that it requires a great ideal
to produce a great crime.

The basic structure of this tragedy falls into three acts, as the
socialist quest moved from Marx to Lenin to Stalin. Marx's fantasy of
socialism as noncapitalism was supposed to have been realized by the
inescapable logic of history—of which violent revolution was nonetheless the "locomotive." Logically putting the social logic before the
political locomotive, Second International Social Democracy failed to
transcend capitalism or to prevent the First World War. In consequence, after the peace the ambitions of the parties of the old International dwindled down into welfare state reformism—which is all the
term "social democracy" now means, and which has proved to be the
only civilized outcome of the Marxist quest. Yet the war made original, maximalist Marxism appear even more compelling, and at the
same time gave Lenin the occasion to put the locomotive of revolution, in the form of the coercive will of the Party, before the logic of
history. Yet despite this inversion of Marx's priorities, Lenin's War
Communism, like mere Social Democracy before it, failed to transcend capitalism. Thus within Lenin's Party the temptation to trust
again in the logic of history was reborn as Bukharin's quasi-social-
democratic hope of "growing into socialism through the market." But
when this course threatened to slow the Party locomotive to a "snail's
pace," Stalin returned to original Leninism and ordered "full steam
ahead" to socialism in five years; and he applied the full measure of
coercion necessary to reach, at last, original Marxism's goal of full
noncapitalism. And so the logic of history was completely replaced by
the locomotive of Party will. Thus, the unfolding of the Soviet tragedy
occurred as a constant debasement, a "primitivization" of both Marx's
logic and the socialist ideal, and a degradation of a would-be egalitarian ideocracy into crass partocracy.

But this outcome was by no means a "betrayal." Rather, it was the
fulfillment of the perverse logic of an impossible utopia. For throughout the entire quest there never existed any "third way" that would
lead to integral socialism as noncapitalism and *yet* would be democratic. At each point in the escalation of the drama, the only alternative road was to abandon the Marxist fantasy and settle for a welfare

state that "capitalism" could produce less painfully and more efficiently. Thus the awful truth of the experiment is that the integral Marxist program could be realized only by Leninist means, and the Leninist means could reach their socialist objective only by Stalinist methods.

And the contribution of Russia to this drama? Her role was hardly to pervert the experiment, as a convenient scapegoat theory of history, would have it. Rather, Russia's role was to provide to the experiment with a social *tabula rasa* in the form of a civil society pulverized by modern war, thereby creating a void of countervailing power that permitted the Party to realize its fantasy. This contribution, however, was a necessary but not a sufficient condition of the Communist adventure. Russian chaos alone could have produced a national authoritarianism of purely regional significance; but it was ideological socialism that proved to be the sufficient condition for precipitating the world-historical Soviet tragedy. Nothing as lethal as the Leninist *Oresteia* could have occurred anywhere outside the House of Marx.

Epilogue
THE LEGACY

These poor villages, these humble fields,
O native land of long suffering,
Land of the Russian people!

—Fedor Tiutchev, 1855

The gradual development of the principle of equality is . . . a Providential fact . . . it is universal, it is durable, it constantly eludes all human interference, and all men as well as all events contribute to its progress. Would it, then, be wise to imagine that a social movement, the causes of which lie so far back, can be checked by the efforts of a single generation? Can it be believed that democracy, after having overthrown aristocracy and the kings, will stop short before the bourgeoisie and the rich?
—Alexis de Tocqueville, Democracy in America, *1838*

RUSSIA AFTER SOCIALISM

The end of "real socialism" in Central Europe in 1989, and then in Russia in 1991, unleashed a wave of euphoria in the affected countries and in the outside world, as if in a replay of the "Springtime of the Peoples" of 1848. In the East, citizens anticipated living at last in a "normal society," by which they meant not just Western-style affluence—although they meant that in part—but also an existence free from the omnipresent distortions of ideological politics. And in the West, there was a surge of triumphalism in anticipation of the universal victory of liberal "market democracy." In Central Europe the euphoria lasted perhaps a year and a half, and in the former Soviet

505

Union not even half a year; and the West in unison took alarm. Indeed, Communism was not yet cold in its grave when prophecies were heard of a looming fascist future—the scenario of "Weimar Russia," as the new refrain went.

And the problems were indeed staggering throughout the whole ex-Soviet world: the economy continued to deteriorate, a nasty form of nationalism led to bloody strife in some areas, and the populations were disoriented by inflation, growing lawlessness, and general insecurity. As for the West, triumphalism waned when it began to dawn that no neat "transition to democracy" was taking place and that whatever positive change was occurring would cost the West much money and many headaches. Even East Germany, which once looked like the easiest area to revive, proved so burdensome that it plunged the Gibraltar-like West German economy into deep recession. It soon became apparent that the end of the Cold War would yield no "peace dividend" and that it had indeed left the world with grave new possibilities of nuclear proliferation.[1]

Yet, though everyone in both the East and the West was surprised, this outcome should not in fact have been surprising, given what real socialism had been in its day. For Sovietism, after all, had been a "mono-organizational" system in which everything, from Party to Plan to political police, had been structurally and functionally interrelated. Thus, it was only to be expected that a total system should collapse totally, and hence leave behind a total problem: The Party dissolved into near administrative anarchy; the Plan imploded into near barter; and the Union fragmented into multiple contending national sovereignties—and all of these implosions occurred simultaneously. So to climb out from under this universal "rubble," to use Solzhenitsyn's metaphor, everything would have to be done at once, thus creating an impossible situation where everything, logically, had to be done first. This is the historical particularity of antisocialist revolution by implosion (rather than breakthrough), and hence the source of the ambiguity surrounding the revolutionary status of August 1991. And so the logic of the system continued to operate even from beyond the grave.

This dilemma is the meaning of an oft-quoted witticism so universally applicable to Sovietism that it has been variously attributed to Lech Walesa and to the Russian humorist Mikhail Zhvanetskii: It is easy to make fish soup out of an aquarium, but no one has yet found a way to make an aquarium out of fish soup. Lenin minced Russian civil society into a marketless, lawless puree in eight months under War Communism in 1918; Boris Yeltsin—and his successors—will require a generation to make Russia once again into a living, vertebrate aquarium. Such a situation, and such a conundrum, is without precedent in world history; and no one knows the recipe for the reverse transformation. Thus Russia will have to improvise, while still in the soup, her return to a "normal society." And the outside world should brace itself for a very long haul of empathy and aid.

The nature of this "normal" society is conventionally defined as a "market democracy" (an expression, incidentally, that would have amazed any economist from Smith to Keynes, or any advocate of democracy from Jefferson to Wilson: it took the Soviet collapse to give it meaning). But the transition to such a society is probably more difficult now for Russia than it would have been in 1914.

The historical evidence indicates that it is a much more arduous task to create the myriad institutions that make a mature market economy than it is to fashion a political democracy. Russia in 1914 already had the basic ingredients of a market society; adding to these a constitutional regime would not have been an intrinsically difficult matter if the hazards of the revolutionary break with autocracy could have been negotiated successfully. The main internal impediment to a successful transition was, as already indicated,[2] Russia's sociological immaturity in 1914, and in particular the inordinate weight of a peasantry largely without private property or a developed sense of modern civil law. And it is this factor, of course, in conjunction with the dislocations of the war, that cancelled out the promise of Russia's market-cum-civil-society and permitted the Bolsheviks to seize power.

After 1991, however, Russia, though fortunately free of the pressures of international war, faces a far more difficult set of internal problems. She has to build a liberal economic order while simultaneously devising a democratic polity; and into the bargain she has to create a Russian nation-state. For we should not forget that no such entity as the post-1991 Russian Federation existed before the fall of Communism.

Ever since Ivan the Terrible conquered the Volga Khanates of Kazan and Astrakhan in the sixteenth century, the state that was ruled from Moscow and St. Petersburg never was a nation-state; it was a multinational empire whose principle of cohesion until 1917 had been dynastic, and after that date had been the Party. Out of this rump of empire a modern nation must be formed, one that will at the same time be decentralized and federal, to undo the damage done by the hypercentralization of the Soviet pseudofederation. These multiple tasks of rebuilding and of new creation, moreover, are functionally interrelated, and so must be pursued simultaneously if they are to succeed individually. This is the staggering effort necessary to reconstitute the civil aquarium smashed in 1917.

In such difficult circumstances, the shortcut of authoritarian rule is not to be excluded as a means of forcing the pace of marketization and nation building, a path that has been called either the Pinochet or the Chinese scenario. But would such an eventuality negate the necessary relationship between the market and democracy that long-time advocates of free enterprise have triumphantly proclaimed to be the lesson of the Soviet collapse? This matter is certain to be hotly debated as advocates of democratic socialism challenge the initial rapid pace of economic liberalization in post-Communist Europe and urge a slower, "centrist" approach to economic conversion—a line of argument advanced with the mixture of scholarly and political concerns noted in the previous chapter.

In regard to this vexed issue, the empirical record strongly suggests a number of generalizations: First, it is now obvious that there are not, and never can be, any examples of political democracies with command economies. Second, there have indeed been examples of successful market economies under authoritarian regimes without political democracy, but this does not prove that the market has an organic affinity with authoritarianism; it only demonstrates that authoritarian regimes can accommodate a space of freedom that totalitarian ones cannot. Third, there are no examples of political democracies *without* a market-driven economy; and this includes all so-called democratic socialisms, such as Sweden's, which only regulate but do not suppress the market or private property. Fourth, extreme regulation and mega-welfare programs do tend to shade off into outright command, and over time they have proved detrimental to efficiency and growth. We therefore must conclude that there does exist a continuum of democratic socialism with the full, statist brand.

But if we trace the continuum of statism in reverse, historical experience from Spain to Chile to South Korea to Taiwan indicates that the market without democracy is a temporary condition, and that in the long run a market society requires constitutional government and political pluralism in order to function in optimal fashion. Sooner or later almost all societies that achieve sustained growth have also democratized. Thus, if Russia is to be truly modern, she will have to complete all of the multiple tasks that the August Revolution has set for her. So-called "centrist" attempts to recycle part of the Soviet heritage will only slow, and perhaps subvert, this process of modernization. The real question is not whether Russia should take a liberal or "centrist" exit from Communism, but, rather, how good are her chances of achieving the logical combination of the market with democracy without an intermediate authoritarian stage.

In this undertaking the chief advantage that Russia possesses after the Soviet hiatus, as compared with 1914, is a new sociological profile. The country is now industrialized, literate, and 75 percent urban; moreover, it has a skilled labor force and a first-class technical intelligentsia. The "middle classes" of this society constitute a broader potential constituency for a market democracy than what the country offered in 1914. And in this respect modernization theory has something of a point.

But only something of a point. For contrary to social-scientific supposition, post-Communist Russia is not a "developed" or a "modern" society, as modernization theory itself generally defines that status. To make matters worse, as modernization theory has been applied to Russia by socialists, "development" was supposed to put a "base" under the Party "superstructure" and thereby at last permit Leninism to democratize[3]—something that of course did not happen. So the whole problem of Russia's skewed modernity must now be thought through anew.

Russia is indeed industrial and urban, but this does not mean that she partakes of the full complex of modernity. To begin with, there is a radical disequilibrium between an elephantine industrial—or rather military-industrial—sector, a dysfunctional agricultural sector, and a barely eveloped service sector. At the same time, Russia's onetime main asset, the industrial sector, is essentially noncompetitive in the modern world market; and insofar as she does participate in that market, she does so as a producer of arms or, like some Third World country, as an exporter of raw materials. Moreover, post-Communist Russia is stricken with the worst ecological blight of the modern age, a circumstance that will necessitate massive investment and rebuilding. Thus, overall, the post-Soviet economy is in a state of collapse comparable to that of the German and Japanese economies after the Second World War; indeed, Russia's situation is worse, since her obsolete physical plant is still intact and still environmentally lethal.

Furthermore, a modern market society requires a whole network of institutions, over and above factories, that Russia lacks. A short list of such institutions would include a variegated banking system with checkbooks and credit cards, independent research and statistical institutions, insurance companies, and of course a genuine service sector. Just as important is a body of commercial and contract law and a legal system capable of administering it. Developing each of these takes much time, as does educating the people in the new mental habits needed to make them work.

And on this score the most debilitating and antimodern aspect of Sovietism has been its effect on the population's mentality: It left behind an envious egalitarianism, a suspicion that entrepreneurship is "speculation," the reflex of responding to administrative commands rather than to market incentives, and the dulling pall cast by Marxist-Leninist dogma over habits of critical thought. To these must be added the depressing awareness that boundless sacrifices had only produced a national failure, and that the country had wasted, in the folk phrase, "seventy years on the road to nowhere."

Thus, Soviet "development," in proportion with the effort expended, has left the new Russia with distressingly little to build on; and much of what is left will have to be rebuilt to make the country functional. It will not be enough to liberate prices and privatize existing industry to arrive at a market society: a panoply of new economic institutions must be built and whole new industries must be created. Moreover, although Communism is gone, the Communists are still there, and the *nomenklatura* of factory managers, kolkhoz chairmen, and local soviet functionaries still manages most of the economy and administers much of the country. Thus, the "transition" will not be a continuum from Soviet to "normal" development; rather, it will amount to a gigantic, generation-long phasing out of old plants and personnel, and a simultaneous reindustrialization of the country and a reeducation of the population in the ways of really existing modernity. The inordinate cost of socialist construction was in significant measure wasted, and post-Soviet Russia—and indeed long-developed post-Communist East Germany and Bohemia as well—will, like Sisyphus, have to start its labors all over again near the bottom of the hill.

* * *

All of this leads one to wonder what Russian development might have been like without Bolshevism. So we may resume the excursus—interrupted as of 1914 for a peacetime Russian revolution—into conterfactual history conducted from a liberal perspective.[4] If we suppose the best-case scenario of a constitutionalist victory, there is no difficulty in imagining an uncollectivized peasantry—but one with no lack of cooperatives, as the dying Lenin had dreamed—for agricultural cooperatives had in fact existed before he came to power and destroyed them. And we may also suppose a state-guided market industrialization in accordance with the tested pattern of overcoming backwardness through government and foreign investment already established by Witte and Stolypin. In these circumstances, Russia would have continued to develop as a major industrial power steadily closing the gap with the West.

Even if we suppose the more likely worst-case scenario of a Russian Franco and a national authoritarianism, the economic result would have been roughly the same: much social inequality, but also much raw growth, though certainly setbacks and recessions, yet at the end of seventy-four years a basically "urban, industrial, and literate" society, as the developmental litany goes, but *with* property and pluralism added—in short, a genuinely modern culture. Nor would a Russian Franco have lasted all those decades, and the country would now quite probably be, like most of Europe, a constitutional democracy.

There is absolutely no way a country of European culture as huge and as rich in natural resources as Russia would not have been a major industrial power by the end of the twentieth century, whatever its non-Communist government. It is absurd to argue—as is almost invariably the case when we start from modernization theory, especially when it is overlaid with socialist expectations—that Communism was necessary to bring Russia from backwardness to modernity. Such reasoning reflects the real determinist fallacy in Sovietology, to wit, that because industrialization in fact happened the Communist way, it could only have happened that way. On the contrary, the Bolshevik road to "development" was a very poor imitation of the real thing; indeed, it was largely counterproductive in almost every sphere—the economy, culture, and morality—and left behind after its failure a crippled, stunted, and, in Yeltsin's term, a "sick" society.

At the same time, what is inconceivable in either of the above non-Communist scenarios is anything so inane and destructive as

Soviet collectivization and the Gulag, or any form of state intervention in the market as stifling and wasteful as Stalinist planning. And this stricture applies also to the original Menshevik-leaning version of the First Five-Year Plan, which was once vaunted along with Bukharin; for after Stalin the Soviet Union returned to planning roughly of that type, and the results were still bad.[5] To produce the distinctive Soviet institutions of Plan, kolkhoz, and Gulag, the illusions of maximalist socialism and the lawlessness of the Leninist Party were indispensable.

So once again we return to the primacy of ideology and politics in the Soviet phenomenon. As Solzhenitsyn put the matter with respect to the unique dimensions of the Soviet terror: "The imagination and inner strength of Shakespeare's villains stopped short at ten or so cadavers, because they had no *ideology*. . . . It is thanks to *ideology* that it fell to the lot of the twentieth century to experience villainy on a scale of millions."[6] And Solzhenitsyn's proposition is also valid, and was intended, of course, for Hitler's Final Solution and his camps. But in the Communist case the primacy of ideology holds not just for camps but for the entire Soviet endeavor, from its socioeconomic base to its cultural superstructure.

To these claims for the "model" of ideocratic partocracy it has, of course, been objected that after the first generation, the Soviet leaders were not ideologues but pragmatic politicians, and, in particular, that it is absurd to view the Brezhnev regime as motivated by ideology.[7] Indeed, the direct relevance of ideology to decision making did steadily decline over the course of Soviet history, to where Brezhnev frankly admitted that he could not understand Suslov's disquisitions. But viewing ideology in terms of direct relevance to current policy is a very shallow way to assess its role: Marxism-Leninism acted in a much more profound manner.

For all the basic institutions of the Soviet order, as they had emerged by 1935 at the latest, were the creations of ideology; they were nothing less than the Party program set in steel, concrete, and the omnipresent apparat. Once these basic structures of socialism had been "built," they hardly required active ideological commitment—or even simple belief—from the human cogs that operated them. All that was required to keep the system was that no one dare to think too critically about it; so until the very end of the regime its institutions were glorified, and the population was benumbed, by an unrelenting barrage of agitprop proclaiming that the country was on the road to the "radiant future." Yet never, until the end, was this ossified ideology completely dead. Indeed, its cardinal coordinates—the superiority of "socialism" over "capitalism," the unending class struggle between the two, and the omnipresence of "enemies"—were in fact operative at the highest levels of government in setting the broad lines of national and international policy. Nothing so fantastic as really existing "sots-ism" (in Aleksandr Zinoviev's *mot*) would have been possible without the all-encompassing and institutionalized intoxication of "scientific Communism."

The result of its collapse, therefore, was to leave a great absence of belief and values in Russian society. Into this void has moved a variety of faiths and pseudofaiths, from traditional religion and patriotism to millenarian cults and rabid nationalism to an aggressive cynicism and nihilism and, yes, to a commitment to Western-style democracy. As the euphoria of 1989–1991 waned, Western commentary on the new Russia shifted the focus of its attention from the positive democratic and traditional elements in this confused spectrum to the negative and threatening ones. Yet we should not exaggerate the dangers they present. For none of these movements has the potential for generating the zeal and drive of Communism; in particular, a militant Russian fascism is hardly in the offing. And this is so precisely because of the three-quarter-century Communist experience.

For one of Russia's few advantages in attempting "to return to Europe," as the democrats frame their goal, is that this experience has inoculated the population against all ideological politics and removed the temptation of any further totalitarian adventures. For the first time since the rise of the radical intelligentsia at the time of Chernyshevskii and the Populists in the last century, Russia is now a post-ideological, even an anti-ideological, society. And this factor, in conjunction with her dearly bought urban and educated sociological profile, may at last make it possible for Russia to resume the narrowing of the gap with Europe that was interrupted by war and revolution in 1917.

SOCIALISM AFTER SOVIETISM

But if Russia after socialism was a disaster area, what was the state of socialism after the "experiment"? At a superficial glance, it would seem that socialism as such should have been discredited, and that mankind could now get on with the practical business of business. And indeed in the immediate wake of 1989–1991, there was much triumphalist talk that History, after having overcome the illusions of both fascism and Communism, had at last arrived at a safe harbor in market democracy. But a post-Marxist vision of the end of history is no more likely to prove accurate than its Marxist predecessor was in 1917. The socialist idea will surely be with us as long as inequality is, and that will be a very long time indeed. Yet socialism can hardly persist in its previous forms.

The discourse on socialism has thus far gone through two great phases. The first extended from the birth of the moral idea of socialism in the 1830s to the Bolshevik attempt after 1917 to at last give it instrumental expression. This phase consequently produced a theoretical discourse centering on the negation of existing reality, with only an anticipation of the just society of the future. Thus socialism meant, above all, the critique of what Brezhnev might have called "really existing capitalism." The second phase of socialist discourse was demarcated by the lifespan of the Soviet experiment, when for the first time a postcapitalism allegedly existed. This phase produced a more practical discourse centering on the instrumental programs of the experiment, since these were viewed as relevant to all forms of socialism, whether in or out of power, and whether "democratic" or dictatorial. For these programs were hardly the idiosyncratic product of Russian backwardness; they were the prime logical deductions from the socialist idea itself: nationalization, collectivization, and planning.

So the dilemma that will stalk the third, coming phase of the discourse on socialism is how to cope with the fact that these programs were the obvious expression of the core idea, and at one and the same time a monumental failure. There is no going back to the innocent days before 1917 and pretending that the Soviet experiment never happened, or that its record is irrelevant because it was not genuine socialism anyway. Much ballast will have to be jettisoned if the socialist aspiration is to survive in credible form. And in one or another form, survive it will.

There has already been a major move to revisionism on the Left with regard to the key matters of centralized planning and nationalization. With hardly any soul-searching Western and Third World socialist parties suddenly dropped their advocacy of such measures. At the same time, in the wake of 1989–1991, and almost overnight and without debate, there emerged an astonishing worldwide consensus that the market and private property were indispensable features of any functioning economy; that they were indeed the basis of constitutional democracy and the rule of law; and that this amalgam constituted the natural order of civilized modernity. To be sure, there were, as we have seen, degrees of acceptance of the market and private property, since some social thinkers held out for a "centrist" course in liquidating Communism, as if in the hope that the ever elusive "third way" might yet emerge from its wreckage. But after the crash of 1989–1991, almost no one would any longer deny property and the market outright. Thus the Great Depression syndrome regarding "capitalism" was largely overcome; Karl Polanyi appeared to be refuted; and Friedrich Hayek's contention that integral socialism was a form of neoserfdom seemed essentially vindicated. Clearly, an epoch in the history of social thought was now closed.

At the same time, though somewhat less clearly, the meaning of the elusive term "socialism" itself was fleshed out. In retrospect it should be evident that we were dealing all along with a continuum of equally "socialist" programs, one extending from "democratic" socialism to Communism and graduated according to the degree of statization of property and the market. All of these programs stemmed from the same moral idea, and they ranged in their instrumental means from mere voluntary cooperatives at the soft end of the spectrum to the Leninist Party-state at the hard end.

Yet October marks a great caesura in the socialist continuum, one cut by the choice of political means employed to effect the hoped-for exit from capitalism. This caesura falls between majority-rule constitutional democracy and "scientific" avant-garde revolution from above, that is, between social democracy and Communism; and this difference of political means determines the degree to which the statization of property and market relations is possible. In short, the two great wings of the socialist continuum differ over means but not ends, and this is the source of their love-hate relationship: to the democratic socialists, Communists are traitors to the cause because of their coercive means; and to the Communists, social democrats are traitors because they never attain their avowed end.

But let us not forget that of the two *frères ennemis* of generic socialism, only the Communists actually reach socialism in its full meaning of noncapitalism. The social democrats of the world, after a generation

or two of waiting for an electoral majority in favor of abolishing capitalism, lose the faith and renounce the vestiges of their Marxism. In
this they follow the example of the senior party, the German SPD, at
Bad Godesberg in 1958, for their commitment to political democracy
eventually kills their commitment to full economic socialism.

Yet all the changes in outlook within the socialist continuum, major
though they were, were only instrumental and programmatic: they did
not touch the core moral ideal of all forms of socialism—the primacy of
equality in determining the just society. What is more, these changes
did not undermine the deep structures of the specifically Marxist paradigm of socialism, which exalts the oppressed and the deprived as
quintessential humanity and thereby grounds politics on the self-
enriching, redemptive character of alienation and suffering. Thus the
immanent logic of that Providential force which Tocqueville called
"democracy"—that is, social levelling—can only be expected to drive
the modern world as inexorably as it has ever since 1789.

So long as inequality exists, society will continue to be divided into
a Left and a Right, a "party of movement" and a "party of resistance," the camp of politics as morality and the camp of politics as the
ethic of prudence and pragmatism. This syndrome, moreover, will
continue to be surrounded with the same emotional charge and
parareligious aura as before. And the former camp will continue to be
called "socialism," for the discredit cast upon that magical word in the
immediate wake of the Soviet disaster will not last beyond the next
crisis of "capitalism"—that is, of the real world. So in one form or
another, the lion of "capitalism" and the unicorn of "socialism" will
no doubt contend inconclusively until the end of modernity.

But what will be the new instrumental program of the coming
phase of the socialist quest? And what social group, or groups, will
constitute the new universal class? Hitherto, socialism centered on the
industrial proletariat, and hence on a program of nationalization and
centralized planning. But this putatively universal class even in its
heyday never numbered more than a third of the population of any
industrial country, and after the Second World War the Western world
witnessed the progressive dismantling of industrial society together
with the withering away of the proletariat and the "embourgeoise-
ment" of its unionized, home-owning remnants. As current social
science now puts it, the developed world is thus in the "postindus-

trial" era with an increasingly "service-dominated" economy driven by the "information revolution" of the computer age. In such a world the toiler at the factory bench is no longer a credible candidate for exemplar of the universal class. Indeed, he has become the symbol of retrograde, hard-hatted prejudice: August Bebel has given way to Archie Bunker—or he has come to power as the all-too-human and very antisocialist Lech Walesa.

But the idea of a universal class of the suffering and the deprived, of a class to end all classes, is still very much with us. Its prime locus, however, is no longer within the developed economies and welfare-state societies of Western Europe and North America. Rather, the old Marxist paradigm has completed the migration it began when Lenin, in his theory of imperialism, privileged the semicolonial and colonial worlds as the vanguard of redemptive revolution (a transformation carried still further by Mao). Now that Lenin's Second World of Communism is defunct, it is the Third World viewed as victim of the First that constitutes the great collective underclass of humanity. And so the eternal polarity of exploiter and exploited has been transformed from the dichotomy of bourgeoisie and proletariat into that of the Northern and Southern Hemispheres.

But this geographical division between the European minority of the North and the multitudinous remainder of the planet overlaps with inequalities founded on race and color, a division reproduced in the "internal Third World" of the North itself. And this in turn is related to the universal biological division of gender. So in the late twentieth century there has emerged a new continuum of liberation movements spreading out from class to race to gender—and latterly to sexual orientation. And this variegation has spawned a series of successor syndromes of oppression to capitalism and imperialism—classism, racism, and sexism.[8] This development is most advanced in the United States, a precocity that derives in part from successive adaptations since the 1960s of the politics of the American civil-rights movement. But everywhere this movement reflects and amplifies the redemptive dialectic of the slave over the master, universalized first by Stoicism and especially by Christianity, and reformulated most powerfully for the modern age in the "deep structure" of Marxism.

Of course, these post-proletarian liberation movements are not direct derivations from Marxism. Nonetheless, they all developed in a cultural atmosphere permeated by residual Marxist categories, as in the Frankfurt School's conflation of Marx, Nietzsche, and Freud into a "critical theory" of repressive bourgeois society, or in Michel Foucalt's post-structuralist transformation of brute economic exploitation into the subtler alienation produced by the discourses of domination secreted by rationalistic bourgeois culture. To be sure, all the problems of inequality and injustice associated with these new "minorities" are quite real, just as the problems of the industrial working class in its day were real. Yet at the same time, these problems have been inserted into an agonistic metaphysic of total "human emancipation" that transcends any of its concrete manifestations.

Still, these transmigrations of the Marxist paradigm yield a multiplicity of universal classes, but none of them is as potent or potentially revolutionary as the old-time proletariat. Any socialist programs erected on these new forms of alienation, therefore, can only be correspondingly more diffuse than the old dictatorship of the proletariat. Nonetheless, it is not difficult to foresee that all future instrumental programs of socialism will converge, like homing pigeons, on suspicion of property and the market; for wealth will always be power, and inequalities of wealth will always allot power unequally. Consequently, there will always be social pressure to use political power to correct economic power in the name of the common good. At the same time, society will always confront the dilemma that without a division of labor, and therefore without enduring inequality, there will not be economic growth—also for the common good.

Thus the practical question of the modern age comes down to the degree of state intervention in economic and social processes. There has never been a purely market-driven economy of the type that nineteenth-century Manchester liberals urged, and that present-day libertarians, Hayek in hand, still dream about. This integral liberalism is as much a utopia as is integral socialism. Yet it should be emphasized that such ultraliberalism, by its very antiauthoritarian nature, can never produce a coercive polity, as integral socialism invariably has done. Thus in the "normal" world—that which is located between the two utopias—the Soviet failure has demonstrated that the market is part of the social order of nature. Despite the vagaries of the business cycle and the recurrence of depressions, the market is absolutely necessary to give us a productive and functioning society, and any attempt to dispense with it leads both to economic disaster and political oppression. Yet the market cannot give us the just society. The just society, insofar as it can be approached, must be the product of the moral and political will of the community acting on the amoral forces of the market. And this means that state intervention in the market's operation for moral and political ends is also part of the social order of nature.

It is this *via media* that became the normality of mature "capitalism" in the developed countries in the wake of the Great Depression. (Indeed, Hitler and Mussolini produced their own, quite comprehensive versions of the welfare state in the same period.) And this new normality of modernity reached its prime during the Great Prosperity that emerged from the reconstruction after the Second World War. Thus the politics of normality came to be a matter of give-and-take between a Left-Center and a Right-Center over the proportions of the American welfare state, the German "social market," or the French "indicative plan." The metahistorical transition from "capism" to "socism" is no longer a real issue, even though vestiges of maximalist vocabulary remain. And the incarnation of maximalist programs in the coercive instrument of a Leninist-type Party seems to have been discredited for the duration of modernity. Thus, Western socialist parties have abandoned Marx and even socialism, and Communist parties have largely switched to the more anodyne label "socialist."

But does this mean that the maximalist temptation is once and for all behind us? Almost certainly not. Candidates for the role of universal class abound; and, although gender-cum-sexual orientation will surely never get the brass ring, some combination of a young, prolific, but poor Third World arrayed against an opulent but graying North could conceivably do so: Peru's surreal Sendero Luminoso is a hint of this possibility. And the potential for an attempted return to the superstate also exists everywhere: the normal Western wrangling over the size of the social safety-net could escalate towards comprehensive statization if a sufficiently compelling concern for the common good appeared.

Indeed, there is already a potent candidate for this catalytic role in the luminous cause of ecology. This is a movement that claims to speak for the collective, planetary interest of mankind against the selfish pursuit of profit and growth by the rich. In all too familiar terms, it challenges the "anarchy" of the market and subordinates individual property rights to pursuit of the common good; and eco-planning is clearly in the wings. Ecology's practical causes, moreover, are invariably presented as moral ones; and in its more extreme forms, ecology shades into a movement for nothing less than the salvation of the species.[9]

To be sure, the practical issues raised by the ecology movement are very real—as were the earlier problems of the working class, and as are the more recently recognized problems of social minorities—and the politics of normality will certainly have to deal with them. Yet once again, and in a familiar pattern, these practical problems have been subsumed in a salvation metaphysics that transcends them all. For utopia springs eternal in an imperfect world, and it would be foolish to conclude that because the greatest utopia of our age has ended in disaster, utopian politics as such are finished.

Nor is it desirable that they should be, for utopias are as necessary as they are dangerous. Without the goad of exaggerated hope and excessive zeal, very little democratic reform would be launched in this world. The Right, despite occasional forays into Tory democracy, usually fears taking the initiative in promoting necessary egalitarian change, and so this task devolves on the rasher forces of the Left. The overstatements of visionary socialism were necessary to produce the welfare state, which is the present point of equilibrium between the two forces that now define the politics of normality. And perhaps the late, great Soviet disaster has definitively defined the extreme form of the utopian danger, and so inoculated us against any further such adventures.

But who knows? The unprecedented Leninist phenomenon appeared because of the unprecedented world crisis of 1914–1918. Any analogous global crisis could drive dormant socialist programs once again towards maximalism, and consequently towards the temptation of seeking absolute power in order to achieve absolute ends. So long as the utopian aspiration of socialism exists, it will always wear a dual face: It will serve as a needed goad to ameliorating an eternally imperfect world, and it will offer the temptation of forcibly replacing that world with an allegedly perfect one. And the perverse Cunning of Contingency will determine, as in the past, how these two competing logics work out.

NOTES AND SOURCES

INTRODUCTION TO NOTES AND SOURCES

This book is not a work of research or erudition, but of interpretation and conceptualization, or more exactly of reconceptualization. For with the demise of Soviet Communism, the great body of analysis generated during the three-quarters of a century since the October Revolution has become in large part superannuated. The time has arrived for a major rethinking of the meaning of the Soviet experience—and of all that we had previously thought we understood about its meaning.

Soviet history may now at last be written entirely in the past tense. Until 1991, the Soviet presence was a daily part of our lives, and indeed a major touchstone of political life throughout the world. One reason was that the Soviet Union had pretensions that were unique in twentieth-century politics. Most major nations make claims to have exceptional significance for the rest of the planet—the United States as the "city on a hill" of liberal democracy, Britain as the mentor to "lesser breeds without the law," and France as the bearer of a *"mission civilisatrice"* to less enlightened nations. The Soviet Union, however, went beyond this and claimed to be the sole model of the good society, the gold standard of human affairs, and the perfect polity at the end of history; and it found millions throughout the world to believe in these pretensions. It was thus a challenge that no one could refuse to meet. One could therefore say of anyone: "Tell me what he thinks about the Soviet Union, and I will tell you what he thinks about his own society." And the proposition could just as easily be reversed: "Tell me his domestic politics, and I will tell you his perception of the Soviet Union." Thus all of our commentaries on the Soviet phenomenon were also implicitly commentaries on ourselves, and hence our objectivity was at its lowest point in tracing the Soviet record. Now, for the first time, we are liberated from the pressure of the Soviet presence in our daily lives, and it should be possible to raise the level of objectivity a great notch.

But in the first instance this change will not come about through the accumulation of new empirical knowledge. New facts will of course emerge—and in abundance—as a result of the opening of the old Soviet archives. But the evidence of the past is never enough to change the conceptualization of a problem or an event; such a change comes from a change of our perspective in the present. Thus no amount of research can decide whether the French Revolution was a bourgeois revolution, or the Russian Revolution a proletarian one; the resolution of such matters depends on whether or not present political concerns make such problems relevant issues. In the French case, as François Furet has argued, for two hundred years after the event the French Revolution remained a living divide in French politics, its heritage separating Left from Right, and socialists from liberals, with each viewing it after 1917 as the prelude to October.* The French Revolution was therefore "over" only in the 1970s, when the Soviet myth faded, draining the passion from the prospect of socialism at home. Hence the issue of the Revolution's bourgeois character, after generating mountains of monographs, simply faded away and ceased to orient research. Though the Russian Revolution is not yet "over," at least not to this extent, and the passion surrounding it has far from abated, it assumed a new visage after 1991. Its conceptualization, therefore, will automatically change, whatever materials come out of the archives, as we progressively disentangle the Soviet past from our own changing present.

Yet the present rethinking of the Russian Revolution will be quite different from that of the French case. This is so not because October became a divide within Russian society—Russian politics simply ceased after 1917—but because it divided the international community and the domestic politics of all its members. Thus one of the anomalies of Soviet history is that most of the relevant interpretative literature is not in Russian but in Western languages, and in particular in English. The reason, of course, is that in the former Soviet Union historical writing, like everything else, was "nationalized" by the regime. As explained in chapters 5 and 7, this process began in ad hoc

---

* François Furet, *Penser la Révolution française* (Paris: Gallimard, 1978).

fashion with Pokrovskii in the 1920s and culminated in Stalin's official *Short Course* in 1938; that canon, though amended in detail, lasted in its main outlines down to *perestroika*. This circumstance left the burden of genuine debate on issues of interpretation largely to foreign scholars.

Moreover, now that the Soviet regime has collapsed, Russian historical scholarship, like everything else in the resulting rubble, must be rebuilt *de novo*. And this leads to a further anomaly: in this task of reconstruction, Russian scholars are now turning to the Western literature for guidance in understanding their own history. For example, in the first—and so far the only—post-Soviet history of Russia from the beginnings to the present, the preponderance of scholarly reference is to Western works for the Soviet period, and such references are frequent even for the prerevolutionary period.* The same imbalance will appear in the citations below. Most of the references in this book are to foreign works, and the reconceptualization it advances is largely a critique of the Western historiography.

Furthermore, since the emphasis is on conceptualization, not coverage, extensive bibliography and annotation are unnecessary. Accordingly, the notes for each chapter begin with mention of the principal relevant secondary works as guidance to readers who wish to refer to the sources and principal commentaries. Following this, more precise annotations are provided only to reference the more important specific points in the text.

Introduction

There are as yet no extensive studies of the development of Western Sovietology, although the events of 1989–1991 have already provoked the beginning of a reassessment that will eventually produce analyses of this interesting branch of intellectual history. For the moment, we have Kenneth Jowitt, *The New World Disorder* (Berkeley: University of California Press, 1992); Andrew Janos, "Social Science, Communism, and the Dynamics of Political Change," *World Politics* 44 (October 1991): 81–112; Martin Malia, "From Under the Rubble, What?" *Problems of Communism* 41 (January–April 1982): 89–106; George Breslauer et al., "In Defense of Sovietology," *Post-Soviet Affairs* 3 (July–September 1992): 197–238. A part of this introduction first appeared as "The Hunt for the True October," *Commentary* 92 (October 1991): 21–28.

---

* S. V. Kuleshov, O. I. Volobuev, and E. I. Pivovar, *Nashe Oteschestvo: opyt politicheskoi istorii* [Our Fatherland: An Essay in Political History], 2 vols. (Moscow: Terra, 1991).

Notes

1. For an elaboration of the concept of the "short twentieth century," see John Lukacs, *The End of the Twentieth Century and the End of the Modern Age* (London: Ticknor and Fields, 1993).

2. G. W. F. Hegel, *The Philosophy of Right*, trans. T. M. Knox (Oxford: Oxford University Press, 1967), p. 13.

3. Max Weber, *Economy and Society*, vol. I (New York: Bedminster Press, 1968), pp. 223–225; Emile Durkheim, *Le socialisme, sa définition, ses débuts, la doctrine Saint-Simonienne* (Paris: no pub., 1925).

4. Richard Lowenthal, "Development versus Utopia in Communist Policy," in *Change in Communist Systems,* ed. Chalmers Johnson (Stanford: Stanford University Press, 1970); for the origins of this approach, see W. W. Rostow, *The Dynamics of Soviet Society* (New York: Norton, 1952); C. E. Black, *The Dynamics of Modernization: A Study in Comparative History* (New York: Harper and Row, 1966).

5. For a more complex genealogy of this term, see Abbot Gleason, " 'Totalitarianism' in 1984," *Russian Review* 43 (1984): 145–159; see also Leonard Schapiro, *Totalitarianism* (New York: Praeger, 1972).

6. Leopold Haimson, "The Problem of Social Stability in Urban Russia, 1905–1917," *Slavic Review* 23 (1964): 619–642, and 24 (1965): 1–22; William Rosenberg, "Conclusion: Understanding the Russian Revolution," in *The Worker's Revolution in Russia, 1917: The View from Below*, ed. Daniel Kaiser (Cambridge: Harvard University Press, 1987), pp. 132–141; Ronald Suny, "Towards a Social History of the October Revolution," *American Historical Review* 88 (1983): 31–52.

7. Alexander Rabinowitch, *The Bolsheviks Come to Power: The Revolution of 1917 in Petrograd* (New York: Norton, 1978).

8. Moshe Lewin, *Lenin's Last Struggle*, trans. A. M. Sheridan Smith (New York: Random House, 1978), hereafter cited as *Struggle;* Stephen F. Cohen, *Bukharin and the Bolshevik Revolution: A Political Biography, 1888–1938* (New York: Knopf, 1973), hereafter cited as *Bukharin;* Stephen F. Cohen, *Rethinking the Soviet Experience: Politics and History Since 1917* (New York: Oxford University Press, 1985), especially chapters 2 and 3 (hereafter cited as *Rethinking*).

9. Moshe Lewin, *The Making of the Soviet System: Essays in the Social History of Interwar Russia* (New York: Pantheon, 1985), chapter 12 (hereafter cited as *Making*); and Cohen, *Bukharin*, p. 378 and p. 382 (quoting Roy Medvedev).

10. Sheila Fitzpatrick, *The Russian Revolution 1917–1932* (New York: Oxford University Press, 1982), pp. 8, 157.

11. Jerry F. Hough and Merle Fainsod, *How the Soviet Union Is Governed* (Cambridge: Harvard University Press, 1979). This book turns on its head Merle Fainsod, *How Russia Is Ruled* (Cambridge: Harvard University Press, 1963), which offered the classic statement of the totalitarian model.

12. Moshe Lewin, *Stalinism and the Seeds of Soviet Reform: The Debates of the 1960s* (London and Armonk, N.Y.: Pluto Press and M. E. Sharpe, 1991); Lewin's book was first published as *The Political Undercurrents of Soviet Economic Debates: From Bukharin to the Modern Reformers* (Princeton: Princeton University Press, 1974), hereafter cited as *Political Undercurrents*. See also his *The Gorbachev Phenomenon* (Berkeley: University of California Press, 1988) and the updated 1991 edition.

13. Adam Michnik, "Towards a Civil Society: Hopes for Polish Democracy," *Times Literary Supplement* (February 19–25, 1988), pp. 188, 198–199.

14. This model can be found in Carl J. Friedrich and Zbigniew K. Brzezinski, *Totalitarian Dictatorship and Autocracy* (Cambridge: Harvard University Press, 1956).

15. See, for example, Merle Fainsod, *Smolensk Under Soviet Rule* (Cambridge: Harvard University Press, 1958); Leonard Schapiro, *The Communist Party of the Soviet Union* (New York: Random House, 1960), hereafter cited as *Communist Party;* Adam Ulam, *The Bolsheviks: The Intellectual and Political History of the Triumph of Communism in Russia* (New York: Macmillan, 1965), hereafter cited as *Bolsheviks.*

16. Mikhail Heller and Aleksandr Nekrich, *Utopia in Power: The History of the Soviet Union from 1917 to the Present*, trans. Phillis B. Carlos (New York: Summit Books, 1980), hereafter cited as *Utopia.*

Chapter 1. Why Socialism?

Far and away the most important assessment of Marxist thought is Leszek Kolakowski, *Main Currents of Marxism*, 3 vols., trans. P. S. Falla (Oxford: Clarendon Press, 1978); it is cited extensively throughout this book. The most comprehensive treatment of the socialist movement is Carl Landauer, *European Socialism*, 2 vols. (Berkeley: University of California Press, 1959). See also: Shlomo Avineri, *The Social and Political Thought of Karl Marx* (Cambridge: Cambridge University Press, 1968); G. D. H. Cole, *A History of Socialist Thought*, 5 vols. (New York: St. Martin's Press, 1953–1960); George Lichtheim, *Marxism: A Historical and Critical Study* (New York: Praeger, 1961); Kostas Papaioannou, *Marx et les marxistes* (Paris: Flammarion, 1972); Kostas Papaioannou, *De Marx et du marxisme* (Paris: Gallimard, 1983), preface by Raymond Aron.

Notes·

1. The matter of possible connections between the socialist idea and religon is of course controversial, and it is related to the broader and equally controversial matter of whether modern culture generally contains secularized elements of antecedent Christian values and doctrines. This book takes a stand on this issue that is basically in favor of the secularization thesis. It does so because of the obvious prominence of Christian themes and vocabulary both in German classical philosophy and in socialist thought during the formative period of socialism in the 1830s and 1840s, a few examples of which are given in the text.

   Some of the more relevant works in the debate on this issue are: Karl Löwith, *Meaning in History* (Chicago: University of Chicago Press, 1957); Hans Blumenberg's response to Löwith, *The Legitimacy of the Modern Age*, trans. Robert M. Wallace (Cambridge: MIT Press, 1983); Laurence Dickey, "Blumenberg and Secularization: Self-Assertion and Problems of Self-Realizing Teleology in History," *New German Criticism* 41 (Spring/Summer 1987): 151–165; Martin Jay, "Blumenberg and Modernism: A Reflection on *The Legitimacy of the Modern Age*," *History and Theory* 24 (1985): 183–190; William Bouwsma, "Review of Blumenberg," *Journal of Modern History* 56 (1984): 698–701. Although not part of this particular debate, two important works develop the secularization thesis with respect to Marxism-Leninism and are thus immediately relevant to this book: Raymond Aron, *L'opium des intellectuels* (Paris: Calmann-Levy, 1955); and Alain Besançon, *The Intellectual Origins of Leninism*, trans. Sarah Matthews (Oxford: Basil Blackwell, 1981). Kolakowski's *Main Currents* also advances a form of the secularization thesis; the protagonist, however, is not religion but philosophy in the form of neo-Platonism, a doctrine of course often associated with Christianity, especially in the German tradition. For an attempted rebuttal of this approach, see David Joravsky, "Kolakowski's Long Goodbye," *Theory and Society* 10 (1981): 293–305. The genealogy of Kolakowski's type of approach to the transmutations of philosophy goes back at least to Arthur O. Lovejoy, *The Great Chain of Being* (Cambridge: Harvard University Press, 1933).

2. For example, see Walt Whitman Rostow, *The Stages of Economic Growth: A Non-Communist Manifesto* (Cambridge: Cambridge University Press, 1975); Louis O. Kelso, *The Capitalist Manifesto* (New York: Random House, 1958).

3. For example, see David Brion Davis, *The Problem of Slavery in Western Culture* (Ithaca, N.Y.: Cornell University Press, 1966).

4. For the full story of this concept, see Walt Whitman Rostow, *Theorists of Economic Growth from David Hume to the Present* (New York: Oxford University Press, 1990).

5. For Hegel as a theologian *manqué*, see Karl Löwith, *From Hegel to Nietzsche*, trans. David E. Green (New York: Doubleday, 1967); Laurence Dickey, *Hegel: Religion, Economics and the Politics of Spirit* (Cambridge: Cambridge University Press, 1987). Perhaps the first statement of the radical implications of German "classical philosophy" as a kind of secular religion equivalent in potency to the French Revolution was given by Heinrich Heine in *De l'Allemagne depuis Luther*, first published in *Revue des deux mondes* (December 1834).

6. G. W. F. Hegel, *Reason in History: A General Introduction to the Philosophy of History*, trans. Robert Hartman (New York: Macmillan, 1987), p. 24.

7. Georges Duby, *The Three Orders: Feudal Society Imagined*, trans. A. Goldhammer (Chicago: University of Chicago Press, 1980).

8. Kolakowski, *Main Currents*, vol. 1, p. 1.

9. Raymond Williams, *Keywords: A Vocabulary of Culture and Society* (New York: Oxford University Press, 1976).

10. For a discussion (unfortunately inadequate) of the similarities and differences between ancient and modern democracy, see the work of a major Hellenist: M. I. Finley, *Democracy Ancient and Modern* (New Brunswick, N.J.: Rutgers University Press, 1973).

11. Benjamin Constant, "De la liberté des anciens comparée à celle des modernes," in *De la liberté chez les modernes: écrits politiques*, ed. Marcel Gauchet (Paris: Hachette, 1980); for an English translation, see *The Political Writings of Benjamin Constant*, trans., and ed. Biancamaria Fontana (New York: Cambridge University Press, 1988). For early liberalism in general, see Pierre Manent, *Histoire intellectuelle du libéralisme* (Paris: Calmann-Levy–Pluriel, 1987).

12. See the first line of Tocqueville's own introduction to *Democracy In America* in *Oeuvres complètes* (Paris: Gallimard, 1951), vol. 1, *De la démocratie en Amérique*, "Avertissement de la douzième édition," p. 43. For Tocqueville's thought in general, see Pierre Manent, *Tocqueville et la nature de la démocratie* (Paris: Julliard, 1982).

13. See Peter Clavert, *The Concept of Class: An Historical Introduction* (London and New York: Hutchison, 1982); William H. Sewell, Jr., *Work and Revolution in France: The Language of Labor from the Old Regime to 1848* (Cambridge: Cambridge University Press, 1980); Dallas L. Clouatre, "The Concept of Class in French Culture Prior to the Revolution," *Journal of the History of Ideas* 45 (1984): 219–244.

14. See the translation in *The Marx-Engels Reader*, ed. Robert Tucker, 2nd

ed. (New York: Norton, 1978), p. 484. Unless otherwise noted, all citations of Marx's work will be made to this edition.

15. Wolfgang Scheider, "Sozialismus," in *Geschichtliche Grundbegriffe: historische Lexikon zur politisch-sozialen Sprach in Deutschland,* eds. O. Brunner et al., 7 vols. (Stuttgart: Klett-Cotta, 1972–1992), vol. 5, pp. 923–998; and Irving Fetscher, "Socialism," and Horst Stuke, "Socialism, Early," both in *Marxism, Communism, and Western Society,* ed. C. D. Kernig (New York: Herder & Herder, 1973), vol. 7, pp. 422–446.

16. See note 8 in Marx, *The Marx-Engels Reader,* p. 475. A modern effort to fuse the English and French cases into a single historical logic is Eric J. Hobsbawm, *The Age of Revolution: 1789–1848* (Cleveland: World Publishing Co., 1962).

17. It was Engels who first gave empirical content to Marx's already elaborated concept of the proletariat as universal class. See his *The Condition of the Working Class in England,* trans. and ed. W. O. Henderson and W. H. Chaloner (Stanford: Stanford University Press, 1968), originally published in 1845. The thesis of the book is that socialist revolution was imminent in England.

18. Wolfgang Scheider, "Kommunismus," in *Geschichtliche Grundbegriffe,* vol. 3, pp. 455–529.

19. See, for example, Marx, *The Marx-Engels Reader,* p. 477.

20. Werner Conze, "Proletariat, Pobel, Pauperismus," in *Geschichtliche Grundbegriffe,* vol. 5, pp. 27–68.

21. See Marx, *The Marx-Engels Reader,* pp. 64–65.

22. Alain Besançon, *The Intellectual Origins of Leninism,* p. 9.

23. David Caute, *The Left in Europe* (New York: McGraw-Hill, 1966).

24. Marie-Elisabeth Hilger, "Kapital, Kapitalist, Kapitalismus," in *Geschichtliche Grundbegriffe,* vol. 3, pp. 399–454; Richard Passow, *Kapitalismus: Eine begrifflich-terminologische Studie* (Jena: Verlag von Gustav Fischer, 1927).

25. See Marx, *The Marx-Engels Reader,* p. 474.

26. The program is reproduced in *Arkhiv "Zemli i Voli" i "Narodnoi Voli"* (Moscow: Izdatelstvo Politkatorzhan, 1932), pp. 54–63. For the precocious development of awareness in Russia of capitalism as a national problem, see Andrzej Walicki, *The Controversy over Capitalism* (Oxford: Clarendon, 1969).

27. The story of our evolving concept of economic modernity from Smith to Weber is given in R. J. Holton, *The Transition from Feudalism to Capitalism* (London: Macmillan, 1985).

28. See Hegel, *The Philosophy of History,* trans. J. Sibree (New York: Dover, 1956), p. 33.

Chapter 2. And Why in Russia First?

A few of the more useful general works for understanding old-regime Russia are: Hugh Seton-Watson, *The Russian Empire 1801–1917* (Oxford: Clarendon Press, 1967); Anatole Leroy-Beaulieu, *L'empire des tsars et les russes*, 3 vols., 3rd ed. (Paris: Hachette, 1889–1893), which, despite its age, is still perhaps the most vivid survey of the old-regime world; Wladimir Weidle, *La Russie absente et présente* (Paris: Gallimard, 1949); William L. Blackwell, ed., *Russian Economic Development from Peter the Great to Stalin* (New York: New Viewpoints, 1974); G. T. Robinson, *Rural Russia Under the Old Regime* (London: Collier-Macmillan, 1967), a reprint of the 1932 edition; Jerome Blum, *The End of the Old Order in Rural Europe* (Princeton: Princeton University Press, 1978). For a *marxisant* historical sociology presenting the "awkward class" of the peasantry as the decisive factor in Russia's peculiar path to modernity, see Teodor Shanin, *The Roots of Otherness: Russia's Turn of Century*, vol. 1: *Russia as a "Developing Society"* (New Haven: Yale University Press, 1986). For Russia as a form of Oriental despotism, or "patrimonialism," radically different from all Western polities, see: Richard Pipes, *Russia Under the Old Regime* (New York: Charles Scribner's Sons, 1974).

Notes

1. Jan Kucharzewski, *The Origins of Modern Russia* (New York: The Polish Institute of Arts and Sciences in America, 1948).
2. Karl Marx, *Secret Diplomatic History of the Eighteenth Century, and the Story of the Life of Lord Palmerston* (New York: International Publishers, 1969).
3. Richard Pipes, *Russia Under the Old Regime;* Tibor Szamuely, *The Russian Tradition*, ed., Robert Conquest (New York: McGraw-Hill, 1974).
4. See Federico Chabod, *Storia dell'idea d'Europa* (Bari: Editori Laterza, 1962); Jean-Baptiste Duroselle, *L'Idée d'Europe dans l'histoire* (Paris: Les Editions Denoël, 1965); Denys Hay, *Europe: The Emergence of an Idea* (Edinburgh: Edinburgh University Press, 1968).
5. Dieter Groh, *Russland und das Selbstverständnis Europas: Ein Beitrag zur europäischen Geistesgeschichte* (Neuwied: Hermann Luchterhand Verlag, 1961), part 2.
6. Alexander Gerschenkron, *Economic Backwardness in Historical Perspective* (Cambridge: Belknap Press of Harvard University Press, 1962), hereafter cited as *Backwardness*.
7. Ernest Barker, *Church, State and Study: Essays by Ernest Barker* (London: Methuen, 1930).

8. The most influential statement about the peculiarities of Russia's historical development was given by Pavel N. Miliukov in the first volume of his *Ocherki po istorii russkoi kultury* [Outlines of the History of Russian Culture]. First published in 1894, this work went through six editions before the revolution. Its central themes were taken up by the intellectual leader of Russian Marxism Georgii Plekhanov. From this source Lenin derived the underpinnings of his later diatribes against Russia's "Asiatic" lack of "culture" (see chapter 5 below).

9. Marc Raeff, *The Well-Ordered Police State: Social and Institutional Change through Law in the Germanies and Russia, 1600–1800* (New Haven: Yale University Press, 1983).

10. Otto Hintze, *The Historical Essays of Otto Hintze*, ed. Felix Gilbert (New York: Oxford University Press, 1975); Otto Hintze, *Staat und Verfassung: Gesamelte Abhandlungen zur Allgemeinen Verfassungsgeschichte*, ed. Gerhard Oestreich (Göttingen: Vandenhoeck & Ruprecht, 1962); Perry Anderson, *Lineages of the Absolutist State* (London: New Left Books, 1974); André Corvisier, *Armées et sociétés en Europe de 1494 à 1789* (Paris: Presses Universitaires de France, 1976).

11. Natan Eidelman, *Revoliutsiia sverkhu v Rossii* (Moscow: Izdatel'stvo "Kniga," 1989).

12. V. O. Kliuchevskii, *A History of Russia*, trans. C. J. Hogarth, 5 vols. (New York: Dutton, 1911–1931), vol. 1, pp. 1–2.

13. Marc Raeff, *The Origins of the Russian Intelligentsia: The Eighteenth-Century Nobility* (New York: Harcourt and Brace, 1966).

14. Nicholas V. Riasanovsky, *A Parting of Ways: Government and the Educated Public in Russia, 1801–1855* (Oxford: Clarendon Press, 1976).

15. Franco Venturi, *Roots of Revolution: A History of Populist and Socialist Movements in Nineteenth-Century Russia* (Cambridge: Harvard University Press, 1983). See also Martin Malia, *Alexander Herzen and the Birth of Russian Socialism, 1812–1855* (Cambridge: Harvard University Press, 1961); E. H. Carr, *Michael Bakunin* (New York: Vintage Books, 1961); W. F. Woehrlin, *Chernyshevsky: The Man and the Journalist* (Cambridge: Harvard University Press, 1971).

16. Theodore H. Von Laue, *Sergei Witte and the Industrialization of Russia* (New York: Columbia University Press, 1963).

17. Nicholas V. Riasanovsky, "The Emergence of Eurasianism," *California Slavic Studies* 5 (Berkeley and Los Angeles: University of California Press, 1967).

18. John L. H. Keep, *The Rise of Social Democracy in Russia* (Oxford: Clarendon Press, 1963).

19. Allan K. Wildman, *The Making of a Worker's Revolution: Russian Social Democracy: 1891–1903* (Chicago: University of Chicago Press, 1967);

Victoria Bonnell, *The Roots of Rebellion* (Berkeley: University of California Press, 1983); Tim McDaniel, *Autocracy, Capitalism, and Revolution in Russia* (Berkeley and Los Angeles: University of California Press, 1988).

20. Abraham Ascher, *The Revolution of 1905* (Stanford: Stanford University Press, 1988–1992). For a sociological view of 1905, see Shanin, *Russia as a "Developing Society,"* vol. 2: *Russia, 1905–07: Revolution as a Moment of Truth.*

21. Geoffrey Hosking, *The Russian Constitutional Experiment: Government and Drama, 1907–1914* (Cambridge: Cambridge University Press, 1973); Terence Emmons, *The Formation of Political Parties and the First National Elections in Russia* (Cambridge: Harvard University Press, 1983).

22. Albert Loren Weeks, *The First Bolshevik: A Political Biography of Peter Tkachev* (New York: New York University Press, 1968).

23. For the meaning of the concept of civil society in history, see Manfred Riedel, "Gesellschaft, Bürgerliche," in *Geschichtliche Grundbegriffe*, vol. 2, pp. 719–800; and Adam Seligman, *The Idea of Civil Society* (New York: The Free Press, 1992).

24. Ulam, *The Bolsheviks*, remains the best biography and political assessment of Lenin; see also Robert Service, *Lenin: A Political Life*, 2 vols. (Bloomington: Indiana University Press, 1985).

25. The key writings of Lenin can be found in Robert C. Tucker, *The Lenin Anthology* (New York: Norton, 1973).

26. Robert Michels, *Political Parties: A Sociological Study of the Oligarchical Tendencies of Modern Democracy* (New York: The Free Press, 1962).

27. For an interesting analysis of Lenin's reduction of politics to sociology, see A. J. Polan, *Lenin and the End of Politics* (Berkeley: University of California Press, 1984).

28. "Contribution to a Critique of Hegel's *Philosophy of Right:* Introduction," *Marx-Engels Reader*, p. 59.

Chapter 3. The Road to October

The most important general works on the Russian Revolution, narrowly defined either as the year 1917 or the years 1917–1921, are: William H. Chamberlin, *The Russian Revolution*, 2 vols. (New York: Macmillan, 1931), reprinted in 1965 by Grosset & Dunlap; John L. H. Keep, *The Russian Revolution: A Study in Mass Mobilization* (London: Weidenfeld & Nicolson, 1975), the most satisfactory social history of 1917; Richard Pipes, *The Russian Revolution* (New York: Knopf, 1990), a relentless demonstration of the point that October was a coup, not a proletarian revolution; Leon

Trotsky, *The History of the Russian Revolution*, trans. Max Eastman (New York: Simon & Schuster, 1932), which remains the best Marxist treatment of 1917; and Marc Ferro, *La Révolution de 1917*, 2 vols. (Paris: Aubier-Montagne, 1967–1976). See also: Dietrich Geyer, *Die Russische Revolution, Historische Probleme und Perspektiven* (Stuttgart: W. Kohlhammer Verlag, 1968).

Notes

1. Jacob Walkin, *The Rise of Democracy in Pre-Revolutionary Russia: Political and Social Institutions Under the Last Three Tsars* (New York: Praeger, 1962).
2. Haimson, "The Problem of Social Stability."
3. Emmons, *Political Parties*, gives a more optimistic assessment of Russia's chances for constitutionalism before 1914.
4. For the devastating political impact of modern war, see Michael Eliot Howard, *The Franco-Prussian War: The German Invasion of France, 1870–1871* (New York: Macmillan, 1961).
5. Michael T. Florinsky, *The End of the Russian Empire* (New York: Collier Books, 1961).
6. T. Hasegawa, *The February Revolution, Petrograd, 1917* (Seattle: University of Washington Press, 1981).
7. Robert V. Daniels, *Red October: The Bolshevik Revolution of 1917* (London: Secker & Warburg, 1968); Sergei P. Melgunov, *The Bolshevik Seizure of Power*, trans. James S. Beaver (Santa Barbara, Calif.: ABC-Clio, 1972); Richard Pipes, *The Russian Revolution*.
8. Alan Wildman, *The End of the Russian Imperial Army*, 2 vols. (Princeton: Princeton University Press, 1980).
9. John L. H. Keep, *The Russian Revolution: A Study in Mass Mobilization* (London: Weidenfeld & Nicolson, 1976).
10. Richard Sakwa, *Soviet Communists in Power: A Study of Moscow During the Civil War* (Houndsmill: Macmillan Press, 1988).
11. Bonnell, *Roots of Rebellion*, and McDaniel, *Autocracy, Capitalism, and Revolution*.
12. Kolakowski, *Main Currents*, vol. 2, pp. 384–393.
13. T. H. Rigby, *Communist Party Membership in the U.S.S.R., 1917–1967* (Princeton: Princeton University Press, 1968).
14. Rabinowitch, *The Bolsheviks Come to Power*.
15. Daniels, *Red October*; Melgunov, *Seizure of Power*.
16. Ronald Suny, "Towards a Social History of the October Revolution."
17. Orlando Figes, *Peasant Russia, Civil War: The Volga Countryside In Revolution (1917–1921)* (Oxford: Clarendon Press, 1989).

Chapter 4. A Regime Is Born

The most important general works for this period are: E. H. Carr, *A History of Soviet Russia*, vol. 1: *The Bolshevik Revolution, 1917–1923*, 3 vols. (New York: Macmillan, 1951–1953); Leonard Schapiro, *The Communist Party of the Soviet Union*, 2nd ed. (New York: Random House, 1971); Merle Fainsod, *How Russia Is Ruled* (Cambridge: Harvard University Press, 1965); and Alec Nove, *An Economic History of the U.S.S.R.* (London: Penguin, 1989), hereafter cited as *Economic History*.

Notes

1. For a different assessment of War Communism, see the most comprehensive attempt at viewing the Civil War period from the perspective of social history: Diane P. Koenker, William Rosenberg, and Ronald Grigor Suny, *Party, State, and Society in the Russian Civil War* (Bloomington: Indiana University Press, 1989), especially parts 1 and 4. See also Abbott Gleason, Peter Kenez, and Richard Stites, eds., *Bolshevik Culture: Experiment and Order in the Russian Revolution* (Bloomington: Indiana University Press, 1985).
2. George Leggett, *The Cheka: Lenin's Political Policy* (London: Oxford University Press, 1981).
3. Oliver H. Radkey, *The Election to the Constituent Assembly of 1917* (Cambridge: Harvard University Press, 1950).
4. The major work on the Soviet economy under War Communism is Silvana Malle, *The Economic Organization of War Communism, 1918–1921* (Cambridge: Cambridge University Press, 1985).
5. Vladimir N. Brovkin, *The Mensheviks After October: Socialist Opposition and the Rise of the Bolshevik Dictatorship* (Ithaca, N.Y.: Cornell University Press, 1987). For the full story of the elimination of rival parties during the Civil War, see Leonard Schapiro, *The Origin of the Communist Autocracy: Political Opposition in the Soviet State* (New York: Praeger, 1965).
6. Richard Sakwa, *Soviet Communists in Power: A Study of Moscow During the Civil War, 1918–1921* (Houndsmill: Macmillan, 1988).
7. D. Fedotoff White, *The Growth of the Red Army* (Princeton: Princeton University Press, 1944); Mark von Hagen, *Soldiers in the Proletarian Dictatorship: The Red Army and the Soviet Socialist State, 1917–1930* (Ithaca, N.Y.: Cornell University Press, 1990).
8. David Footman, *Civil War in Russia* (London: Faber & Faber, 1961); W. Bruce Lincoln, *Red Victory: A History of the Russian Civil War* (New York: Simon & Schuster, 1989); Evan Mawdsley, *The Russian Civil War* (Boston: Allen & Unwin, 1987).

9. Orlando Figes, *Peasant Russia, Civil War: The Volga Countryside in Revolution* (Oxford: Clarendon Press, 1989).

10. Alec Nove, *Economic History*, chapter 3; Malle, *The Economic Organization of War Communism*, throughout. See also Thomas F. Remington, *Building Socialism in Bolshevik Russia: Ideology and Industrial Organization, 1917–1921* (Pittsburgh: University of Pittsburgh Press, 1984). For a perceptive, if somewhat dogmatic, libertarian analysis of the genesis of the Soviet economy, see Peter J. Boettke, *The Political Economy of Soviet Socialism: The Formative Years, 1918–1928* (Boston: Kluwer Academic Publishers).

11. Lars Lih, *Bread and Authority in Russia, 1914–1921* (Berkeley: University of California Press, 1990).

12. Nikolai Bukharin and Eugenii Preobrazhensky, *The ABC of Communism* (Harmondsworth: Penguin Books, 1969).

13. For an early and still cogent assessment of the problem, see Barrington Moore, *Soviet Politics: The Dilemma of Power* (Cambridge: Harvard University Press, 1950).

14. David Mitrany, *Marx Against the Peasant* (Chapel Hill: University of North Carolina Press, 1951).

15. See, for example, Karl Kautsky, *Die Agrarfrage* (1899), translated as *The Agrarian Question*, trans. Peter Burgess (Atlantic Highlands, N.J.: Zwan Publications, 1988).

16. Rigby, *Party Membership*, pp. 68–87; Fainsod, *How Russia Is Ruled*, pp. 248–250.

17. Victor Chernov, quoted in "Orlando Figes on Peasant Rebellions," *London Review of Books* 13 (September 25, 1991): 8–9.

18. Abdurakhman Avtorkhanov, *Proiskhozhdenie partokratii*, 2 vols. (Frankfurt: Possev-Verlag, 1973).

19. Nicholas Berdiaev, *The Origin of Russian Communism*, trans. R. M. French (Ann Arbor: University of Michigan Press, 1960).

20. One of the few works of Sovietology to advance a position similar to the one given here is Carl A. Linden, *The Soviet Party-State and the Politics of Ideocratic Despotism* (New York: Praeger, 1983).

Chapter 5. The Road Not Taken

The following are the important general works for the period of the NEP. E. H. Carr, *A History of Soviet Russia*, vol. 2: *The Interregnum, 1923–1924* (published in 1954); vol. 3: *Socialism in One Country, 1924–1926*, 3 vols. (published in 1958); with R. W. Davies, vol 4: *Foundations of a Planned Economy, 1926–1929*, 2 vols. (published in 1969–1979); all volumes published in New York by Macmillan. Also, Isaac Deutscher's three volumes on *Trotsky:* vol. 1, *The Prophet Armed. Trotsky: 1879–1921* (published in 1954); vol. 2, *The Prophet Unarmed. Trotsky: 1921–1929* (published in 1959); vol. 3, *The Prophet Outcast. Trotsky: 1929–1940* (published in 1963); all volumes published in New York by Oxford University Press. Also, Stephen F. Cohen, *Bukharin;* Moshe Lewin, *Russian Peasants and Soviet Power: A Study of Collectivization,* trans. Irene Move, with the assistance of John Biggart (London: Allen & Unwin, 1968), hereafter cited as *Russian Peasants.*

Notes

1. Richard Pipes, *The Formation of the Soviet Union,* rev. ed. (Cambridge, Harvard University Press, 1964); Hélène Carrère d'Encausse, *The Great Challenge: Nationalities and the Soviet State, 1917–1930,* trans. Nancy Festinger, foreword by Richard Pipes (New York and London: Holmes and Meier, 1992).
2. Israel Getzler, *Kronstadt 1917–1921: The Fate of a Soviet Democracy* (Cambridge: Cambridge University Press, 1983).
3. Oliver H. Radkey, *The Unknown Civil War in Soviet Russia: A Study of the Green Movement in the Tambov Region, 1920–21* (Stanford: Hoover Institution Press, 1976).
4. Nove, *Economic History,* chapter 4.
5. Lewin, *Political Undercurrents,* p. 124. The same idea is expressed by a historian with a very different attitude toward the USSR: Alain Besançon, *Court traité de soviétologie à l'usage des autorités civiles, militaires, et religieuses* (Paris: Hachette, 1976).
6. During his long stay in North America, Aleksandr Yakovlev became quite familiar with American Sovietological literature; he put it into circulation within IMEMO (Russian acronym for "Institute of the World Economy and International Relations"), the principal social-science think tank in Moscow, when Gorbachev made him its director in 1983. According to members of IMEMO, the American revisionist Sovietological perspective reached Gorbachev by way of Yakovlev.
7. Cohen, *Bukharin,* pp. 270–276.
8. Lewin, *Making,* chapter 12.
9. Gerschenkron, *Backwardness,* p. 64.
10. Dorothy Atkinson, *The End of the Russian Land Commune, 1905–1930* (Stanford: Stanford University Press, 1983).
11. Alan M. Ball, *Russia's Last Capitalists: The NEPmen, 1921–1929* (Berkeley: University of California Press, 1987).
12. Lewin, *Struggle,* chapter 4.
13. See chapter 2, note 8, for the sources of Lenin's views.

14. V. I. Lenin, "On Co-operation," in *Collected Works*, 4th ed. (Moscow: Progress Publishers, 1970), vol. 33, p. 473 (hereafter cited as Lenin, *Works*).

15. Lenin, *Works*, vol. 32, p. 8.

16. The fullest discussions of the economic debate of the twenties can be found in Lewin, *Russian Peasants;* and A. Ehrlich, *The Soviet Industrialization Debate* (Cambridge: Harvard University Press, 1960). See also Nove, *Economic History*, chapter 5; and Cohen, *Bukharin*, chapter 6. Marx's famous analysis of primitive accumulation is in *Capital*, vol. 1, chapter 24.

17. William J. Chase,*Workers, Society, and the Soviet State: Labor and Life in Moscow, 1918–1929* (Urbana: University of Illinois Press, 1987).

18. Isaac Deutscher, *Stalin: A Political Biography* (New York: Oxford University Press, 1949; second edition, 1966).

19. Robert Davies, *The Socialist Offensive: The Collectivization of Soviet Agriculture, 1929–1930* (London: Macmillan, 1980).

20. Lewin, *Making*, pp. 258–285; *The Gorbachev Phenomenon*, p. 194.

21. Kolakowski, *Main Currents*, vol. 3, pp. 218–219.

22. See Ball, *NEPmen*, chapter 6.

23. Nove, *Economic History*, p. 132.

24. See his *Notes of an Economist*, republished as *Izbrannye proizvedeniia* (Moscow: Politizdat, 1988).

25. R. Daniels, *The Conscience of the Revolution: Communist Opposition in Soviet Russia* (Cambridge: Harvard University Press, 1960).

26. Rigby, *Party Membership*, chapters 3–5; Fainsod, *How Russia Is Ruled*, pp. 249–259.

27. Robert C. Tucker, *Stalin as Revolutionary: 1879–1929* (London: Chatto & Windus, 1974); Boris Souvarine, *Stalin: A Critical Survey of Bolshevism* (New York: Alliance Book Corporation, Longmans, Green, 1939).

28. Deutscher, *Stalin*, p. 278.

29. Boris Nicolaevsky, *Power and the Soviet Elite: "Letter of an Old Bolshevik" and Other Essays*, ed. Janet D. Zagoria (New York: Praeger, 1965).

30. For the NEP seen from below, as a culture and a society, see Sheila Fitzpatrick, Alexander Rabinowitch, and Richard Stites, eds., *Russia in the Era of NEP: Explorations in Soviet Society and Culture* (Bloomington: Indiana University Press, 1991), especially chapters 1 and 18. For the utopian flowering, see Richard Stites, *Revolutionary Dreams* (London: Oxford University Press, 1989). See also Cohen, *Bukharin*, chapter 9.

31. For the initial hopes, and the disappointing results, of Soviet policy for improving the status of women during the first decade of the

regime, see Richard Stites *The Women's Liberation Movement in Russia: Feminism, Nihilism, and Bolshevism, 1860–1930* (Princeton: Princeton University Press, 1978), part 3. For the position of women throughout Soviet history, see Gail Lapidus, *Women in Soviet Society: Equality, Development, and Social Change* (Berkeley: University of California Press, 1978).

32. J. C. Curtiss, *The Russian Church and the Soviet State, 1917–50* (Boston: Little, Brown, 1953); W. C. Fletcher, *The Russian Orthodox Church Underground, 1917–70* (Oxford: Oxford University Press, 1971).

33. Peter Kenez, *The Birth of the Propaganda State: Soviet Methods of Mass Mobilization, 1917–1929* (London and New York: Cambridge University Press, 1985).

34. Alec Nove, *Economic Rationality and Soviet Politics, Or, Was Stalin Really Necessary?* (New York: Praeger, 1964).

35. Lewin, *Political Undercurrents*, p. 124.

Chapter 6. And They Built Socialism

The most important general works on Stalin are: Boris Souvarine, *Stalin: A Critical Survey of Bolshevism* (New York and London: Alliance Book Corporation; Longmans, Green, 1939), new French edition, *Staline: aperçu historique du bolchevisme* (Paris: Editions Champ Libre, 1977); Deutscher, *Stalin;* Adam Ulam, *Stalin: The Man and His Era* (New York: Viking Press, 1973); Robert C. Tucker, *Stalin in Power: The Revolution From Above, 1928–1941* (New York and London: Norton, 1990), hereafter cited as *Stalin in Power;* Robert McNeal, *Stalin: Man and Ruler* (New York: New York University Press, 1988); Robert Conquest, *Stalin: Breaker of Nations* (New York: Viking, 1991); Dmitri Volkogonov, *Stalin: Triumph and Tragedy*, trans. and ed. Harold Shukman (New York: Grove Weidenfeld, 1991). The most important works dealing with major aspects of the revolution from above are: E. H. Carr and R. W. Davies, *A History of Soviet Russia*, vol. 4: *Foundations of a Planned Economy, 1926–1929*, 2 vols. (New York: Macmillan, 1971–1972); Robert Conquest, *The Harvest of Sorrow: Soviet Collectivization and the Terror Famine* (London and Oxford: Hutchinson, 1986); R. W. Davies, *The Industrialization of Soviet Russia*, 2 vols. (London: Macmillan, 1980); R. W. Davies, *The Socialist Offensive: The Collectivization of Soviet Agriculture, 1929–1930*, 2 vols. (Cambridge: Harvard University Press, 1980); Naum Jasny, *The Socialized Agriculture of the U.S.S.R.* (Stanford: Stanford University Press, 1949); Naum Jasny, *Soviet Industrialization, 1928–1932* (Chicago: University of Chicago Press, 1961); Lewin, *Russian Peasants;* Nove, *Economic History.*

Notes

1. Nikolai Valentinov in *Sotsialisticheskii vestnik* (New York, April, 1961).
2. Robert C. Tucker, *Stalinism: Essays in Historical Interpretation* (New York: Norton, 1977), pp. 77–108.
3. Ulam, *Stalin*, p. 307.
4. Gerschenkron, *Backwardness*, passim. See also Igor Kliamkin, *"Kakaia doroga vedet k khramu," Novyi mir* (November, 1987), pp. 67–92.
5. See above, introduction.
6. Cohen, *Bukharin*, p. 322.
7. Robert M. Slusser, *Stalin in October: The Man Who Missed the Revolution* (Baltimore and London: Johns Hopkins University Press, 1987).
8. The foundations of the Austrian School's critique of socialist economies were laid before the First World War and derived from experience with both the German statist tradition in economics and the German opposition tradition of the Social Democrats. The founding work of this critical school is Friedrich von Wieser, *Social Economics*, trans. A. Ford Hinrichs (London: Allen & Unwin, 1927), originally published in 1914.
9. See Ludwig von Mises, *Socialism: An Economic and Sociological Analysis*, 2nd ed., trans. J. Kahone (New Haven: Yale University Press, 1951), original German edition, 1922. This book builds on his "Die Wirtschaftsrechnung im sozialistischen Gemeinwesen," *Archiv für Sozialwissenschaften* (Tübingen) 47 (1920): 86–121.
10. Marx, *Capital*, various editions, vol. 1, chapter 24.
11. Lewin, *Russian Peasants*, chapter 13.
12. Kendall E. Bailes, *Technology and Society Under Lenin and Stalin: Origins of the Soviet Technical Intelligentsia, 1917–1941* (Princeton: Princeton University Press, 1978), hereafter cited as *Technology and Society*.
13. Nina Tumarkin, *Lenin Lives! The Lenin Cult in Soviet Russia* (Cambridge: Harvard University Press, 1983).
14. Lewin, *Russian Peasants*, chapter 14.
15. Lynne Viola, *The Best Sons of the Fatherland: Workers in the Vanguard of Soviet Collectivization* (New York: Oxford University Press, 1987).
16. Viktor Danilov, *Rural Russia Under the New Regime*, trans. and intro. Orlando Figes (Bloomington: Indiana University Press, 1988); Boris Mozhaev, *Muzhiki i baby* (Moscow: Sovremennik, 1988); Mikhail Sholokhov, *Virgin Soil Upturned* (Moscow: Progress, 1979); Vasilii Grossman, *Forever Flowing*, trans. Thomas P. Whitney (New York: Harper & Row, 1972).
17. Conquest, *Harvest of Sorrow*.
18. Dorothy Atkinson, *The End of the Russian Land Commune, 1905–1930* (Stanford: Stanford University Press, 1983).

19. Jasny, *Industrialization*, p. 73.
20. Eugene Zaleski, *Planning for Economic Growth in the Soviet Union, 1928–1932*, trans. and eds. Marie-Christine MacAndrew and G. Warren Nutter (Chapel Hill: University of North Carolina Press, 1971); Eugene Zaleski, *Stalinist Planning for Growth, 1933–1952*, trans. and eds. Marie-Christine MacAndrew and John H. Moore (Chapel Hill: University of North Carolina Press, 1980).
21. For the degree of Soviet dependence on the West, particularly America, for the process of industrialization, see Anthony C. Sutton, *Western Technology and Soviet Economic Development, 1930–1945*, 3 vols. (Stanford: Hoover Institution Press, 1971), especially vols. 1 and 2.
22. Nove, *Economic History*, p. 199.
23. Hiroaki Kuromiya, *Stalin's Industrial Revolution: Politics and Workers, 1928–1932* (New York: Cambridge University Press, 1988).
24. See second epigraph in this chapter.
25. Sheila Fitzpatrick, *Education and Social Mobility in the Soviet Union, 1921–1934* (New York: Cambridge University Press, 1979); Bailes, *Technology and Society*, part 3.
26. Bailes, *Technology and Society*, pp. 95–140.
27. Lewis H. Siegelbaum, *Stakhanovism and the Politics of Productivity in the U.S.S.R., 1935–1941* (New York: Cambridge University Press, 1988).
28. Mikhail Heller, *Mashina i vintiki, Istoriia formirovaniia sovetskogo cheloveka* (London: Overseas Publications, 1985).
29. Quoted by Seweryn Bialer in *Stalin's Successors: Leadership, Stability, and Change in the Soviet Union* (Cambridge: Cambridge University Press, 1980), p. 22.
30. The term "command economy" was put into general circulation by Franz Neumann, *Behemoth: The Structure and Practice of National Socialism* (London: Gollancz, 1942); it was first applied to the Soviet system by Gregory Grossman in his "Notes for a Theory of the Command Economy," *Soviet Studies* 15 (October 1963).
31. Abram Bergson, *The Real National Income of Soviet Russia Since 1928* (Cambridge: Harvard University Press, 1961).
32. Nikolai Shmelyov and Vladimir Popov, *Na Perelome* (Moscow: Novosti, 1989).
33. David Landes, *The Unbound Prometheus* (Cambridge: Cambridge University Press, 1972), pp. 114–115.
34. Alexander Yanov, *The Origins of Autocracy: Ivan the Terrible in Russian History* (Berkeley and Los Angeles: University of California Press, 1981).
35. See above, chapter 2.
36. Ulam, *Stalin*, p. 290.

Chapter 7. Purge and Consolidation

In addition to the works cited at the beginning of the notes to chapter 6, the following are the most crucial for the matters treated here. The indispensable work on the purges is Robert Conquest, *The Great Terror* (New York: Macmillan 1968), and Robert Conquest, *The Great Terror: A Reassessment* (New York: Oxford University Press, 1990). The great literary monument on the subject is Aleksandr I. Solzhenitsyn, *The Gulag Archipelago, 1918–1956*, 3 vols. (New York: Harper & Row, 1973–1978). For a Reform Communist perspective on Stalinism, see Roy Medvedev, *Let History Judge: The Origins and Consequences of Stalinism* (New York: Knopf, 1972). See also Abdurakhman Avtorkhanov, *Stalin and the Soviet Communist Party: A Study in the Technology of Power* (Munich: Institute for the Study of the USSR, 1959); Alexander Dallin and George Breslauer, *Political Terror in Communist Systems* (Stanford: Stanford University Press, 1970); Merle Fainsod, *Smolensk Under Soviet Rule* (Cambridge: Harvard University Press, 1958); Nikita Khrushchev, *Khrushchev Remembers: The Last Testament*, trans. and ed. Strobe Talbott, 1st ed. (Boston: Little, Brown, 1974); Leon Trotsky, *The Revolution Betrayed: What Is the Soviet Union and Where Is It Going?*, trans. Max Eastman (London: Faber & Faber, 1937); R. C. Tucker and S. F. Cohen, eds., *The Great Purge Trial* (New York: Grosset & Dunlap, 1965); Amy Knight, *Beria, Stalin's First Lieutenant* (Princeton: Princeton University Press, 1993).

Notes

1. See Sheila Fitzpatrick, *Russian Revolution*.
2. Medvedev, *Let History Judge*.
3. See the debate between Fitzpatrick and the "New Cohort" in *Russian Review* 45 (October 1986): 357–413, and 46 (October 1987): 379–431.
4. The term "nationalization of culture" is that of Heller and Nekrich, *Utopia*, pp. 287–301.
5. Lynne Malley, *Culture of the Future: The Proletkult Movement and the Russian Civil War* (Berkeley: University of California Press, 1990).
6. Richard Stites, *Revolutionary Dreams: Utopian Vision and Experimental Life in the Russian Revolution* (London: Oxford University Press, 1989).
7. George M. Enteen, *The Soviet Scholar-Bureaucrat: M. N. Pokrovskii and the Society of Marxist Historians* (University Park: Pennsylvania State University Press, 1978); John Barber, *Soviet Historians in Crisis, 1928–1932* (London: Macmillan, 1981); Marin Pudeff, ed., *History in the U.S.S.R.: Selected Readings* (San Francisco: Chandler, 1967).
8. Kolakowski, *Main Currents*, vol. 3, pp. 63–76.

9. Edward J. Brown, *The Proletarian Episode in Russian Literature, 1928–1932* (New York: Columbia University Press, 1953).

10. Sheila Fitzpatrick, ed., *Cultural Revolution in Russia, 1928–1931* (Bloomington: Indiana University Press, 1988).

11. See above, chapter 1.

12. Kolakowski, *Main Currents*, vol. 3, pp. 91–105.

13. Nicholas Timasheff, *The Great Retreat: The Growth and Decline of Communism in Russia* (New York: Dutton, 1946).

14. John and Carol Garrard, *Inside the Soviet Writers' Union* (New York: The Free Press, 1990); Katarina Clark, *The Soviet Novel: History as Ritual* (Chicago: University of Chicago Press, 1985); Boris Groys, *Stalins Gesamtkunstwerk* (Munich and Vienna: Carl Hanser Verlag, 1988).

15. D. Jorovsky, *The Lysenko Affair* (Cambridge: Harvard University Press, 1970); Zhores Medvedev, *The Rise and Fall of T. D. Lysenko* (New York: Columbia University Press, 1969).

16. Loren R. Graham, *The Soviet Academy of Sciences and the Communist Party, 1927–1932* (Princeton: Princeton University Press, 1967), and *Science and Philosophy in the Soviet Union* (London: Allen Lane, 1973); Alexander Vucinich, *Empire of Knowledge: The Academy of Sciences of the USSR (1917–1970)*. (Berkeley and Los Angeles: University of California Press, 1984). See also Loren R. Graham, *Science in Russia and the Soviet Union: A Short History* (New York: Cambridge University Press, 1993).

17. Lewin, *Making*, pp. 269–276 and 300–314; Medvedev, *Let History Judge*, chapter 11, section 14.

18. See above, chapter 5.

19. Boris Pasternak, *Doctor Zhivago*, trans. Max Hayward and Manya Harari (London: Collins & Harvil Press, 1958), p. 422.

20. McNeal, *Stalin*, pp. 184–186.

21. Medvedev, *Let History Judge*, chapter 5; Schapiro, *History of Party*, chapter 23.

22. Ulam, *Stalin*, chapter 10.

23. Fainsod, *How Russia Is Ruled*, pp. 260–269; Rigby, *Party Membership*, chapters 5 and 6; Merle Fainsod and Jerry Hough, *How the Soviet Union Is Governed* (Cambridge: Harvard University Press, 1979), chapter 5.

24. See chapter 6, note 16.

25. Conquest, *Great Terror*, chapter 1; J. Arch Getty, *Origins of the Great Purges: The Soviet Communist Party Reconsidered, 1933–1938* (New York: Cambridge University Press, 1985).

26. Sheila Fitzpatrick, *Education and Social Mobility in the Soviet Union, 1921–1934* (Cambridge: Cambridge University Press, 1979).

27. Deutscher, *Stalin*, chapter 9.
28. See Jonathan Haslam, *Soviet Foreign Policy, 1933–1939* (London: Macmillan, 1986); and especially Haslam, "Political Opposition to Stalin and the Origins of the Terror in Russia, 1932–1936," *Historical Journal* 29 (1986): 395–418.
29. Deutscher, *Trotsky*, vol. 3, pp. 269–277.
30. Heller and Nekrich, *Utopia*, pp. 278–279.
31. See Cohen, *Bukharin*, pp. 369–372; Conquest, *Terror*, pp. 259–267.
32. Roy A. Medvedev and Zhores A. Medvedev, *Khrushchev: The Years in Power* (New York: Columbia University Press, 1976), part 1.
33. John Dornberg, *Brezhnev: The Masks of Power* (Delhi and London: Vikos Publishing House, 1974), part 2.
34. Fitzpatrick, *Russian Revolution*, p. 8.
35. Fitzpatrick, *Russian Revolution*, p. 157.
36. For example, see Victor Kravchenko, *I Chose Freedom: The Personal and Political Life of a Soviet Official* (New York: Scribners, 1946).
37. Getty, *Origins of the Great Purges*, p. 8; for similarly deflated figures, see Fainsod and Hough, *How the Soviet Union Is Governed*, pp. 176–177.
38. Alec Nove gives 10 million to 11 million for the 1930s, and a "deficit" of 27 million for 1939–1945. See Alec Nove, "The Scale of the Purges," in *The Stalin Phenomenon*, ed. Alec Nove (New York: St. Martin's Press, 1993), pp. 29–33; Nove, "Victims of Stalinism: How Many?" in *Stalinist Terror: New Perspectives*, eds. J. Arch Getty and Roberta Manning (New York: Cambridge University Press). (Most of this book is not convincing in its radical revisionism of the Stalin era.) See also another update of revisionist positions based on very selective sampling of Soviet archives: J. Arch Getty, Gábor T. Rittersporn, and Viktor N. Zemskov, "Victims of the Soviet Penal System in the Pre-War Years: A First Approach on the Basis of Archival Evidence," *American Historical Review* 98 (October 1993): 1017–1049.
39. McNeal, *Stalin*, p. 198.
40. Kolakowski, *Main Currents*, vol. 3, pp. 77–91.
41. Schapiro, *History of Party*, chapter 22.

Chapter 8. The Fortunes of War

The literature on post-1941 Soviet history is less voluminous than that on the 1920s and 1930s, and in particular it is of a different character. Because the more recent period poses no such pivotal problems as the proletarian nature of October or the "necessity" of Stalin, the corresponding literature tends to be less analytical and more occupied with expository narrative. This fact will be reflected in the present and following chapters, and bibliographical annotations will accordingly be briefer.

The principal works relevant to the present chapter are: Adam Ulam, *Expansion and Coexistence: Soviet Foreign Policy, 1917–73* (New York: Praeger, 1968); Jonathan Haslam, *Soviet Foreign Policy, 1930–33: The Impact of the Depression* (London: Macmillan, 1983), and *The Soviet Union and the Struggle for Collective Security in Europe, 1933–1939* (New York: St. Martin's Press, 1984); Robert Conquest, *Power and Policy in the U.S.S.R.: The Study of Soviet Dynastics* (London: Macmillan 1961); Vladimir Petrov and Aleksandr Nekrich, *"June 22, 1941": Soviet Historians and the German Invasion* (Columbia: University of South Carolina Press, 1968); John Erickson, *The Road to Stalingrad* (New York: Harper & Row, 1975), and *The Road to Berlin: Continuing the History of Stalin's War with Germany* (Boulder, Colo.: Westview Press, 1983); Timothy J. Colton, *Commissars, Commanders, and Civilian Authority: The Structure of Soviet Military Politics* (Cambridge: Harvard University Press, 1979); Alexander Dallin, *German Rule in Russia, 1941–1945* (London: Macmillan, 1957); George Fischer, *Soviet Opposition to Stalin: A Case Study in World War II* (Cambridge: Harvard University Press, 1952).

Notes

1. George Kennan, *Soviet Foreign Policy, 1917–1941* (Westport, Conn.: Greenwood Press, 1978).
2. Franz Borkenau, *World Communism* (Ann Arbor: University of Michigan Press, 1962).
3. Ruth Fischer, *Stalin and German Communism: A Study in the Origins of the State Party* (Cambridge: Harvard University Press, 1948).
4. See above, chapter 7; D. T. Cattell, *Communism and the Spanish Civil War* (Berkeley and Los Angeles: University of California Press, 1955); Paolo Spiriano, *Stalin and the European Communists* (London: Verso, 1988).
5. Gerhard L. Weinberg, *Germany and the Soviet Union, 1939–1941* (Leiden: E. J. Brill, 1954).
6. Heller and Nekrich, *Utopia*, chapter 7.
7. Heller and Nekrich, *Utopia*, chapter 8; see especially pp. 371–374, 383–393, 399–403, and 442–446.
8. Dallin, *German Rule*,
9. L. Gouré and H. Dinerstein, *Moscow in Crisis* (Glencoe, Ill.: The Free Press, 1955).
10. Fischer, *Opposition to Stalin*.

11. Ulam, *Stalin*, p. 567

12. Nove, *Economic History*, chapters 10 and 11.

13. Robert Conquest, *The Nation Killers: The Soviet Deportation of Nationalities* (London: Sphere Books, 1972); Aleksandr Nekrich, *The Punished Peoples: The Deportation and Fate of the Soviet Minorities at the End of the Second World War*, trans. George Saunders (New York: Norton, 1978).

14. Fainsod, *How Russia Is Ruled*, pp. 269–275; Rigby, *Party Membership*, chapters 7 and 8.

15. Norman Davies, *God's Playground: A History of Poland*, vol. 2: *1795 to the Present* (New York: Columbia University Press, 1982), chapters 20 and 21.

16. François Fejtö, *Histoires des démocraties populaires*, vol. 1: *L'ère de Staline, 1945–1952* (Paris: Seuil, 1952); Vojtech Mastny, *Russia's Road to the Cold War: Diplomacy, Warfare, and the Politics of Communism, 1941–1945* (New York: Columbia University Press, 1979).

17. Adam Ulam, *Titoism and the Cominform* (Cambridge: Harvard University Press, 1952).

18. Adam Ulam, *Expansion and Coexistence*, chapter 9.

19. Ulam, *Expansion and Coexistence*, chapter 10, section 1.

20. Werner Hahn, *Postwar Soviet Politics: The Fall of Zhdanov and the Defeat of Moderation* (Ithaca, N.Y.: Cornell University Press, 1969); Louis Rappaport, *Stalin's War Against the Jews* (New York: The Free Press, 1990).

21. Sergei Goncharov, John Lewis, and Xue Lital, *Uncertain Partners: Stalin, Mao, and the Korean War* (Stanford: Stanford University Press, 1992) gives interesting if inconclusive evidence that Stalin contemplated major international war at the end of his career.

Chapter 9. Reform Communism I

The most important works on the Khrushchev years are: Robert Conquest, *Power and Policy in the U.S.S.R.: The Study of Soviet Dynasties* (London: Macmillan, 1961); Carl A. Linden, *Khrushchev and the Soviet Leadership* (Baltimore: Johns Hopkins University Press, 1966), hereafter cited as *Khrushchev*; Michel Tatu, *Power in the Kremlin: From Khrushchev to Kosygin*, trans. Helen Katel (New York: Viking, 1969); George W. Breslauer, *Khrushchev and Brezhnev as Leaders* (Boston: Allen & Unwin, 1982). See also Roy Medvedev, *Khrushchev* (New York: Doubleday, 1984); Roy and Zhores Medvedev, *Khrushchev: The Years in Power* (New York: Columbia University Press, 1976); Nikita Khrushchev, *Khrushchev Remembers*, trans. and ed. Strobe Talbott (Boston: Little, Brown, 1970), *Khrushchev Remem-*

bers: The Last Testament, trans. and ed. Strobe Talbott (Boston: Little, Brown, 1974), and *Khrushchev Remembers: The Glasnost Tapes*, trans. and ed. Jerrold L. Schecter, with Vyacheslav V. Luchkov (Boston: Little, Brown, 1990); Fedor Burlatskii, "Khrushchev," *Literaturnaia gazeta* (Moscow), February 24, 1982; Adam Ulam, *The Rivals: America and Russia Since WW II* (New York: Viking, 1971); Edward J. Brown, *Russian Literature Since the Revolution*, rev. ed. (Cambridge: Harvard University Press, 1982).

Notes

1. This is contrary to the view of Stephen Cohen, *Rethinking*, and of Moshe Lewin, *Political Undercurrents*, who see Reform Communism as the fulfillment of the system's potential. Another example of this view is Seweryn Bialer, *Stalin's Successors: Leadership, Stability, and Change in the Soviet Union* (New York: Cambridge University Press, 1980).
2. Solzhenitsyn, *Gulag*, vol. 3, part 4, chapters 11 and 12.
3. Nikita Khrushchev, *The Crimes of the Stalin Era* (New York: New Leader, 1962), p. 248.
4. Roy Medvedev, *Khrushchev*, pp. 91–92.
5. Charles Gati, *The Bloc That Failed: Soviet–East European Relations in Transition* (Bloomington: Indiana University Press, 1990).
6. Fejtö, *Histoire des démocraties populaires*, vol. 2: *Après Staline, 1953–1971* (Paris: Seuil, 1969), chapter 5; Davies, *God's Playground*, vol. 2, chapter 23.
7. Fejtö, *Histoire des démocraties populaires*, vol. 2, chapters 5 and 8; Miklos Molnar, *Budapest 1956: A History of the Hungarian Revolution*, trans. Jennetta Ford (London: Allen & Unwin, 1971); Paul Zinner, *Revolution in Hungary* (New York: Columbia University Press, 1962).
8. Robert Conquest, *Courage of Genius: The Pasternak Affair* (London: Collins/Harvill, 1961); Hugh McLean and Walter M. Vickery, eds., *The Year of Protest, 1956: An Anthology of Soviet Literary Materials* (New York: Vintage, 1961).
9. Adam Ulam, *Expansion and Coexistence* (New York: Praeger, 1968), chapters 9 and 10; Klaus Mehnert, *Peking and Moscow: Soviet Foreign Policy, 1917–73*, trans. Leila Vennewitz (New York: Putnam, 1963).
10. Ulam *Expansion and Coexistence*, chapters 9 and 10.
11. Fejtö, *Histoire des démocraties populaires*, vol. 2, chapter 10.
12. Ulam, *The Rivals*.
13. Linden, *Khrushchev*.
14. Nove, *Economic History*, chapter 11; K. E. Wadekin, *The Private Sector in Soviet Agriculture* (Berkeley: University of California Press, 1973);

Jerzy F. Karcz, ed., *Soviet and East European Agriculture* (Berkeley: University of California Press, 1967).

15. Martin McCauley, *Khrushchev and the Development of Soviet Agriculture: The Virgin Lands Programme* (London: Macmillan, 1976).

16. Nove, *Economic History*, pp. 332–355; Linden, *Khrushchev*, chapters 2 and 4.

17. George Breslauer, *Khrushchev and Brezhnev*, parts 1 and 2.

18. Linden, *Khrushchev*, chapters 2 and 4; Breslauer, *Khrushchev and Brezhnev*, part 2.

19. For the battle to publish *Ivan Denisovich*, see Aleksandr Solzhenitsyn, *The Oak and the Calf: Sketches of Literary Life in the Soviet Union*, trans. Harry Willets (New York: Harper & Row, 1980).

20. Ulam, *Expansion and Coexistence*, chapters 10, 11, and 12; Mehnert, *Peking and Moscow*, part 4.

21. Ulam, *Expansion and Coexistence*, chapter 10, section 2, and chapter 11; Ulam, *The Rivals*, part 3, chapters 8 and 9.

22. David Holloway, *The Soviet Union and the Arms Race* (New Haven: Yale University Press, 1983).

23. Fainsod, *How Russia Is Ruled*, pp. 275–282; Rigby, *Party Membership*, chapters 9 and 10. Fainsod and Hough, *How the Soviet Union Is Governed*, chapter 9.

Chapter 10. And the Bill Came Due

With the Brezhnev era, the bibliography of Soviet history dwindles drastically. Among the more important general works are: John Dornberg, *Brezhnev: Masks of Power* (New York: Basic Books, 1974); Abdurakhman Avtorkhanov, *Sila i bessilie Brezhneva* (Frankfurt: Posser Verlag, 1979); Hélène Carrère d'Encausse, *Decline of an Empire: The Soviet Socialist Republics in Revolt*, trans. Martin Sokolinsky and Henry A. La Farge (New York: Newsweek Books, 1979); John Dunlop, *The Faces of Contemporary Russian Nationalism* (Princeton: Princeton University Press, 1983); Igor Birman, *Personal Consumption in the USSR and the USA* (London: Macmillan, 1989); Adam Ulam, *Dangerous Relations: The Soviet Union in World Politics, 1970–1982* (New York: Oxford University Press, 1983); Raymond L. Garthoff, *Détente and Confrontation: American-Soviet Relations from Nixon to Reagan* (Washington, D.C.: Brookings Institution, 1985); David Holloway, *The Soviet Union and the Arms Race* (New Haven: Yale University Press, 1983); Andrei Sakharov, *My Country and the World* (New York: Knopf, 1975); Ludmilla Alekseeva, *Soviet Dissent: Contemporary Movements for National, Religious, and Human Rights* (Middletown, Conn.: Wesleyan University Press, 1985).

Notes

1. Roy Medvedev, *All Stalin's Men*, trans. Harold Shukman (Oxford: Basil Blackwell, 1983), chapter 3; Serge Petroff, *The Red Eminence: A Biography of Mikhail A. Suslov* (Clifton, N.J.: Kingston Press, 1988).
2. Dornberg, *Brezhnev*, part 4; see also above, chapter 7.
3. See above, chapter 1.
4. Peter Reddaway, trans. and ed., *Uncensored Russia: Protest and Dissent in the Soviet Union: The Unofficial Moscow Journal "A Chronicle of Current Events"* (New York: American Heritage Press, 1972); Stephen Cohen, ed., *An End to Silence: Uncensored Opinion in the Soviet Union— From Roy Medvedev's Underground Magazine "Political Diary"* (New York: Norton, 1982), see especially Roy Medvedev, "The Danger of a Revival of Stalinism," pp. 153–161.
5. Kostas Papaioannou, *L'Idéologie froide, essai sur le dépérissement du marxisme* (Paris: J. J. Pauvert, 1967); Alain Besançon, *L'Eloge de la corruption* (Paris: Calmann-Levy, 1977).
6. Nove, *Economic History*, pp. 362–367.
7. Nove, *Economic History*, pp. 362–363.
8. Moshe Lewin, *Political Undercurrents in Soviet Economic Debates: From Bukharin to the Modern Reformers* (Princeton: Princeton University Press, 1974), chapters 6, 7, 8.
9. See his essay in Cohen, *An End to Silence*, pp. 223–227.
10. Naum Jasny, *The Socialized Agriculture of the USSR* (Stanford: Stanford University Press, 1949); Naum Jasny, *Soviet Industrialization, 1928– 1952* (Chicago: University of Chicago Press, 1960); Igor Birman, *Personal Consumption in the USSR and the USA* (London: Macmillan, 1989).
11. Dmitri Steinberg, "The Real Size and Structure of the Soviet Economy: Alternative Estimates of Soviet GNP and Military Expenditures for 1987," paper presented at the American Enterprise Institute conference "Comparing the Soviet and American Economies: Overall Output, Levels of Consumption, Military Expenditures," Warrenton, Virginia, April 19–22, 1990, p. 3.
12. Murray Feshbach, *The Soviet Union: Population, Trends, and Dilemmas* (Washington, D.C.: Population Reference Bureau, 1982).
13. Seweryn Bialer, *The Soviet Paradox: External Expansion, Internal Decline* (New York: Knopf, 1986); Richard Pipes, *Survival Is Not Enough: Soviet Realities and America's Future* (New York: Simon & Schuster, 1984); Marshall I. Goldman, *U.S.S.R. in Crisis: The Failure of an Economic System* (New York: Norton, 1983).
14. Solzhenitsyn, *Gulag*, vol. 3, pp. 506–514.

15. Gregory Grossman, "The Second Economy: Boon or Bane for the Reform of the First Economy?" in Stanislaw Gomulka, Yong-Chool Ha, and Cae-One Kim, eds., *Economic Reforms in the Socialist World* (Armonk, N.Y.: M. E. Sharpe, 1989); Gregory Grossman, "The 'Second Economy' in the U.S.S.R.," *Problems of Communism* 26 (September–October 1977): 25–40; Konstantin Simes, *The Corrupt Society: The Secret World of Soviet Capitalism*, trans. J. Edwards and M. Schneider (New York: Simon & Schuster, 1982).

16. See Dmitri Steinberg, "Soviet Economy," for a full discussion of this issue.

17. Abel Aganbegyan, *The Economic Challenge of Perestroika* (Bloomington: Indiana University Press, 1988).

18. John Lewis Gaddis, *Russia, the Soviet Union, and the United States* (New York: McGraw, 1978), chapter 9. See also his *The Long Peace: Inquiries into the History of the Cold War* (New York: Oxford University Press, 1987).

19. Gaddis, *U.S.–Soviet Relations*, p. 276.

20. Jonathan Haslam, *The Soviet Union and the Politics of Nuclear Weapons in Europe, 1969–1987: The Problem of the SS-20s* (London: Macmillan, 1989), hereafter cited as *Nuclear Weapons;* David Holloway, *The Soviet Union and the Arms Race* (New Haven: Yale University Press, 1983).

21. Heller and Nekrich, *Utopia*, chapter 9.

22. Zhores A. Medvedev, *Andropov* (New York: Norton, 1983), part 2, chapters 7, 8, 9.

23. Max Hayward, ed., *On Trial: The Case of Sinyavsky and Daniel* (London: Collins/Harvill, 1967).

24. Andrei Sakharov, *Sakharov Speaks*, ed. Harrison E. Salisbury (New York: Knopf, 1974).

25. Roy Medvedev, *Let History Judge: The Origins and Consequences of Stalinism*, trans. Colleen Taylor (New York: Knopf, 1972).

26. See Cohen, *An End to Silence*, pp. 317–327.

27. J. J. Marie and Carol Head, eds., *L'Affaire Guinzbourg-Galanskov*, trans. J. J. Mare and Nadine Marie (Paris: Seuil, 1969).

28. Valery Chalidze, *To Defend Those Rights: Human Rights and the Soviet Union*, trans. Guy Daniels (New York: Random House, 1975); Peter Reddaway, ed., *Uncensored Russia: Protest and Dissent in the Soviet Union* (New York: American Heritage Press, 1972).

29. Andrei Amalrik, *Will the Soviet Union Survive Until 1984?* (New York: Harper & Row, 1970).

30. *Letter to the Soviet Leaders*, trans. Hilary Sternberg (New York: Harper & Row, 1974).

31. Georgii A. Arbatov, *The System: An Insider's Life in Soviet Politics* (New York: Times Books/Random House, 1992).

32. A particularly revealing example of this symbiosis is provided in Aleksandr Tsipko, "Kontrrevoliutsia v Tska KPSS" [Counterrevolution in the Central Committee of the Communist Party] (unpublished, untranslated. typescript).

33. Edward Brown, *Russian Literature Since the Revolution* (Cambridge: Harvard University Press, 1982), chapters 11–13.

34. Fainsod and Hough, *How the Soviet Union Is Governed*, chapters 9–14.

35. Aleksandr Zinoviev, *Homo Sovieticus*, trans. Charles Janson (Boston: Atlantic Monthly Press, 1985).

36. Arbatov, *The System*, pp. 218–235.

37. Mikhail Voslenskii, *Nomenklatura: The Soviet Ruling Class*, trans. Eric Mosbacher, preface by Milovan Djilas (New York: Doubleday, 1984), first published in German four years earlier (Vienna: Molden, 1980).

38. See Fejtö, *Histoire des démocraties populaires*, vol. 2, chapters 11 and 12; H. Gordon Skilling, *Czechoslovakia's Interrupted Revolution* (Princeton: Princeton University Press, 1976), p. 532; Ivan Svitak, *The Czechoslovak Experiment, 1968–1969* (New York: Columbia University Press, 1971); Zdenek Mlynar, *Nightfrost in Prague* (New York: Karz-Cohl, 1980).

39. Janos Kornai, "The Hungarian Reform Process: Visions, Hopes, and Reality," *Journal of Economic Literature* 24 (December 1986): 1687–1737.

40. J. Karpinski, *Countdown: The Polish Upheavals of 1956, 1968, 1970, 1976, 1980 . . .* (New York: Karz-Cohl, 1982); Abraham Brumberg, ed., *Poland: Genesis of a Revolution* (New York: Random House, 1983); Martin Malia, "Poland's Eternal Return," *New York Review of Books* 30 (September 29, 1983): 18–27.

41. Jan Jozef Lipski, *KOR* (London: Aneks, 1983).

42. Timothy Garton Ash, *The Polish Revolution: Solidarity, 1980–82* (London: Jonathan Cape, 1983); Jerzy Holzer, *"Solidarnosc": 1980–1981* (Paris: Instytut Literacki, 1984); Martin Malia, "Poland's Winter War," *New York Review of Books* 29 (March 18, 1982): 21–26.

Chapter 11. Reform Communism II

The chapter is based in large part on my reading of the Soviet press and on periodic visits to the Soviet Union, including attendance at the First Congress of Peoples Deputies in 1989 and the Twenty-seventh Party Congress in 1990.

Most of the principal works relevant to the *perestroika* years were composed by direct observers of the events described. For the politics of *perestroika*, see Hedrick Smith, *The New Russians* (New York: Random House, 1991); Robert Kaiser, *Why Gorbachev Happened: His Triumphs, His*

Failure, His Fall (New York: Touchstone, 1991, revised edition 1992); David Remnick, *Lenin's Tomb* (New York: Random House, 1993); John B. Dunlop, *The Rise of Russia and the Fall of the Soviet Empire* (Princeton: Princeton University Press, 1993); Alec Nove, *Glasnost in Action: Cultural Renaissance in Russia* (Boston: Unwin Hyman, 1989).

For the economics of *perestroika*, see Anders Aslund, *Gorbachev's Struggle for Economic Reform* (Ithaca, N.Y.: Cornell University Press, 1989, revised edition 1991); Marshall I. Goldman, *Gorbachev's Challenge: Economic Reform in the Age of High Technology* (New York: Norton, 1987); Marshall I. Goldman, *What Went Wrong with Perestroika* (New York: Norton, 1992); Michael Ellman and Vladimir Kontorovich, eds., *The Disintegration of the Soviet Economic System* (London: Rutledge, 1992).

Among Soviet participants in *perestroika*, see especially: Abel Aganbegyan, *The Economic Challenge of Perestroika* (Bloomington: Indiana University Press, 1988); Tatyana Zaslavskaia, *The Second Socialist Revolution: An Alternative Soviet Strategy*, trans. Susan M. Davies and Jenny Warren (London: I. B. Tauris, 1990); Nikolai Shmelev and Vladimir Popov, *The Turning Point: Revitalizing the Soviet Economy*, trans. Michele A. Berdy, preface by Richard Erickson (New York: Doubleday, 1989); Aleksandr Yakovlev, *The Fate of Marxism in Russia*, trans. Catherine A. Fitzpatrick (New Haven: Yale University Press, 1993).

See also Isaac J. Tarasulo, ed., *Gorbachev and Glasnost: Viewpoints from the Soviet Press* (Wilmington, Del.: SR Books, 1989); Stephen F. Cohen and Katarina vanden Heuvel, eds., *Voices of Glasnost: Interviews with Gorbachev's Reformers* (New York: Norton, 1989).

Notes

1. Zhores A. Medvedev, *Andropov* (New York: Norton, 1983).
2. Seweryn Bialer, ed., *Politics, Society, and Nationality Inside Gorbachev's Russia* (Boulder, Colo.: Westview Press, 1988), p. 18.
3. Tatiana Zaslavskaia, "The Novosibirsk Report," *Survey* 28 (1984): 88–108.
4. Michel Tatu, *Gorbachev: L'U.R.S.S., va-t-elle changer?* (Paris: Le Centurion–Le Monde, 1987).
5. Zdenek Mlynar, *L'Unita*, April 9, 1985; English translation in *FBIS* (Foreign Broadcast Information Service), June 4, 1990.
6. For an assessment of Gorbachev's early intentions, see Gail Lapidus, "Gorbachev and the Reform of the Soviet System," *Daedalus* 16 (Spring 1987): 1–30.
7. *Zhivoe tvorchestvo naroda* (Moscow, 1984), summarized in Kaiser, *Why Gorbachev Happened*, pp. 75–80.

8. Sergei Kuleshev, "Gorbachev Kak Lenin Segodnia" (Gorbachev as the Lenin of Today), manuscript, 1990.

9. Haslam, *Nuclear Weapons*.

10. Seweryn Bialer, *The Soviet Paradox: External Expansion, Internal Decline* (New York: Knopf, 1988), chapter 5.

11. Haslam, *Nuclear Weapons*, pp. 143–145.

12. Gaddis, *Russia, the Soviet Union, and the United States*, p. 235.

13. For the early stages of economic *perestroika*, see above all Aslund, *Gorbachev's Struggle*, chapters 2, 3, and 4. See also Goldman, *Gorbachev's Challenge*, chapters 4 and 5; Edward A. Hewett, *Reforming the Soviet Economy* (Washington, D.C.: Brookings Institution, 1988).

14. CIA, *Handbook of Economic Statistics*, 1987.

15. Kaiser, *Why Gorbachev Happened*, p. 96.

16. The best analysis of the literature of *glasnost* is Alec Nove, *Glasnost in Action*.

17. Aleksandr Yakovlev, public lecture and conversations in Berkeley, California, February 1993; see also his memoirs, *Predislovie, obval, posleslovie* (Moscow: Novosti, 1992).

18. Nikolai Shmelev, "Avansy i dolgi," *Novyi mir* (June 1987): 142–158.

19. John Morrison, *Boris Yeltsin: From Bolshevik to Democrat* (New York: Dutton, 1991), chapter 6.

20. Yegor Ligachev, *Inside Gorbachev's Kremlin: The Memoirs of Yegor Ligachev*, trans. Catherine A. Fitzpatrick, Michele A. Berdy, and Dobrochna Dyrcz-Freeman, introduction by Stephen F. Cohen (New York: Pantheon, 1993).

21. Andranik Migranyan, "Dolgii put k evropeiskomu domu," *Novyi mir* (July 1983): 183.

22. Quoted in Kaiser, *Why Gorbachev Happened*, p. 256.

23. Vasilii Grossman, *Life and Fate*, trans. Robert Chandler (London: Collins/Harvill, 1985), introduction.

24. Anna Larina, *This I Cannot Forget: The Memoirs of Nikolai Bukharin's Widow*, trans. Gary Kern, introduction by Stephen F. Cohen (New York: Norton, 1993).

25. See above, chapter 6, note 16.

26. Gavriil Popov, "O romane Aleksandra Beka 'Novoe naznachenie,'" *Nauka i zhin* (April 1987): 54–65.

27. See above, chapter 6.

28. Fedor Burlatskii, "Khrushchev: Shtrikhi k politicheskomy portretu," *Literaturnaia gazeta* (February 24, 1988): 14.

29. Vasilii Seliunin, "Istoki," *Novyi mir* (May 1988): 162–198.

30. Aleksandr Tsipko, "Istoki Stalinizma," *Nauka i zhizn* (November 1988): 45–55; (December 1988): 40–47; (January 1989): 46–56; and

(February 1989): 53–61. See also his *Is Stalinism Really Dead?* trans. E. A. Tichina and S. V. Nikheev (San Francisco: Harper, 1990).

31. Igor Kliamkin, "Kakaia ulitsa vedet k khramu," *Novyi mir* (November 1987): 150–188.

32. Iurii Afanasiev, *Russkaia mysl* (March 14, 1989).

33. Quoted in *Le Monde*, December 20, 1988.

34. Quoted in Kaiser, *Why Gorbachev Happened*, pp. 376 and 400.

35. Geoffrey Hosking, *The Awakening of the Soviet Union* (Cambridge: Harvard University Press, 1990).

36. Bahdan Nahaylo and Victor Swoboda, *Soviet Disunion: A History of the Nationalities Problem in the USSR* (New York: The Free Press, 1990).

37. See above, chapter 5.

38. Victor Zaslavsky, *The Neo-Stalinist State: Class, Ethnicity, and Consensus in Soviet Society* (Armonk N.Y.: M. E. Sharpe, 1982).

39. See above, chapters 7 and 10.

40. Hélène Carrère d'Encausse, *The End of the Soviet Empire: The Triumph of the Nations*, trans. Franklin Philip (New York: Basic Books, 1993).

Chapter 12. From *Perestroika* to Collapse

The present chapter is based, even more than the preceding one, on personal impressions and reading of the contemporary press. The basic bibliography is the same as that of the previous chapter. See also John Morrison, *Boris Yeltsin: From Bolshevik to Democrat* (New York: Dutton 1991); Wlodzmierz Brus and Kazmierz Laski, *From Marx to the Market: Socialism in Search of an Economic System* (Oxford: Clarendon Press, 1989); Janos Kornai, *The Socialist System: The Political Economy of Communism* (Princeton: Princeton University Press, 1992); Murray Feshbach and Alfred Friendly, Jr., *Ecocide in the USSR: Health and Nature Under Siege* (New York: Basic Books, 1992).

Notes

1. Text of Congress debates, *Izvestiia*, June 7, 1989.

2. Andrei Sakharov, "A Speech to the People's Congress," in *New York Review of Books* 36 (August 17, 1989): 25–26.

3. Iurii Kariakin, *Izvestiia*, June 9, 1989.

4. A remark in private conversation.

5. Ivan Drach, the leader of Ukraine's "Rukh," private conversation, September 1989.

6. Timothy Garton Ash, *The Magic Lantern* (New York: Random House, 1990), p.78.

7. Charles Gati, *The Bloc That Failed: Soviet–East European Relations in*

Transition (Bloomington: Indiana University Press, 1990), part 3; hereafter cited as *Bloc That Failed.*

8. Private conversation, February 1993.

9. Remark in private conversation, September 1988.

10. Garton Ash, *Magic Lantern,* pp. 47–60; and Gati, *Bloc That Failed,* pp. 170–174.

11. Garton Ash, *Magic Lantern,* pp. 25–46.

12. Andrei Codrescu, *The Hole in the Flag: A Romanian Exile's Story of Return and Revolution* (New York: Morrow, 1991).

13. Bill Keller, in *New York Times,* January 22, 1989.

14. The author's article, "To the Stalin Mausoleum," *Daedalus* 119 (Winter 1990): 295–344. Published under the pseudonym "Z"; translated at this time by "White Tass" (that is, confidentially for only the government and the Party) and distributed during the Central Committee meeting. Participants in the meeting later told the author that it had the effect of increasing awareness of the gravity of the crisis, and thus of helping Gorbachev.

15. Morrison, *Yeltsin.*

16. Mikhail Souloukhin, "Chitaia Lenina," *Rodina* (December 1990).

17. Aslund, *Gorbachev's Struggle,* chapters 7–9; Goldman, *Gorbachev's Challenge,* chapters 5–7.

18. It is analyzed in detail in Ed A. Hewett, "The New Soviet Plan," *Foreign Affairs* 69 (Winter 1990–1991): 146–167.

19. Martin Malia, "A New Russian Revolution?" *New York Review of Books* 38 (July 18, 1991): 29–32; and Malia, "Yeltsin's Revolution," *New York Review of Books* 38 (September 26, 1991): 22–29.

20. Graham Allison and Robert Blackwill, "America's Stake in the Soviet Future," *Foreign Affairs* 70 (Summer 1991): 77–97.

21. Victor Zaslavsky, "Nationalism and Democratic Transition in Post-Communist Societies," *Daedalus* 121 (Spring 1992): 97–123.

Chapter 13. The Perverse Logic of Utopia

Notes

1. For example, see Alexander Dallin, "Causes of the Collapse of the USSR," *Post-Soviet Affairs* 8 (1992): 279–302; and Abraham Brumberg, "The Road to Minsk," *New York Review of Books* 39 (January 30, 1992): 21–26.

2. As might be expected, adherents of these positions in the West usually consider themselves "democratic socialists," and in the East they are often to be found in reconstructed Communist parties that

now use the name "socialist" or "Left." Some representative samples of this position are Robert V. Daniels, *The End of the Communist Revolution* (London and New York: Routledge, 1993); Peter Reddaway, "Russia on the Brink?" *New York Review of Books* 40 (January 28, 1993): 30–35, and "Yeltsin," *New York Review of Books* 40 (December 2, 1993): 16–21. See also Stephen F. Cohen, "American Policy and Russia's Future," *The Nation* 256 (April 5, 1993): 476–485; Moshe Lewin, "Russia: Nationalism & Economy," *Dissent* (Spring 1992): 172–175.

3. See above, chapter 5.
4. For a similar perspective, see Martin Malia, "From Under the Rubble, What?" *Problems of Communism* (January–April 1992): 89–106.
5. See Karl Griewank, *Der neuzeitliche Revolutionsbegriff* (Frankfurt: Europaische Verlagsanstalt, 1969).
6. See above, chapter 1.
7. See, for example, Shlomo Avineri, "Capitalism Has Not Won, Socialism Is Not Dead," *Dissent* 39 (Winter 1992): 7–11.

Epilogue

Notes

1. For an early and accurate assessment of the extent of the disaster, see Pierre Briançon, *Les héritiers du désastre: précis de décomposition de l'univers soviétique* (Paris: Calmann-Levy, 1992).
2. See above, chapter 3.
3. See, for example, Moshe Lewin, *The Gorbachev Phenomenon;* and *Making.*
4. See above, chapter 3.
5. See above, chapter 6.
6. Solzhenitsyn, *Gulag Archipelago*, vol. 1, p. 181.
7. See for example, Alec Nove, "Ideology, Planning and the Market," *Critical Review* (Fall 1991): 559–572.
8. See, for example, Joan Wallach Scott, "Gender: A Useful Category of Historical Analysis," *American Historical Review* 91 (1986): 1053–1075.
9. For the illiberal potential of the ecology movement, see Garrett Hardin, *Living Within Limits: Ecology, Economics, and Population Taboos* (New York: Oxford University Press); and Donald Worster, *The Wealth of Nature: Environmental History and the Ecological Imagination* (New York: Oxford University Press).

ACKNOWLEDGMENTS

Among the persons who have made this book possible, one name leads all the rest; he indeed would have been the subject of the dedication, if the dissidents from Communism had not furnished my first inspiration. This person is Stephen Graubard, long-time friend and editor of the journal of the American Academy of Arts and Sciences, *Daedalus*. In 1989, at a time when commitment to Gorbachev's Reform Communism was the regnant orthodoxy in the West, Stephen Graubard gave prominence to the vigorously dissenting views I expressed in my article "To the Stalin Mausoleum," views which I had not been able to publish in unadulterated form in any journal of comparable stature. Without him this book, and the belated Sovietological career which preceded it, would have been impossible.

Once the book was near completion, I benefited from thoughtful readings of the entire manuscript by Professor Nicolas Riasanovsky of the History Department of the University of California at Berkeley and Professor Terence Emmons of the Stanford History Department. A similar benefit derived from critical readings of certain key chapters by two non-Russianist graduate students in history at Berkeley, Warren Breckman and the late Veselin Skekic. I wish also to thank Arthur McKee and John Randolph, graduate students of Russian history at Berkeley, for research assistance and help in composition. Finally, at various stages of this project I received valuable aid with assorted tasks of typing, advice with editing, and the verification of references from still other students: Kenneth Hodges, Xavier Thomas, David Shapard, Ilya Vinkovetsky, and John Grandy. Needless to say, all of these persons are absolved of any responsibility for the views expressed in this study, and warmly thanked for having helped it to completion.

INDEX